DOS 5 User's Guide

DOS 5 User's Guide

A Comprehensive Guide for Every PC User

Dan Gookin

M&T Books
A Division of M&T Publishing, Inc.
501 Galveston Drive
Redwood City, CA 94063

© 1991 by M&T Publishing, Inc.

Printed in the United States of America

Limits of Liability and Disclaimer of Warranty
The Author and Publisher of this book have used their best efforts in preparing the book and the programs contained in it. These efforts include the development, research, and testing of the theories and programs to determine their effectiveness.

The Author and Publisher make no warranty of any kind, expressed or implied, with regard to these programs or the documentation contained in this book. The Author and Publisher shall not be liable in any event for incidental or consequential damages in connection with, or arising out of, the furnishing, performance, or use of these programs.

Library of Congress Cataloging in Publication Data

Gookin, Dan.
DOS 5 User's Guide / by Dan Gookin.
    p.   cm.
Includes index.
ISBN 1-55851-188-1
1. Operating systems (Computers)   2. MS-DOS.   3. PC-DOS.
I. Title
QA76.76.063G666   1991
005.446—dc20   91-17417
                                                                  CIP

Trademarks:
All products, names, and services are trademarks or registered trademarks of their respective companies.

Project Editor: Christine de Chutkowski

Cover Design: Lauren Smith Design

94 93 92 91   5 4 3 2 1

Contents

Why This Book Is For You

This book contains information for all levels of DOS users. Where you start depends on your familiarity with DOS:

Part One is background information on your computer and its hardware. It's primarily orientation material, identifying certain important terms and how to use some of the equipment in your computer system.

Part Two explores DOS, including its history, DOS 5 installation, and working with DOS. With the exception of Chapters 6 and 7 (what's new with DOS 5 and DOS 5 installation), this material is very introductory.

Part Three covers simple DOS use. This section covers basic file management, disk management, and using the MS-DOS Editor and DOS Shell programs.

Part Four is about hard-disk management and includes a discussion of batch files, CONFIG.SYS and AUTOEXEC.BAT, and system maintenance.

Part Five is about advanced DOS, including the ANSI.SYS file, using pipes and I/O redirection, and some new features with DOS 5: DOSKEY, memory management, and running Windows.

Part Six is troubleshooting, including correction and prevention of some problems. DOS 5's new maintenance, problem prevention, and undo features are reviewed.

Part Seven is the DOS reference, including the complete command reference and several useful and handy appendices.

Introduction

There has never been a DOS upgrade as exciting as version 5.0. Whether you're coming from DOS 3.3, DOS 4.01 or DOS 0.0 and you're a total novice, this is the book that tells you how things are done, why they work, and what secrets exist beyond that forbidding facade of:

```
C:\>
```

Assumptions

This book assumes that you already own a computer. Further, you should have a computer that has a hard drive installed. While a hard drive is not mandatory for DOS 5, in order to get the most from DOS, your computer, and your software, you will need a hard drive.

As the title of this book implies, I'm assuming that you also have a copy of DOS. DOS 5 is actually the first version of DOS widely available at software stores as well as at traditional computer dealers. You can also order it directly from Microsoft at (206) 882-8080.

Where to Start

If you're just starting out with DOS, fine. This book will bring you up to advanced speed in no time. Start your reading with Chapter 1.

Part Three is where most intermediate users should begin. This doesn't imply that Parts One and Two contain useless information, but they're written in a more relaxed, tutorial style—which might easily bore an experienced DOS user.

If you already have a version of DOS installed on your computer and are just interested in learning about and using DOS 5, then follow this path:

Read Chapter 6, the section titled "What's New With DOS 5."

Read Chapter 7 if you haven't yet installed DOS on your system.

Start reading at Part Four, "Hard Disk Management."

If you consider yourself an "expert" and are interested in finding out new information, then begin reading at Part Five, "Advanced DOS."

Before darting off, you should note that this book is covered with various TIP and INFO sections that contain important and useful information about DOS. Because these are scattered throughout the text, consider leafing through the entire book to make sure there's nothing you missed.

How to Use this Book

Text you will see on your screen or text used to reference a command or message appears like this:

```
MS-DOS version 5.00
```

Text you should type appears like this:

```
TYPE IN THIS COMMAND
```

Generally you'll be told what to type and, up until Chapter 11 or so, when to press Enter. Also, note that what you type can be entered in upper- or lowercase; DOS doesn't care. (This book uses uppercase throughout.)

This is an active book. You'll be both reading and doing as you travel through these pages. The tone here is light and entertaining, with lots of information and plenty of chances to type things in and test things out. This is a fun book, and you're going to learn a lot. Don't be afraid to do anything, and consider all the possibilities. Soon you'll be an old hand at DOS 5.

PART ONE

About DOS and Your PC

Welcome to *DOS 5 User's Guide*. This part of the book contains basic information about DOS and your computer. The topics in these chapters are designed for first-time computer users and folks who are not familiar with DOS. If you're already comfortable with your MS-DOS PC, skip ahead to Part Two.

Chapter 1 describes your basic computer hardware and tells you where all the parts are located. Chapter 2 defines the differences between the various PC models and discusses microprocessors, memory, and disk storage. Chapter 3 is about the other parts of your computer: input/output ports and the video system. Chapter 4 is devoted to software. Finally, Chapter 5 introduces the ubiquitous ASCII computer code.

Your Computer and Its Parts

Ancient Eastern philosophers have told us that everything in the universe is composed of two equal but opposite natures. There is good and evil, life and death, yin and yang. Had they had access to a computer, the masters might have added to the list of opposites hardware and software—the body and soul of a computer.

This chapter will answer the following questions for you:

- What is the difference between hardware and software?

- Which is more important?

- What are all the different parts of a computer called?

Hardware and Software

Hardware is the physical aspect of the computer. It consists of everything you can touch: the computer itself, the keyboard, a monitor, and a printer. Anything you can pick up, drop, thump, or spill coffee in or on is hardware.

Software is the mental aspect of the computer—the collection of electronic instructions that tell the hardware what to "think" and "do." Typically, software is stored on floppy diskettes, just as music is recorded on tapes and CDs. The musical metaphor is a good way to think of software: The music in Beethoven's Ninth may be written on sheets, and a performance may be recorded on a reel of tape, but neither the paper nor the tape is the music. Similarly, the software is the data on the diskette, not the diskette itself.

Note: In a computer, software controls hardware.

A lot of people are puzzled that software is the priority. After all, you see the computer hardware; you can't see software. And your computer hardware probably cost more than any piece of software you own. But that doesn't mean it's more important. In fact, without the software to control it, the computer is only an expensive art object.

If you own an IBM-compatible personal computer, you can choose from literally thousands of software packages, or applications. The most important software of all, however, is DOS, your Disk Operating System.

DOS is the PC's main control program. It's the first one your computer runs; it manages the complex interactions of all the basic hardware in the system, and it governs the behavior of every other application you use. Once you understand DOS, you're well on the way to getting more from your computer.

Hardware Terminology

Although this is a book about software, we can't ignore the importance of hardware. You use hardware—such as your keyboard or a mouse—to communicate with software, and that software in turn uses hardware—such as your monitor or printer—to provide you with important information. Before you can take advantage of your software, you'll need to become familiar with the hardware.

Learning to use a computer means dealing with a barrage of new buzzwords and acronyms. Some humans take to foreign languages effortlessly; others never get used to it. When it comes to computers, you'll need a basic vocabulary to comprehend all the material you'll learn throughout this book. It isn't overly technical stuff, and it will give you a bounty of trendy terms to drop at cocktail parties.

Most PCs look pretty much alike, yet there are literally thousands of subtly different ways to build a computer. The PC shown in Figure 1-1 is typical, although a few of the items illustrated may be in different locations or missing altogether from your system.

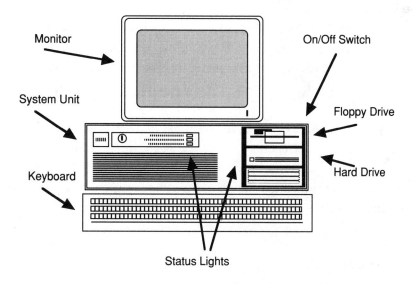

Figure 1-1. Your PC and Its Parts.

Info: Most PCs are designed in a desktop configuration, like the one shown in Figure 1-1. A popular design variation is the tower PC, which is essentially a desktop model that sits on its side. Tower models have room for more internal components—such as disk drives and add-in cards—than most desktop models. Another increasingly popular PC design is the laptop or notebook computer. Modern laptop designs pack virtually all of the power and disk storage of a standard PC into a small, lightweight package.

Three pieces of hardware are essential to every PC: the monitor, the keyboard, and the system unit.

The Monitor

Your computer monitor looks like a TV set without a tuner knob. In fact, in the early days of personal computing, many PC makers allowed you to attach a TV set directly to a computer. The results were painfully fuzzy, and these days computer monitors and televisions use very different technologies to display information on a screen.

A typical monitor has an on/off switch and an assortment of controls that allow you to adjust brightness, contrast, image size and position, and other attributes of the image on the screen. The topic of monitors is covered in depth in Chapter 3.

It's important to distinguish between the monitor and the display. The monitor is the equipment itself, a piece of hardware. The display, on the other hand is the information—letters, numbers, pictures, and so forth—that you see on the monitor.

The Keyboard

The keyboard is your direct line of communication to the computer, just as the monitor is how the PC sends important messages to you. For virtually any job you can imagine, a keyboard is essential—that's why all computers have a keyboard.

Generally speaking, a computer keyboard looks and works like the one you'll find on an electric typewriter. The keys are arranged in a pattern similar to the familiar IBM Selectric layout, with a handful of extra keys clustered around it. In addition to the standard typewriter keys, there is a numeric keypad, arrow (or cursor) keys, and special keys called function keys, which serve a variety of purposes.

The typical PC keyboard layout is shown in Figure 1-2. Take a moment to look at that keyboard, and then compare the areas highlighted with those on your own computer keyboard.

Info: The original PC had a frustrating keyboard, with only 83 keys—some in unexpected arrangements—and the Enter key was just too small. The PC/AT came with a different keyboard layout, and then the clone manufacturers started offering subtle improvements. Things got really crazy, until the PC industry more or less settled on the keyboard layout you see in Figure 1-2. Laptops and some other systems, however, still march to the beat of their own key-click.

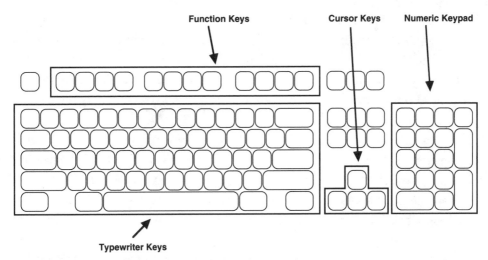

Figure 1-2. The typical PC keyboard.

Most DOS computers sold these days use the "Enhanced 101-key" keyboard shown in Figure 1-2. Older DOS computers may use different layouts, but the essential areas are still present. No matter what the layout of your keyboard, all PC keyboards work pretty much the same. In fact, if you don't like the arrangement or the feel of your keyboard, you can replace it.

The System Unit

The system unit is the box that houses all the electronic parts in your PC—disk drives, memory chips, circuit boards, expansion cards, and the power supply. Some people prefer to think of the system unit itself as the computer, and consider the monitor, keyboard, printer, and whatever else you have hooked up to the system unit to be peripherals.

Most of the system unit is hidden inside the case, where you'll never touch it. The parts of the system unit that you're likely to see and touch are the status lights, the on/off switch, and the disk drives.

Status lights can be found in a number of places on your computer. You'll usually find one status light on each of your disk drives; depending on your PC's design, you may also find a few on the front panel of the system unit.

Rule: Never take a floppy disk out of the drive until the drive light goes out.

11

The status light on a disk drive is important. It lights up whenever the computer is reading from or writing to the disk. Read the light as a warning; the computer is telling you, "I'm using the drive—don't take the disk out." If you interrupt the read/write process, you may hopelessly scramble an important file. When the PC has finished working with the disk, the light will go out and you can safely remove the disk.

Status lights on the system unit's front panel are less critical. Depending on what the manufacturer deems important, a status light may glow brightly whenever your computer is on, another may indicate the speed at which your PC is running, and a few computers incorporate digital readouts that tell you which sector of the hard disk is currently being accessed. (It's all for show and sales; none of that really matters when you use the computer.)

Finally, there's the on/off switch. On most PCs, it's a big red switch located inconveniently on the back right side of the system unit. This switch is simple to operate, but there are a few rules that are well worth remembering:

Rule: Never turn the computer off when a drive light is on. The effect can be even more devastating to your important files than yanking a disk from the drive at the wrong time.

Rule: After turning a computer off, always wait 15 seconds or so before turning it back on again.

There may be a separate switch that turns the monitor's power on and off. Indeed, almost every computer peripheral has its own power switch.

Info: Chapter 8 has more details about how to safely turn your PC on and off.

The Disk Drives

With a few specialized exceptions, every computer has at least one floppy-disk drive. You typically access the disk drive from the front of your system unit. That first disk drive is called drive A. If you have a second floppy disk drive, it's most likely located below or alongside drive A and is named (not surprisingly) drive B.

Most modern computers also come with a hard drive (the details of which are covered in the next chapter). Regardless of how many floppy drives are installed in your system, the first hard drive is always called drive C. Additional hard drives are letters D, E, F, and on up the alphabet through Z. (These drives may be separate physical drives, partitions of a single physical drive, or logical drives on a computer network.)

Info: Drive A is always your first floppy-disk drive.

Drive B, if available, is reserved for a second floppy-disk drive.

Drive C is your first hard drive.

Drives D through Z represent additional hard drives or network drives.

Figure 1-3 shows the locations of various drives in a typical computer system. The hard drive C may be visible from the outside, or it may be hidden away inside the system unit. Drive A is usually installed on top, although there's no law that says a PC has to be configured this way.

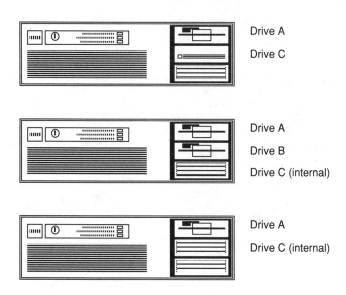

Figure 1-3. The locations of various disk drives.

Summary

Your computer is made up of hardware and software. Hardware is the "physical" aspect of the computer. Anything you can touch—the system unit, monitor, keyboard, as well as assorted peripheral devices—is hardware. Software represents the "mental" aspect of the computer. Hardware is nothing without the software to tell it what to do.

The most important piece of software is DOS, the Disk Operating System. DOS manages your hardware and controls all the other software you use. You need to learn DOS before you can effectively use your computer.

Every computer consists of three essential components: a monitor, to display information; a keyboard, to let you communicate with the computer; and the system unit, which houses the main computer components. The disk drives, which are your computer's main storage devices, are installed in the system unit. The first floppy drive is drive A, the second (if available) is drive B, and the hard disk is always drive C.

CHAPTER 2

Microprocessors, Memory, and Storage

Inside your PC's system unit is a veritable electronic salad of parts. If you take the cover off your PC, you'll probably be amazed at the detail and complexity of what you see. Perhaps you'll even be intrigued enough to pick up a technical book and discover what it's about. To make the most of DOS, you should learn about the microprocessor (the "brain" of the computer), memory, and disk storage. Some important concepts of DOS 5 are directly linked to these items.

This chapter answers the following questions:

- What is a microprocessor or CPU?

- Which microprocessors does the PC use?

- What are bits and MHz, and how do they relate to PC power?

- What is RAM?

- How can you visualize what a byte is?

- What is a K, a megabyte, and a gigabyte?

- How is information stored long term?

- What is the relationship between disk density and disk capacity?

- How can you prevent a disk from being written to or changed?

- How can hard drives store more information than floppy disks?

About Microprocessors

Your computer's motherboard sits deep inside the system unit, on a rigid sheet coated with micro-thin wire tracings. It contains an assortment of integrated circuits, resistors, capacitors, and other microcircuitry, making it resemble a dinner presentation at a high-tech sushi bar.

The motherboard contains a set of control chips that direct your peripherals; RAM (random-access memory); a set of chips called the BIOS (Basic Input-Output System), which gives your PC its personality; and expansion slots for adding options to your computer. At the heart of everything is your computer's brain—the microprocessor.

Info: The motherboard inside your system unit contains:

Control circuitry

Memory

The BIOS

Expansion slots

The microprocessor

The microprocessor is a thin, black, flat computer chip—an after-dinner mint with metal legs. You might hear it called a microprocessor, a central processing unit (CPU), or just "the processor." This book uses the term "microprocessor."

While this book calls a DOS computer a PC, every computer sold to the individual is, in reality, a personal computer. An Apple Macintosh or a Commodore Amiga, for example, can each legitimately be called a personal computer. However, since IBM called its first microcomputer the "PC," every compatible machine since produced has been given the same designation.

Info: Before it was designated a personal computer, the system atop your desk was called a "microcomputer"—as opposed to the larger minicomputer and the still larger mainframe computers that have been used for the past 40 years.

Over the years, microprocessors and the computers built around them have become progressively faster and more powerful. Today there are four popular varieties of Intel chips found in DOS computers. Table 2-1 lists these computer systems and the microprocessors used by each.

Computer	Microprocessor(s)
IBM PC, PC/XT	8088, 8086, 80C86, V20, V30
IBM PC/AT	80286
'386	80386, 80386SX
'486	80486

Table 2-1. DOS computers and their microprocessors.

The IBM PC and PC/XT were built around the Intel 8088 microprocessor. (The V20 and V30 are clones of the Intel chip designed and sold by NEC Corporation.) IBM's PC/AT was the first system to use the more powerful 80286 CPU. The '386 and '486 microprocessors are not associated with an official IBM designation; other manufacturers came out with computers using those chips before IBM did.

Every one of these chips, up to and including the 80486, is compatible with the original IBM PC and its 8088 CPU; in other words, any software that runs on older PCs will run on a newer model. However, the reverse is not true—more and more software these days includes features that take advantage of the special capabilities of advanced chips like the 80386 and 80486 families. DOS 5, for example, has a handful of commands that will only work on a system with a '386 or higher CPU.

Measuring Microprocessor Power

A microprocessor is essentially a tiny calculator. It performs basic math functions—addition, subtraction, multiplication, and division—as well as an array of logic functions that would enchant Mr. Spock.

By human standards, the microprocessor does its calculations very quickly, with the relative speed being measured in cycles per second or megahertz (MHz). The larger the MHz value, the faster the microprocessor. Table 2-2 lists the MHz value of some of the typical microprocessors found in a DOS computer. The low and high values indicate the range of speeds available for the different chips.

CPU	System	MHz low/high	Bits	Memory (megabytes)
8088	PC	4.77 / 10	8/16	1
80286	PC/AT	6 / 20	16/16	16
80386SX	'386SX	16 / 20	16/32	4,096
80386	'386	16 / 33	32/32	4,096
80486	'486	25 / -	32/32	4,096

Table 2-2. PC microprocessor statistics.

The speed of a CPU is a practically meaningless value when considered by itself. In fact, over the past few years, the PC-buying public has become so sophisticated on the subject of speed that most computer manufacturers use the MHz value simply to define the power of different models in their product lines. To compare performance of different machines, you should measure the actual work you can do during a given time.

An additional measurement of a microprocessor's power is the maximum number of bits it can work with at one time. Each bit represents one of the millions of tiny electronic switches inside the microprocessor. Computers can count from only 0 to 1. In a microprocessor, 1 means "on" and 0 means "off." Since this describes the binary (base two) counting system, each on or off switch in a computer is called a "binary digit," a term which has been shortened to "bit."

Trying to think or speak in ones and zeros will drive you nuts. To make it easier to deal with bits, the microprocessor handles eight bits at a time, in a group known as a byte. (Get it?) It's the bytes on which the microprocessor performs all its calculations.

Info: A bit is a tiny on/off switch, represented by a 1 or a 0. "Bit" is short for binary digit, binary being the base two counting system. A byte is a group of 8 bits.

As the microprocessor evolved, it was able to handle more and more bits at once. While a byte is still only eight bits, newer microprocessors can work with 16, 32, or even 64 bits (that is, 2, 4, or 8 bytes) at a time. The more bits a microprocessor can work with, the faster it can process instructions from software and the more work it can do.

These bits aren't anything to concern yourself with, although they do play a role in determining the amount of memory your microprocessor can access. Memory is covered later in this chapter.

From the 8088 to the 80486—and Beyond

For the sake of tradition (and really for no other reason), microprocessors are named after numbers. The first microprocessor was named the 4004, because it contained the equivalent of 4,004 transistors. Later microprocessors doubled, split, and then swapped the various numbers, and trying to make sense of this labeling is like learning how to keep score in bowling.

Intel, the architect of all the PC's microprocessors, came up with the 80x86 numbering scheme. The x in that number stands for a successive generation of the original 8086 chip, which was the model for the original IBM PC. Thus, the 80286 was replaced by the 80386, which in turn was followed by the 80486. By the time you read this, Intel will have introduced its next-generation chip, the 80586.

In IBM's original design, the 8086 was too expensive, so the microprocessor used in the first IBM PC was the 8088, which ran at a speed of 4.77 MHz. Internally, the 8088 could process 16 bits at once, but it could only communicate with the outside world 8 bits at a time. (For this reason, Table 2-2 shows "8/16" in the bit column.)

As the PC's popularity increased, other microprocessors were developed and used in newer models. The first 80286 chip operated at 6 MHz; later versions ran as fast as 20 MHz. The 80286 PC is a 16/16-bit machine, meaning it can process 16 bits at a time and send and receive data at the same rate, which makes it more powerful than a PC with an 8088.

The 80386 was introduced in 1987. Its speed at that time was only 16 MHz, yet it really worked several times faster than any 80286 chip—more proof that CPU speed alone is not a reliable way to compare the speed of two computers. The 80386 was the first 32/32-bit processor, which made it a veritable speed demon when compared with the original 8088.

The 80386SX chip is a curiosity in that it's actually the little brother of the 80386. Internally, the 80386SX works exactly like the 80386. The single difference is that it talks with the outside world 16 bits at a time. This makes the 80386SX cheaper than the full 80386 (also called the 80386DX), but slightly less powerful.

The latest chip to appear in a PC is the 80486. Essentially it's a faster 80386 that also contains a built-in math coprocessor and memory cache, which speed up processing. (Math coprocessors and memory caches for an 80386 are separate, expensive add-on chips.) As far as DOS is concerned, the 80386 and 80486 microprocessors are considered to be the same; throughout this book, we will refer to members of both families as '386 chips.

Why Is All This Important?

Bits and bytes and megahertz are technical terms, yet they're important to DOS. Aside from their speeds, these microprocessors determine the different options a DOS user can choose from. This is most obvious when we look at how much memory the microprocessor is capable of handling.

The original 8088–based IBM PC can access only so much memory. A PC/AT, thanks to its 80286 CPU, can access 16 times as much memory. A DOS computer with an 80386 chip can access 4,096 times as much memory as an original PC. More memory means more potential for the machine.

Although you'll probably never pack your computer with all that memory, it's important to note that each system is different in the way it treats memory. For standard DOS programs, this may not be an issue. But if your future plans include graphics, desktop publishing, animation, sound, or any of a number of "advanced" PC applications, then the amount of memory, as well as the type of microprocessor you have in your computer, will be very important to you.

About RAM

The microprocessor by itself can do only so much. It can add, subtract, divide, multiply, and perform all those logical operations, but it has nowhere to store its results. In a way, the microprocessor is like a person who has to keep track of thousands of little pieces of paper but has only a few pockets to store them in. If we're willing to completely disregard considerations of fashion, it's possible to add many more pockets to a microprocessor for holding information.

To temporarily store bits and bytes while it's performing calculations, the microprocessor uses random-access memory, or RAM. (Disk storage, covered in the next section, is a more permanent way of storing information.) The amount of RAM you can install in your computer is directly related to the number of bits your microprocessor can process at one time. The more RAM you have, the more useful the work you can do with your PC.

Why Is RAM Needed?

A microprocessor needs RAM to store bytes. But at this point the concept of a byte is still abstract. It might be accurate to think of a byte as a row of eight light switches; a simpler way is simply to think of a byte as a character. The letter A is a byte. The word byte contains four bytes. For the computer to store the word spaghetti, it would need 9 bytes of RAM.

Since a microprocessor can access huge quantities of RAM, bytes are measured in increments of 1,024—called kilobytes and abbreviated as "KB" or simply "K." Again, you could think of one kilobyte as half a page of text—about 1,000 characters. Why are there 1,024 bytes in a kilobyte? Why not use a nice round number like 1,000? The reason is that 1,024 is the closest "power" of 2 to the number 1,000. The number 1,024 is really 2 raised to the 10th power. So (at least where RAM is concerned) 1K is really 1,024 bytes.

Early computers could access only 64K of memory. That's exactly 65,536 bytes—64 times 1,024—or enough characters for a short story. The 8088 could access sixteen times that amount, or 1,024 kilobytes. That much memory, 1,024K, is referred to as one megabyte, or one million bytes. That's more than the total number of characters in this book—a lot of information.

Info: A byte is one character—a letter, number, or symbol. A kilobyte, or K, is 1,024 bytes—about half a page of text. A megabyte is 1,024K or 1,048,576 bytes—*War and Peace.*

The actual number of bytes in a megabyte is really 1,048,576—1,024 x 1,024—close enough to one million to satisfy the definition of "mega."

The final term used to describe literally gobs of memory is "gigabyte." That's one billion bytes, or 1,024 megabytes, or 1,048,576 kilobytes, or 1,073,741,824 bytes. As J. Paul Getty said, "A billion here, a billion there. It all adds up after a while."

When you consider memory in your computer, it's easiest to think in terms of kilobytes. A megabyte is also a useful measure, but for most of us it's a little beyond the scope of everyday work. (Just think of it as an impressive value.) Above all, consider memory in your computer as potential. The more you have, the more you and your microprocessor can do.

About Disk Storage

RAM is only temporary storage, the result of electronic impulses. When you turn off the computer's power, the contents of this memory disappear—poof! When you want to store computer information in a more lasting fashion, you'll need to use a disk drive.

Because DOS stands for Disk Operating System, you can assume that working with disks is central to using and understanding DOS. By itself, your computer doesn't know how to store information on disk drives. The microprocessor is designed only to work with the temporary storage provided by RAM. To use disk drives, you need a special type of control program—DOS.

Info: RAM is temporary storage. In order to maintain the contents of RAM, the computer requires electricity. Turn the power off, and the bytes stored in RAM are lost. Disk drives are permanent storage. Bytes recorded on disk stay there, even when the computer has been turned off.

Disk drives are storage devices. The drive itself is the mechanism that reads and writes information, in a fashion that is similar to a cross between a CD player and a tape recorder. The storage medium, where the information is actually contained, is the disk itself.

To read or write information on the disk, the disk drive uses a special read/write head much like the one in a tape recorder. Using magnetic impulses, the read/write head electronically stores patterns of ones and zeros on the disk. The microprocessor has to work a bit to get access to bytes stored on disk, but unlike the contents of RAM, those bytes stay there when the power goes off.

Disk storage comes in two major varieties on a PC: floppy diskettes and hard drives.

Floppy Diskettes

Today's floppy diskettes aren't really floppy. But yesterday's variety were. They measured 8 inches by 8 inches and really had some flop to them.

In the late 1970s, before the birth of the IBM PC, the minifloppy appeared. It looked similar to the 8-inch floppy diskette but measured only 5-1/4 inches on each side. It had less flop, but was still flexible—especially when compared with the rigid hard drive systems available on larger computers. Because the 8-inch floppy has landed in the dustbin of electronic history, the term "minifloppy" has disappeared. Now, a 5-1/4-inch diskette is a floppy disk. People would look at you strangely if you called it a minifloppy.

The 3-1/2-inch diskette was introduced in 1983. Its rigid shell makes the 3-1/2-inch diskette look something like a plastic coaster; it also makes it more durable and longer lasting than a 5-1/4-inch floppy diskette. Originally used in the Apple Macintosh, the 3-1/2-inch disk gained popularity in PC laptops and in IBM's PS/2 line. Since it stores more information and is easier to insert into a disk drive (or shirt pocket) than a 5-1/4-inch diskette, the 3-1/2-inch disk is becoming increasingly popular on desktop models. Figures 2-1 and 2-2 show the details of the 5-1/4- and 3-1/2-inch diskettes.

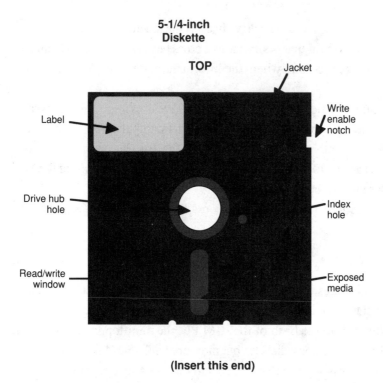

(Insert this end)

Figure 2-1. A 5-1/4-inch floppy diskette.

Tip: You cannot stick a 5-1/4-inch disk into a 3-1/2-inch drive, or vice versa. When you buy software, make sure it comes on disks that are the right size for your drive.

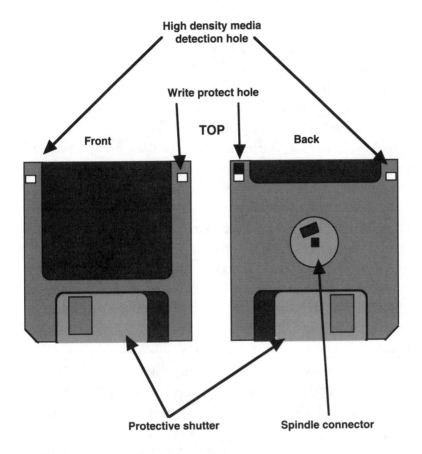

High density media
detection hole

Write protect hole

Front   TOP   Back

Protective shutter   Spindle connector

(Insert this end)

Figure 2-2. A 3-1/2-inch diskette.

Floppy Disk Capacity

The surface of a floppy diskette is composed of the same substance, or medium, as that found on a cassette tape. In the case of a floppy diskette, of course, the medium is flat like a pizza instead of in a long ribbon like a cassette, and it's of much higher quality. Information is recorded on the diskette and read back by the disk drive, which spins the diskette as it's being accessed.

Disk capacity is typically measured in kilobytes. See Table 2-3 for a summary of common diskette formats and their capacities.

Another measurement of capacity is the density of a diskette. Density is a terribly abused term when applied to floppy-disk storage. Generally speaking, the higher a diskette's density, the more information it can store.

Today, the most widespread PC floppy diskette is the 5-1/4-inch double-sided double-density format, which is capable of storing 360 kilobytes of information. A 5-1/4-inch high-capacity diskette can store 1.2 megabytes of information. Other densities of 5-1/4-inch diskettes exist, but the 360K and 1.2M diskettes are the most popular.

Info: The first PC diskettes were the single-sided, single-density format. The disk drive could write on only one side of the disk, hence the "single-sided" label. Later, when technical improvements allowed more information to be written on a diskette, PC marketing types called the new format "double density." The older format became known as "single density." As storage technology advanced, drive makers found ways to read and write to both sides of a diskette, thus creating the double-sided diskette. For a brief time, high-density diskettes were called quadruple-density diskettes.

All this density madness proves nothing, really—except perhaps that the people who name PC products often don't plan ahead.

Which diskette is which? It depends on the hardware and the diskettes you buy. If you buy a PC with a 5-1/4-inch drive today, the odds are it's configured with a high-capacity drive, which is capable of using both 360K and 1.2M diskettes. Older computers came with drives that could read only 360K diskettes; stick in a 1.2M diskette and the drive wouldn't know it from a piece of cheese.

Disk Size	Capacity (bytes)	Capacity
5 1/4-inch	368,640	360K
5 1/4-inch	1,213,952	1.2M
3 1/2-inch	737,280	720K
3 1/2-inch	1,457,664	1.4M

Table 2-3. Disk capacities in bytes and kilobytes.

To take advantage of the 1.2M of capacity of a high-density diskette, you need the right hardware, and you also need the right type of diskette. Even though all 5-1/4-inch diskettes look pretty much alike, there are significant differences in the storage media themselves. A 1.2M diskette will usually be labeled as "high-capacity" or "high-density." The 360K diskettes are labeled as "double-sided/double-density"—and they typically cost much less.

> **Tip:** When you buy diskettes, they're labeled according to their capacity: DSDD for double sided, double density and HD for high density (or capacity). Out of the box, you can tell a 5-1/4-inch high-density disk from a DSDD disk by looking for the hub ring; it's present on a 360K diskette but absent from a 1.2M diskette. On 3-1/2-inch diskettes, the high capacity models have the letters HD on them, plus an extra hole in one corner.

Today's 3-1/2-inch diskettes come in three flavors: The double-sided variety stores 720K of information; the high-density type holds 1.44M; and a new format lets you pack up to 2.88M of information on a diskette (which slips into your shirt pocket more easily than War *and Peace*). As with the 5-1/4-inch diskettes, you must have the proper hardware and invest in higher-priced high-capacity diskettes to be able to use the extra storage capacity.

Confused? Table 2-4 should clear the air on capacity, density, and disk sizes.

Diskette size	Format	Byte storage capacity
5-1/4-inch	Double-sided/ double-density	360K
5-1/4-inch	High capacity	1.2M
3-1/2-inch	Double-sided/ double-density	720K
3-1/2-inch	High capacity	1.44M

Table 2-4. Diskette density and capacity.

Tip: Always buy the highest capacity diskettes your computer can use; don't buy lower capacity diskettes just to save a few dollars.

Info: If you do format a low-density disk at a higher density (provided that the diskette can fool the disk-formatting program in the first place), you'll get quite a few "bad sectors," and the disk will be marginally useful. A few companies offer devices that purport to magically transform low-density 720K diskettes into high-capacity 1.44M diskettes. The devices work—but any data you place on such diskettes is at risk. If you lose an important data file while using one of these doctored diskettes, you'd no doubt consider it a pretty expensive way to save a few pennies.

The Care and Handling of Diskettes

Treat diskettes carefully. Sure, they're durable, but they're not as robust as some other parts of the computer. You should never set them down where they might be spilled on, trampled, or chewed by kids or critters. The following is a list of do's and don'ts for handling floppy diskettes with care:

When handling a diskette, pick it up by its top—the part that's nearest to you when you insert the disk in the drive. Keep 5-1/4-inch diskettes in protective paper sleeve when they're not in use.

Never touch any exposed media on the diskette. Even your thumb print can damage the information on the diskette.

Don't write directly on the diskettes—especially with a ball-point pen or pencil. Write on a label first, then peel and stick.

Never pinch diskettes with paper clips. Never fold them. Never put them in the toaster or feed them to farm animals.

Magnetic fields can scramble data beyond repair, so keep diskettes well away from magnets. Don't lay a disk on your phone (there's a magnet in the handset). Be on the alert for magnetic clasps on purses and briefcases.

Avoid sunlight and extreme heat; on a hot summer day, disks can melt into a gooey mess if left in the trunk of your car.

Write Protection

One way to protect the data on your disks is to use write protection. This feature allows you to essentially "lock" the disk, preventing the computer from changing any information already on the disk or from writing new information to it. There are two methods of write protecting a diskette, as seen in Figures 2-1 and 2-2.

Every 5-1/4-inch diskette includes a write-protect tab. Inside a new box of diskettes you'll usually find a sheet of tiny self-adhesive tabs. To protect the diskette, fold the label over the notch on the side of the diskette (see Figure 2-1). Remove the tab to allow information to be written on the disk.

The 3-1/2-inch diskettes use a sliding tile for write protection. Slide the tile away from the hole to protect the diskette from being accidentally or deliberately overwritten; move the tile over the hole and you can once again write to the diskette (see Figure 2-2).

Info: If you can see through the write-protect hole in a 3-1/2-inch diskette, you can't write to the disk.

The tile method is a neater and more elegant write-protection technique than the sticky tabs. When you want to write-protect a 5-1/4-inch diskette, you'll have to search for the sticky tabs; later, if you change your mind and remove the tab, the adhesive leaves a sticky residue everywhere.

Hard Disks

A hard disk—or "fixed disk," as it's referred to in IBM manuals—is a faster version of a floppy drive and can store greater quantities of information. But unlike a floppy, the hard disk is not removable. Believe it or not, this used to bother early PC owners, who were accustomed to removing their diskettes of valuable data from the computer at the end of the day.

Although some of the basic principles are the same, there are many differences between a hard disk and a floppy disk. For example:

A hard disk is constantly spinning; a floppy disk spins only when it's being accessed.

A hard disk is rigid. Its "platters" are made of metal or glass and are coated with a magnetic recording medium.

A hard disk is contained in a sealed, super-clean environment, and the read/write head sails along at high speeds a microscopic distance from the disk surface—closer than the breadth of a human hair or a particle of smoke.

A hard disk is fast. Not only does it spin much faster, but the close tolerances in the drive unit mean that information is written to and read from the hard drive many times faster than it is with a floppy.

A hard disk stores hundreds of times the information held on a floppy. The typical PC hard drive holds 40 megabytes; some can hold as much as 600 megabytes, and gigabyte-size drives will soon be commercially available.

In short, a hard disk is a fast device, ideally suited for long-term storage. It's no wonder then that it's an overwhelmingly popular choice among business people and serious PC users.

Like a floppy diskette, a hard disk must be formatted. But this is something you want to do only once. An accidental format of the hard drive can destroy many megabytes of priceless information in an instant. Because of this potential for disaster, DOS makes it difficult to inadvertently reformat a hard drive.

Rule: After its initial formatting, do not format the hard drive.

Hard drives are almost always internal and are usually nonremovable. And unlike floppy disks, there is no write-protect tab or sliding tile to let you protect the data on a hard drive. Later in this book we'll explore tips and techniques you can use to protect your hard-disk information from being erased.

Summary

The three items central to every computer are the microprocessor, memory, and storage.

The microprocessor, or CPU, is the computer's brain. The speed at which it processes instructions is measured in millions of cycles, or MHz; the number of bits it can process at a time also affects its performance. The higher the speed (in MHz), the more bits it can process at a time, and the faster and more powerful the microprocessor.

Random access memory (RAM) is where the microprocessor temporarily stores information while it performs calculations and logical operations. The contents of RAM are volatile—information disappears the instant you turn off the power.

For long-term storage, PCs use floppy disks and hard drives. These devices store the same type of information that you'll find in RAM, although it is not as easily accessible by the microprocessor. DOS is the disk control program that allows the microprocessor access to information stored on disks.

Computers store information in the form of bytes. A kilobyte (K) equals 1,024 bytes; a megabyte (M) is the same as 1,024K, or 1,048,576 bytes. It's convenient to think of a byte as a character. There are about 1,000 characters (or a half page of text) in a kilobyte; a megabyte contains the equivalent of a hefty novel.

CHAPTER 3

Expanding the System

Your computer is more than the system unit and all the data stored within it. It's expandable, both internally and externally. Everything plugged in, attached to, and used by your computer is part of your computer system. These expansion options are what gives a DOS computer its potential.

This chapter answers the following questions:

- What is I/O?

- Which is the serial and which is the parallel port?

- How are expansion slots used?

- What is a peripheral?

- How are the varieties of video systems different?

- What is the relationship between graphics color and resolution?

- Which printer is best for use with DOS?

- How does DOS work with all these peripherals?

Input and Output

With the help of your computer, you can manipulate information all day long. The computer churns numbers, makes calculations, and fills the system's memory with prodigious quantities of data. But all this work is for nothing unless there is a way to get new information into the computer, or to get the information processed back out.

Input and Output, or I/O, is a big part of all computers. You input information, the computer processes it and then outputs a result.

Info: A popular saying in computerology is "garbage in, garbage out." Computers are fast, but they can't work miracles; the output is only as good as the input.

To handle the input and output, the computer uses a variety of devices. Traditional I/O devices such as the keyboard, monitor, and disk drives—your basic system—are all input and output devices. Refer to Table 3-1:

Device	Input	Output
Keyboard	X	
Monitor		X
Disk drives	X	X

Table 3-1 The basic devices and their input/output capabilities.

The keyboard is an input device that sends your input to the computer. The monitor is an output device displaying information generated by software controlling the computer. The computer cannot send information to the keyboard, and you cannot tell the computer what to do by using the monitor. These devices are either for input or output, exclusively.

The disk drive is an example of a device that's capable of both input and output. DOS saves information on a disk and can later transfer that information back into the computer's memory.

By themselves, these basic devices—the keyboard, monitor, and disk drives—don't give your computer enough I/O abilities. How can you show someone your work? After all, you can't drag the computer around from publisher to publisher and ask them to read your Great American Novel on the screen.

Ports

To assist the computer in its input and output abilities, other devices—peripherals—are used. These peripherals attach to the computer by means of ports.

A port is basically a connector on the back of your computer. You plug a peripheral into a port, which connects it to your system unit and, ultimately, the microprocessor. Then you, the peripheral, DOS, and the computer can all work together in synchronous harmony.

The typical PC has two types of ports into which a variety of devices can be plugged. These ports are the "parallel" and "serial" ports.

The Parallel Port

The parallel port, also called a Centronics port, is where you plug in your printer. The printer is, by far, the most popular device currently used in this port, which is why the parallel port is often called a "printer" port. Every computer will have at least one printer port, with up to three available in some configurations.

The term "parallel" indicates how data is sent out the port. A byte is sent out the port all at once, with each of its eight bits traveling along eight different wires. The bytes are sent in parallel—like a marching band standing eight abreast in a parade (although they move much faster and without the music).

The Serial Port

The second—and possibly the most useful—common connector on the back of a PC is the serial port, also known as the modem port or sometimes referred to as the RS-232 port (which sounds like a Radio Shack part number, but isn't). Unlike the parallel port, the serial port allows the hook-up of a variety of peripheral devices.

As with parallel, the term serial refers to the way data is sent through the port. Each byte is sliced into its eight separate bits, and each bit is sent out one at a time—as if being squirted through a garden hose. The technology of the serial port disassembles and then reassembles the bits into bytes. Serial ports are two-way communicators; they're capable of both input and output. You can hook up a mouse, modem, printer, or any number of devices to a single serial port. The current design of the PC allows for as many as four serial ports, so that's quite a number of peripherals you can add.

Ports and DOS

The best part about the parallel and serial ports is that DOS knows about them. DOS knows about memory, your disk drives, the keyboard, and the monitor. It also knows about the parallel port (and therefore, your printer) and the serial port. Attaching devices to these ports means they're immediately recognized by DOS.

Internal Expansion

IBM really wanted its first PC to be successful. To achieve that end, they borrowed the expansion slot concept from the early Apple II computer. This "opened the box," allowing just about anyone to easily add an item to the inside of the computer, thus upgrading its power and potential.

Inside the system unit, on the back of the motherboard, are a row of slots. Into those slots you can plug circuit boards called expansion cards. An expansion card is like a little motherboard (sometimes called a daughterboard). It contains circuitry that adds one or more features to those already available. This system of expansion slots and cards allows you to expand and customize your computer as you see fit, adding devices that could not be attached by means of a parallel or serial port.

For example, if you want to add more memory, you buy a memory card and plug it into an expansion slot. Hundreds of such cards are available, giving PC owners an endless variety of options for customizing their computers.

The best part about internal expansion is that you can do it yourself. Other computers have forbidden internals. Apple purposefully made the original Macintosh a sealed unit; internal expansion was prohibited. But on a PC, you can scour the dealers and magazine ads, looking for just the expansion card you need. Buy it, install it yourself, and you have upgraded the power and capability of your computer.

The drawback to this internal expansion is that, after time, there are 50 million differently configured PCs. DOS is able to deal with all those different configurations. But for the typical DOS user, it means making some extra effort to set it all up. It's easier to configure DOS today than it was several years ago, true. Still, all those expansion options must be integrated. Fortunately, it's something you need to do only once (or whenever you add a new option). This book will explain the gorier aspects of doing so in a friendly and helpful manner.

Peripherals

A peripheral is a device external to the system unit attached to the computer.

A peripheral assists in the operation of your computer, or somehow improves its function. If a TV set were a computer, then your VCR, cable box, and Nintendo would be considered peripherals; they enhance the performance of the basic item (the TV), giving it more capabilities and features.

Info: Your monitor and keyboard aren't considered true peripherals. Early computers had the keyboard, monitor, and system unit all built into one case, so there wasn't debate over this point. However, while keyboards and monitors are often separate parts, you need the keyboard to "talk" to the computer and it needs the monitor to "talk" back to you.

One true peripheral is the computer printer. Other examples are the computer mouse, a modem, or a scanner. These either plug into a parallel or serial port, or into their own custom expansion card.

Peripherals add to your system. They expand upon what you already have, allowing the computer to do more. As long as you have the expansion slots or space on your desktop, you can add an endless variety of devices to your system.

The two most important peripherals you'll use are your video system and printer. These items are discussed in the following two sections, with additional peripherals mentioned toward the end of the chapter.

The Video System

The monitor is a standard part of any personal computer—hardly a peripheral in the traditional sense. On a DOS computer, however, there are many different types of monitors available. Each of them displays text, but the graphics capabilities of each varies. This used to be a trivial consideration; graphics on a PC were of poor quality and largely ignored. Several years ago that changed.

The monitor on top of (or alongside or near) your system unit is actually only one half of your video system. The monitor's cable is connected to an expansion card plugged into your PC's motherboard. That expansion card is called a graphics adapter. In your video system, it's the graphics adapter that's in charge—even governing which type of monitor can be attached to the system.

The type of monitor and graphics card you have determines two things about your video system:

Whether or not you can display text in color.

Whether or not your computer is capable of producing graphics.

Text and graphics are two different items. Text is readable characters. Graphics are lines, circles, squares, little men who dodge aliens tossing spears, and pie charts.

Text and Graphics

IBM thought its first PC would be used only to display text. At the time, personal-computer graphics were used only by kids playing video games. Little did they know...

Eventually, programs took advantage of the PC's primitive graphics capabilities. Then Lotus released 1-2-3 and showed the world how graphics could be used to print charts, graphs, and business forecasts. PC graphics exploded. Today, PCs are largely sold based on the graphics they produce. Just stop by any computer store and look at the floor models; all of them will be running some type of graphics demo program.

Currently there are four different levels of text-and-graphics systems you can use on a PC. Each is listed below in chronological order:

- MDA
- CGA
- EGA
- VGA

The first monitor-adapter video system available to the PC was the monochrome system. It was a basic green-on-black monitor and a monochrome adapter card, the MDA (Monochrome Display Adapter). All you saw were text characters; there were no graphics.

Later, a company named Hercules improved upon the IBM monochrome system. They provided a compatible monochrome display adapter card that also offered graphics. Today it's referred to as the Hercules or monographics standard. But while you can still produce graphics with the card, you can do so only in two colors. And the card isn't compatible with any of the other color-graphics cards available.

CGA stands for Color Graphics Adapter, and it refers to the first color text-and-graphics standard available for the PC. The text on a CGA screen is fuzzy and not well-suited for long-term text use, which is why a lot of early PCs came with monochrome rather than color video systems. CGA graphics, while offering 16 colors from which to select, were limited and slow. When IBM saw the graphics potential possible with applications such as 1-2-3, they quickly developed a graphics standard superior to the CGA.

EGA stands for Enhanced Graphics Adapter. EGA was designed to offer more color and better-looking text than the CGA system. Text on an EGA system was almost as crisp and easy to view as that on a monochrome display, and the system offered more colors than CGA.

VGA stands for Video Graphics Array. This adapter produces text that some say is better looking than a monochrome display—and it offers color graphics with more colors than the EGA standard. Currently, VGA, or its cousin, the SuperVGA standard, is the most popular, widely supported graphics standard for a DOS computer.

Monochrome DOS computers still exist. Seriously—they are the best and most economical choice for text-only work. The only problem with having a monochrome video system is that it locks you out of the color graphics that many programs offer.

DOS could care less about graphics. DOS was designed to be a text-only operating system. However, many applications offer features that can be used only with the proper graphics systems. Some applications even require a minimum graphics adapter in order to run; and DOS can get graphic by running such applications.

Resolution and Colors

Graphics on a PC are measured by resolution and color.

Resolution is the number of individual dots, or "pixels," on the screen, measured in terms of horizontal and vertical values.

Together, the monitor and graphics adapter card in the computer can control only a specific amount of pixels. The more you have, the better looking the image—the less "jagged" it is. But the more pixels there are, the more time it takes the microprocessor to deal with them all—and the more the video system costs.

Colors refers to the maximum number of colors the video system can display. From the time of the CGA, all graphics adapters can display colored text with up to 16 different colors for the text and 8 different background colors. You can even mix and match them using DOS (a process which will be covered in a later chapter).

In the graphics mode, the number of colors you can use is actually less than the total number of colors the video system can produce at one time. The higher the resolution, the fewer colors you get to choose from; the lower the resolution, the more colors available to you. But this works in an interesting way; with more colors on the screen, the eye is fooled into seeing a better image. For example, a TV set has very poor resolution but a virtually unlimited amount of colors. That's why the picture doesn't look "jagged."

Monitor/ Adapter	Max. Resolution (Horz. x Vert.)	Total Colors
Mono	80 x 25 characters	2
CGA	640 x 200 pixels	16
EGA	640 x 350	64
VGA	640 x 480	262,144

Table 3-2. The major video systems for the PC.

Table 3-2 lists the major video systems available for the PC, their maximum resolution, and total number of colors available. Generally speaking, all color modes available with the CGA work on the EGA, and all EGA and CGA modes will work on a VGA system.

These values for color and resolution only come into play when you select color graphics software to use under DOS. DOS itself can control only the color of the text; DOS doesn't "do" graphics.

Printers

In the old days, computer printers cost a lot of money—almost as much as the computer itself. The price was so prohibitive that many computer systems were often sold without printers. Now, every PC has a printer—almost to the point where it's not considered to be an expansion option or a peripheral.

Printers plug into your computer's parallel port, which is also conveniently called the printer port. All PCs have at least one parallel port, and DOS can handle up to three of them. (You add extra parallel ports by buying them on an expansion card.)

The basic PC printer is a dot-matrix printer. IBM makes its own brand but, unlike their video systems, it's not an industry standard. Instead, there are hundreds of printers available, each of which conforms to a handful of standards. All of them tackle the basic printing job.

A more advanced PC printer is the laser printer. It works like a copy machine, but creates the image on paper using a laser beam instead of mirrors and a reflected image. Laser printers are faster, quieter, and produce better results than a dot-matrix printer, yet they are quite a bit more expensive.

The type and model of printer that will work best for you depends on the software you use and the output you want. There are thousands of printers that can work with a PC. The best software programs only support a couple of hundred different printers at the most (WordPerfect supports over 700; my favorite mailing list program supports only five). Some standards exist: the Epson, Panasonic and IBM dot-matrix printers, and the Hewlett Packard Laserjet laser printers.

The only crucial consideration for using a printer and DOS is whether or not the printer is capable of producing IBM's character graphics. If the printer is compatible with IBM's line of printers, then this isn't a problem. Otherwise, your printer may not be able to print some of the special characters displayed on the screen. (The subject of IBM's character graphics is covered in Chapter 5.)

Of Mice and Modems

There are so many peripherals you can plug into or attach to a computer that the list would fill a book. In addition to monitors and printers, other popular peripherals worth mentioning include:

The Computer Mouse

A mouse is a small object, the size of a deck of cards. It's rounded and has two or more buttons on top. A cable extends out the back of the mouse (giving it that "mouse" look), and attaches either to a serial port or a special "mouse expansion card" inside the computer.

The computer mouse is classified as an "input device." Moving the mouse around on your desk moves a corresponding pointer or cursor on the screen. Using the mouse's buttons, you can point at, grab, pull, and stretch graphics objects and manipulate them in other ways. If you're planning on using graphics, a mouse will be a necessary peripheral.

A Modem

Modem stands for modulator-demodulator. It plugs into a serial port in the computer, although some modems come on expansion cards that have built-in serial ports.

The modem is a device that translates electronic bits in a computer into audible signals that you can send over a phone line. Two computers, each equipped with a modem, can call each other on the phone and exchange information. Using a modem opens up a new window into the world of computer communications.

Networks

As with modems, a network provides another means by which computers can communicate. A network, unlike a modem, is a direct line of communication between two or more computers. Computers hooked up to a network can exchange information, send files back and forth, or share other peripherals such as printers.

A Scanner

A scanner is an input device that works a lot like a photocopy machine. The difference is that the material you scan is translated into a graphic image you can manipulate in the computer. If you use special Optical Character Reader (OCR) software, you can even scan in pages of text and have that text input into your computer.

Each of these devices, and the thousands of other peripherals you can hook up to your PC share one thing in common: DOS doesn't know they exist. DOS was written at a time when a mouse was a rodent and a network was ABC, CBS or NBC. While DOS can be set up to deal with these devices, DOS by itself doesn't use them. The real power to peripherals is the software you run on the computer that takes advantage of them. That's the subject of the following chapter.

Summary

Your computer needs I/O, input and output, to help it communicate with the outside world. All devices attached to the computer are capable of either input or output or both. The keyboard handles input only, the monitor handles output only, and the disk drives handle both input and output.

To attach another device to the computer, you either plug it into a port or an expansion card inside the system unit.

There are two types of ports: the parallel or printer port, and the serial port.

To expand the power of your basic computer system, you can either add an expansion card internally or attach a peripheral, port, or an expansion card.

Internal expansion is achieved by taking a circuit board—and expansion card—and plugging it into an expansion slot on your PC's motherboard. A wide variety of options can be added to the basic computer this way, allowing you to customize your PC.

External expansion is provided by peripherals. These are devices external to the computer attached to a port or by means of a custom expansion card.

Your PC's video system is composed of an internal graphics expansion card and an external monitor. The monochrome video system is capable of displaying only text—no graphics. Color video systems—the CGA, EGA, and VGA—are capable of displaying color text as well as color graphics. The varying degrees of graphics are measured by the resolution in pixels and the total number of colors that can be displayed.

Printers are a peripheral used for output. Two popular types of printers are available—dot matrix and laser. Printers plug into your PC's parallel port.

Other peripherals exist, allowing you to further expand and customize your system, but note that all peripherals must plug into something—either a serial or parallel port or an expansion card inside the computer.

CHAPTER 4

Software

Software is the most important part of your computer. A PC can be bustling with potential—a powerful microprocessor, packed full of RAM, lots of hard disk space, graphics, all the latest peripherals—something really worth boasting about. But all that gloating means nothing; without software to seize the advantage, hardware goes unused.

- This chapter answers the following questions:

- What is the most important program on your PC?

- How is information stored using DOS?

- How is a program file different from other files?

- What can applications do for the computer?

- Which is the best way to learn and use an application?

- How is DOS like an application?

DOS

Central to all software is DOS, the most important piece of software you use.

Believe it or not, DOS is a software program. DOS works like other software on your computer, but DOS is loaded into memory first. Why? Because DOS controls the disk drives. It tells the microprocessor how to access the drives, store bytes there, and retrieve them later. Without DOS or some similar operating program, your computer would lack its most basic form of input and output.

DOS controls other aspects of the computer as well: DOS works with memory (although not as well as other operating systems); it organizes information on disk; it controls other programs and applications; and it coordinates keyboard and screen activity, as well as activity on the serial and parallel ports. But the main purpose for DOS is dealing with information on disk.

Information Storage

DOS stores information on disk in the form of files. It helps to think of a disk drive as being similar to a file cabinet. In that file cabinet are files which contain information—bytes stored on disk. DOS manages those files, keeping all the bytes for one file separate from another, saving information from RAM into a specific file, loading information from a file back into memory, and so on. DOS manages hundreds of files, never losing track of the information in any of them.

There are different types of files on disk, and DOS treats each differently. Most programs contain what's generally referred to as data. Data could be anything: readable text, numbers stored in a special format, a catalog of your baseball card collection, a customer mailing list, raw bytes used for some program in some unknown capacity—just about anything can be stored in a file.

An important type of file is the program file. As with all other files, a program file is simply a collection of bytes on disk. What makes it different is that the bytes are actually instructions for the microprocessor.

When DOS transfers—or "loads"—a program file from disk into the computer's memory, the next thing it does is run that program. It finds the start of the instructions, then tells the microprocessor, "Here, this is a program. Start following these instructions." The microprocessor does so, and the program runs on your computer.

Info: Using a program on a computer is referred to as "running" a program. You say to a colleague, "Run that program that produces the handicaps for the third race." Other terms for running a program include "execute," "start," and "launch."

Note that the program file is the only type of file a computer will "run." Data files, which include just about everything but a program file, are loaded (also known as being "retrieved" or "fetched") into memory. Information in the computer (in memory) is saved (also known as being "stored" or "recorded") to a "file one" disk. These three terms—run, load, and save—are common computer vernacular.

When a program runs, DOS drops out of the picture. The program then has control of your computer and can access your printer, monitor, or do whatever it is you paid for the program to do. When the program needs to access the disk drives again, it uses DOS—but only to save or load information to or from the disk.

When you're done using the program, you tell it you want to quit and DOS takes over again. At that point, you can run another program, work with DOS and manipulate files on disk, or turn the computer off and go to the store to buy Häagen Dazs.

Briefly, that's the way DOS and your software work on the computer. You can see how DOS is central to everything: It's the first program your computer runs, it controls the disk drives and other devices in the computer, and it lets other programs run. Control always returns to DOS when an application quits; indeed, DOS is boss. This is why learning about DOS is important, to allow you to get the most from your computer.

Applications

Certainly it would be a dull life if all there ever was to a computer was its DOS operating system. What makes a PC worthwhile is the software you use.

A program is software is an application. The terms refer to the same thing, but they aren't really interchangeable.

An application is one or more programs that accomplishes some task. Popular application classifications are:

Word Processor
Spreadsheet
Data Base
Graphics
Communications
Educational
Entertainment/Games

Your word processor is the application you use to compose text. This book was written on a word processor. The office memo, a letter home, a form letter you get from your member of Congress—they were all composed on a word processor.

WordPerfect is an example of a word-processing program. The application is word processing and the program is WordPerfect. WordPerfect itself is a program file on disk (actually several dozen files and programs).

Lotus produces a spreadsheet called 1-2-3. The application is spreadsheet and 1-2-3 is the software. The program is named 123.

Software refers to all programs that run on your computer. DOS isn't an application, but it's a program and it's software. WordPerfect is a word-processing application, 1-2-3 is a spreadsheet application, and both are software.

Ah, semantics...

You'll work with applications more than you work with DOS. But keep in mind that DOS is the launching pad. Also, DOS makes it easier to juggle several applications on a single computer system. This book will show you how in Part Four.

Using Applications

Most DOS books concentrate only on what DOS does. They rattle off commands and procedures, but ignore applications. This book is about DOS, but the chapter subject is applications. Though all applications can't be mentioned, the following are five general steps you should take when using an application.

1. Make sure it works under DOS.

Applications are available for all computers. But make sure the one you buy is for the computer you own. WordPerfect, Microsoft Excel, and several other programs have versions for both the Macintosh and DOS computers.

2. Make sure you have the required equipment.

On the back of the application's package you'll see a list of system requirements. It will mention that you need a DOS computer, a type of microprocessor, a given minimum of RAM, a hard drive, maybe a specific version of DOS, graphics, a special type of printer and so on. Make sure your system has all those items, as well as any options mentioned.

3. Install the application.

Applications come on floppy diskettes but must be installed onto your computer's hard drive. This process is done either by following step-by-step instructions in the manual or by running a special install or setup program or some combination of both.

Rule: Even if you only have a floppy-drive system, don't use the original program diskettes. *Always* make copies. This book will show you how to make copies of diskettes in a later chapter. Otherwise, use the application's installation procedure as recommended in the manual.

4. Learn the application.

A lot of people buy software and never give themselves time to learn it. Almost any program seems terrible and difficult to use if you don't first learn how it works. Tutorials are included in the computer's manual, and you can buy books for major applications that contain how-to's and offer instructions and advice.

Sometimes it's difficult to give yourself all the time you need to learn an application. Typically, the boss wants something "yesterday," so you must slug it out the first few days. But after that, go back and read through the tutorial. You'll be surprised what you figure out on your own and what new abilities lie lurking under the application's exterior.

5. Use the application.

Part of learning an application requires using it. Thanks to competition, applications offer more features than you'll probably ever use. But you paid for them! After working with a program, leaf through the manual and check out some of its more esoteric features. Some you may find more useful after you get to know the software.

The First and Most Important Step

While you buy a computer to run applications, at the center of everything will always be DOS. This is true even if you're using a program like Microsoft Windows, which purportedly makes a DOS computer easy to use. Knowledge of DOS is still required.

Know DOS and you know your computer. Know your computer and you become more productive with it. The key to getting the most from your investment in time and money is to learn DOS and use your computer to its fullest possible potential.

Since DOS is a program on your computer, the same steps for learning an application also apply to DOS:

1. Make sure it works under DOS.

Of course.

2. Make sure you have the required equipment.

You probably do. But make a note of what you have. In the preceding chapters you read about microprocessors, memory, and disk storage; now you should know which and how much of each you have. Maintain a chart near your computer telling you what and how much of what you have in your system. Keep the chart near your computer, preferably with the computer's hardware manual.

3. Install the application.

DOS is installed on your computer just like any other application. Starting with DOS 4, the procedure became sophisticated—as much as you'd expect from any other application. DOS 5 has the smoothest installation process of all. It's covered in Part Two of this book.

4. Learn the application.

Learning DOS requires a good book on the subject. I'd suggest a few, but why buy them when you have this one?

5. Use the application.

It's hard not to use DOS and using it will make you better at it. This book is full of tricks. A few of these you'll be using right away. Others may not become apparent until you've played with DOS a few weeks.

DOS isn't scary. In fact, DOS is a lot more stable than some other applications. I remember working with early word processors that would "forget" parts of my text. There were certain things you had to remember not to do in order to keep your writing intact. DOS is much more reliable.

There is little you can do with DOS to damage your files—nothing, in fact, that it doesn't first prompt you for a decision on. If ever DOS is about to do something with even semi-grave consequences, it will let you know. Often you can press any key to back away from the operation and then proceed safely. Only the truly careless experience DOS disaster—and even that can be repaired with the proper knowledge of DOS.

Approach learning DOS as an exploration. It's exciting. And soon you'll be the one telling the computer what to do. It's obedience will astound you!

Summary

DOS is the main piece of software on your computer. It controls the disk drives, memory, the keyboard, monitor, printer—anything attached to the computer. It's also in charge of running other applications; all software pays its respects to DOS.

DOS stores information on disk in the form of files. A file is basically a collection of bytes. DOS keeps track of each file, keeping them individual and separate. It can load a file into memory or save memory to disk in a file.

A special type of file is the program file. A program file contains bytes like any other file, but the bytes in a program file are actually instructions for the microprocessor. When DOS loads the program file into memory, it tells the microprocessor to start executing the instructions held in the program file.

An application is a general category for a type of program known as "software." To get the most from an application, you need to do the following: Make sure the program works under DOS; make sure you have the required equipment; install the application; learn the application; use the application. These same steps apply to DOS as well.

CHAPTER 5

About ASCII

Computers have colorful acronyms buzzing around them like wasps. DOS is the most popular acronym, as are the CGA, EGA, and VGA graphics standards. Another one you'll soon see all the time is ASCII. It's not a term critical to understanding DOS, but it's in common use. Normally a DOS book wouldn't devote a whole chapter to the subject, but knowing what ASCII is and how it fits in will help you later as you explore DOS and your PC.

This chapter answers the following questions:

- What is ASCII?

- What is an ASCII file?

- How do the Extended ASCII characters fit in?

- What's the difference between a text and ASCII file?

- How does ASCII allow information to be exchanged between computers?

What is ASCII?

ASCII is an acronym for the American Standard Code for Information Interchange. A technical description could appear right now, but a more pressing issue is:

Just how does one pronounce ASCII?

The temptation is to say "ask-two," which is what I did when I first saw the acronym. Of course, I never said it aloud for fear of chastisement. It was only later that I learned the proper pronunciation:

ASCII is pronounced ASK-ee.

Once you have that down, learning about ASCII is a snap.

Bytes and ASCII

ASCII defines a code for representing characters, including letters, numbers, punctuation, and other symbols. This works a lot like the secret decoder rings of yore; every character has its own ASCII code value.

For example, code 33 is the code assigned to the exclamation point (!) symbol. Code 65 is the capital letter "A." If you were a Secret Agent, you could use the ASCII codes to send your accomplice the following:

```
77, 97, 108, 116, 45, 111, 45, 109, 101, 97, 108
```

When you look up the characters those ASCII codes represent (in Figure 5-1), they spell out the letters: Malt-o-meal.

Notice how 45 represents the hyphen character? Also, 77 is the code for a capital "M," whereas 109 is the code for a lower case "m." In ASCII, the codes for upper and lower case characters are different. If the decoded phrase had been "Malt o meal" instead, code 32 would have replaced code 45. ASCII 32 is the code for the space character.

There's no need to memorize these codes or their assigned letters—thank goodness. Internally, the computer will use the ASCII codes to represent characters. Computers think in numbers, after all, not in the letters you're now reading. It's convenient for the computer to represent characters using some type of symbolic code. Because ASCII is the character/code standard, IBM decided to use those codes to represent characters; when you type an A, your computer doesn't see the letter "A," it sees the ASCII code for a capital A, 65.

Info: Note that the first 32 ASCII codes, 0 through 31, are different. They are referred to as control characters. The ^ (carat or hat) next to a letter means "control," so ^L is Control-L.

All the ASCII codes are listed in Figure 5-1:

0 ^@	32	64 @	96 '
1 ^A	33 !	65 A	97 a
2 ^B	34 "	66 B	98 b
3 ^C	35 #	67 C	99 c
4 ^D	36 $	68 D	100 d
5 ^E	37 %	69 E	101 e
6 ^F	38 &	70 F	102 f
7 ^G	39 '	71 G	103 g
8 ^H	40 (	72 H	104 h
9 ^I41)	73 I	105 i	
10 ^J	42 *	74 J	106 j
11 ^K	43 +	75 K	107 k
12 ^L	44 ,	76 L	108 l
13 ^M	45 -	77 M	109 m
14 ^N	46 .	78 N	110 n
15 ^O	47 /	79 O	111 o
16 ^P	48 0	80 P	112 p
17 ^Q	49 1	81 Q	113 q
18 ^R	50 2	82 R	114 r
19 ^S	51 3	83 S	115 s
20 ^T	52 4	84 T	116 t
21 ^U	53 5	85 U	117 u
22 ^V	54 6	86 V	118 v
23 ^W	55 7	87 W	119 w
24 ^X	56 8	88 X	120 x
25 ^Y	57 9	89 Y	121 y
26 ^Z	58 :	90 Z	122 z
27 ^[	59 ;	91 [	123 {
28 ^\	60 <	92 \	124	
29 ^]	61 =	93]	125 }
30 ^^	62 >	94 ^	126 ~
31 ^_	63 ?	95 _	127

Figure 5-1. Standard ASCII codes and characters.

Control characters define some special keyboard functions, but most of them held significance only in the old Teletype days.

The Extended ASCII Characters

There are 128 ASCII codes, numbered 0 through 127. These numbers, 0 through 127, fit easily into a byte, which is handy because that's how the computer stores information. Yet a byte can store a value of up to 256. (There are 256 possible positions for the eight on/off bits in each byte.) If a byte can hold up to 256 values, and the ASCII codes range from 0 through 127, what fits into the other 128 values?

The answer is "it depends." ASCII doesn't define characters for codes 128 through 256. All personal computers display characters for those values, but there is no standard.

On IBM-compatible computers, the codes from 128 through 256 are assigned to IBM's special extended ASCII character set. These codes describe foreign language characters, mathematic symbols, and special line-drawing characters, which can be seen in Figure 5-2.

ASCII and DOS

In DOS, the term ASCII is used to describe a file that contains only ASCII characters. Essentially, this is a text file, containing characters you can read. There are no special characters, foreign characters, or any other mess. Thus, an ASCII file contains text you can read.

For example, the text you're reading now could be stored in a file on disk. Since all the characters here have ASCII codes, the file would be an ASCII, or text, file.

Why bring it up? Because you'll see ASCII all over the place when you start using the computer. In DOS, it's more customary to refer to a readable file as a text file, or better still, a "formatted text file." An ASCII file is the same thing.

128Ç	160á	192└	224α
129ü	161í	193┴	225ß
130é	162ó	194┬	226Γ
131â	163ú	195├	227π
132ä	164ñ	196─	228Σ
133à	165Ñ	197┼	229σ
134å	166ª	198╞	230μ
135ç	167º	199╟	231τ
136ê	168¿	200╚	232Φ
137ë	169⌐	201╔	233Θ
138è	170¬	202╩	234Ω
139ï	171½	203╦	235δ
140î	172¼	204╠	236∞
141ì	173¡	205═	237φ
142Ä	174«	206╬	238ε
143Å	175»	207╧	239∩
144É	176	208╨	240≡
145æ	177	209╤	241±
146Æ	178	210╥	242≥
147ô	179│	211╙	243≤
148ö	180┤	212╘	244⌠
149ò	181╡	213╒	245⌡
150û	182╢	214╓	246÷
151ù	183╖	215╫	247≈
152ij	184╕	216╪	248°
153Ö	185╣	217┘	249·
154Ü	186║	218┌	250·
155¢	187╗	219█	251√
156£	188╝	220▄	252ⁿ
157¥	189╜	221▌	253²
158₧	190╛	222▐	254■
159ƒ	191┐	223▀	255

Figure 5-2. IBM Extended ASCII codes and characters.

Info: It's important to know that most word processors don't produce ASCII text documents. Word processors usually insert special non-ASCII codes to represent underline, bold, justification, and other format items. Those codes foul up the ASCII text. So to produce a pure ASCII file on some word processors, you must specifically save it in the ASCII format.

Information Interchange

The last part of the ASCII acronym is II, for Information Interchange. This is what establishes ASCII as a useful standard. Nearly all personal computers (and even some larger computers) use the ASCII codes to describe characters. Because of this, information can be exchanged between the two computers without translation.

For example, the Macintosh uses the ASCII standard. If you were to send a Mac the phrase, "You may look pretty, but I cost hundreds of dollars less," it would receive it—no problem. All those characters are defined by standard ASCII codes, which both the PC and the Mac understand.

Info: The ASCII code 65 represents a capital "A" on the IBM PC, Macintosh, Apple II, Atari ST, Amiga, TRS-80 Model 16, Timex Sinclair, and so on and so on and so on. Each ASCII-compatible computer understands that 65 equals "A."

A Final Word

Remember that you don't need to memorize the ASCII codes in order to use your computer. All this translation between the ASCII code and the characters is taken care of by the computer. You simply type; the computer stores your keystrokes as ASCII code values in its memory.

No one needs to know that ASCII 109 is lower case "m." In fact, even the computer gurus wouldn't know that off the top of their heads. Your computer will automatically generate the code necessary to produce an "m" character. Your job is just finding the "M" key on the keyboard.

Summary

ASCII is an acronym for the American Standard Code for Information Interchange. It defines 128 codes, 0 through 127, which represent letters, numbers, symbols, and other characters.

Since there are 256 possible values of a byte, a computer uses a byte to store an ASCII character. The first 128 characters are defined by the ASCII codes. In a PC, the remaining 128 characters follow the extended ASCII codes, as set by IBM.

In DOS, the term ASCII refers to a file that contains only ASCII characters, or readable text. That type of file is also referred to as a text file.

The ASCII code is a standard for many computers, not just those that run DOS. The ASCII code is the same on all those computers. Therefore, an ASCII file created on a Macintosh can sent to a PC without any translation.

PART TWO

Introduction to DOS

This part of the book is an introduction to DOS 5, exploring what DOS does as well as how to install and become familiar with the operating system.

Chapter 6 talks about DOS's history and what you can expect from DOS 5. Chapter 7 deals with DOS 5 installation. Chapters 8 through 10 provide beginners with an introduction/tutorial to DOS. It you're just starting out, this part of the book will gently guide you until you become comfortable with using DOS 5 and your computer. Old hands may want to read only Chapters 6 and 7 and then move on to Part Three of this book.

CHAPTER 6

Chronicles of DOS

"I wasn't born yesterday."—MS-DOS

In order to appreciate some types of art, it helps to sit in front of it—epoxied to your chair. To understand DOS, get some old time computer buff to wax monotonous on its history. You'll learn about the good old days, antique versions of DOS, steam-powered disk drives, and programs from hell. But why bother? Because DOS changes. It's updated. Knowing about the existence of older versions isn't important, but understanding why they changed is. Taking this lesson from history also raises important questions: When—and should—you update DOS or any piece of software for that matter?

This chapter answers the following questions:

- What are DOS versions?

- What's the difference between PC-DOS and MS-DOS?

- How has DOS improved?

- Which version of DOS do I need?

- When should I update my version of DOS?

- What new features are available with DOS 5?

Info: This book assumes that you have DOS 5. If not, you should upgrade. Instructions for upgrading DOS are given in the following chapter.

In the Beginning...

All microcomputers with disk drives have some type of a disk-operating system available. In the early 80s, the term DOS referred to the operating system for the Apple II computer. The TRS-80 used the TRSDOS operating system. Other microcomputers, primarily those used in business, used an operating system called CP/M.

Info: DOS stands for Disk Operating System. What does CP/M stand for? No one knows. Some say it's Control Program/Microprocessor, others say Control Program/ Monitor. Since the people who made CP/M don't remember, this may end up on some future TV mystery series.

When IBM first thought of making a microcomputer—their PC, or Personal Computer—they approached Digital Research, the developers of CP/M. IBM wanted to attract all the business people who used CP/M, as well as all the software that ran under the CP/M operating system.

Well, things didn't work out for one reason or another. So IBM went to Microsoft, the company that was making the BASIC programming language for the first PC. Microsoft created an operating system named PC-DOS (Personal Computer Disk Operating System) for the first IBM PC. (Remember, Apple computers used the term "DOS" at the time.) Later, Microsoft developed its own version of PC-DOS, called MS-DOS for Microsoft Disk Operating System.

PC-DOS and MS-DOS—What's Different?

PC-DOS and MS-DOS are essentially the same; your applications can't tell one brand from another. There are subtle differences:

PC-DOS is available only from IBM. MS-DOS is available through Microsoft, but is usually acquired from the original manufacturer of your computer.

Some commands in MS-DOS and PC-DOS serve the same function, but share different names. PC-DOS calls their RAM drive software VDISK, MS DOS calls it RAMDRIVE. (RAMDRIVE is covered in Chapter 21.) PC DOS uses the

COMP command to compare files, MS-DOS uses FC (and DOS 5 uses them both).

PC-DOS comes with a BASIC programming language that's specific to IBM's line of computers; it won't run on anything else.

Other than those few differences, PC-DOS is simply MS-DOS under an IBM label. You can run either PC-DOS or MS-DOS on a computer with no ill effects. In fact, I've run PC-DOS on non-IBM computers for years without a hitch.

DOS Versions

DOS, and all other microcomputer software, comes in various versions and releases. This will drive you nuts; keeping track of version numbers and, more importantly, keeping up to date is central to getting the most from DOS—and any other software that uses the same version/number scheme.

Version 1.0, August 1981: Primordial DOS

When it first appeared, DOS was labeled as version 1.0 (one-point-zero). The 1 stands for the first version of DOS, the 0 means the initial release. These can also be referred to as the major and minor release numbers, with 1 being the major release number and 0 being the minor.

Info: DOS 1.0 looked a lot like CP/M. IBM really wanted a version of CP/M for its new microcomputer, so Microsoft made DOS 1.0 act just like CP/M. This smoothed the transition for a lot of new PC users and also made some CP/M programs quickly available for the new machine.

Version 1.1, October 1982: 640K RAM, 320K floppies

DOS 1.1 appeared soon after 1.0. The 1.1 indicates the first version of DOS, second release. This release ironed out some wrinkles found in the initial release, and it introduced a new format for floppy disks.

Note: New floppy-disk formats are one of the primary reasons for a new version of DOS—at least through version 3.3. The "disk-density madness" weaved its way through DOS, making the job of dealing with different disks and preparing them for use a frustrating task.

Version 2.0, March 1983: The PC/XT Hard Drive

Version 2.0 of DOS heralded the arrival of the hard disk in IBM's PC/XT computer. Before that, DOS was a floppy-disk-only system. This version of DOS offered new commands and features for using the hard disk, ways for using external "devices," and international support.

Version 2.1, November 1983: The PCjr

When IBM announced its PCjr computer, an update to DOS version 2.1 was produced to support it. The PCjr was actually the funniest thing IBM ever did— a marketing blunder IBM would just as soon forget about, which is why I'm reminding everyone about it here.

Version 3.0, August 1984: The PC/AT

Version 3.0 of DOS came out to support the IBM PC/AT and networks. It also supported the AT's new 1.2M, high-capacity floppy drives and higher capacity hard drives.

Version 3.1, November 1984: Improved Network Support

DOS 3.0 was quickly replaced by version 3.1. (Version 3.0 was on the market for only three months—the shortest lived version of DOS ever.)

Version 3.2, January 1986: The PC/Convertible Laptop

Version 3.2 supported the new IBM laptop and its 3.5-inch disk drive. But a major problem existed: Version 3.2 made lousy use of hard-disk space. Also, it was rumored to have lots of bugs, which made some people stick with version 3.1 until version 3.3 was available. (This is when the "should I upgrade DOS" question hit home.)

Version 3.3, April 1987: The PS/2

For the longest time, version 3.3 of DOS reigned supreme. Released in April 1987 with the new IBM PS/2 line of computers and 1.4M floppies, DOS 3.3 was the most stable and feature-rich version of DOS yet. Given the problems with versions 3.0 through 3.2, a lot of users stayed with DOS 2.1 for a long time. But the stability of DOS 3.3 made them upgrade. (DOS 3.3 has remained the most popular version of DOS until now.)

Version 4.0, July 1988: "We Were Bored"

DOS 4.0 was released in July of 1988. This surprised everyone: A new version of DOS? People thought DOS was dead because Microsoft and IBM were pushing their new operating system, OS/2. But version 4.0 offered many new features, including support for large hard drives, a new DOS "shell" program, and several interesting commands and functions.

The big disappointment with DOS 4.0 was that it didn't work with a lot of existing DOS applications. After initially becoming attached to the new version, a lot of DOS users rejected DOS 4.0. The industry pundits screamed about it, and most users decided to stick with DOS 3.3.

Info: DOS 4.0 was quickly fixed to DOS version 4.01. The "01" implies only bug fixes and minor repairs. Had there been a DOS 4.1, it would be considered a minor upgrade and not a "fix."

Version 5.0, June1991: Adios 640K

DOS version 5.0 was announced in April, 1991. Unlike the DOS 4.0 disaster, DOS 5 was more thoroughly tested to ensure that it would work well with all applications. DOS 5 kept all of DOS 4.0's features and improved upon each of them, and also added improved memory support, a better version of the BASIC programming language, and lots of features you'll soon be reading about.

Odd Version Numbers

Not all versions of DOS are whole numbers. In fact, the first version of MS DOS available to COMPAQ computers was 1.25. Is that 1-1/4 or 1/2 the distance between DOS release 1.2 and 1.3? Hmmm...

There are no real, hard and fast rules for sub-version (subversion?) numbers. The first number is the major version, the second the minor version or release. But often times you'll see values such as 2.11 or 4.01. In the case of 4.01, it was simply a minor improvement to DOS 4.0; it fixed the bugs. The renovation didn't carry the impact of a full release, so "01" was used instead of point-one.

Applications

Applications use a numbering scheme similar to that of DOS. The first version of WordPerfect that I bought was 4.1. That's the fourth version of the program (supposedly), second release; 4.0 was the first release of the fourth version.

WordPerfect 4.2 soon came out, with better features and a new manual. Version 5.0 was a complete update of the program, with new features and new options. And version 5.1 added many new features, but wasn't different enough to warrant a new major version number.

This can get confusing.

Generally speaking, a minor, minor release of an application (or of DOS) just means a new manual wasn't printed. The upgrade from version x.0 to x.01 means bugs were fixed and things were made to work properly, but no features were added.

Some developers will also use a three-dot system. When Tandy first came out with their MS-DOS-compatible Tandy 1000, they used version 2.11.35 of MS DOS. The explanation given was the 2.11 was the version of DOS—plus some 35 odd improvements made in the south tower at One Tandy Plaza.

For DOS, the major and minor release numbers don't get too crazy. However, if you're using what's called an OEM version of DOS (essentially MS-DOS with your computer manufacturer's name on it), you'll get into odd numbering schemes. For MS-DOS itself, there is usually only a major and minor release number.

Upgrading Questions

If you've ever used computer software or dabbled in programming you can understand why there are version numbers attached to programs: Things don't always work right the first time. Users clamor for new features. Those features are added and, voila, you have a new version of DOS or some application. And let us not forget the greed factor: Money can be made by selling a software upgrade. "If you have an older version great! But hey, look at the new improved version 3.5. Isn't it worth $75 to upgrade?"

Upgrading has benefits:

You get a newer version of the program.

The new program lacks the bugs found in the first program.

The new program offers new features you may need.

On the other hand, upgrading:

Costs money.

You may not need the highly touted new features.

New versions spawn new bugs.

My recommendation: If you're happy and productive with the application, why mess with it?

On Upgrading DOS

The answer to the upgrading question becomes less clear when dealing with DOS. Users stuck with DOS 2.1 for the longest time... because it worked. Only after "everyone else" started using DOS 3.3 did some people upgrade. Of course, soon there came DOS 4.0. DOS 2.1 users wanted to know which way to go: To 3.3 or 4.0?

The industry magazine columnists, consultants, and user-group leaders eventually decided that DOS 4.0 wasn't worth the hassle, so version 3.3 was settled upon. But that took time. By then, there were thousands of bewildered DOS 4 users.

For upgrading DOS, follow this advice:

1. Wait. The new version of DOS will be snatched up by a few users right away. Fine. Let them play with it. If they have any problems, you'll hear or read about it in a few months.

2. After hearing about any problems (or lack of problems), make the decision as to whether or not to upgrade.

3. Keep a copy of your current version of DOS around "just in case." It has always been possible to undo a DOS upgrade. With DOS version 5, de-installation is now a feature.

Tip: Everyone using this book should be using DOS version 5.0. Most will be coming from a DOS 3.3 environment, or will be a new computer owner. If a new version of DOS appears, consider the upgrade question only if it fixes bugs that have been bothering you or offers features you need. Even then, wait and hear what others have to say before making the Big Decision.

What's New With DOS 5?

After three years of no new DOS versions and no hope of one thanks to Microsoft and IBM's affair with OS/2 and "the future," DOS 5 came as a pleasant surprise. And after the DOS 4 debacle, the fifth version of DOS was long overdue and highly anticipated.

If you're new to DOS, then all DOS 5's features will be new to you; just glance at the following material, smile and nod. If you've used DOS before, the following lists some of the new features added, as well as existing features updated:

Easy Installation (Chapter 7)

DOS 4 came with the first true installation program for DOS. DOS 5 improves upon it—even to the point of saving your original version of DOS and allowing you to un-install DOS 5 if need be.

Memory Management (Chapter 26)

The big problem with DOS is its use of memory—specifically above the 640K memory barrier. While you're still limited to 640K for using programs, you get more of that memory under DOS 5.

Info: DOS can now be loaded into "high" memory, freeing up some 50K of RAM. You can also load your device drivers and memory-resident programs into high memory, freeing up more space. Using the third-party utilities covered in this book, you can get even more memory free—sometimes up to the full 640K.

Command Line Editing (Chapter 22)

The DOSKEY utility replaces the old function key method of editing a command line. Using DOSKEY you have full cursor control and visible editing right at the command prompt. A command history is kept, allowing you to retrieve, edit and use older DOS commands, or review all commands in a DOS session. DOSKEY also allows for the creation of macros and multiple commands on a single line.

Anti-Disaster Utilities (Chapter 28)

DOS 5 now has built-in file and disk resuscitation. You can un-delete files and un-format disks. Additional utilities, and improvements to the FORMAT command, allow for even quicker recovery of dead files and damaged disks.

No more EDLIN! (Chapter 12)

EDLIN, DOS's text editor, was feeble and gross—a ten-year-old awkward program that most DOS users hated and ignored. Ta-da! DOS 5 comes with the EDIT program, a full-screen text editor with mouse support.

On-line Help (All over this book)

DOS now has extensive help facilities. Type /? after any DOS command and you see a screenful of helpful information and available options. The new HELP command provides a list of all DOS commands, as well as instant access to their helpful information.

Improved DOS Shell (Chapter 16)

DOS 4 introduced the DOS Shell program, an alternative "menu" system for running the computer. DOS 5 improves upon DOS Shell, giving it better mouse support, cleaner graphics, and making it more functional.

More than a simple menu system, DOS Shell offers task switching. This allows you to run several applications at once and quickly switch between them. (The speed of this is limited by the amount of memory in your system.)

Improved DIR Command (Chapter 17)

The DIR command can now sort files, display files by attribute, and can display all files in the current directory as well as in all subdirectories. (Several other DOS commands have been improved with this subdirectory-searching feature.) Additionally, the DIRCMD environment variable can be used to store default DIR command settings.

Improved ATTRIB Command (Chapter 17)

The ATTRIB command can now be used to set all attributes for a file—even making files invisible.

Version Fooling Utility

Some applications run only under a specific version of DOS. With DOS 5's SETVER command, you can pre-arrange to have DOS fool those applications into thinking they're running under another DOS version.

Quick BASIC Interpreter

Since the earliest days of microcomputing, nearly all computers have come with the BASIC programming language. For years, DOS came with the ancient and dated GW BASIC program. DOS 5 offers QBASIC, a full-screen, mouse supported, BASIC programming environment and debugger.

Support for Windows (Chapter 27)

Microsoft really likes Windows. DOS 5 really likes Windows. If you elect to run your computer under the Windows environment—or any of the other Extended DOS environments—DOS 5 won't get in your way.

Summary

DOS, and all computer software, appears in various version numbers. A system of major and minor release numbers is used to indicate the version and release of the software.

All software starts with version 1.0. A minor upgrade is labeled version 1.1. Major upgrades, such as the addition of hard drive to support to DOS, is marked by a new major version number, 2.0.

The most popular version of DOS was 3.3, which also survived longer than any other version.

The question of upgrading is an important and often frustrating one. Upgrade only if the new version offers features you need, solves problems you have, or fixes bugs bugging you. For DOS, wait until the industry experts have given their ruling before making the upgrade.

DOS 5 is the first major upgrade to DOS in four years. It offers quite a few new features plus improved memory support. Everyone reading this book should have DOS 5 and be ready to upgrade or install it—a topic which is covered in the next chapter.

CHAPTER 7

Installing DOS

DOS is software. Don't forget that. Even though DOS always runs automatically each time you start your computer, it's still a program just like any other on your computer. And like every other program, DOS needs to be installed. This chapter tells you how.

This chapter answers the following questions:

- How is a hard drive set up?

- How is DOS installed onto a new hard drive?

- How is an older version of DOS upgraded to version 5?

- What does the SETUP program do?

- Can DOS 5 be uninstalled?

Note: DOS 5 may already be installed on your system. Almost every PC sold today will have some version of DOS already on the hard drive. As long as you're certain that it's DOS version 5, you can skip ahead to the next chapter.

Checking Your System

Set up your computer: Attach the monitor, keyboard, printer, and any other device that completes your system. If this is already done, then re-check everything. Make sure all the connections are sound. Also, make sure the thing is plugged in. I'm serious. Double check the plug. You may be surprised.

Remove any disks from your floppy-disk drives. If the computer is new, it may have a cardboard or plastic holder in the drives.

Turn on your computer.

After a few seconds the system will warm up. The monitor may display a message, a copyright notice, or some other information. What happens next depends on how most of your computer has been set up to run DOS.

Note: If you don't have a hard drive (and you really should), it's possible to run DOS 5 and your system off of floppy diskettes. Proceed to the section entitled "Installing DOS."

If nothing happens after two or three minutes, then you need to set up your hard drive and install DOS. Go to the section titled "Hard Drive Setup."

If you see either of the following two messages, or anything resembling them, go to the section titled "Hard Drive Set Up"

```
Non-system disk or disk error
Replace and strike any key when ready
No boot device available
```

If the computer asks for the date ("Enter new date") press the Enter key. When it asks for the time, press the Enter key. Eventually you'll see the DOS prompt, which may look something like this:

```
C>/
```

Type the following:

```
VER
```

Press the Enter key. DOS displays its version number. If you see any number less than 5.00, proceed to the section titled "Upgrading DOS." If you see version 5.00 displayed, move on to the next chapter; you already have DOS 5 installed on your system.

If the computer does anything else, (e.g., you see a "Main Menu" or "Start Programs" or some interesting graphics display,) then you have a shell installed on your computer. Select an option that says "DOS prompt"or "Command prompt" or "Exit to DOS." (Read any information on the screen that may tell you how this is done.) For example if you're in the DOS Shell program, press the F3 key to exit. In Microsoft Windows, press the Alt key and the F4 key together, or use the mouse to close all the windows on the screen. Once you've reached the DOS prompt, type the following:

```
VER
```

Press the Enter key. DOS displays its version number.

```
MS-DOS Version 5.00
```

If you see any number less than 5.00, proceed to the section titled "Upgrading DOS." If you see "Version 5.00" displayed, move on to the next chapter.

Hard Drive Setup

A great majority of the computers sold today come with hard drives. Those hard drives are installed and ready to roll, usually coming with some version of DOS already on them. If your system has a hard drive installed but it hasn't been prepared, here are the steps you should take:

1. Get a professional to set up your hard drive.

Setting up a hard drive isn't hard, but it's complex. Anyone who's done it once can do it a second time, which is how some amateur computer consultants pick up a quick $50. If you have a local computer dealer, chances are they can set up your hard drive and install DOS for less than $50 (more if they wear a nice suit). If you're just starting out, this is the recommended course.

2. Setup your hard drive yourself.

To set up your hard drive for use with DOS 5 you'll need to make sure it's low-level formatted. Most of the more expensive drives will already have this done to them. The cheaper drives may come with instructions on how to do this, or come with special software that lets you perform the low level format.

After the low level format comes the partitioning step. For this, you need to run a program named FDISK. What FDISK does is to prepare the hard drive for DOS plus any other operating systems you may install. (Normally, only DOS is installed.) To work with FDISK, simply select the suggested options; FDISK is great at assuming things. As long as you select your entire hard drive (100 percent) to be used as the primary DOS partition, you'll be in good shape. After running FDISK, you should reset the system.

After running FDISK, you need to do the high level format. This is done by the DOS FORMAT command. For example (and only type this in if you're doing a high level format):

FORMAT C: /S

The above command formats the new hard drive, plus it transfers the DOS boot files that make the hard drive a bootable DOS disk. After formatting is complete, you're ready to proceed with installing DOS.

Note: As an alternative to the above, you can buy a special OEM (Original Equipment Manufacturer) version of DOS that does the hard drive setup for you. Normally only dealers have this version of DOS. So if these instructions leave you in a fog, consider having your dealer setup DOS for you.

Upgrading DOS

Upgrading to DOS 5 is totally automatic—and reversible. Part of the benefit of using DOS 5 is that you can un-install it and easily recover your previous version of DOS.

Requirements

To use DOS 5 on your computer, make sure your system has at least the following minimum requirements:

256K of RAM

A hard drive with at least 4 megabytes of storage available.

DOS version 2.1 or later already installed

Additionally, it helps to know what type of video system you have, the maximum amount of RAM in your system, and whether or not you have any expanded or extended memory. It's okay if you're unsure about these things. The SETUP program that installs DOS is fairly smart.

Upgrading Overview

The SETUP installation program will do the following to update your PC to DOS Version 5:

Perform a full inventory of your system's hardware, displaying the results and allowing you to make changes.

Allow for an optional backup of the entire system.

Modify and update your CONFIG.SYS and AUTOEXEC.BAT files to work with DOS 5. (The originals will be saved.)

Save the original system information on a "Uninstall" diskette.

Place DOS 5's files onto your system, in your DOS directory.

Save your old DOS programs and files in a new subdirectory named OLD_DOS.

The reason for all the backup, Uninstall, and OLD_DOS steps is to give you the chance to change your mind. Normally, that won't be necessary. DOS does so, however, "just in case."

Getting Started

Turn on your computer if it's not already on.

Info: Your PC should boot up using your current version of DOS. Perform whatever steps are necessary to get to the DOS prompt; if you're using Windows or running the DOS Shell or menu program, exit from it. If you can, unload or disable any memory-resident programs.

To proceed with the upgrade, make sure you have one or two floppy diskettes handy. Label the diskettes "Uninstall 1" and "Uninstall 2."

Tip: If you want to do a full backup of your system, you'll need an appropriately sized stack of diskettes. This step is optional, but if you have the time, do it. If you're already using a third-party backup program, then do a full hard-disk backup before the installation. (The SETUP program uses DOS 5's BACKUP.)

Running the SETUP Program

Locate the DOS 5 diskette labeled "Disk 1." Place it into your computer's A drive. Close the drive door.

Type the following at your DOS prompt:

```
A:SETUP
```

Press Enter. If you're installing DOS 5 from your system's B drive, then substitute "B" for "A" above.

After a moment, the DOS 5 installation program, SETUP, will run. SETUP will evaluate your system and then proceed with the installation.

During installation, various text screens will be displayed, informing you of your options. The keys you can press and what they do will be listed at the bottom of the screen. In summary, they are:

ENTER	Continue the installation
F3	Exit to DOS, stop the installation
F1	Display help
Y	Answer a question "Yes"
N	Answer a question "No"
Up Arrow	Move the selection bar up
Down Arrow	Move the selection bar down

Tip: Always read the screens (!)—even if you're an "expert" and don't need to bother with "meaningless text." I personally know of one expert (yes, you Jerry!) who neglected to do so and had to rework the entire installation.

Proceed through installation. Follow the instructions on the screen. In summary, here are the steps you'll go through:

Introduction

Networking question/preparation

Optional hard drive backup

System summary (equipment list)

Note: For this book, make sure the option "Do not run MS-DOS Shell on startup" is selected.

Actual setup; disk swapping.

Tip: Keep your stack of diskettes in order, from Disk 1 through the highest numbered diskette. The SETUP program will ask you to remove and insert each diskette, one at a time. As you remove diskettes, place them face down in a second stack.

You will be asked to insert your UNINSTALL diskette(s) after starting installation. Follow the instructions on the screen; remove the UNINSTALL diskette and re-insert Disk 1 when it tells you to do so.

Completion

When SETUP is done, a message appears on the screen. Remove the final installation diskette from your A drive. Put all the diskettes away in a safe place.

Press Enter to end installation and reset your computer. DOS 5 will then load from your hard drive. The installation process is complete.

If You Need To Uninstall

If you change your mind, you can uninstall DOS 5 and restore your previous version of DOS. This can be done by using the "Uninstall" diskette, created by the DOS 5 SETUP program. Why you would wish to do this is up to you. But if the need arises, do the following:

1. Put the "Uninstall" diskette (or the first Uninstall diskette) into your A drive.

2. Reset the computer; press Ctrl-Alt-Del.

3. As the Uninstall diskette boots, it will run the UNINSTAL program. Follow the instructions on the screen to restore the previous version of DOS.

Tip: The sooner you uninstall DOS 5, the better. Waiting a while lessens the chances that it will be effective. (Of course, the longer you wait, the more you'll like DOS 5.)

As a bit of advice, if you've been using DOS a while consider the following before you think about uninstalling DOS 5:

Use, at once, all your favorite programs, especially those central to your work. Make sure they all function well under DOS 5. If not, contact the manufacturer about any DOS 5 compatibility problems. Follow the manufacturer's advice before you consider uninstalling.

Do not repartition your hard drive before uninstalling. The Uninstall diskette(s) contain information about your hard disk's partitions. Any re-partitioning or re-formatting of the hard drive will make the Uninstall process less successful.

Keep your original copy of DOS in the OLD_DOS subdirectory. If you delete those files, move that subdirectory, or run the DELOLDOS program, you will not be able to recover your original version of DOS by uninstalling.

Follow those steps and an un-installation of DOS 5 is possible. Personally, I don't think you'll want to.

All Done

Once the installation process is complete, you're ready to start using DOS 5.

If you're an advanced user, you may want to take a peek at your AUTOEXEC.BAT and CONFIG.SYS files. Unlike other applications that modify those files upon installation, DOS 5 makes only minor (and important!) changes. Your original files will be saved with the OLD extension, and you can use them under DOS 5 with relatively little problems.

Info: This book will explain what the changes to your AUTOEXEC.BAT and CONFIG.SYS files mean in Chapters 19 and 20.

Summary

DOS 5 is either installed by your dealer before you buy the computer, or it's installed via an upgrade kit for those who are already using DOS.

The name of the installation program is SETUP. It examines your system and installs DOS to work best with the way your PC is already setup.

Information about any previous version of DOS is saved on an Uninstall diskette; the previous version of DOS on disk is stored in a new subdirectory named OLD_DOS. If you want to undo the DOS 5 installation, you simply reset your system, booting from the Uninstall diskette in drive A. Though this is a nice feature to have, you'll probably never do it.

Once DOS 5 is installed, you're ready to start using it. Eventually you may want to delete the older, original version of DOS on your system. This is done using the DELOLDOS command.

CHAPTER 8

Booting DOS

Every day you put on your shoes. If the weather is nice, you may wear sandals. Writers who never leave the house wear fuzzy slippers. And DOS, when it first starts in the morning, puts on its boots. Actually, the process of starting your computer and running DOS is referred to as booting. It has nothing to do with footwear, but since it's the first thing you and DOS do together, it's covered here in this chapter.

This chapter answers the following questions:

- What happens after you flip the power switch on?

- Why does DOS ask for the date and time?

- How does DOS tell you it's ready to work?

- How do you properly turn off a computer?

- What is a warm boot?

- Should you leave your computer on all the time?

Turning It On

Your computer's day starts when you turn on the power switch (your's would too if someone sent 120 volts into your sleeping body). Make sure your computer is all plugged in, setup, and ready to go.

Tip: Make sure your computer is kept in a clean, well-ventilated area. Don't worry about all the cables and connectors; there isn't a computer alive that doesn't suffer from cable pasta salad.

To turn on your computer, follow these general steps:

Turn on all necessary peripherals

Turn on the computer/system unit

Enter the date and time

Start working with DOS

Painless. In fact, you'll be doing this so often you won't even think about it. (Anyone remember the acronym you learned in driver's ed for changing lanes? Me neither.)

Info: Before hard drives were commonplace, you had to insert a special "boot disk" after turning on the computer/system unit. Since DOS is already installed on your computer's hard drive, that step is no longer needed.

The only necessary peripheral at this point is your monitor, which may come on automatically when the system unit is turned on. However, if you were planning on printing or using any other external device, now would be the time to turn on your printer or any other external device.

Believe it or not, there is major debate in the computer world about whether the system unit should be turned on last or first. This is similar to the debate in Gulliver's Travels on whether an egg goes big end or little end down in the egg cup. (But at least no one's started a war over this—yet!)

Personally, I turn my monitor on first. That gives it time to warm up, just like the TV sets of old. Others turn on the computer first, then the monitor.

Tip: If you have an IBM-compatible printer, turn it on before the computer. The computer will send it a special startup instruction if the printer is on.

If the question is really burning, then invest in a power strip or one of the fancier "computer power control centers." Just plug everything into one box and turn it all on with a master switch. My old boss plugged everything into a power strip on the floor and turned on his computer using his big toe (right through the hole in his sock!).

Start your computer now (if it's not already on). Turn on all the peripherals, and then the system unit. You'll hear the fan warble up to power and the hard drive spin up to speed.

Tip: Keep all diskettes out of your floppy drives until you need to use them. If you forget, DOS will attempt to boot from your A drive, which may not be what you want.

Welcome to Your Computer

A brief second after flipping the power switch, your computer will display a message. This is usually a brand name, copyright notice, or some cryptic BIOS version number. Figure 8-1 shows such a message, though what you see on your computer will, doubtless, be different.

```
Phoenix ROM BIOS Version 3.11
Copyright (c) 1984-1990 Phoenix Technologies Ltd.
All Rights Reserved

Mondo Turbo Deluxe 386
```

Figure 8-1. Good morning from your PC!

Some computers may display no message but instead a flashing cursor. Others may add some type of memory scan, which you'll see as one or more numbers rapidly increasing in size.

Then there is a pause. During that time, the computer is performing an inventory of its parts—and the all-important self test. When the test passes, you'll hear a beep. If not, you'll see a message or instruction code on the screen. (Refer to your hardware manual for assistance, or contact your dealer for service if that ever happens.)

After the beep, the computer tries to load DOS from disk. DOS is software, and as such it lives on a disk. The computer knows enough to look for DOS on disk— but that's it. If DOS isn't found, you'll see a message such as:

```
Insert system diskette and press any key.
```

If you have a hard drive, this means DOS isn't installed. Refer to Chapter 6. Or if DOS is installed, then there may be a problem with the hard drive. Panic, then contact your dealer for assistance.

Loading DOS

The computer looks for DOS in two places: First, your computer's A drive, and second, the hard drive.

The A drive is your first floppy drive. DOS looks there first because of tradition. "I must look on drive A first to remind me of the suffering of my pre-hard drive ancestors."

The first version of DOS only worked on floppy-disk PCs; hard drives were rare and not directly supported. Even today, if you just have a floppy-only machine, you must boot by sticking your boot disk into drive A after turning on the computer.

The computer will usually find DOS on your hard drive. DOS is loaded into memory in several steps, which are covered in their full technical glory at the end of this chapter (if you're interested).

Loading DOS is part of your computer's built-in instructions—what's called the BIOS or ROM. Your computer contains a lot of smarts all by itself—otherwise it wouldn't know what to do when you first turn it on. But DOS isn't a part of those smarts. DOS must be loaded from disk.

Enter the Date and Time

Prior to DOS 5, your first encounter with DOS was to enter the date and time. This is traditional: Since the earliest days of microcomputers, the system has always wanted to know the date and time. The PC is no exception. Early PCs lacked a built-in clock. They always assumed it was midnight, January 1st, 1980 each time you started the computer. Nearly every computer sold today, however, comes with a built-in clock. Because of this, DOS 5 no longer asks for the time—unless you tell it to.

Note: Some older PCs may still see the date and time prompts displayed when the computer first starts. If so, check the date and time displayed. If it's current, just press the Enter key when asked for the new date or time. Otherwise, type in the new date and press the Enter key, then type the new time and press the Enter key.

Welcome to DOS

DOS may display more information before the entire boot process is complete. You may see several cryptic messages. One of them may be a DOS copyright message. Whatever, eventually you'll see the DOS prompt. Your screen may look something like Figure 8-2:

Down toward the bottom of your screen locate the last little bit of DOS text displayed. It should look something like this:

```
C:\>
```

That whatchamacallit is the DOS prompt. It's the letter C, a colon, a back slash, and a greater-than sign. The DOS prompt is the place where you'll be entering DOS commands and running your computer's software.

The DOS prompt may also be referred to as the command prompt. It shows you the spot on the screen where you control DOS by entering commands. That subject is covered in the next chapter.

The computer has booted; DOS is loaded and ready for your first command. (It's very obedient.) Congratulations! You've successfully—and effortlessly—booted your computer and started DOS.

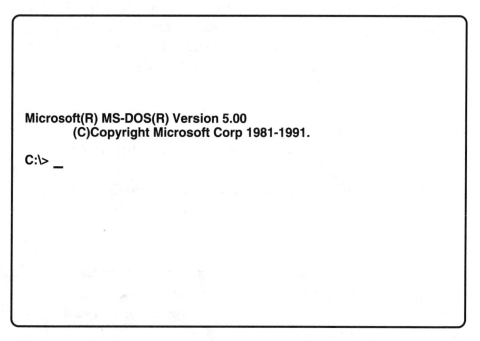

Microsoft(R) MS-DOS(R) Version 5.00
        (C)Copyright Microsoft Corp 1981-1991.

C:\> _

Figure 8-2. DOS's copyright notice and general welcoming information.

Turning It Off

Turning off a computer only poses a problem for heroes of science fiction epics. Who can't recall those times when Mr. Spock dallied while Captain Kirk tried to shut down a computer by reasoning with it? But no matter how good your knowledge of space folklore, nothing beats a big red ON/OFF switch.

Turning off a PC does involve a few steps, plus several rules. First the rules:

Rule: Don't turn off the computer when the disk drive light is on.
Rule: Always turn off the computer when you're at the DOS prompt.

That second rule is important: Try not to turn off the computer when you're in the middle of a program. Most programs have a "quit" function, which returns control of the computer to DOS. After doing so, you'll see the DOS prompt on your screen again. At that time, it's safe to turn the PC off.

Note: There are times when the computer will run amok. (Nothing is perfect.) Only at those times can you wrest control from the computer by turning it off with a drive light on or in the middle of some maniacal program.

To turn off your computer, follow these steps:

1. Quit your application—if you're currently using one. Make sure you're at the DOS prompt.

2. Remove any floppy diskettes from the floppy drives.

This step isn't crucial. The computer won't put bite marks or anything into a disk left in a drive. The problem comes when you turn on the computer again. If a disk is in drive A with the drive door shut, the PC will try to load DOS from that disk. It will be unsuccessful.

If you do remove any diskettes, make sure the drive light is off.

3. Turn off all peripherals first.

Again, there's the argument of "which comes first." But for turning off a computer, I recommend shutting down the peripherals first—unless you have a power strip or control center. In that case, just punch the master OFF button.

4. Turn off the PC.

Flip the big red switch to the OFF position.

If you need to turn the computer on again, wait at least 15 seconds before doing so. This gives the components, especially the disk drives, time to wind down. Flipping a power switch on and off rapidly is the worst thing you can do to a good computer.

Info: Turning a computer on and off is referred to as cycling the power. This is something some beginners do to quit one application and start another. This is not the way the computer was meant to be operated.

Why Turn Off? Just Reset!

There are times when you may want to turn the computer off and on again. If so, you should try a reset, or warm boot, instead.

Turning the computer on is referred to as a cold boot. You're starting the computer cold, like starting a car on a frost-covered morning. A warm boot, on the other hand, is a restart of the computer. With the power on, you press a special combination of keys on the keyboard or a Big Red Reset Switch, and it's almost the same thing as turning the power off and on again.

Your computer is now on and the DOS prompt, "C:\>", is on the screen. Look for the keys labeled Ctrl (for Control), Alt, and Del (for Delete) on your keyboard. Figure 8-3 shows their location for the common, "enhanced 101" keyboard layout.

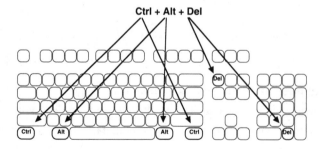

Figure 8-3 The location of the Ctrl, Alt, and Del keys.

Press and hold the Ctrl and Alt keys (only one of each). Traditionally, people use the Ctrl and Alt keys on the left side of the keyboard. Now type the Del key.

Ka-chinka!

Ctrl-Alt-Delete is the "three-finger panic button"—the keyboard's built-in reset switch. After a few moments, your computer will start again, doing the same things described earlier in this chapter. Enter the date and time (if necessary), and soon you'll be at the DOS prompt.

Info: Some computer models have a Big Red Reset Switch on them. Pressing that switch does the same thing as pressing Ctrl-Alt-Delete—with an exception: There are times when Ctrl-Alt-Del will not reset your computer. At those times, the Big Red Reset Switch will. (If your computer lacks a reset switch, then turning it off, waiting 15 seconds, and turning it on again will serve the same purpose.)

As with turning the computer off, you should reset only if you're at the DOS prompt, the drive light isn't on, and there are no disks in the drive. However, there are certain situations where this can't be avoided. (After all, it is a reset switch, not a panic button.)

Keep your computer on and warm for the next chapter. As a suggestion, you may want to earmark this chapter when the time comes to turn off your computer at the end of the day.

Should You Leave it on all the Time?

A debate rages in the computer industry: Should you ever turn off a computer?

Computers like being on all the time. The reason is air conditioning. Inside the computer is a fan (which makes the noise you hear when the computer is on). That fan regulates the temperature inside the PC, keeping everything not-too-hot. When you turn off a computer, it cools. Turn it on again, and it gets warm.

Turning a computer off and on a lot increases the cycling between warm and cold. This will fatigue the computer's innards after a time, leading some of the soldering points to crack and break. The long-term result is a malfunctioning computer after a time.

If you leave the system on all the time, it will last longer. A common saying is "every time you turn the computer off you subtract a day from its life span." Whether or not that's true, we'll never know. My advice is to turn off the computer only if you're going to be away for several days. Even over the weekend, it's okay to leave the system on.

If you do leave your system on all the time, turn off the monitor if you're going to be away for more than a few hours. Leaving a monitor on causes the image displayed to burn into the screen—a peril called "phosphor burn-in." After a time, the same image appears even when the monitor is turned off. (A lot of older, monochrome PCs have a permanent image of Lotus 1-2-3 etched on their screens. No, it's not a Lotus marketing ploy.)

Tip: If you leave your computer on all the time, turn the monitor off while you're away.

The Booting Process: A Technical Description

The process of turning on a computer is called booting and it has nothing to do with kicking the machine.

"Booting" comes from the old phrase, "pulling up your boot straps." For non-boot-wearing folk, boot straps are little loops on the sides of a boot that help you pull the boot on (unlike the "fruit loop" on the back of a dress shirt, which serves no known function other than to annoy awkward teenage boys).

Programmers have applied the term "bootstrapping" to the set of programming routines that start a computer. Therefore, the phrase "boot your computer," could also apply to a reset as well as a power-on.

Booting consists of the following in a DOS computer:

1. The memory test and self test.

2. The disk scan

3. Loading DOS

The memory test and self test are performed to make sure the computer is in working order. Also, the computer will take an inventory of its parts, counting how many serial ports and printer ports its has, the type of monitor hooked up, and so on. If anything is wrong, the computer will display a message, or more often, a cryptic code.

The disk scan is where the computer looks for DOS. This is the first part of the boot process. Programming code inside the computer is designed to look for a disk in drive A and then the hard drive. The computer will take the first 512 bytes of any disk it finds and load that part into memory. That part of disk is called the loader.

The loader is actually a tiny program. On a non-DOS disk, the loader is a program that displays a message saying essentially, "I'm not a DOS disk." On a DOS disk—one that you can use to start the computer—the loader will load a second program into memory. That second program is the DOS BIOS.

The DOS BIOS is basic, bare-bones DOS. This program in turn will look for and load up to three other programs:

1. The DOS Kernel

The kernel is a second, basic set of routines that make up DOS.

2. CONFIG.SYS

CONFIG.SYS is the name of a file that contains information for configuring your system. What can be done with this file is covered in Chapter 19 of this book.

3. The Command Interpreter

The command interpreter is another program DOS uses. Its job is to accept your input and translate those instructions into commands the computer understands. When you started your computer earlier in this chapter, the command interpreter may have displayed DOS's copyright notice and the DOS prompt. An optional program run by the command interpreter is AUTOEXEC.BAT. It's a special type of program file called a batch file. AUTOEXEC.BAT and batch files are covered in Part 4 of this book.

Why go through all these steps? It does seem complicated. But the reason is variety. Your PC can run a number of operating systems besides DOS. There's OS/2, UNIX, XENIX, and other operating systems. Each of them follows the same type of bootstrapping pattern.

Note: DOS 5 does come on a chip, which can be installed into some computers, particularly laptops. When that's the case, DOS is a part of the computer's basic instructions and is never loaded, or bootstrapped, from disk.

These steps describe how your computer starts, but this isn't information you need to memorize to get the most from DOS 5. Later, after you've explored DOS, learned about the files named COMMAND.COM, CONFIG.SYS, and AUTOEXEC.BAT, you may want to return here to review these steps.

Summary

DOS is software on disk. As such, your computer must load it each time you start the system. That process is referred to as booting.

To load DOS and run your computer, first turn on all the necessary peripherals, hen turn on the computer (system unit) itself. It will warm up, display some messages, and eventually display the DOS prompt, which is where you get your work done.

To turn off the computer, quit your application, remove disks from the disk drives, turn off all peripherals, then turn off the system unit. If you need to turn the computer on again, wait at least 15 seconds before doing so.

It's okay to leave the computer on all the time. If you do so, turn off the monitor if you're going to be away for any length of time. This will prevent phosphor burn in.

CHAPTER 9

Using the DOS Prompt

The DOS prompt works like an air-raid siren. Mention it, and normal, well-adjusted humans will run screaming into their closets. The mind freezes. People making massive amounts of money would rather clamp their thumb in a three ring binder than work at a DOS prompt.

The DOS prompt is cryptic; it's text and ugly characters. This causes most people to immediately block out how useful the DOS prompt can be. Instead of seeing a forbidding omen you should view the DOS prompt as the computer saying "Here I am! Tell me what I can do for you?" This chapter will show you how it's done.

This chapter answers the following questions:

- What is the DOS prompt and what does is mean?

- How does the command line work?

- What does the CLS command do?

- What do the DATE and TIME commands do?

- What do the VOL and VER command do?

- What does the HELP command do?

At the DOS Prompt

Start your computer if it isn't already on. (Refer to Chapter 8 for instructions if you have yet to do this.) Enter the date and time, or just press the Enter key if the correct date and time are displayed. Soon you'll be at the DOS prompt.

The DOS prompt is foreboding. True, it's not friendly, or happy, but it's not mysterious either. Figure 9-1 shows the DOS prompt broken down into its individual parts. When you look at it this way, you can see how informative the DOS prompt can be.

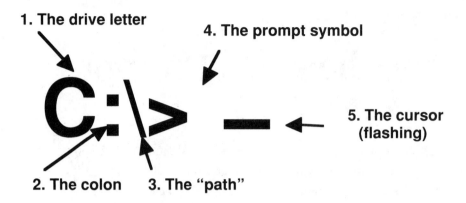

1. The drive letter

4. The prompt symbol

5. The cursor (flashing)

2. The colon   3. The "path"

Figure 9-1 The DOS prompt.

There are five parts to the DOS prompt, three of which are important at this stage in learning about DOS:

The drive letter

The prompt symbol

The flashing cursor

For now, consider the colon and backslash character as being there for effect. What's important in the prompt is the drive letter, the prompt symbol, and the flashing cursor.

The drive letter is how DOS tells you which drive you're currently using. (DOS sees each drive individually.) On your screen you should now see the letter "C," which is DOS's way of saying you're using, or logged onto, drive C. If you saw an "A" in the prompt, it would indicate that you were using drive A. The same holds true for drive B and so on. So the first part of the prompt is useful in that it tells you where you are.

The prompt symbol is a greater-than sign, ">," also called the right angle bracket. The greater-than sign is the traditional computer prompt for input. It implies, "Here is where you are, type something on the keyboard and it will appear, starting at this spot."

Finally, there is the flashing underline—the cursor. Cursor is Latin for "runner," not for someone who curses (though quite a few users do curse their computers). On the screen, the cursor shows you where each character you type will appear. The prompt shows you where you start, but as you type, the cursor will move forward with each character.

The Command Line

If the DOS prompt represents a door, what you type following the prompt is the door's key. Actually, what you type at the DOS prompt are DOS commands, instructions that tell DOS what to do. The whole line of instructions is referred to as the command line.

With the flashing cursor awaiting your input, type the following:

```
I LOVE MY DOS COMPUTER
```

Check your typing carefully. If you make a mistake, use the Backspace key to backup and erase.

Tip: You can type in upper- or lowercase; DOS doesn't mind. This book shows all input as being in uppercase. To type in uppercase on your computer, press the Caps Lock key once.

As you typed, you noticed the cursor moving forward with you. The cursor always indicates where the next character will appear on the screen. Presently it should be positioned after the R ending "computer." That whole line, "I love my DOS computer," is considered a command line. To send that information to DOS, you press the Enter key. Do it now.

```
Bad command or file name
```

Nothing is wrong with this; nothing blew up or has been damaged. DOS is simply telling you (rather rudely) that it didn't understand the command line you sent. (A friendlier message such as "Well, I love you too" would have been nicer.)

After displaying the error message, a second DOS prompt appears. DOS always returns after you execute any command. The prompt is sitting there and the cursor is flashing, awaiting your next command.

This exercise is designed to get you familiar with using the DOS prompt and command line. So far you know the following:

The DOS prompt tells you information about DOS, primarily about the current disk drive. (Other symbols will be explained later.)

The greater-than sign prompts for input.

The cursor shows your position on the screen; as you type, characters appear at the cursor's position and the cursor moves forward.

The command line is text you type at the DOS prompt—a command or instruction for DOS.

Command lines can be typed in upper- or lowercase.

To correct a typing mistake, use the Backspace key. Backspacing moves the cursor back, erasing characters to the left of the cursor.

To send the command line to DOS, press the Enter key.

DOS will either carry out the instructions on the command line or, as you experienced in the example above, display an error message.

After DOS performs its command (or displays an error message), another DOS prompt appears.

Command Line Typing Skills

The biggest complaint people have about DOS is that you must type in commands and what you type must be on the mark. DOS doesn't assume anything. If you make a typing error, even when entering a legitimate command, DOS will respond with a message like "Bad command or filename." Because of this, learning how to type messages to DOS is important.

A second DOS prompt should now be visible on your screen. Press the Enter key:

```
C:\>
C:\>
```

Pressing Enter sends the command line to DOS. But you didn't type a command line. Therefore, DOS did nothing. DOS is saying "Okay, I won't do anything; here's another DOS prompt for when you do decide to type something."

Now press and hold the "I" key. Release it after you see about two dozen or so I's on the screen.

Pressing and holding any key for a period of time activates the computer's typematic feature. The key is repeated for as long as you hold it down. The same applies with the Backspace key. Hold it down to erase all the I's on your screen. Another handy way to erase a line is the Escape key, that is, the key labeled Esc on your keyboard.

Type in the following command line:

```
ARE YOU SMARTER THAN I AM?
```

Check your typing. Use Backspace to backup and correct anything.

Don't bother pressing Enter here. You know what the answer will be. (Don't get excited; DOS doesn't understand "Who is smarter," so it will respond again with "Bad command or filename.") Since you know the answer, do away with the entire line. This can be done by holding down the Backspace key, or by pressing the Esc key. Press Esc now.

You should see something like the following on your screen:

```
C:\>ARE YOU SMARTER THAN I AM?\
    _
```

When you pressed Esc, a backslash appeared at the end of the command line. Then the cursor dropped down to the next line and is flashing under the "A" in "are."

What the Esc key does is to cancel a command line. Essentially the line is erased and you're allowed to start over.

Right now you could enter another DOS command, but instead press Enter. This produces a new DOS prompt and makes the screen look more appropriate for entering another command line.

In summary, there are three important keys you can use at the DOS prompt:

Enter, to send the command line to DOS.

Backspace, to backup and erase.

Esc (Escape), to cancel a command line.

Also, remember that if you send DOS a command line that it doesn't understand the world won't come to an end, nothing will be lost, and the computer won't spew out smoke and sparks. DOS will politely display a message, then you'll see another DOS prompt and be given a chance to repair the situation or start over.

DOS Commands

Typing at the DOS prompt is fun! In fact, nearly every new DOS user delights in flinging a few insults the PC's way via the DOS prompt. The excitement wears thin after the several hundredth "Bad command or filename" message. So instead of dallying, why not use the command line as Microsoft intended?

There are two legitimate things you can type at the DOS prompt—two types of command lines that DOS will understand:

DOS commands

The names of programs

DOS commands are instructions for DOS. These commands are what you'll learn throughout this book. They're usually simple one-word (and often English words!) instructions that tell DOS what to do, how to act, or to carry out some function. You tell DOS what to do, and it does it.

Info: All DOS commands do something, performing some task that's part of the computer's operation. Most commands deal with files—information—stored on disk. Other DOS commands control the way the computer works and acts.

When you type the name of a program at the DOS prompt, DOS will find the corresponding program file on disk, load that file into memory, and then tell the microprocessor to execute the instructions.

DOS commands and program names are the only two things DOS understands as a command line. Sure, you can type other things at the DOS prompt; but the usual result is "Bad command or filename." To be constructive, you need to know a few DOS commands and have a few programs to work with.

The next few sections will introduce you to a few basic DOS commands. This will give you an idea of how the DOS prompt and command line work "for real."

The CLS Command

If you've been typing away at the DOS prompt, the screen is probably fairly cluttered; there are command lines visible, maybe some insults, and various "Bad command or filename" errors.

When you get to the bottom of the screen, the text already on the screen scrolls up; old text moves up and off the top of the screen and new text or blank lines appear on the bottom. If you haven't yet filled the screen, press the Enter key a few times. A new DOS prompt appears each time you press Enter and, eventually, the screen will scroll up.

Info: The Scroll Lock key on your keyboard has nothing to do with the scrolling screen. Actually, come to think of it, the Scroll Lock key isn't used for much of anything on a PC.

If you don't want someone to see what you've been typing—especially if it's littered with error messages—then you can continually press Enter to scroll that stuff off the screen. A better way to do it is to erase the display using DOS's CLS command. Type the following at the DOS prompt:

```
CLS
```

Double check your typing; that's three letters, no quotes, and no period at the end. Remember you can type in upper- or lowercase. Press the Enter key.

Zap! The screen is cleared. All the old text is gone, and a new DOS prompt appears at the top of the screen. It's like DOS has given you a blank page on which to begin anew.

The CLS command is used to clear the screen. CLS stands for Clear the Screen. You type CLS at the DOS prompt, press enter to send the command line to DOS, and DOS says, "Oh, you want me to clear the screen. Here: Voosh!" And it does it. You don't need to use CLS all the time. For example, most people just enter commands lines and DOS keeps scrolling the screen. But when you want to clear the screen, erase sensitive information or embarrassing mistakes, or just start over with a clean screen, CLS comes to your rescue.

CLS is your first DOS command, and possibly the easiest to use. To use it again, type CLS at the DOS prompt and press Enter.

For this, and all other DOS commands mentioned in this book, a corresponding information box will appear:

COMMAND: CLS (Internal)
                    Function: To clear the screen.
                    Format: CLS

After you type CLS, the screen will clear and a new DOS prompt will appear at the top of the display.

This box contains reference information for a command—in this case CLS. The "(Internal)" comment (next to "CLS" in the box) will be explained in a later chapter.

The DATE and TIME Commands

DOS always wants to know the current date and time. You may have been asked to enter the correct date and time when you started the computer. This is really part of PC tradition; today nearly all computers come with built-in clocks that automatically keep track of the time. You only need to enter the correct date or time during daylight savings or if the battery is slow or dies.

DOS has two commands that allow you to change the date or time after the computer has started. They are called, surprisingly, DATE and TIME.

The DATE command displays the current date and gives you a chance to enter a new date. At the DOS prompt, type the following:

```
DATE
```

Check your typing; use the Backspace key to correct any mistakes. When you're certain the command is entered correctly, press the Enter key. You'll see something like the following:

```
Current date is Thu 02-25-1993
Enter new date (mm-dd-yy):
```

The date you see will be the current date, which is either tracked by the computer's internal battery, or which you entered when the computer first booted.

The second line is a prompt, allowing you to enter a new date. If you press Enter, then the date won't be changed and you'll return to another DOS prompt. Otherwise, you can enter a new date in the format listed: mm for the month, dd for the day, and yy for the year. You must enter all three values, each separated by a hyphen, and then press Enter. If you make a mistake, DOS replies "Invalid date" and you get another chance to enter a new date.

For now, press Enter. Another DOS prompt will appear.

The TIME command works just like the DATE command and is exactly the same as the time prompt you see when you start the computer. At the DOS prompt, type the following:

```
TIME
```

Check your typing, then press the Enter key. You'll see something like the following:

```
Current time is 11:21:48.01a Enter new time:
```

As with the DATE command, the time you see will be different. Note that the time is displayed in hours, minutes, seconds and hundredths of seconds. A final "a" or "p" indicates A.M. or P.M.

At the prompt, you can enter a new time or just press the Enter key to return to the DOS prompt. The time is entered in the format HH:MM, where HH is the current hour, MM is the minute, and a colon is sandwiched between them. You don't need to enter seconds or hundredths of seconds (often the computer doesn't need to be that precise). Unless you know military (24-hour) time, follow the MM value with a little "a" or "p" to denote A.M. or P.M. For example, suppose it's 2:05 in the afternoon. You could type the following:

```
2:05p
```

Press Enter, and then at the DOS prompt type the TIME command again. You'll see:

```
Current time is 2:05:01.33p Enter new time:
```

Type the TIME command again:

```
TIME
```

Press Enter. In military time, 2:05 is 14:05. Enter the following at the prompt:

```
14:05
```

Press Enter, and then type the TIME command again. You'll see:

```
Current time is 2:05:01.00p Enter new time:
```

Press Enter to return to the DOS prompt or enter the current time, and then press Enter.

Tip: If you're in a hurry, you can enter a new date or time after typing DATE or TIME at the DOS prompt. For example:

```
DATE 2-25-93
```

The above command changes the current date to February 25, 1993. Also:

```
TIME 2:05p
```

The above command changes the current time to 2:05 in the afternoon.

Change the date on your PC to July 4th, 1995. Type the following at the DOS prompt:

```
DATE 7-4-95
```

Double check your typing. Press the Enter key. (If you enter an incorrect date, DOS displays the "Invalid date" message and a prompt for you to enter the correct date.)

After pressing Enter, another DOS prompt appears. No fuss, no muss. To verify that the date has been changed, type the DATE command again:

```
DATE
```

Press the Enter key. You'll see:

```
Current date is Tue 07-04-1995 Enter new date (mm-dd-yy):
```

Go ahead and enter today's date at the prompt, resetting the computer back to the present. Press Enter.

Perhaps the only drawback to the DATE and TIME commands is that, while they display the current date and time, they always ask for a new one. It would be nice if they just displayed the current date and time, but they don't. So we have to live with being prompted each time DOS tells us the date or time.

COMMAND: DATE (Internal)
                Function: Displays the date/sets a new date
                Format: DATE [mm-dd-yy]

mm-dd-yy is the current month, day, and year, each separated by a hyphen. DOS is aware of the proper number of days in each month. If you enter an incorrect value, the message "Invalid date" is displayed, and you're prompted for the date again.

mm-dd-yy is optional. If not specified, the DATE command will prompt for the current date.

COMMAND: TIME (Internal)
                Function: Displays the time/sets a new time
                Format: TIME [hh:mm:ss][a|p]

hh:mm:ss is the current hour, minute, and second (although you really only need to enter the current hour and minute). If you're not entering the hour in military (24-hour) format, a little "a" or "p" can be used to indicate A.M. or P.M.

hh:mm:ss is optional. If not specified, the TIME command will prompt for the current time.

Note: Several DOS commands have optional information, just as DATE and TIME do. When this is the case, the optional information will be displayed in square brackets, as in the DATE and TIME command boxes.

If a pipe character (|) appears in the brackets, it means "or"; you can use one or the other items in the brackets. For example, [a|p] means that "a" or "p" is optional in the TIME command.

The VER Command

Another simple DOS command is VER, which is short for version. The VER command displays the current DOS version on the screen. Type the following:

```
VER
```

Check your typing. Press the Enter key. You'll see:

```
MS-DOS Version 5.00
```

Other versions of DOS display their own unique version numbers. Since this book is keyed to DOS version 5, you'll see the above (or something close to it).

Why is this a command? After all, you know which DOS you bought for your PC. Nevertheless, the VER command is used when you're on some alien PC. If you've learned DOS 5 and suddenly you find out all your secrets and tricks don't work, type the VER command. Since all versions of DOS look the same superficially, you may surprised to find that the computer is using some older version of DOS.

> COMMAND: VER (Internal)
> Function: Displays the DOS version number
> Format: VER

The VOL Command

VOL is another short and quick DOS command. It's usually lumped with the VER command, more because they both have that nifty V-sound than anything else they share in common. The VOL command displays the name of a disk, also called the disk's label. In more ancient times, disks were called volumes. DOS uses the term "volume" to refer to disks in some of its commands. The VOL command itself displays a name assigned to a disk, as well as the disk's unique serial number.

Type the following at the DOS prompt:

```
VOL
```

Press the Enter key. DOS may display something like this:

```
Volume in drive C is DOS 5
Volume Serial Number is 1621-49A7
```

Your drive C may have a different label. In the example above the volume is labeled "DOS 5". If it doesn't have any label, you'll see:

```
Volume in drive C has no label
Volume Serial Number is 1621-49A7
```

Note that the serial number contains both letters and numbers. This is the unique identification for your disk.

VOL really holds no practical purpose for DOS; the volume name and serial number values are rarely used—if ever. For floppy disks, it's much better to write on one of the labels that comes in the disk box, then peel and stick it on the diskette. But VOL is a good basic DOS practice command.

COMMAND: VOL (Internal)
               Function: Displays a disk's volume label and serial number
               Format: VOL [drive]

Drive is optional, specifying the drive containing the disk you want to examine. If omitted, VOL returns the label and serial number for the current drive.

In the format for the VOL command, note that you can tell DOS which disk drive to examine. DOS can be very specific. If not, DOS always assumes you mean the current drive—the one whose letter is displayed in the DOS prompt. (More information about accessing other drives is covered in Chapter 13.)

Note: Remember that a disk's volume label is in no way related to the sticky label you apply to the disk. The volume label is an electronic code put on the disk; the visible label you write on, peel and stick on the diskette itself.

Getting Help

So far, you've been introduced to five honest-to-goodness DOS commands:

```
CLS—Clears the screen
DATE—Displays/resets the date
```

```
TIME—Displays/resets the time
VER—Displays the DOS version
VOL—Displays a disk's volume name and serial number
```

Here's another handy command to know: Help! Type the following at the DOS prompt:

```
HELP
```

That's four letters, HELP. There is no period or exclamation point at the end (no need to get goofy here—having help with DOS is nice enough). After checking your typing, press the Enter key.

On your screen you'll see a list of every DOS command along with a short description of what it does. Take at look at the screen and locate the CLS and DATE commands. The description tells you what the command does.

Take a second and find the word "More" at the bottom of the screen.

"---More---" is the DOS more prompt. It tells you that there is more information to display, however, DOS is being nice and only showing you a screenful at a time. To see the next screen, press the Spacebar. Do it now.

Tip: The normal "more prompt" instruction given to DOS users is to press any key. But look at your keyboard. There is no ANY key! Instead, whenever a program or manual mentions pressing ANY key, press the Spacebar.

The second screen appears after you press the Spacebar, showing you even more DOS commands and descriptions. Press the Spacebar a few more times until you see a DOS prompt again (but take time to glance at some of the commands; don't worry about memorizing anything). After you've seen the last screen and are sitting at the DOS prompt, take a look at the top of the HELP display. It says:

```
For more information on a specific command,type HELP command
    name.
```

This means if you follow the word HELP with the name of a DOS command, you'll see even more helpful information. Type in the following command line:

```
HELP CLS
```

This command tells DOS to display more helpful information on the CLS command. Check your typing; there's a space between HELP and CLS. Press the Enter key. You'll see:

```
Clears the screen.

CLS
```

Rather blunt, isn't it? The HELP command displays two or more lines for each command; the first is a description, the second is the format of the command—the same as you've been seeing throughout this chapter in the "Command" boxes. Above, the description for CLS is "Clears the screen." The format of the command is just CLS.

Try this again for the DATE and TIME commands. Type the following:

```
HELP DATE
```

Check your typing (remember the space between HELP and DATE) and press the Enter key. You'll see the following:

```
Displays or sets the date.
DATE [date]

TYPE DATE with no parameters to display the current date setting
    and prompt for a new one. Press ENTER to keep the same date.
```

The first line tells you about the command, the second gives the format, and the third describes the format. Granted, it's terse, but it's better than no help at all. In fact, DOS's HELP command is really only of use if you already know the command but maybe forgot how it works or what its options are. Now enter the following line. Let's try to toss DOS a curve and see what happens. (This is all part of your you-can't-blow-up-the-computer training.)

```
HELP BLECH
```

Check your typing—but not too closely. "BLECH" is not a DOS command. It's a nonsense word. Let's see how DOS reacts to it. Press Enter.

```
Help not available for this command.
```

BLECH isn't a DOS command, and DOS lets you know it. In fact, any command DOS isn't familiar with produces the same results. You'll also see the above message if you mistype a command. (And, of course, using the command will produce the now legendary "Bad command or filename" message.)

Tip: The HELP command is a major improvement to DOS, something that didn't exist before DOS version 5. Another improvement is the help option switch. This is an optional item, or parameter, that you can type after a DOS command specifically in order to get help: /?

Type the following at the DOS prompt:

```
CLS /?
```

That's the CLS command followed by a space, a slash, and finally a question mark. (The slash and question mark are both on the same key on your keyboard.) Check your typing. Press the Enter key.

Wow—instant help! DOS displays the same helpful information you saw when you typed the HELP CLS command line. But note that the screen wasn't cleared. Whenever you get help on a command, the command itself will not be executed by DOS; DOS will instead display helpful information.

The /? optional parameter is referred to as a switch. A switch is simply any optional parameter that starts with a slash character. The best thing about the /? switch is that it's available for all DOS commands. Try typing in the following, each at its own DOS prompt and follow each with the Enter key:

```
DATE /?
TIME /?
VER /?
VOL /?
```

So there are two ways to get help on a DOS command:

```
1. HELP command
2. command /?
```

Either way, you'll see the same information. (And, of course, you can always look the command up in this book for even more help.)

Summary

The DOS prompt is where you enter DOS commands. It also tells you which disk drive you're using and prompts you for input.

There are three important keys you can use at the DOS prompt: Enter, to send the command line to DOS; Backspace, to backup and erase; and Esc (Escape), to cancel a command line.

The CLS command is used to clear the screen.

The DATE and TIME commands allow you to view and optionally change the DATE and TIME, respectively.

The VER command displays the DOS version number.

The VOL command displays a disk's electronic label or volume name.

The HELP command is used to display a list of all DOS commands and a description of what they do. If you follow the word HELP with the name of a command, more helpful information about that command is displayed.

Any optional (or required) information after a DOS command is called a parameter; if that information starts with a slash, it's referred to as a switch.

CHAPTER 10

Using the Keyboard

To round out your basic introduction to DOS, here is some information about using the keyboard—your main line of communication to DOS. The keyboard has more buttons on it than anything else on the computer. But it's just the alphabet as well as a few special keys you'll soon master.

There are secrets lurking in your keyboard, stuff that's not that obvious at a glance. This chapter tells you about those secrets and how to use them and clues you in on a few interesting tricks no one else will ever tell you.

This chapter answers the following questions:

- How does the keyboard work?

- Do I need to know how to type?

- What do some of the more unusual keys do?

- What's a control-key combination?

- How can I get something to print?

- How can I pause long displays of text?

- How can I stop a command run amok without resorting to resetting?

Note: To better follow some of the examples in this chapter you may want to hook your computer up to a printer and have the printer ready to print.

Exploring the Territory

Before getting started, a few words about learning how to type:

No, you don't need to learn how to type to use a computer—but it helps! Most computer programmers (and these are the computer geniuses, remember) type with two fingers, hunched over the keyboard, never looking at the screen. It's ugly, but it works.

As an aside, there's the story about a software developer who saw how his programmers were typing. So he stopped work for two weeks while everyone learned how to type. (There is a computer program that does this, which is handy.) Afterwards, he noted that the programmers had increased their output tremendously. So it doesn't hurt to know—or to learn—how to type. Here endeth the lesson.

The Great Key Hunt

Before 1987—the dark ages—PCs came with a variety of weird and wacky keyboards. You'd think IBM, creator of the patented Selectric electric typewriter— the touch typist's friend—would have built a decent keyboard for their PC. But no. Since the PCs first birthday, each computer has had a different, funky keyboard. And important keys kept moving around.

After 1987, the keyboard design stabilized. Nearly all PCs now use the enhanced 101-key keyboard. If yours is not one, locate the following important keys on your own keyboard. Their locations on the enhanced 101-key keyboard are shown in Figure 10-1.

Enter

Esc

Spacebar

Backspace

Backslash, \

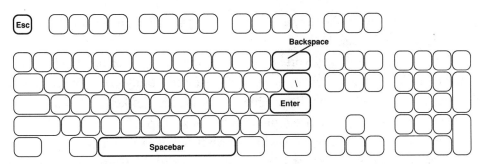

Figure 10-1 The locations of some important keys.

The Enter key appears twice, once on the main typewriter keyboard and again on the numeric keypad. Both keys have the same result; use whichever is handy.

Esc (Escape) is important because many applications use it as their cancel key. Even in DOS, the Esc key cancels a command line, allowing you to start over. Note the position of the Esc key. Some keyboards will place it by the Backspace key.

The Spacebar is good as a general purpose "any" key. If an application says to "press any key" or you're waiting at a "more" prompt (as with the HELP command earlier in the last chapter), press the Spacebar.

The Backspace key is used to back up and erase characters.

The Backslash key seems trivial, but it's important to the way DOS works. This key more than any other, moves around on the various PC keyboards. Figure 10-1 shows its location on the standard enhanced 101-key keyboard. On other keyboards its location will be different.

Keys of State

A state key affects the way the keyboard operates. The typical typewriter has only one state key, the Shift key. When you press and hold the Shift key, the letter keys come out in upper case and the number keys produce symbols. The PC's keyboard has three such state keys:

Shift

Ctrl (Control)

Alt (Alternate)

The Shift key works just like the shift key on a typewriter; press Shift plus a letter to produce an uppercase letter.

The Ctrl, or Control, key works similarly to the Shift key. You press and hold the Ctrl key and then type a letter key or some other key on the keyboard. The end result is a control key combination. For example, pressing the Ctrl key and typing a "C" produces the Control-C character, often abbreviated "Ctrl-C."

The Alt, or Alternate, key works like the Shift and Ctrl keys. Press and hold Alt, and then type a numeric keypad key on the keyboard. The result is an alt key combination: Alt-F1 means to press and hold the Alt key and then press the F1 key.

Unlike Shift keys, the Ctrl and Alt key combinations are used to produce special commands and functions; they normally don't display anything. However, you will often see Ctrl abbreviated using the ^ (carat or hat) character. For example, ^C means Control-C.

Three other state keys exist:

Caps Lock

Num Lock

Scroll Lock

The Caps Lock key works like the Shift Lock key on a typewriter. Press Caps Lock and all the text you type will be in upper case. But, unlike the Shift Lock key, the number keys will not be shifted. On some keyboards, Caps Lock has a corresponding light. When the light is on, the Caps Lock key has been activated. Press it again to turn it off.

Note: If you use the Shift key when Caps Lock is on, the result will be a lowercase letter.

The Num Lock key is used to lock in the keyboard's numeric keypad. Take a close look at the keypad. You'll see two sets of symbols on every key (except for the 5 key): The 2, 4, 6, and 8 keys have arrows on them; the 1, 3, 7, and 9 keys have the words End, Pg Dn, Home, and Pg Up on them, respectively. Those symbols and words identify the cursor movement keys. On the enhanced 101-key keyboard, those same keys are duplicated to the left of the keypad.

The numeric keypad on a PC's keyboard serves two purposes: The first is as the cursor pad, the second is as the numeric keypad. If you want to use the numbers, press the Num Lock key. If you want to use the arrow keys, press Num Lock again. As with the Caps Lock key, some keyboards have a tiny lamp which tells when you Num Lock is on or off. Figure 10-2 shows the two different states of the numeric keypad:

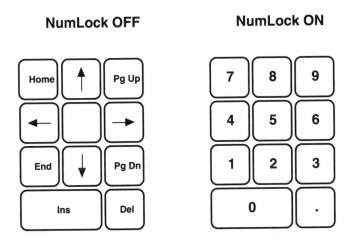

Figure 10-2 How Num Lock affects the numeric keypad.

Finally, there's the Scroll Lock key.

Although Scroll Lock can be on or off, and it may even have its own little light, it doesn't do much. DOS ignores it—most applications ignore it. One of the few kinds of applications that does use the Scroll Lock key is computer games. Even then, the key's function has little to do with the screen scrolling.

Special Keys

Your keyboard has a few special keys that allow you to perform some interesting tricks. The first of these is the Pause key.

The Pause key is used to suspend computer operations; press Pause and everything stops. To continue, press any key (okay, the Spacebar). This key is necessary because information will often scroll on and up the screen before you get a chance to read it. If you're quick with the Pause key, you can read all the text.

Tip: Some older keyboards lack a Pause key. If that's the case, the key combination to press is Ctrl-Num Lock; press and hold the Ctrl key and quickly press the Num Lock key. That produces the same effect as the Pause key.

To test the Pause key, type the HELP command at the DOS prompt. But be ready to hit the Pause key. Type in the following:

```
HELP
```

Press Enter, then quickly press the Pause key. The screen should be frozen, somewhere about halfway through the first page of the HELP command's display (depending on how fast you are with the Pause key). Press the Spacebar to continue.

The second special key is the Print Screen key. This key may be cryptically labeled on your keyboard. Look for a key named "Print Scrn" or "PrtSc" or any combination thereof.

What the Print Screen key does is to send a copy of the text on your screen to the printer. This action has the uncomfortable term screen dump attached to it. (In the olden days, a computer that could produce a screen dump was considered a notch above the rest. Ah, nostalgia...) If you have a printer, make sure it's properly hooked up to the PC and ready to run. Turn the printer on. If it's a laser printer, give it time to warm up.

Tip: If you don't have a printer, or it's not hooked up or turned on, don't press the Print Screen key. With some computers, doing so will cause the computer to wait and wait and wait until you eventually hook up a printer. Other computers are more tolerant and will simply ignore the Print Screen order when a printer isn't hooked up or ready to print.

Press the Print Screen key.

If you have a dot-matrix printer, you'll see all the text on your screen dutifully produced on your printer. If you have a laser printer, the screen dump is inside the printer. To see it, press the Form Feed button on the printer's control panel. (You may have to first press the On Line or the Select button before pressing Form Feed.)

The Print Screen key is a handy way to get a hard copy of what you see on the screen. But it doesn't work miracles! If you're looking at a graphics image, don't expect the Print Screen key to properly render it on your printer. Also, some programs have their own methods of printing, which usually produce results that are much better than those gained by using the Print Screen key. But for a quick screen dump, nothing beats it.

Control-Key Combos

One of the most handy keys you'll find is the Alt key, which is used in many applications to activate certain commands. But DOS ignores the Alt key. Instead, when you're using the DOS, you'll find the Ctrl (control) key has many interesting and surprising uses.

Control-C, or Stop!

The Ctrl key is often used in combination with other keys on the keyboard. Pressing the Ctrl key by itself is a lot like pressing the Shift key on a typewriter; nothing happens. Press the Ctrl key right now on your keyboard. Nothing happens.

Now, press and hold the Ctrl key and type a C.

```
^C
```

You've just pressed the Ctrl-C key, which is DOS's cancel key. Ctrl-C is the mini-panic button. Pressing that key stops DOS from doing whatever it was doing and returns you safe and happy to the DOS prompt.

When typed at the DOS prompt, ^C simply produces another DOS prompt; there's nothing to cancel. Type the following command line:

```
HELP
```

The HELP command, when used by itself, displays four or five screens of DOS commands and descriptions. Press the Enter key.

Suppose the command you wanted help on was the ATTRIB command. Right now, it's there on your screen. You can read its description, but why press the Spacebar four more times to see the rest of the list? Instead, type a Ctrl- C: Press and hold the Ctrl key and type a C.

DOS displays ^C—Control-C—and you're back at the DOS prompt.

In addition to Ctrl-C, the Ctrl-Break key combination works as well. The Break key is often labeled on the front of a key; on the enhanced 101-key keyboard, the Break key is on the front of the Pause key. Pressing Ctrl-Break (actually Ctrl-Pause) cancels a DOS command just like Ctrl-C.

Control-S, or Pause

Another interesting Ctrl key is Ctrl-S. Ctrl-S works exactly like the Pause key; press Ctrl-S and DOS freezes the display. Press the Spacebar to continue. (Refer to the earlier tutorial on the Pause key if you want to practice using Ctrl-S; just substitute the Ctrl-S key combination for Pause and it will work the same.)

Control-P, Printer Echo

Control-P invites a plethora of puns...Ahem...Here, the "P" stands for Printer.

The Ctrl-P key is used to turn on DOS's printer-echo feature. Make sure your printer is connected to the computer and turn the printer on. Then press and hold the Ctrl key and type a "P." Although nothing happens, DOS's printer-echo feature has been activated. Now all text displayed on the screen will also be printed. Press Enter twice.

The DOS prompt re-appears—but it also appears on the printer! (If you have a laser printer, you won't see the DOS prompt until an entire page is printed.)

Let's put the printer-echo feature to good use. Type the following:

```
HELP
```

That's the help command again. Press Enter.

As the commands and descriptions appear on the screen, a duplicate appears on the printer. Keep pressing the Spacebar until every screen is displayed. (After the final screen, press the Form Feed button on your printer.)

Now you have a hard copy of DOS's help list, as well as all of DOS's commands and their descriptions.

Turn printer echo off by typing a Ctrl-P again.

Info: Ctrl-P is what's known as a toggle. That's one key (or switch or command) that both turns something on and later turns it off. Press Ctrl-P once to turn printer echo on, press it again to turn it off.

Press Enter a few times to display a few DOS prompts. If they don't appear on the printer, then you know echo to printer is off.

Control-Alt-Delete

Another interesting Ctrl-key combination is Ctrl-Alt-Del, pronounced Control-Alt-Delete. That's the keyboard reset switch, which was discussed in Chapter 8. Press that combination if you want to reset your computer.

When is a good time to reset your computer? There are actually several times when you're supposed to reset the computer. Sometimes after installing a new program you need to reset. If so, press and hold the Ctrl and Alt keys and then the Del (Delete) key. Other times, your computer may freeze or something may run berserk (it happens). In those rare instances, Ctrl-Alt-Del is often the only way to regain control of the machine.

Interesting Ctrl-key Combos

The ASCII code was discussed in Chapter 5. The first part of the code, the first 32 code numbers, are referred to as control codes. These codes directly correspond to keys you press in combination with the Ctrl key. Some of the control codes are obscure, having no practical use on a computer. But some of them have functions that directly correspond to keys already on your keyboard. Consider the following:

Ctrl key	Keyboard key
Ctrl-H	Backspace
Ctrl-M	Enter
Ctrl-I	Tab
Ctrl-]	Esc

Just as pressing Ctrl-H is the same as pressing the Backspace key, pressing each of the other four control keys corresponds to pressing a keyboard key. Of course, it's easier to type the real keyboard key. But this does give you a chance to see the relationship between some control keys and how other keys on the keyboard work.

Later in this chapter you'll experiment with other Ctrl keys. Few of them have any true DOS function, other than what's been mentioned so far. But it's interesting to use them "for effect."

Command Line Editing

The keyboard tricks discussed in this chapter aren't something you'll use every day, but it's nice to know they're available. One additional keyboard trick, which you can use all the time at the DOS prompt, is command line editing.

Every command line you send to DOS is kept inside the computer's memory, in a special location known as the template. You can recall that command line or edit it in the template, which allows you to reuse a command line with a minimum amount of typing. To demonstrate how this works, try the following stopwatch trick using the TIME command.

Type the following at the DOS prompt:

```
TIME
```

That's the TIME command, which displays the current time. Press Enter once to send the command to DOS.

The current time is displayed and you'll be prompted to enter a new time. Don't bother, just press Enter again. You're now back at the DOS prompt.

To see how fast it took you to enter the TIME command, type the TIME command a second time at the DOS prompt:

```
TIME
```

Press Enter.

Now compare the two times displayed (which will both still be on your screen). On my system the first time was 11:37:20 and the second time displayed was 11:37:41 (it's okay to ignore the hundredths' value—which may only be accurate on a handful of PCs anyway). According to my calculations, it took me 21 seconds to complete the stopwatch test. Your time will probably be faster, because you're not writing a book while you're running the test.

Because the TIME command is now prompting for a new time, press Enter again. You should be at the DOS prompt.

Whenever DOS asks for input, special command line editing keys are available. What these keys allow you to edit is the previous DOS command, which is held in memory in the template.

Press the F1 key once.

```
T
```

Press the F1 key three more times.

```
TIME
```

The F1 key is used to re-display the previous DOS command, one character at a time. But there's more; press the Backspace key four times to erase the TIME command.

```
C:\>
```

The DOS prompt is now sitting there, sans command line ("sans" is French for "without." People think you're smart when you use it, but if you pronounce it, ditch the second "s.") However, the previous command line is still in the template.

Press the right arrow key four times:

TIME

Tip: Both the right arrow key and F1 are used to redisplay the previous command line (stored in the template), one character at a time.

Press Enter now. The TIME command will again be sent to DOS, and you'll see the current time displayed on the screen. Press Enter again to return to the DOS prompt.

Now you know that to re-display a previous command line, you press the F1 or right arrow key. And if you want to enter a new command, or modify the one in the template, you can do that as well. For example, you could press the right arrow key three times to display TIM. Typing "BER" after TIM would create the TIMBER command; press Enter and that command is sent to DOS.

But the best DOS command line editing key—the most popular one—is F3. At the DOS prompt, press the F3 key:

TIME

Info: F3 re-displays the previous command line in one fell swoop.

When you have to use the same command a lot, F3 really helps. Since the TIME command is displayed on the screen, press Enter to see the current time. Press the Enter key again.

Now press F3 and Enter.

Compare the two times displayed. On my screen, the difference is now only three seconds.

Command line editing can boost your speed at the DOS prompt. Even better, DOS 5 comes with a utility named DOSKEY. This program enhances your command line editing abilities to unbelievable heights. DOSKEY is covered later in this book, in Chapter 22.

Summary

Keys that serve special functions in DOS are as follows:

Ctrl-C or Ctrl-Break is used to stop or cancel the current DOS command, returning you to a fresh DOS prompt. Ctrl-S or Pause is used to pause the display; press the Spacebar to continue.

Ctrl-P turns on DOS's printer-echo feature. Make sure your printer is on and ready to print. Type Ctrl-P a second time to turn printer echo off.

Ctrl-Alt-Del is used to reset the computer.

To speed up entering commands, you can use DOS's command line editing keys. These keys help you re-use the previous command line, which DOS keeps in a template. Three of the keys are: F1 and right arrow, which display the previous command one character at a time; and F3, which displays the previous command all at once. Press F3 and Enter to duplicate any previous DOS command.

This marks the end of the learning phase of DOS. Right now you have enough knowledge to forge ahead to some beginning and intermediate DOS topics. Helpful information will always be available in the Info and Note sections if you need assistance.

PART THREE

Using DOS

This section covers the fundamentals of how DOS works. These are the basic concepts and everyday commands every DOS user needs to know. Once we've gone over this ground, you'll be ready to put DOS to work.

Chapter 11 deals with information and files, which are at the heart of your computer and DOS itself. Chapter 12 introduces the MS-DOS Editor, a simple word processor that lets you create notes, memos, and DOS batch files. In chapters 13, 14 and 15, we'll discuss techniques you'll use when storing and manipulating files on disk. Finally, Chapter 16 covers the DOS Shell program, which provides an easy-to-use interface between you and your computer.

CHAPTER 11

Information and Files

We live in the "information age." With computers, you can store and manipulate information. It's still up to you to create or gather the information, and to interpret the results. But the computer and DOS make it easy to store and manipulate vast quantities of information.

This chapter answers the following questions:

- How does DOS keep track of information on disk?

- How can I see a list of the files on my computer?

- What are the rules for naming a file?

- How can a filename reflect the file's contents?

- How can I display a file's contents?

Storing Information

Inside a computer, information is represented by bytes. The computer's microprocessor manipulates the bytes—storing, sorting, and sifting through them as you and your software direct it. At your command, DOS transfers information from its memory to a file on disk.

Info: A file can contain any information. There are actually different types of files—ASCII text, formatted text, and program files—that store different types of information. This subject will come up again when we discuss files in detail.

Erase the idea of bits and bytes from your head for a second. Instead, think of a file as a collection of information. A file could contain text for a memo, a letter, or a report, or the first chapter in your Great American Novel. A file might include a list of employees, customers, or creditors, or it might itemize your mollusk collection. This month's budget, your company's general ledger, or a portfolio of Depression-era stocks counts as information that can be stored in a file. Pictures of interesting primates, your church newsletter, even your all-time high scores from the company bowling league can also be stored in a file.

DOS is in charge of all this information. It takes the information (in the form of bytes) from RAM and carefully stores it on disk, marking its location so that nothing else interferes with it. Later, DOS can retrieve the same information, loading it back into memory so you can work with the file again.

Files can also come from sources besides RAM. When you buy software, it comes on one or more disks that contain files; DOS copies those files to your hard drive when you install the program. You can transfer files from one PC to another using floppy disks. If you own a modem, you can dial up national on-line services or hook up to a remote computer or bulletin board system (BBS). Once you've made the connection, you can download program and data files to your own computer as fast as your modem will allow.

Just about anything can be a file! To use an office metaphor, a file contains information just as a folder contains a sheaf of papers; your disk is like a filing cabinet filled with drawers (directories) and DOS is the faithful file manager. Of course, this all happens electronically inside the computer. The only way you can see a list of your files, look at their contents, or use them is by asking DOS the proper questions.

The DIR Command

A disk may contain hundreds or even thousands of files, but you'll never see one. The files and filenames are recorded magnetically on the disk by the electronic components in the disk drive. Trying to find a file with your eyes is like trying to listen to a CD by placing it against your ear; it can't be done. But DOS can tell you which files are on a disk. To see a file listing, you use the DIR command.

DIR is short for directory. On each disk, DOS reserves space for a record of all the files on the disk. Think of the directory you typically find near the elevator in a large office building. That directory includes a list of the building's occupants, along with their floors and suite numbers. The DOS directory works in the same way: It tells you the file's name, where on the disk the file begins, its size (in bytes), and the date and time it was stored on disk.

To see a list of files on disk, type the following command:

```
DIR
```

Press Enter.

You should see a list of files, along with some disk information. If the current directory contains a large number of files, the beginning of the list may scroll right off the screen. The exact contents of this directory listing will be unique to your computer. Figure 11-1 shows an example of what the DIR command might display:

Volume in drive C is DOS 5
Volume Serial Number is 1621-49A7
Directory of C:

DOS   <DIR>   10-19-90 5:47a
AUTOEXEC BAT   501 02-24-93 10:53a
CONFIG SYS   64 02-24-93 11:04a
COMMAND COM   46246 05-01-91 12:00p
**   4 file(s)   46811 bytes**
**   16140288 bytes free**

C:\>

Figure 11-1. Typical output from the DIR command.

There's a lot of information in a directory listing, but don't let it intimidate you. Everything is organized into neat rows and columns. With a bit of practice, you'll be able to sift through the display quite easily.

The directory listing on your screen consists of the following information:

General information about the disk

Information about the files on disk

The file's name, size, date, and time

Let's tackle these one at a time.

Disk information

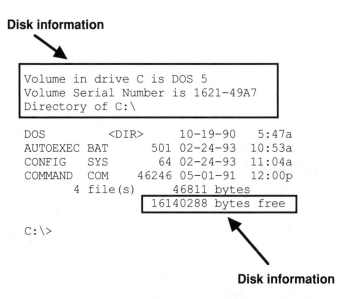

```
Volume in drive C is DOS 5
Volume Serial Number is 1621-49A7
Directory of C:\

DOS          <DIR>        10-19-90    5:47a
AUTOEXEC BAT        501 02-24-93   10:53a
CONFIG   SYS         64 02-24-93   11:04a
COMMAND  COM      46246 05-01-91   12:00p
        4 file(s)        46811 bytes
                     16140288 bytes free

C:\>
```

Disk information

Figure 11-2. Disk information in a directory listing.

In the output of the DIR command, the first three lines and the last line of the resulting display provide disk information.

The first line gives you information about the current volume—just like the VOL command (see Chapter 9). In the example shown in Figure 11-2, the current drive is C: and the volume name is DOS 5. The second line tells you the disk's serial number—again, just as the VOL command does. Together, the first two lines simply identify the disk drive you're examining; no file information is listed.

The third line tells you where the files are located on the disk. In Figure 11-2 the third line reads "Directory of C:\". The backslash (\) tells you that the files are located in the root directory. "C:" is the drive letter. (The colon is used by DOS to identify C as a disk drive.)

Info: Since hard drives can store so much information, they're usually divided into separate subdirectories. The subject of subdirectories and the root directory is covered in Chapter 14.

The final line of the display—"16140228 bytes free"—tells you the amount of storage space still available on the entire disk. In this case, about 16 megabytes is free. If this drive had a total storage capacity of 40 megabytes, you could assume that some 24 megabytes were currently filled.

Info: It's a good idea to check the amount of free space on your hard disk regularly, using the DIR or CHKDSK command. If that number gets too small, you may have trouble saving an important file. When necessary, you can delete some old files or archive them to floppy disks.

All of this information about your disk is nice, but it's really just an added benefit. The real purpose of the DIR command is to list the files on a disk. This essential information is contained in the central part of the directory listing.

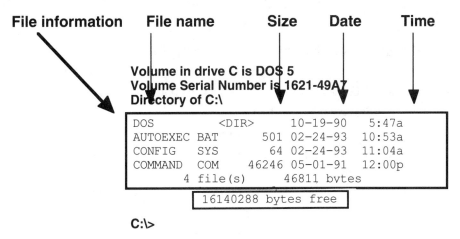

Figure 11-3. File information in a directory listing.

The sample directory listing shown in Figure 11-3 is typical. Four columns of information describe the files: From left to right, they show the file's name, the size of the file, and the date and time the file was last saved to disk.

As you can see from the listing in Figure 11-3, a DOS filename actually has two parts. The name itself can be up to eight characters long, while the optional extension can be up to three characters long. When you refer to the filename, you'll typically include both parts of the name. In the directory listing, however, names and extensions are shown in separate columns.

The next column tells you the file's size in bytes. In Figure 11-3, the word DOS appears in the same column as the other filenames, but the entry doesn't include a size. Instead, the word "<DIR>" is displayed. In this case, the directory listing identifies a special storage area on disk called a subdirectory. Although they're not at all like the program and data files you're used to, subdirectories are an essential part of the DOS filing system. That's why DOS displays their names in the directory listing. (For more information on subdirectories, see Chapter 14)

The final two columns tell you when the file was last saved. DOS reads the PC's system clock and stamps the file with the current date and time when the file is first created. Every time you modify the file and save it to disk again, these settings are updated.

Info: The date and time stamps on your files are only as accurate as your system's clock. It's a good idea to check the internal clock every so often to make sure it's keeping accurate time. If you notice that a recently created file is stamped 1-1-80, your PC's internal battery is probably dead.

The last line of the directory listing, following the file information, gives you a summary of the files listed and their total size. In the example shown in Figure 11-3, there are four files listed, with a combined size of 46,811 bytes.

Now take another look at the DIR command's output on your screen. See if you can identify the following:

The disk's volume label and serial number.

The number of files displayed.

The total number of bytes available on the disk.

The names of the files displayed.

Any files that are subdirectories (denoted by "<DIR>" in the size column).

The smallest file displayed.

The oldest file displayed.

The most important item shown is the name of each file. The name helps you to identify the file's contents and can tell you how the file is used.

Note: Normally, a command box would appear here, detailing the DIR command. So far, though, we've only scratched the surface of what DIR can do. The full format of the DIR command, with all its options, is shown in Chapter 17, as well as in the Reference section.

All About Filenames

Imagine what a nightmare it would be to use a computer in which files were identified only by code number. Think how frustrating it would be if you had to tell the computer how to find a file using an address scheme more complicated than ZIP+4. Fortunately, the developers of DOS decided to identify files using simple names. But there's a catch...

Let's say you've created a file that contains your monthly budget. Wouldn't it be nice to name the file "Monthly budget"? After all, that accurately describes the information in the file. Unfortunately, DOS isn't that convenient. There are rules for naming files and, as we'll see, creating descriptive filenames that follow the rules can be a challenge.

Info: File naming rules

1. DOS filenames are limited to a maximum of 11 characters, arranged in an 8-dot-3 pattern—i.e., up to 8 characters for the filename, followed by an optional period (the dot), and up to three characters for the filename's extension.

2. Filenames may contain any letter of the alphabet (A–Z), numbers (0–9), or the following symbols:

' ~ ! @ # $ % ^ & ( ) - _ { } '

DOS does not distinguish between lowercase and uppercase letters when you specify a filename; in directory listings and other displays, DOS shows all filenames in upper case.

3. A filename may not contain any of the following characters:

" / \ [ ] : * | < > + = ; , ?

The period character is also forbidden, except where it is required to separate a filename from its extension. Spaces are prohibited as well.

The following are filenames you may see in a directory listing:

```
123      EXE
AUTOEXEC BAT
COMMAND  COM
READ     ME
TEST
WIN      COM
```

These six files all follow the DOS rules. Each has up to eight characters as the filename, plus up to three characters for the optional extension. Note that a filename can (legally) have fewer than eight characters; in addition, an allowable filename can have an extension with fewer than three characters, or it may have no extension at all. Also, the format of the directory listing differs from the format you would use when typing the filename as part of a DOS command—the directory listing omits the dot between a file's name and its extension and it pads the area between the two with spaces.

The following table shows how the same six filenames would appear in a DOS display and how you would type them as part of a DOS command.

Filename Displayed	Filename on the Command Line
123 EXE	123.EXE
AUTOEXEC BAT	AUTOEXEC.BAT
COMMAND COM	COMMAND.COM
READ ME	READ.ME
TEST	TEST
WIN COM	WIN.COM

The dot is required only when a filename has an extension. If the filename has no extension, there's no need to type the dot, as with the file named TEST above.

Info: There are times when you should specify the dot after a filename, particularly in applications that assume a filename extension. For example, to load the file TEST above into Microsoft Word, you need to specify the period, indicating that the file has no extension.

Tip: With the DIR command, if you type the filename and a period, DIR will match all files with that same name and any extension.

Testing Your Filename I.Q.

Ideally, a filename should tell you what's in the file. (Remember, the DIR command simply lists the names, sizes, and date/time stamps of your files; it doesn't tell you what's in them or even what application they're associated with.) Before you can devise a useful file-naming system, however, you need to become familiar with the rules.

The following are all valid names for files:

A	A filename can be one character long.
MUSIC	"Music" gives a description of the file's contents.
TESTFILE	An eight-character filename, no extension.
NEW_FILE	The underline character is permitted.
B.1	A one-character filename with a one-character extension—perfectly legal.
5-9-92	Filenames can contain numbers (they can even start with a number) and the hyphen character.
READ.ME	A file that someone wants you to read.
READ.ME!	A file that someone wants you to read right now.
TEMP.$$$	The dollar sign is a valid character.

The following are not valid filenames. See if you can figure out why before looking at the reason:

STATEMENTS	This filename is too long.
"QUOTES"	Double quotation marks are not an acceptable character.
I.LOVE.YOU	There are too many periods in this name; a filename may have only one extension with a maximum of three characters.
MY DIARY	This filename contains a space—no good.
.TXT	The minimum size for a filename is one character.
ED.COM.	An extension must not be followed by a period.

File Naming Smarts

Even within the limitations of the 8-dot-3 format, it's possible to come up with interesting and informative filenames. Generally speaking, it's a good idea to follow two general rules:

Use the filename to describe the contents of the file.

Use the file extension to define the file's type.

Using extensions consistently can help you make sense of even the most crowded file listings. DOS itself uses extensions to identify certain types of files. For example, program files (those that contain instructions telling the computer to do something) end in one of three extensions: COM, EXE, or BAT.

COM is the extension for a command file, EXE for an executable file. Both types of files contain instructions for the microprocessor, with COM files typically being smaller than EXE files. The BAT extension is used with batch files—ordinary text files that contain DOS commands and instructions. (Batch files are covered throughout this book, starting with Chapter 18.)

While all programs will have either a COM, EXE, or BAT extension, the filenames themselves will be different. For example, the following files could be programs on your computer:

WP.EXE	A word processor
DB.EXE	A data base
TALK.COM	A communications program
CAPNZOOM.COM	A game

Each name reflects what the program does: WP for a word processor; DB for a database manager; TALK for a communications program; CAPNZOOM for a game, probably called Captain Zoom. (See how the eight-character filename is used to truncate a longer name?)

In naming and creating your own files, you can use similar schemes. A popular one is to associate all files with a specific program by using the extension. For example, the default extension for Microsoft Word documents is DOC. If you were writing a book like this one, you might name your files INTRO.DOC, CHAP01.DOC, CHAP02.DOC, and so on.

When you create a worksheet in Lotus 1-2-3, the program adds a WK1 extension to the file (some versions of the program use WKS or WK3). If you're putting together budgets for July, you might name your files BUDGET.WK1, JULY.WK1, 07BUDGET.WK1, 07-93.WK1, etc.

Using the same extensions consistently helps you see at a glance which files belong to which programs. Some applications insist on certain extensions; others let you create and assign your own filenames. As you gain more experience with DOS, you'll no doubt develop your own scheme.

Just for fun, I've assembled the following list of filename extensions. Nothing is etched in stone here; these are simply extensions that various software developers have chosen for use with various applications. The only extensions reserved by DOS are the COM, EXE, and BAT endings used by programs.

Extension	Meaning
ARC	Archive file (used by a number of data-compression programs)
ASM	Assembly language source code (text file)
BAK, BK!	Backup file
BIN	Binary image file
BMP	Windows' bit-map graphics format
C	C language source code (text)
CAL	SuperCALC spreadsheet data file
CFG	Configuration file
DAT	Data file
DB	Paradox database file
DBF	dBASE database file
DEF	Definition file

DIF	Data Interchange Format file, used for transferring information between otherwise-incompatible spreadsheets and databases
DLL	Microsoft Windows Dynamic Link Library
DOC	Text file containing documentation or Microsoft Word document
DRV	Driver file
FON, FNT	Font file
GIF	Graphic Interchange Format file
HLP	Help file
INI	Microsoft Windows initialization file
LIB	Library file
MNU	Microsoft Mouse menu file
NDX, MDX	dBASE index file
OVL, OVR	Overlay file
PCX	PC Paintbrush graphics file
PIC	Lotus 1-2-3 graphic file
PIF	Microsoft Windows Program Information File
PM3, PM4	PageMaker document
PRG	dBASE program file
PT3, PT4	PageMaker template file
RBF	R:base database file
SET	Lotus 1-2-3 configuration file
SYS	DOS device driver
TFF	TIFF formatted graphics file (Tagged Image File Format)
TXT	Text file
TMP	Temporary file
WKS, WK1, WK3	Lotus 1-2-3 spreadsheet
WPM	WordPerfect macro
WRI	Windows Write document
XLS	Microsoft Excel spreadsheet (other Excel extensions are XLA, XLC, XLM, XLW)
ZIP	PKZIP compressed file

The TYPE Command

While the DIR command shows you a list of the files on a disk, the TYPE command actually lets you view the contents of those files. But TYPE isn't particularly smart. It works best only on plain ASCII text files (see Chapter 5 for a detailed discussion of text files). While it will try to display the contents of any file on disk, only text files will be consistently readable.

The TYPE command is the first DOS command introduced in this book that requires a parameter; after the TYPE command you must supply the name of the file you want DOS to display. For example, type the following at the DOS prompt:

```
TYPE CONFIG.SYS
```

This command displays the DOS system configuration file, CONFIG.SYS (covered in Chapter 19). All DOS 5 computers should have a CONFIG.SYS file, created and saved as an ASCII text file, and the above command will display (or type) it on the screen.

Press Enter. You'll see the contents of your CONFIG.SYS file displayed. The contents will vary, but they may look something like the following:

```
DEVICE=C:\DOS\HIMEM.SYS
DOS=HIGH
FILES=10
SHELL=C:\DOS\COMMAND.COM C:\DOS\ /p
STACKS=0,0
```

If you're new to DOS, this file's contents will likely be nearly inscrutable, but at least it will be readable. The fact that the CONFIG.SYS file contains plain ASCII text makes it ideal for use with the TYPE command. A data file or a program file, on the other hand, looks like gibberish on the screen. At the DOS prompt, enter the following command line:

```
TYPE COMMAND.COM
```

The file COMMAND.COM is a program file (It ends with the COM extension, which tells both you and DOS it's a program file.) COMMAND.COM contains no readable text. To prove it, press Enter.

Beep! Perhaps the resulting muddle of symbols means something in some language somewhere, but it's all Greek to me!

The TYPE command is diligent. You told DOS to display the contents of COMMAND.COM and it did so. What you see on your screen is the computer's visual representation of that file. Those are commands for the microprocessor, not text you can read.

You can also type the AUTOEXEC.BAT file. Remember, although filenames with the BAT extension are program files, they contain readable text. Enter the following at the DOS prompt:

```
TYPE AUTOEXEC.BAT
```

Press Enter. The contents of your AUTOEXEC.BAT file will display on your screen.

What happens when you issue the TYPE command without specifying a filename? Let's try it and see. Enter the following:

```
TYPE
```

That's the TYPE command by itself. Press Enter and you'll see:

```
Required parameter missing
```

That error message is DOS's way of telling you there needs to be more information for the command to work; something was required and you didn't type it. When you forget any part of a command, remember how to get help:

```
HELP TYPE
TYPE /?
```

These are the two commands for getting help with the TYPE command. (Refer to Chapter 9 for more information on the HELP command.) Both display:

```
Displays the contents of a text file.
TYPE [drive:][path]filename
```

As long as we're experimenting, what happens if you try to display a nonexistent file? Type the following:

```
TYPE NONSENSE
```

Press Enter. DOS responds:

```
File not found - NONSENSE
```

Next to "Bad command or file name," the most common DOS error message is "File not found." In this case, the file you entered doesn't exist. More often, "File not found" appears when you've mistyped a filename. DOS is persnickety. You must enter a filename exactly (although you can use upper- or lower-case letters).

COMMAND: TYPE (Internal)
                Function: Displays a file's contents.
                Syntax: TYPE filename
                                Filename is the name of a file to display.

The TYPE command displays any file you specify with a filename. It is most useful for displaying ASCII text files.

Summary

DOS stores information in files on disk. The most common file types are plain (ASCII) text, formatted text, data files, and program files, which contain instructions for the computer's microprocessor.

The DIR command displays general information about the disk and lists the files in the specified directory. For each file in the directory listing, DOS provides its name, size, and the date and time it was saved.

A DOS filename may consist of no more than 11 letters in an 8-dot-3 format: up to eight characters for the filename, followed by an extension of no more than three characters. A dot or period separates the filename and the extension. Any alphanumeric character can be used in a filename, as can a number of symbols. The following symbols may not be used in a DOS filename:

" / \ [ ] : * | < > + = ; , ? .

The TYPE command displays a file's contents. The TYPE command must be followed by the name of the file to be displayed. While TYPE will display any file on disk, only ASCII text files will be consistently readable. DOS will attempt to display other files, but the results will be unpredictable.

CHAPTER 12

Using the MS-DOS Editor

The MS-DOS Editor is an advanced tool that's built right into DOS. Not really a DOS command, the Editor is actually a remarkably complete program that lets you create and edit text files. It is most useful for creating notes, memos, or short documents, as well as for dealing with the many text files DOS uses.

This chapter answers the following questions:

- How do you start the Editor?

- With what types of files does the Editor work?

- How can text be changed?

- Which mouse and keyboard shortcuts are available in the Editor?

- How are the Editor's menus used?

- How do you load, save, print, and quit a file?

Welcome to the Editor

Sooner or later, everyone who works with a PC needs a simple editor to create and edit text files. On the surface, a text editor resembles a word processor minus the fancy formatting and page layout features, spell checkers, and other bells and whistles that you pay real money for.

Given its power and ease of use, the Editor could really be packaged and sold as a separate program. Similar text editors sell for between $20 and $200, but the MS-DOS Editor is built right into the operating system.

There's nothing remarkable about DOS coming with a text editor. Since the very first version, DOS has had a text editor: EDLIN. EDLIN is short for "line editor," and like its name, the utility was downright backward—ugly and awkward to use. Its one saving grace? Because every version of DOS (even DOS 5) includes EDLIN, you can count on having a common text editor on any PC.

EDLIN is painful to use. Nearly all DOS books include an obligatory chapter on it, but only the most dedicated DOS users ever master it. Thankfully, DOS 5 makes EDLIN irrelevant by providing the MS-DOS Editor.

Learning the Editor

The MS-DOS Editor lets you create and edit text files. These might be notes to yourself, memos, or letters. You could even use the Editor to write the Great American Novel that's burning within you (although a real word processor would be a better tool). The real purpose of the Editor, however, is to work with the many text files that DOS itself uses. The Editor makes it easy to modify those files, allowing you to control the way DOS behaves.

Info: All DOS's batch program files can be created or changed using the Editor. You'll be doing that starting with Chapter 18.

If you have experience using other MS-DOS applications, you may already be familiar with the basics of the Editor. There's no hard-and-fast strategy that you should follow when learning to use the Editor. If you're the hands-on type, you may want to just dive in: Start up the Editor, create and edit a simple file, save it to disk, print it, and exit to DOS. More conservative types may prefer to preview the program by first reading the manual. But the DOS manual itself has no tutorial instructions in it, so you've come to the right place.

Running the Editor

At the DOS prompt, you'll recall, you can enter a DOS command or the name of a program. True, EDIT is a DOS command, but it's not one of the internal commands built into DOS; the Editor is an external command, which is simply a DOS command that is contained in a separate program file in the DOS directory. The name of the MS-DOS Editor is EDIT.COM; to run the Editor, therefore, type the following at the DOS prompt:

```
EDIT
```

(There's no need to enter the COM extension; DOS knows to look for it.) Press Enter. The Editor's startup screen is shown in Figure 12-1.

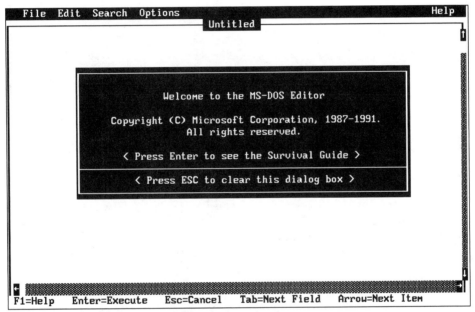

Figure 12-1. The Editor's startup screen.

Press the Esc key. This erases the dialog box from the screen and puts you right into the Editor. (If you press Enter, you'll see the Editor's "Survival Guide," which gives you hints for using the Editor. You'll do that later in this chapter.)

You should be staring at a screen that looks like Figure 12-2. This is every writer's nightmare—the dreaded blank page. Rather than suffer from writer's block, stop to take a moment to get familiar with the territory. The major elements of the Editor screen are labeled in Figure 12-2 and discussed below. For now, just note the location of each of these six items. As you use the Editor, each element's purpose will become apparent.

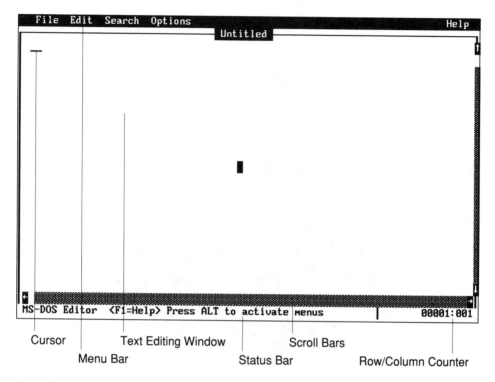

Figure 12-2 The Editor's editing screen.

The menu bar

Along the top of the screen is a menu bar containing five selections: File, Edit, Search, Options, and Help (to the right). Each of these selections contains a menu of commands that direct the Editor to do something. You can use the keyboard or a mouse to pull down the menus and select individual commands.

The text-editing window

The large blank space below the menu bar is the text-editing window. The name of the document currently open appears in the top center of the window; if no document is open, this label reads "Untitled."

The cursor

In the upper left-hand corner of the text-editing window is the flashing cursor. Just like the DOS prompt, it shows you where text will appear as you type. If you're using a mouse, you will also see the block-shaped selection cursor. As you move the mouse along your desktop or mouse pad, you'll see the selection cursor move. You can use the mouse to position the cursor by pointing and clicking in the text-editing window. To select a menu item, position the selection cursor over the item and click the left mouse button.

The scroll bars

Running along the bottom and the right-hand side of the text editing window are scroll bars. These are devices or "gadgets" that let you use the mouse to move quickly through large text files.

The status bar

At the bottom of the window (the last line below the bottom scroll bar) is the status bar. It states the name of the program, tells you that the F1 key can be used to get help, and informs you that the Alt key activates the menus at the top of the screen.

Tip: The F1 key displays helpful information. It lets you quickly look up keyboard shortcuts and command-line options or review the basics of menus and dialog boxes. The Help function is context-sensitive—if you press F1 when a pull-down menu is selected or a dialog box is open, you'll get detailed, specific help about the operation you're trying to perform.

The row/column counter

At the extreme right of the status bar are two numbers separated by a colon. These values tell you the row and column position of the cursor, which gives you an idea of where you are within a document. When you first start a new document, the counter reads "00001:001," meaning you're in the first column of the first line. (If Num Lock or Caps Lock is on, you'll see the letter N or C to the left of this value.)

Getting Help

When you first start the Editor, it asks if you want to view the Survival Guide. Normally, you'll press the Esc key to get right to work. Pressing the Enter key, however, displays a screen full of tips and other valuable information about using the Editor.

You can access the Survival Guide at any time within the Editor. Make sure no dialog boxes are open or menu items selected and press the F1 key.

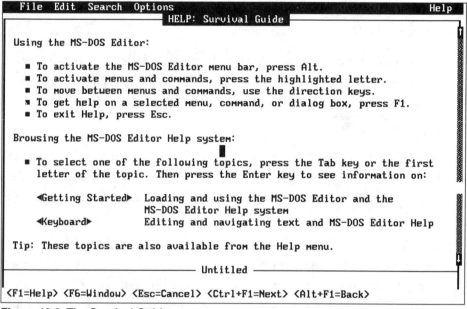

```
 File  Edit  Search  Options                                   Help
                    HELP: Survival Guide

Using the MS-DOS Editor:

  ■ To activate the MS-DOS Editor menu bar, press Alt.
  ■ To activate menus and commands, press the highlighted letter.
  ■ To move between menus and commands, use the direction keys.
  ▪ To get help on a selected menu, command, or dialog box, press F1.
  ■ To exit Help, press Esc.

Browsing the MS-DOS Editor Help system:

  ■ To select one of the following topics, press the Tab key or the first
    letter of the topic. Then press the Enter key to see information on:

    ◄Getting Started►  Loading and using the MS-DOS Editor and the
                       MS-DOS Editor Help system
    ◄Keyboard►         Editing and navigating text and MS-DOS Editor Help

Tip: These topics are also available from the Help menu.

 ─────────────────────────── Untitled ───────────────────────────

<F1=Help> <F6=Window> <Esc=Cancel> <Ctrl+F1=Next> <Alt+F1=Back>
```

Figure 12-3. The Survival Guide.

Editor's text-editing window splits, as shown in Figure 12-3. The text window shrinks and moves to the bottom of the screen. The top of the screen fills with the Help window, containing some tips and a summary of how to use the Help system.

Within the Help system, you can move around using the following keys:

Tab   Move to the next Help topic.

Enter   Select the highlighted Help topic, displaying additional information.

Esc   Cancel Help, return to the Editor

Up   Scroll upward through the text displayed

Down   Scroll downward through the text displayed

If you have a mouse, you can point to an item with the selection cursor and click on it to see more information. To move the text display in the editing window, point to the scroll box (the dark box in the middle of the scroll bar), hold down the left mouse button, and drag the scroll box up and down in the scroll bar.

Make sure the cursor is sitting under Getting Started. Press Enter.

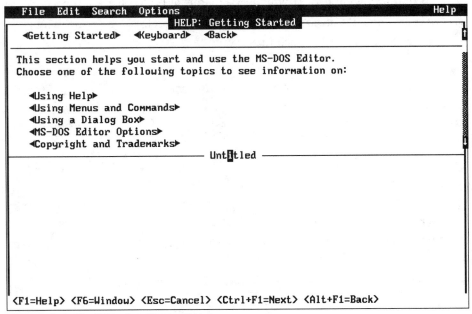

Figure 12-4. The "Getting Started" Help screen.

Your screen should look like the one in Figure 12-4. At the top of the screen are three choices: "Getting Started" is not a choice, because you're already looking at this screen; "Keyboard" uncovers a new Help menu offering details about the various keyboard shortcuts available; "Back" always returns you to the previous screen.

Take a second to explore the Help system, pressing the Tab and Enter keys (or using the mouse) to move through the available options. Be sure to look at Using Menus and Commands and Using a Dialog Box.

When you're done exploring, press Esc to return to the Editor.

Working with Text

When you use the MS-DOS Editor, anything you type appears in the text-editing window, with characters appearing at the cursor's position just like a typewriter. The commands, the editing tools and other tricks the Editor does are accessed by using special Ctrl and Alt key combinations.

Type the following text. If you make any mistakes, use the Backspace key to backup and correct. If you notice a mistake on a previous line, leave it there for now.

Press Enter at the end of each line:

```
I am considering an investment in a dairy farm near Jackson
Hole, Wyoming. It is my purpose to start rather small, with
about one thousand head of cattle. Each cow averages about
1,200 gallons of milk a year. This should give me a total of
about 1,200,000 gallons of milk. At a wholesale price of .50
a gallon, I should be making around $600,000 my first year.
```

Info: Each line in the Editor can be up to 256 characters long. You must press Enter at the end of each line; unlike a word processor, the Editor lacks the "word wrap" feature.

If you type a line that is too long to be displayed in the editing window, use the Ctrl-PageUp and Ctrl-PageDown key combinations to move one screen at a time to the left and right, respectively. You can also use the scroll bars and the mouse to move around in the window.

When you use a text editor, you spend half your time entering text and the other half editing the text. To edit the text, move the cursor to a position in the text, then insert or delete characters. For example, suppose you want to change the first line to read "cows" instead of "head of cattle." Follow these steps:

1. Move to the first line in the document.

Press the Up arrow key until the first number in the row/column indicator (bottom left corner of the screen) reads "00004."

2. Move to the words "head of cattle."

You could press and hold the right arrow key to move there, but there's an easier shortcut. Press and hold the Ctrl key, then type the right arrow seven times.

Note: Ctrl-Right Arrow moves the cursor right one word at a time. Ctrl-Left Arrow moves the cursor left one word at a time.

---

3. Type the word "cows" and a space.

The word "cows" is inserted into the text.

Now change the word "start" at the end of line 2 to "begin":

1. Move the cursor up two lines.

Press the Up Arrow key twice.

2. Move to the word "start."

You could press Ctrl-Right Arrow twice. Instead, press the End key, which moves you to the end of the line. Now press Ctrl-Left Arrow, which moves you back one word.

3. Switch from insert mode to replace mode.

Press the Ins key. The cursor changes from an underline to a large flashing block. This means any new text you enter will overwrite existing text.

4. Type "begin."

The word "begin" replaces "start" in the text. Press the Ins key again to return to insert mode.

The purpose of this exercise is to get you familiar with using the keyboard to move around and edit your text. Complete books have been written on this subject, and other DOS books will probably tarry too long on it with the MS DOS Editor.

A full list of the key combinations you can use to move around, delete, and edit text in the Editor is provided in Appendix K. If you wish to experiment, turn there and try out some of the combinations. Since you're working with nonsense text, don't worry about making any goofs. However, you may want to save the text before moving on.

Tip: The Editor uses many of the standard WordStar text editing keys. If you're familiar with WordStar, you can use those control-key combinations to move around and edit text. A full list is presented in Appendix K.

Saving to Disk

As you typed, the Editor translated each character that you entered into a byte in memory. At this point, the text you've entered is stored in RAM only. If you turn off your computer, those words are gone forever. To keep your information around, you need to store it on a disk using the Editor's Save command.

1. Press the Alt key to activate the menu bar.

Note that the word "File" is highlighted. The program is anticipating that you'll select a command from the menu bar.

2. Press F for File.

The File menu includes the commands you use to create, open, and save files. When you press F, the File menu drops down and you can see the available choices. You can now save this delightful text to disk.

Tip: You can press Alt-F to access the File menu more quickly. If you have a mouse, position the mouse cursor over the word "File" on the menu bar and click the mouse's left button.

3. Select the "Save" menu item.

The Save menu item saves your text to a file on disk. Use the arrow keys or the mouse to highlight the word "Save," or press the S key. This activates the Save dialog box, as seen in Figure 12-5.

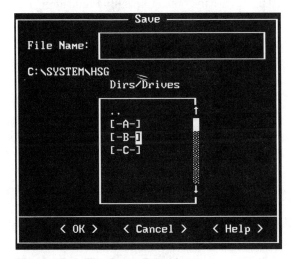

Figure 12-5. The Save dialog box.

4. Enter a name for the file.

The cursor is now flashing in the File Name input box. We'll call the file COWS.TXT—note that the Editor does not automatically supply the TXT extension. Type the filename:

```
COWS.TXT
```

Press Enter. The dialog box disappears; the file is now saved on disk. Notice that the title of the text window now reads COWS.TXT, reflecting the name of the file on disk.

Info: Working with Dialog Boxes

Dialog boxes, such as the Save dialog box shown in Figure 12-5, have a number of features in common. Among the most useful are the buttons usually found along the bottom of the dialog box: OK lets you accept the dialog box's settings; Cancel allows you to quit the dialog box and return to the Editor; Help starts the context-sensitive Help facility to provide detailed information about the current action.

You can use the keyboard to move from button to button by pressing the Tab key; when a button is highlighted, press Enter to activate it. If you have a mouse, move the selection cursor over the button and click the left mouse button once.

Printing

If there is no printer hooked up to your computer, skip ahead to the section titled "Quitting."

After you've created a literary masterpiece like COWS.TXT, you'll no doubt want to share it with your friends. The best way to see that this treasure gets the audience it so richly deserves is to produce a hard copy of it. Fortunately, the Editor makes it easy to accomplish this task, which is handled by the Print command on the File menu.

To Print, follow these steps:

1. Press Alt-F to drop down the File menu.

2. Press P to select Print.

The Print dialog box appears, as shown in Figure 12-6:

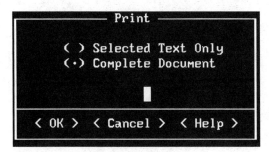

Figure 12-6. The Print dialog box.

Make sure the Complete Document option is selected. (Use the Up or Down Arrow keys to move the selection between the two options.)

3. Press Enter to print the entire document.

Note: If you see a second dialog box which says "Device fault," check to see that your printer is turned on. After fixing the problem, press Enter. In some cases, you may need to start over. Your creation is now in hard copy for all the world to see.

Tip: Some printers—laser printers, for example—may not eject the last page after a document has printed. If this happens, take the printer off-line, press the Form Feed button, and then put the printer back on-line. If you'd like, you can add a form-feed character to your documents. Hold down the Ctrl key and tap P. The characters ^P will appear just to the left of the row/column counter. Now hold down the Alt key, tap 0 1 2 on the numeric keypad, and release the Alt key. The form-feed character (it resembles the medical symbol for a female) will appear in your document; whenever this character is fed to your printer, it will cause the current page to eject.

Quitting

The Editor is fun to use—especially if you've ever worked with its ugly predecessor, EDLIN. But all good things must end eventually. To quit the Editor and return to the DOS prompt, follow these steps:

1. Press Alt-F to pull down the File menu.

2. Press X to select Exit.

Ta-da! You're back at the DOS prompt.

Note: If you haven't saved the current file, or if you've made changes since the last time you saved, the Editor will display a dialog box when you attempt to quit. This dialog box gives you the opportunity to save the file, quit without saving, or return to the Editor.

You've just created a text file named COWS.TXT on disk. You can verify its existence by displaying a directory of the files on your disk. Type the following:

```
DIR
```

Press Enter. Somewhere in the list you'll see an entry for the COWS.TXT file. Locate it. It should look something like this:

```
COWS    TXT   522   2-24-93       4:05p
```

Since COWS.TXT is a text file, you can use the TYPE command at the DOS prompt to display its contents. Type the following:

```
TYPE COWS.TXT
```

Press Enter to view your creation.

Loading a File

The MS-DOS Editor can also be used to edit a text file already on disk. To edit the COWS.TXT file, run the Editor a second time. At the DOS prompt, type:

```
EDIT
```

Press Enter.

Upon entering the Editor, press Esc to bypass the Survival Guide. You'll find yourself back in a blank editing window, where the cursor awaits your inspired thoughts. This time, however, instead of spontaneously composing, you can load the COWS.TXT file from disk by following these steps:

1. Press Alt-F to pull down the File menu.

2. Press O to select Open.

Note: "Open" and "load" mean the same thing—to open a file on disk and load it into memory for editing.

The Open dialog box appears. As you can see from the example in Figure 12-7, this dialog box includes an assortment of gadgets that let you select a file from any drive or directory in your system. (We'll explore exactly how this works later.) For now, note the top of the dialog box, where the cursor is flashing and *.TXT is highlighted.

In DOS, the asterisk is called a wild card. The MS-DOS Editor assumes you want to edit only text files, so by default only those files with the TXT extension initially appear in the Open dialog box (even though there are almost certainly files with different extensions on the disk). COWS.TXT appears in the Files box.

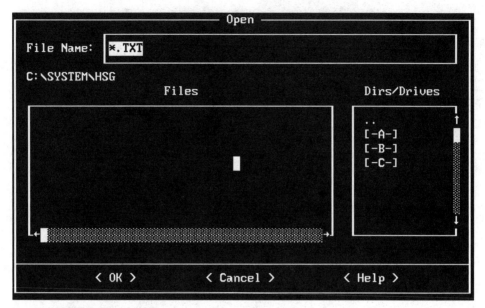

Figure 12-7. The Open dialog box.

There are three ways to load a file into the Editor using the Open dialog box. Here's how it works using the example of COWS.TXT:

1. Type "COWS.TXT" to enter it into the File Name box. Press Enter and COWS.TXT is loaded and ready for editing.

2. Press the Tab key. This moves you from the File Name box to the Files box. Use the cursor keys to highlight the filename COWS.TXT (even if it's the only file listed, you'll need to press one of the arrow keys to highlight it). Press Enter.

3. If you have a mouse, point to the filename COWS.TXT and double-click with the left mouse button.

After selecting the file, the Open dialog box disappears and your text is once again in the Editor.

Note: There is a quicker way to load a file into the Editor: When you first start the Editor, type the name of the file you want to edit after EDIT on the command line. For example:

```
EDIT COWS.TXT
```

This starts the Editor and immediately loads the file COWS.TXT for editing.

Changing the Text

The search-and-replace capability is a common feature in text editors and word processors.

1. Press Alt-S to pull down the Search menu.

2. Press F (or Enter) to select Find.

The Find dialog box appears, as shown in Figure 12-8.

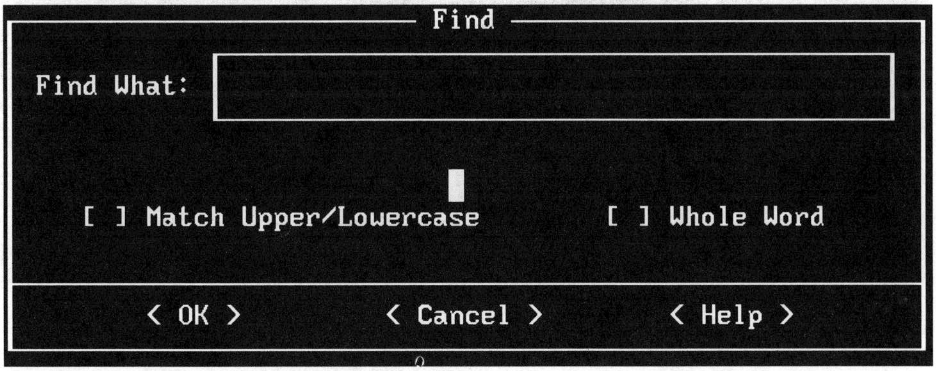

```
┌──────────────────────── Find ────────────────────────┐
│                                                       │
│  Find What:  ┌───────────────────────────────────┐    │
│              │                                   │    │
│              └───────────────────────────────────┘    │
│                                                       │
│                            ▌                          │
│      [ ] Match Upper/Lowercase        [ ] Whole Word  │
│                                                       │
│        < OK >         < Cancel >        < Help >      │
│                                                       │
└───────────────────────────────────────────────────────┘
```

Figure 12-8. The Find dialog box.

Type:

```
cow
```

Press Enter.

The Find dialog box disappears and the first instance of the word "cow" is highlighted on the third line.

To find additional instances of "cow," press F3. Each time you press F3, the Editor locates "cow" in the text and highlights it.

Now let's change each instance of the word "head of cattle" to "cows." This is referred to as a global change; it will affect all text in the window.

1. Press Ctrl-Home to move the cursor to the top of the document.

2. Press Alt-S to pull down the Search menu.

3. Press C to select Change.

The Change dialog box appears, as shown in Figure 12-9.

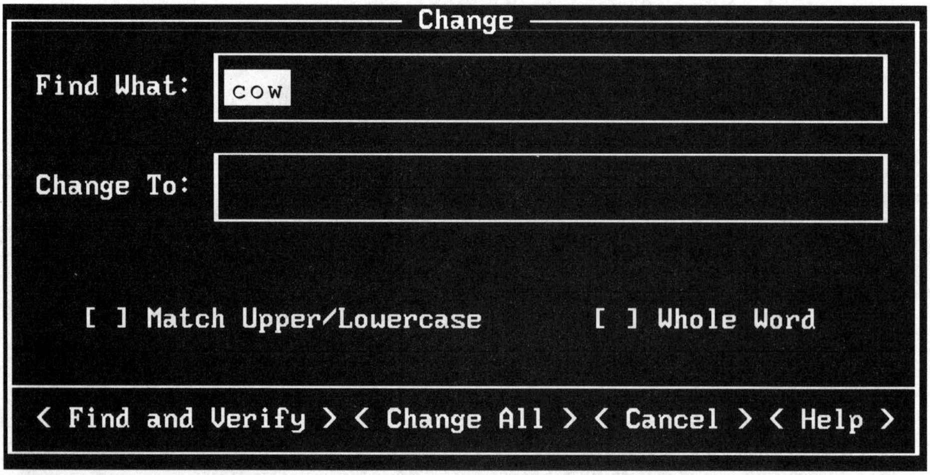

```
┌──────────────────────────── Change ────────────────────────────┐
│                                                                 │
│   Find What:  ┌──────┐                                          │
│               │ cow  │                                          │
│               └──────┘                                          │
│                                                                 │
│   Change To:  ┌─────────────────────────────────────────────┐  │
│               │                                             │  │
│               └─────────────────────────────────────────────┘  │
│                                                                 │
│      [ ] Match Upper/Lowercase           [ ] Whole Word        │
│                                                                 │
│   < Find and Verify > < Change All > < Cancel > < Help >       │
└─────────────────────────────────────────────────────────────────┘
```

Figure 12-9. The Change dialog box.

Because the Editor remembers your previous search request, the word cow already appears in the Find What box. Press the Tab key once to move to the Change To box. Type:

```
cattle
```

Press the Tab key until the "Change All" button is highlighted at the bottom of the dialog box. Press Enter. A dialog box tells you that all the changes have been made. Press Enter to clear the screen

Figure 12-10. The Change complete dialog box.

Selecting, Cutting and Pasting

Among the Editor's most useful features is its ability to copy, cut, and paste blocks of text. For starters, let's learn how to select blocks of text.

Start over with a new file; give yourself a blank sheet of screen on which to work:

1. Press Alt-F to pull down the File menu.

2. Press N to select New.

Note: If the text already in the Editor has not been saved, you'll see a dialog box asking if you want to save it. Use the Tab key and Enter to select Yes to save or No to discard the file without saving.

The top of the text editing window again says "Untitled."
Enter the following text:

```
Violets are blue
Roses are red
Sugar is sweet
And M&Ms are round
```

It's obvious that the first two lines are reversed; "Roses are red" traditionally comes first. To move that line above "Violets are blue" you could just retype it and then delete the duplicate. However, this section is about selecting, cutting and pasting.

Start by selecting the line "Roses are red." If you have a mouse, this task is easy: Just point to the beginning of the line, hold down the left mouse button, and drag the selection cursor to the beginning of the next line.

With the keyboard, the process is a bit more complicated:

1. Use the Up Arrow key to position the cursor on the second line ("Roses are red").

2. Press the Home key to move the cursor to the start of the line.

3. Hold down either Shift key and press the Down Arrow key. This highlights the entire line "Roses are red."

Info: Selecting Text.
To select text, you use the same keys as you'd use to move the cursor—with one difference. Move the cursor to one end of the block to be highlighted, and then press and hold either Shift key and move the cursor to the other end of the block. All selected text will appear in inverse video.

To move "Roses are red" above "Violets are blue," you need to cut the selected text out of its original position and store it temporarily, then move the cursor to the new position and paste the text back into the document.

Info: Cutting deletes the text, copying it to an area in memory called the buffer. From there, the text can be pasted back into the document. When you copy text, the original is not deleted. Note that you can paste the same text any number of times; it stays in the buffer until you cut or copy another block of text or exit the Editor.

To cut the text, do the following:

1. Press Alt-E to pull down the Edit menu.

2. Press Enter or T to cut the selected text.

Note: From the keyboard you can press Shift-Del to cut selected text.

The line vanishes from the screen. Your text should now look like this:

```
Violets are blue
Sugar is sweet
and M&Ms are round
```

Press the Up Arrow key once to move the cursor up to the first line.

The text you just cut is now in the storage buffer. To paste it back into the document, do the following:

1. Press Alt-E to pull down the Edit menu.

2. Press P to select Paste from the menu.

Note: From the keyboard, press Shift-Ins to paste text.

Ta-da! The line is back in the text, in the proper position.

Info: The original cut text is still in the buffer. If you wish, you can move the cursor and paste the text into a new place in the document. The pasted text will always appear at the cursor's position.

You can now exit to DOS by pressing Alt-F and then X. Type Y if you want to save the document or N to exit straight to DOS without saving.

COMMAND: EDIT (External)
                  Function: The MS-DOS Editor program
                  Format: EDIT filename

filename is the optional name of a text file to edit. If omitted, the Editor will start with a clean screen.

A summary of the keystrokes and commands available in the Editor is listed in Appendix K.

Summary

The MS-DOS Editor is a handy, full-screen text editor you can use to create or modify DOS text files, batch files, and any text files of your own.

To start the Editor, type EDIT. When the Editor first loads, you'll see the Survival Guide screen. Press Esc to clear the screen and begin editing text.

Files are created by typing on the keyboard; Each line can be up to 256 characters long, but note that there is no "word wrap." You should press Enter at the end of each line.

The Editor's commands are contained in five pull-down menus: File, Edit, Search, Options, and Help.

You can load a file quickly by typing its name after EDIT at the DOS prompt.

To edit text, you use the keyboard's cursor keys plus special commands found in the pull-down menus. To select text, hold down the Shift key as you move the cursor, or click on the text and drag with the mouse.

Special commands in the Edit menu allow you to cut, copy, and paste text. Text can be copied or cut to a temporary storage buffer, then pasted into another location in the document.

CHAPTER 13

Working With Disks

DOS's first function is dealing with disks and storing information on them. To understand how it's done, you need to know how DOS views your disk drives, how it prepares the diskettes for use by formatting them, and how DOS accesses those disks once they've been prepared.

This chapter answers the following questions:

- How does DOS refer to drive A, B, C, etc.?

- Can you use drive B if you don't have a second floppy drive?

- What is diskette formatting and why is it necessary?

- How does the FORMAT command prepare a diskette for use?

- What do the volume label and serial number do?

- How is the hard drive formatted?

- Can a volume label or serial number be changed?

- What is "logging?"

- How can the current drive be changed?

DOS and Disks

Every PC has at least one disk drive, the first floppy drive, A. The majority have two drives, the floppy drive, A, and a hard drive, C. Then there's the three drive systems—two floppy drives A and B plus drive C—and systems that have all three basic drives plus even more hard drives: D, E, F, and so on. Yet DOS sees all these storage devices as being the same; to DOS they're disk drives used for long-term storage of information.

Info: Drive A is your first disk drive—a floppy drive

Drive B, if available, is your second disk drive—a floppy drive

Drive C is your first hard drive, even if you lack a drive B

Drives D through Z are additional hard drives or network drives

Phantom Drives

Even if your computer has only one floppy drive and a hard drive, you still have a B drive—a phantom drive! This drive evolved from the early days of the PC when one floppy drive was all you could afford. DOS became adept at faking a second floppy drive, so every computer has a B drive whether or not it is physically present. (And this also explains why the hard drive is always C.)

There are really two types of disk drives that DOS deals with—the physical and logical. This is different from the concept of a floppy or hard drive.

Info: A physical drive is physically present: it's your A drive or your hard drive C. A logical drive isn't there, but it can still be used. DOS "fakes" the drive by using another physical device.

Suppose you have only one floppy drive, A. DOS will still let you access drive B, but only as a logical drive; there is no physical disk drive for B, so DOS pretends for a moment that drive A is really drive B. Internally, DOS remembers which drive is which, so it can tell if you're using the physical drive A as logical drive B or just as drive A.

The same thing holds true with a hard drive. Your system can have one physical hard drive C. That drive may hold millions of bytes of information. To manage it more efficiently, you can divide the single hard drive into several logical drives, so that the one hard drive may actually contain drives C, D, and E. Unlike the phantom floppy drive B, logical drives D and E do actually occupy space on the hard drive.

Don't let it get to you if this subject is confusing. Just put it in the back of your head for a few minutes. Later you'll see how the logical/physical roles come into play under DOS.

Referencing Drives Under DOS

DOS can store information in a file on any drive. But you need to tell it which drive to use. The same holds true with some DOS commands; unless you tell DOS otherwise, it always assumes you mean the current drive. You can use the commands on other drives, but you have to tell DOS where to look.

Under DOS, a disk drive is known as a device. The keyboard, screen, printer port, and serial port are also devices under DOS. DOS gives a unique name to each device, referring to disk drives by the same letters you use. There is one difference:

Rule: DOS refers to a disk drive by its letter followed by a colon.

If you want DOS to refer to drive A, you use A: (A-colon). The colon tells DOS that A is really a disk drive—not a filename. (A by itself is a valid name for a file.)

Info: A: refers to drive A

             B: refers to drive B

             C: refers to drive C, and so on

This lettering scheme applies to all drives in your system, up to the highest lettered hard drive or network drive (which can go all the way up to Z:). But every system with a hard drive has access to A:, B:, and C:. (Remember that drive B can always be accessed as a logical drive.)

Preparing Diskettes for Use

When you buy a box of diskettes, you want to check for a few things: Make sure the disk is the right size (5-1/4- or 3-1/2-inch) and the proper density for your disk drive (double-density diskettes for those drives, and preferably high density diskettes for high-density drives—which will be more expensive).

No matter which diskettes you buy, they all share one thing in common: they're naked. In a sense, a new diskette is like a tube sock: You can buy it no matter whether you're a man or a woman and no matter how big your feet are; the sock will eventually "learn" your foot. The same thing works (kind of) with diskettes; one type of diskette works with a variety of computers. To make that diskette work with your PC, you need to prepare it for use. That's done by formatting the diskette.

Info: Formatting is preparing a diskette for use.

All new diskettes are blank—like blank cassettes, white paper, or a record without the groove. To use the diskette, DOS has to prepare it for holding data: DOS must create places on the diskette where the bytes will sit in an organized fashion. Other computers' DOSes will prepare the same diskettes for use on their systems, which is why all diskettes come blank.

Tip: You can buy preformatted DOS diskettes, which is more efficient than formatting them yourself. Preformatted DOS diskettes will cost more than unformatted diskettes. But when you consider that it takes from 20 to 30 minutes to format a box of 1.4M diskettes, your time may be worth it.

What Formatting Does

Think of a new diskette as a newly paved, unmarked parking lot around a stadium: Both are blank. An unmarked parking lot is not very good for parking cars. Eventually, right before game time you'd have a zillion cars wedged in there with no hope of anyone getting home in time to watch the TV highlights.

Most parking lots, however, have rings and rows of painted parking spaces. You can locate any car in the lot by its row and section number, and all cars are parked in their own stalls (save for those rude RV or Porsche owners who ignore the lines).

To prepare a disk for use, DOS formats it. This works along the same lines of painting parking stalls around a stadium parking lot. In the case of formatting, DOS divides a diskette up into tracks and sectors.

Unlike a stadium parking lot, DOS formats both sides of a disk, putting tracks and sectors on each side. When two tracks exist on different sides of the disk, DOS refers to them collectively as a cylinder (because that's the geometric shape they define).

176

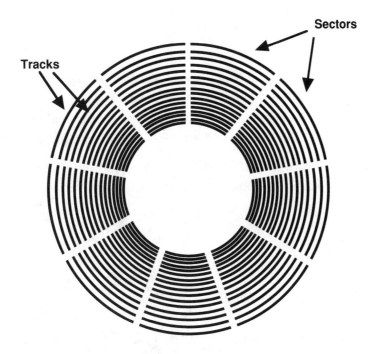

Figure 13-1. Tracks and sectors on a diskette.

Info: A track is a circle, like a circle of car slots around a stadium. A sector is a pie slice of tracks, like section A in a stadium parking lot. A cylinder refers to two tracks on either side of a diskette. (The term cylinder was popular for DOS version 3, but you may still encounter it today.)

After the disk is prepared with these tracks and sectors, DOS can then put files on that disk. The files will sit in the areas defined by tracks and sectors, just as cars fit in parking stalls around the stadium. DOS will remember where the files are, occupying which sectors on which tracks, thus allowing you to recall the files later.

But before any of that can be done, the diskette must be formatted. That's the job of the FORMAT command.

Formatting a Diskette

FORMAT is a DOS command that prepares a diskette for use. It creates the tracks and sectors on the diskette, allowing DOS to store files there.

Formatting is something you will do for each diskette you buy (unless you buy them pre-formatted). DOS just can't use the diskette until it's formatted.

Tip: Always format all diskettes in the box as soon as you open it. Sure, this takes time, but it's good to have a formatted disk handy when you need one.

To format a diskette, you should take the following steps:

1. Insert a diskette into the drive.

2. Use the FORMAT command

3. Remove the diskette and label it.

Obtain a blank diskette, one suitably sized for your computer's A drive. Make sure the diskette matches the capacity for the drive: If you have a high-capacity drive, then use a high-capacity diskette; for a low-capacity drive use a low-capacity (double-density) diskette.

Info: You don't always have to use a new diskette. The FORMAT command will format any diskette whether or not it already contains information. This requires care, because you will eventually need to reformat already formatted diskettes. This is fine as long as the diskette doesn't contain any important information.

Insert the new diskette into the A drive, label up. Make sure you stick the diskette into the drive; don't wedge it into the space below the drive (which I've done more than once).

Note: A 3-1/2-inch diskette fits only one way into the drive: label up, metal shutter forward. Push the diskette far enough in and the drive will eventually snatch it from you, locking it into place. If this doesn't happen, the diskette is improperly oriented.

A 5-1/4-inch diskette is square on all sides. While there are conceivably eight different ways to put the disk into the drive only one is correct: Keep the label up and toward you. (Refer to Figure 2-1). Slide the disk in all the way. Close the drive door latch.

The FORMAT Command

The FORMAT command has a required parameter; you must specify the drive containing the diskette to be formatted. At the DOS prompt type the following:

```
FORMAT A:
```

Following the FORMAT command is a space, then A: (A colon). This tells DOS to format the diskette in drive A. (Note how the colon follows A? This is what tells DOS that "A:" is a disk drive.)

Check your typing and press Enter. You'll see:

```
Insert new diskette for drive A: and press ENTER when ready...
```

The new diskette is already in the drive. Press Enter. DOS responds with the following:

```
Checking existing disk format
```

DOS is checking the drive's highest capacity.

Info: DOS will always try to format a diskette of the highest capacity. If you've accidentally inserted a low-capacity (double-density) diskette in a high capacity drive, DOS responds:

```
Invalid media or Track 0 bad—disk unusable
Format terminated
Format another (Y/N)?
```

Remove the diskette and replace it with a high-capacity one; press N, and then Enter, and proceed.

Later you'll see how to format a low-capacity diskette in a high-capacity drive.

After the capacity is verified, the disk formatting continues. You'll see:

```
Formatting xxxx xxxx percent of disk formatted
```

In "Formatting xxxx," the xxxx will be replaced by the size of the diskette you're formatting: 1.44M, 1.2M, 720K, or 360K. The value in "xxxx percent of disk formatted" will increment in size, from zero to 100 percent, as DOS creates tracks and sectors on the disk.

Note: If you're formatting a diskette that has already been formatted ("re-formatting"), you'll see additional information displayed.

After a time, depending on the capacity of the diskette, you'll see:

```
Format complete
Volume label (11 characters, ENTER for none)?
```

DOS is prompting you to enter an electronic label—a volume name for the diskette. This is optional; if you press Enter, the diskette won't have a label. Any other text you enter, up to 11 characters, will then be the diskette's label. For example, type:

```
TEST DISK
```

Info: A disk's volume label can be from 1 to 11 characters long. It can include letters, numbers, spaces, and all symbols except for those forbidden in a filename. Forbidden characters include: " / \ [ ] : * | < > + = ; , ? ( ) & ^

Note: All lowercase text will be converted to uppercase when DOS creates the filename.

If you put a period in the name, DOS will only use the next three characters. (The volume label is essentially a special filename, so a period is treated the same as the filename-extension separator.)

After typing the Volume label, press Enter. The following is then displayed:

```
xxxxxxx bytes total disk space
xxxxxxx bytes available on disk

    xxx bytes in each allocation unit
   xxxx allocation units on disk

Volume Serial Number is xxxx-xxxx

Format another (Y/N)?
```

The first two values tell you how many bytes are available for storage on the diskette. The two numbers will match—unless bad sectors were found during the formatting process. This only happens rarely, and it's okay; DOS has recognized the bad sectors and locked them out. However, since most new diskettes are guaranteed, you can take it back and get a replacement if you like. (Older diskettes just wear out with use, which is why bad sectors appear on them.)

The "allocation unit" information refers to the minimum number of bytes DOS assigns to each file on disk. This information is explained in Chapter 2.

A volume serial number is a unique I.D. that DOS gives each diskette. It can contain both numbers and the letters A through F. (The serial number is displayed along with the volume label using the VOL command, explained below.)

The final item is a prompt, "Format another (Y/N)?" DOS is asking if you'd like to format another diskette: Press Y to proceed or N to return to the DOS prompt.

```
Press N, then Enter.
```

You're now back at the DOS prompt and have a fully formatted diskette ready for use in drive A.

> COMMAND: FORMAT (External)
>   Function: To format disks, preparing them for use.
>   Format: FORMAT drive

Drive is the letter of the drive containing the disk to be formatted. It must be specified. The FORMAT command has many other optional parameters. They will be detailed in Chapter 28.

Applying the Label

A diskette's volume label is optional, but a requirement for all diskettes should be a sticky label, which either names the disk or lists its contents.

Tip: Label all your formatted diskettes—even if you don't write anything on the label. This will help you to quickly differentiate formatted diskettes from the unformatted (and unlabeled) ones.

Remove the newly formatted diskette from drive A:

You eject a 3-1/2-inch diskette by pressing on a button below or to the side of the drive's door. This spits the disk out just so far; you can then pull it out the rest of the way using your fingers.

Remove a 5-1/4-inch diskette by opening the drive-door latch, and then pinching and pulling the diskette out. Always put the diskette back into its protective paper sleeve when it's not in the drive.

Grab one of the peel-and-stick labels that came with the box of diskettes. Write "Test Disk" on it, matching the diskette's electronic-volume label. You can also date the diskette if you like.

Tip: If you have more than one type of computer in the office, you may also want to write "IBM" or "DOS 5" on the diskette. Indicating the diskette's size and capacity (1.4M, 1.2M, 720K, or 360K) is also a good idea.

Peel and stick the label on the diskette.

Testing the Format

Reinsert your freshly formatted and labeled diskette into drive A. If you have a 5-1/4-inch drive, then remember to close the drive's door latch after inserting the diskette.

The diskette is really formatted—honest! The FORMAT command isn't wishy washy. But you can verify that the diskette is formatted by accessing with DOS. This is an old trick many users will pull to see if an unlabeled diskette is formatted (which is another argument why you should label diskettes after they've been formatted).

There are two DOS commands commonly used to test the format of a diskette:

```
VOL DIR
```

The VOL command displays a disk's volume label. In Chapter 9, the VOL command displayed the label on the hard disk, which was also the current disk or the currently logged disk.

The DIR command displays a list of files on disk, as well as other information about the disk. As with the VOL command, unless you tell it otherwise, the DIR command only displays information about the current drive. With either command, however, you can display information about other drives simply by specifying the drive letter.

Type the following at the DOS prompt:

```
VOL A:
```

That VOL, the VOL command, followed by a space and A: (A colon). With the VOL command, the drive letter is optional. If not specified, then VOL assumes you mean the current drive (which is also reflected in the DOS prompt). But when you specify a drive letter, VOL displays information about that drive.

Press Enter. DOS displays:

```
Volume in drive A is TEST DISK
Volume Serial Number is xxxx-xxxx
```

Both the volume label and serial number will be identical to those applied by the FORMAT command. Also, the positive results of this command tell you that the diskette is formatted and ready for use. This can be further verified using the DIR command. Type the following:

```
DIR A:
```

As with the VOL command, when you specify a drive letter after the DIR command DOS displays a directory of files stored on that drive. The diskette in drive A is newly formatted, so there will be no files.

Press Enter. DOS displays:

```
Volume in drive A is TEST DISK
Volume Serial Number is xxxx-xxxx
Directory of A:\
File not found
```

"File not found" is DOS's way of telling you the diskette is empty; it contains no files. But the test proved positive: the diskette in drive A is formatted and ready to store files.

Info: Both DIR and VOL, as well as other DOS commands always assume you mean the current drive, the one reflected in the DOS prompt. As an optional parameter, you can specify another drive. Just follow the command with a space, the drive letter and a colon, and the command will work on the indicated drive.

What if the disk is unformatted? Try this: obtain another blank diskette from the box. Insert it into your A drive. (Remember to shut the door latch on a 5-1/4-inch drive.) Type the following at the DOS prompt:

```
VOL A:
```

Press Enter. You'll see one of the nastiest error messages DOS displays.

```
General failure reading drive A
Abort, Retry, Fail?
```

Gulp! This nasty message basically means you're trying to access an unformatted diskette. You can press the following keys:

A, to "abort" and cancel the DOS command, returning you to the DOS prompt.

R, to try again. Press this key only if you know what the problem is, can fix it, and then want to retry.

F, to fail—essentially ignore the DOS command and steam on ahead.

Tip: When you get an "Abort, Retry, Fail?" error, press A. If you know what the problem is and can repair it, press R. Rarely should you press F.

Press the A key now. Remove the unformatted diskette from drive A.

Formatting Drive B

Insert another unformatted diskette into your B drive. If you have a drive B, make sure that the diskette is of the proper size and capacity.

Note: In a quandary? If you lack a drive B, then stick the properly sized diskette into your physical drive A. Keep on reading.

Type the following at the DOS prompt:

```
FORMAT B:
```

Press Enter—even if you know the diskette is in your A drive and that the above command is likely to make the computer explode.

The formatting will continue as it did earlier in this chapter (refer back to the heading "The FORMAT Command" if you need assistance). Watch the formatting process, and then enter a volume label of your own choice (something like "B TEST" would be fine). Type N and Enter when asked if you want to format another. Remove the diskette and label it accordingly.

Now verify the format with the VOL command. Reinsert the diskette into drive B (or your A drive if you lack a drive B). Type the following:

```
VOL B:
```

Press Enter. You'll see something like:

```
Volume in drive B is B TEST
Volume Serial Number is xxxx-xxxx
```

If you have a drive B, then everything makes sense. Please continue reading at the section titled "Formatting the Hard Drive."

If you don't have a drive B, stop scratching your head for a second. Remember the first section in this chapter where we talked about physical and logical drives? Right now, DOS is treating your A drive as a logical drive B. All references to drive B are conveniently redirected to drive A. This is why FORMAT, VOL, DIR, and a number of DOS commands you haven't yet used will treat your physical drive A as a logical drive B.

Type the following at the DOS prompt:

```
VOL A:
```

Press Enter.

```
Insert diskette for drive A: and press any key when ready
```

Ah-ha! Now DOS is letting you know that the internal change has taken place. Physical drive A and logical drive A are about to meet. If you're simulating a two-drive system, you can swap diskettes now. There's no need in this case, however, so press your "any" key (the spacebar).

```
Volume in drive A is B TEST
Volume Serial Number is xxxx-xxxx
```

You can move back and forth between logical A and logical B simply by specifying A or B in a DOS command. Usually this is done only rarely, but it is possible. DOS handles the changes by prompting you to swap diskettes at the right moment.

Formatting the Hard Drive

The FORMAT command works on all drives in your system, including those with letters higher than B—the hard drive. But first, a healthy tip:

Tip: Don't format your hard drive.

The hard drive is formatted only once, usually by the dealer before you walk out of the store with the computer, or when you're first setting up the machine. After that you should never format or reformat the hard drive. There's no need to.

If you do accidentally type "FORMAT C:" DOS will provide you with ample warning about what you're doing. Unlike older versions of DOS (when FORMAT didn't require a drive letter), there are many warnings you go through before formatting begins. In any event, be careful.

Working With Volume Labels

Volume labels are really a silly topic. Most DOS users just press Enter when asked to "enter volume label." But it's a good idea to name diskettes, even if the names don't reflect the disk's contents.

The volume label pops up every time you use the DIR command, as well as appears with the VOL command. If you want to change the label after the disk is formatted, you use the LABEL command.

Info: The LABEL command allows you to examine a disk's volume label and optionally change or delete it.

Insert the B test diskette into your drive B or into drive A if you lack a B drive. Remember to close the door latch if you have a 5-1/4-inch drive.

Type the following at the DOS prompt:

```
LABEL B:
```

Press Enter.

Note: If you don't have a B drive, DOS may prompt you to "Insert diskette for drive B: and press any key when ready." Press the spacebar to continue.

```
Volume in drive B is B TEST Volume Serial Number is xxxx-xxxx
Volume label (11 characters, ENTER for none)?
```

The LABEL command is giving you the chance to change or delete the volume label. Here are your options at this point:

Enter a new label, from 1 to 11 characters. You can use letters, numbers, symbols, and spaces. (A list of what's kosher or not for a label is given at the end of this section.) Press Enter after entering the new label. DOS changes it and you're back at the DOS prompt.

Press Enter. This erases the label. After pressing Enter, DOS asks:

```
Delete current volume label (Y/N)?
```

Press Y and Enter to delete it; press N and Enter to cancel and return to the DOS prompt. If you press Y, then when you ask for the diskette's label, DOS will respond with a "has no label" message.

Note: Press Ctrl-C. This immediately cancels the LABEL command and returns you to the DOS prompt.

For a new label, you can type what you like or take one of the above three actions. Instead, why not get creative? Type the following:

```
DIRTY
```

Press Enter. Now type the VOL command to verify your label:

```
VOL B:
```

Press Enter.

```
Volume in drive B is DIRTY
Volume Serial Number is xxxx-xxxx
```

Tip: With the LABEL command, the drive letter is optional. If you don't specify a drive, DOS assumes the current drive and will let you change/delete that drive's label.

Another optional item with the LABEL command is the new label itself. Type the following:

```
LABEL B: TOO LOUD
```

Press Enter to change the label to "TOO LOUD." Enter the VOL command again for drive B to have a chuckle.

COMMAND: LABEL (External)
               Function: To change or delete a disk's volume label.
               Format: LABEL [drive] [label]

Drive is optional. It indicates the disk drive containing the disk you want to label. If omitted, the current drive is assumed.

Label is optional. It's the new label to apply to the disk. If omitted, the LABEL command will prompt for a new label. Note that the new label cannot contain the following characters:

" / \ [ ] : * | < > + = ; , ? ( ) & ^

Drive Logging

When DOS is using a disk drive, it's said to be logged to that drive. So far you've been using only the hard drive. You've been logged to the hard drive, even though you've accessed drives A and B by means of some DOS commands. It's possible to access those drives directly by logging to them. This is done by telling DOS to use (or log to) another drive.

To log to another drive, you type that drive letter at the DOS prompt followed by a colon.

Tip: Always make sure a diskette is in the drive before you log to it.

Stick your recently formatted diskette labeled TEST DISK into drive A. At the DOS prompt, type:

```
A:
```

Press Enter.

Note: If you've been using drive B and you don't have a drive B, DOS will prompt you to "Insert diskette for drive A: and press any key when ready." Press the spacebar to continue. You're now logged to drive A. The DOS prompt will reflect this:

```
A:\>
```

Now type the VOL command:

```
VOL
```

Press Enter. The volume label for drive A is displayed; since you're currently logged to drive A, there was no need to specify it. However, if you now want to see the volume label for drive C, type the following:

```
VOL C:
```

Press Enter. If you're not logged to a drive, you must specify its letter in order for a DOS command to look there. (If not, DOS will always assume you mean the current drive.)

Log to drive B. Type the following:

```
B:
```

Press Enter.

Note: Again, if you only have one floppy drive, DOS will prompt for you to "Insert diskette for drive B: and press any key when ready." Press the spacebar to continue.

```
B:\>
```

Now you're looking at the world from drive B. Now all the VOL, DIR and LABEL commands will assume you mean drive B unless another drive letter is specified. Log back to drive C by typing the following:

```
C:\>
```

Press Enter.

```
C:\>
```

Drive C is now the currently logged drive.

Info: To change or log to another drive, type the drive's letter followed by a colon. Remember: When followed by a colon, DOS assumes the letter identifies a disk drive, not a filename.

Now you will know what to do when an installation manual (or maybe even this book) tells you to "log to drive A." But remember that colon! According to DOS, "A:" is your drive A.

Summary

This has been a busy chapter, with lots of things to do and lots of information to learn. Here are the high points:

All PCs have three basic drives: A, the first floppy; B, the second floppy; and C, the hard drive. Even if you lack a second floppy as a physical device, DOS will simulate it as a logical drive.

DOS refers to each disk drive in your system by its letter, followed by a colon: Drive A is A:; B is B:; C is C:; and so on. Whenever DOS sees a letter followed by a colon, it assumes you mean a disk drive.

Formatting is the process of preparing a diskette for use. DOS creates magnetic "parking places"—which are organized into tracks and sectors—for bytes and files on disk.

FORMAT is the DOS command that carries out the formatting process. You must follow the FORMAT command with the letter of the drive containing the disk to be formatted—either A or B. Do not format the hard drive, C (or any drives greater than C).

The FORMAT command lets you assign a volume label (electronic name) to the disk. It can be from 1 to 11 characters in length, or it can be nothing. Additionally, a serial number or I.D. is given to the disk.

A disk's volume label and serial number can be viewed using the VOL and DIR commands.

The LABEL command can be used to add, change, or delete a disk's volume label after the disk has been formatted.

Accessing a new disk is referred to as "logging to" that disk. When you log to a new disk, you enter the drive's letter followed by a colon. That disk then becomes the current disk.

CHAPTER 14

Using Subdirectories

Massive amounts of information can be stored on a disk. Managing all that information is your job. DOS gives you the tools to organize and store your information, but DOS isn't going to do everything for you. Organization of disks, files and information is an important job, and how you do it is up to you.

This chapter answers the following questions:

- What are the disadvantages to storing many files on a disk?

- How can subdirectories help with file organization?

- What is the "root" directory?

- How are directories created?

- What are the two functions of the CD command?

- What is a pathname?

- What are the dot and dot-dot directories?

- How do you remove a directory?

- What is the "tree structure"?

Getting Organized

A hard disk is a magnificent thing—one storage device capable of holding megabytes of information. All your programs and files are kept in one compact—not to mention fast and reliable—unit. But things weren't always that way.

Before hard drives were cheap, everything was put on floppy disks. Users would put a program disk in drive A and a data diskette in drive B. To change programs they changed disks, to access another data file, they found that disk and stuck it in drive B.

Program and file management was as simple as keeping a stack of the right disks handy—and labeled appropriately. Life was simple... but not convenient.

The hard drive made life better for PC owners. Not only is it faster than floppy disks, it eliminated the need for the "disk shuffle." All programs and data files can be kept on one big disk. And therein lies the rub: Imagine one disk with hundreds of files on it. Imagine looking for the file you lost in a directory listing several dozen screens in length. This is potential for chaos.

The typical 40-megabyte hard drive has room for hundreds of files. If you forget a filename you can look it up using the DIR command—but that would be like locating a name in an unalphabetized phone book. And eventually, given the limitations of the 8-dot-3 filename pattern DOS uses, you'd run out of interesting and clever names for files. It would be a mess.

Disk Limitations

Adding files and information to a large-capacity disk without a thought to organization leads to trouble. Here is what you encounter:

Chaos

A disk drive with hundreds of files is a mess; it would take the DIR command several minutes to list them all. Files of one type would be listed in with files of another type; word processing files and spreadsheet files—you wouldn't know which files belonged to which programs or projects.

Filename limitations

After a while, you'd run out of filenames. True, there are millions of combinations for the 8-dot-3 pattern. But after a while, the good descriptive ones would be used up and you'd have to resort to odd filenames that would give no clue as to the file's contents.

Filename conflicts

DOS won't let you have two files with the same name on the same disk. If you decide to make a new file named STUFF, it will replace any file already named STUFF.

Note: Usually an application will warn you that a file with the same name already exists. At that point, you can choose between replacing the old file or giving the new file another name. Sometimes, however, the original file is just over-written by the new file. This may happen without warning.

DOS limitations

The way a disk is formatted means that it can only hold so many files. DOS makes room for anywhere from 64K to 512K on a disk. Once that limit is exceeded, DOS reports that the "disk is full," and you can add no more files. This happens even though there may be megabytes of space available.

Info: A 360K or 720K floppy diskette has room for 112 files. A 1.2M or 1.4M floppy diskette has room for 224 files. The typical hard drive has room for 512 files. These are maximum values. However, using DOS's organizational commands, you can put many, many more files on a disk.

The Solution

In order to work best with a hard drive, DOS comes with special disk-organizational commands. These tools allow you to divide the disk into individual work areas, called directories or subdirectories.

Info: If you think of a disk as a file cabinet, the subdirectories are drawers in the cabinet; they organize your files (folders) by category and type. But you can subcategorize your disk further by creating subdirectories within subdirectories—in essence, creating drawers within drawers (to continue with the file cabinet analogy.)

Files in one subdirectory are separate from those elsewhere on the disk. That way you can have many files on disk with the same name, as long as each is in its own subdirectory.

Although a disk is limited in the number of files it can have, it's not limited to the number of subdirectories and files within those subdirectories. A hard drive may only have room for 512 files, but only two subdirectories on that drive can hold thousands of files—or more. You'll never see a "disk full" error message if you use subdirectories properly.

The subdirectories also give you an organizational edge: All your word-processing files can be kept in their own subdirectory adjacent to the word-processing program. Furthermore, you can go a level deeper and put individual projects in their own subdirectories.

DOS is quite flexible with its subdirectory-organization tools, but shallow on recommendations for using them. It's up to you to place files into subdirectories and to organize them. This is all done with the subdirectory commands, as well as with DOS's file-management and manipulation commands.

Working with Subdirectories

Subdirectories are used to organize the files on your hard drive. How you organize them is up to you. Since each PC is different and has different software on it, there is no correct way to do this. For now, the subject is learning about the tools that help you make and use subdirectories.

Subdirectories organize your files into different areas on disk. The organization scheme looks like an upside-down tree when you visualize it. Refer to Figure 14-1.

This system of subdirectory organization is actually referred to as the tree structure (albeit upside-down). The subdirectories are compartments, or work areas, where you can store files. And, as you can see from the Figure, subdirectories can have subdirectories.

Definition: Individually, a subdirectory is simply a directory. It's only when you refer to a directory below another directory that it's a subdirectory. There are no hard-and-fast rules about this. In fact, most DOS users use the two terms interchangeably.

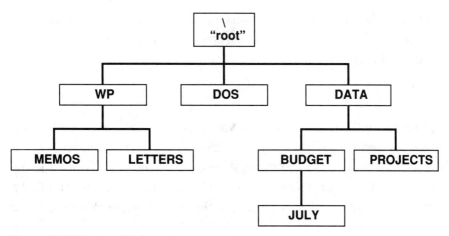

Figure 14-1 The upside-down tree structure.

To work through the remainder of this chapter, have your computer up and running. If the computer is off, refer to Chapter 8 for how to turn it on. Also, you should have your formatted "Test Disk" handy.

The Root Directory

Subdirectory organization starts at the root, just as a tree grows from its root. All disks have a root directory. It's from this directory that subdirectories branch.

Note: The root directory is the main directory on every disk.

Every disk—whether it's a 160K floppy or a 600M hard drive—has a root directory. As with everything, DOS has a name—actually a symbol—for the root directory. It's the backslash character, \.

Note: The backslash character, \, is the symbol for the root directory.

You've already been using the root directory—and haven't known it, although DOS has told you so several times. Turn your computer on if it isn't on already. Take a look at the DOS prompt:

```
C:\>
```

The first part of the DOS prompt tells you where you are. (This was discussed in Chapter 9.) Specifically, it tells you which drive you're using and which subdirectory on that drive you're using. Above, "C:" refers to drive C, and the backslash, \, tells you you're using the root directory; you are logged to drive C, the root directory. (The greater-than symbol, >, is still just a prompt marking where you enter the command line.)

The DIR command has also been telling you about the root directory. At the DOS prompt, type the following:

```
DIR
```

Press Enter. DOS displays a list of files in the root directory. How do you know that? Take a look at the top of the directory listing:

```
Volume in drive C is DOS 5
Volume Serial Number is xxxx-xxxx
Directory of C:\
```

That third line says you're looking at the directory of drive C, the root directory. "C:\" means drive C, root directory. When you used the DIR command on another drive, the root directory of that drive was also displayed.

DOS commands can also reference the root directory, just as you reference different drives in the system. Type the following:

```
DIR \
```

This command reads, "give me a directory of the root." Press Enter. The files in the root directory are displayed. This is nothing new; since you were logged to the root directory all the time, the DIR command was just assuming that's what you wanted. (DOS assumes a lot.)

Info: It's actually the root directory that has a limitation on the number of files it can hold. A 360K diskette's root directory has room for only 112 files; a hard drive's root directory has room for only 512. However, one of those "files" can be a subdirectory, into which you can put an almost unlimited number of files. That's how a hard drive is able to hold thousands of files.

Making Subdirectories

The root directory is only the name given to a disk's main directory. Before DOS version 2, there was no such thing as a root directory. All disks had only a main directory, which didn't have a name.

Subdirectories are directories you create beneath the root directory. They sprout from the root, like branches in the upside-down tree. It's these subdirectories into which you'll be placing your files and organizing them. The root is only the starting point.

Each disk's root directory is created when the disk is first formatted. To make the subdirectories, you need to use a special DOS command, MKDIR.

Note: Subdirectories can be created on any disk, not only on the hard drive. They are the key to organizing your files, although that aspect of using subdirectories will be covered in a later chapter.

The MKDIR Command

The MKDIR command creates a new subdirectory. MKDIR stands for Make

Directory and that's what it does. An abbreviated version of the command is MD, which does the same thing. Since it's easier to type, this book uses MD.

Insert your Test Disk (formatted in the previous chapter) into your A drive. Log to drive A by typing:

```
A:
```

Press Enter. The DOS prompt changes, reflecting your new location—the root directory on drive A:

```
A:\>
```

To create a new directory, you follow the MD command with the name of the new subdirectory. Type the following:

```
MD DATA
```

Check your typing: That's the MD command, a space, and the name of the new subdirectory, DATA. Press Enter.

Info: Subdirectories are named just like files. As such, the file naming rules apply:

A subdirectory follows the 8-dot-3 naming pattern: an eight-character name followed by an optional dot and up to three characters for an extension. Note, however, that subdirectories are rarely given an extension.

Valid characters for a subdirectory include letters, numbers, and symbols. You cannot include a period, unless it's identifying an extension, nor can you include a space or any of the following characters:

```
" / \ [ ] : * | < > + = ; , ?
```

Note that a Subdirectory can start with a number or any character.

A subdirectory is essentially a file on disk—and the DIR command displays them that way. As such, you cannot give a subdirectory the name of a file that already exists. Each name must be unique.

The disk spins for a few seconds and then... there's the DOS prompt again. The MD command is one of those silent DOS commands; you won't get any visual feedback. However, type the following:

```
DIR
```

Since a subdirectory is listed by the DIR command, you can see it now by pressing Enter:

```
Volume in drive A is TEST DISK
Volume Serial Number is xxxx-xxxx
Directory of A:\

DATA     <DIR>     02-27-93    7:00a
  1 file(s)          0 bytes
                xxxxxx bytes free
```

The directory of drive A, root directory, shows one "file" present—your subdirectory, DATA. That subdirectory occupies zero bytes on the disk.

Info: When you see "<DIR>" in a directory listing, it indicates a subdirectory, not a file.

Now your Test Disk has one subdirectory, into which you can eventually put all sorts of files. You can create as many subdirectories in the root directory as there is room for. On the typical floppy diskette that's 112 files total for low capacity and 224 files for high capacity. Of course no one will ever need that many; with good organization, only a few subdirectories branching off the root are necessary.

Create two more subdirectories on your Test-Disk floppy. Name the first DOS and the second WP. Into DOS you can assume you would put DOS files; WP may be for word processing. (This is only an example of good naming tactics; there's no real need to set up a floppy disk this way.) Go ahead and do this on your own using the MD command. The answers are listed below.

Note: The MD command doesn't give any feedback; use the DIR command to verify that the directories have been created.

To create the DOS subdirectory, you should have typed the following:

```
MD DOS
```

The WP subdirectory is created with:

```
MD WP
```

The directory listing will now show three files:

```
Volume in drive A is TEST DISK
Volume Serial Number is xxxx-xxxx
Directory of A:\

DATA      <DIR>      02-27-93      7:00a
DOS       <DIR>      02-27-93      7:04a
WP        <DIR>      02-27-93      7:05a
        3 file(s)    0 bytes
                     xxxxxxx bytes free
```

What's in those subdirectories? Nothing. You haven't put anything there—you haven't even used the subdirectories yet. But you can take a peek at them. The DIR command will show you what's in any subdirectory. You just follow the DIR command with the name of the subdirectory. Type the following:

```
DIR DATA
```

Press Enter. You'll see:

```
Volume in drive A is TEST DISK
Volume Serial Number is xxxx-xxxx
Directory of A:\DATA

.       <DIR>      02-27-93      7:00a
..      <DIR>      02-27-93      7:00a
      2 file(s)       0 bytes
                      xxxxxxx bytes free
```

This is a directory of "A:\DATA," drive A, DATA subdirectory of the root directory. There are two files present—actually two directories—but they have quite unusual names (you'll learn about those dots later).

Following the DIR command with the name of a subdirectory is just like following DIR with the name of another drive. DIR will always bend over and take a peek in wherever you tell it to look.

Info: Later in this chapter you'll read about pathnames, which is what the DIR command really uses when it looks elsewhere on disk.

COMMAND: MKDIR (Internal)
MD
Function: To create or make a new subdirectory.
Format: MKDIR pathname
MD pathname

Pathname is the name of the new directory to create. The naming rules are the same as for naming a file. Unless otherwise specified, the new directory is created under the current directory.

Changing Directories

To use another directory you must log to it, just as you log to another disk drive to use it. Logging to another disk drive is done by typing the drive letter (followed by a colon) at the DOS prompt and then pressing Enter. Typing the name of a subdirectory at the DOS prompt produces a "Bad command or filename" error. To change to that subdirectory, you must use the Change Directory command, CHDIR.

The CHDIR Command

The CHDIR command is used to change to, or log to, another directory or subdirectory. CHDIR stands for Change Directory. An abbreviated version is CD, which is more popular and, yes, easier to type.

Info: The CHDIR command actually does two things. Changing directories is only one of them. The command's other function is covered in the next section.

To change to another directory, you follow the CD command with that directory's name. This is your main way of navigating through a subdirectory structure. Type the following:

```
CD DOS
```

That's the CD command, a space, and the name of the subdirectory to change to, DOS. Press Enter.

```
A:\DOS>
```

The only feedback you have is the DOS prompt, which now reflects your new location. The CD command was successful; you're now logged to the subdirectory DOS on drive A.

Since DOS is now the current directory, all DOS commands will assume you mean it instead of the root directory. Prove this by typing the DIR command:

```
DIR
```

Press Enter and the following is displayed:

```
Volume in drive A is TEST DISK
Volume Serial Number is xxxx-xxxx
Directory of A:\DOS

  .      <DIR>    02-27-93     7:00a
  ..     <DIR>    02-27-93     7:00a
     2 file(s)           0 bytes
                  xxxxxxx bytes free
```

The DOS directory is empty, just as the directory listing for the DATA subdirectory was earlier. However, it still contains those curious dot files. Hang on— they'll be explained shortly.

Tip: To display the contents of the root directory from the DOS subdirectory, you would enter the command:

```
DIR \
```

Or to be more specific, you could type:

```
DIR A:\
```

Log back to the root directory. Type:

```
CD \
```

The name of the root directory is \. The above command logs you to the root. Press Enter.

```
A:\>
```

If you were to visualize the directory structure created so far, a picture you could form would be like Figure 14-2. To make the directory structure more complete (more like Figure 14-1) you need to use both the CD and MD commands to add new directories.

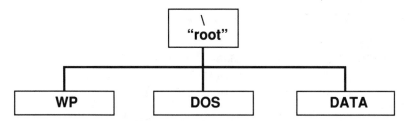

Figure 14-2 The directory structure so far.

First, add two subdirectories to the WP directory. Start by changing to the WP subdirectory:

```
CD WP
```

Press Enter. The DOS prompt changes to reflect your new location:

```
A:\WP>
```

When you create a directory using MD, it's placed in the current directory. Using MD now would make subdirectories off of the WP subdirectory—a sub-subdirectory (although it's still referred to as a "subdirectory").

Create the MEMOS subdirectory by typing the following:

```
MD MEMOS
```

Press Enter. Create the LETTERS subdirectory by typing:

```
MD LETTERS
```

Press Enter. Use the DIR command to verify your work:

```
DIR
```

Press Enter.

```
Volume in drive A is TEST DISK
Volume Serial Number is xxxx-xxxx
Directory of A:\WP

.           <DIR>    02-27-93    7:00a
..          <DIR>    02-27-93    7:00a
MEMOS       <DIR>    02-27-93    7:21a
LETTERS     <DIR>    02-27-93    7:21a
    4 file(s)        0 bytes
                xxxxxxx bytes free
```

There are the two curious dot entries, plus your two new subdirectories, MEMOS and LETTERS, each earmarked by "<DIR>."

COMMAND: CHDIR (Internal)
          CD
          Function: To change to a new subdirectory.
          Format: CHDIR [drive:]pathname
                      CD [drive:]pathname

Drive is optional. If specified, CD will change directories on that drive to the one specified by pathname. You will not, however, be logged to that drive.

Pathname is the name of the directory to change to.

Pathnames

The second function of the CD command is to "tell you where you are." When typed by itself, the CD command displays the currently logged disk drive and subdirectory. Type the following:

```
CD
```

Press Enter.

```
A:\WP
```

What the CD command displayed is the pathname. You see the currently logged drive as well as the currently logged directory—the same thing the DOS prompt displays.

Definition: A pathname is a precise location on disk—the disk drive letter and subdirectory name.

At present you're logged to the WP subdirectory. Use the CD command to log to the LETTERS subdirectory you just created:

```
CD LETTERS
```

Press Enter and you're in the LETTERS subdirectory. This is already reflected by the DOS prompt, but can be verified by the CD command. Type:

```
CD
```

Press Enter:

```
A:\WP\LETTERS
```

What CD displays is a full pathname—your current location. CD tells you where you are—but where are you? What does A:\WP\LETTERS mean? Take a look at it in pieces. Refer to Figure 14-3.

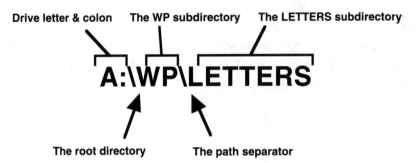

Figure 14-3 Anatomy of a pathname.

The pathname displays the exact subdirectory you're logged to. Above, you're logged to the subdirectory LETTERS, which is a subdirectory of WP, which is a subdirectory of the root directory on drive A.

Info: You can think of a pathname as a "path" to a specific location on disk. For example, to get to A:\WP\LETTERS, you must first log to drive A, then use the CD command to log to the \WP and then the LETTERS subdirectory.

A:	The A drive
A:\	The root directory
A:\WP	The WP subdirectory
A:\WP\LETTERS	The LETTERS subdirectory

Note how the backslash character is used to separate the different subdirectories. In addition to identifying the root directory, the backslash also keeps the names of the various subdirectories from running together.

Info: The backslash is used in a pathname to separate the subdirectories. Why a backslash? Microsoft really wanted to use the forward slash, which is an easier key to find and type. But the slash character had already been assigned a purpose under

DOS version 1. So for DOS version 2, the backslash character was used.

There is a limit to a pathname. DOS allows for no more than 63 characters in a pathname, which includes the drive letter, colon and all the backslashes. This also defines the limit of how "deep" you can go with subdirectories.

Info: As you become clever at this, you can create a subdirectory that's 30 levels deep; 30 one-letter subdirectory names will fit into a 63-character pathname. In practice, however, even the most organized of PC users never get more than three or four subdirectory levels deep.

Pathnames are used all the time in DOS. Usually, a pathname will end with a filename, which makes sense because it tells you exactly where a file is located on disk. However, pathnames can also describe directories. Change back to the root directory. Go there directly, do not pass WP, do not collect $200. Instead, type:

```
CD \
```

Press Enter. Now use the DIR command to display the files in the A:\WP\MEMOS subdirectory. Type:

```
DIR \WP\MEMOS
```

Press Enter.

The DIR command accepts a full pathname as its optional parameter. You can list any pathname after DIR to see which files are there.

The CD command is also capable of "looking elsewhere." Type the following:

```
CD C:
```

When followed by a drive letter, the CD command will display the currently logged subdirectory for that drive. Press Enter. Unless you've been messing around, the root directory on drive C will be displayed. If you have other drives, use the CD command on them to see which subdirectory they're using.

COMMAND: CHDIR (Internal)
                   CD
                   Function: To display the pathname of the current directory.
                   Format: CHDIR [drive:]
                               CD [drive:]

Drive is optional. If specified, CD displays the current directory (pathname) for that drive.

Parent and Child Directories

Another way to look at the tree structured directory is to view it like a family tree. Right now, you're logged to the root directory on drive A. That directory has three children: DATA, DOS, and WP.

The WP subdirectory has two children: MEMOS and LETTERS. It also has a parent directory, the root directory. (The root directory has no parent—it's an orphan!)

This concept of parent-and-child directories explains a few things. For example, when you create a subdirectory with the MKDIR, you're really creating a child directory in the current directory. Also, it explains the purpose behind those two unusual directory entries you see in each subdirectory.

Log to the DATA subdirectory. Type:

```
CD DATA
```

Press Enter. Now pull a directory. Type:

```
DIR
```

Press Enter.

Info: The term "pull a directory" means to list a directory, or to use the DIR command.

```
Volume in drive A is TEST DISK
Volume Serial Number is xxxx-xxxx
Directory of A:\DATA

    .        <DIR>      02-27-93    7:00a
    ..       <DIR>      02-27-93    7:00a
     2 file(s)           0 bytes
                    xxxxxxx bytes free
```

Every subdirectory on disk has these two files in it: dot and dot-dot. Both files have the "<DIR>" notation by them, indicating they're subdirectories. But you didn't create them with MD. Or did you?

The dot and dot-dot entries are indeed subdirectories. Actually, they're abbreviations. The single dot is an abbreviation for the current directory; the dot-dot is an abbreviation for the parent directory. Prove this by typing the following:

```
DIR .
```

Press Enter. The DIR command displays the directory for the pathname listed. In this case, you see the directory of A:\DATA—the current directory. Now do the same with dot-dot:

```
DIR ..
```

Press Enter. The DIR command displays the root directory, the parent of the DATA directory.

Tip: Here's a handy trick:

```
CD ..
```

This CD command always moves you up to the parent directory—regardless of its name.

Building a Structure

Change directories to the root. Type the following if you're not already there:

```
CD \
```

Press Enter.

The DATA subdirectory pictured in Figure 14-2 has two child directories: BUDGET and PROJECTS. Additionally, BUDGET has a subdirectory JULY. You can make those directories using the MD command in two ways:

1. Change to the future parent directory and use the MD command.

2. Use the full pathname of the new directory with the MD command.

Use step one to create the PROJECTS subdirectory. Type the following:

```
CD DATA
```

Press Enter. This logs you to the DATA subdirectory. To create PROJECTS, type the following:

```
MD PROJECTS
```

Press Enter. Use the DIR command to verify that the subdirectory PROJECTS has been created. Then change back to the root directory:

```
CD \
```

Press Enter.

Now, use step two to create BUDGET and put the JULY subdirectory under BUDGET. This will use the full pathname with the MD command, as opposed to moving to the parent directory.

To create BUDGET under the DATA subdirectory, enter the following:

```
MD \DATA\BUDGET
```

Double check your typing. DOS requires precision: The MD command is followed by a space, then a backslash to represent the root directory, the DATA subdirectory, a backslash (separator), and finally the new directory, BUDGET. Look it over to confirm what you're doing. Press Enter.

Info: Successfully creating a subdirectory doesn't produce any messages. If you make a mistake, DOS may display the message "Invalid function," "Path not found," or "Unable to create directory." Check your typing and try again.

The subdirectory BUDGET has been created remotely by using a full pathname. Before getting any concrete proof, create the JULY subdirectory under BUDGET now.

Tip: Press the F3 key!

Type the following:

```
MD \DATA\BUDGET\JULY
```

Note: If you already see "MD\DATA\BUDGET" at the DOS prompt, then just type the final backslash and JULY. Press Enter.

How is that for remote control? Why not do the same thing to create a JUNE subdirectory under BUDGET? Type the following:

```
MD \DATA\BUDGET\JUNE
```

Tip: Press the F3 key, backspace twice, then NE.

Press Enter.
Verify your work using the DIR command. Type the following:

```
DIR \DATA\BUDGET
```

Press Enter.

```
Volume in drive A is TEST DISK
Volume Serial Number is xxxx-xxxx
Directory of A:\DATA\BUDGET

   .      <DIR>    02-27-93    7:00a
   ..     <DIR>    02-27-93    7:00a
JULY     <DIR>    02-27-93    7:40a
JUNE     <DIR>    02-27-93    7:41a
     4 file(s)         0 bytes
                  xxxxxxx bytes free
```

The directory of A:\DATA\BUDGET shows two new subdirectories: JULY and JUNE. The operation was a success.

Navigating the Disk

To visit your new subdirectories, use the CD command. First, travel on down to the JULY subdirectory. From the root you need to enter the following commands, pressing Enter after each:

```
CD DATA
CD BUDGET
CD JULY

A:\DATA\BUDGET\JULY>
```

Wait a second! That was three commands—definitely a waste of time. Go back to the root directory. Type:

```
CD \
```

Now log to the new JULY subdirectory by typing:

```
CD \DATA\BUDGET\JULY
```

Press Enter. Ta-da! Much faster.

Tip: You can move anywhere in your subdirectory structure by typing the full pathname. This avoids the time wasted by "climbing the tree."

Now log to the JUNE subdirectory. This can be done with two commands:

```
CD \DATA\BUDGET
```

or

```
CD .. CD JUNE
```

Or just one command:

```
CD \DATA\BUDGET\JUNE
```

To move to the MEMOS subdirectory under WP, type the following:

```
CD \WP\MEMOS
```

Press Enter. See how you moved from one branch of the subdirectory tree to another? There was no need to first go to the root directory, then log to \WP\MEMOS. The CD command takes you directly to any place on the current drive directly.

The RMDIR Command

The final subdirectory command is RMDIR, which removes a subdirectory. RMDIR stands for Remove Directory. Like MKDIR and CHDIR, an abbreviated version of the RMDIR command is available: RD.

Info: DOS's subdirectory commands are:

MKDIR	MD	Make a subdirectory
CHDIR	CD	Change to another subdirectory
CHDIR	CD	Display the pathname/a subdirectory's location
RMDIR	RD	Remove a directory

The RD command isn't used that often. Of the three subdirectory commands, CD is the most popular. You'll only use MD as you build the subdirectory structure. If you've planned things right, there will be little need to use RD to remove subdirectories.

To remove a subdirectory you specify its name or a full pathname after the RD command. But before removing a subdirectory you must make sure of the following things:

1. There can be no child directories in the subdirectory you're removing.

2. There can be no files in the subdirectory you're removing.

3. You cannot delete a subdirectory if you're logged to that subdirectory (which would be like destroying the building you're in, when you think about it).

Tip: A subdirectory must be "empty" before you can remove it with the RD command.

The only two files allowed in a subdirectory you're about to remove are dot and dot-dot. If not, DOS displays the following error message:

```
Invalid path, not directory, or directory not empty
```

Although you can follow the RD command with a full pathname, it's recommended to delete a subdirectory from its parent. Log to the \DATA\BUDGET subdirectory by typing:

```
CD \DATA\BUDGET
```

Press Enter. Carefully type the following:

```
RD JUNE
```

Press Enter. The JUNE subdirectory is gone. No fanfare, no bleeps, no warnings. Use the DIR command to confirm that it's gone, or try changing to that directory:

```
A:\DATA\BUDGET>CD JUNE
Invalid directory

A:\DATA\BUDGET>
```

Again, you won't be using RD that often. When you do, remember the rules about deleting a subdirectory. Most often, people forget about removing all files and subdirectories before using RD. (And, yes, that implies that you must use the RD command on any child directories of the directory you want to delete—kill off the whole family, so to speak.)

COMMAND: RMDIR (Internal)
                RD
                Function: To remove or delete a subdirectory.
                Format: RMDIR pathname
                               RD pathname

Pathname is the name of the directory you want to remove. It must be empty (contain no files or subdirectories). You cannot be logged to the *pathname* you're about to delete.

The TREE Command

The figures in this chapter have given you a good idea of what your subdirectory structure looks like. But there's a DOS command that's just as handy.

The TREE command is used to display all or part of your directory structure. Log to the root directory by typing:

```
CD \
```

Press Enter. Now type in the TREE command:

```
TREE
```

Press Enter. The TREE command gives you a graphic representation of the subdirectory structure on disk. You should see something like this:

```
Directory PATH listing for Volume TEST DISK
Volume Serial Number is xxxx-xxxx
A:.
+ _ _ _ DATA
|     + _ _ _ PROJECTS
|     + _ _ _ BUDGET
|           + _ _ _ JULY
+ _ _ _ DOS
+ _ _ _ WP
      + _ _ _ MEMOS
      + _ _ _ LETTERS
```

The subdirectory structure is referred to as a "PATH listing" by the TREE command. You'll notice that it starts with drive A:, the root directory. But the root directory is represented by a single dot. This is because you didn't specify a directory for the TREE command to start with. The TREE command therefore assumed you meant the current directory, which is represented by a dot.

Type the following:

```
TREE \
```

Press Enter. The output will be identical—however, because you specified the root directory, "A:\" appears at the top of the output. Type the following command to view the structure of your hard drive:

```
TREE C:\
```

Press Enter. What you see will vary, depending on how your hard drive is set up.

The TREE command also has a two optional parameters or switches. (They're switches if they start with a slash.)

The /A switch is used to have TREE produce its output using ASCII characters. Above, the TREE command displays your subdirectory structure using IBM's extended ASCII line-drawing characters. Type the following:

```
TREE \ /A
```

This TREE command has two optional parameters. First is the backslash, indicating the root directory. That's followed by a space, then the /A switch. Press Enter.

```
Directory PATH listing for Volume TEST DISK
Volume Serial Number is xxxx-xxxx
A:\
+ _ _ _ DATA
            +_ _ _PROJECTS
            \_ _ _BUDGET
                    \_ _ _JULY
+_ _ _DOS
\_ _ _WP
        +_ _ _MEMOS
        \_ _ _LETTERS
```

ASCII characters are used instead of the line-drawing characters. If you're just viewing the TREE command's output on the screen, then the /A switch is unnecessary. However, if you wanted to print the output and your printer cannot print the IBM extended ASCII line drawing characters, you should specify the /A switch.

Tip: To print the output of the TREE command, turn on DOS's echo-to-printer function by pressing Ctrl-P. (Make sure your printer is ready to print.) Then type in the TREE command, with the optional /A switch if necessary. When you're done, turn off echo-to-printer by typing Ctrl-P again.

The second optional parameter is the /F switch. When specified, the TREE command will list all the files found in the various subdirectories. Type the following:

```
TREE \ /F
```

Tip: Press F3, backspace, then F.

Press Enter. The output will be the same, since the diskette in drive A has no files, only subdirectories. However, your hard drive is probably packed full of files. Type the following:

```
TREE C:\ /F
```

Check your typing; remember the space between the drive parameter (C:\) and the optional switch (/F). Press Enter.

Depending on how many files are on your hard drive, you could be looking at them for quite a time. Quickly scroll by.

Tip: Press the Pause key to temporarily freeze the display. Press the Spacebar to continue. If your keyboard lacks a Pause key, use the Ctrl-S key to pause the display.

COMMAND: TREE (External)
    Function: To display the subdirectory structure for a drive.
    Format: TREE [drive:][pathname] [/A][/F]

Without any parameters, the TREE command displays your subdirectory structure from the currently logged directory down through any subdirectories it has.

Drive specifies a disk drive you wish the TREE command to examine. If not specified, DOS assumes you mean the current drive.

Pathname specifies the starting subdirectory. The TREE command will display your subdirectory structure from that *pathname* downward. If not specified, DOS assumes you mean the current directory (which is specified by a dot).

/A is the ASCII switch. When specified, the output of the TREE command is produced using ASCII characters.

/F is the Files switch. When specified, the TREE command lists any files found in the subdirectories.

Working with Subdirectories in the Editor

The MS-DOS Editor has the ability to save and load files to and from any subdirectory on any disk. Start the Editor by typing:

```
EDIT
```

Press Enter, and then Esc to skip over the Survival guide. From the File menu, choose the Open item. You'll see the Open dialog box displayed.

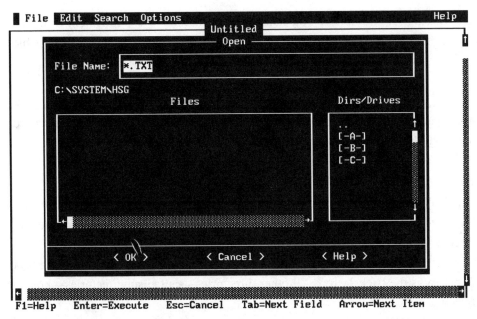

Figure 14-4 The Editor's Open dialog box.

At the right center of the dialog box is a smaller box entitled "Dirs/Drives." You can use the box to log to any other disk drive or subdirectory in your system.

Subdirectories are listed in the box by their name and the parent subdirectory is shown as dot-dot. Drives are listed by their letter and enclosed in square brackets.

To change to another drive or directory, press the Tab key until the "Dirs/Drives" box is highlighted. Then use the arrow keys to select the directory or drive you want. Press Enter.

This isn't the most logical or obvious way to negotiate a subdirectory structure in an application, but it is common. You can always type in the text file's full pathname by the "File Name:" prompt.

Press Esc to close the dialog box, then exit from the Editor: Press Alt-F, then X.

Subdirectory Limitations

There are some things DOS won't let you do with subdirectories. These include:

Renaming subdirectories. Once it's created, you cannot change a subdirectory's name. (This is odd because it is possible to rename a file once it's created.)

Moving subdirectories. You cannot pickup and move a subdirectory from one branch to another. This is referred to as "pruning and grafting," and it is possible using some DOS programs and utilities—but not with DOS directly.

As you keep reading this book, you'll discover how to perform hard disk management. If you do it right (and this book will show you how), you won't need to worry about renaming or moving subdirectories.

Summary

DOS lets you organize megabytes of disk storage by using subdirectories. Subdirectories solve the problems of the limited number of files on disk (in the root directory), file-naming conflicts, and organization.

Each disk has one main directory, the root directory. The symbol for the root directory is the backslash, \. All other directories—called subdirectories—branch from the root.

The MKDIR or MD command is used to create subdirectories. MD is followed by the name of the new subdirectory, which is named just like a file.

The CHDIR or CD command is used to change or log to another subdirectory. Also, the CD command by itself displays the full pathname of the subdirectory.

A pathname gives the exact location of a subdirectory or file. It starts with the drive letter, colon, root directory (\), and all the subdirectories that lead to the current directory. Each subdirectory in the pathname is separated by a backslash.

The directory above the currently used directory is referred to as the parent directory, and its symbol is dot-dot. The current directory's symbol is the single dot. Subdirectories in the current directory are referred to as child directories.

The RMDIR or RD command is used to remove a subdirectory. To be removed, a subdirectory must be empty, containing no files or subdirectories of its own. Also, you cannot remove a directory if you're currently logged to it.

The TREE command displays a disk's directory structure.

Finally, you cannot rename a subdirectory or move it using conventional DOS commands. Certain third-party programs and tools called utilities will allow you to "prune and graft" subdirectories.

CHAPTER 15

File Manipulation

DOS is a file manipulator. Behind the scenes it moves information (bytes) from memory to disk, storing it in convenient files. But the manipulation doesn't end there. DOS has several commands that help you manage the files once they're on disk: You can copy files, rename them, and delete them.

This chapter answers the following questions:

- How do files get on disk?

- What does the COPY command do?

- What does the RENAME command do?

- What does the DEL command do?

- How is it possible to work with more than one file at a time?

Creating Some Sample Files

In order to practice manipulating files, you need some files to manipulate. Normally these would be files you created or were using on the hard drive. But since all this is practice, you're going to use the MS-DOS Editor to create some sample files on the Test-Disk floppy. You'll manipulate those expendable files instead.

Start your computer if it's not already on. Enter the date and time. Insert your floppy diskette labeled "Test Disk" into drive A and log to it. Type:

```
A:
```

Press Enter.

Now you're going to create three text files using the Editor:

ABOUT.ME, which contains information about yourself

FOOD.TXT, which contains a list of food to eat

TIPS.TXT, which lists some handy DOS tips

Fire up the editor by typing the following at the DOS prompt:

```
EDIT
```

Press Enter.

Info: This chapter assumes you've used the Editor and know how it works. For a review of using the Editor, refer to Chapter 12.

Press Esc to skirt around the Survival Guide and dive right into the Editor.

Creating ABOUT.ME

The first file you're going to create should tell a little bit about yourself. If you're totally lost, then just create a file with your name and address, and possibly what you do for a living. For example:

```
Dan Gookin
Writer
P.O. Box 24296
San Diego, CA 92124
```

You can type the above (if you like), or create your own "about me" file. Remember to press Enter after each line.

Save your file to disk, naming it ABOUT.ME. Follow these steps:

1. Drop down through the File menu—press Alt-F.

2. Select the Save As menu item—press A.

3. Type ABOUT.ME in the box—the filename is ABOUT, followed by the filename separator (the dot), and the extension is ME.

4. Press Enter and the file is saved. Note that the title of the text-input window is now "ABOUT.ME".

Creating FOOD.TXT

The file ABOUT.ME is saved on disk, but its contents are still in the Editor. To create the FOOD.TXT file, you need to clear the text-editing window and start over. (This is much more efficient than restarting the Editor to create a new file.)

To start editing a new file, follow these steps:

1. Drop down through the File menu—press Alt-F.

2. Select the New menu item—press N or Enter.

The Editor is now cleared and ready for you to type in a new file.

Note: If the text in the Editor has not been saved and you select New, you'll be given a warning and a last chance to save the file.

The FOOD.TXT file will contain a list of your favorite foods. If you can't think of any, or are afraid to document on the computer what you really like to eat, then type in the following. Press Enter at the end of each line:

```
Pizza
M&Ms
Ice Cream
Twinkies
Peanut Butter
Pretzels
Coffee
Pringles
Ding Dongs
Oreos
```

Mmm, mmm. Save this file as FOOD.TXT. Follow the same steps as you did for creating ABOUT.ME file above.

Clear out the Editor (New) and get ready to create the final text file.

Creating TIPS.TXT

The TIPS.TXT file will contain a list of some handy DOS tips, stuff that you've been learning throughout this part of the book, and information which cannot be told by the HELP command.

Enter the following, pressing Enter after each line. To create the blank lines, just press Enter. If you want to add your own tips and suggestions or things you keep forgetting, feel free to do so.

```
A filename uses the 8-dot-3 pattern.
The following characters cannot be used in a filename:
(space) . " / \ [ ] : * | < > + = ; , ?

To log to another drive, type its drive letter followed by a
     colon.
To log to drive A, type A:
To log to drive B, type B:
To log to drive C, type C:

The root directory is named \.

To log to another subdirectory, use the CD command,
followed by the subdirectory's name.

You can log to any subdirectory directly by typing CD
followed by the pathname.

The . directory entry indicates the current directory.
The .. directory entry indicates the parent directory.
```

Save the file as TIPS.TXT, using the same commands and keystrokes mentioned earlier.

After saving the file, quit to DOS:

1. Drop down the File menu, press Alt-F.

2. Select the Exit menu item, press X.
You're back at the DOS prompt.

Checking Your Work

At the DOS prompt, type the following:

```
DIR
```

Press Enter. You should see something that looks similar to the following:

```
    Volume in drive A is TEST DISK
    Volume Serial Number is xxxx-xxxx
    Directory of A:\
DATA   <DIR> 02-27-93  7:00a
DOS    <DIR> 02-27-93  7:08a
WP <DIR> 02-27-93  7:09a
ABOUT   ME    62 03-01-93 10:40a
FOOD   TXT    98 03-01-93 10:52a
TIPS   TXT   648 03-01-93 10:57a
    6 file(s)    808 bytes
    xxxxxxx bytes free
```

The three files you created are shown in the directory listing, along with their sizes (which may vary, depending on what you put in your files), and dates and times. The DIR command also tells you there are "6 file(s)" listed, and the total amount of disk space they occupy is 808 bytes. The remainder of space available on the diskette will be listed in the last line.

Another way to verify the files is by using the TYPE command. To see your file's contents, type the following:

```
TYPE ABOUT.ME
```

Press Enter to see the ABOUT.ME file.

```
TYPE FOOD.TXT
```

Press Enter to see the contents of FOOD.TXT.

```
TYPE TIPS.TXT
```

Press Enter to see TIPS.TXT.

Using the COPY Command

Files accumulate on disks like coat hangers multiply in closets. The difference is, we know how files appear:

Files—such as ABOUT.ME, FOOD.TXT, or TIPS.TXT—are created by applications.

Files are generated by software. Although you may not order a program to save information, the program itself may save information to disk for later retrieval.

Files are duplicated or copied from an original. This is how you install software or files on your system: You use a DOS command to make a duplicate of the file, placing the copy on your hard drive.

The DOS command that duplicates or copies files is named, appropriately, COPY.

The COPY command needs to know two things: The original file, called the source file, and the name of the duplicate file, called the destination file.

When you copy a file from one drive to another, or from one subdirectory to another, you tell the COPY command the location of the original file and where you want the duplicate. The original (the source) is then copied to the duplicate (the destination). (The COPY command creates the duplicate file.) In the end you have two of the same files on disk in different locations.

You can also use the COPY command to make a duplicate of a file in the same directory. But when you do so, the duplicate must have a new name; no two files in the same directory can share the same name.

Info: The source file is the file you're copying—the original, like an original in a photocopying machine. The destination file is the name and location of the duplicate file. That duplicate will have the same contents as the original, but it may not necessarily have the same name.

Duplicating a File

To make a copy of the ABOUT.ME file, type the following at the DOS prompt:

```
COPY ABOUT.ME MYSELF
```

The source file is ABOUT.ME, the destination file is MYSELF. The COPY command will take the contents of ABOUT.ME and place them into a new file named MYSELF which it creates. Since another location for MYSELF isn't specified, DOS will place that file into the current directory.

Info: When you duplicate a file with the COPY command, DOS creates a new file on disk. Because of this, the duplicate must follow the same naming rules as all other files. Refer to Appendix F for the file-naming rules.

Press Enter. The disk drive spins for a moment (check the drive light, confirming that there's activity on the drive). Then you see:

```
1 file(s) copied
```

The "1 file(s) copied" message is DOS's way of telling you that one file was just copied successfully. Verify this with the DIR command, type:

```
DIR
```

Press Enter and you'll see the MYSELF file in the listing. Note that it gives the same size as the ABOUT.ME file—but a different time since it was created later than ABOUT.ME. You can verify that both files contain the same information by typing the following:

```
TYPE MYSELF
```

Press Enter. You'll see the contents of the MYSELF file, which are identical to the ABOUT.ME file. Indeed, it is a copy.

Tip: You can quick-compare any two files on disk using the COMP command. Type the following:

```
COMP ABOUT.ME MYSELF
```

This tells DOS to compare the contents of the file ABOUT.ME with the contents of the file MYSELF. Press Enter and you'll see:

```
Comparing ABOUT.ME and MYSELF...
Files compare OK
Compare more files (Y/N) ?
```

Type N and Enter to return to DOS.

Some Limitations

You can go around making copies of any file on disk. DOS isn't fussy about this. Files can be duplicated until you fill up the disk. But there are some things the COPY command won't do. Type the following:

```
COPY MYSELF
```

Press Enter.

```
File cannot be copied onto itself
0 file(s) copied
```

Oops. The DOS command "COPY MYSELF" doesn't tell DOS where you want the file MYSELF copied to. So DOS assumes you mean the current directory. Yet, DOS is smart enough to see that MYSELF is already there, which makes the operation redundant. In the end, no file was copied. But don't overestimate DOS's I.Q. Type the following:

```
COPY FOOD.TXT MYSELF
```

Press Enter.

```
1 file(s) copied
```

It's true, the file MYSELF already existed. Yet the COPY command will diligently overwrite that file, replacing it with a copy of the FOOD.TXT file now named MYSELF. Prove this by typing:

```
TYPE MYSELF
```

Press Enter and you'll see a duplicate of the FOOD.TXT file. The original file, MYSELF, was overwritten; you told DOS to COPY the file FOOD.TXT to a file named MYSELF. DOS didn't bother to warn you that a file already named MYSELF was on disk. Instead, it diligently created a duplicate of FOOD.TXT using the name MYSELF. The original MYSELF file is now gone.

Info: The COPY command does not warn you when it overwrites a file.

Although it's true that "a file cannot be copied onto itself," it's equally true that a file can be copied onto any other file—as long as it has a name that's different from the original or that is in a different directory. Be aware of this or you might accidentally overwrite some files.

COPYing to Another Drive

To make a duplicate of a file in the same directory, you only need specify a new name for the duplicate. When you copy a file to another drive or subdirectory, the new name is optional.

Type in the following:

```
COPY FOOD.TXT C:
```

Press Enter.

```
1 file(s) copied
```

The file FOOD.TXT has been copied to drive C. FOOD.TXT is the source and the destination is drive C. Since a filename wasn't specified, DOS gives the duplicate the same name as the original. To prove this, pull a directory of drive C. Type the following:

```
DIR C:
```

Press Enter. In the directory listing for drive C you'll find the FOOD.TXT file. (You may have to press the Pause key or Ctrl-S to stop the listing so that you can locate FOOD.TXT.)

Info: When copying a file to another drive, you can get as specific as you like. For example, copying a file to "C:" doesn't mention which subdirectory on drive C, so DOS assumes you mean drive C's current subdirectory. If you want to get specific, follow C: with the pathname where you want the file to go. For example:

```
COPY FOOD.TXT C:\
```

The above command copies the FOOD.TXT file to the root directory on drive C.

Unless you specify a new name for the duplicate file, the COPY command will give the duplicate the same name as the original. Type the following:

```
COPY FOOD.TXT C:EATS.TXT
```

232

Press Enter.

```
1 file(s) copied
```

The file FOOD.TXT has again been copied to drive C. This time, the copy has the new name, EATS.TXT. Pull a directory of drive C:

```
DIR C:
```

Press Enter and look for both files, FOOD.TXT and EATS.TXT.

The Optional Destination

DOS assumes a lot. One thing it assumes with the COPY command is the destination file's location. Only the source location of the original file is important. If you leave out the location of the destination file, DOS will assume you mean the current directory. Type the following:

```
COPY C:EATS.TXT
```

It looks like something is missing, but it's not. The source file is EATS.TXT on drive C. The destination? DOS assumes you mean the current directory. Press Enter.

```
1 file(s) copied
```

Info: The COPY command only requires a source filename. If a destination isn't specified, the file will be copied to the current drive and directory. But be aware of the following:

Using just the source file with the COPY command only works when you're copying to the drive or directory you're currently logged to.

If the file already exists, DOS will overwrite it.

You cannot use this trick to duplicate a file. If you do, DOS displays the "file cannot be copied onto itself" error. To duplicate a file in the same directory, you must specify a new name.

233

COPYing to Another Directory

Copying files to other directories works just like copying a file between two drives. You must specify the source file and then the destination subdirectory. Type the following:

```
COPY TIPS.TXT \DATA\PROJECTS
```

Press Enter. The file TIPS.TXT is copied to the PROJECTS subdirectory under the DATA subdirectory. Since a new name wasn't specified, DOS uses the same name. Prove it by typing the following:

```
DIR \DATA\PROJECTS
```

Press Enter and you'll see the file TIPS.TXT in the directory listing.

To specify a new name for the file copied to another subdirectory, you separate the new filename from the subdirectory with a backslash. Type the following:

```
COPY ABOUT.ME \DATA\PROJECTS\MYSELF
```

The file ABOUT.ME will be copied to the \DATA\PROJECTS subdirectory. It will be given a new name, MYSELF. Note how MYSELF is separated from the subdirectory by the backslash character. Press Enter.

```
1 file(s) copied
```

Info: \DATA\PROJECTS\MYSELF is really a pathname, ending in a filename. It gives the exact location of the file on the disk. To be a full pathname, the drive letter and colon would be at the beginning. Since you're already logged to drive A, the drive is assumed.

The COPY Command and Concatenation

Concatenation is a big fancy word meaning to stick two things together. The COPY command can stick two text files together, producing a third file that contains the contents of both originals. This is done by using the plus sign, +.

Change directories down to the \DATA\PROJECTS subdirectory on drive A. Type:

```
CD \DATA\PROJECTS
```

Press Enter.

Two files in this subdirectory are TIPS.TXT and MYSELF. You can glue, or concatenate, both of these together using the COPY command and the plus sign. Type the following:

```
COPY MYSELF+TIPS.TXT COMBO
```

This command reads, "Take the contents of MYSELF, glue them to the contents of TIPS.TXT, and place the result into a file named COMBO."

Note: The original files, MYSELF and TIPS.TXT are not changed by this command. The COPY command never alters the source file.

Press Enter.

```
MYSELF TIPS.TXT
1 file(s) copied
```

Pull a directory to see the new file listed on disk. Type:

```
DIR
```

Press Enter.

```
Volume in drive A is TEST DISK
Volume Serial Number is xxxx-xxxx
Directory of A:\DATA\PROJECTS

              <DIR>    02-27-93    7:00a
              <DIR>    02-27-93    7:00a
TIPS      TXT    648   03-01-93   10:57a
MYSELF            62   03-01-93   10:40a
COMBO            711   03-01-93    1:42a
        5 file(s)      1421 bytes
                 xxxxxxx bytes free
```

The COMBO file contains the contents of both MYSELF and TIPS.TXT. Note how neither file was changed by the COPY command. Type the following:

```
TYPE COMBO
```

Press Enter. Ta-da! There's the concatenated file, your name and the tips.

Info: Using the COPY command for concatenation is rare, but it can be done. Above all, note that it can only be done with text files. You cannot make a large spreadsheet by concatenating two spreadsheet files. For this reason, the COPY command is usually only used to copy files.

Keep in mind that concatenation glues files together. It does not copy more than one file to another disk, although there is a way to copy several files at once to another location. This is covered later in this chapter, under the section entitled "Wildcards."

COMMAND: COPY (Internal)
           Function: To duplicate a file, to copy a file to another drive or
                          subdirectory.
           Format: COPY source[+source] [destination] [/a][/b][/v]

Source is the file to be copied. If source isn't in the current directory then it will be copied to the current directory.

+source are any additional files that will be concatenated (stuck to) the first source for creation of the copy.

Destination is the destination pathname for the file. If a new filename isn't specified, the destination will have the same name as the original file.

/A and /B are two optional switches, either of which may follow the source or destination. These tell DOS how to copy the files; whether to treat them as ASCII (text) files or as binary (non-ASCII) files. You can specify the /A switch after text files and the /B switch after binary files. In practice, this is rarely done.

/V is an optional switch that forces the COPY command to doubly verify that the contents of the duplicate are identical to the original. If you specify /V, the COPY command will take slightly longer to complete the copying, due to the verification. Normally /V isn't used.

Point of View

DOS makes a lot of assumptions. For example, if you use the CD command, DOS assumes you mean to change directories on the current drive. If you type "DIR", DOS assumes you mean "list files in the current directory." With the COPY command (as well as other file manipulation commands), unless you tell DOS otherwise, it will always assume you mean the current disk drive and subdirectory.

You can get as specific or as general as you want with any DOS command, particularly the COPY command. For example, each of the following commands does the same thing:

```
COPY ABOUT.ME \DATA\PROJECTS\MYSELF
COPY \ABOUT.ME \DATA\PROJECTS\MYSELF
COPY A:\ABOUT.ME A:\DATA\PROJECTS\MYSELF
```

They all copy the file ABOUT.ME from the root directory of drive A to the subdirectory \DATA\PROJECTS, also on drive A. If you're currently logged to drive A's root directory, any of the above commands will do the job. But supposed you're logged to drive C? In that case, you must be specific:

```
COPY A:\ABOUT.ME A:\DATA\PROJECTS\MYSELF
```

237

Any other command may assume that you mean to locate the file ABOUT.ME on drive C, which is incorrect.

If you're currently logged to the \DATA\PROJECTS subdirectory on drive A, you can get away with any of the following, moving in order from specific to general:

```
COPY A:\ABOUT.ME A:\DATA\PROJECTS\MYSELF
COPY \ABOUT.ME \DATA\PROJECTS\MYSELF
COPY \ABOUT.ME MYSELF
```

In the final example, DOS assumes you mean the current directory. If you didn't want to rename the copy to MYSELF, then the following command would work:

```
COPY \ABOUT.ME
```

Here, DOS assumes you mean the destination to be the current drive and subdirectory. Although DOS makes assumptions, make sure you don't fall into the same trap. Sometimes it pays to be precise.

These assumptions—and how detailed you can get with the COPY command— apply to nearly all DOS commands. It's also part of what I call "DOS's point of view." In DOS, you're always logged to a disk drive and directory. It's from that location—that perch—that DOS sees the rest of the drives and subdirectories in your system. This can be used to your advantage in several situations, a few of which are detailed throughout the remainder of this chapter.

Renaming Files

Once you create or COPY a file, its name can be changed. Just as a volume label of a disk can be changed, you can use a DOS command to change or rename a file— any file on disk. The command that does that is the RENAME command.

Info: The RENAME command—like CHDIR, MKDIR, and RMDIR—has an abbreviated version: REN. Most people use REN instead of RENAME.

The RENAME command requires two things: the file's original name and the new name. Log to the root directory of drive A. Type:

```
CD \
```

Press Enter.

Rename the file EATS.TXT to SNACKS (without an extension). Type the following:

```
REN EATS.TXT SNACKS
```

Press Enter. As with some other DOS commands, the REN command offers no feedback. But if you list the directory, you'll see that the file EATS.TXT has been changed to SNACKS. The contents of the file are the same, as are its size, date, and time. Type the following:

```
TYPE SNACKS
```

Press Enter. The file is essentially the same, but its name has changed (just like they used to do on Dragnet to protect the innocent).

Info: The new name you give a file must follow the file naming rules. Refer to Appendix F for a review of those rules and a list of which characters you cannot include in a filename.

You can use the REN command to remove a filename's extension. Type the following:

```
REN TIPS.TXT TIPS
```

Here you're removing the TXT extension by renaming the file to just TIPS. Press Enter. Use the DIR command to verify the change; use TYPE to confirm that the file retains its same contents.

Tip: In a like manner, you can use the REN command to give a file an extension. Just use the opposite format as the previous command, for example:

```
REN FILE FILE.TXT
```

RENAME and Brains

In a way, the REN command is smarter than COPY; you cannot rename a file with a name that already exists. Type the following:

```
REN MYSELF SNACKS
```

This will rename the file MYSELF to SNACKS—which already exists. Press Enter.

```
Duplicate file name or file not found
```

DOS is telling you no two files can share the same name in a directory. (And this error also appears when you try to rename a file that doesn't exist.)

Because a subdirectory is listed like a file in the directory listing, you cannot rename a file with a subdirectory's name either. Type the following:

```
REN MYSELF DATA
```

Press Enter.

```
Duplicate file name or file not found
```

Info: And, sadly, the REN command will not rename subdirectories. If you try it, you'll get an "Invalid path or file name" error.

If the file to be renamed isn't in the current directory, then you should specify a full path to it. Type the following:

```
REN \DATA\PROJECTS\COMBO FUSION
```

Note that the new name doesn't require a path, but only the new filename.

Press Enter. There's no feedback, but you can verify the change by typing the following:

```
DIR \DATA\PROJECTS
```

COMMAND: RENAME (Internal)
                     REN
                     Function: To rename files; give them a new name.
                     Format: RENAME oldname newname
                                       REN oldname newname

Oldname is the file's original name. If the file isn't in the current directory, then a full path to that file must be specified.

Newname is to be the file's new name; it's the filename only—not a path. *Newname* must follow the standard DOS file-naming rules, as listed in Appendix F.

Deleting Files

The final file manipulation command is the one that deletes files. Actually, DOS uses two commands used to delete files: DEL and ERASE. The ERASE command isn't as popular as DEL, which like REN and CD is quicker to type than ERASE. This book uses the DEL command, though you can use either DEL or ERASE on your system.

Deleting files is a natural part of file maintenance. Some files you just don't need any more. Sometimes you may copy files to a floppy diskette, in which case you can delete the originals on the hard drive. This is all done to free up space on disk, which disappears at a remarkable rate. DOS is designed to make the most efficient use of disk space. So when you delete a file, new files can move into the empty spaces. This is all considered file maintenance.

Tip: Deleting files is serious business. Once you delete a file—it's gone! DOS 5 does come with tools that will let you recover files you've accidentally deleted. Still, you should always be careful as to which files you delete.

Your Test Disk is full of files and subdirectories that can be deleted. Start in the root directory by removing the SNACKS file. Type the following:

```
DEL SNACKS
```

Press Enter. The DEL command is quiet and deadly. The DOS prompt appears again with no feedback. Type:

```
DIR
```

Press Enter and the SNACKS file is no where to be seen.

As with other commands, DEL can accept a pathname if the file to delete isn't in the current directory. Earlier in this chapter you copied two files to drive C— EATS.TXT and FOOD.TXT. Delete them with the following two DEL commands:

```
DEL C:EATS.TXT
DEL C:FOOD.TXT
```

This is a prime example of using the DEL command for cleanup; you don't need those two files on the hard drive, so use DEL to whisk them away.

COMMAND: DEL (Internal)
               ERASE
               Function: To delete files.
               Format: DEL pathname [/P]
                             ERASE pathname [/P]

Pathname is the name of the file to delete.

/P is an optional switch. When specified, DOS will ask you before it deletes a file or group of files.

Wildcards

A computer is designed to make work easier. Yet using COPY, REN, or DEL on one file at a time doesn't seem too efficient. DOS has a method of letting you manipulate several files at once with only one command. This is done by using a DOS wildcard.

A wildcard can be anything. Often you encounter them in card games, specifically the occasional dining-room-table poker game. Since Saturday night gamblers don't know how to play poker (a game of bluffs and calls), they typically assign some card as "wild." For example: All deuces, one-eyed jacks, and sixes are wild. It makes the game more interesting, and gives everyone a chance at a good poker hand.

In DOS, wildcards can be used as part of a filename. While they won't help you win that massive 30-cent poker pot, they will help you manipulate groups of files at one time using a single DOS command.

Using Wildcards

Log to your DOS subdirectory on drive C. First, log to drive C:

```
C:
```

Press Enter. Then log to the DOS subdirectory. Normally this can be done by typing the following:

```
CD \DOS
```

Press Enter. If you see a message saying "Invalid directory," then your DOS files have been installed into another directory. (It's usually named DOS—it may simply be a sub-subdirectory.)

Tip: You can use the TREE command to help you locate the DOS subdirectory; refer to Chapter 14 for more information.

The reason for logging to the DOS subdirectory is that it contains a wealth of interesting files—some of which share similar names (which is good for practicing with wildcards).

DOS has two wildcards you can sandwich into a filename. They are the question mark (?) and asterisk (*) wildcards.

The ? Wildcard

The question mark wild card can be used to represent any single character in a filename.

Info: The ? wildcard is used to represent a single character either in the filename or its extension.

Type in the following:

```
DIR MO?E
```

Press Enter. The DIR command will list all files in the DOS subdirectory that match MO—any character—E. You may see something like the following displayed:

```
    Volume in drive C is DOS 5
    Volume Serial Number is xxxx-xxxx
    Directory of C:\DOS

MODE     COM   23313    4-01-91  12:00a
MORE     COM   2547     4-01-91  12:00a
         2 file(s)      25860 bytes
                    xxxxxxx bytes free
```

What you see on your display may look different, but all the filenames will match the pattern MO?E. Above, both MODE and MORE match the pattern.

Type in the following:

```
DIR ????.COM
```

The single question mark represents one character. Above, the DIR command will list all files that are up to four characters long—but only those with a matching COM extension. Press Enter.

The DIR command will display a number of files (six on my computer) that match the ????.COM filename wildcard. See how ????.COM treats all those files as a single unit? That's where you can take advantage of the file-manipulation commands.

Insert your "Test Disk" diskette into drive A if it's not already there. Type the following command:

```
COPY ????.COM A:\
```

The above command reads, "Copy all the files matching ????.COM to drive A's root directory. " Press Enter.

```
KEYB.COM
MODE.COM
SYS.COM
MORE.COM
TREE.COM
EDIT.COM
    6 file(s) copied
```

As the COPY command moved each file, its name was displayed on the screen. Each of the files now has a duplicate on drive A. All the duplicates have the same name as the original; you cannot give a group of files new names using a single COPY command. Verify that the files are there. Type:

```
DIR A:
```

Press Enter and you'll see the files on your Test Disk.

The * Wildcard

The asterisk wildcard is used to represent a group of characters in a filename. It's much more powerful and widely used than the question mark wildcard.

Info: The * wildcard is used to represent a group of characters either in the filename or its extension.

Type in the following:

```
DIR D*.COM
```

Press Enter. The DIR command will list all files that start with D, followed by any number of characters, and ending with the COM extension. This includes all combinations of files from D.COM through any other COM file that begins with D, although your output may look just like this:

```
Volume in drive C is DOS 5
Volume Serial Number is xxxx-xxxx
Directory of C:\DOS

DOSKEY   COM     5693  04-01-91 12:00a
DOSSHELL COM     4505  04-01-91 12:00a
DISKCOMP COM    10428  04-01-91 12:00a
DISKCOPY COM    11393  04-01-91 12:00a
         4 file(s)       32019 bytes
                     xxxxxxx bytes free
```

The DIR command displayed four files, each of which starts with D and has the COM extension. Try this:

```
DIR *.COM
```

Press Enter to see a list of all files with the COM extension. This is the most powerful use of the asterisk wildcard.

Info: The wildcard *.COM is pronounced "star-dot-COM." It's shorthand for all the COM program files in the current directory.

A few pages ago, if you were told to copy all the files with the SYS extension from the hard drive to your Test Diskette, you would have given up computers for llama herding. But with wildcards, you can do all that with one command. Type the following:

```
COPY *.SYS A:\
```

Press Enter.

```
EGA.SYS
DISPLAY.SYS
ANSI.SYS
HIMEM.SYS
COUNTRY.SYS
KEYBOARD.SYS
PARTDVR.SYS
RAMDRIVE.SYS
SMARTDRV.SYS
DRIVER.SYS
PRINTER.SYS
    11 file(s) copied
```

DOS sought out and matched 11 files on disk with *.SYS. Each of them was then copied to drive A. This was done with a single DOS command.

Even more powerful than the single asterisk, is the double asterisk: *.*, which is pronounced star-dot-star. It's shorthand for every file in the current directory, no matter what the name, no matter how many files.

Using Wildcards with REN

Log to drive A. Type:

```
A:
```

Log to the root directory:

```
CD \
```

Pull a directory of the files in the root directory:

```
DIR
```

Drive A contains quite a few interesting files in its root directory, in addition to the original three you created at the start of this chapter. Because these are all practice files on a test disk, you can safely perform the following commands. First, use the REN command to rename a group of files using wildcards. Type in the following:

```
REN *.SYS *.TEM
```

Press Enter. The REN command gives no feedback, yet all the files ending in SYS now end in TEM. The asterisk wildcard acted as a place holder for the filename of each file. All that was changed was the extension. Verify this by typing:

```
DIR
```

You'll notice that your former SYS files now have the TEM extension.

The REN command can also be used with a wildcard to remove or add an extension to a group of filenames. Type the following:

```
DIR *.
```

That's the DIR command followed by an asterisk and a dot. This directs the DIR command to list only those files that lack an extension. Press Enter. You should see something like the following:

```
Volume in drive A is TEST DISK
Volume Serial Number is xxxx-xxxx
Directory of A:\

DATA        <DIR>       02-27-93    7:00a
DOS         <DIR>       02-27-93    7:08a
WP          <DIR>       02-27-93    7:09a
TIPS             648    03-01-93   10:57a
MYSELF            98    03-01-93   10:52a
        5 file(s)           746 bytes
               xxxxxxx bytes free
```

The "*." wildcard matches all the subdirectories (which generally lack extensions) and two filenames without extensions. Give them extensions by typing the following:

REN *. *.EXT

Press Enter. Now type:

DIR *.EXT

Press Enter and there are the two files, now with an extension.

Tip: The command "DIR *." is a quick way to list all subdirectories in the current directory. Since subdirectories are usually not given an extension, "*." will match them all.

To remove the extension for a group of files, use the REN command in the opposite format. Type the following:

REN *.EXT *.

Here you're taking all the EXT files and renaming them—but the renaming wildcard lacks an extension. All the files will retain their filenames, but will lose the extensions. Press Enter. Type the following to verify that the extensions are gone:

DIR *.

Using Wildcards with DEL

The DEL command can also accept a wildcard. That way you can delete a whole slew of matching files with one command. Doesn't that sound deadly? In truth, it is. So be careful.

On the test disk, it's safe to type the following:

DEL *.TEM

In one fell swoop, the DEL command will delete all files with the TEM extension. Press Enter. You won't see any feedback, but you've just "zapped" several files from your disk.

Change directories to the \DATA\PROJECTS subdirectory. Type:

```
CD \DATA\PROJECTS
```

This directory contains several files, all of which have been copied from the root. (Use the DIR command to view the files if you wish.) With one DOS command you're going to delete all those files. Type in the following:

```
DEL *.*
```

This is the famous "Del star-dot-star," which probably heard about in the computer folk songs of yore. This command removes every file in the current directory. (It doesn't remove subdirectories, RMDIR does that.) Press Enter.

```
All files in directory will be deleted!
Are you sure (Y/N)?
```

Through the ages, too many people have accidentally typed DEL *.* and press Enter. DOS was formerly lame about this action. On your screen now you see a subtle warning message; you're given a chance to resend your decision. But this is all for practice, so type Y and press Enter. The files disappear.

Change back to the root directory. Type:

```
CD \
```

Try DEL *.* again. But this time you'll use the DEL command's optional /P switch. When specified, the /P switch forces the DEL command to prompt you before deleting each file. Type the following:

```
DEL *.* /P
```

DEL is followed by two parameters: the name of the file to delete, above *.* or every file in sight, and the /P switch. Press Enter. Instead of seeing a warning message, you'll see something like this:

```
A:\ABOUT.ME,  Delete (Y/N)?
```

DOS asks the "Delete (Y/N)?" question for each file matching the wildcard. Press N to skip it or Y to delete it. If you want to stop, press Ctrl-Break or Ctrl-C.

Tip: If you're going to use a wildcard with the DEL command, use the optional /P switch. This prompts you for each file to be deleted in the format:

```
filename, Delete (Y/N) ?
```

Press Y to delete the file, N to keep it on disk.

Wildcards and Pathnames

Wildcards fit nicely into pathnames. But you can only specify the wildcard as the last part of a path, the part that contains the filename. For example:

```
A:\*.*
```

The above wildcard represents every file in the root directory of drive A. It does not represent any subdirectories.

```
C:\DOS\*.COM
```

Above, the pathname represents all files in the DOS subdirectory with the COM extension on drive C. This could be used with the DIR command. Type:

```
DIR C:\DOS\*.COM
```

If you know that the DOS files are held in another subdirectory, substitute it for \DOS above. Press Enter to see all the COM files.

The following are improper uses of the wildcard in a pathname:

```
*:\
```

It would be nice if the this wildcard represented all the root directories of all your disk drives. Unfortunately, DOS just sees it as hieroglyphics.

```
C:\*\FILE
```

Again, the wildcard above doesn't represent all subdirectories on drive C. It would be nice, but it just ain't so.

Info: You can use wildcards in a pathname, but only as part of the filename or extension.

Wildcards and Common Sense

DOS's wildcards fall far short of being logical. In fact, they're pretty dumb. Consider the following:

```
M*.*
```

This wildcard represents all files in the current directory that start with M.

```
*M.*
```

It would appear that the above wildcard would match all files on disk that have an M as the last character in their name. That's not the case. DOS interprets the above as *.*—you never get to the M.

Info: The asterisk wildcard stands for the group of characters from its first-character position to the dot or to the end of the extension.

It would be nice if wildcards like T*NG would stand for TRYING, TYPING, and TANG. But T*NG is the same as T* as far as DOS is concerned.

Summary

File manipulation is a major part of DOS. It's part of a larger picture called Hard-Disk Management, which you'll be learning about in the next part of the book. The following represents the key points of this chapter.

The DOS command that copies or duplicates files is the COPY command. COPY makes a duplicate of a file either in the current directory or in any other drive or directory in your system. The file created either receives a new name or keeps the same name as the original. Note that the COPY command will not warn you if the new file overwrites an existing one. The RENAME or REN command is used to give a file a new name.

The ERASE or DEL command is used to delete a file.

Using Wildcards you can manipulate groups of files at a time. DOS's two wildcards are: ?, which represents any single character in a filename and *, which represents a group of characters in a filename. Using these wildcards you can copy, rename, or delete a whole set of matching files.

CHAPTER 16

The DOS Shell

Because most people find DOS so cryptic, a great effort is made to make DOS easier to use. Third-party developers have produced DOS shells for years. These are simple-to-use menu systems that let you control your computer and manipulate files without using DOS directly. Starting with DOS 4, DOS Shell comes with the DOS operating system. Version 5 of DOS has an even better Shell program, which is the subject of this chapter.

This chapter answers the following questions:

- What is a "shell?"

- How does the DOS Shell manipulate subdirectories and files?

- How can I change the look of the Shell?

- What are program groups?

- How can an application be installed in the shell?

- What is task swapping?

- How can I run more than one program at a time?

Exploring the Shell

A DOS shell works like a sea shell. A sea shell protects the soft, gooey creature inside from the harsh reality of other gooey creates in the ocean who would like to eat it. In DOS, you are the gooey creature and the shell is protecting you from DOS. That's kind of how it works.

DOS is gross. Even though you know commands such as COPY, TIME, and FORMAT are plain English words, some people would rather not type anything when they use a computer. For them, the DOS shell provides a comfortable environment in which they can use the computer and not be bothered by the operating system. Other users may prefer a shell for convenience; it's just easier to manipulate files in the shell. Personally, I like DOS shells because they can often do things DOS cannot—work with dozens of irregularly named files (which wildcards can't match), rename subdirectories, and view two directories at a time.

There are plenty of reasons to look into the DOS Shell program. Professional DOS shells have existed since the first version of DOS. Some of them are free and some you pay up to $150 for. Each offers different ways of using DOS as well as ways to customize the shell to suit your tastes. The DOS Shell is no exception. In fact, a whole book could be written on the DOS Shell alone. Rather than do that, however, this chapter shows you the DOS Shell in two steps: First there is an introduction and a tour showing how the Shell works and its best features. And second, the new addition to the Shell is covered—task swapping, which is something worth taking a look at.

The $1.98 Tour

The DOS Shell program is located in your \DOS subdirectory, installed there when you first set up DOS. To run the DOS Shell, type the following on the command line:

```
DOSSHELL
```

Press Enter and the DOS Shell takes over, becoming the file-and-program manager for your system. You'll see a screen similar to that shown in Figure 16-1, although it's possible to alter the display to suit your tastes.

As DOS Shell loads, it counts the subdirectories and files on your current drive. The directories are then placed into the Directory Tree portion of the display. The files in that directory are placed to the right of that display, in the File List window.

The top of the screen contains drop-down menus just like the MS-DOS Editor. (In fact, operation of the DOS Shell is very similar to that of the Editor.) Below the menus is your current directory, C:\ (C-root) in Figure 16-1, and a list of available disk drives in your system.

The bottom of the display shows one of DOS Shell's more handy features, the Program List window. "Main" is the title of a list of programs or program groups. From that list you can select applications on your system and instantly run them. The

256

program groups are subcategories of programs, such as "Disk Utilities." You can add your own applications and program groups to the list, making the DOS Shell your center of operations while you run your PC.

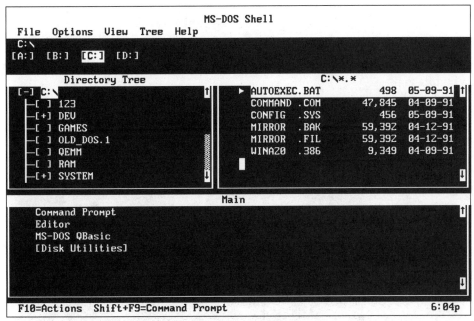

Figure 16-1. The DOS Shell program's main screen.

Some basic control keys you can use in the Shell are:

Key	Function
F1	Activate the Help system
Tab	Move forward between the different areas/windows
Shift-Tab	Move backward between the different areas/windows
Arrow keys	Move around within an area/list window
Esc	Cancel
F10	Activate the menus
Alt	Activate the menus
Alt+letter	Activate the menu starting with letter
F3	Quit; return to DOS
Alt-F4	Quit; return to DOS

Working with Subdirectories

The Shell is a handy place in which you can deal with files. For some, this beats the heck out of using the command line.

The currently logged drive and directory is right below the word "File" on the menu bar. You change drives by pressing Tab until a drive letter is highlighted and then use the arrow keys and Enter to make your selection.

Below the driver letter is your subdirectory tree. Press the Tab key until that area is highlighted.

You select directories using the Up and Down Arrow keys. As you move between the directories (much more easily than with the CD command), the files in those directories are displayed to the right, in the File List window.

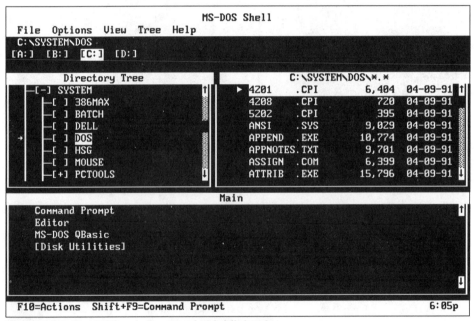

Figure 16-2. The DOS subdirectory is highlighted.

Some directories have a plus sign in them. That indicates that the directory contains subdirectories. Pressing the + key will open the directory, revealing its subdirectories. When that happens, the + changes to a - (minus). You can use the arrow keys to explore that open subdirectory branch, or use the - (minus) key to close it up again.

Tip: While a subdirectory is highlighted you can use some of the commands in the File menu to manipulate it. Most notably, you can use the Rename command to give the subdirectory a new name. This is the only way to rename a subdirectory in DOS.

In the subdirectory tree, locate your DOS subdirectory. Highlight it using the Up and Down Arrow keys. The list of files in your DOS subdirectory will be displayed in the File List window.

Working with Files

To work with a group of files, highlight the File List window on your screen; press the Tab key.

You can scroll through the list of files using the Up and Down Arrow keys or by using the mouse on the scroll bar. The Home, End, PgUp, and PgDn keys will also move you through the list in greater leaps.

When a file is highlighted, the commands in the File menu will affect it. You can copy, move, delete, and rename any file by highlighting it, dropping down through the File menu with Alt-F, and selecting the proper command. (A list of all the commands is provided at the end of this chapter.)

A nice thing about the Shell is that you can select a number of files to manipulate at once. The currently highlighted file is always selected.

Info: A selected file has a large triangle by it.

To select more than that one file you can do the following:

Press Shift and use the Arrow keys to select a group of consecutive files

Press Ctrl-/ to select all files in the list

Use the Add function to select non-consecutive files. You can use the Shell to select a number of files, which—for the most part—couldn't be manipulated as a group with wildcards. To use this handy Shell feature, use the Add function: Press Shift-F8. The word "Add" appears on the bottom of the screen. Select files using the arrow keys; mark the ones you want to group using the Spacebar; select a file a second time to unselect it.

Once you've selected a group of files, each of the commands in the File menu will manipulate the group as a whole. To unselect files, drop down through the File menu and choose Deselect All.

New Looks

You can customize the Shell to reflect the way you work. For example, if you want to work with only subdirectories and their files, pull down the View menu and select Single File List. Your screen will look like Figure 16-3.

If you want to work between two file lists at once (such as when copying files between two disks or two different subdirectories) pull down the View menu and select Dual File Lists. The Shell then appears as in Figure 16-4:

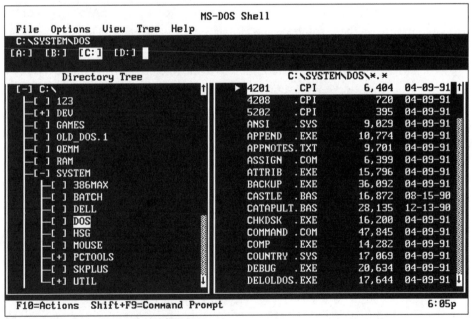

Figure 16-3. The single-file list display.

The All Files option lets you deal with all files on your drive as if it lacked subdirectories. Select All Files from the View menu. Your screen will look something like Figure 16-5.

Information about the file, its subdirectory, and disk drive are displayed to the left of the File List window. In the File List window itself you'll find all files on the current drive.

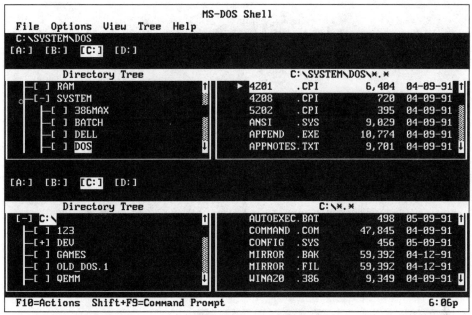

Figure 16-4. Dual file lists.

The Program/File-Lists item under the View menu returns the Shell to its initial display—the subdirectory tree, file list, and the program list on the bottom of the screen. If you choose the Program List item from the View menu, you'll see only the program list. Other ways to configure the display depend on what type of graphics adapter you have installed on your system. Pull down the Options menu and choose the Display item. A dialog box like that shown in Figure 16-6 will be displayed.

```
                              MS-DOS Shell
     File  Options   View  Tree  Help
     C:\WORK\CRYSTAL
     [A:]  [B:]  [C:]   [D:]

                                                 *.*
                              06                3,555   10-22-90   10:15a ↑
     File                     07                5,825   10-22-90    3:04p
       Name  : 06             08                4,258   10-23-90   10:10a
       Attr  : ....           09                  830   10-23-90   10:14a
     Selected          C      10                2,646   10-22-90    5:02p
       Number:         1      11                1,018   10-22-90    5:04p
       Size  :     6,404      12                  375   10-22-90    5:04p
     Directory                123     .CMP    138,783   07-19-89    1:23a
       Name  : CRYSTAL        123     .CNF        376   07-19-89    1:23a
       Size  :    79,322      123     .DLD      5,148   07-19-89    1:23a
       Files :        14      123     .DYN     12,436   07-19-89    1:23a
     Disk                     123     .EXE     15,392   09-17-90    9:37a
       Name  : DOS 5          123     .HLP    199,499   07-19-89    1:23a
       Size  : 42,366,976     123     .RI      36,319   07-19-89    1:23a
       Avail : 12,800,000    · 123    .SET     38,623   09-17-90    9:49a
       Files :     1,008      13                  813   10-22-90    5:05p
       Dirs  :        48      14                1,622   10-22-90    5:05p ↓

     F10=Actions   Shift+F9=Command Prompt                         6:06p
```

Figure 16-5. All files are displayed.

```
          ┌─────────Screen Display Mode───────────┐
          │                                        │
          │      Current Mode: Text (25 lines)     │
          │   → Text     25 lines  Low Resolution   ↑│
          │     Text     43 lines  High Resolution 1 ▓│
          │     Text     50 lines  High Resolution 2 ▓│
          │     Graphics 25 lines  Low Resolution   ↓│
          │                                        │
          │                                        │
          │    ▆OK▆      ▆Preview▆     ▆Cancel▆     │
          └────────────────────────────────────────┘
```

Figure 16-6. The Screen Mode dialog box.

From the list in the Screen Mode dialog box you can select how many lines of text you want the Shell to display, as well as whether you want a graphics or text display. The number and variety of displays that your system can produce are determined by your video system. VGA systems can display up to 60 lines on a screen in the high-resolution graphics mode.

If you like, select a new graphics mode from the dialog box or press Esc to cancel.

Associating Files

One of the more powerful features of the Shell is its ability to recognize data files and launch them; the Shell will figure out which application is associated with the data file, and then run that program and load in the data file—all in one step.

To associate a file with an application, look for the file in the File List window. For example, locate a TXT file. (A few can be found in the DOS subdirectory.) Highlight, for example, the TXT file README.TXT.

Info: To associate files with an application, the files should all have the same file extension, such as TXT, DOC, XLS, etc. Data files without extensions cannot be associated.

Drop down through the File menu and select Associate. The Associate dialog box appears. For TXT files, it says:

```
'.TXT' files are associated with:
```

This is followed by a line with a program name. In the case of TXT files, the program is EDIT, the MS-DOS Editor. When you select a TXT file in the File List window and open that file (using the Open command in the File menu or by pressing Enter), the Shell will run the Editor and automatically load the selected file.

Association can be done with any application provided all its data files have similar extensions. This gives you an easy way to run your applications and programs—and does something that DOS can't do by itself.

Getting Help

Using the Shell should seem logical, especially if you're already familiar with several DOS commands (most notably, the ones mentioned in this part of the book). If you need to know shortcuts or information about certain commands, the Shell's Help system will show you the ropes.

The Help command is context-sensitive, meaning that the helpful information you see will always pertain to whichever area of the program you're in or the command you're currently using. Just press F1 to see the help.

To get started with the Help command, select the Using Help menu item from the Help menu. The MS-DOS Shell Help dialog box is displayed.

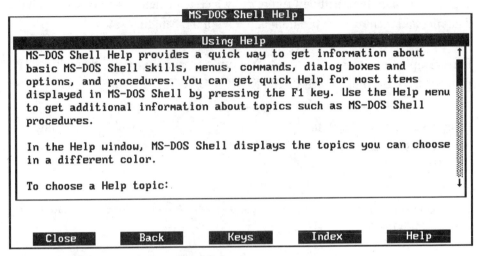

Figure 16-7. The MS-DOS Shell Help dialog box.

Use the arrow keys to scroll through the information displayed; the Tab key selects highlighted text to view other topics, as well as the buttons on the bottom of the dialog box.

Use the Tab key to select the Index button, and press Enter. You'll see the Help index, which contains a master list of topics. Some you might wish to check out include "General Shell Keys" and "Movement Keys." At the end of the list you'll see all the menus and their commands displayed.

Press Esc to cancel Help when you're done poking around.

Working with Applications

One of the most useful features of the Shell is its ability to store applications in groups. When you want to run an application, you can select it from the group and run it right from the Shell. This saves some users the pain and agony of using DOS to run programs. (Although if you know DOS, there doesn't seem to be much pain or agony involved.)

Restore your screen to the Program/File list option; select Program/File Lists from the View menu if you need to.

Press the Tab key until the Program List area "Main" is highlighted, or click in that area using your mouse.

The Main Group

"Main" is the name of the first program group. When you installed DOS, it put three applications into the Main group: Command Prompt, Editor, and MS DOS QBasic. Any items displayed in square brackets—such as "[Disk Utilities]"—indicates a subgroup of programs.

To run a program, move the highlight over the program's name and press Enter. For example, to start the Editor, move the highlight bar over "Editor" and press Enter. A dialog box appears, asking for a file to edit. Just press Enter for now.

In a few moments the Editor is up and running on your screen. You've just launched the Editor from the DOS Shell. This can be done with any program on your system (which is covered in the next section).

Exit the Editor: Press Esc, Alt-F, then X.

Move the highlight bar down to the Disk Utilities group. Press Enter.

A list of DOS disk utilities appears: Disk Copy, Backup Fixed Disk, Restore Fixed Disk, and so on. The [Main] item atop the list will return you to the Main group—just like CD'ing to the root directory (although these are program groups, not subdirectories).

Return to the Main group by highlighting [Main] and pressing Enter.

Creating Program Groups

DOS gives you only a small sampling of program groups—primarily because it doesn't know what you do with your computer or what applications you have installed. Ideas for program groups include:

Utilities
Programming
Word Processing
Spreadsheets
Data Bases
Communications
Games

...and on and on. For example, suppose you use several word processing programs. Or, better yet, you have WordPerfect, PageMaker, and a small editor, and you would like to place them into a group. To create that group, make sure you're in the Main group (or whichever group will contain your "Document processing" group), and select New from the File menu. The New Program Object dialog box appears.

Use the Up Arrow key to select the Program Group Item, and press Enter or click OK with the mouse. The Add Group dialog box appears, as shown in Figure 16-8.

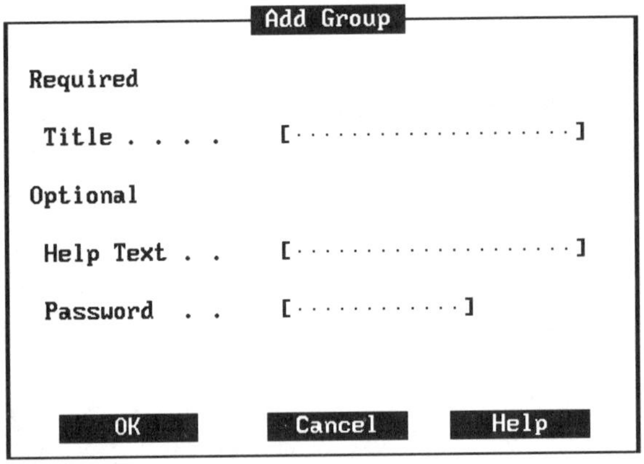

```
┌──────────────┤ Add Group ├──────────────────┐
│                                              │
│  Required                                    │
│                                              │
│   Title . . . .    [···················]    │
│                                              │
│  Optional                                    │
│                                              │
│   Help Text . .    [··················]      │
│                                              │
│   Password  . .    [···········]            │
│                                              │
│                                              │
│      ▓▓OK▓▓       ▓Cancel▓      ▓Help▓       │
└──────────────────────────────────────────────┘
```

Figure 16-8. The Add Group dialog box.

Type:

```
Document processing
```

Info: The group name can be up to 23 characters long, including spaces and ornamental characters.

Press Tab. Any Help Text you enter will appear when the user has "Document Processing" highlighted and presses the F1 key. Type:

Use word processor, page layout and other text-oriented programs Notice how the text slides left as you type. It will all be nicely formatted by the Help command when it's displayed.

Info: You can type up to 255 characters for the help description. Be brief and descriptive.

Press the Tab key. You now have the option of entering a password for the program group. Only those who know the password will be able to access the programs in that group. For now, leave the password line blank.

Press Enter.

The new [Document processing] group appears in the Program List window. Select it by pressing Enter.

Info: You can change the order of the items in the Program List window using the Reorder command under the File menu.

If you want to change anything in a program group after it's been created, highlight that group and then select the Properties item from the File menu.

Change to the Document processing group; highlight it using the Up or Down Arrow keys, and press Enter. When that group is active, note how the title of the Program List window changes to "Document processing."

Adding Applications

Applications are added to a group in the same manner as new groups are created. Pull down the File menu and select New. Use the Down Arrow key to highlight Program Item. Press Enter. The Add Program dialog box appears.

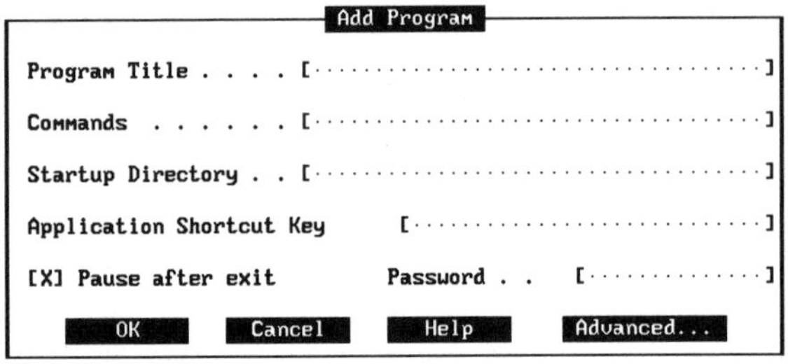

```
┌──────────────────── Add Program ────────────────────┐
│                                                      │
│  Program Title . . . . [·······························] │
│                                                      │
│  Commands  . . . . . . [·······························] │
│                                                      │
│  Startup Directory . . [·······························] │
│                                                      │
│  Application Shortcut Key   [························]   │
│                                                      │
│  [X] Pause after exit      Password . .  [··············] │
│                                                      │
│      ███ OK ███   ███ Cancel ███   ███ Help ███   ███ Advanced... ███ │
└──────────────────────────────────────────────────────┘
```

Figure 16-9. The Add Program dialog box.

Type a title for the Application you're adding. This is different from the program's actual name on disk. For example, if you're adding WordPerfect, you could type:

```
WordPerfect 5.1
```

Info: You can type up to 23 characters for the program's title.

Press the Tab key.

At the Commands prompt you can type the DOS command that actually starts the program—as well as any options or parameters required. For WordPerfect, the command is:

```
WP
```

Press the Tab key.

The Startup Directory is the name of the subdirectory which contains WordPerfect and its files. For WordPerfect, that would be C:\WP51 (although it varies from system to system, refer to the Subdirectory Tree if you need to locate a subdirectory on your system). Type:

```
C:\WP51
```

Press the Tab key.

The Application Shortcut Key is a special key combination you can use to activate that application primarily for use with the Shell's Task-Swapping function. For example, if you want to start WordPerfect by typing Alt-W, press Alt-W. You won't see the key displayed right away, but if you edit the program entry again ALT-W (or whatever) will be displayed.

Press the Tab key.

"Pause after exit" directs the Shell to display a "press any key" message after you quit the application; type Spacebar to toggle the "X" on or off. (Keep it off if you find it annoying.) Press the Tab key.

And finally, you can enter an optional password for the item. Press Enter when you're done, or use the TAB or arrow keys to move the items and make editing changes. Back in the Program-List window you'll see the new item added: WordPerfect 5.1. If you have WordPerfect and have entered the correct items, then highlighting that item and pressing Enter will run WordPerfect. If not, you can delete the application entry with the Delete item in the File menu. (This only deletes the entry, not the program file on disk.)

Task Swapping

One of the Shell's most powerful features—and something that should be appealing to advanced DOS users—is its ability to swap between several programs at a time.

Most of your time wasted in DOS is spent leaving one program and running another. The typical DOS user will do the following:

1. Run DOS.

2. Run a word processor to create a memo.

3. Quit back to DOS.

4. Load the spreadsheet to print some data.

5. Quit back to DOS.

6. Rerun the word processor and copy in the data. Print.

7. Quit back to DOS.

8. Run the database program to print a list of mailing labels.

9. Quit back to DOS.

You have used nine steps to run three programs. What the shell does is to eliminate most of those steps, particularly any that say "Quit back to DOS." Using the Shell, you can run several applications at a time without quitting one to start the other. While all the programs don't work at once (which is called multitasking), you can switch between them easily. It's called task swapping.

Activating the Task Swapper

You must tell the Shell that you want to use it as a task swapper. Otherwise, it just operates as a mortal DOS Shell program.

To activate task swapping, pull down the Options menu and select the Enable Task Swapper item. The bottom of the screen splits into two parts as shown in Figure 16-10.

Info: Task swapping stays active in the Shell until you turn it off.

The Active Task list contains programs that the Shell currently has open and working. (But remember that they don't "run" when they're not active.) To add a program to the list, thus starting a new task, select it from the left side of the window, or choose an EXE or COM program from the File List window.

For example, select the MS-DOS Editor from the Main group. Press Enter when it asks you for a file to edit.

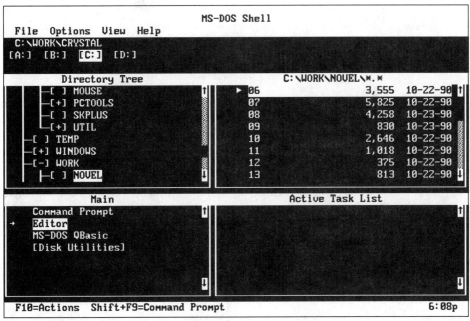

Figure 16-10. Task swapping has been activated.

After a few seconds, the Shell disappears and you're running the Editor. Press Esc to skip over the Survival Guide, and then type the following in the Editor:

```
This is my first task
```

Suppose you wanted to quit to DOS right now to, say, pull a directory. Instead of quitting, press the Ctrl-Esc key combination. A few spins of the drive and—ta da!—you're back in the Shell.

Info: What's happened to the Editor? It's still there, but it's "frozen" in time. You haven't really quit the editor, you've simply swapped it out to disk and swapped back into the Shell. You can juggle a number of programs in this manner, switching between them with the press of a key.

Back in the Shell, you see the Editor listed in the Active Task List. You wanted to pull a directory, so fire up the Command Prompt item; select it and press Enter.

```
Microsoft(R) MS-DOS(R) Version 5.00
(C)Copyright Microsoft Corp 1981-1990.
```

```
C:\>
```

Now you're sitting at the DOS prompt—actually a copy of the DOS prompt run by the Shell program. Type your directory:

```
DIR
```

Now, to switch back to the Editor, press the Ctrl-Esc key to return to the Shell. Once in the Shell, select the Editor item from the Active Task list; highlight it and then press Enter. Zip! You're back in the Editor—with the same contents on the screen.

Info: Task-Swapping Keystrokes

Alt-Tab	Switch to the next application
Shift-Alt-Tab	Switch to the previous application
Alt-Esc	Switch to the next application
Ctrl-Esc	Return to the Shell

You can load and switch between a number of applications. The Shell will juggle everything and save you from having to quit to DOS all the time. The only programs you can't do this with are communications programs; they will not function after being swapped out and may cause the system to crash. Otherwise, just about any program—even graphics—can be swapped in and out.

Info: If your display doesn't return to normal after running a graphics program and you have an EGA display, then you need to install the EGA.SYS device driver into your CONFIG.SYS file. Installing device drivers is covered in Chapter 19.

When you want to remove a program from the list, just quit it as you normally would. In the Editor, drop down through the File menu and select the Exit item. Save the file, if you want. Otherwise, when you quit you'll be back in the Shell and that application will be removed from the Active task list.

To quit from the Command Prompt task, activate it, and then type the following at the DOS prompt:

```
EXIT
```

Press Enter.

You should quit all active tasks before leaving the shell. (It won't let you quit without doing so.)

Shell Menu Overview

As with the Editor, DOS Shell puts its commands and functions in drop down menus, which appear along the top of your screen. There are five menus:

File	File, application, and directory commands; Exit
Options	Controls the way the Shell looks and behaves
View	Controls which parts of the Shell you can see
Tree	Opens/closes your view of the subdirectory tree
Help	The Help system

If you have a mouse, then you can select a menu by hovering the mouse cursor over the menu's title, and then clicking the mouse button. From the keyboard, menus are activated by pressing the Alt key, F10, or Alt and the first letter of the menu you want.

Info: The menus change as you move around various areas of the Shell; certain menu items will be available only in some areas. For example, when you're working with files, the File menu contains items dealing with files as well as a Tree menu. When you move to the "Main" area (containing applications and program groups), the Tree menu disappears and the File menu's contents change.

The following is an overview of the menus, their items, and functions. Use of those commands is covered in the following sections.

The File menu contains options for dealing with files, applications, and subdirectories on disk. When any area of the Shell—except for the "Main" area—is active, the file menu contains the following items:

Menu Item	Function
Open	Runs the highlighted program file; runs and loads a data file into a program file if it's been associated
Run	Allows you to run a program by typing its name
Print	Prints the selected file or group of files
Associate	Associates the highlighted file or all files with a similar extension to a given application. Associated files can be run automatically with their applications
Search	Scans your disk system for the file or files you specify
View File Contents	Displays the contents of a file in either text or "raw" (binary) mode.
Move	Moves the file or a group of files from one directory to another (combination COPY and DEL commands)
Copy	Copies a file or group of files (the COPY command)
Delete	Deletes a file, group of files, or a subdirectory
Rename	Renames a file, group of files, or a subdirectory

Change Attributes	Changes the attributes for a single file or group of files
Create Directory	Makes a new subdirectory
Select All	Selects all the files in the file list part of the display; all the files can then be controlled as a group (like *.*)
Deselect All	Unselects all the files selected.
Exit	Quits the Shell, returns to DOS

Note that these commands also work on subdirectories when they're highlighted in the Shell—especially the Rename command.

When the program list at the bottom of the screen is activated, the File menu changes to contain the following items:

Menu Item	Function
New	Creates a new program item in the current group
Open	Runs the highlighted program file; runs and loads a data file into a program file if it's been associated
Copy	Copies an application into a program group
Delete	Deletes an application or program group
Properties	Sets/changes the information about an application Reorder Changes the position of an application in the group
Run	Allows you to run an application by typing in its name
Exit	Quits the Shell, return to DOS

The Options menu contains items that control how the Shell works and how it looks on the screen.

Menu Item	Function
Confirmation	Asks for confirmation upon deleting or moving files
File Display Options	Controls the order in which files are displayed (alphabetically by name or extension, size, or date and time), and which files are displayed
Select Across Directories	Allows you to select files from different subdirectories and treat them all as one group
Show Information	Displays information about the disk driver, subdirectory, or file, whichever is currently selected
Enable Task Swapper	Switches the Shell's task-swapping function on or off (covered later in this chapter)
Display	Switches the display from text to graphics; allows you to specify the number of lines on the screen (covered later in this chapter)
Colors	Allows you to set or change the colors the Shell displays

The Tree menu contains options which control the display of subdirectories in the Shell. Each of these options has a keyboard equivalent as noted by each menu item and in the following table.

Menu Item	Key	Function
Expand One Level	+	Open the [+] directory to reveal any subdirectories
Expand Branch	*	Display all subdirectories in the current [+] directory
Expand All	Ctrl-*	Expand all directories on the current drive
Collapse Branch	-	Collapse (close) the current part of the subdirectory tree

The Help menu grants you access to the Help system, displaying all sorts of helpful information about the DOS Shell.

Menu Item	Function
Index	Displays an index of all Help topics
Keyboard	Displays a list of all keyboard functions and shortcuts
Shell Basics	Displays a list of basic skills for using the Shell
Commands	Displays a list of the menus, menu items, and the functions of each item.
Procedures	Displays a summary of what the Shell can do and how it's done.
Using Help	Displays information on using the help system
About Shell	Displays the About dialog box

Other menus may come or go or change contents as you use the Shell. The major points of menus are noted above. If you need additional help, select the Index help item. In the list, all of the Shell's menus are displayed. Select the menu you're interested in and its items and descriptions of what they do will be displayed.

Summary

The Shell comes in extremely handy as a file manipulator, menu program, and application swapper. It's primarily designed for new DOS users, although the so-called "power user" can get mileage from the easy-to-use commands and task swapping.

To start the DOS Shell, type DOSSHELL. The Shell is kept in your DOS subdirectory, and it can be used with the keyboard or the mouse.

The Shell contains separate areas for viewing subdirectories and files, and it has a menu of applications from which you can select. You can rearrange these areas according to how you use the Shell.

You can associate data files with programs in the Shell. By matching a filename extension to an application, you can select that application in the shell and automatically run that program and load that file.

Applications can be stored individually or in groups. In this way, the Shell works like a menu system, allowing you to select items and run programs with the touch of a key. Password protection can be added for security.

Task Swapping is the Shell's special ability to hold more than one active program in memory at a time. You can "run" several programs at once, hopping between them without returning to DOS. (Note that programs do not run unless they're currently being used.)

Like the Editor, the Shell contains its commands in drop-down menus, each menu containing similar commands and functions. The five menus in the shell are: File, Options, View, Tree, and Help. Note that some menus appear and disappear, depending on which part of the Shell you're in.

PART FOUR

Hard-Disk Management

This part of the book is about using your hard disk, a subject given the title of "hard-disk management." It deals with organizing and maintaining all your files and information on disk. There is a definite strategy to using a hard drive, one that will keep you and your computer productive and happy, but it requires some effort and more knowledge of how DOS works.

This part of the book also breaks with the simple tutorial style of the previous chapters. It's now assumed that you know DOS and have the background necessary to move into this subject. This doesn't mean anything's getting harder to do. If you're new to DOS and have read the previous parts of this book, this is material you're now ready for.

Chapter 17 explores how hard drives work and how they are used, with emphasis on subdirectory and file organization. Chapter 18 is about batch files, a concept central to using a hard drive. Chapters 19 and 20 explore the subject of configuring DOS, first using the CONFIG.SYS file and second using the all-important AUTOEXEC.BAT file. Chapter 21 wraps up the subject of hard-disk management with a discussion of system maintenance, along with some performance-boosting tips.

CHAPTER 17

Disks & Storage

DOS provides commands for file management, as well as subdirectory commands for file organization. Other than that, using the commands, organizing your disk storage, and file maintenance is all up to you. Since each user is different, there is no one solution, but the suggestions and hints provided in this chapter will help you choose a file-management method that works best in your situation.

This chapter answers the following questions:

- How is a hard drive prepared for use?

- What is low-level formatting?

- Does a disk need to be partitioned?

- How are files stored on disk in clusters?

- What are good hard-disk file-organization strategies?

- How weird can a filename get?

- What does the ATTRIB command do?

- How many different ways can the DIR command list files?

Disks and File Storage

If there were no such thing as hard disks, hard-disk management wouldn't be a concern. Comparatively speaking, floppy-disk management was simply organizing a stack of disks. It worked like the old Wurlitzer jukeboxes: You found the disk containing your program, slid it into the slot, and played it. But with a hard drive and its massive storage space, the issues of organization and optimization crop up. Handling both those items properly is the cornerstone of hard disk management.

Anatomy of a Hard Drive

A hard drive consists of two separate items: The hard-disk controller, which is an expansion card plugged into an expansion slot, and the hard disk itself. Both of these items work together to give you your "hard drive."

The hard disk actually consists of several physical disks—typically two, four, or six platters—all on a common spindle. The platters are contained in a hermetically sealed environment, which cuts down on the introduction of dust and debris that could damage the disk. The issue here is tolerance: A hard drive is an extremely delicate thing. The read/write heads are only microns above the rapidly spinning hard-disk platters. They might actually be called "floating heads" because, in aerodynamic terms, they literally fly over the surface of the disk. In fact, the distance is so close that a human hair would be like a log in comparison; a finger print is a speed bump; particles of dust or smoke won't fit under the read/write head and if they did the head would "crash" and render part of the disk unusable.

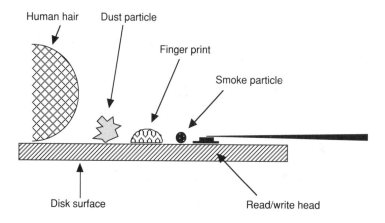

Figure 17-1. Nasty things that can crash your disk.

The advantages of the rapidly spinning disk and close proximity of the read/write head are speed and capacity. Hard drives store much more information than floppies and can access it more quickly, thanks to their unique environment.

The Low-level Format

The disks themselves are usually created of some special type of aluminum, coated with a magnetic oxide—essentially the same stuff you find on a floppy disk's media or on a cassette tape. The read/write head is used to change the magnetic orientation of the magnetic particles. It can both read and change their orientation.

The read/write head is controlled by the hard-disk controller, which may be located on the controller card (hence the name), or be a part of the drive itself (in which case the controller card is merely an interface between the hard drive and the computer). The controller moves the read/write head in and out over the surface of the disk. The read/write head organizes the magnetic particles in a series of concentric rings—not in a spiral like a record. Those rings, illustrated in Figure 17-2, are known as tracks.

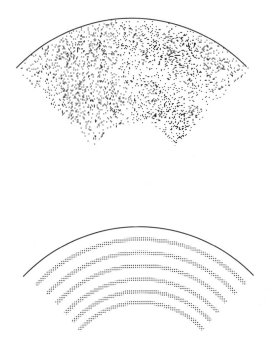

Figure 17-2. How the read/write head organizes the magnetic particles on your disk.

Because a hard drive has many disks or "platters," each disk has two read/write heads—one on the top and one on the bottom. When you picture all the tracks on either side of the disk, plus all the tracks on all the disks, the image is of several cylinders in space. Because of this, all tracks on the disk are referred to as cylinders. (The first track on the first platter, top and bottom, plus all other platters' first track, is collectively known as the first cylinder.)

Info: A hard disk's capacity is a measure of how many cylinders it has. This is directly related to the number of platters in the hard drive, as well as to the density at which tracks can be recorded on each platter.

Knowing about the magnetic particles, tracks, and sectors isn't something that should keep you up nights. Organization of the particles, moving the read/write head, and creating the tracks and cylinders is the hard-disk controller's job. Eventually somewhere down the line, DOS will take control of all the thinking.

The basic organization of the magnetic particles on your hard drive, and the creation of tracks and cylinders are referred to as low-level formatting. It's the responsibility of the hard-drive's controller to create the low-level format, which is the first step in preparing a hard drive for use by DOS.

Info: There is more than one way to organize the information stored on disk. Switching the orientation of the magnetic particles is how the controller reads and writes ones and zeros—the basic bits of information the computer users—to the hard drive. But how that's done depends on the drive's controller. Some standards for organization of disk information include: MFM (modified frequency modulation); RLL (run length limited); and ERLL (extended run length limited). Several schemes for moving information between the disk and the PC include: ESDI (enhanced small device interface); SCSI (or "scuzzy," for small computer serial interface); and IDE (integrated drive electronics).

Partitioning a Disk

The low-level format of a disk is achieved by running special software stored in the controller's ROM. This can be done by using DOS's DEBUG program, but more commonly it's done at the factory—especially with today's combination hard-drive/controller units. To continue preparing the disk for DOS, it needs to be partitioned.

Partitioning is an interesting concept. You can divide one physical hard drive into several smaller "logical" drives. One reason for doing this is to store more than one operating system on the drive. For example, the first partition could be used for DOS, the second for Xenix or some other operating system.

Formerly, partitioning was done because of DOS's limitations. DOS could handle only a 33M hard drive. If you had a 100M drive, you had to split it into three partitions because DOS couldn't "see" the full 100M. DOS 5, however, can deal with hard drives up to two gigabytes in size.

Why is partitioning important? Why is it the second step? Because you must tell DOS how much of the disk it can use. This information, called the partition table, is kept at the very front of the disk. Later, when the disk is formatted by DOS, it will examine the disk's partition table and determine which part of the disk it's allowed to format.

Using FDISK

Under DOS, the partitioning is handled by the FDISK program. FDISK is menu driven. It allows you to select a hard drive in your system and examine its partition information, create a new DOS partition, or delete an existing partition. To understand this, boot up your PC and run the FDISK program. Type:

```
FDISK
```

You should see FDISK's main screen, as shown in Figure 17-3.

Your hard disk is already formatted and set up, so there's nothing to add with FDISK—and you certainly don't want to delete anything at this point! Instead, you can use FDISK to see how DOS is treating your hard drive, and to bring home some of the information covered so far. Type the number 4 and press Enter.

The "Display partition information" item tells you about the hard drive already set up on your system. A 40M hard drive under DOS 5 appears in Figure 17-4.

```
                    MS-DOS Version 5.00
                  Fixed Disk Setup Program
            (C)Copyright Microsoft Corp. 1983 - 1991

                       FDISK Options

Current fixed disk drive: 1

Choose one of the following:

1. Create DOS partition or Logical DOS Drive
2. Set active partition
3. Delete partition or Logical DOS Drive
4. Display partition information



Enter choice: [1]



Press Esc to exit FDISK
```

Figure 17-3. FDISK's main screen.

There can be any number of hard drives hooked up to your system. The "current fixed disk drive" number on your screen indicates the physical hard drive you're examining. Below that are columns of information and a list of the partitions on the physical drive. In Figure 17-4, there is only one partition. It's a "PRI DOS" (or Primary DOS) partition taking up 40M of space—the whole drive. Any additional partitions would be listed below along with their types. For example, if a drive has two partitions, both used by DOS, the second would be partition 2, an "EXT DOS" or Extended DOS partition—and it would be assigned drive letter D.

Press Esc twice to exit FDISK and return to DOS.

If you were adding a new drive to your system, FDISK is one of the first steps you'd take to prepare that drive for DOS. After the low-level formatting (which may already have been done), you would step through FDISK. The program is very logical and normally you need only to press Enter to select the proper options. Under most circumstances, you simply specify "100 percent" of the disk for use by DOS and FDISK does the rest. The next step is to perform the DOS format, also called the high-level format.

```
                 Display Partition Information

Current fixed disk drive: 1

Partition  Status   Type   Volume label  Mbytes  System  Usage
  C: 1        A    PRI DOS    DOS 5          40    FAT16    98%




Total disk space is   41 Mbytes (1 Mbyte = 1048576 bytes)



Press Esc to continue
```

Figure 17-4. The Display Partition Information Screen.

Info: Partitioning is only needed in two circumstances: When you're using another operating system aside from DOS on the same hard drive, and when you have such a large hard drive that partitioning it into a drive D, E, or F makes sense.

Partitioning a drive for organizational purposes is silly, although most people do it for that reason. For practical organization, use the DOS subdirectory commands instead. Even on a 100M drive, subdirectories are a much more flexible and logical method than organizing the drive by partitioning it.

The High-level Format

The low-level format creates the tracks and cylinders on a hard drive. FDISK does the partitioning. But DOS still cannot use the drive. The hard disk must be formatted by the FORMAT command before DOS can use it—just like a floppy disk. This is usually done with the following FORMAT command:

```
FORMAT C: /S
```

The above command does three things with the hard drive:

Places information on disk for DOS

Creates sectors on each track and verifies each track

Creates the boot sector, FAT and root directory

The FORMAT command is used on a hard drive as it is on a floppy, although usually only once (on purpose, at least). FORMAT creates the disk's boot sector, which either loads DOS from elsewhere on the disk or displays the "I'm not a boot disk" error message. The boot sector also contains information about the disk, its size, and the location of some important items.

Each track created with the low-level format is double-checked by DOS's FORMAT command. Additionally, the track is divided up into 512-byte-long sectors. The typical track on the typical hard drive has 17 sectors per track. DOS creates the sectors, numbers them, and places special information between each sector.

If the FORMAT command locates a sector it cannot verify, that sector is flagged as "bad." DOS makes a note of all bad sectors on a disk in the disk map, stored in the FAT (file allocation table). Don't be alarmed if you see bad sectors after a disk formatting, just about every disk has a few. And there's nothing to worry about either—no data will be stored in bad sectors by DOS.

Info: Using math, you can figure out the capacity of a disk based on the number of sectors per cylinder and the total cylinders. For example, consider the classic 20M hard drive. It has two disks with four sides and four tracks per cylinder. If there are 17 sectors per track that's: 17 times 4, or 68 sectors per cylinder. If the drive has 612 total cylinders, that's 41,616 sectors. At 512 bytes per sector, that's 21,307,392 bytes—20M (plus change.)

Finally, after formatting is complete, DOS creates the File Allocation Table (FAT) and root directory. The FAT tells DOS where files are located on the disk, as well as how much disk space is used. And the root directory is the main directory on disk.

If FORMAT's /S switch is specified (as is usually the case with a hard disk), boot information will be placed on the boot sector, and DOS's boot files—the DOS kernel—will be placed in the root directory. The disk is then ready for use.

Putting Files on Disk

Files are placed on disk by DOS. But DOS doesn't put files on disk on a byte - by-byte basis. Instead, files are put on disk in pre-allocated storage areas (or "allocation units") called clusters.

On a floppy diskette, DOS uses a sector as an allocation unit; one sector equals one cluster. When you save a file to disk, it's placed into various sectors. Even if the file is two bytes long, it occupies the full 512-byte sector. It sounds inefficient, after all, twelve 2-byte files will take up 6K of disk space. But it's even more inefficient for DOS to keep track of files by the byte on a large-capacity disk.

On a hard drive, DOS uses an average of four sectors per cluster. True, a 2-byte file instantly uses up 2K of disk space. But there are really more 5K and 10K files, and many more larger than that. And you're still able to store millions of files using clusters instead of sectors. It's a compromise.

When DOS stores a file, it first looks to the File Allocation Table (FAT) for space to locate the file. The FAT is really a map of all the clusters on a disk. It's a coded shorthand for disk space used, disk space free, and space unusable by the FORMAT command.

If DOS finds enough space in the FAT, the file is physically located on the indicated part of the disk. If the space is noncontiguous, then DOS splits the files into small pieces and fits it into the available space. (DOS always makes the best of available space.) And if it can't fit, you get a "disk full" error.

After writing the file to disk, its entry in the directory is created, along with information on where DOS can find the file again using the FAT. That's how a file can be split into pieces on disk without any concern on your part. DOS reassembles the file when needed. However, access to the file is notably quicker when it's all in one piece.

Tip: The process of splitting a file into several pieces is known as fragmentation. It occurs naturally as you use your disk, update and delete files. To eliminate fragmentation, occasionally use a special defragmentation utility. Examples include Norton's Speed Disk and PC Tools' Compress, which are discussed in Chapter 21.

To check to see if any files are split or fragmented on disk, use the CHKDSK utility followed by the *.* wildcard.

```
C:\>CHKDSK *.*

Volume DOS 5        created 09-21-1990 1:26p
Volume Serial Number is 1668-BE65

   42366976 bytes total disk space
      73728 bytes in 2 hidden files
      96256 bytes in 44 directories
   26050560 bytes in 893 user files
   16146432 bytes available on disk

       2048 bytes in each allocation unit
      20687 total allocation units on disk
       7884 available allocation units on disk

     655360 total bytes memory
     636608 bytes free

C:\COMMAND.COM Contains 10 non-contiguous blocks
```

The output you see may be different. Normally, CHKDSK reports just the upper part of the listing you'll see. Note the information on allocation units. Those are clusters. Above, a 2K cluster is used and there are 20,687 of them on that hard drive. (If you divide the "bytes total disk space" by "bytes in each allocation unit" you get 20,687.) The disk has room for 7,884 files.

At the bottom of the listing, CHKDSK will show you any files that have been fragmented. Above, COMMAND.COM is the victim of fragmentation. It exists in 10 noncontiguous blocks, or clusters. That's okay—DOS can handle it, but it is inefficient. In fact, it's probably a good sign that this drive could use a sweep over with a defragmentation utility (which I'll hop on as soon as I'm done with this chapter.)

If all the files in the directory are in one piece, you'll see the message "All specified file(s) are contiguous." That means DOS has yet to encounter a situation where it must split a file between two or more clusters.

Setting up a Hard Drive

The process of describing how a disk stores information parallels the same process of installing a hard drive into your system. On the software side, you do three things to a hard drive once you've bolted it into your PC:

1. Low-level formatting

2. FDISK (partitioning)

3. High-level formatting with FORMAT C: /S

Normally, a low-level format is done by the factory. You simply run FDISK, stepping through the options displayed, to partition your drive. The high-level format is done by DOS's FORMAT command. Once completed, the disk is prepared and ready for use. The next issue is organizing your programs and files in the best possible manner.

File Organization Strategies

Dozens of books exist on hard-disk management. Thick books, too. But the subject can be summarized in two words: Subdirectories and Backup. Subdirectories are governed by the concept of file organization. Backup is file security.

DOS lays down no laws for subdirectories concerning how to name them, where to put them, or what to put in them. Other operating systems have definite subdirectory rules. For example, Unix has numerous required subdirectories into which certain files must be stored. On the Macintosh, all system files go into a special "folder" named SYSTEM. The PC? No rules—which is why file organization and hard disk management are important issues.

Info: The only rules DOS makes about subdirectories are the following:

Every disk has a root directory, \ .

Subdirectories are created using the MKDIR/MD command.

Subdirectories are named just like files.

You cannot rename a subdirectory (although you can in DOS Shell).

You cannot move a subdirectory.

To delete a subdirectory, it must be empty of files and subdirectories and you cannot be logged to it.

The Rules of Hard-Disk Management

In the DOS manual there are some hints about how to organize files into subdirectories. But a few lame examples won't help you create a system that obeys what I call the rules of hard-disk management.

RULE #1: Keep the root clean

The root directory should never scroll off the screen. This is a constant battle—something you really need to control. Here's why:

Each new application you install will specify the root as the location for its own directory.

Programs that create instant-run batch files will put them in the root directory.

Device drivers you add to your system will plop themselves down in the root directory.

Disk utilities save their temporary and information files in the root directory.

It's maddening! There is really a place for all those files and subdirectories. If you build a usable system, there should never be more than a dozen files in the root.

RULE #2: Create an organized tree structure

Organization can just happen. If you now have 18 subdirectories off your root, note how some of them are similar. Consider placing similar subdirectories into one master subdirectory. This usually happens first with a GAMES subdirectory. But why not a UTIL subdirectory for utilities or a PROJECT subdirectory for projects?

To create an organized tree structure you need a plan of attack. The following are methods of subdirectory organization. Nothing is gospel here. These are only suggestions for setting up your hard drive. Follow one, borrow from another, or create your own.

In the end, the best system is what works best for you. You'll want to have a system where any possible program you add to your hard drive will have a definite place. There should be no need to create new subdirectories off the root, nor will you ever have to move a subdirectory branch. Everything will fall into place with proper forethought and organization.

The Basic System

Think about what you need subdirectories for. The first thing that comes to mind is DOS. DOS should always be in its own subdirectory. Note that the DOS subdirectory need not branch immediately off the root directory. For a basic system, however, that's okay.

Other subdirectories can be created off the root as well; for example, one for Microsoft Word or your word processor, one for Lotus 1-2-3 or your spreadsheet, and so on. Adding a subdirectory for temporary files—a TEMP or JUNK subdirectory—is also part of a basic organized system.

That much takes care of your applications. Next you need to install subdirectories for your data files. A convenient place is immediately under each of the application subdirectories.

Tip: In the figure, the subdirectories are named DATA. In practice, you would want to name your subdirectories to reflect their contents. Good subdirectory names include BUDGET, NOVEL, MEETING, MEMOS, or any of a number of eight-letter combinations that accurately reflect the subdirectory's contents.

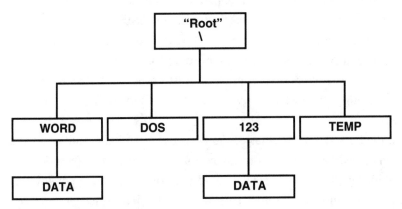

Figure 17-5. The basic organized system.

Provided you don't plan on adding too many other applications, the basic system works just fine. In fact, it's an ideal setup for most laptop computers or other systems that don't see a lot of work.

The Project System

The project system expands upon the basic system primarily by adding a special PROJECT directory. The actual projects being worked on are then contained in their own subdirectories under PROJECT—as many as you can add, since they're all special projects.

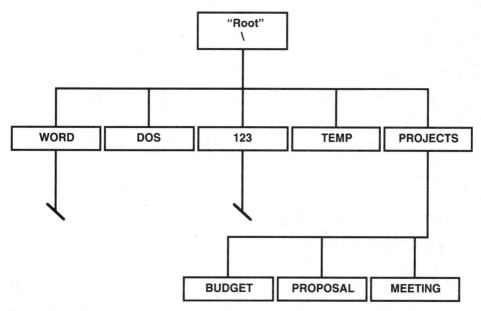

Figure 17-6. The project system.

In Figure 17-6, note that the application directories continue to have their own subdirectories. But all the major projects, regardless of which application created them, will be put under the PROJECT directory. For example, the BUDGET subdirectory may contain Lotus 1-2-3 files, a presentation document written in Microsoft Word, and so on.

Need to add another application? Fine, create another subdirectory off the root. Remember to give that application's subdirectory its own data subdirectories. But, if you find yourself doing this too often, you'll need to find a better approach.

The Main Branches System

The Main Branches system—typically found on a "power user" system, a diverse multipurpose computer, or a home system—is built for expansion. The idea behind this strategy is to create a system that can be expanded without intruding on the root directory. Instead, major directories are used to contain all applications and secondary subdirectories are added under them.

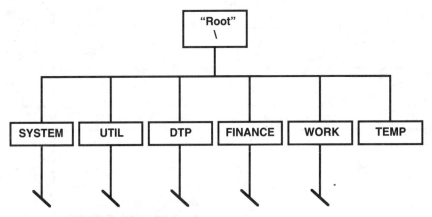

Figure 17-7. The Main Branches system.

Figure 17-7 shows six main subdirectories off the root: SYSTEM, for system files, DOS, and so forth; UTIL, for utility programs; DTP, for this computer's desktop publishing system; FINANCE, for 1-2-3, accounting software, etc.; WORK, which contains current projects, each in their own subdirectory; and TEMP for temporary files. Additional subdirectories you might consider adding off the root could be: GAMES, for—well, you know; WINDOWS, if you installed Microsoft Windows on this system; and a general-purpose MISC subdirectory. In fact, you could place GAMES under MISC if you're wary of someone concluding that they like GAMES better than 1-2-3.

Underneath each main branch would go individual subdirectories, which again may have subdirectories. Figure 17-8 shows some possibilities:

Under the SYSTEM subdirectory are DOS, BATCH, MOUSE, and DEVICE— items generally associated with the computer system. If you added anything else such as an expansion card with its own software, you could place all that into a subdirectory of the SYSTEM directory. That's the essence of the branch system; you add new directories to subdirectories, not the root.

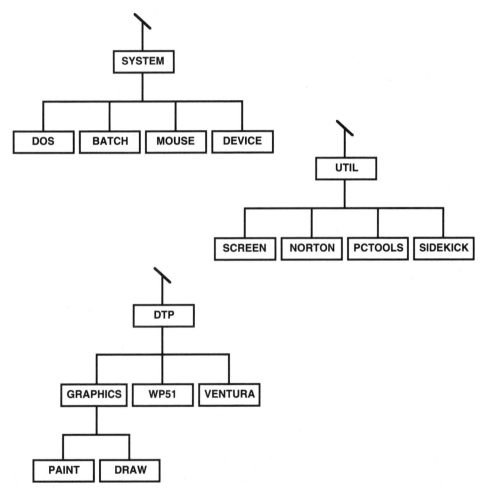

Figure 17-8. Subdirectories for each branch.

Other subdirectory trees have similar subdirectories within them. The DTP subdirectory contains all things relating to desktop publishing. Note that the PAINT and DRAW directories may contain additional subdirectories, each with its own painting or drawing program. If you had more than one word processor, the WP51 subdirectory could be changed to WORDS, and under it you would put individual directories for each of your word processors.

The BIN System

The BIN system is unique because all files and programs—or batch files that run those files and programs—are kept in a single BIN subdirectory. The data files and other information is then kept in other subdirectories similar to the Main Branch system.

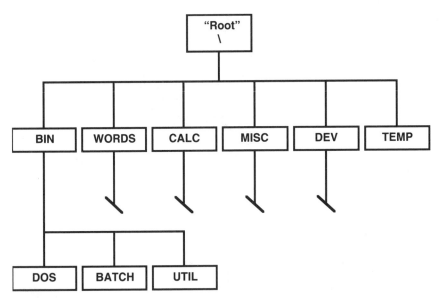

Figure 17-9. The BIN system.

The BIN directory can contain other subdirectories, usually consisting of crucial files or system information. In Figure 17-9, subdirectories for DOS, batch files, and utilities are stored under BIN.

Other subdirectories in the BIN system work like the Main Branches system. Again, the object is to have a place—a subdirectory off the root—into which additional programs can be put. For example, QBASIC and the Turbo C programming languages could each be placed into subdirectories of the DEV directory. But all programs central to this system can be launched from the BIN directory.

Running the System

Creating a usable subdirectory structure is only building the house. To live in it, you need more DOS commands and some utilities. For now, you can subsist by using the CD command to change directories and then type in program names. Later you'll discover the PATH command and batch files. The importance of these techniques for making the above systems usable is explained over the next few chapters. If you're anxious to rearrange your hard drive into a better system, hold off until you've been briefed on batch files and the PATH command, as well as general system configuration.

Files and Information

There are three types of files on your system:

Program files, which end in COM, EXE, or BAT

Data files, which include all non-program files

Text files, which you can read

Actually, there are only two types of files—program and data. A text (or ASCII) file is only a data file that contains formatted, readable text. You can read it using the TYPE command.

Program files are easily recognizable, thanks to their filename extensions; they're all going to be COM, EXE, or BAT files. By eliminating those, you can assume everything else is a data file. And it's a good bet that if a file ends in TXT, it's probably a text file. Other than that, you have to rely on a file's name to judge its contents. Since DOS only gives you eight letters for naming a file, things get interesting.

File-Naming Secrets

DOS filenames follow the classic 8-dot-3 file-naming convention. That's up to eight characters, followed by an optional dot and up to three characters of an optional extension. DOS forbids only the following characters in a filename:

```
"  /  \  [  ]  :  *  |  <  >  +  =  ;  ,  ?
```

Add to that list the space character and the period, which can only be used to separate a filename from its extension, and the 31 control characters. (Refer to Chapter 5 and Appendix B for more information on ASCII.) Yet that's only 48 characters out of a possible 128 ASCII characters. Since both upper case and lower case are treated the same, that leaves you 54 characters with which to name files, including some interesting symbols.

For example, to name tables, figures, or any numbered items, you can use the following scheme:

```
TBL01-01 TBL01-02 TBL02-01 TBL02-02 etc...
```

"TBL" means table; the numbers could be chapter numbers followed by a hyphen and the table number. You could also take advantage of the dot and make the number an extension:

```
FIG01.01 FIG01.02 FIG02.01 FIG02.02 etc...
```

Above, the figures ("FIG") are given chapter numbers as the filename and figure numbers as an extension. However, this foils the concept of an extension for manipulating groups of files. Instead, consider the following:

```
01-01.FIG 01-02.FIG 02-01.FIG 02-02.FIG etc...
```

Now all figures can be manipulated using the *.FIG wildcard.

Another key character to use is the underline. In a way, this lets you put more than one "word" into a filename if you treat the underline like a space character. Consider the following:

```
READ_ME.TXT BACK_UP.BAT MY_STUFF.WP CAR_FIX.WKS
```

Other interesting characters let you produce filenames as follows:

```
WOW! S&P.500 (SHH) ANNUAL% CO$T_EST.WKS
```

Later in this chapter you'll discover how to display a sorted directory using the DIR command. Some applications do this automatically, sorting files when displayed internally by the program. To put files toward the top of the list, name them using low ASCII codes; to put files toward the end of the list, name them using high ASCII codes. For example, files starting with numbers are always listed first in order. Files with letters are listed next in alphabetical order.

```
!FIRST 0SECOND 9THIRD A-FOURTH Z_FIFTH ~LAST
```

Above, the files created will be listed in that order when sorted by the DIR command or inside an application. Note that files starting with an exclamation point (!) will always be listed first; those starting with the tilde (~) are always listed last.

In addition to the standard ASCII characters, DOS lets you use the 128 Extended ASCII characters in a filename as well. This puts some real flexibility in filenames, allowing you to secretly code filenames using graphics characters, blanks (like the space character), and foreign language characters. Imagine, a filename that actually is Greek!

Tip: The Extended ASCII characters aren't available on the keyboard. To produce them, look up their numbers and then type them using the Alt key and the numeric keypad. Refer to Figure 5-2 or Appendix B for the numbers. To enter a number, press and hold the Alt key, and then type that number on the keypad. Release the Alt key, and the character matching that code appears.

A neat character to use in naming files is 255, the blank. This isn't a space character, but its effect is the same as in a filename. For example:

```
READ ME.TXT
```

That filename is created by typing READ, then Alt-2-5-5, then ME.TXT. Alt-2-5-5 creates the blank character.

You can't have a period in a filename, but you can have a hovering dot, character code 249:

```
JUST·FOR.YOU
```

The dot between JUST and FOR is produced by typing Alt-2-4-9. Other examples of interesting files are listed in Table 17-4. Their code combinations are at the right.

Filename	Interesting Codes
$9^1/_2$	171
¥en	157
├╫┤	195, 196, 215, 196, 197, 180
πr^2	227, 253
∞	236
ΦΩΘ	232, 234, 233
Olé	130
ZERO±10°	241, 248

Table 17-1. Weird filenames that you too can create.

Files and Their Attributes

Various items describe a file on disk. The DIR command displays a file's name, extension, size, date, and time. Information not displayed includes the file's location on disk and its attributes. Only DOS needs to know where a file sits on disk, but its attributes are something you can view and manipulate.

There are four attributes used to describe a file on disk, as shown in Table 17-2. Not every file will have an attribute. For example, after doing a system backup, each file's A, or Archive, attribute is reset. But if you change the file, the A attribute is set again. (This is how some backup programs can select only those recently modified files to backup.)

Attribute	Effect/Meaning
R, Read-only	File is read-only, cannot be changed or deleted
A, Archive	File has been modified since last backup
S, System	System file, invisible and cannot be deleted
H, Hidden	File is invisible

Table 17-2. File attributes and their meanings.

The Read-only attribute prevents a file from being changed or deleted. It offers a simple method of file security since a read-only file cannot be accidentally removed with a DEL *.* command. (It also prevents a file from being infected by some viruses.)

The System attribute is assigned to system files, those that DOS needs to operate. By default, a file with its System attribute set will be invisible; the DIR command will not display it. Also, you cannot delete a System file using the DEL command.

The Hidden attribute makes a file invisible. While you can still access the file, you cannot see it in a directory listing and no other DOS commands will be able to locate it.

Tip: To get at an invisible file, specify its full name in your application. But DOS utilities cannot access the file even when you specify a full name.

To see which attributes are assigned to which files, the ATTRIB command is used. You simply follow ATTRIB with the name of the file to examine it, or a wildcard to see all files.

Log to the root directory on drive C and type the following:

```
ATTRIB *.*
```

You'll see something like:

```
SH    C:\IO.SYS
SH    C:\MSDOS.SYS
A     C:\AUTOEXEC.BAT
A     C:\COMMAND.COM
A     C:\CONFIG.SYS
   R  C:\WINA20.386
```

IO.SYS and MSDOS.SYS are the two DOS files that make your hard drive a boot disk. They are System files and Hidden.

Info: IO.SYS and MSDOS.SYS compose the DOS kernel, the core files that actually make up MS-DOS.

AUTOEXEC.BAT, COMMAND.COM, and CONFIG.SYS all have their Archive attributes set. This means that these files have been modified since the last full-disk backup. In the case of COMMAND.COM, it means that the file has been copied to the root directory since the last backup.

The file WINA20.386, used by Windows, is a Read-only file. It cannot be modified, renamed, or deleted. (But you can remove it from the root directory using the SWITCHES command, which is discussed in Chapter 19.)

An optional switch specified with the ATTRIB command is /S. This is the subdirectory switch, which causes ATTRIB to display the attributes of all files in all subdirectories under the current directory. If you type ATTRIB /S in the root directory, you'll see the attributes of all files on your hard drive—but be prepared to press Ctrl-S to pause the display; it will whip by pretty fast.

Changing a File's Attributes

In addition to displaying a file's current attributes, you can use the ATTRIB command to change a file or group of files' attributes. The same attribute letters as those shown in Table 17-2 are used, preceded by a plus or minus sign. For example, to remove the A attribute for all files in the root directory, type the following:

```
ATTRIB -A C:\*.*
    Not resetting hidden file C:\IO.SYS
    Not resetting hidden file C:\MSDOS.SYS
```

ATTRIB will avoid changing the two hidden/system files, and it will tell you so on the screen. Otherwise, you won't see any feedback. Use the ATTRIB *.* command again to verify that the A attribute has been removed from the other files.

Info: Changing the Archive attribute is normally done after a backup operation. This is covered in Chapter 21.

For a little security, set the Read-only attribute on COMMAND.COM. Type the following:

```
ATTRIB +R COMMAND.COM
```

Again, no feedback. But if you type ATTRIB COMMAND.COM you'll see that its Read-only attribute has been set. Now, be bold, and type the following:

```
DEL COMMAND.COM
```

Normally this course of action wouldn't be advised. But upon pressing Enter, you'll see:

```
Access denied
```

Isn't that reassuring!

You can combine two or more switches to set the options for a group of files. For example, if you wanted to remove the Read-only and System attributes of the IO.SYS and MSDOS.SYS files, you could type: ATTRIB -R -H *.SYS. Don't type that in! It just shows how more than one attribute can be set with a single command.

It's interesting to use the +H switch to hide various things on your system—including subdirectories. The only reason to do this is security. After all, if you forget you've hidden something, only the ATTRIB command will tell you about it—and for a subdirectory, you must remember the subdirectory's exact name (*.* after ATTRIB doesn't list subdirectories).

For example, to hide the SECRET directory, you would type the following:

```
ATTRIB +H SECRET
```

SECRET is now invisible; the DIR command will no longer list it. You can still CD to that directory, and use RD to remove it. But to anyone else using your system, it's invisible.

COMMAND: ATTRIB (External)
                Function: To examine or change a file's attributes.
                Format: ATTRIB $\pm$ A $\pm$ R $\pm$ H $\pm$ S filename /S

ATTRIB by itself displays the attributes for all files in the current directory.

$\pm$ A is used to set or reset the Archive attribute; + sets the attribute and - resets it. (This holds for all the following options.)

$\pm$ R is used to set or reset the Read-only attribute.

$\pm$ H is used to set or reset the Hidden attribute.

$\pm$ S is used to set or reset the System attribute.

Filename is an optional filename, wildcard, or the name of a subdirectory. When specified, ATTRIB shows the attributes for that *filename*, group of files, or subdirectory.

/S is the subdirectory switch. When specified, ATTRIB carries out its duties in all subdirectories under the current subdirectory, matching whichever files and setting or resetting whichever attributes are specified.

The DIR Command Revisited

It's now time to introduce you to the full power of the DIR command, perhaps the most common DOS command after COPY. With DOS 5, the DIR command has grown in stature. It does some tremendous things that DOS users have been clamoring for—including sorting, displaying files by their attributes, and displaying an entire directory tree with a single command.

The Optional Switches

The DIR command has a throng of optional switches. You can specify one or more switches on the command line after the DIR command to customize its output. This armada of options follows the optional pathname used with the DIR command. They're listed in Table 17-3.

Switch	Function
/P	Pauses the listing after each screen
/W	Displays the files in the wide format (doesn't work with the /B switch)
/B	Display only filenames
/L	Display filenames in lower case
/S	Display all filenames in any subdirectories under the current directory
/A	Displays files according to their attributes
/O	Sort the filenames

Table 17-3. The DIR command's optional switches.

To test these switches, use a directory on your disk that contains a lot of files. A good one would be your DOS subdirectory, which should contain some 90 or so files. Actually, to see how many files it contains, type DIR once you get to the DOS subdirectory.

The first problem with the DIR command is that it scrolls too fast. If you're quick with Ctrl-S, that's okay, but, after all, this is a computer designed to make life easier. Try the DIR command again, but this time use the /P switch:

```
DIR /P
```

The P in this case stands for pause (or page). Every 24 lines, the directory listing pauses and DOS says:

```
Press any key to continue . . .
```

Press the Spacebar and you see "(continuing C:\DOS)" and another 22 directory entries are displayed. (Keep pressing the Spacebar until the entire directory is displayed—or press Ctrl-C to cancel.)

The /W switch shows you a directory in the W-i-d-e format. Type:

```
DIR /W
```

The filenames are shown in their 8-dot-3 format, and only the names are displayed. Note that any subdirectories are listed in square brackets.

You can combine the two switches if the display still scrolls off the screen:

```
DIR /W /P
```

The /B switch, new to DOS 5, is the Brief switch. It displays only filenames, similar to the /W switch, but in only one column. Often you must combine the /B and /P switches to see the filenames. Type:

```
DIR /B /P
```

Info: If you try to use both the /B and /W switch, only the /B switch will be recognized.

The /L switch is also new to DOS 5. It displays the filenames in a directory in lower case. Type:

```
DIR /L /P
```

The output is unusual—especially if you've been using another version of DOS and have never seen lower-case filenames in a directory. (Remember, DOS doesn't care if a filename is upper or lower case; but the DIR command normally displays them in upper case.)

The DIR command's /S switch finds itself with several other commands, including the ATTRIB command covered earlier in this chapter. The /S switch simply repeats the current command for all subdirectories under the current or specified directory. Log to the root directory and type the following:

```
DIR /W /P /S
```

This reads, "Display the files in wide format, pause every page, and display all files in all subdirectories." An alternative would have been to specify the root directory directly, as in: DIR C:*.* /W /P /S. Press Enter and you'll see every file on your hard drive displayed. (Press Ctrl-C if you feel the need to cancel.)

The /A switch allows the DIR command to display files with or without a certain attribute. Prior to DOS 5, the DIR command wouldn't tell you anything about a file's attribute—nor could it display hidden or system files. You needed the ATTRIB command to locate read-only and archive files. Now DIR does it all.

The /A switch without any options displays all files in the directory, no matter what their attribute. In the root directory, type:

```
DIR /A
```

You'll see all files displayed—including the system files IO.SYS and MSDOS.SYS. To see files of only one type, follow /A with an optional colon and the letters of the attributes you want to see. The letters are:

A—Archive files
D—Directories
H—Hidden files
R—Read-only files
S—System files

Note the addition of the D attribute, which DOS uses to identify directories. If you want to see only subdirectories in the current directory, type:

```
DIR /A:D
```

To see all the read-only files in the root directory, type:

```
DIR /A:R
```

You'll see the WINA20.386 file and COMMAND.COM (if you made it Read-only earlier in this chapter). Now how about finding those hidden files? Type:

```
DIR /A:H
```

Now the DIR command helps you to locate hidden files. If you see "File not found," then there are no hidden files in that directory.

Tip: Are there any hidden files on your hard drive? Type the following command to find out:

```
DIR C:\*.* /A:H /P /S
```

A hyphen in front of an attribute letter displays files that lack those attributes. For example:

```
DIR /A:-S
```

The command above displays only nonsystem files. If you combine options, then do not separate the attributes letters with spaces. For example:

```
DIR /A:A-RH
```

That reads, "Display files in the current directory that have their Archive attribute set, are not read-only but are hidden." Did you find any on your system?

Note: Don't forget that "/A:" is the attribute switch and "A:" is a drive letter. It's a common mistake.

The /O switch is perhaps the best switch of all. It determines the sorting order for files listed in the directory. Normally, DOS displays files in the same order they were added to the disk—haphazardly! But if you use the /O switch, your files will be sorted alphabetically. Type:

```
DIR /O
```

The files appear as before, but in alphabetical order. Now it's not that hard finding files in a large directory.

As with the /A switch, you can follow /O with an optional colon and several other letters to control the sort order. The letters are:

D—By date and time, oldest first
E—Alphabetically by filename extension
G—Subdirectories first
N—Alphabetically by filename (the default)
S—By size, smallest first

Putting a hyphen in front of an item reverses the sort order. So -N is reverse alphabetical, -S lists the largest files first, and so on. And you can combine options to sort at various levels—but no spaces should come between the letters and hyphens.

Change back to your DOS subdirectory or a directory containing a number of files of different names, dates and sizes. Type:

```
DIR /O:-S
```

You'll see a sorted directory by size, largest files first. To sort by filename extension and secondarily by filename, type:

```
DIR /O:EN
```

See how the BAS, COM, and EXE files are listed in order and then by their filenames alphabetically?

To see a sorted list of the subdirectories in the current directory, type:

```
DIR /O /A:D
```

Any or all of the DIR command's switches can be combined in any number of ways. Only the /B and /W commands don't function together (with the /B command taking priority.

Tip: If you're an experienced DOS user and would prefer a certain sorting order, or would like to always see filenames in lower case, you can permanently set your DIR command switches using the environment variable DIRCMD. Set DIRCMD equal to the switches you always want the DIR command to use. For example, if you always want your directories displayed in alphabetical order in lower case, type:

```
SET DIRCMD=/O/L
```

To override the DIRCMD variable, you must specifically turn an item off with the DIR command at the DOS prompt, using the hyphen. For example, DIR /-O /-L would undo what the DIRCMD variable has done above.

More information on using the SET command and environment variables is covered in Chapter 20.

COMMAND: DIR (Internal)
               Function: To display files on disk.
               Format: DIR pathname /P /W /B /L /S /A:attrib /O:sort

Without any options, the DIR command displays a list of all files in the current directory.

Pathname is an optional drive letter, pathname, wildcard, or individual filename. DIR will list only those files matching the *pathname* description.

/P is the pause or page switch. When specified, the DIR command will list a screenful of files, then pause for you to press any key before continuing.

/W is the wide switch. When specified, the DIR command displays only directories and filenames in a five-column format. No information on size, date, or time is displayed.

/B is the brief switch. When specified, the DIR command lists only directories and filenames in one column.

/L is the lower-case switch. When specified, the DIR command displays all filenames in lower case.

/S is the subdirectory switch. When specified, the DIR command will seek out the files indicated and display them in all subdirectories under the current directory.

/A:attrib is the attribute switch. The DIR Command will display only those files that match the attribute(s) listed, according to the following letters:

A—Archive attribute
D—Directory attribute
H—Hidden attribute
R—Read-only attribute
S—System attribute

If a hyphen precedes an attribute letter, then all files except for that attribute are displayed. More than one letter can be combined after the /a switch but they must not be separated by spaces.

/O:sort is the sort order switch. The DIR command sorts the files in the order specified, according to the following letters:

D—Date and time, oldest first
E—Alphabetically, by file extension
G—Directories first
N—Alphabetically, by filename
S—By size, smallest first

/O:n is the default. Placing a hyphen before a letter reverses the sort for that letter. Specifying more than one letter sorts on more than one level, but note that no spaces should come between the letters.

Summary

Disks store information electronically by manipulating magnetic particles on the disk's media. Those particles are organized into tracks and cylinders by the low-level format, partitioned for use by DOS, then organized into sectors and clusters by the DOS format.

Files are placed on disk by the cluster. A cluster can be one or more sectors and it becomes the "allocation unit" DOS uses to store files on the drive. Each file occupies a minimum of one allocation unit.

Hard-disk management is the art of organizing and maintaining files and programs on a hard drive.

The first part of hard-disk management is organization. That involves using DOS's subdirectory commands to build a usable and flexible file system. The object is to create a system that keeps the root directory clean but still provides expansion flexibility.

The second part of hard-disk management is file maintenance, which is accomplished via DOS commands, batch files, and backing up you files every so often.

While filenames are limited to the 8-dot-3 format, there are some 48 ASCII characters and 128 extended ASCII characters you can use to name a file. To get at the extended ASCII characters, you hold the Alt key and type the character's code on the numeric keypad. Release the keypad and the character appears.

Every file on disk has certain attributes associated with it: Archive, Read-only, System, and Hidden. The ATTRIB command is used to both view and change a file's attributes.

The DIR command displays files in a number of manners using its optional switches. Files can be displayed by their attributes, wide across the screen, in lower case, or they can be sorted.

CHAPTER 18

Batch Files

Of the three types of programs that run under DOS, one is actually a text file that you can create. Batch files are great little tools for running your hard-disk system. And although they're kind of like a programming language, you don't need to be a genius at math or know anything more than DOS commands in order to create them.

This chapter answers the following questions:

- How do batch files fit into a hard-disk system?

- How are batch files created?

- What types of things are put into a batch file?

- How do the special batch-file commands work?

- What is a batch-file variable and how can it be used?

- After batch files, what's next?

Building a Batch File

A batch file is any text file that ends with a BAT extension. It contains DOS commands—the stuff you normally type on the command line. But rather than type those commands one at a time, they're all stored one after another in a convenient batch file. When you type the batch file's name at the DOS prompt, DOS executes all the commands contained inside the batch file—just as if you typed each one on the command line yourself. That's what makes batch files so handy.

Info: A batch file can consist of three things—special batch file commands, DOS commands, and the name of programs on your computer. Anything you can type on the command line can be placed into a batch file.

Batch files become part of a sophisticated hard disk system in that they run everything for you. With a well-designed system, you can forget about typing CD-this or remembering where files are located or recalling bizarre options on commands and applications. With batch files, everything can be done automatically. It's like having a TV remote-control that automatically remembers at what time to change the channel.

Simple Batch Files

A batch file is a stack of DOS command lines—a batch of them. This is how batch files started out. IBM wanted DOS to contain a batch-file language, one which would allow the early PC to run a series of tests over and over. From that simple beginning grew the batch files that you'll soon use to run your hard-disk system.

Consider the following simple DOS commands:

```
C:
CD \
CLS
VER
VOL
```

After entering each of those five commands at five different DOS prompts, you'll be logged to drive C's root directory, the screen will clear, and you'll see the DOS version and disk-volume label displayed. But that's five steps! To do it all in one step, you can place each of those commands into a single batch-file program.

To create this sample batch file, you'll use what's called the COPY CON command.

Info: DOS knows your keyboard as the CON device. Since the COPY command copies between DOS devices, you use a filename to copy text from the keyboard to a file on disk:

```
COPY CON filename
```

To end the copying, you press the F6 key or type Ctrl-Z. The Ctrl Z character marks the end of a text file and DOS stops copying. Note that you cannot use COPY CON to edit a file already on disk; the COPY command will simply overwrite the file. COPY CON is best used to create quick-and-dirty text files. If you really want to edit a batch file or any text file, use the MS-DOS Editor.

DOS's COPY command will be used to copy information from the keyboard directly to a file on disk. For now, create the file in the root directory on drive C. Type:

```
COPY CON SAMPLE.BAT
```

Press Enter. The cursor drops down to the next line and awaits your input. You're now in a simple editing mode. All text you type will be sent to a file by the COPY command; you're copying text directly from the keyboard (the "CON" device) to a file (SAMPLE.BAT). Type the five DOS commands:

```
C:
CD \
CLS
VER
VOL
```

After the last command, press Ctrl-Z. You'll see "^Z" displayed on the screen. That's the end-of-file marker, which tells the COPY command you're finished creating a file from the keyboard. Press Enter.

```
1 file(s) copied
```

You've just created the text file SAMPLE.BAT, but because it's a batch file, it's also a program that DOS can run. Type:

```
SAMPLE
```

One after the other, you'll see each DOS command in the batch file "typed" onto the screen.

Info: If you see any errors, or something doesn't look right, then you've probably made a typo in the batch file. You cannot use the COPY CON technique to edit the file, but you can load it into the MS DOS Editor and make corrections. Save the file back to disk and then try to run it again.

The true power of a batch file is apparent when it issues commands that you normally type over and over. By creating the proper batch files, you can greatly cut down on your time using the DOS prompt.

Consider the commands you use to start your word processor. Every day you may type the same thing:

```
CD \WP
WP
```

Those commands could be placed into a batch file, WP.BAT. That would make life much easier on you every time you run your word processor.

Info: As your knowledge of DOS increases, you'll be able to do more with DOS and batch files. In fact, the rest of this book uses batch-file examples to show you how quickly things can be accomplished under DOS.

The BATCH Subdirectory

Take another look at that SAMPLE.BAT file. Call in your friends and show them the first computer "program" you've written. But SAMPLE.BAT is in the root directory. And, as you know by now, it's not a good hard-disk management practice to clutter up the root. ("Keep the root clean.")

The best place to put batch files is in their own subdirectory. Every computer I own has a BATCH subdirectory somewhere. On the laptop, \BATCH is right off the root. On my writing system (which uses the Main Branches method of organization covered in the previous chapter), BATCH is under a general SYSTEM subdirectory.

Wherever you decide is best, create a BATCH subdirectory. Use the MD command and be thoughtful about its location. As you continue to organize your hard-disk system, various batch files will find their way into the BATCH subdirectory. For now, it will be home to all your sample batch files created in this chapter.

Copy SAMPLE.BAT into your BATCH subdirectory once you've created it. Then delete the copy in the root directory.

Batch File Commands

DOS's batch files work like a programming language of sorts. On one level, you can create batch files that simply contain the DOS commands and program names necessary to start your word processor, spreadsheet, database, and so on. Beyond that, you can build batch files that can make decisions, repeatedly perform tasks that would bore you to tears, or do any number of amazing things.

Aside from all the DOS commands and programs on your computer, there are eight simple batch-file commands that you can use to give a batch file more smarts. They are:

```
CALL
ECHO
FOR
GOTO
IF
PAUSE
REM
SHIFT
```

Not all the batch-file commands are covered here in great detail. After all, entire books are dedicated to the subject of using DOS's batch programming language. Those commands central to this book and important to using your system are illustrated below. The ECHO, PAUSE, and REM commands are illustrated in detail, followed by the IF and GOTO commands. The others—FOR and CALL—are documented here, although they aren't as central to hard-disk management batch-file programming as are the others.

Info: Batch-file commands are really DOS commands, albeit with a special purpose. All of these batch-file commands can also be used at the DOS prompt, although they lack any real practical use outside of a batch file.

The ECHO Command

ECHO is perhaps the most useful and popular of all the batch-file commands. It does two things: It turns the echoing of batch-file commands on or off, and it echoes text to the screen.

Run your SAMPLE.BAT file. (Log to your BATCH subdirectory if you haven't already.) See how all the commands are echoed to the screen? See all the DOS prompts? Isn't that ugly?

Using the ECHO command you can turn off the echoing a batch file does. This doesn't prevent DOS commands and programs from displaying information, it just turns off the batch file's own redundant echoing to the display.

Use the MS-DOS Editor, or your own favorite text editor or word processor, to load and edit the SAMPLE.BAT file. (If you're using a word processor, remember to save all batch files in the unformatted, nondocument, text, or ASCII format.)

Insert a line at the top of the file, ECHO OFF. That's the ECHO command followed by its OFF parameter, which turns echoing in the batch file off. The batch-file commands that follow ECHO OFF will run silent and smooth.

Your final SAMPLE.BAT file should look like this:

```
ECHO OFF
C:
CD \
CLS
VER
VOL
```

Save it to disk, exit the Editor, and then run SAMPLE.BAT at the DOS prompt again:

```
SAMPLE
```

It's much more professional looking with the ECHO OFF, don't you think? You can turn on echoing again with ECHO ON, although few batch file programs ever use it.

DOS normally echoes all batch-file commands, unless you do one of two things—turn ECHO OFF, or begin a line in the batch file with an At Sign, @. For example, you could edit the SAMPLE.BAT file to read as follows:

```
@C:
@CD \
@CLS
@VER
@VOL
```

Since each line starts with an @, nothing will be echoed to the screen. A more practical use of the @ is to put it in front of the initial ECHO OFF. That prevents that ECHO OFF from being displayed, making the entire batch file run "silent." Edit your SAMPLE.BAT file, putting an @ in front of the first line, ECHO OFF. Save it to disk and run it again.

Tip: Start all your batch files with @ECHO OFF.

Aside from the initial @ECHO OFF, batch files use the ECHO command to display text on the screen. Log to your batch-file subdirectory and use the MS DOS Editor to create the following batch file, WHERE.BAT:

Tip: Start the Editor by typing: EDIT WHERE.BAT

```
@ECHO OFF
CLS
ECHO You are on the volume:
VOL
ECHO And logged to the directory:
CD
ECHO.
```

Save the file to disk. Name it WHERE.BAT if it isn't already named. At the DOS prompt, type:

```
WHERE
```

Echo displays several two lines of text, describing the batch file's output. This is the primary use of the ECHO command: To tell the user what's going on. You should always be informative when creating a batch file, especially when someone else will be using the computer.

The final line in WHERE.BAT is ECHO followed immediately by a period. It's used to ECHO a blank line to the screen. If you just type ECHO alone, then the ECHO command displays "ECHO is on" or "ECHO is off," depending on the state of the ECHO command.

COMMAND: ECHO (Internal/Batch)
               Function: Displays text, controls the echo state
               Format: ECHO [ON|OFF] text

By itself, the ECHO command displays the current state of echoing in a batch file, either on or off.

When followed with either ON or OFF, ECHO in a batch file will turn on or turn off the echoing of the batch file's commands.

Text is optional text to be echoed to the display.

To echo a blank line, follow ECHO immediately with a period, as in "ECHO."

The PAUSE Command

Oftentimes you'll want a batch file to stop, giving the user a chance to read text on the screen or an opportunity to "break out" of a batch file. That's done with the PAUSE command. Type the following at the DOS prompt:

```
PAUSE

Press any key to continue . . .
```

The PAUSE command simply displays the message "Press any key to continue" and waits for you to press a key. Press the Spacebar. Edit the SAMPLE.BAT file using the MS-DOS Editor. Change it to read as follows:

```
@ECHO OFF
ECHO I'm about to clear the screen
PAUSE
CLS
VER
VOL
```

Save it back to disk, then run the batch file.

```
C:\BATCH>SAMPLE
I'm about to clear the screen
Press any key to continue . . .
```

Press the spacebar and the screen clears.

A good use for the PAUSE command is to give the user time to reflect before the batch file does something well-intended but potentially disastrous. Use the MS-DOS Editor to create the following batch file, named CRASH.BAT:

```
@ECHO OFF
ECHO This program causes your computer to explode.
ECHO To cancel, press Ctrl-C, or
PAUSE
ECHO Boom!
```

Don't worry about any fireworks; enter the program and save it to disk as CRASH.BAT. Exit to DOS and type:

```
C:\BATCH>CRASH
This program causes your computer to explode.
To cancel, press Ctrl-C, or
Press any key to continue...
```

See how the PAUSE command's message fits right into the scheme of things? It naturally follows the ECHO command before it. To continue with the batch file, press the Spacebar.

Boom!

The second ECHO command in CRASH.BAT states that you can press Ctrl-C to cancel. That's the way any batch file can be stopped. When you press Ctrl-C, the batch file will ask if you want to "terminate." Press Y to return to DOS or N to continue with the batch file.

Tip: To stop a batch file, press Ctrl-C or Ctrl-Break. Press Y to return to DOS or N to continue with the batch file.

Run CRASH again, but type Ctrl-C when asked. You'll see:

```
^C

Terminate batch job (Y/N)?

Press Y to stop or N to continue.
```

COMMAND: PAUSE (Internal/Batch)
Function: Pauses a batch file, waits for any key to continue.
Format: PAUSE text

Text is optional text the PAUSE command will display. However, when ECHO is turned OFF (as it is in most batch files), the *text* will not be displayed.

The REM Command

The REM command is used to put remarks into the batch file. These are just notes to yourself about the batch file, and they're not displayed on the screen when ECHO is off.

Edit the SAMPLE.BAT program again. Insert the following line after the initial @ECHO OFF:

```
REM This here is the ancestor of my first batch-file program
```

Save the file to disk and then run SAMPLE again. You won't notice any difference; the REM command has no effect. But it did allow you to insert a note inside the batch file. As your batch files grow more complex, you can use the REM command to tell you what the batch file is doing. (You'll see examples of this later in the book.)

You can also use the REM command to "comment out" certain parts of a batch file. This is better than deleting lines in a batch file; the line is still there, but because you put a REM in front of it, the command won't be executed.

Edit the WHERE.BAT file again. Put a REM command in front of the CLS command on the second line. Change that line to read:

```
REM CLS
```

Note the space after the REM; if you don't include it, then DOS will look for the program named REMCLS. Save the file to disk and run WHERE.BAT again. The effect is the same as before, but the screen doesn't clear. The CLS has been commented out. If you wanted the screen to clear again, simply cut out the REM command.

COMMAND: REM (Internal/Batch)
              Function: Allows for remarks in a batch file.
              Format: REM comments

Comments are optional comments after the REM command. Those *comments* are not executed by DOS nor are they displayed when ECHO is turned off.

The Intermediate-level Batch Commands

The following batch-file commands, GOTO, IF, FOR, and CALL, are used primarily in intermediate- and advanced-level batch files. The commands are documented here, but not really necessary for building a simple batch-file system for your hard drive.

Using GOTO

Normally, commands in a batch file run from top to bottom. You don't need an END or STOP command at the end of the batch file to tell it when it's done; after the last command line is run, control reverts to DOS. Using the GOTO command, however, you can make the batch file jump around a bit as it executes.

The GOTO command requires a label. That's a line in the batch file that starts with a colon, followed by a one-to-eight-character-long label or comment. When you use the GOTO command, you follow it with the name of a label to go to. The batch file then begins executing commands after that label.

Info: The label can be upper or lower case; GOTO matches any case label. Also, GOTO searches for the label from the top of the batch file down. If two labels have the same name, GOTO always goes to the first one. If the label cannot be found, the batch file halts immediately and a "Label not found" error message is displayed.

Enter the following batch file, named POEM.BAT. Check your typing and read it over twice before saving it to disk:

```
@ECHO OFF
GOTO FIRST
:THIRD
ECHO Sugar is sweet
GOTO FOURTH
:FIRST
ECHO Roses are red
GOTO SECOND
:FOURTH
ECHO And so are you
GOTO END
:SECOND
ECHO Violets are blue
GOTO THIRD
:END
```

Save the file to disk, then run POEM.BAT at the DOS prompt:

```
C:\BATCH>POEM
Roses are red
Violets are blue
Sugar is sweet
And so are you
```

Though the batch file looks severely messed-up, the end result is not. Figure 18-1 explains how it works:

See how the GOTO commands work with the labels to execute the ECHO commands in order? This is a silly example, granted. But when combined with other batch file commands, most notably the IF command, GOTO can do some pretty powerful stuff.

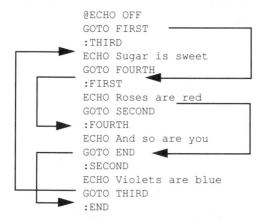

```
@ECHO OFF
GOTO FIRST
:THIRD
ECHO Sugar is sweet
GOTO FOURTH
:FIRST
ECHO Roses are red
GOTO SECOND
:FOURTH
ECHO And so are you
GOTO END
:SECOND
ECHO Violets are blue
GOTO THIRD
:END
```

Figure 18-1 How the POEM batch file uses GOTO.

COMMAND: GOTO (Internal/Batch)

                   Function: Branches batch-file execution to a label elsewhere

                             in the batch file.

                   Format: GOTO label

Label is required. It's a one-to-eight letter label elsewhere in the batch file to which GOTO sends batch-file execution.

The format for *label* elsewhere in the batch file starts with a colon. You can specify as many characters after the colon as you like, but only the first eight (up to a space character) are part of the *label*.

Note that the colon can also be used to replace the REM command, seeing that DOS ignores all text after a colon in a batch file.

The IF Command

The IF command is the batch file's decision maker. It works on an "if-something-then-do-this-command" basis. If the something is true, the command is executed. In a batch file, IF is used to test a condition and then execute a command if that condition is true. There are three conditions IF evaluates:

Comparison
Errorlevel test
File existence

Using IF for comparison requires understanding batch-file variables. There are two types of variables—command-line variables and environment variables. We cover the use of the IF command with a command-line parameter later in this chapter. Environment variables are introduced in Chapter 20.

The Errorlevel IF test relies on certain programs that return a code to DOS when they quit.

The IF command can also be used to test for a file's existence. If the file is present the IF command passes the test and will optionally run a DOS command. The format is:

```
IF EXIST filename command
```

If the filename represented by *filename* exists, then the command is executed. *Filename* can be a single file, pathname, or wildcard. *Command* can be a DOS command, program name, or a batch file command.

Create the following batch file, named HELLO.BAT:

```
@ECHO OFF
IF EXIST C:\COMMAND.COM ECHO I found COMMAND.COM here!
```

Save the file to disk and run it. IF-EXIST test for the file COMMAND.COM in the root directory of drive C. If found, the ECHO command displays "I found COMMAND.COM here!" Otherwise, nothing is displayed.

To display something if there is no COMMAND.COM in your root directory, edit the file and change its contents to the following:

```
@ECHO OFF
IF EXIST C:\COMMAND.COM GOTO FOUND
REM No COMMAND.COM was found
ECHO I can't find COMMAND.COM!
GOTO END
:FOUND
ECHO I found COMMAND.COM here!
:END
```

The batch file gets more complex, thanks to the GOTO statements and labels. But now it displays one of two messages, depending on if COMMAND.COM is found. Note how the REM command is used to tell you what's going on. Also, trace the flow of the GOTO statements and their labels.

Save the file to disk and then run it. If the program can't find COMMAND.COM, it tells you so.

You can use the optional NOT keyword with the IF command to reverse the results of the condition. Edit the HELLO.BAT file again and change line 2 to read:

```
IF NOT EXIST C:\COMMAND.COM GOTO FOUND
```

Save the file back to disk, and then run it. The results will be opposite from those you had before because you've reversed the condition of the test.

Later examples in this book will show you how the IF command works evaluating its other conditions.

COMMAND: IF (Internal/Batch)

        Function: Test for certain conditions in a batch file, executing an optional DOS command if the conditions are true.

        Format: IF [NOT] %var%==text command

        Format: IF [NOT] errorlevel value command

        Format: IF [NOT] exist filename command

[NOT] is optional and used to reverse the results of the test.

%var%==text is used to test an environment variable, var, against a word or string, text. If the two compare, command is executed. Note that there are two equal signs used.

Errorlevel is used to compare a DOS command or program's return code with the specified value. If the return code is greater than or equal to the value, command is executed.

Exist is used to test for the existence of filename. Filename can be a single file, pathname, or a group of files specified with wildcards. If filename exists, command is executed.

Command is a DOS command, program name, or batch-file command.

Using the FOR Command

The FOR command is the most unusual batch-file command. Basically it allows you to define a group of files and then run them all through one DOS command. For an example, consider the TYPE command.

The TYPE command lets you display only one file at a time; you cannot specify wildcards with the TYPE command. However, you can use the TYPE command with the FOR command to display a group of files. Type the following at the DOS prompt:

```
FOR %A IN (*.BAT) DO TYPE %A
```

Press Enter and DOS will use the TYPE command to display all the batch files in the current directory. Figure 18-2 illustrates how the FOR command works.

The FOR command consists of three elements: A FOR command variable, a group or "set" of programs and a DOS command. The FOR command variable will take on the files represented by the set, and it can then be used with the DOS command. In the above example, %A takes on the name of each batch file in the current directory. It is then used with the TYPE command to represent each of those files individually.

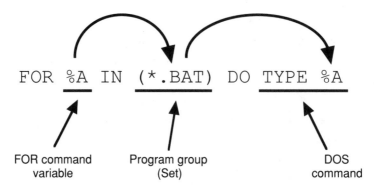

Figure 18-2 How the FOR command works.

Info: The FOR variable is a single percent sign followed by a letter of the alphabet. Do not follow the percent sign with a number.

In a batch file, you must use two percent signs with the FOR command's variable.

The set can contain any group of files. Consider the following FOR command:

```
FOR %E IN (*.TXT *.BAT *.DOC) DO TYPE %E
```

Above, %E represents each file in the current directory that has a TXT, BAT, or DOC extension. All those files will be displayed using the TYPE command.

```
FOR %B IN (*.BAT) DO %B
```

Above, %B represents all batch files in the current directory. The DOS command following DO is simply "do %B." The end result? The above FOR command will run all the batch files in the current directory.

The FOR command has limited use in a batch file, although it's listed as a batch-file command. If you do find a use for it, remember to specify two percent signs—instead of one—for the FOR variable.

COMMAND: FOR (Internal/Batch)

                      Function: Performs a single DOS command on a group of files.

                      Format: FOR *var* IN (*set*) DO *command*

Var is a FOR variable. At the DOS prompt it starts with one percent sign, followed by a letter of the alphabet. In a batch file, var is preceded by two percent signs. Var is used to represent each file matched by the set.

Set is a group of file names, pathnames, or wildcards.

Command is a DOS command. You can specify var in the command just as you would any single file in the set.

The CALL Command

You can put anything in a batch file that you would normally type at the DOS prompt; batch files contain DOS commands and the names of programs. That also includes the names of batch files, because you run them from the DOS prompt as well. But what happens when you put one batch file inside another? Create the following batch file, RUN1.BAT:

```
@ECHO OFF
ECHO Now trying to run the HELLO batch file:
HELLO
ECHO  How did that work?
```

Save the file to disk as RUN1.BAT. Exit to DOS and run the RUN1 batch file.

```
C:\BATCH>RUN1
Now trying to run the HELLO batch file:
I can't find COMMAND.COM
```

That's it! The last ECHO command in RUN1.BAT isn't executed. Why? Because DOS only runs one batch file at a time. When you tell DOS to run a second batch file, it says "Okay, here we go" and forgets totally about the original batch file. You can change this, however, with the CALL command.

Info: If you specify a batch-file program as a line in a batch file, it will run. But unlike other programs, control doesn't return to the original batch file. To change that, run the second batch file using the CALL command.

Edit the RUN1.BAT file using the MS-DOS Editor. Change the line that runs the HELLO batch file to read:

```
CALL HELLO
```

Save the file to disk, and then type RUN1 again:

```
C:\BATCH>RUN1
Now trying to run the HELLO batch file:
I can't find COMMAND.COM
How did that work?
```

Cool! Now it works.

Later examples in this book will show you how to use the CALL command to have several batch files share common batch-file cores.

COMMAND: CALL (Internal/Batch)
             Function: Runs a second batch file and then returns control to the first.
             Format: CALL batch_file

Batch_file is the name of a batch-file program. It's followed by any options or required parameters of the batch file—just as if it were entered on the command line.

After *batch_file* is executed, control returns to the current batch file, at the line following the CALL command.

Variables in Batch Files

A variable is a storage place for information. All programming languages use them. For example, if a program asked your name, it would store the results in a variable—say the "name variable." Because people have different names, the same name variable can be used to store any number of names.

There are two types of variables used in batch-file programming. The first are variables that represent any information typed after the batch file's name on the command line. These are command-line variables or replaceable parameters. The second type of variable is the environment variable, which deals with information stored in DOS's environment. Environment variables are covered in Chapter 20.

Command Line Variables

When you start some programs, they allow you to specify optional parameters or switches. For example, you can list a whole parade of optional parameters after the DIR command. The FORMAT command has a similar procession of options. With the MS-DOS Editor, you can specify a filename to edit as the optional parameter. And with batch files, you can specify any number of optional parameters, each of which can be examined inside the batch file using the IF command.

Inside a batch file, optional parameters are referred to as command-line variables. They're given the numbers zero through nine, and they start with a percentage sign. Each variable, %1 through %9, represents the first through ninth items typed after the batch-file name on the command line. Variable %0 represents the batch-file name as typed at the DOS prompt.

Info: All variables in a batch file start with a percent sign. Command line variables, environment variables (which are covered in Chapter 20), and the FOR command's variables all begin with a percent sign. In the case of the FOR command's variables, two percent signs are used.

The ECHO command can be used to display the command-line variables. Use the MS-DOS Editor to enter the following batch file, VARSHOW.BAT:

Tip: Use the Copy and Paste commands to create the repetitive lines in VARSHOW.BAT.

```
@ECHO OFF
ECHO %%0=%0
ECHO %%1=%1
ECHO %%2=%2
ECHO %%3=%3
ECHO %%4=%4
ECHO %%5=%5
ECHO %%6=%6
ECHO %%7=%7
ECHO %%8=%8
ECHO %%9=%9
```

Info: When the ECHO command displays a batch-file variable, it expands it out to its equivalent text. However, to avoid confusing ECHO when you display a percent sign, two percent signs are used. In VARSHOW.BAT, "%%" will display a single percent sign. However, "%6" displays the sixth item typed after VARSHOW on the command line.

Run the program, but type a few items after VARSHOW at the DOS prompt. For example:

```
C:\BATCH>VARSHOW APPLE BANANA COCONUT
%0=VARSHOW
%1=APPLE
%2=BANANA
%3=COCONUT
%4=
%5=
%6=
%7=
%8=
%9=
```

The content of each command-line variable is displayed by the ECHO command above. Note how variables %0 through %3 are equal to items typed at the DOS prompt. If you had typed "ONE TWO THREE" after VARSHOW, those words would be assigned to variables %1, %2, and %3 and then displayed above. Since the variables %4 through %9 aren't equal to anything, nothing was displayed.

Tip: To see how ECHO expands variables, edit the batch file and put a REM command in front of the initial @ECHO OFF. Run it again and watch how the variables are replaced as the batch file runs.

Using Command-Line Variables

Turn back to the beginning of this chapter and refer to the batch file that runs your word processor, WP.BAT. That's an excellent example of how to use a command-line variable in a batch file. Suppose your word processor allows you to specify a filename to edit, for example:

```
WORD CHAPTER1
```

You can pass along that information using the WP batch file. It would look like this:

```
@ECHO OFF
REM Run the word processor
C:
CD \MSWORD
WORD %1
```

Above, the first command line variable, %1, is used to pass a filename to Microsoft Word for editing. You could start the batch file like this:

```
WP CHAPTER1
```

"CHAPTER1" would be assigned to the %1 variable and successfully passed to Microsoft Word for editing.

Tip: Since most applications allow more than one option or switch to be specified, create your application-running batch files with as many command-line variables as possible. For example, the following could be used to run Windows:

```
WIN %1 %2 %3 %4 %5 %6 %7 %8 %9
```

This would allow you to run a batch file with as many as nine parameters, each of which would pass through safely to Windows. Apply this to all of your application-running batch files for the best results.

Command-line variables are also used with the IF command for comparison purposes. Enter the following batch file, IAM.BAT:

```
@ECHO OFF
IF %1==SMART GOTO OFCOURSE
ECHO I don't know what you're thinking.
GOTO END
;OFCOURSE
ECHO Of course you are!
:END
```

Save the file, then exit to DOS. Type the following (make sure you type "SMART" in upper case:

```
C:\BATCH>IAM SMART
Of course you are!
```

The reason for typing SMART in upper case is that the IF command is dumb. It will only match "SMART" if you type in "SMART". "Smart" just ain't the same. (You can edit the batch file to read "smart" if you always type in lowercase.)

If you follow IAM with anything else, the IF test will fail and "I don't know what you're thinking" is displayed. However, if you just type IAM by itself, you'll see a rare Syntax error.

The Syntax error means something went wrong in the batch file, usually with an IF command. In this case, %1 is equal to nothing and you're asking IF to compare nothing with "SMART"—which it can't do.

Info: Normally, DOS expands command-line variables into something. But if nothing is there, the IF command assumes you didn't type anything, and hence the error.

To fix this up you must do a trick known as "balancing the IF command." Two equal items must be placed on either side of the double equal signs. Normally, this is done by enclosing both items in double quotes. Edit IAM.BAT, and change the IF command to read:

```
IF "%1"=="SMART" GOTO OFCOURSE
```

Save it, then exit to DOS. Now you can type IAM by itself, but the program will still tell you it doesn't know what you're thinking!

Info: If the first command-line variable doesn't exist:

```
%1==SMART evaluates to ==SMART
"%1"==SMART evaluates to ""=="SMART"
```

If **SMART** is the first command line variable:

```
%1==SMART evaluates to SMART==SMART
"%1"==SMART evaluates to "SMART"=="SMART"
```

The SHIFT Command

The final batch-file command is the SHIFT command. SHIFT handles the problem of more than nine items typed after the batch-file name on the command line. What it does is to shift variable %1 into variable %0, variable %2 into variable %3, and so on. Any items beyond %9 are then shifted into item %9—one at a time for each SHIFT command. Enter the following batch file, SHIFTY.BAT:

```
@ECHO OFF
REM Shift test; type several items after SHIFTY
:LOOP
IF "%1=="" GOTO END
ECHO %1
SHIFT
GOTO LOOP
:END
```

The "%1"=="" IF test is used to see if the %1 variable exists. If it doesn't, then the test is true and, as in the above example, the batch file goes to the END label and stops. If %1 does exist, it's ECHOed. The variables are then shifted, and variable %2 becomes variable %1. The GOTO command then branches batch-file execution up to the LOOP label and the process repeats.

Save the file to disk as SHIFTY.BAT, exit to DOS, and type the following at the DOS prompt:

```
SHIFTY 1 2 3 4 5 6 7 8 9 10 11 12 13 14 15 16 17 18
```

That's twice as many command-line variables as the batch-programming language can handle. Yet, SHIFTY displays them all—and all through the %1 variable. If you want to see how all this works, remove the initial ECHO OFF command and watch the batch file execute one line at a time. (Press Ctrl-S to pause the display.)

Beyond Batch Files

Batch files can be a lot of fun—and practical too, as you'll see throughout the rest of this book. But some people will get really excited about batch files. If that's you, then batch files have ignited the spark of computer programming within you. Think about it: If you learn to program, you can tell the computer exactly what to do.

But batch files can only do so much. Microsoft hasn't made much headway toward expanding or improving the batch language, which means you have several choices available to you if you wish to pursue batch file programming further:

Pick up a good book on batch-file programming

There are dozens out there, from small handbooks to extensive texts on working with batch files, to volumes of sample batch-file programs that "you too" can create.

Consider working with third-party utilities

Since any DOS command or program can be part of a batch file, a lot of people have written batch-file augmenting utilities. These do an amazing number of useful things, all of which can be incorporated into your batch files.

Expand the batch-file language

Batch-file extenders give real muscle to batch files. One of them, Hyperkinetix Builder, adds dozens of commands to the batch-file repertoire—it even lets you compile a batch file into a real COM or EXE file.

Consider another programming language

The next step up from writing batch files would be to explore the BASIC programming language. BASIC naturally follows batch files on the programming scale. And the best advantage it has is that you already have it: The QBASIC interpreter comes with DOS.

Whichever path you take, there are ample ways to explore programming beyond the use of batch files. Or, for now at least, you can be satisfied with the interesting little things they can do for you and your hard-disk system. Be prepared to start filling that BATCH subdirectory with some interesting little programs.

Summary

Batch files are programs that DOS runs. They're text, consisting of DOS commands and program names—anything you'd normally type at the DOS prompt. These commands are stacked into a single batch file and are then run one after another when you type the batch-file name at the DOS prompt.

In addition to DOS commands and program names, there are special batch-file commands you can put into a batch file. DOS has eight of them:

ECHO, which turns batch-file echoing on or off as well as displays information on the screen.

PAUSE, which pauses batch-file execution, displaying a "press any key" message.

REM, which allows you to insert comments into a batch file.

GOTO, which branches batch-file execution to a corresponding label.

IF, which is used to make decisions in batch files.

FOR, which will execute a single DOS command for a group or set of programs.

CALL, which runs one batch file from within another.

SHIFT, which shifts command-line variables down by one.

Most batch files start with the command @ECHO OFF. Normally, batch files display all their commands as they run. ECHO OFF disables the echoing of commands. Additionally, any line in a batch file that starts with an @ sign isn't displayed, so the @ECHO OFF makes the batch file totally "silent."

Items typed after a batch file name become command-line variables. They're represented in a batch file as %1 through %9, for the first through ninth items typed after the batch-file name (which is variable %0). The SHIFT command is used to shuffle in any additional items.

CHAPTER 19

System Configuration

DOS allows you to control its behavior and customize its appearance. You get your chance as the system boots: Two special text files can be created on the boot disk to tell DOS how you want the system configured. The first is CONFIG.SYS, the system-configuration file—the subject of this chapter. The second file is a batch file, AUTOEXEC.BAT, and it's covered in the following chapter.

This chapter answers the following questions:

- How does the CONFIG.SYS file fit into the big picture?

- What does the CONFIG.SYS file do?

- What are CONFIG.SYS file's configuration commands?

- What is the importance of the FILES and BUFFERS commands?

- What are device drivers?

- How is CONFIG.SYS file customized for each computer?

The Computer Comes to Life

What really happens as the hard disk begins to spin and the BIOS desperately looks to the disk for an operating system—or anything—to load and run the computer? Here's a behind-the-scenes look at how DOS starts.

A disk's boot sector contains a tiny program that the BIOS loads into memory. The program is only 512 bytes—on sector—long. If the disk has DOS on it, the tiny program will search out the file named IO.SYS on disk and load it into memory. If it's a non-DOS disk, the program displays the following message:

```
Non-System disk or disk error
Replace and press any key when ready
```

The file IO.SYS is the DOS BIOS. It contains basic DOS-to-hardware code and the simple instructions that let DOS communicate with the PC's BIOS, the system's hardware itself. Additionally, IO.SYS contains a software routine called SYSINIT, which is responsible for loading the rest of DOS into memory.

The next program SYSINIT looks for and loads into memory is MSDOS.SYS, the DOS kernel and the essence of DOS. MSDOS.SYS contains the bulk of DOS's instructions and routines—all the disk routines, file management, memory management, hardware support, the whole bailiwick. That's all put into memory for your DOS applications to use.

After MSDOS.SYS, the SYSINIT routine looks for your system-configuration file, CONFIG.SYS, located in the root directory of your boot disk. If found, SYSINIT reads the commands in CONFIG.SYS and sets up DOS accordingly. CONFIG.SYS may also contain device drivers, which are special programs used to control DOS devices or to interface DOS with nonstandard equipment. For example, if your computer has a mouse, CD-ROM, extra memory, or an external drive, a device driver will be loaded into memory so that your software can control it.

Info: If SYSINIT can't find CONFIG.SYS, DOS makes some assumptions about your computer and sets it up accordingly. The problem is that those assumptions usually aren't too good, which is why a well-written CONFIG.SYS file is critical to running your system at optimum performance.

After CONFIG.SYS, the SYSINIT routine looks for a file named COMMAND.COM in the root directory of the boot disk. If found, COMMAND.COM is then run. If not, you'll see the dreaded "Bad or missing command interpreter" message—a true heart-stopper. Then the system will not boot.

COMMAND.COM is DOS's command interpreter. It's the program that runs when you see the DOS prompt. COMMAND.COM contains all the internal DOS commands—COPY, REN, DIR, TYPE, CLS, and so on. It reads your input and then translates that text into instructions for the DOS kernel in memory.

When COMMAND.COM starts, it looks for one additional program to run: a batch file named AUTOEXEC.BAT. If found, the instructions in AUTOEXEC.BAT are executed, allowing you to further configure the system, run setup programs, and so forth. Once AUTOEXEC.BAT is finished running, you're at the helm, using COMMAND.COM's interface to control DOS and your PC.

Info: The basic files that run DOS are (in order) as follows:

IO.SYS	The DOS-hardware-interface program, starts the SYSINIT routine.
MSDOS.SYS	The DOS kernel, contains the meat of DOS.
CONFIG.SYS	DOS's configuration file, controls the way DOS behaves and loads device drivers.
COMMAND.COM	The command interpreter, the interface between you and DOS
AUTOEXEC.BAT	An automatically executed batch file, which you can use to further configure your system.

CONFIG.SYS and AUTOEXEC.BAT are important, but optional. Without them, DOS will make assumptions and configure your system accordingly (which is boring and not the best situation) and will let the computer boot if you lack those files.

Following the hard-disk philosophy of keeping the root clean, note that the three files—CONFIG.SYS, COMMAND.COM, and AUTOEXEC.BAT—will always be in your root directory. It's possible to move COMMAND.COM into a subdirectory; however, CONFIG.SYS and AUTOEXEC.BAT can only be in the root.

The CONFIG.SYS File

When DOS boots, it looks for and reads your system configuration file, CONFIG.SYS, which is located in the root directory of your boot disk.

CONFIG.SYS is a text file containing special configuration commands. It's used to direct DOS to do certain things, use certain system resources (such as memory and disk storage), and to perform general configuration. A well-thought-out CONFIG.SYS file can boost the performance of your system tremendously.

There are 15 configuration commands used in CONFIG.SYS. Here is a summary of what each one does:

Command	Function
Break	Turns extended Ctrl-C checking on or off
Buffers	Sets aside memory for DOS to use when reading and writing files
Country	Defines country- and language-specific information for DOS
Device	Loads a device driver
Devicehigh	Loads a device driver into upper memory
Dos	Loads DOS into the high-memory area, helps create the upper-memory area
Drivparm	Sets a disk drive's configuration
FCBS	Old-style file-control block allocation
Files	Sets the number of files DOS can have open at once
Install	Loads a memory-resident program at boot-up
Lastdrive	Defines the highest possible drive letter in the system
Rem	Used for comments
Shell	Defines the name and location of the command interpreter
Stacks	Sets aside space for DOS's internal interrupt stacks
Switches	Regulates the enhanced-101 keyboard, allows the WINA20.386 file to be removed from the root directory

These commands each configure a certain aspect of DOS: how much memory is used for certain operations; the standard way of displaying the date and currency symbols; how files are accessed on disk; how extra memory in the computer is used; and how DOS will interact with the hardware in your system and any extra hardware you may add.

Info: The configuration commands do not work like a programming language or like batch-file commands. Instead, they configure DOS and determine how your computer works.

Your Own CONFIG.SYS File

The best thing about CONFIG.SYS is that it's a text file you can create, edit, and later update, if needed. When DOS 5 was installed, it may have created a sample CONFIG.SYS file on your system. For example:

```
DEVICE=C:\DOS\HIMEM.SYS
DOS=HIGH
FILES=10
SHELL=C:\DOS\COMMAND.COM C:\DOS\ /p
STACKS=0,0
```

To see the contents of your own CONFIG.SYS file, enter the following command:

```
TYPE C:\CONFIG.SYS
```

The following sections will describe the CONFIG.SYS commands and may give you an idea of what your CONFIG.SYS file is doing. They may also assist you when you need to update your CONFIG.SYS file, offering suggestions on creating the best possible system configuration for your PC.

Note: Examples of complete CONFIG.SYS files are given at the end of this chapter, along with explanations. You can pattern your own CONFIG.SYS file after one of them, updating and editing it if you like.

Configuration Commands

The following sections describe all 15 configuration commands. Note that no one computer will use all of them. In fact, the most common are the FILES, BUFFERS, and DEVICE commands. Other commands worth looking into are LASTDRIVE, SHELL, and DOS.

Break

The BREAK command is used to monitor Ctrl-C and Ctrl-Break. It has one of two settings:

```
BREAK=ON
```

or

```
BREAK=OFF
```

Normally, Ctrl-C—the break key—is monitored only when you're typing in DOS, or when DOS is writing to the screen or printing. That's the BREAK=OFF condition. When you set BREAK=ON in CONFIG.SYS, DOS does extra Ctrl-C checking. In addition to monitoring the keyboard, screen, and printer, DOS also checks for the Ctrl-C key press when it writes to disk.

The advantage of turning BREAK=ON is that you can break out of some operations that you couldn't with BREAK=OFF. However, BREAK=ON degrades system performance slightly, and non-DOS commands generally ignore the Ctrl-C Break anyway.

Tip: The DOS BREAK command can be used to set Break "on" or "off" after the computer has started. To see the current Break setting, type BREAK at the DOS prompt.

Buffers

BUFFERS is a key configuration command, closely linked to the FILES configuration command. What BUFFERS does is to allocate memory for DOS to use when reading files from disk. On systems that have disk-intensive software (such as databases and graphics), having a lot of BUFFERS can help the computer run faster. The format is:

```
BUFFERS=buffs,read_ahead
```

Buffs is the number of buffers, ranging from 1 to 99. Each buffer uses over 500 bytes of memory, so the value you use has to establish a happy medium between making the disk run fast and not eating up 50K of memory. A good value to set BUFFERS to is 32.

Read_ahead is optional. It's a value from 1 through 8 and is used as a special "read-ahead" type of buffering. On some systems, specifying the read-ahead value will boost system performance, although in practice *read_ahead* is rarely specified. If both *buffs* and *read_ahead* are used, a comma must separate them.

It's a good idea to include a BUFFERS command in CONFIG.SYS. In fact, the following line works best for the majority of PCs:

```
BUFFERS=32
```

If you omit buffers, DOS assigns them based on how much memory your computer has and the capacity of your disk drives. Values range from 2 for a system with less than 128K of RAM up to 15 if you have the maximum of 640K.

Country

The COUNTRY configuration command is used to tell DOS-formatting information for specific countries and languages. DOS displays the date and time, currency symbol, and even Extended ASCII characters differently, based on the country code and code page you specify. The format for the COUNTRY configuration command is:

```
COUNTRY=country_code,code_page,pathname
```

Country_code is a three-digit code representing the country, region, or language under which DOS will format the date and time, upper- and lower-case conversions, alphabetical-sorting order, punctuation rules, and currency symbols. (Don't get excited—it doesn't translate DOS into Greek or anything. COUNTRY only provides minor cultural assistance, not unlike a FODOR's guidebook.)

Code_page is a three-digit code representing an Extended ASCII-character set. When specified, DOS will load that character set into memory and use it, which allows some special foreign language characters to be displayed under DOS. When *code_page* isn't specified, DOS uses the United States code page.

Pathname is the full pathname of the COUNTRY.SYS file, usually kept in your DOS subdirectory. COUNTRY.SYS contains the information that the COUNTRY command needs to set its country code and code-page values.

Info: Appendix C lists the country codes and code pages for countries supported by the DOS 5 COUNTRY configuration command as well as the KEYB command covered later in this book.

If you wanted to set up DOS to run as if you were in the United Kingdom, you could include the following command in your CONFIG.SYS file:

```
COUNTRY=044,437,C:\DOS\COUNTRY.SYS
```

The country code for Britain is 044 (which is also its international phone-dialing code). The code page is 437, which is the standard English-speaking world code. The COUNTRY.SYS file is located in the DOS subdirectory. After issuing the above command, DOS will display the date as day-month-year instead of month-day-year (as we do in the colonies). Also, the computer will now have the annoying tendency to drive on the left side of the road.

Info: A companion command to the COUNTRY configuration command is the KEYB command. It's covered in Chapter 22.

Device

The DEVICE configuration command is used to load a device driver. The format is:

```
DEVICE=pathname options
```

Pathname is the full pathname of a device driver. You should always include the drive letter, subdirectory, and the filename extension in the *pathname*.

Options are any options, parameters, or switches as required by the device driver.

Device drivers are special types of programs that tell DOS about extra hardware you may have added to your system, or load a program that gives you extra control over the hardware you already have.

Tip: Normally all device drivers end in with the SYS extension. However, a few end in EXE. Be aware of them! Don't make the mistake of typing EMM386.SYS when you mean EMM386.EXE.

DOS comes with ten device drivers. They and their functions are listed below:

Device Driver	Function
ANSI.SYS	Provides added control for the screen and keyboard
DISPLAY.SYS	Specifies certain code pages for use with certain video systems
DRIVER.SYS	Allows you to re-configure a physical driver for use as an additional logical drive
EGA.SYS	Allows the system to regain control over the EGA graphics screen when you switch between text and graphics modes (used by DOS Shell & Windows)
EMM386.EXE	An expanded-memory device driver for '386 computers
HIMEM.SYS	An extended-memory device driver for 80286 and '386 computers
PRINTER.SYS	Specifies code pages to be used with certain printers

RAMDRIVE.SYS	Sets up a RAM drive—an electronic disk drive—in memory
SETVER.EXE	Offers additional support for the SETVER command
SMARTDRV.SYS	Sets up a disk cache in memory (used to improve disk performance)

Note: There may be other files that come with DOS that are not device drivers. COUNTRY.SYS, KEYBOARD.SYS, and PARTDRV.SYS all end with the SYS extension. Do not use them with the DEVICE command.

A common device driver is the mouse driver, although it comes with your mouse hardware and is not a part of DOS. If you've added a mouse to your system, you need to load a device driver for it, telling software that can use a mouse how to interact with the not-so-furry pointing device. A DEVICE command such as the following might be used:

```
DEVICE=C:\MOUSE\MOUSE.SYS /C1
```

The DEVICE command is followed by an equal sign, and then the full pathname of the mouse device driver, MOUSE.SYS. The optional switch, /C1, which sets up a serial mouse, is then specified.

Devicehigh

The DEVICEHIGH configuration command is identical to the DEVICE command in almost every way. The difference is that the device driver will be loaded into the upper-memory area instead of into conventional memory. This increases the amount of memory available to DOS and to your programs.

The format for DEVICEHIGH is:

```
DEVICEHIGH [size=hex] pathname options
```

Size=hex is optional. It's used to specify the size of a device driver that may expand after it's been loaded into memory.

To use the DEVICEHIGH command you need an 80386, 386SX, or 80486 computer with at least 350K of extended memory. You must also configure the system so that it has upper-memory blocks, or UMBs. This subject is covered in detail in Chapter 26. For now, use the DEVICE configuration command instead.

Dos

The DOS configuration command is used to load DOS's own programs (the kernel) into a special part of memory known as the high-memory area, or HMA. This is only possible on 80286 or later computers that have extended memory installed.

The format of the DOS configuration command is:

```
DOS=location,umbs
```

Location is either high or low. It specifies the location for DOS and whether it will be loaded into the HMA or into conventional memory. If *location* is high, then DOS is loaded into the HMA. If *location* is low, DOS is loaded into conventional memory (as it usually is). The default is low.

Umbs is either umb or noumb. It specifies whether DOS should maintain links to the upper-memory blocks created by the EMM386.EXE device driver. If umb is specified, DOS maintains the links, and device drivers and memory-resident programs can be loaded into upper-memory blocks. If noumb is specified, device drivers and memory-resident programs cannot be "loaded high." Noumb is the default. Note that this option has an effect only on 80386 and later computers.

The DOS command requires that the HIMEM.SYS device driver be loaded elsewhere in CONFIG.SYS. And to use the umb option, the EMM386.EXE device driver must also be loaded. This subject, as well that of using all DOS's memory device drivers, is covered in detail in Chapter 26.

Drivparm

DRIVPARM is an interesting command. It allows you to specify parameters for what DOS calls "block devices." These are typically your disk drives. The DRIVPARM configuration command can be used to set certain aspects for disk drives and other drive-like devices attached to your system. Here is its format:

```
DRIVPARM /drive /e /form /heads /i /n /sectors /tracks
```

Setting these options depends on the type of device you're adding to your system. The device's hardware manual should provide suggestions for each of these options. For example, if you added a 3-1/2-inch 720K drive to an older PC that didn't normally work with that size drive, you could configure it as drive D using the following command in your CONFIG.SYS file:

```
DRIVPARM /D:3 /F:2 /I
```

The device is defined as drive 3, which translates to drive D. (Drive A is drive zero.) The form factor is 2, which signifies a 720K 3-1/2-inch drive. And the /I switch is specified to maintain compatibility with older systems' BIOSs that cannot recognize the 3 1/2-inch drive format.

FCBS

FCBS is an acronym for File Control Blocks. Prior to DOS 2.0, files were accessed using the FCBs. The FCBS configuration command was used to set aside memory for use with FCBs. (The FILES configuration command is now used instead.)

The only circumstance in which you should be using FCBS under DOS 5 is if some arcane program on your system still requires an FCBS statement in your CONFIG.SYS command. If so, retain that command, which should already be in your CONFIG.SYS file from a previous version of DOS. If not, forget it; use the FILES configuration command instead.

Files

The FILES configuration command is used to tell DOS how many files it can have open at one time. It's closely tied to the BUFFERS configuration command and, although the two commands are related, what they control is different. The format for FILES is:

```
FILES=n
```

N is the total number of files DOS can access at one time. Values for *n* range from 8 through 255.

To set FILES to 20, you'd put the following command into your CONFIG.SYS file:

```
FILES=20
```

If you don't have a FILES configuration command in your CONFIG.SYS file, DOS assigns you 8. That value is way too low for most DOS applications. In fact, some applications insist on a FILES value equal to that of the BUFFERS configuration command. Some databases require you to set both FILES and BUFFERS equal to 32. For most CONFIG.SYS files, however, the following two commands work well:

```
FILES=20
BUFFERS=32
```

Install

The INSTALL configuration command is used to load a memory-resident program into memory. Normally, memory-resident programs are loaded at the DOS prompt or with a batch file such as AUTOEXEC.BAT, but by using the INSTALL command, you can load them with CONFIG.SYS, which saves a few bytes of memory. The format is:

```
INSTALL filename options
```

Filename is the full pathname of a memory-resident program. It must be a memory-resident program (or "TSR") or the results could be unpredictable. Also, it must be an "INSTALL configuration command approved" memory-resident program (which should be stated in the program's manual).

Info: The following are memory-resident programs that come with DOS. These are okay to use with the INSTALL configuration command:

APPEND.EXE	GRAPHICS.COM
DOSKEY.COM	KEYB.COM
DOSSHELL.COM	MIRROR.COM
FASTOPEN.EXE	NLSFUNC.EXE
GRAFTABL.COM	SHARE.EXE

Note that the SHARE.EXE program is okay to use with INSTALL, and might already be in your CONFIG.SYS file from DOS 4. However, DOS 5 does not require SHARE.EXE and you should delete it.

Options are any options or switches that could follow the filename at the DOS prompt.

Early versions of DOS were fond of using the following INSTALL command in CONFIG.SYS:

```
INSTALL C:\DOS\FASTOPEN C:
```

If you have this command in your CONFIG.SYS file, however, I'd recommend that you delete it. DOS's SMARTDrive disk cache is a better way to improve disk speed. It's discussed in Chapter 21.

Tip: If you're using an 80386 or later microprocessor with DOS 5, don't bother with the INSTALL configuration command. Instead, you can load the program using the LOADHIGH command in AUTOEXEC.BAT and thus save lots of memory. This technique is covered in Chapter 26.

Lastdrive

The LASTDRIVE command lets you tell DOS which drive letter will be the highest drive letter allowed in your system. The format is:

```
LASTDRIVE=drive
```

Drive is a drive letter, ranging from A through Z. Realistically, it should range from the highest lettered drive in your system on up through Z. For example, if you have two hard drives, C and D, then you can specify a *drive* value from E through Z with LASTDRIVE.

Normally, DOS allows for drives A through E on every DOS system. But suppose you're running a computer network, which adds drive letters up through N. To allow DOS access to drive letters up through N, put the following command in your CONFIG.SYS file:

```
LASTDRIVE=N
```

Each drive letter you add above E gobbles up about 80 bytes of memory. But if you have memory to spare, consider putting the following command in CONFIG.SYS:

```
LASTDRIVE=Z
```

It's not that you never know when another drive will pop up. But certain DOS commands do let you access "phantom" drives on your system. For example, the SUBST command can be used to shorthand a drive letter for a subdirectory in your system. Also, you can create a RAM drive, which requires another drive letter. (The SUBST command is covered in Chapter 20; RAM drives are covered in Chapter 21.)

Rem

The REM configuration command works exactly like the REM batch-file command. You can use REM to include comments in your CONFIG.SYS file, or to "comment out" certain configuration commands. The format is:

```
REM comments
```

Comments are notes or instructions to be included in your CONFIG.SYS file. For example:

```
REM CONFIG.SYS File, dated 3-27-93
REM Start by loading some device drivers...

DEVICE=C:\DOS\HIMEM.SYS
Etc....
```

To comment out a command, simply put REM in front of it (followed by a space). This prevents the command from running, but keeps it in CONFIG.SYS should you want add it again later:

```
REM DEVICE=C:\MOUSE\MOUSE.SYS /C1
```

Above, the MOUSE.SYS device driver will not be loaded. But if you edit CONFIG.SYS and delete the REM command, it will be reloaded.

Shell

The SHELL configuration command is used to specify a command interpreter for DOS. The format is:

```
SHELL=pathname options
```

Pathname is the full pathname of a command interpreter to use with DOS. Normally COMMAND.COM is used. In the same vein, you can specify a subdirectory other than the root directory of the boot disk for COMMAND.COM. Other command processors, such as JP Software's 4DOS, can also be specified using the SHELL configuration command.

Options are any options that would follow the command processor. Since COMMAND.COM is often used, the following are its options:

```
COMMAND.COM pathname device /e:size /p
```

Pathname is the location of COMMAND.COM on disk. It must be specified whenever you put COMMAND.COM in a subdirectory other than the root. If not, then when some programs quit, you may see the message "Cannot load COMMAND, system halted." (So it's a good idea to specify a pathname.)

Info: COMMAND.COM has two portions—the resident and the transient. To save on memory, only a small part of COMMAND.COM—the resident part—is kept in memory at all times. The second part—the transient part—is loaded high in memory. When some large programs run they may overwrite the transient portion. In that case, DOS needs to reload COMMAND.COM's transient portion back into memory when you quit the application.

Device is optional. It's used to specify a DOS device—other than the keyboard and screen—that COMMAND.COM will use for input and output. Normally the device is CON, the console. However, you could specify another device, say AUX for your serial ports (although this isn't recommended—refer to Chapter 24 and the CTTY command.)

/E is a switch that controls the size of the DOS environment. Normally, DOS gives you 256 bytes of environment storage. The *size* parameter can be used with the /E switch to specify a larger environment, if possible. Values for *size* range from 160 through 32768 (although DOS will round the number to the nearest multiple of 16).

/P is a switch that tells COMMAND.COM to look for and run a batch file named AUTOEXEC.BAT in the root directory of the boot disk.

Tip: If you're running a DOS "window" in DESQview or Windows, specify the /P switch when you start COMMAND.COM. That makes the command interpreter permanent, preventing the window from being closed with an EXIT command.

Consider the following SHELL configuration command:

```
SHELL=C:\DOS\COMMAND.COM C:\DOS\ /E:1024 /P
```

COMMAND.COM is located in the C:\DOS subdirectory; its full pathname is specified after SHELL=. The directory in which DOS should look for COMMAND.COM is specified next, C:\DOS\. The /E switch sets the size of the environment to 1,024 bytes, or 1K. And the /P switch is used to make COMMAND.COM permanent and to run AUTOEXEC.BAT in the root directory.

Stacks

The STACKS configuration command is used to set aside memory for DOS's internal interrupts. The format is:

```
STACKS=stacks,size
```

Stacks are the number of stacks to create. Values for stacks can be the number 0 and numbers from 8 through 64. The default is 9 unless you have an original 8088-based IBM PC, in which case 0 is used.

Size is the size of each stack, in bytes. Values for size can be 0, and the numbers from 32 through 512. The default is 128, unless you have an original 8088-based IBM PC, in which case 0 is used.

The STACKS command is a big memory waster on most PCs. To find out how much memory is uses, multiply the value of stacks by size. That can be quite a hefty amount. DOS's internal interrupts seldom require the extra memory STACKS provides. By default, DOS sets STACKS to the following:

```
STACKS=9,128
```

That eats up over 1K of memory for something most computers don't need. Instead, put the following command in your CONFIG.SYS file:

```
STACKS=0,0
```

If you experience problems running your system, such as the message "Internal stack overflow; System halted," then remove the above command from your CONFIG.SYS file.

Switches

The SWITCHES command serves two purposes, depending on whether you use it with the /K switch or the /W switch. The /K switch is used to maintain keyboard compatibility with older DOS programs.

```
SWITCHES=/K
```

/K is not an optional switch; it's the full format of the SWITCHES configuration command. When you specify SWITCHES as above, DOS will suppress the extended keyboard functions that take advantage of your Enhanced-101 keyboard. If you're experiencing problems with some applications that misinterpret some key functions (such as the cursor keys or F11 or F12), then install the above SWITCHES command into your CONFIG.SYS file.

Tip: If you use the SWITCHES=/K configuration command and you're using the ANSI.SYS console device driver, specify the /K switch when starting ANSI.SYS. For example:

```
DEVICE=C:\DOS\ANSI.SYS /K
```

The /W switch can be specified to allow the WINA20.386 file to be removed from the root directory (which helps keep the root clean.)

Info: WINA20.386 is a file required when you run Windows 3.0 in the 386 Enhanced mode under DOS 5. If that doesn't describe your situation, you can delete the file. Otherwise, refer to Chapter 27 for more information on Windows.

```
SWITCHES=/W
```

You must combine the above command with a modification to your Windows' SYSTEM.INI file. In the section titled [386Enh], add a DEVICE command such as:

```
DEVICE=C:\WINDOWS\WINA20.386
```

Be sure to specify the proper directory; above C:\WINDOWS is assumed. Save the SYSTEM.INI file to disk, move the WINA20.386 file from the root to its designated directory, and then reset.

Note that you can specify both switches, as in:

```
SWITCHES=/K /W
```

Building Your Own CONFIG.SYS File

A CONFIG.SYS file isn't created. Batch files are created, but CONFIG.SYS files evolve. Every PC's CONFIG.SYS file has the basic elements: the FILES and BUFFERS commands and a few device drivers. Nothing exciting. Anything else present usually depends on the software you use or hardware device drivers that must be installed. Because of that, there is no Magna Carta of CONFIG.SYS files. But there are some guidelines you can follow when creating a custom CONFIG.SYS for your system.

Making the Perfect System Configuration

CONFIG.SYS files usually go unchanged for long stretches of time. However, you can modify your CONFIG.SYS file at any time, adding or deleting commands if your system's needs change. In order for the changes to take effect you must reset; the commands in CONFIG.SYS are only executed when the computer boots, so resetting after saving to disk is the only way to test out your new configuration.

Rule: Any changes you make to the CONFIG.SYS file only take place after you boot the computer.

Other than remembering the reset rule, here are some general suggestions about your CONFIG.SYS file:

Use a text editor, such as the MS-DOS Editor, to work with CONFIG.SYS. If you use a word processor, remember to save CONFIG.SYS in the unformatted, non-document, text, or ASCII mode.

It's a good idea to start CONFIG.SYS with a few REM commands listing information about the CONFIG.SYS file, the machine it's for, and the date. For example:

```
REM CONFIG.SYS file for Marketing's Deskpro
REM Written by Mike Rowsoft
REM Last updated 12/19/93
```

If you update or change the CONFIG.SYS file, change the date as well.

Order in a CONFIG.SYS file is important. DOS reads the commands in CONFIG.SYS from top to bottom. Some commands and device drivers must come before other commands. For example, if you're using a special hard-disk device driver, it must be installed first. After that usually come memory management device drivers. The position of all other commands is arbitrary.

To make your CONFIG.SYS file more readable, you can insert some blank lines. This avoids that condensed, confusing look and it also helps group various similar and companion configuration commands together. (This same suggestion can also apply to batch files.)

If you decide to remove a command, instead of deleting it, stick a REM command in front of it. This has the same effect as removing the command, because DOS ignores anything after the REM command. But if you wish to add the command again at some future date, it's as easy as removing the REM.

The CONFIG.SYS file does produce errors if you make a typo or specify a device driver that doesn't exist. DOS is nice enough to tell you about the type of error as well as give you the line number where the error took place. Make a note of it, and then use your text editor to make repairs, reset, and continue.

Sample CONFIG.SYS Files

Just about every DOS machine should have the following three commands in its CONFIG.SYS file:

```
FILES=20
BUFFERS=32
STACKS=0,0
```

Around that base you can build a custom CONFIG.SYS file that reflects the needs of the machine.

SAMPLE #1, DOS 5's SUGGESTION

Here is the CONFIG.SYS file DOS 5's SETUP program creates on systems without a CONFIG.SYS file:

```
DEVICE=C:\DOS\HIMEM.SYS
DOS=HIGH
FILES=10
SHELL=C:\DOS\COMMAND.COM C:\DOS\ /p
STACKS=0,0
```

This computer has an 80286 or later microprocessor plus at least 350K of extended memory. The HIMEM.SYS device driver is used to control extended memory, as well as create an extra 64K bank of memory for use by DOS. The DOS=HIGH command loads DOS's resident programs into high memory, which increases the amount of memory available to programs. (This is covered later, in Chapter 26.)

The FILES command allows DOS to access up to ten files at once; SHELL sets the location of COMMAND.COM and adds the /P switch to run AUTOEXEC.BAT; and the STACKS configuration command sets aside zero bytes for DOS's interrupt stacks.

All in all, it's a fair CONFIG.SYS file. On a system with lots of hard-disk activity, I'd recommend increasing FILES to 20 and adding a BUFFERS=32 command. This system might also require some device drivers, which would be added using the DEVICE configuration command.

SAMPLE #2

```
BUFFERS = 32
FILES = 40
LASTDRIVE = Z
SHELL=C:\DOS\COMMAND.COM C:\DOS\ /E:1024 /P
DEVICE = C:\DOS\HIMEM.SYS
DOS = HIGH
DEVICE = C:\DOS\ANSI.SYS
DEVICE = C:\MOUSE\MOUSE.SYS
DEVICE = C:\DOS\RAMDRIVE.SYS 2048 /E
```

This CONFIG.SYS file contains the basic FILES, BUFFERS, and SHELL configuration commands. The LASTDRIVE command is used to set the highest drive letter to Z. That could be for installation of a network or use of the SUBST command.

Four device drivers are installed here: HIMEM.SYS, for controlling extended memory; ANSI.SYS, to give extra control over the keyboard and display; MOUSE.SYS, to control a mouse attached to the computer; and RAMDRIVE.SYS, which creates a 2M RAM drive in extended memory.

Info: Additional information on the SUBST command can be found in Chapter 20 Information on HIMEM.SYS and the DOS configuration command is in Chapter 26; ANSI.SYS is the subject of Chapter 23; and RAM drives are covered in Chapter 21.

SAMPLE #3

```
REM Windows 80386 System with four megabytes of memory
REM August 14, 1992
DEVICE=C:\BIN\DOS\HIMEM.SYS
DOS=HIGH,UMB
DEVICE=C:\BIN\DOS\EMM386.EXE /NOEMS
DEVICEHIGH=C:\MOUSE\MOUSE.SYS
DEVICEHIGH=C:\WINDOWS\SMARTDRV.SYS 512 0
FILES=32
BUFFERS=32
STACKS=0,0
```

This CONFIG.SYS file is used on a '386 Windows system. Memory is organized first using the HIMEM.SYS and EMM386.EXE device drivers. DOS is loaded high and the upper-memory blocks (UMBs) are specified by both the DOS configuration command and the EMM386.EXE device driver.

Because the UMBs are created, the DEVICEHIGH command is used to load the MOUSE.SYS device driver into upper memory. Windows' SMARTDrive disk cache is created, and then loaded into upper memory as well.

The CONFIG.SYS file finishes with the standard FILES, BUFFERS and STACKS commands. Since a SHELL configuration command isn't included, it's assumed DOS will find COMMAND.COM in the root directory.

SAMPLE #4

```
REM This is my DOS 5 CONFIG.SYS file
REM Dell 320LT, 386SX system
REM September 20, 1993
REM Boot 386MAX version
DOS=HIGH,UMB
DEVICE=C:\386MAX\386MAX.SYS PRO=C:\386MAX\386MAX.PRO
DEVICEHIGH=C:\MOUSE\MOUSE.SYS /C1
DEVICEHIGH=C:\DOS\ANSI.SYS
DEVICEHIGH=C:\DOS\SETVER.EXE
SHELL=C:\DOS\COMMAND.COM C:\DOS\ /E:1024 /p
FILES=32
BUFFERS=32
STACKS=0,0
```

This example uses the REM command to describe the CONFIG.SYS file, the computer, the date, and to tell that this CONFIG.SYS file runs the third-party memory manager, 386MAX.

The DOS command is used to load DOS high and help establish the upper-memory blocks (UMBs). Next, the DEVICE configuration command loads the 386MAX memory device driver, which takes the place of DOS's HIMEM.SYS and EMM386.EXE device drivers.

The ANSI.SYS and SETVER.EXE device drivers are loaded into upper memory using the DEVICEHIGH command instead of DEVICE. This frees up some 5K of conventional memory—not much, but better than nothing.

Finally, the standard SHELL, FILES, BUFFERS, and STACKS configuration commands are used.

A Sample Exercise

After you get the basics down, there may come a point in time when you need to update your CONFIG.SYS file. For example, suppose you added a new device to your system. The device will require a special device driver to interface it with DOS and your software. That device driver will come on a disk with the device and will, most likely, be installed by means of some sort of INSTALL or SETUP program. If not, you'll have to place the device driver in CONFIG.SYS. Consider these instructions:

The warp-field generator attached to your computer requires the WARP.SYS file in order to work. Install WARP.SYS into your CONFIG.SYS file using the DEVICE configuration command. The format is:

```
DEVICE=pathname\WARP.SYS /system /gravity
```

Pathname is the location of the WARP.SYS file on your hard drive, usually in the \WFG subdirectory.

/System is the type of computer you have. Values are 8088, 80286 and 80386.

/Gravity is the ratio of your planet's gravity to Earth's, where one Earth gravity is equal to 1.0.

To setup the WARP.SYS device driver, you would first edit CONFIG.SYS, then insert the appropriate DEVICE command. Since nothing is mentioned in the instructions about the driver's position, just put it anywhere. For example, at the end of your present CONFIG.SYS file:

```
DEVICE=C:\DOS\HIMEM.SYS
DOS=HIGH
FILES=10
SHELL=C:\DOS\COMMAND.COM C:\DOS\ /p
STACKS=0,0
DEVICE=C:\WFG\WARP.SYS /80286 /1.0
```

Save the changes in CONFIG.SYS to disk, exit to DOS, then reset to load and start using the new device driver.

All Done!

Once you've created your CONFIG.SYS, you leave it alone! Nothing feels as good as a well-written CONFIG.SYS—one that really works. In some cases, you can actually see improved system performance. After that, there's no sense in messing with CONFIG.SYS anymore.

Tip: Once you have your CONFIG.SYS file perfect, make a copy of it. For example, I put a copy of my CONFIG.SYS file in the TEMP subdirectory. You could put a copy of yours in your DOS subdirectory, a Temporary Files subdirectory, or save it to a disk for safekeeping.

Summary

CONFIG.SYS is your system configuration file and is located in the root directory of your boot disk. It contains commands that tell DOS how to use the computer and how much memory can be used for certain functions and disk operations, and it loads special control programs called device drivers into memory.

CONFIG.SYS is a text file. Into it you place the special configuration commands. If you need to modify or update CONFIG.SYS, you must reset your system in order for the changes to take effect.

Of the 15 configuration commands, seven will appear most often in the typical CONFIG.SYS file:

BUFFERS   Reserves memory for DOS to use when reading information from disk. A good value is BUFFERS=32.

DEVICE   Loads device drivers into memory. Popular device drivers include ANSI.SYS, EGA.SYS, EMM386.EXE, HIMEM.SYS, MOUSE.SYS, and SETVER.EXE.

DOS   Used with HIMEM.SYS to load DOS's kernel into upper memory as well as to create upper-memory blocks.

FILES   Tells DOS how many files it can have open at a time. A good value is FILES=20.

REM   Used to insert comments into CONFIG.SYS or to comment out certain commands.

SHELL   Specifies the location for COMMAND.COM (or another command interpreter).

STACKS   Should be set as STACKS=0,0 to save 1K of memory.

CHAPTER 20

DOS Configuration

Where CONFIG.SYS handles system configuration AUTOEXEC.BAT handles DOS configuration. In CONFIG.SYS you really don't get a chance to do such things as change the DOS prompt, set a system search path, or run some of your favorite startup programs or utilities. That job is left for AUTOEXEC.BAT, a special batch file DOS runs when you start your computer.

This chapter answers the following questions:

- What can go into an AUTOEXEC.BAT file?

- How does DOS use the PATH command to search for programs?

- What can the APPEND command do?

- How does the PROMPT command alleviate the dull DOS prompt?

- How many different things can the MODE command do?

- How can disk drives become subdirectories and vice versa?

- What is the environment and how is it used?

- What is the best command to put at the end of an AUTOEXEC.BAT file?

Your AUTOEXEC.BAT File

AUTOEXEC.BAT is a batch file that's automatically executed (hence the name) when your computer first starts. COMMAND.COM looks for the batch file AUTOEXEC.BAT in the root directory of your boot disk, loads it, and runs it as the last step of starting your computer.

Info: If you use the SHELL configuration command in CONFIG.SYS, remember to specify the /P switch after COMMAND.COM. Otherwise, AUTOEXEC.BAT will not run.

Without an AUTOEXEC.BAT file, DOS will ask you for the date and time, then plop you down at a simple and boring DOS prompt. It's like being in a house with no furniture, plants, or decorations. Yawn.

With an AUTOEXEC.BAT file, you can run a whole slew of interesting little programs that help customize the way DOS works. This moves a level beyond what CONFIG.SYS does. AUTOEXEC.BAT lets you set parameters and run programs that give your computer personality, and anything you would normally type when you first start the computer can be entered automatically in AUTOEXEC.BAT. If you create the proper AUTOEXEC.BAT file, you can save yourself a lot of time and have your system just the way you want it each time you boot.

What Goes in an AUTOEXEC.BAT File?

Some people write inordinately long AUTOEXEC.BAT files, some running more than 15 minutes. (It keeps the computer busy and gives you an excuse to wander about and forage for coffee.) Other AUTOEXEC.BAT files can be quick and to the point. Of course, the long ones started that way and eventually snowballed to their massive proportions.

What can be done in an AUTOEXEC.BAT file? Any of the following items:

Set the date and time

Set a search path

Create a new prompt

Set up the screen

Set up the printer

Configure the serial ports

Substitute or join drives and directories

Create environment variables

Maintain files

Run memory-resident utilities and programs

Run startup programs

Run an application or shell

This is just a suggested list—it shows you the possibilities; no one AUTOEXEC.BAT file needs to contain all those items. The following sections describe each item individually, as well as introduce you to some popular commands that weave their way into an \AUTOEXEC.BAT file.

Setting the Date and Time

Without an AUTOEXEC.BAT file present, COMMAND.COM asks you for the date and time when you boot the computer. This was necessary with older PCs because they didn't come with an internal clock, and so you either used the DATE and TIME commands in AUTOEXEC.BAT or, more likely, used a program that read the time from a clock card installed into an expansion slot.

Older PCs may still require that the time be set. If so, AUTOEXEC.BAT is the best place to do it. Simply put the command to set the time in AUTOEXEC.BAT and you won't have to mess with it for the rest of the day.

Today's systems have internal clocks, which DOS reads when it boots. With these systems there is no need to set the date and time or use the DATE or TIME commands in AUTOEXEC.BAT.

The PATH Command

When you type a program name at the DOS prompt, DOS looks in the current directory for a matching COM, EXE, or BAT file. If you specify a full pathname for a file, then DOS looks in the specified directory for the COM, EXE, or BAT file. Otherwise, you get a "Bad command or filename" error.

Using the PATH command, you can tell DOS to look for program files in subdirectories listed on the search path. From any drive or directory on your system, you can run programs stored in directories on the search path. DOS will find them.

The format of the PATH command is:

```
PATH directory;directory;..
```

Directory is the full pathname of a subdirectory on your system. It should be a subdirectory containing programs you often run, commonly used utilities, or batch files. You can specify more than one directory by separating their pathnames with semicolons.

The PATH command is tightly linked to the organized directory structure you create. By placing key directories on the path, you can run your important programs from anywhere on your hard drive. For example, consider the following path:

```
PATH C:\DOS;C:\UTIL;C:\BATCH
```

The DOS directory contains DOS's commands and programs. The UTIL subdirectory may contain miscellaneous utilities. A BATCH directory is used to hold batch files that can run other programs on your system. On most systems, if you write enough batch files, this will be all the path you need (although you'll have to put in the proper subdirectories used on your system).

To see your current path, type the PATH command at the DOS prompt:

```
C:\>PATH
PATH=C:\DOS
```

To reset a path, you specify PATH followed by the directories you want. The new path will replace the old in DOS's memory-storage area, the environment. (The subject of the environment is covered later in this chapter.)

To set a path to nothing, type PATH followed by a single semicolon:

```
PATH ;
```

This erases the search path in memory. If you use the PATH command again to display the search path, DOS responds, "No Path."

Setting a proper path is central to the concept of hard-disk management. Here are some rules you should follow:

The search path, including all subdirectories, drive letters, colons, semicolons, and backslashes, cannot exceed 127 characters (the maximum number of characters you can type at the DOS prompt). Keeping that in mind:

Specify full pathnames, including the drive letter. That way DOS can locate program files on the hard drive when you're logged to a floppy diskette.

Try to keep as few directories on the search path as possible. If you have any more than three or four, you slow down DOS.

Info: DOS must search through each directory on the path every time you type a command. If you have seven subdirectories on the search path, then DOS scans each one for a matching COM, EXE, or BAT file. The more subdirectories you have, the longer it takes.

To cut down on the search path, consider creating batch files to run some of your applications, particularly those that may be the only program in a particular directory.

Remember that dot-dot (..) is an abbreviation for the parent directory. If you're using a subdirectory-organization scheme that has data subdirectories under application directories, then dot-dot will always indicate the parent (application) directory no matter which subdirectory you're logged to. For example:

PATH=C:\DOS;C:\BATCH;..

The dot-dot entry above means all parent directories. No matter where you're logged, DOS will search in the current directory, the DOS directory, the BATCH subdirectory, and then the parent directory to look for programs.

Consider using the SUBST command to reduce the search-path size. SUBST is covered later in this chapter.

Tip: Put the PATH command toward the front of your AUTOEXEC.BAT file. That way you can run DOS commands and programs without specifying a full pathname. If the DOS subdirectory is already on the path, there's no need to do so.

The PATH command can be changed at any DOS prompt to suit your needs. Better still, consider writing some batch files that could reset the path to something else. For example, the batch file to start your word processor could use the PATH command to add its own subdirectory to the path. After the batch file is run, the PATH could be reset to normal again:

```
@ECHO OFF
REM Run the word processor
REM First reset the path:
PATH=C:\WP;C:\DOS;C:\UTIL;C:\BATCH
C:
CD \WP
WP
REM Put the path back:
PATH=C:\DOS;C:\UTIL;C:\BATCH
```

COMMAND: PATH (Internal)
               Function: Sets a search path which DOS uses to locate programs.
               Format: PATH directory;directory;..

Without any options, the PATH command displays the current search path.

Directory is the full pathname of a subdirectory containing programs to which you always want to have access. More than one subdirectory can be specified by separating each with a semicolon.

When PATH is followed by a lone semicolon, the search path is reset to zero (no directories).

The APPEND Command

DOS only looks for program files in directories on the search path. If you want to use any data files, DOS will still look for them only in the current directory—unless you specify a full pathname.

To search for data files in directories other than the current directory, the APPEND command is used. APPEND works like the PATH command, although what it allows DOS to search for are data files.

APPEND is used like the PATH command. For example, the following AP-PEND command places two directories on the data-file search path:

```
APPEND C:\PROJECTS\PROPOSAL;C:\123\JUNE
```

DOS will now search for data files in the PROPOSAL and JUNE subdirectories as specified above. This will work for all DOS commands and programs you run, although the DIR command will still display only files in the current directory.

Unlike the PATH command, APPEND doesn't store its data-file search path in the environment. However, you can force APPEND to use the environment. To do so, use these two commands in your AUTOEXEC.BAT file:

```
APPEND /E
APPEND C:\PROJECTS\PROPOSAL;C:\123\JUNE
```

The first APPEND command uses the /E switch. APPEND is loaded into memory, and it uses the environment to store the data-file search path. The following APPEND command sets the data-file search path, which will now be in the environment.

To add or delete directories, specify another APPEND command. To remove the data-file search path, type APPEND followed by a semicolon—just like the PATH command.

Info: APPEND is best suited for data files that are not to be modified. If you load a file into a program from an APPENDed subdirectory and then save that file back to disk, it will be saved in the current directory—not in its original subdirectory

APPEND is a memory-resident program. It occupies some 9K of RAM. To make APPEND use less memory, refer to Chapter 26 on the LOADHIGH command.

COMMAND: APPEND (External)
     Function: Creates search path for DOS and applications to look for data files.
     Format: APPEND pathname;pathname... /x /path /e

By itself, APPEND displays the current data directory search path.

Pathname is a list of subdirectories, separated by semicolons, which DOS and your applications will now search through to locate data files.

/X is used to extend APPEND's power to your applications. When */x:on* is specified, your application can search APPENDed directories in the same manner as DOS. When */x:off* is specified, your application will not be able to search the APPENDed directories (though you can still specify a full pathname to any file).

/Path is used when you specify a data file with a full pathname. When */path:on* is specified, DOS will continue to look through the APPENDed directories even when you specify full pathnames. When */path:off* is specified, DOS will not examine the directories when you specify a full pathname.

/E directs APPEND to place its data-directory search path into DOS's environment. Otherwise, APPEND stores its data directory in its own memory storage.

The PROMPT Command

One of the standard AUTOEXEC.BAT procedures is to define the DOS prompt. This is done with the PROMPT command. Without it, the DOS prompt would be boring: the drive letter followed by a greater-than sign. Dull. Dull. Dull.

The PROMPT command allows to you define the system prompt. You can include special symbols, the date and time, DOS version, currently logged drive and directory, and any text or symbols the computer can produce. Prompts can be exciting!

The PROMPT command is followed by any text you want to appear in the prompt, plus special PROMPT command characters. Type the following:

```
PROMPT Yes, Master?
```

The DOS prompt now says "Yes, Master?" It can say any text you specify, although the true power of the PROMPT command lies in its special command characters. The following table lists the PROMPT command characters and what each will display in the system prompt.

Command	Displays
$$	$, dollar sign character
$b	|, pipe character
$d	The date (according to the system clock)
$e	The ESCape character, ASCII 27
$g	>, greater-than character
$h	Backspace (erase previous character)
$l	<, less-than character
$n	The currently logged disk drive (letter)
$p	The current path (disk drive and subdirectory)
$q	=, equal-sign character
$t	The time (according to the system clock)
$v	DOS version
$_	Carriage return/line feed (new line)

These commands can be entered in upper or lower case. Note that they all start with a $, dollar sign.

Most of the special commands are used to display "forbidden" DOS characters. In the PROMPT command, you can include those characters only by prefixing them with a dollar sign. The same holds true for other characters difficult to produce from the keyboard: The ESC character; Backspace; Enter key; and the dollar sign itself.

Some special PROMPT commands are used to display system information (the date, time, disk drive, current path, and DOS version). These can be combined to create interesting and informative system prompts. Feel free to experiment by typing in the following examples, or create your own interesting system prompt.

Without any options, the PROMPT command creates the dull system prompt, showing the current drive and a greater-than sign:

```
PROMPT
C>
```

The traditional DOS prompt, which DOS 5's SETUP may have created for you, is the currently logged drive and subdirectory followed by a greater-than sign:

```
PROMPT $P$G
C:\>
```

The following is the informative date and time prompt. Note how the $_ command is used to display information on different lines.

```
PROMPT $D$_$T$_$P$G
Tue 03-26-93
 9:06:58.97
C:\>
```

When the PROMPT command displays the time, it displays seconds and hundredths of seconds. To erase that display, you can use the backspace command, $H. Six backspaces are required to erase the seconds and hundredths of seconds:

```
PROMPT $D$_$T$H$H$H$H$H$H$_$P$G
Tue 03-26-93
 9:08
C:\>
```

382

The $E PROMPT command character is used to include ANSI escape sequences in the prompt. This allows you to change the prompt's color, move the cursor to various locations on the screen, and so on. ANSI is covered in Chapter 23, along with several interesting system prompts you can use.

Setting up the Screen

Some displays may require special configuration commands. In that case, you can specify them in your AUTOEXEC.BAT.

Your display came with a configuration utility (such as VGAPROF, which comes with the Paradise VGA Professional card), or perhaps it's a custom utility—such as the STRETCH.COM program—for a laptop that displays text in an easy-to-read font. These custom programs can be run in AUTOEXEC.BAT to configure your display.

DOS has a multi-purpose command that can also be used to configure the screen. The MODE command, which controls many aspects of the computer, can be put into AUTOEXEC.BAT to change or establish the video mode. The following are several examples of the MODE command and how they configure the assorted video systems on the PC.

Info: MODE is a general-purpose command which configures several parts of the computer. Note that it has many options and parameters, and will probably be a common command in your AUTOEXEC.BAT file.

MODE Command	Function
MODE 40	Sets the number of columns on the screen to 40 on color/graphics systems.
MODE 80	Sets the number of columns on the screen to 80 on color/graphics systems.
MODE CO80	Commonly used to configure color systems. Note that it's C-Oh-80, not C-zero-80.
MODE MONO	Configures monochrome systems.

For EGA and VGA graphics systems, you can specify the number of rows and columns on the screen by using the MODE command in the following format:

```
MODE CON: COLS=columns LINES=rows
```

Columns are the number of columns on the display (characters per line). Values for columns are 40 and 80.

Rows specifies the number of lines on the screen. Values can be 25, 43, and 50, with 25 the default. In order to support the 43- or 50-line mode, you need a compatible graphics adapter plus the ANSI.SYS device driver installed in your CONFIG.SYS file. (ANSI.SYS is covered in Chapter 23.)

```
MODE CON: COLS=80 LINES=43
```

The above command in your AUTOEXEC.BAT file sets your graphics adapter to 80 columns by 43 rows of text. To reset back to 80 by 25, you can use the following command:

```
MODE CO80
```

Typing the MODE command followed by CON, the console device, will display the current status of the display:

```
C:\>MODE CON
Status for device CON:
-------------
Columns=80
Lines=25

Code page operation not supported on this device
```

Info: Your graphics adapter may support more rows and columns than the MODE command recognizes. Utilities that came with your hardware may be more versatile than the MODE command, and may work without support from the ANSI.SYS file. If so, use them instead of the MODE command in your AUTOEXEC.BAT file.

For example, the Hercules Monographics card comes with the HGC utility. To configure your Hercules adapter in the full-graphics mode, the following command could be placed into your AUTOEXEC.BAT file:

```
HGC FULL
```

Other things you can do with your display include using ANSI.SYS commands in AUTOEXEC.BAT to spice up the display, as well as running graphics startup commands or programs that change your Hercules, EGA or VGA screen font.

Configuring the Serial Ports

One of the MODE command's many functions is to configure the computer's serial ports. This action is required only if you're going to be using the serial ports under DOS; your communications program will probably configure the serial ports by itself. Using the MODE command is only required when you use the serial-port device under DOS.

Info: DOS's device names for your serial ports are:

```
COM1   Your first serial port
COM2   Your second serial port
COM3   Your third serial port
COM4   Your fourth serial port
```

AUX can also be specified for COM1, although the MODE command doesn't recognize AUX as a proper device.

A serial port is configured by setting four values:

Term	Describes
Baud	The communications speed, usually measured in bits per second.
Parity	The type of error checking used to verify the data, transmitted, usually Odd, Even, or None.
Data	Also called the "word size," it's the number of bits in each byte sent, which can be 5, 6, 7, or 8.
Stop bits	The number of bits sent after the data, instructing the serial port that a byte has been transmitted.

The MODE command is used to set those values for a given serial port in the following format:

```
MODE COMx: BAUD=b PARITY=p DATA=d STOP=s RETRY=r
```

X is the serial port, 1 through 4.
B is the Baud rate. Values are:

> 11 for 110 Baud
> 15 for 150 Baud
> 30 for 300 Baud
> 60 for 600 Baud
> 12 for 1200 Baud
> 24 for 2400 Baud
> 48 for 4800 Baud
> 96 for 9600 Baud
> 19 for 19,200 Baud

P is the Parity, which can be the letters N for none, E for even, O for odd, M for Mark, or S for Space.

D specifies the word size. Values are 5, 6, 7, and 8.

S specifies the number of stop bits: 1, 1.5, or 2.

R determines how the computer will react if the serial port times out. This is primarily used when the serial port is connected to a printer. For *r* you can specify the following letters:

B—Return a "busy" status
E—Return an error
N—Take no action
P—Continue trying
R—Return ready

The following MODE command can be used in AUTOEXEC.BAT to configure the first serial port to 9600 Baud, no parity, 8-bit word, and one-stop bit:

```
MODE COM1: BAUD=96 PARITY=N DATA=8 STOP=1
```

The MODE command has an abbreviated format that can do the same thing:

```
MODE COM1: 9600,N,8,1
```

These commands are normally used to configure a serial port for use with a printer. This technique is continued in the following section. Under DOS, however, you can also use the CTTY command after configuring the serial port. CTTY is used to specify another device for DOS's input and output.

Normally, DOS uses the CON device, the screen, and the keyboard. By using CTTY, you can reassign input and output to another device—most often a serial port.

```
CTTY AUX
```

The above command redirects all DOS's output to the serial port. DOS also looks to the serial port for input. Unless you have a remote terminal hooked up to the first serial port, don't type the above command.

The practical uses for CTTY AUX are rare. But it does show DOS's flexibility in using devices.

Setting up the Printer

There are two ways you could set up a printer in AUTOEXEC.BAT. The first is to run some utility that prepares your printer for use. For example, a utility such as Metro Software's LaserTwin allows incompatible printers to emulate the Hewlett Packard LaserJet. The second way to setup a printer is to use the MODE command.

The MODE command has three functions for setting up a printer:

Initializing IBM- and Epson-compatible printers

Assigning a code page to a printer

Configuring a serial printer

Since the early PC was closely linked with Epson printers, and IBM printers use the Epson printer commands, you can use the MODE command to configure an IBM- or Epson-compatible printer. The format is:

```
MODE LPTx: COLS=cols LINES=lines RETRY=r
```

X is the printer port, 1 through 3.

Cols are the number of columns on the printer, or characters per line. Values for cols are 80 and 132.

Lines indicates the vertical line spacing, or number of lines per inch. Values for lines are 6 and 8.

R determines how the computer will react if the printer port times out. You can specify the same letters for RETRY here as for the serial port, covered earlier in this chapter.

The following MODE command in AUTOEXEC.BAT will set up your first printer to print in the condensed mode when the computer starts:

```
MODE LPT1: COLS=132
```

The MODE command can be abbreviated as:

```
MODE LPT1:132
```

Note: The MODE command will only have effect if the printer is IBM- or Epson-compatible and if the printer is on when the MODE command is issued.

Finally, the MODE command is used to configure a serial port for use as DOS's PRN device. PRN is often equated with LPT1, your first printer. However, you can assign a printer connected to a serial port for use as PRN. This "fools" some programs into using the serial printer as a standard DOS printer, and allows you to use certain DOS commands with the serial printer. The two steps are:

Configure the serial port

Assign the serial port to PRN

The serial port must be configured to match the serial-port settings on the printer. Most printers use 9600 Baud, 8-N-1. If yours is so, you could use that printer by putting the following two commands in your AUTOEXEC.BAT file:

```
MODE COM1: BAUD=96 PARITY=N DATA=8 STOP=1
MODE LPT1:=COM1:
```

The final command, MODE LPT1:=COM1:, does the reassignment.

Other Uses for the MODE Command

The MODE command can control the keyboard's delay and repeat—the pause after which you press and hold a key so that it starts repeating characters—and the rate at which it repeats. This feature is known as the Typematic Rate. The format for the MODE command is:

```
MODE CON: RATE=r DELAY=d
```

R is the rate at which a key, when held down, will repeat. Values range from 1 through 32 for 2 through 30 characters per second, respectively. The default value is about 20.

D sets the delay, the time after you press the key up until the time it repeats. Values range from 1 through 4 for .25 through 1 second, respectively. The default value is 2.

Rule: You must set both the RATE and DELAY values for the typematic.

```
MODE CON: RATE=32 DELAY=1
```

The above MODE command in AUTOEXEC.BAT will make your keyboard light to the touch and quickly responsive—maybe too quick for some. The following MODE command sets the keyboard back to normal:

```
MODE CON: RATE=20 DELAY=2
```

The MODE command has almost 101 uses. As it's final trick, MODE can be used to display the status of a device and whether or not a code page is assigned to it. Simply follow the MODE command with the device name (CON, COMx, or LPTx). If you follow LPTx with the /status switch, you can check the status of any serial printers reassigned to LPTx devices. (Note that although this is interesting, it's doesn't need to be part of an AUTOEXEC.BAT file.)

The SUBST and JOIN Commands

SUBST and JOIN were introduced with DOS 3.1, which made people believe it was a special networking command. (DOS 3.1 was lauded for its "network support.") In fact, SUBST and JOIN can be used on any hard-drive system with subdirectories. Both are useful, and both can make organizing and running your system easier.

The SUBST command is used to substitute a drive letter for a subdirectory on your system. In essence, you fool DOS into thinking that some subdirectory, say C:\MISC\GAMES, is really a drive, say drive G. When you log to the substituted drive, it's like logging to the subdirectory—but according to DOS you're on the root directory of another drive.

Tip: To get the most from the SUBST command, use the LASTDRIVE configuration command in CONFIG.SYS. Set the highest drive letter to Z, allowing you the full 26 drive letters for use with the SUBST command.

```
SUBST W: C:\WINDOWS
```

The above SUBST command assigns drive letter W to the Windows subdirectory on drive C. If you type W: to log to drive W, you'll really be logged to the C:\WINDOWS directory—but from your perspective, you'll be on the root directory of drive W.

Several drive substitutions can be made in AUTOEXEC.BAT, each on its own line:

```
SUBST M: C:\MISC
SUBST U: C:\BIN\UTIL
SUBST T: C:\COMM\SCOM
SUBST G: C:\DTP\GRAPHICS
SUBST
```

At the end of the above commands, SUBST is used by itself. That displays the list of drives currently substituted on the system.

To remove a drive from the list, the following format is used:

```
SUBST drive /D
```

Drive is the letter of the substituted drive to remove. Note that the subdirectory is merely unassigned or "unsubstituted"; nothing is deleted from your system by using the /D switch.

The advantages to the SUBST command are many:

It cuts down on typing time for changing between long subdirectory names.

It allows you to specify full pathnames to programs, using only a drive letter.

It cuts down on the search path size: SUBST your subdirectories first in AUTOEXEC.BAT, and then use only those substituted drive letters in your PATH command.

Note that you cannot use the following DOS commands on a substituted drive letter:

BACKUP   LABEL
CHKDSK   MIRROR
DISKCOMP   RECOVER
DISKCOPY   RESTORE
FDISK   SYS
FORMAT

COMMAND: SUBST (External)
           Function: Assigns a disk drive letter to a subdirectory.
           Format: SUBST drive pathname [/d]

Drive is the drive letter to be assigned to a subdirectory. It's in the range from the next-highest unused drive letter in the system, through the highest drive letter defined by the LASTDRIVE configuration command (in CONFIG.SYS).

Pathname is the full pathname of the subdirectory.

/D is used to unsubstitute a drive. When the /d switch is used, the pathname isn't specified.

The JOIN command does the opposite of the SUBST command: It takes a disk drive in your system and assigns it as a subdirectory on another drive. Once done, DOS believes the disk drive not to exist; however, you can access is as the subdirectory to which it was joined.

```
JOIN D: C:\DRIVED
```

The above JOIN command assigns drive D to a subdirectory on drive C, DRIVED. If \DRIVED doesn't exist, DOS creates it. Logging to \DRIVED is now the same as logging to drive D—all drive D's subdirectories will be there, but now as subdirectories of C:\DRIVED.

Info: JOIN will let you assign a drive to a subdirectory that already exists. However, that subdirectory must be totally empty for the operation to work.

You can JOIN your drives in AUTOEXEC.BAT as follows:

```
JOIN D: C:\DRIVED
JOIN E: C:\TEMP\RAM
JOIN
```

Above, drive E is possibly a RAM drive. Note that the directory C:\TEMP should exist; DOS will create the RAM subdirectory if it's not already there. JOIN used by itself, as with SUBST, displays the summary of JOINed drives.

To remove a JOINed drive from the list, the /D switch is used:

```
JOIN drive /D
```

Drive is the drive letter of a JOINed drive—not the pathname to which it was assigned. After the above command, DOS will once again recognize the drive, and you can access it as before. Note that the directory the drive was previously joined to still exists. (Do not add files or subdirectories to that directory if you want to use the JOIN command with it again.)

The advantages to the JOIN command are that it:

Allows partitioned hard drives to be treated as one unit. By JOINing a drive D or E partition to drive C as subdirectories, you never have to log to another drive to access your programs and files.

Allows RAM drives to be integrated into a subdirectory structure.

Note that you cannot use certain DOS commands with a JOINed subdirectory. These are the same as those listed for the SUBST command above. Also, don't mess with JOINing a substituted drive or vice versa. Our system is too important to mess with that silliness.

COMMAND: JOIN (External)
            Function:
            Format: JOIN drive pathname [/d]

Drive is the drive letter of the drive you want to assign to a subdirectory.

Pathname is the full pathname of the directory to which the drive will be joined. If the directory doesn't exist, DOS creates it. If it does exist, it should be totally empty.

/D is used to un-JOIN the drive. When the /d switch is used, the pathname isn't specified. After using the /d switch, you can once again access the drive.

Creating Environment Variables

The environment is DOS's memory scratch pad. Into the environment you can store special variables, which can be used by DOS and other applications to modify the way they work.

The subject of the Environment and its variables is covered toward the end of this chapter. But note that environment variables are usually set in your AUTOEXEC.BAT file.

File Maintenance Routines

An important part of AUTOEXEC.BAT is cleaning up unfinished business. Because there is no program that does things when you turn the computer off (unless you're wise enough to write a SHUTDOWN.BAT or similar batch file, and you remember to run it at the end of the day), you can leave the cleanup job to AUTOEXEC.BAT. This is like putting off doing the dishes until you get up the morning, but as long as the job gets done, it's okay.

If you have any file-maintenance utilities, consider running them in AUTOEXEC.BAT. For example:

```
SWEEP DEL *.BAK
```

The above command runs the SWEEP utility, which removes all *.BAK (backup) files from your disk drive. To get rid of temporary files, use the following command:

```
IF EXIST \TEMP\*.* DEL \TEMP\*.*
```

The IF command tests to see if any files exist in your TEMP directory. If so, they're deleted with the DEL command.

The following command can be used to delete any of Windows' temporary files left over in the root directory:

```
IF EXIST ~*.* DEL ~*.* > nul
```

Running disk-compression or hard-drive optimization programs can be done in AUTOEXEC.BAT. Just about any file maintenance command or utility that aids in computer performance can be done every time the computer starts. And they don't need to be third-parity utilities. DOS commands such as CHKDSK can be used as well. Simply put the proper commands into your AUTOEXEC.BAT file.

Memory-Resident Utilities and Startup Programs

The old way to describe a memory-resident program, or "TSR," was that it "attached itself to DOS." These programs stayed in memory, actually becoming part of the operating system—like the APPEND command covered earlier in this chapter. Other memory-resident programs can be run in AUTOEXEC.BAT to expand the power of DOS and the capabilities of your system.

A few popular DOS commands can be loaded and made resident in AUTOEXEC.BAT: the DOSKEY program extends your command line editing ability and the power of the DOS prompt; the MIRROR program can be used as a method of disaster recovery; and the KEYB program changes the way the keyboard behaves. These programs can be loaded as resident using AUTOEXEC.BAT, as well as third-party programs such as SIDEKICK or other "pop-up" utilities.

395

Info: More information on DOSKEY and KEYB is in Chapter 22. MIRROR is covered in Chapter 28. Also refer to Chapter 26 for information on loading memory-resident programs into upper memory.

You can run non-memory-resident programs in AUTOEXEC.BAT as well. For example, a day planner or appointment book could be run, automatically printing out the day's schedule for you. If your normal duties involve running two or three programs in a row first thing in the morning, those programs can be put in AUTOEXEC.BAT.

Run an Application or Shell

AUTOEXEC.BAT can finish in two ways: It just ends, leaving you at the DOS prompt to run whichever programs you wish; or it could end by running an application, DOS environment, or a shell.

If you're using a DOS environment such as Windows or DESQview, you can put the commands to start those environments at the end of your AUTOEXEC.BAT file. Every time you start your computer, it will automatically run Windows or DESQview for you.

If you're not a Windows or DESQview fan, you can run a menu program at the end of AUTOEXEC.BAT. The perfect example is DOS Shell, which the SETUP program already asked you if it was okay to install in AUTOEXEC.BAT.

A third option is to run a program you normally run when you start your PC. For example, suppose that after AUTOEXEC.BAT runs, you automatically run your MCI Mail program to get the morning's letters. Why not make the MCI Mail program part of your AUTOEXEC.BAT file? Or if you automatically type WP to start your word processor, stick that at the end of AUTOEXEC.BAT.

The Environment

The environment is a special storage place used by DOS. It's the part of the computer's memory where DOS keeps the PATH, the PROMPT, the location of COMMAND.COM, as well as information used by other applications. Batch files can also take advantage of the environment using it for temporary storage of information.

In the environment you'll find two types of items: Environment variables and the character strings assigned to them. The SET command is used to create the variables and assign strings to them, as well as to display all variables currently in the environment. DOS, applications, and batch files can examine the environment variables and use the information stored in their character strings.

The SET Command

Your key to the environment is the SET command. SET works in two manners. First, SET is used to view the contents of the environment. Secondly, SET is used to place or remove items in the environment.

To view the contents of your environment, type the SET command at the DOS prompt. You may see something like the following:

```
COMSPEC=C:\DOS\COMMAND.COM
PROMPT=$p$g
PATH=C:\DOS
TEMP=C:\DOS
```

Each environment variable is shown, followed by an equal sign and the character string assigned to that variable. That's the format for all variables in the environment:

```
variable=string
```

Above, you can recognize the PROMPT and PATH variables. These are placed in the environment by the PROMPT and PATH commands.

The COMSPEC variable is used by DOS to locate the command interpreter, COMMAND.COM. DOS will read the value of COMSPEC when it needs to reload the resident portion of COMMAND.COM.

Info: The COMSPEC variable is created by DOS or the SHELL configuration command in CONFIG.SYS. If you don't have a SHELL command in CONFIG.SYS, DOS assumes COMMAND.COM is in the root directory of the boot disk and it creates the COMSPEC variable to reflect that. If you do use a SHELL command, then the pathname option is used by DOS to properly set the COMSPEC variable.

TEMP is a variable that tells DOS where to put its temporary files. Above, TEMP is telling DOS to use the C:\DOS directory for temporary files.

DOS allows you to specify other environment variables; DIRCMD, DOSSHELL, and certain applications will use environment variables. For the PATH and PROMPT variables, the PATH and PROMPT commands are used to create them. For everything else, you use the SET command in the following format:

```
SET variable=contents
```

Variable is the name of the environment variable. It can be any length and can contain any characters. A short, descriptive variable is best (and takes up less memory). Note that DOS will convert a variable to upper case when it's placed into the environment.

Contents are the text assigned to variable. It can be any length and can contain any characters (except for an equal sign). Note that the DOS command line accepts only 127 characters of text (and long variables take up more memory).

```
SET COLOR=BLUE
```

The above command places "COLOR=BLUE" into the environment. The SET command by itself can be used to verify the addition.

Info: You can also manipulate the PATH and PROMPT variables using the SET command in the following format:

```
SET PATH=C:\DOS;C:\BATCH
SET PROMPT=$p$g
SET COLOR = BLUE
```

This command looks similar to the previous one, but they're not the same. DOS defines the variable name as everything up to the equal sign. Above, that includes the space after COLOR. Also, the character string assigned to COLOR is " BLUE"— which starts with a space.

Tip: Don't "pad" the equal sign in a SET command with spaces.

```
SET COMPILER OPTIONS=/A /G+ /T:\TEMP /X
```

The above creates a variable named "COMPILER OPTIONS" complete with its embedded space character. This variable is probably used by a programming language to automatically set command-line switches.

Variables can also be removed by the SET command. To do so, use SET to set the variable equal to nothing:

```
SET COLOR=
```

The above command removes the COLOR variable and its contents from the environment.

It's a good idea to remove all variables you no longer use. The issue here is memory; the environment uses one byte of conventional memory for each character you put into it. By default, DOS sets aside 256 bytes for the environment—but that can go quickly. When it does, you'll see the message:

```
Out of environment space
```

This usually happens when you use that one last SET command. If so, DOS will try to put the variable in the environment, but it usually ends up truncated. To remedy the problem in the short term, delete variables you're no longer using, and consider shortening your PATH. For the long term, use the SHELL configuration command in CONFIG.SYS. Load COMMAND.COM and specify a larger environment size using its /E switch. (Refer to Chapter 19.)

> COMMAND: SET (Internal)
> Function: To view the environment, create, or delete environment variables.
> Format: SET variable=contents

Without any options, the SET command displays the current contents of the environment.

Variable is the name of the environment variable. It can be any length and can contain any characters, although a short, descriptive variable is best. Variable is converted to upper case when placed into the environment.

Contents become the string assigned to variable. It can be any length and can contain any characters (except for an equal sign). If variable already exists, then contents replaces its current contents.

When contents are omitted, the variable is removed from the environment.

DOS 5's Environment Variables

If you never use the PATH, PROMPT, or SET commands, DOS will automatically creates two environment variables: the PATH, which is set equal to nothing; and COMSPEC, which is set to the location of COMMAND.COM. Normally, a PATH—as well as the PROMPT—is set in AUTOEXEC.BAT. That makes three environment variables. There are three additional variables DOS will recognize and use:

TEMP
DIRCMD
DOSSHELL

TEMP is used to identify a directory DOS can use for its temporary files. Additionally, programs such as Windows will take advantage of a TEMP environment variable—and you can use it in your batch files as well (see below). A typical command in AUTOEXEC.BAT may set TEMP as follows:

```
SET TEMP=C:\TEMP
```

Tip: If you've set up a RAM drive, consider assigning the TEMP variable equal to the RAM drive.

DIRCMD can be used to hold optional switches for the DIR command. For example, say you've grown fond of DIR with its /O and /L switches to always display a sorted directory in lower case. You can use the DIRCMD variable to make those options a permanent part of the DIR command:

```
SET DIRCMD=/O /L
```

Every time you use the DIR command, DOS looks for the DIRCMD environment variable and automatically sets any specified options for you.

Note: To temporarily override the options, respecify the switches on the command line with a hyphen in front of each. For example:

```
DIR /-O /-L
```

This DIR command will override the switches set by the above DIRCMD variable.

The DOSSHELL variable is used to set a location for the DOS Shell DOSSHELL.INI (configuration) file. For example:

```
SET DOSSHELL=C:\DOS\
```

The above command tells DOSSHELL to look for its DOSSHELL.INI file in the C:\DOS subdirectory.

Some applications running under DOS may allow you to specify your own environment variables. Now's the time to go back to your manuals and look up Environment Variables in the index. Make any necessary modifications to your AUTOEXEC.BAT file. Also, if you need more space in the environment, modify CONFIG.SYS's SHELL configuration command by specifying an environment larger than 256 bytes. (Refer to Chapter 19.)

Using Environment Variables in Batch Files

Environment variables can be assigned in any batch file simply by using the SET command. You can create and delete environment variables all day, if you like. Additionally, environment variables can be used with ECHO and other DOS commands. When specified, they will expand into their assigned contents, which makes them valuable shorthand. Further, the IF command can be used to test and compare environment variables.

To use an environment variable in a batch file, it must be surrounded by percent signs. When the batch file runs, DOS expands the environment variable out to its equal its assigned text string. For example:

```
ECHO Your path is %PATH%
ECHO Your prompt is %PROMPT%
```

In a batch file, the above commands display the contents of the PATH and prompt commands, something like:

```
Your path is C:\DOS;C:\UTIL;..
Your prompt is $p$g
```

Info: Percent signs around an environment variable expands it when the batch file runs. To see this at work, remove the batch file's initial @ECHO OFF and watch it run. Note that environment variables will not expand when used at the DOS prompt, but only when used in batch files.

Consider the following:

```
COPY *.* %TEMP%
```

Above, the TEMP variable will be expanded into its contents. If TEMP is assigned to C:\TEMP, the end result in the batch file will be:

```
COPY *.* C:\TEMP
```

COPY will copy all files (*.*) into the C:\TEMP subdirectory, which is how the %TEMP% variable expands when the batch file runs.

When used with the IF command, an environment variable can be examined to test (compare) its contents. The following is a test to see if the TEMP environment variable exists:

```
IF "%TEMP"=="" ECHO A temporary directory is not assigned.
```

If TEMP doesn't exist, it's not expanded into anything. In the batch file, that would read as:

```
IF ""=="" ECHO A temporary directory is not assigned.
```

Because "" equals "", the ECHO command would display a message. (More likely, a GOTO would be used or, better still, a SET command could assign a value to TEMP.) If TEMP is already equal to something, it expands as follows:

```
IF "C:\DOS"=="" ECHO A temporary directory is not assigned.
```

Above, IF wouldn't pass the test. Since TEMP is equal to C:\DOS, it's expanded in the IF command.

Sample AUTOEXEC.BAT Files

As with CONFIG.SYS, there is no universal AUTOEXEC.BAT file. There are basic elements in all AUTOEXEC.BAT files. But the one on your system will reflect your own tastes, the software you run, and the way you use your computer.

Almost all AUTOEXEC.BAT files will contain commands to set the PATH and the PROMPT, not to mention that initial @ECHO OFF. Beyond that, the following are examples of various AUTOEXEC.BAT files with explanations of what they do. Note that the line numbers are included here for reference purposes only.

DOS 5's Suggested AUTOEXEC.BAT

Here is a basic AUTOEXEC.BAT file. It doesn't do much beyond the minimum requirements of setting a PATH and PROMPT and a temporary directory for DOS:

```
1: @ECHO OFF
2: PROMPT $p$g
3: PATH C:\DOS
4: SET TEMP=C:\DOS
```

This AUTOEXEC.BAT file doesn't really exploit the full power that AUTOEXEC.BAT offers. Either that, or it's a new system and the user doesn't really know what AUTOEXEC.BAT is capable of.

Windows AUTOEXEC.BAT

A Windows system requires some—but not much—setup. Most of the advantages to running an environment like Windows mean you don't need to go over jumps and through hoops to get your system started. The following AUTOEXEC.BAT file does some minimum maintenance, but then leaves the job of running your system up to Windows:

```
 1: @ECHO OFF
 2:
 3: PROMPT $p$g
 4: PATH C:\WINDOWS;C:\DOS;C:\BATCH
 5: SET TEMP=C:\TEMP
 6:
 7: REM Destroy any Windows temporary files...
 8: IF EXIST ~*.* DEL ~*.*
 9:
10: REM do some disk maintenance before starting Windows
11: C:\UTIL\VOPT C: /F
13:
14: CD \WINDOWS
15: WIN
```

Lines 3, 4 and 5 set the environment variables. Note that the PATH is set with the WINDOWS subdirectory first; when you run Windows its subdirectory should be listed on the path. Also, the TEMP variable is both by DOS and Windows.

Line 8 does some cleanup. Sometimes Windows exits with temporary files in the root directory, each of which starts with a tilde (~). Line 8 uses the IF EXIST test to see if any temporary files are present and, if so, it deletes them.

Line 11 runs Golden Bow System's VOPT, a disk-optimizer program. VOPT cleans up the drive—but note that this is done before Windows starts. (You shouldn't run drive-optimizing utilities from within Windows.)

Finally, Lines 14 and 15 change to the WINDOWS subdirectory and Windows is run, which is how all good Windows AUTOEXEC.BAT files will end.

Tip: Windows is big on the path; almost every discrete Windows application you install will request that its own subdirectory be on the path. If you're not practicing good hard-disk management, that's okay; just toss everything into one big WINDOWS subdirectory. But if everything is in its own unique subdirectory, it means you must put that directory on the path for it to run under Windows.

The solution is to use the SUBST command to assign your important Windows applications subdirectories to drive letters. The drive letters will take up less space on the path and are easier to manipulate. Remember to set the LASTDRIVE configuration command to the appropriate value.

BIN System AUTOEXEC.BAT

A hard disk organized along the BIN system can really get complex. The following sample shows you just how much an AUTOEXEC.BAT file can do each time your system boots:

```
 1: @ECHO OFF
 2: REM Set system variables...
 3: PROMPT $p$g $a
 4: PATH C:\DOS;C:\BATCH;C:\UTIL
 5: SET MPATH=%PATH%
 6: SET TEMP=C:\TEMP
 7:
 8: REM Set your DOSKEY macros
 9: DOSKEY /INSERT
10: C:\DOS\DOSKEY D=DIR /W
11: C:\DOS\DOSKEY H=DOSKEY /HISTORY
12: C:\DOS\DOSKEY M=DOSKEY /MACROS
13:
14: JOIN D: C:\RAM
15: ECHO JOINed drives:
16: JOIN
17:
18: COPY C:\AUTOEXEC.* %TEMP% > NUL
19: COPY C:\CONFIG.* %TEMP% > NUL
20:
21: DOSSHELL
```

The standard system variables are set in lines 3, 4, and 6. But take a look at line 5. It creates the MPATH variable, assigning it equal to the contents of the PATH; when the batch file runs, it will expand %PATH% out into the search path, and then set the variable MPATH equal to the PATH. In the end, two variables will contain the search path: PATH, which DOS uses, and MPATH, which can be used as a backup PATH.

Info: The MPATH variable is simply part of running the BIN system. Some batch files may run other applications and may, at times, change the PATH. To restore the original path, a line such as the following could be included in such a batch file:

```
SET PATH=%MPATH%
```

That restores the original path, and cuts down on typing.

Lines 8 through 12 set up the memory-resident DOSKEY program. Line 9 loads DOSKEY into memory, specifying the Insert mode. Lines 10, 11, and 12 create three DOSKEY macros. (DOSKEY is covered in Chapter 22, but note that you need to use the DOSKEY command several times to create macros. Ideally, this is done in AUTOEXEC.BAT.)

Lines 14, 15, and 16 JOIN a RAM drive D into the main hard-disk system as a subdirectory \RAM on drive C. Line 14 is the JOIN command, line 15 ECHOes a message, and line 16 displays the results of the JOIN operation:

```
D: => C:\RAM
```

Lines 18 and 19 are used to make safety backups of the CONFIG and AUTOEXEC files in the root directory. Both COPY command a duplicate of each file, storing it in the temporary-files directory specified by %TEMP%. Why? Because some programs modify CONFIG.SYS or AUTOEXEC.BAT when they install. This COPY trick helps to maintain the originals.

Info: Both lines 18 and 19 end with "> NUL". That's used to suppress the "1 file(s) copied" message the COPY command displays. An explanation of how that works is given in Chapter 24.

Finally, the file ends by running the DOSSHELL program in line 21. It could end with another shell being run, such as PC Tool's PCSHELL or Direct Access, or DESQview, or whichever program is normally run first on the system.

Batch File/RAM Drive Example

This is another variation on the BIN system. But here, a 32K RAM drive, D, has been created. All the batch files on this system will be copied to the RAM drive, and the path will be set up accordingly. Pay attention to the steps involved:

```
 1: @ECHO OFF
 2:
 3: SET COMSPEC=C:\DOS\COMMAND.COM
 4: PATH=D:\BATCH;C:\DOS;C:\UTIL
 5: PROMPT=$p$g
 6: SET TEMP=D:\TEMP
 7:
 8: REM Set up RAM Drive
 9: MKDIR D:\BATCH
10: MKDIR D:\TEMP
11: ECHO Moving Batch Files...
12: COPY C:\BATCH\*.* D:\BATCH > NUL
13:
14: NUMOFF
```

Lines 3 through 6 set various environment variables. But note that line 3 is redundant. If you've already specified a pathname for COMMAND.COM in your CONFIG.SYS file with the SHELL command, setting the COMSPEC variable is no longer needed. If your AUTOEXEC.BAT file was created under DOS 3.3, then it may still linger; it's okay to delete it, providing the SHELL configuration command is properly set up. (Refer to Chapter 19.)

Lines 8 through 12 prepare the RAM drive. Lines 9 and 10 create two subdirectories on the RAM drive, one for batch files and another for the TEMP variable.

Line 12 copies the batch files from their subdirectory on drive C to the BATCH subdirectory on the RAM drive.

Note that the RAM drive is first on the path. Running your system using batch files is important for hard-disk management, especially with a complex hard drive tree structure. Putting your batch files into a RAM drive speeds things up immensely. (RAM drives are covered in the next chapter.)

Info: DOS reads batch files from disk one line at a time. If you have a 23-line batch file, DOS reads the disk 23 times to run that batch program. Putting all your batch files on a RAM drive, which is faster than any hard drive, means they'll run faster.

Summary

The batch file AUTOEXEC.BAT allows you to configure your system, run special startup programs, and perform "early morning" chores every time your computer starts. It must be in the root directory of your boot disk, and if you use the SHELL configuration command, be sure to specify COMMAND.COM's /P switch to run AUTOEXEC.BAT.

There are several useful commands which become a part of most AUTOEXEC.BAT files. They are:

PATH   The PATH command is used to set a program search path. DOS will look in directories listed on the search path for program files to run—no matter which directory you're currently logged to.

APPEND The APPEND command creates a search path for data files. (PATH is only used by DOS to look for program files.)

PROMPT The PROMPT command is used to customize the DOS prompt. Special PROMPT commands are used to produce interesting characters and test on the display. The most popular prompt is PROMPT pg, the currently logged drive and directory, followed by a greater-than (>) sign.

MODE   The MODE command is used to configure the screen, serial ports, and printer ports. Other custom commands may also be used in AUTOEXEC.BAT, especially those specific to the hardware in your system.

SUBST   The SUBST command can be used to assign a drive letter to a subdirectory. After using the SUBST command, accessing the substituted drive is the same as logging to the subdirectory; it's shorthand, ideal for CD shortcuts and tightening up a long search path.

JOIN   The JOIN command does the opposite of the SUBST command: It assigns a disk drive to a subdirectory on another drive. This can be put to use integrating partitioned drives and RAM drives into one hard-disk subdirectory system.

409

SET   The SET command is used to place variables into DOS's environ-
             ment. DOS can use six variables: COMSPEC, which tells DOS
             the location of COMMAND.COM; PATH, which lists the search
             path; PROMPT, which stores the system prompt definition;
             TEMP, which defines a subdirectory for temporary files;
             DIRCMD, which contains options for the DIR command; and
             DOSSHELL, which tells the DOS Shell program where to find its
             DOSSHELL.INI file. In addition, other applications may require
             their own environment variables, as well as those you can create
             on the fly for batch files.

In addition to these commands, you can put special startup programs, pop-up
programs, memory-resident utilities and DOS enhancers, disk optimizers and so on
in AUTOEXEC.BAT. The final line should contain the name of the first program you
run, such as Windows, DOS Shell, PC Shell, DESQview, or whichever application
you normally run first.

CHAPTER 21

System Maintenance

The most important aspect of on-going hard-disk management is system maintenance—the upkeep of your files and file system. To meet that end, there are certain procedures and special tools you can use to keep your hard drive and its files working at top efficiency, and make you a happy PC owner.

This chapter answers the following questions:

- How can batch files be used to run applications?

- What can batch files do to give DOS more power?

- How are subdirectories moved and maintained?

- What does the XCOPY command do?

- How can disk performance be improved?

- How do BACKUP and RESTORE work?

- What is a good backup routine to follow?

- What else can BACKUP and RESTORE do?

- How does a RAM drive help the hard-disk system?

- What does a disk cache do?

Working with Applications

A computer isn't about playing with DOS, or building subdirectories or silly little batch files. It's about running applications. Everything else is important, but secondary; good hard-disk management is designed to support your applications.

To get the most out of your applications, you should accomplish the following hard-disk management tasks:

- Build an effective subdirectory structure

- Establish a worthy PATH

- Create batch files to assist the running of applications

- Perform routine file maintenance

- Back up

Info: An additional task on some systems may be PC security. On single-user systems, only the most paranoid user will bother with slapping on a password and encrypting files. But in an office situation, or any time there is sensitive information on a computer, security is an important issue.

DOS provides no methods of security other than the data security created by giving you the BACKUP command to make a safety copy of the information on your hard drive. You can hide files with the ATTRIB command, but if you can hide them, others can find them.

Third-party packages are available that provide system security, passwords, and data encryption. (The DOS Shell program has password protection at some levels, but it doesn't prevent someone from accessing programs outside of the shell.)

You should have already built an effective subdirectory structure, or at least modified your present subdirectory system to make it more flexible. (Refer to Chapter 17 for more information.) Creating a worthy PATH is closely linked to your subdirectory structure. But don't forget that it's possible to change the PATH for some programs by running batch files. That's more or less the subject of the next topic—running applications with batch files. The final two subjects—file maintenance and backup—are covered later in this chapter.

Batch Files to Run Your System

Batch files can do anything on your system. Any series of commands you normally type can be stuffed into a batch file for convenience. Put that batch file in a BATCH directory on the path, and you can access those commands from anywhere on your hard drive. That's the essence of using batch files with DOS.

Commonly there will be many types of batch files on your system. Consider two types for running your system:

Those that run applications

Those that do something DOS doesn't (or do it better)

It's almost too easy to mention how batch files run applications. Consider the following, 123.BAT, which runs the Lotus 1-2-3 spreadsheet:

```
@ECHO OFF
C:
CD \123
123
```

There's nothing to it. Generally speaking, all application-running batch files do the same thing: They change to the proper drive and directory, and then issue the command to run the program. Some can get slightly more complex than that. The following is a batch file that runs WordPerfect:

```
@ECHO OFF
SET PATH=%MPATH%
D:\WP51\WP %1/R
```

The approach here is a bit different. First, the PATH is reset using the MPATH variable (refer to Chapter 20). Next, WordPerfect is run using its full pathname. After that comes a command-line parameter, possibly a filename to load, as well as WordPerfect's /R switch telling the program to use expanded memory.

The whole world doesn't spin around Windows. The following batch file sets up DESQview to run, and it also preps Lotus' Magellan file-management utility to work under DESQview. This is an example of a batch file that runs a computing environment, as opposed to running an application:

```
 1: @ECHO OFF
 2: C:
 3: CD \SYSTEM\MAGELLAN
 4: MG /TSR
 5: CD \SYSTEM\DV
 6: BREAK OFF
 7: DV %1 %2 %3 %4 %5
 8: CD \SYSTEM\MAGELLAN
 9: MG /NOTSR
10: CD \
```

Magellan must be started in its own subdirectory; lines 2 and 3 see to that. Magellan is run with its /TSR switch in line 4, which makes it operate better under DESQview. Next, it's off to the \SYSTEM\DV subdirectory where DESQview is run. (Lines 6 and 7 were actually created by DESQview's INSTALL program, but later expanded upon in this batch file.)

After the user quits from DESQview, line 8 takes you back to the Magellan subdirectory, shuts of the memory-resident mode, and then logs back to the root directory in line 10.

The following batch file runs Borland's Turbo C programming environment. This is an example of changing a computer's mode of operation, for example, on a system that's not dedicated to programming 100 percent of the time.

```
@ECHO OFF
E:
CD \TC\BIN
SET PATH=C:\TC\BIN;%PATH%
PROMPT @$p$g
```

This batch file doesn't run any program; it simply sets the computer up in a Turbo C mode. Note how the PATH is set to reflect the TASM subdirectory; the original path is appended to C:\TASM using %PATH% as a variable. Also, notice the At Sign (@) in the prompt? If you run a system such as this that changes modes, it might be a good idea to change the prompt as well. Above, an @ in the prompt may tell the user that they're in "programming mode."

A companion batch file on such a "modal" system would be one that returns the mode to normal. Consider the following, NORMAL.BAT file:

```
@ECHO OFF
MODE C080
PROMPT $P$G
SET PATH=%MPATH%
```

Above, the screen mode is reset to standard 80-by-25 color, the PROMPT is reset, and the PATH is restored using the %MPATH% variable. Again, the batch file doesn't run any program, it simply sets a mode of operation.

Making Life Easier—Expanding DOS

Batch files don't always need to run applications. The following batch files make things easy on you, as well as do some things DOS cannot.

There are four popular sizes for disk drives in a PC: 360K and 1.2M 5-1/4-inch, and 720K and 1.4M 3-1/2-inch. If you have the higher density drives, then the FORMAT command will always format diskettes in those drives for the higher capacity. Otherwise, you need to specify FORMAT's "do a low capacity" switches, which are hard to remember—unless you write a batch file that remembers them for you.

The following is AFORMAT.BAT, a batch file that formats a 360K diskette in drive A:

```
@ECHO OFF
ECHO Formatting 360K diskette in Drive A. . .
FORMAT A:/4
```

The only information needed here is the /4 switch, which directs FORMAT to make a 360K diskette in a 1.2M drive. But it's easier to type in AFORMAT than to remember that trivia. The following batch file does the same thing, but assuming it's a 1.4M 3-1/2-inch drive and you want to format a 720K diskette in it:

```
@ECHO OFF
ECHO Formatting 720K diskette in Drive A. . .
FORMAT A:/N:9 /T:80
```

The following batch file creates a new DOS command: MOVE.BAT is a combination file-copy/delete utility. The end result: files are moved from one location to another. Look this over closely:

```
 1: @ECHO OFF
 2: REM MOVE FILES FROM %1 TO %2
 3: IF "%1"=="" GOTO WARNING
 4: IF "%2"=="" GOTO WARNING
 5: ECHO Moving Files. . .
 6: COPY %1 %2 >NUL
 7: DEL %1 <C:\BATCH\YES >NUL
 8: ECHO Files moved
 9: GOTO END
10: :WARNING
11: ECHO Please specify a source and destination filename
12: :END
```

The format for this "MOVE command" is:

```
MOVE source destination
```

Source is a file or group of files specified with a wildcard.

Destination is a pathname to where you want the files moved. You must specify both, and the batch file uses the IF command to test for that in lines 3 and 4.

Line 6 does the initial COPY. Line 7 deletes the originals once they've been copied. The "<C:\BATCH\YES" and other uses of the less-than and greater-than symbols is covered in depth in Chapter 24.

Note how a WARNING label is used at line 10. If either a source or destination is omitted, the IF test executes a GOTO command that branches to the WARNING label. A message is then displayed (line 11). Notice how line 9 skips over this with a GOTO END command.

Batch files are really capable of doing anything you need. Like the MOVE.BAT example, they can even perform tasks DOS is unable to handle. The next few sections concentrate on disk and file maintenance. Batch files can be used there as well. In fact, there is no limit to their usefulness.

Maintaining Your Subdirectories

Provided that you designed a workable subdirectory structure, there should be no reason to do major subdirectory maintenance. You should never have doubt as to the location for new applications, where new subdirectories should be added, or what goes where.

For example, if you add some new recreational software (a game), place it in a new subdirectory in your general GAMES directory. On my system, I have a major subdirectory for Microsoft Windows and its programs. Adding a Windows program, such as Excel or Word for Windows is as easy as adding a new subdirectory in the general Windows subdirectory. But sometimes, life just isn't that easy.

Pruning and Grafting

The process of deleting and moving subdirectories is referred to as pruning and grafting, which sort of keeps with the subdirectory tree-structure metaphor (but let's not get carried away with that).

There is no MOVE command in DOS. If you suddenly discover that a particular subdirectory, or a branch of directories, would better suit your purposes if it were elsewhere in the tree structure, you have some work cut out for you.

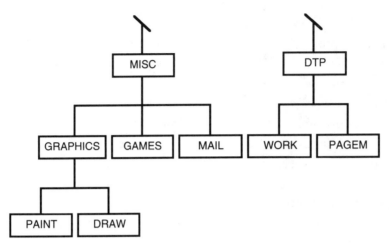

Figure 21-1. Moving part of the tree structure.

Consider Figure 21-1. After working with that system for a while, you decide that your GRAPHICS directory would better suit you if it were placed under the DTP subdirectory. You need to prune GRAPHICS and its two subdirectories, grafting it under the DTP subdirectory. Here are the commands you could use in DOS to do that:

First, create the new structure:

```
MD DTP\GRAPHICS MD DTP\GRAPHICS\PAINT
MD DTP\GRAPHICS\DRAW
```

Second, copy over the files:

```
COPY MISC\GRAPHICS\*.* DTP\GRAPHICS
COPY MISC\GRAPHICS\PAINT\*.* DTP\GRAPHICS\PAINT
COPY MISC\GRAPHICS\DRAW\*.* DTP\GRAPHICS\DRAW
```

Third, remove the old structure:

```
DEL MISC\GRAPHICS\PAINT\*.*
DEL MISC\GRAPHICS\DRAW\*.*
RD MISC\GRAPHICS\PAINT
RD MISC\GRAPHICS\DRAW
DEL MISC\GRAPHICS\*.*
RD MISC\GRAPHICS
```

That's a lot of work to move a subdirectory branch. DOS has a command, XCOPY, that makes the first two steps easier. But you must still go through the steps of deleting the old files and subdirectories.

Info: This procedure is also the way the DOS manual recommends you rename as subdirectory. Yeah, right. It's much easier to use a shell like DOS Shell to rename directories. This is covered in a later section.

The XCOPY Command

The XCOPY command is an extended version of the COPY command. Basically they work the same; you specify a source and destination and XCOPY moves or duplicates the files. But the first major difference you'll notice is that XCOPY reads in all files in a group at once, and then copies them all at once. This makes XCOPY faster than COPY, which reads in a group of files one at a time.

XCOPY also comes with a parade of optional switches. These switches are what gives XCOPY its power, and makes it ideal for moving around branches in a subdirectory structure. As an example, look at the first two steps required to move the GRAPHICS subdirectory in the previous section. First, the new structure was created, and second, the files were copied. The following XCOPY command does both those steps:

```
XCOPY MISC\GRAPHICS\*.* DTP\*.* /S /E
```

The /S switch is the subdirectory switch. XCOPY will copy all files and subdirectories under the source (MISC\GRAPHICS*.*) and duplicate them on the target. The /E switch insures the XCOPY will also copy and set up any empty subdirectories. This causes XCOPY to duplicate the entire structure, and not skip over a subdirectory because it lacks files.

Info: Generally speaking, it's always best to use XCOPY rather than the COPY command, especially when you're copying a group of files. It's just faster.

Of course, you still need to manually delete the old subdirectory structure from the disk. That will again require all the DEL and RD commands listed earlier.

COMMAND: XCOPY (External)
> Function: A better COPY command; moves subdirectory structures in addition to files; moves a group of files at once instead of one at a time; can move files based on their Archive attribute or on or after a certain date.
> Format: XCOPY source destination switches

Source is the source filename, pathname, or a group of filenames specified with a wildcard.

Destination is the target pathname to which XCOPY will duplicate the source file(s). If destination is omitted, XCOPY assumes you mean the currently logged drive and directory.

Switches are the optional switches for the XCOPY command. They are:

/A copies only files with their Archive attribute set. This switch does not affect the Archive attribute after the files are copied. (See the /M switch.)

/D copies only those files created after a specified date. For example, the following command copies only those files created after November 12, 1990:

```
XCOPY *.* /D:11-13-90
```

/E copies subdirectories, even if they're empty. (Used with the /S switch.)

/M copies only files with their Archive attribute set. After the XCOPY command, the Archive attribute will be reset.

/P causes XCOPY to display a prompt (Y/N) before copying each file.

/S copies subdirectories under the source as well as all files in those subdirectories. (See the /E switch.)

/V turns on verification; as each file is copied, it will be verified against the original. This somewhat increases the amount of time XCOPY takes.

/W displays an initial pause message before XCOPY begins to copy files.

Although the XCOPY command has some switches that make it "feel" like the BACKUP command, XCOPY is not BACKUP. You cannot use XCOPY to copy a large group of files across several floppy disks. Once a disk is full, the XCOPY command displays an error and returns you to the DOS prompt.

Using DOS Shell

If you want to get really semantical about things, "pruning and grafting" is actually a term used in the XTree program, a hard-disk shell that's big on subdirectory maintenance. Other shells and programs—PC Tools, the Norton Commander, and so on—have similar commands. All of them will let you move and copy subdirectory structures with differing degrees of ease. DOS Shell will let you do the same, although not in as few keystrokes.

In DOS Shell you can do the following with subdirectories:

Create new directories

Select the directory in the Directory List Window, pull down the File menu, and then select Create Directory. Give the new directory a name in the Create Directory dialog box, and DOS Shell creates it.

Rename directories

Select the directory, pull down the File menu, and then select Rename. Enter the new name for the directory in the Rename Directory dialog box.

Delete directories

Select the directory, pull down the File menu, and then select Delete. You can also highlight the directory and press the Del key. But note that a directory must be empty before you can delete it (just like the RD command).

Note that although there is a MOVE command in the File menu, it's not available when you're in the Directory List Window. The DOS Shell has no prune or graft functions.

Beyond these commands you'll have to look to third-party programs such as the three mentioned at the start of this section. XTree Pro Gold is currently the best, with separate Prune and Graft commands. However, PC Tools and Norton Commander both offer more features than the basic file-manager functions of XTree Pro Gold. If subdirectory-and-file management is important to you, then buy one based on your own needs and evaluations.

File Maintenance

File maintenance can be routine. Consider the following things you should do regularly without giving a thought to official File Maintenance:

Delete files you no longer need

Archive (copy or compress) seldom used files to floppy disks

Move similar files from general directories into specific directories

These tasks can be done regularly or in batch files. Beyond them, you can use DOS and third-party utilities to do file maintenance DOS cannot. DOS does offer the CHKDSK command. But for major disk tune-ups, you need something with more options and more brains.

The CHKDSK Command

CHKDSK is the check disk command. Many users treat it like some occult ceremony, going through it as some sort of sacred ritual without knowing exactly what it does or how it benefits.

On the surface, the CHKDSK command gives you statistics about your disk and the files on it. It also informs you if it's found any fragmented files or lost clusters. The fragmented files you cannot fix using CHKDSK. Lost clusters can be deleted, however, which will improve disk efficiency.

When you type CHKDSK at the DOS prompt, it gives you a summary of disk and file usage on the drive:

```
C:\>CHKDSK
Volume DOS 5   created 09-21-1990 1:26p
Volume Serial Number is 1668-BE65

 42366976 bytes total disk space
    73728 bytes in 2 hidden files
    96256 bytes in 44 directories
 26050560 bytes in 893 user files
 16146432 bytes available on disk

     2048 bytes in each allocation unit
    20687 total allocation units on disk
     7884 available allocation units on disk

   655360 total bytes memory
   636608 bytes free
```

The disk's volume name and serial number are displayed, followed by a summary of disk usage: total disk space, files and directories on the disk and their occupied space, and the number of bytes free. Allocation unit (cluster) information follows, and then a summary of memory is provided.

Info: If CHKDSK reports any "Bad sectors," that information was established by the FORMAT command as it verified the disk surface. CHKDSK doesn't scan the disk for bad sectors at all; it only reports what DOS already knows about the drive.

If any lost chains are found, they're summarized at the end of the display, in a message like:

```
xxx lost allocation units found in xx chains
Convert lost chains to files?
```

If you type Y or N nothing will happen. CHKDSK is only alerting you to the presence of lost chain (file fragments). To actually fix them, you must run CHKDSK with the /F switch:

```
CHKDSK /F
```

When the lost chains message is displayed again, type Y. CHKDSK will create one or more files in the root directory of the drive, each with the name FILExxxx.CHK. The xxxx will be a number from 0000 through however many files were converted.

Sometimes you can examine the files CHKDSK creates, rescuing information from them using some disk tools or other applications. Most of the time, it's safe to just delete the files and move on.

Info: Lost chains are file fragments created by sloppy applications or when you quit or reset in the middle of an application. The files show up in the FAT, but lack directory entries. CHKDSK converts them into files with directory entries, but the results are less than useful; because the fragments were discarded in the first place, they usually don't convert into information worth saving.

To check for fragmented files, follow CHKDSK with a filename or wildcard. CHKDSK will scan the FAT for the number of noncontiguous blocks in each file. Files with more than one segment will be displayed, along with the number of noncontiguous blocks they occupy. This situation can only be remedied by defragmenting the drive—a process covered in the next section. (You can always back up the whole drive, reformat it, and then restore all the files—but, naaaa...)

If all files are contiguous, CHKDSK will inform you:

```
All specified file(s) are contiguous
```

COMMAND: CHKDSK (External)
      Function: Displays disk statistics, lost chains, fragmented files.
      Format: CHKDSK drive: pathname /F /V

Without any parameters, CHKDSK checks the current drive.

Drive is the letter of a drive for CHKDSK to check. It cannot be an assigned (SUBST'd) or JOINed drive, and the drive letter must be followed by a colon.

Pathname is a filename or wildcard; CHKDSK will report if the file is contiguous or split into noncontiguous blocks.

/F is used to fix any lost chains or clusters. Although CHKDSK always reports their presence, only by specifying the /F switch will they be removed to files for clean up.

/V is the verbose switch. When specified, CHKDSK displays the full pathname of every file and directory on disk as it's being processed.

Disk Tune-ups

Oftentimes, to maintain your file system, you need help from outside. Third-party utilities can be used to check the integrity of your file system, optimize disk performance, and defragment your hard drive. While this need not be done as often as general maintenance, it's important.

Disk tune-up programs have a lot to offer, but usually they do only one useful thing that should be done every once in a while: They defragment your hard drive.

When DOS deletes a file, it creates available space on disk for other files. If a file is too big to fit into available space, DOS splits up the file, filling in available space using appropriately sized pieces of the file. This is fragmentation. The more you use your drive (and delete files), the more it will become fragmented. Since it takes DOS longer to locate and assemble the pieces of a fragmented file, fragmentation eventually degrades your disk performance.

DOS provides no tools for defragmenting files. However, many third-party utilities can do so: The Mace Utilities were founded on defragmentation, and the Norton Utilities Speed Disk program, PC Tools' Compress, Prime Solutions' Disk Technician Advanced and Gibson Research's SpinRight, all perform disk defragmentation as well as other disk tune-ups.

Tip: As a rule, defragment your drive when total fragmentation reaches ten percent or more of used disk space.

Some programs—especially the directory listings—compress disk space. When you delete a file, DOS maintains a file "tombstone" in the directory listing. The compress program will usually remove the tombstones, as well as sort the directory entries or, optionally, place COM and EXE program files at the front of the directory for fast access.

Some utilities will also verify the disk's surface, checking for questionable sectors and marking them "bad" as necessary. Whatever the case, do this type of maintenance on a regular basis. But keep in mind software cannot cure all hardware problems. Like CHKDSK, these programs aren't magic. If your disk really starts to go south, consider buying a new one. (And back up regularly!)

Backup

If the flag of hard-disk management has "Keep the Root Clean" as its banner, then the rallying cry is "Backup!" There's no need to waggle fingers here, so I'll be brief: Backup your hard drive system on a regular basis. This is very important. Don't forget it. You'll regret it.

How Often do you Need to Backup?

Backing up your hard drive should be done on a regular schedule. Most people complain because backing up an entire hard drive takes several boring minutes, complete with disk swapping, even with the fastest of third-party backup programs. But you only have to backup the entire hard drive every so often. Daily, however, you should backup the work you do.

There are three types of backup you should use:

Complete hard disk

Incremental

Daily work backups

For personal computer use, backup the entire hard disk once a month, or once every three months if it's not used that often.

An incremental backup simply copies those files that have been added or modified since the last backup. This is the reason behind a file's Archive attribute; DOS sets that flag when you modify or create a file since the last backup. Backing the file up (or using XCOPY) will reset the Archive flag, which lets you and DOS know that a safety copy of the file exists elsewhere.

Daily work backups should be done at the end of each work day. You can then do an incremental backup of the day's work, or do a backup of your work subdirectories. A batch file can be written to use the BACKUP command, COPY, or XCOPY to copy those files to floppy disks "just in case."

To get an idea of when you need to backup, you can use the ATTRIB command to examine the A (Archive) attribute of files on disk. Or, if you're into batch-file programming, type in the following batch file, BACKTEST.BAT, which will give you a summary of files on disk with their Archive attribute set:

```
1: @ECHO OFF
2: ECHO Checking the list of files to backup. . .
3: %1
4: CD \
5: ATTRIB /S > %TEMP%\ARCHIVE
6: ECHO You have this many files in need of backup:
7: FIND /C "A " %TEMP%\ARCHIVE
8: PAUSE
9: DEL %TEMP%\ARCHIVE
```

Line 1 is the initial ECHO OFF and line 2 displays a startup message. Since this program takes some time, the message gives the user something to stare at.

Line 3 is used when BACKTEST is followed by an optional drive letter. If so, line 3 will be used to log to that drive. If not, %1 expands to nothing and the current drive is used. Following that, line 4 logs to the root directory of the drive.

Line 5 issues the ATTRIB command with the /S switch. The net effect of the command is that the attributes for all files on the drive will be displayed. The > symbol is used to redirect ATTRIB's output to a file (this is covered in Chapter 24) The file is created in the temporary directory, as specified by %TEMP%, and named ARCHIVE. Note that if the %TEMP% environment variable isn't defined, the file is created in the root directory. Once ATTRIB is done, all files and their attributes will be in the ARCHIVE file.

Line 6 displays a summary message.

Line 7 uses the FIND command (covered in Chapter 25) to locate the text string "A" (upper case A followed by a space). When ATTRIB displays the archive attribute, it displays A-space. This avoids confusion if the FIND command locates an A in a pathname. The FIND command's /C switch is used to display the number of instances found, which directly translates into the number of files on the drive that have been added or modified since the last backup.

Line 8 pauses the batch file using the PAUSE command.

Line 9 deletes the ARCHIVE file created in the temporary directory.

To run this batch file, type BACKTEST followed by an optional drive letter (and colon) to test a specific drive. If the drive letter isn't specified, then BACKTEST tests only the current drive.

After a few spins of the disk you'll see something like the following displayed:

```
Checking the list of files to backup...
You have this many files in need of backup:

---------- C:\TEMP\ARCHIVE: 845
Press any key to continue . . .
```

Whoa! Time to backup! There are 845 files with their Archive attribute set, which is more than enough to justify a major hard-drive backup. If you do a daily backup or incremental backup on a regular schedule, that number should never be that high (unless you've been very busy!). Time to dust off the BACKUP command.

Using DOS's BACKUP Command

Ever since the days of hard drives, there have been archive—or backup—programs available. These copy all the files from the hard drive to a series of backup diskettes. If anything ever goes wrong with the hard drive, copies of the files exist on the backup diskettes. Or, if you accidentally delete a file or need an older version, it can be fetched from the stack of backup diskettes.

DOS's archiving program is BACKUP.EXE, the external BACKUP command. Other archiving programs that do a better job exist: In addition to making copies of the files, they do so faster than DOS, and they also compress the files, which uses fewer diskettes for the backup. For this book, however, the subject remains DOS's BACKUP program.

Info: There are plenty of third-party backup programs available, from the venerable FastBack to PC Tool's PCBackup to Norton's Norton Backup. They all judge themselves by speed and ease of backup. However, if backup is really important, consider getting a tape backup system. It has the advantage of being easy to use and makes backing up an unattended, early-morning operation.

To begin the backup you need to know what you're backing up. Suppose you've never backed up your hard disk before. Then it's obvious you need a full-disk backup.

Before backing up, you should get an idea of how many diskettes you'll need. If you have high-capacity drives, then by all means use the high-capacity diskettes. Further, use the CHKDSK command to see how many bytes are being used by files on the hard drive. For example, suppose CHKDSK says:

```
26050560 bytes in 893 user files
```

Divide that number by 1,457,664 if you're backing up to 1.4M 3-1/2-inch diskettes, or by 1,213,952 if you're backing up to 1.2M 5-1/4-inch diskettes. For example, 26,050,560 divided by 1,457,664 equals 17.87 (plus change). Figure that the backup will take 18 diskettes, and add one diskette—just in case—for a total of 19.

Info: The value to divide by if you have a 360K floppy is 368,640; for a 720K diskette, the value is 737,280.

The next step is to label the diskettes. Number diskette labels from one through however many you have. Mark them as "Full Disk Backup #1" and so on, with the date. You can format the diskettes if you have time, but the BACKUP command does that automatically. (Note that the FORMAT command must be in a subdirectory on the PATH for BACKUP to format the diskettes.)

To backup the entire hard drive C, the following backup command should be used:

```
BACKUP C:\*.* A: /S
```

A backup is made of all files on drive C's root directory to floppy diskettes in drive A. The /S switch tells BACKUP to include all files in all subdirectories, therefore this is a full-disk backup. After entering the above command, DOS displays the following:

```
Insert backup diskette 01 in drive A:

Warning! Files in the target drive A:\ root directory will be erased
Press any key to continue . . .
```

If the diskette already contains data, the BACKUP command will erase it. If the diskette is unformatted, BACKUP will call upon the FORMAT command to format it. Insert diskette number one and press Enter. You'll see:

```
*** Backing up files to drive A: ***
Diskette Number: 01
```

As the diskette fills, you'll see the pathnames of files copied to it. When the disk is full, BACKUP prompts:

```
Insert backup diskette 02 in drive A:

Warning! Files in the target drive A:\ root directory will be erased
Press any key to continue . . .
```

Remove the first diskette, insert the next diskette, and press Enter. (Backup will always tell you which numbered diskette to insert next, which is why it's a good idea to number your diskettes before you start.)

Tip: Each backup diskette is given a volume label equal to its number in the backup sequence. Use the VOL command to confirm a diskette's backup number if you're in doubt.

The backup is complete when you return to the DOS prompt. Bundle the diskettes and put them away for safekeeping.

Info: If your system has more than one hard drive, then you must issue a BACKUP command for each hard drive in the above format. A batch file can be created to simplify this operation, but note that you should keep each backup diskette set for each hard drive separate. Also, label them as "Full Disk Backup #1, Drive C" etc., to avoid confusion.

The process is the same for backing up only a work subdirectory; simply specify the subdirectory with the BACKUP command. For example, to backup all subdirectories under your 1-2-3 directory, you'd use the following command:

```
BACKUP C:\123\*.* A: /S
```

To backup only a single subdirectory, simply lop off the /S switch.

The incremental backup is what you'll probably do on a daily or weekly basis. That way, only those files modified since the last backup will be copied to the backup disks. To do an incremental backup, the BACKUP command's /M switch is used:

```
BACKUP C:\*.* A: /S /M
```

The above command backs up only those files on the hard drive that have been changed or modified since the last backup. (You can use the BACKTEST program to see how many files need to be backed up, and then make an estimate of the number of disks you need.)

Label your incremental backup sets differently from the full-hard-drive backup set. After a few incremental backups, another hard-drive backup is in order. Of course, the frequency with which you backup is dependent upon how much you use your computer and how important your data is. For example, in my situation, I backup as follows:

A daily backup is made of all work subdirectories.

A weekly incremental backup is made. This catches all files changed or modified that aren't in any work subdirectories.

A monthly full-hard-drive backup is made.

At the most, a disk failure will cause me to loose a day's worth of data and a week's worth of routine changes and maintenance to the hard-disk system.

The only other interesting aspect of this routine is that I use three different backup programs: DOS's BACKUP is okay for a daily backup (it gives me time to put out the cat at the end of the day). The weekly incremental backup is done by Lotus' Magellan. Magellan stores files in a noncompressed format and builds a mini-subdirectory structure on the backup floppies. Also, unlike XCOPY, it can copy files across several diskettes. For the full-disk backup, I use PC Tools. It's fast and uses a compressed backup format, so it takes up fewer disks. Fifth Generation System's Fastback is faster, and the Norton Backup allows you to archive several drives on one disk set, so they too would be useful options, worth considering for your own system.

COMMAND: BACKUP (External)
Function: Archives files from the hard disk to floppy diskettes.
Format: BACKUP source drive switches

Source is the source filename, pathname, or a group of filenames specified with a wildcard.

Drive is a floppy-drive letter and colon. It indicates the drive to which the source files will be backed up.

Switches are the optional switches for the BACKUP command. They are:

/A adds files to an existing backup disk set. When /A is specified, the contents of the existing backup disk will not be erased; the new files will be added.

/D archives only those files created after a specified date. For example, the following command backs up all files with a date later than May 5, 1992:

```
BACKUP C:\*.* A: /S /D:5-5-92
```

/F allows you to backup to diskettes of a different size than those of the drive you're using. Since BACKUP will format new diskettes, this switch can be used to tell the FORMAT command which size to format the diskettes. For example, to backup to 720K diskettes in a 1.4M drive, you could specify /F:720.

/L creates a backup log file. /L is followed by an optional path for the log file. If a pathname isn't specified, the logfile is placed in the root directory and named BACKUP.LOG.

/M archives only files with their Archive attribute set. The Archive attribute will be reset after the backup. (This is the incremental backup switch.)

/S archives all files in all subdirectories under the source.

/T archives files created after a specified time. This switch is used with /D to narrow the field of files to be copied. For example, the following command archives all files with a date later than May 5, 1992, created after noon:

```
BACKUP C:\*.* A: /S /D:5-5-92 /T:12:00
```

Note that the /T switch must be used with the /D switch.

Note: Using the Backup Log

It's a good idea to specify the /L switch when performing a backup. That creates a backup-log file, which contains a list of all files archived by their pathnames, the backup diskette they're on by number, and the date and time of the backup.

Further, you should copy the backup log to the last backup diskette for safekeeping (as long as there's room on the diskette). If anything happens and you need to restore from the backup disk set, the backup log will help you quickly locate the file you need and confirm which diskette it's on.

The RESTORE Command

Every backup program has a lesser-known counterpart, a restore program. The hope is that the restore program will never have to be used. After all, backup is done "just in case," so when you need the restore program it means something nasty must have happened. For this reason, not much emphasis is put on restore. In fact, the major third-party backup programs traditionally have lousy restore operations (although this is starting to change).

DOS has a RESTORE command to complement its BACKUP command. Aside from the obvious restoration of a hard disk after a major disk catastrophe, RESTORE can be used in the following circumstances:

Large file copy

Subdirectory/file recovery

Old version resuscitation

BACKUP and RESTORE aren't just for file security. The BACKUP program is the only way you can copy a large program onto several floppy diskettes and move it to another computer (aside from a network or direct communications link). The RESTORE program is used to recreate the file at the destination, piecing it together from the backup diskettes.

If you ever accidentally delete a file or a complete branch of subdirectories, it's possible to undelete them at once using a recent backup diskette set. (DOS 5 has other disaster recovery tools, which are covered in Chapter 28.)

Finally, RESTORE can be used to resurrect an older version of a file that may have been replaced by a new version. This comes in handy when your client suddenly changes his mind and likes the version you showed him three weeks ago.

DOS's RESTORE command is similar to BACKUP in its format and optional switches. For example, in the ultimate disaster, you can RESTORE all files to a hard drive with the following RESTORE command:

```
RESTORE A: C:\*.* /S
```

The files are kept on backup diskettes which will be inserted into drive A. The files will be restored to drive C. The /S switch tells RESTORE to reconstruct subdirectories as necessary, filling them with proper files.

RESTORE always restores files in their original subdirectories; you cannot specify a new location for the files. For example, suppose you want to recover an older version of the ROCKET.DOC file. The file was originally backed up from C:\WORK\NASA subdirectory. You cannot use the following RESTORE command:

```
RESTORE A: C:\TEMP\ROCKET.DOC
```

There is no file with a pathname "C:\TEMP\ROCKET.DOC" on the backup diskettes. There is, however, a file "C:\WORK\NASA\ROCKET.DOC." The following RESTORE command should be used:

```
RESTORE A: C:\WORK\NASA\ROCKET.DOC
```

The RESTORE command will ask you to insert each backup diskette in order, from one through however many are necessary for it to find the proper ROCKET.DOC file. Sure, that takes time. But RESTORE wasn't design to be elegant; it was designed for "just in case."

COMMAND: RESTORE (External)

Function: Recovers files from diskettes created by the BACKUP command.

Format: RECOVER drive pathname switches

Drive is the floppy-drive letter and colon where RESTORE can locate the backup diskettes.

Pathname is the pathname of the file or group of files to be restored. (If the entire drive or a subdirectory branch needs to be restored, the optional /S switch should be added; see below.)

Switches are the optional switches for the RESTORE command. They are:

/A restores files on the backup diskettes with dates after the date specified. The following command restores all files created after Halloween, 1992:

```
RESTORE A: C:\*.* /S /A:10-31-92
```

/B restores files on the backup diskettes with dates before the date specified. The following command restores all files before Halloween, 1992:

```
RESTORE A: C:\*.* /S /B:10-31-92
```

/D causes RESTORE to display a list of files that match the specified pathname on the backup diskettes. The files will not be restored:

```
RESTORE A: C:\*.* /S /B:10-31-92 /D
```

The above command displays all files on the backup diskettes that would be restored if the /D switch were not used.

/E restores files on the backup diskettes with a time earlier than the specified time. /E is used with the /B switch to further narrow the range of files restored.

/L restores files on the backup diskettes with a time later than the specified time. /L is used with the /A switch to narrow the range of files restored.

/M restores only the original version of files that have been modified after the last backup. Essentially, this switch will undo all changes since the last incremental backup.

/N restores only files that exist on the backup diskette set but not on the hard drive. This is a great way to recover lost files or parts of the tree structure. For example, to recover the JULY tree structure from 1-2-3's subdirectory, you'd use the following RESTORE command:

```
RESTORE A: C:\123\*.* /S /N
```

/S restores all files in all subdirectories under the pathname. The /S switch will recreate subdirectories as needed.

/P causes the RESTORE command to prompt you when a file is restored over one that already exists on the hard drive, providing that file has its Read-only or Archive attribute set.

Improving System Performance

A key part of system maintenance—and hard-disk management in general—is improving system performance. Regular file maintenance, disk maintenance and optimization, and scheduled backup all contribute to improved system performance. Beyond that, you can use two special tools that come with DOS to boost your disk performance, and make file access much faster: RAMDrive and SMARTDrive.

RAMDrive is a RAM drive or electronic disk drive simulated in memory. Using the RAMDrive program, you can tell DOS to treat part of the computer's memory like a disk drive. Since the drive is made up of fast memory, the RAM drive is exceptionally fast—much quicker than the fastest hard drive.

SMARTDrive is a disk cache (pronounced "cash"). It improves disk access on your hard drive for all programs by keeping often-read information on disk in memory. Since most information is read repeatedly from disk, the cache gradually improves your disk performance the more you use your computer.

Using RAMDrive

RAMDrive is a device driver that converts part of your computer's memory into a disk drive. DOS "formats" memory, assigns it a drive letter, and then allows you to use that memory just like a disk drive. You can copy programs and files to the RAM drive, use all DOS commands on the drive (with a few exceptions), and generally treat it like another drive added to your system.

The advantage of a RAM drive is that it's as fast as memory. You can copy disk-intensive programs—such as databases and accounting software—to the RAM drive to improve their performance. Also, you can use a RAM drive to store temporary files and larger files DOS has to access in pieces to fit in memory. If you use graphics files, then storing the graphics images on a RAM drive improves the software's performance.

There are two disadvantages to a RAM drive. The first is that it uses memory—either main memory, which is precious, or any extra memory in your system, called extended or expanded memory. (The different types of memory available in a PC are covered in Chapter 26.) If you have extra memory—great! You can put it to use as a RAM drive. If you don't, then the benefits of a RAM drive dwindle.

The second disadvantage to a RAM drive is that it's temporary. Like all RAM in the computer, when you turn off the power, the contents of the RAM drive disappear. If you're only copying programs to the RAM drive and running them from there, then there's no problem; original copies of the programs still exist on the hard drive. But if you create or modify anything on the RAM drive, you must copy it back to the hard drive before you turn off the computer.

To create a RAM drive, the RAMDRIVE.SYS memory device driver is used. It's installed in your CONFIG.SYS file using the DEVICE configuration command. RAMDRIVE.SYS has the following format:

```
DEVICE=path\RAMDRIVE.SYS size sector entries [/E|/A]
```

Path is the location of RAMDRIVE.SYS, which will probably be your DOS subdirectory.

Size is the size of the RAM drive. Values for size range from 16 through 4096 for a 16K through 4 megabyte RAM drive. A 64K RAM drive is created if you don't specify a size value. Note that you must have enough memory available to create a RAM drive of a given size.

Sector is the sector size the RAM drive will use. Values for sector can be 128, 256, or 512. If you don't specify sector, a value of 512 is used. Note that you must specify a size value if sector is specified.

Entries indicates the number of root directory entries on the RAM drive. Values for entries range from 2 through 1024, with a 64 used if you don't specify anything. Note that you must specify a size and sector value if entries is specified.

If you have extended or expanded memory, you can tell RAMDRIVE.SYS to locate the RAM drive there by specifying the /E or /A switch, respectively. (/E is for extended memory, /A is for expanded.) If neither switch is specified, the RAM drive is created in DOS's conventional memory—which subtracts from the amount of RAM you have for running programs.

When DOS creates the RAM drive it assigns it a letter one higher than the highest logical drive in your system. For example, if you have a hard drive C, the first RAMDRIVE.SYS command in CONFIG.SYS creates the RAM drive D. A second RAMDRIVE.SYS command will create RAM drive E, and so on.

Creating a RAM Drive

The following command in CONFIG.SYS creates a 64K RAM drive in Extended memory on an 80286 or later PC:

```
DEVICE=C:\DOS\RAMDRIVE.SYS /E
```

After the changes are saved to CONFIG.SYS, the system is reset. As it boots, DOS assigns 64K of extended memory to the RAM drive and displays something like the following:

```
Microsoft RAMDrive version 3.06 virtual disk D:
Disk size: 64k
Sector size: 512 bytes
Allocation unit: 1 sectors
Directory entries: 64
```

Drive D is now a usable RAM drive. It's been created using RAMDrive's default values: a 64K drive with 512 byte sectors and room for 64 files in the root directory.

Putting a RAM Drive to Work

RAM Drives have many uses, but in order to get the most from them you must integrate the RAM drive into your system. This usually involves some extra work in AUTOEXEC.BAT, but not much.

The following are examples of things you can do with a RAM drive to improve your system's performance:

Copy disk-intensive programs to the RAM drive

Keep an eye on your hard-disk-drive light. If it flashes quite a bit as you run a program, then you've found a disk-intensive piece of software. Discover how much space the program occupies (use the DIR command) and create a RAM drive large enough for it. In AUTOEXEC.BAT, copy that program and all its files (or as many as will fit) up into the RAM drive. Modify the batch file that runs the program so that the program is run from the RAM drive.

In most cases, your disk-intensive programs may not fit, or they may even recommend against using a RAM drive. Check the manual for any advice pro or con on the subject. Some manuals are extremely helpful and will tell you which files to place on the RAM drive and how to modify the program's setup to integrate in the RAM drive.

Copy batch files to the RAM drive

This is a simple trick, using usually the minimum size for a RAM drive. Batch files run quicker when copied to a RAM drive—and the RAM drive letter is easy to put into your search path. The following creates a 16K RAM drive well suited to storing batch files:

```
DEVICE=C:\DOS\RAMDRIVE.SYS 16 128 144
```

Since batch files are each typically less than 100 bytes, a 16K RAM drive gives you room for over 150 batch files. Since batch files are so small, a sector size of 128 bytes is used, which improves the disk's efficiency. Also, to fit more batch files on the disk, an value of 144 is used for the number of root directory entries. To put the RAM drive in extended memory, specify the /E switch above; specify the /A switch to put it into expanded memory.

The following commands could be added to AUTOEXEC.BAT to move your batch files to the RAM drive:

```
ECHO Moving batch files . . .
XCOPY C:\BATCH\*.* D:\
PATH C:\DOS;D:\
```

Note how the PATH command includes the RAM drive with the batch files? This all works very well and with great speed improvement. Just remember to create and edit the batch files on the hard drive, and then copy them to the RAM drive.

Don't forget that you can have more than one RAM drive on your system. The above 16K RAM drive isn't enough for other applications. However, you can create two or three, each of different sizes, for programs that need them.

Assign the RAM drive as a temporary or overflow file directory

Both DOS and Windows can use a RAM drive as their Temporary Files directory. Some programs, such as Ventura Publisher, can use the RAM drive for its overflow files.

A RAM drive download directory

Communications programs don't run more efficiently on a RAM drive, but if you download files you can specify a RAM drive as your download directory. This has an added bonus in that most downloaded files are in a compressed format. Decompressing the files on the RAM drive works more quickly than on a hard drive. If you want the program, copy it into your hard-drive structure; otherwise leave it on the RAM drive, and it will erase itself when the system resets.

JOINing a RAM drive

Don't forget that you can JOIN a RAM drive to become part of your subdirectory structure. The following JOIN command attaches the RAM drive D as a subdirectory RAM off the root directory of drive C:

```
JOIN D: C:\RAM
```

What is a Disk Cache?

A disk cache is storage place in memory. The caching software duplicates information read from disk, placing it in the copy cache memory. When an application wants to read the disk again, the caching software checks to see if that information is already in cache memory. If so, the information is quickly read from memory, which is faster than disk. Because most disk reads are redundant, after a time the cache will greatly improve its disk access time.

The advantages to a disk cache are that it speeds up all disk access. While a RAM drive is only fast when you're using it, you're always using a disk cache when you're using your hard drive. Also, since the cache always contains a copy of information already on disk, if the power goes you don't lose anything. (RAM drives disappear if the power goes).

The main disadvantage to a cache is that it eats up memory. DOS's SMARTDrive disk cache can only use expanded or extended memory, so if you lack either, that too is a disadvantage. And some programs just don't like disk caches; SMARTDrive appears to be fairly compatible, but if after using it for a time you notice some programs seize, then it's incompatible and you should remove it.

Using SMARTDrive

There are many disk caching programs available, but the one that comes with DOS is SMARTDrive. The SMARTDrive program, SMARTDRV.SYS, is installed using the DEVICE configuration command in your CONFIG.SYS file. SMARTDRV.SYS has the following format:

```
DEVICE=path\SMARTDRV.SYS max min /A
```

Path is the location of SMARTDRV.SYS, most likely your DOS subdirectory.

Max is the size of the cache in kilobytes. Values for max range from 128 through 8192 for a 128K through 8 megabyte cache. If max isn't specified, a 256K cache is created.

Min is the minimum size for the cache. Values for min range from zero though the value specified for max. Why min? Some programs (presently only Windows) can squeeze down the cache size to make more room for themselves. If you don't want this to happen, specify the same values for both max and min.

/A is used to create the cache in expanded memory. If /A isn't specified, the cache is created in extended memory. This means that if you have an 8088 PC with no expanded memory, you cannot use the SMARTDrive program.

Unlike RAMDrive, you only need to specify one SMARTDrive command in your CONFIG.SYS File. The following command creates a 256K disk cache in extended memory:

```
DEVICE=C:\DOS\SMARTDRV.SYS
```

When you reset the system, DOS tells you that the cache has been installed:

```
Microsoft SMARTDrive Disk Cache version 3.13
   Cache size: 256K in Extended Memory
   Room for 30 tracks of 17 sectors each
   Minimum cache size will be OK
```

The only way you can really tell the cache is at work is by using your system. Pull a directory once or twice, or just start using the computer for a while. After a time, you'll notice that the system appears to be running normally, but the hard-drive light isn't flashing as much. And everything will be a lot faster.

Tip: If memory is tight, consider using a cache over using a RAM drive. A 256K (or 512K if you can spare it) cache improves all disk performance; a 256K RAM drive can only go so far and do so much.

Summary

System maintenance is about disk, subdirectory, and file management. Deleting unused files, writing batch files to prepare and run applications, optimization, and improving system performance are all central to system maintenance.

Batch files can be used with DOS to run your applications, perform common chores, and to do some things DOS can't—such as move files.

Moving a subdirectory branch is known as pruning and grafting. Under DOS, this can be done by copying the branch and then deleting the original. Most DOS shell programs have easier methods to accomplish pruning and grafting.

The XCOPY command is like a super COPY command. XCOPY copies files all at once, rather than one at a time. Using XCOPY's many switches, you can be selective about the files copied, and even copy files in subdirectories under the specified directory.

The CHKDSK is used to check your disk. A summary of disk information is displayed, along with any lost chains or clusters. The lost chains or clusters can be deleted with the CHKDSK /F command. When a file or wildcard is specified, CHKDSK will tell you if it has been fragmented and how many pieces it's in.

All files on disk should be examined regularly for fragmentation. A third-party tool must be purchased for this purpose, and the disk must be regularly defragmented.

The BACKUP command is used to archive files on the hard drive for storage on a set of diskettes. Backing up the hard drive, whether by BACKUP or a third-party program, is something that should be done regularly.

The RESTORE command is used to restore archived files from floppy diskettes to the hard drive. RESTORE can be used to recover earlier versions of files, undelete files and subdirectories accidentally erased, or in case of total hard-disk recovery.

The RAMDrive program that comes with DOS creates a RAM drive in memory. You can use a RAM drive to improve the performance of programs copied there. Note that RAM drives are volatile, like all RAM. If files are modified or created on a RAM drive, they should be copied back to the hard drive for permanent storage.

The SMARTDrive program that comes with DOS is used to create a disk cache. Disk caches use memory to improve all hard drive performance. Unlike a RAM drive, the disk cache contains a copy of information already stored on disk. When an application needs to access that information again, it's read from the cache memory instead of disk, improving disk performance.

PART FIVE

Advanced DOS

Advanced DOS isn't as scary as it seems. Instead, consider the subject as an exploration of some powerful, yet seldom used or little-understood DOS topics. DOS is bursting with potential, just waiting for you to exploit it. The chapters in this part of the book introduce you to those "advanced topics," each of which will let you squeeze more power from your system, and help you get the most from DOS.

Chapter 22 covers the DOSKEY command, a keyboard enhancer that extends what can be done at the DOS prompt. Chapter 23 goes over the ANSI.SYS file, which gives extra power to DOS's screen, keyboard, batch files, and the DOS prompt. Chapter 24 is about advanced file manipulation and uses DOS's device I/O commands. Chapter 25 covers DOS's program editor, DEBUG. Chapter 26 is about your PC's memory and DOS 5's memory management, and Chapter 27 discusses Windows and the Extended DOS environments.

CHAPTER 22

Controlling the Command Line

The command line is your communications link with DOS. It's also one of DOS's weak spots; typing a proper command is an exacting form of communication. DOS offers ways to enhance your command-line abilities beyond the basic type-and-backspace you might be using now. There is real power waiting in the command line, and DOS is more than happy to let you plunder it.

This chapter answers the following questions:

- What are the standard DOS editing keys?

- How does DOSKEY improve command-line editing?

- What is the command history?

- How can more than one command be issued at a single DOS prompt?

- How do DOSKEY's macros work?

- What are the limitations of DOSKEY

- How can I easily access foreign-language characters from the keyboard?

Command Line Editing

Typing on the command line is how you communicate with DOS; you type commands, and then press Enter to send the commands to the command interpreter, COMMAND.COM. If it understands what you type, then those instructions are carried out. Otherwise you see an error message such as "Bad command or filename."

If you make a typing mistake, you can use the backspace key to backup and erase. If you've totally flubbed it, press the Esc key and start over. In addition to those two keys, DOS gives you a few (albeit feeble) command-line editing keys. Few users bother with these special keys. One reason you may not is that when you edit the command line you can't see what you're editing. Another may be that you don't know about the special keys or what they can do.

DOS's Standard Editing Keys

The command line isn't totally dumb. DOS remembers the last command you typed. It's stored in a special place in memory called the template. As you type in a new command, you can take advantage of the characters stored in the template to make your typing easier. True, this isn't as nice as having a mini word-processor at the DOS prompt, but it's better than nothing.

On your PC, type the following command at the DOS prompt:

```
DIR *.* /W /O
```

The command displays all files in the current directory—sorted, and in the wide format. But more importantly, as soon as you pressed Enter, DOS stored that command in the template. To view the template again, you can press the F3 key:

```
C:\>DIR *.* /W /O
```

Pressing the Backspace key appears to erase the template, but in fact, it simply moves the cursor back one character in the template. Press the Backspace key three times, and then press the Right arrow key three times:

```
C:\>DIR *.* /W_
```

```
C:\>DIR *.* /W /O_
```

The Right arrow key works like the F3 key, but it displays characters already in the template one key at a time. The F1 key works the same way. Press the Backspace key four times. Type A. Press F3.

448

```
C:\>DIR *.* /_

C:\>DIR *.* /A_

C:\>DIR *.* /A /O_
```

As you type new characters at the DOS prompt, they replace those already in the template. Above, you backspaced to the W, typed an A in its place, and then pressed F3 to complete the template. Press Enter.

Info: Pressing Enter always saves a new command line in the template. Pressing Esc cancels any changes made and allows you to start over again.

The problem with this type of command-line editing is that you can't see what you're doing—you're in the dark! The template is always in memory, but you can't see it at the prompt to know what you're editing.

Press F3 again. Press the F5 key.

```
C:\>DIR *.* /A /O@

    _
```

The F5 key records all changes made on the command line into the template, and then gives you a new command line to start editing. It works like the Enter key does, but it doesn't send the command to DOS. You can now edit the command and see what you're doing on the line above.

Press the F1 key or right arrow four times. Press the Insert or Ins key. This allows you to insert characters into the template. Type a backslash, \. Press the F3 key.

```
C:\>  DIR *.* /A /O@
      DIR _

C:\>  DIR *.* /A /O@
      DIR \_

C:\>  DIR *.* /A /O@
      DIR \*.* /A /O_
```

449

Press Enter.

The F2 key is used to search for a specific character in the template. You press F2 and a character, and then DOS displays the template up to that character. Press F2 and then A.

```
C:\>DIR *.* /_
```

Press the F1 key to move forward one character, and then press Insert and type S. Press F3, and then Enter.

```
C:\>DIR *.* /A_
```

```
C:\>DIR *.* /AS_
```

```
C:\>DIR *.* /AS /O_
```

At the next DOS prompt, type F2 and A again:

```
C:\>DIR *.* /_
```

The F4 key works like F2, but it deletes all characters in the template between the cursor's position and the character you type. Press F4, then type O. Then press F3 to display the remainder of the template (only the letter O in this case):

```
C:\>DIR *.* /_
```

```
C:\>DIR *.* /O_
```

You've sliced out all characters between the A and the O in the original command. Another way to do this would be to use the Delete or Del key. The problem with that is that you can't see what you're deleting to know how many times to press Delete. (You could first press F3 then F5 to see what you're doing.)

Of all these keys, the one you'll use most often is F3. But with the addition of the DOSKEY command, these function keys—which were not that widely used before—are really behind the times. Before discussing DOSKEY, the following table summarizes the basic command-line editing keys DOS uses:

Key	Function
F1	Display the next character in the template
Right arrow	Display the next character in the template
F2, char	Display the template up to the character char
F3	Display the remaining characters in the template
F4, char	Delete characters in the template up to the character char
F5	Store the current line as the template; start over
F6	Ctrl-Z character
Backspace	Move back one character in the template
Left arrow	Move back one character in the template
Delete/Del	Delete the next character in the template
Insert/Ins	Insert characters in the template
Esc	Cancel the line/changes, start over
Enter	End input

Info: Internally, DOS uses a function called Buffered Input for reading a line of text. This function is used at the DOS prompt, in the Edlin text editor, and in the DEBUG program. In fact, nearly any time you need to type in a line of text at a DOS prompt, the Buffered Input function is being used. Because of that, the standard editing keys described in this section apply in those situations.

Using DOSKEY

DOSKEY is a program that expands your editing power at the DOS prompt. It gives you something close to word-processor editing abilities and—ta da!—you can see what you edit as you edit it. If that wasn't enough, with DOSKEY you can type more than you can on DOS command on the command line, recall previous command lines for editing, and create special DOSKEY macros. All this starts by running the DOSKEY program, which is usually done in your AUTOEXEC.BAT file.

The DOSKEY Command

To take advantage of DOSKEY's many features, you must first install it. DOSKEY is a memory-resident program that attaches itself to DOS, augmenting the power of the command line.

Info: Although DOSKEY augments the power of the command line, its editing keys are unavailable in DOS programs such as Edlin and DEBUG; with those programs you must still use the basic-function key editing commands.

The format for starting DOSKEY is as follows:

```
pathname\DOSKEY /reinstall /bufsize=size [/insert|/overstrike]
```

Pathname is the location of DOSKEY on your hard drive, which will usually be your DOS subdirectory.

/Reinstall is optional. When specified, a new memory-resident copy of DOSKEY will be loaded and the old one disabled. This can be used, for example, when running a COMMAND.COM or DOS window in a program such as Windows or DESQview. /reinstall resets all DOSKEY's options and clears its buffer.

/Bufsize is used to set the size of DOSKEY's command history and macro buffer. Normally the buffer is set at 512 bytes. Using the size parameter after /bufsize, you can set the buffer to any size from 256 bytes up to some ridiculous amount (but not too large, say, over 4096 or 4K).

/Insert and /overstrike set the initial editing mode for DOSKEY. You can specify only one or the other, with /overstrike being the default. When /insert is specified, new characters are always inserted into the command line. (Of course, you can use the Insert or Ins key while editing to toggle between insert and overstrike.)

The following command installs DOSKEY in your AUTOEXEC.BAT file:

```
DOSKEY /INSERT
```

If you wanted to have a large buffer, you may want to use the following command:

```
DOSKEY /BUFSIZE=1024 /INSERT
```

Info: If you want to save the 4K of RAM which DOSKEY uses in memory, consider using the LOADHIGH command to start DOSKEY. LOADHIGH is covered in Chapter 26.

After making the changes to AUTOEXEC.BAT, you can reset the system to load DOSKEY. Or, since DOSKEY can be typed on the command line, issue the same command at the DOS prompt. Either way, you'll see the following displayed:

```
DOSKEY Installed.
```

After DOSKEY's initial message is shown, you're ready to try out DOSKEY's editing commands.

Note: If you type DOSKEY again, DOSKEY will not re-load and the above message will not be displayed. DOSKEY is smart enough to locate itself in memory and will not consume extra RAM by installing twice. However, if you start DOSKEY with the /reinstall switch, it will load itself into memory twice.

Editing the Command Line with DOSKEY

Command-line editing with DOSKEY is intuitive to anyone who's used a word processor. The best thing is that you can actually see what you're editing; the cursor slides underneath the characters, not deleting them as you move left or right.

The following table summarizes the basic DOSKEY editing keys now available:

Key	Function
Left arrow	Moves the cursor left one character
Right arrow	Moves the cursor right one character
Ctrl-Left arrow	Moves the cursor left one word
Ctrl-Right arrow	Moves the cursor right one word
Home	Moves the cursor to the start of the command
End	Moves the cursor to the end of the command
Ctrl-End	Delete from the cursor to the end of the command
Ctrl-Home	Delete from the cursor to the start of the command
Backspace	Deletes the character to the left of the cursor
Del	Deletes the current character
Ins	Toggles insert/overwrite (overwrite mode is always active unless DOSKEY was started with the /insert switch)

Note that the regular function keys, F1 through F5, are also in effect while DOSKEY is active. There are two visual exceptions: F5 still records changes to the template, but does not display an @ (At Sign) and drop down one line, and pressing Esc erases the line.

Type the following command at the DOS prompt (substitute the proper name for your DOS subdirectory if it's not C:\DOS as below):

```
DIR C:\DOS\*.EXE /ON
```

Press Enter. Once the command is done, press F3 to redisplay it. Now press the Home and End keys, play with the left and right arrows, and then try Ctrl-Left and Ctrl-Right. The cursor moves gracefully under each character, allowing you to see the command as you edit.

Replace the EXE in the command with COM: Position the cursor under EXE and type COM. If overwrite mode is active, the COM replaces EXE. If the insert mode is active, then press Delete three times to delete EXE. Keep the cursor after the M in COM and press Enter.

Info: The cursor can be anywhere on the command line when you're using DOSKEY; the entire command is sent to DOS as you see it.

Issuing Multiple Commands

A special key you can use in DOSKEY is the command-line separator, Ctrl-T, which shows up as the paragraph symbol on the screen: [¶]. You can use Ctrl-T to put more than one DOS command on a command line.

Type the following, pressing Ctrl-T where you see [¶] below:

```
CLS [¶] DIR
```

Press Enter and two commands are issued, one after the other. (The spaces around the Ctrl-T aren't required; you could have just typed CLS [¶] DIR, but it's not as easy to read.)

Ctrl-T can come in quite handy, but keep in mind it's not like a batch file. For one, you can't turn ECHO OFF when you issue more than one command. As an example, here's a handy way to see all program files in a directory:

```
DIR *.COM [¶] DIR *.EXE [¶] DIR *.BAT
```

But the end result is sloppy; while you only need to press Enter once, the net effect is still as if you entered all three commands at three DOS prompts.

Another raindrop to dim Ctrl-T's candle is that it won't work in a batch file. When a batch file sends a command line to DOS, it circumvents DOSKEY. So a Ctrl-T character in a batch file will be treated as an error.

To stop a multiple command issued with Ctrl-T separators, you must press Ctrl-C once for each command. For example, if the above command were typed, you would press Ctrl-C once to cancel the first DIR command, and then you'd need to type Ctrl-C a second time to cancel the second DIR command, and finally a you'd type Ctrl-C a third time to cancel the last one.

The Command Line History

Without DOSKEY installed, DOS only keeps a copy of the last DOS command in the template. But with DOSKEY installed, a record, which are stored in an area known as the DOSKEY history buffer, is kept of all the commands you type.

Info: The history buffer is 512 bytes in size. It's also shared with any DOSKEY macros you create, so the number of command lines you can put into the buffer is limited. Using the /bufsize parameter, you can change the size of the buffer—but only when you first start DOSKEY.

To recall a previous command from the history buffer, you use the Up Arrow key. Pressing the Up Arrow key once is the same as pressing F3. But press the Up Arrow again and you'll see the next previous command. Keep pressing Up and you'll scroll through all the previous commands, each of them being displayed on the command line and ready for you to edit and re-use.

Pressing the Down Arrow key moves you down through the list. To move to the first command quickly, use the PgUp key; PgDn moves you to the end of the list.

To all the command lines you've typed, enter the following:

```
DOSKEY /HISTORY
```

Tip: The /HISTORY switch can be abbreviated as /H.

You'll see something like the following:

```
DIR C:\DOS\*.EXE /ON
DIR C:\DOS\*.COM /ON
CLS [¶] DIR
DIR *.COM [¶] DIR *.EXE [¶] DIR *.BAT
DOSKEY /HISTORY
```

To see the command history you can also press the F7 key, which has the advantage of being a "hot key" and showing you line numbers for reference. Press F7:

```
1: DIR C:\DOS\*.EXE /ON
2: DIR C:\DOS\*.COM /ON
3: CLS [¶] DIR
4: DIR *.COM [¶] DIR *.EXE [¶] DIR *.BAT
5: DOSKEY /HISTORY
```

If more than one screenful of commands is displayed, DOSKEY even uses its own "more" prompt; press any key to see the next screenful.

You an recall any of these commands quickly, without having to use the Up or Down Arrow keys. There are two shortcuts—the F8 and F9 keys:

The F8 key is a quick-memory search key. Type CL on the command line and then press the F8 key:

```
CLS [¶] DIR
```

F8 uses whatever text you've typed at the DOS prompt as a search parameter. It will match those characters with whatever DOS command it finds. Keep pressing F8 to scan for additional matching commands. To issue that command, press Enter.

The F9 key allows you to select a previous command by number. Press F9:

```
Line number:
```

Now type the number of a previous DOS command. That command line then appears at the DOS prompt (replacing "Line number:"). You can now optionally edit the line, or just press Enter to send the command to DOS. Press Esc if you wish to cancel.

Tip: To use F9, press F7 first and then F9. Remember that after entering the number you have the option of editing the command or pressing Enter to issue it.

457

The following are the cursor and function keys you can use to manipulate DOSKEY's command history:

Key	Function
Up Arrow	Recall previous command line
Down Arrow	Recall next command line
PgUp	Recall the first command line
PgDn	Recall the last command line
F7	List command line history with line numbers
Alt-F7	Erase command line history
F8	Scan history for matching text
F9	Select command by number

As you enter more DOS commands, the command history will fill. Older commands will be removed from the list to make room for new ones. To delete the entire list, press Alt-F7. This frees up the memory used by the command history and allows you to start over. It's also a form of security in that other users can't see what you've been doing or examine passwords once you've cleared the command history.

Tip: You can easily create batch files using the command history. This is a multistep process: First you clear the command history. Second, you type all the commands you'd normally type in the batch file. Third, you use I/O redirection to create the batch file as follows:

```
DOSKEY /HISTORY > DOSHIST.BAT
```

Note that you cannot use I/O redirection with the F7 key, therefore DOSKEY is used with its /history switch.

Further editing is required, for example, to insert the initial @ECHO OFF, as well as to add GOTOs and IF commands as necessary. Refer to Chapter 24 for more information on I/O redirection.

DOSKEY Macros

"Macro" is short for macroinstruction. It means one item—a word or command—that represents many. Macros are shorthand, but they're not batch files. A batch file is a program, a collection of commands complete with some programming (GOTOs, IFs, FORs, etc.). A DOSKEY macro is simply a one-word command to which you can assign a complex DOS command.

You create DOSKEY macros using the following format, similar to the SET command:

```
DOSKEY name=command
```

Name is the name assigned to the macro. It can be from one to any number of characters, except for those forbidden in a filename. Note that that name can be the name of a DOS command or program name if you like.

Command is the DOS command line, command, or program to assign to name, complete with whatever optional parameters are required. Note that some optional parameters must be specified using special characters, which are listed in a table that follows.

When you use DOSKEY to create a macro, it does not load and run a second copy of the DOSKEY program. Instead, the name and command are transferred into DOSKEY's buffer. Keep in mind the size of the buffer is limited, and it can only be set by using the /bufsize parameter when you first start DOSKEY.

You must use DOSKEY in the above format to create each of your DOSKEY macros. This means several commands must be issued to create several macros, which is a job best done in your AUTOEXEC.BAT file. (The macro-creating commands must be specified after the initial command that starts DOSKEY.)

With DOSKEY installed, type the following:

```
DOSKEY D=DIR /W /O /P
```

This creates the D macro. The D macro is assigned to the DIR command, displayed in the wide format, sorted alphabetically, with a pause after every page. At the DOS prompt, type D and press Enter.

It you can still see it, note how the D macro was immediately followed by another DOS prompt and how the contents of the macro were automatically typed. That's how the macros work; they are only a place holder. After you type the macro, DOS expands it to the full command at the next DOS prompt.

Here's a handy macro to create. Enter:

```
DOSKEY H=DOSKEY /HISTORY
```

Now H is equal to the DOSKEY /HISTORY command.

You can create a DOSKEY macro with the same name as a DOS command. The limitation is that the macro only works when it's the first item after the DOS prompt; DOSKEY cannot translate macros that have spaces or any other characters before them. Type the following:

```
DOSKEY PROMPT=PROMPT $$p$$g
```

The PROMPT macro is equal to the PROMPT command, which is actually followed by pg—the standard DOS prompt. (The double dollar signs will be explained in a moment.) Edit the above line using your own system-prompt definition if different from above. Remember to specify two dollar signs for every one in your PROMPT definition.

Tip: If you make a typo or some other mistake, then remember to use the Up Arrow key to recall the previous line for editing.

Now typing PROMPT at the DOS prompt will change your system prompt back to the default. But if you type PROMPT with a space before it, then DOS runs the original PROMPT command. To wit:

```
C:\>PROMPT
C:\>PROMPT $p$g

C:\> PROMPT

C>
```

Above, the first PROMPT command is interpreted as the DOSKEY macro, and the following line expands the macro. The second PROMPT command, preceded by two spaces, is treated as the standard PROMPT command, changing the system prompt back to the boring drive letter-greater-than sign. Type PROMPT again (without any preceding spaces) to restore your system prompt.

The reason for the double dollar signs is that the DOSKEY macro command works similarly to the PROMPT command. If you define a macro (or prompt) with certain characters, notably |, >, or <, DOS interprets those characters as its I/O redirection commands (covered in Chapter 24). To use those and other special characters in a macro definition, substitute the dollar-sign special characters as listed in the following table.

Macro command	Represents
$B	|, pipe character
$G	>, greater-than character
$L	<, less-than character
$T	, Ctrl-T character (command separator)
$$	$, dollar sign
$1	Through
$9	Command line parameters
$*	All parameters

Note the special commands, $1 through $9 and $*. These work like command-line variables in batch files. When the macro runs, they expand out into any parameters typed after the macro. For example, the following macro is used to shorten the FORMAT command to one letter, F:

```
DOSKEY F=FORMAT $*
```

The $* represents all items typed after F at the DOS prompt. They'll be passed as one giant string to the following line, where F expands into the FORMAT command. The $1 through $9 characters can be used similarly to represent the first through ninth items typed after the command.

To see a current list of the macros you have created, use the DOSKEY command with its optional /macros switch:

```
C:\>DOSKEY /MACROS
D=DIR /w /o /p
H=doskey /history
PROMPT=prompt $$p$$g
F=format $*
```

Tip: The /MACROS switch can be abbreviated as /M.

Tip: Once you've created your macros, use the I/O redirection trick to create a batch file that automatically creates your macros. For example, type the following:

```
DOSKEY /MACROS > SETMACRO.BAT
```

Edit the file to place DOSKEY and a space at the start of each line, as well as to add the initial @ECHO OFF. The resulting file can be incorporated into your AUTOEXEC.BAT file, or it can work as a stand-alone batch file.

Macros will stay in memory if you erase them individually or all at once. To erase an individual macro, the same format is used as when you remove an environment variable. For example:

```
DOSKEY PROMPT=
```

The above command erases the PROMPT macro.

To delete all the macros at once, press Alt-F10. That zaps all the macros from memory—without so much as a warning. So use Alt-F10 carefully.

There are only two drawbacks to using DOSKEY macros: The first is that the macro must always be the first item after the DOS prompt. No spaces or other characters can come before the macro, otherwise DOS will interpret what you type to be the same as if you weren't using the macro.

This comes as a major disappointment, especially when you consider how fun the following macro could be:

```
DOSKEY ALL=*.*
```

Unfortunately, the ALL macro cannot be used, as in "DIR ALL"; because it's not the first element after the DOS prompt, it's not expanded.

Secondly, DOSKEY macros will not work in batch files. True, you can create DOSKEY macros in batch files. But the batch-file interpreter does not pass its commands through DOSKEY and therefore the macros won't be executed.

Info: Additional material on getting the most from your keyboard can be found in Chapter 23 on ANSI.SYS.

Going International

Starting with version 5, DOS has really taken on an international flavor. There are many commands that deal with configuring DOS for use in non-English speaking, non-American countries.

Most of the international DOS commands deal with code pages. These are software character sets which can be used instead of the 128 Extended-ASCII characters. They allow PC users in foreign countries access to their own unique, non-Roman characters.

DOS was configured properly for your language and country when you first ran the SETUP program. However, there are times when you may need to access some of these international characters—for example, when writing a report in Spanish, or working on an assignment in French. This is possible with DOS using the KEYB command, which gives you quick access to special characters without your having to memorize oddball code values and then manually punch in the characters using the Alt key and your keypad.

The KEYB Command

The KEYB command allows you to use a keyboard containing keys specific to certain languages. The format of the KEYB command in this instance is:

```
KEYB kb
```

Kb is the code for the keyboard you want to define. It's a two-letter code representing the country or region whose keyboard you want to use. (A full list is provided in Appendix C.)

Info: The KEYB command is memory resident, taking up some 6K of space. Refer to Chapter 26 for information on using KEYB with the LOADHIGH command to save on memory.

For example, suppose you're working in Spanish and need access to special Spanish-language characters. The following command loads in a Spanish keyboard layout:

```
KEYB LA
```

"LA" stands for Latin America—not Los Angeles. After typing the above command, you'll notice a few of the keys seem out of place. Pressing the semicolon/colon key produces the ñ key. The left bracket key is now a prefix key; press it and then the letter A and you see á .

To switch back to the standard keyboard, press Ctrl-Alt-F2. Switching back to the keyboard defined by the KEYB command is done with Ctrl-Alt-F1.

The Ctrl-Alt-F7 combination is used to enter "typewriter mode." In that mode, the keyboard layout will resemble the typewriter layout used in the country defined by the KEYB command. For Latin America, the semicolon key becomes the ñ key, which is where it sits on the standard Spanish typewriter.

COMMAND: KEYB (Extern)
               Function: Defines another keyboard layout for use in DOS.
               Format: KEYB kb codepage pathname /E /ID

Without any options, KEYB displays the two-letter code for the keyboard layout you're using, along with code page information.

Kb is a two-letter code, representing the country, language, or region of a keyboard layout you want to install.

Codepage is an optional code-page value for KEYB to use.

Pathname is the full pathname for the KEYBOARD.SYS file on your system, or a similar file containing keyboard definitions.

/E only required if you're using the Enhanced-101 keyboard with an older, 8088 model PC.

/ID is used to specify the code value for a foreign-language keyboard on a PC. This is a hardware keyboard that's used in another country such as the U.K., France, or Italy. /ID is followed by a colon and the keyboard's three-digit ID number.

Values for kb, codepage, and /ID are in Appendix C.

Setting up a Code Page

If you wish to take advantage of some of the interesting and useful foreign-language characters in the various code pages, you can use the following commands to set them up:

```
COUNTRY
NLSFUNC
CHCP
```

COUNTRY is a CONFIG.SYS configuration command. It prepares DOS for use with a code page, as well as with country-specific information, such as the format for the date and time, currency symbol, and alphabetic sorting order. (The format for the COUNTRY configuration command is given in Chapter 19).

Info: In case you're interested, these are among a few of the items the COUNTRY configuration command sets for DOS:

Date Format

Time Format

Date separator

Time separator

Currency symbol

Currency symbol precedes or follows amount

Space before or after currency symbol

Thousands separator

Decimal separator

Number of decimal places

Data list separator symbol

Alphabetical sorting order

The following configuration command in CONFIG.SYS will set up the computer to work in Italian:

```
COUNTRY=039,437,C:\DOS\COUNTRY.SYS
```

The code for Italy is 039, the code page is 438, and the COUNTRY.SYS file is assumed to be located in the C:\DOS directory.

The next step is the NLSFUNC command. It's a memory-resident National Language Support program. You follow NLSFUNC with the name of the country support file, which is usually the COUNTRY.SYS file that comes with DOS:

```
NLSFUNC C:\DOS\COUNTRY.SYS
```

Once that's loaded into memory, you can use the CHCP (Change Code Page) command to switch to another code page (the one defined with the COUNTRY command in CONFIG.SYS).

By itself, CHCP displays the current code page in use:

```
C:\>CHCP
Active code page: 437
```

Following CHCP with another code-page number directs DOS to use the characters in that code page as the active Extended-ASCII character set. For example, the Italian code pages are 437 and 850. To switch to the 850 code page, the following command is used:

```
CHCP 850
```

If this seems like a lot of work and pre-set, well, it is! Even after all that, your hardware may not allow another code page to be loaded into video memory. If this is the case, loading NLSFUNC before running COMMAND.COM may solve the problem. Use the INSTALL configuration command in CONFIG.SYS to load NLSFUNC.EXE. (This is one of those rare instances under DOS 5 when INSTALL is necessary.)

Note that not all applications may pay heed to the newly defined code page. Your printer may not support a code page, either. The MODE command can be used to load a code page into an IBM-compatible printer (refer to Chapter 20).

Summary

DOS uses the first five function keys as the standard DOS editing keys at the DOS prompt, in EDLIN and in DEBUG. The keys edit a template, which contains a copy of the previous command. They are:

F1—Move forward one character in the template

F2—Search and display up to the indicated character

F3—Display the remaining characters in the template

F4—Delete up to the indicated character

F5—Save the template and start over

DOSKEY is used to augment DOS's own feeble command-line editing skills. On the first level, DOSKEY lets you edit the command line as if it were a mini word-processor.

You can issue multiple commands on the same command line by separating them with the Ctrl-T character. Each command will then be reissued at its own DOS prompt. Note that this technique will not work in batch files.

DOSKEY maintains a command history—a list of all previously typed command lines. You can recall a command from the list using the Arrow keys; F7 displays the list; F8 searches the list; and F9 fetches a command line when you specify a line number.

You can create macros with DOSKEY, which allow you to abbreviate common or complex DOS commands using simple words. Note that DOSKEY's macros cannot be used in batch files.

The KEYB command is used to remap your keyboard for more effective use when typing in foreign languages.

To take further advantage of "international DOS," you can use the COUNTRY configuration command, the NLSFUNC and CHCP commands.

CHAPTER 23

Using ANSI.SYS

ANSI.SYS is an interesting, yet often overlooked, device driver included with DOS. The device it drives is the console (CON), your screen, and keyboard. ANSI.SYS gives you new control over the screen, the cursor position, screen color and graphics mode, and it lets you redefine keys on the keyboard. With the ANSI command ANSI.SYS you can spice up boring old batch files and dull system prompts.

This chapter answers the following questions:

- How can DOS access the ANSI screen and keyboard commands?

- What is an escape sequence?

- How are ANSI commands sent to ANSI.SYS?

- What can ANSI commands do with the DOS prompt?

- Which ANSI commands can be used in a file to move the cursor?

- Which ANSI commands work in a batch file to change the color?

- How does ANSI redefine characters on the keyboard?

- How can ANSI make DOS more useful?

Installing ANSI.SYS

DOS doesn't automatically come with ANSI commands installed. You must setup the ANSI.SYS driver in order to take advantage of the neat things it offers. This is done by installing the ANSI.SYS device driver using the DEVICE configuration command in CONFIG.SYS. The format is:

```
DEVICE=pathnameANSI.SYS /K /L /SCREENSIZE /X
```

Pathname is the directory—typically your DOS subdirectory—in which ANSI.SYS is located.

/K is an optional switch used to maintain compatibility with the configuration command, SWITCHES=/K (see Chapter 19). /K suppresses ANSI.SYS's monitoring of keys on the Enhanced 101 keyboard that don't exist on earlier models. Only specify this switch if you're using the SWITCHES configuration command.

/L is an optional switch that forces ANSI.SYS to restore the number of rows and columns on the screen after an application quits. This switch should only be specified if you're using the MODE command to change the number of rows and columns on the screen.

/SCREENSIZE is used to set the physical size of your screen. It's followed by a row and column value in the following format:

```
/SCREENSIZE:(row,column)
```

The default values for row and column are 25 and 80, respectively. Note that /SCREENSIZE can be abbreviated to just /S.

/X is an optional switch that allows you to redefine duplicate keys on the Enhanced 101 keyboard. The duplicate keys are the Arrow keys and cursor-movement keys between the typewriter keys and numeric keypad. When the /X switch is specified, you can use the ANSI Keyboard Reassignment commands to give those keys new values.

Normally, ANSI.SYS is installed without any optional switches or parameters. For example, the following command loads ANSI.SYS into memory and prepares the PC for some interesting new visual effects and keyboard control:

```
DEVICE=C:\DOS\ANSI.SYS
```

The ANSI Commands

ANSI.SYS is a device driver that controls your console. What ANSI.SYS gives you are ANSI commands that can control your screen and modify the behavior of your keyboard.

All ANSI commands are sent to the ANSI.SYS driver in memory in what's called an escape sequence. Each command starts with the Escape character, ASCII 27 or Ctrl-[(which is where "escape sequence" gets it name). This is followed by a left bracket and various codes, and it ends with a command letter—either upper or lower case. The following is a typical ANSI command and escape sequence:

←[2J

"←[" is the Escape character (which appears as a left arrow when you enter it into the MS-DOS Editor), followed by a left bracket—the start of the escape sequence. "2" is a code value. Note that it's the character "2", not a numeric value. The command letter is "J". What the above command does is to clear the screen and "home" the cursor in the upper left corner.

When the ANSI.SYS driver is installed, it monitors the CON device, looking for the Escape character followed by a left bracket. If found, ANSI.SYS reads in additional codes and then waits for the final command letter. The final command letter tells it how to interpret the codes, whether to move the cursor, or change the text color, or assign a string of characters to a function key.

The problem with this method of sending commands to ANSI.SYS is in the delivery: You cannot type an Escape character at the DOS prompt. When you do so, you erase the command line and start over. This leaves the following methods of sending Escape sequences to ANSI.SYS:

Via the PROMPT command

In a text file

In a batch file

The PROMPT command allows you to specify the Escape character using the $E command. The character is then sent to ANSI.SYS every time the DOS prompt is displayed. For example, enter the following prompt command:

```
PROMPT $e[7m$p$g$e[m
```

There are two ANSI escape sequences in there: $e[7m turns on inverse video and $e[m turns it off. Note that it's a lower case "m" at the end of the command.

Text files can be edited to contain ANSI escape sequences as well. But entering the Escape character is often tricky. The following summarizes how the Escape character can be entered into various text editors and word processors. Note that when you use a word processor, you must save the text in plain ASCII, unformatted, non-document or DOS text mode:

In the MS-DOS Editor, enter the Escape character by typing Ctrl-P then Ctrl-[(or the Esc key). This produces a "←" (left-pointing arrow) in the text, the Escape character. (This technique also works in most WordStar-compatible text editors, such as QEdit.)

In Edlin, enter the Escape character by typing Ctrl-V and then a left bracket. On the screen this looks like ^V[, but when you list the line again, the Escape character appears as ^[. Don't get confused by this; the escape sequence will appear as ^[[in Edlin.

In Microsoft Word, enter the Escape character by holding the Alt key and pressing the 2 and then 7 key on the numeric keypad, release the Alt key. The produces a "←" in the text, the Escape character.

In WordPerfect, enter the Escape character by typing Ctrl-V and then Ctrl-[(or the Esc key). This produces the character ^[in the text. Don't get confused by ^[[, which is how the escape sequence will appear in WordPerfect.

To send the ANSI commands to ANSI.SYS in a text file, the text file must be displayed on the screen. The TYPE command does this quite easily, although you can also copy the file to the screen using the COPY command:

```
COPY filename CON
```

In a batch file, the ANSI escape sequence is entered using whatever text editor or word processor you use to create the batch file. (Note that COPY CON doesn't work in this instance.) The ANSI command is sent to the console using the ECHO command. For example:

```
ECHO ←[2J
```

The above ECHO command echoes the Erase Display ANSI command to the console, clearing the screen.

Controlling the Screen

For controlling the screen, ANSI commands are divided into three categories:

Cursor movement

Erasing the screen

Setting color and graphics

The following tables summarize each of the commands. Full descriptions of all ANSI commands are given in Appendix A.

Cursor Movement Commands:

Locate Cursor	←[row;colH
Position Cursor	←[row;colf
Move Cursor Up	←[nA
Move Cursor Down	←[nB
Move Cursor Right	←[nC
Move Cursor Left	←[nD
Erase Display	←[2J
Erase Line	←[K
Save Cursor Position	←[s
Restore Cursor Position	←[u

Row represents a row number ranging from 1 through the number of rows on the screen. *Col* is a column number ranging from 1 through the number of columns on the screen. The upper left corner of the screen is row 1, column 1. The maximum values are 25 for row and 80 for col, unless redefined using the MODE command.

N is a value indicating the number of rows or columns to move the cursor.

Erasing the Screen Commands:

Erase Display	←[2J
Erase Line	←[K

Setting Color and Graphics Commands:

Set Graphics Mode	←[nm
Set/Reset Mode	←[=modeh

N is one or more color or attribute values that affect the color or attributes of text displayed after the Set Graphics Mode command. If more than one n value is specified, each is separated by a semicolon: ←[n;n;nm

There are two types of attributes: character attributes and color.

Character	Attribute Values
0	Normal text
1	High-intensity
2	Low-intensity
4	Underline on (monochrome displays only)
5	Blinking on
7	Inverse video on
8	Invisible text

Color	Values	
	Foreground	Background
Black	30	40
Red	31	41
Green	32	42
Yellow	33	43
Blue	34	44
Magenta	35	45
Cyan	36	46
White	37	47

Mode is a text or graphics mode for the display. All of the modes are listed in Appendix A.

Of all these commands, you'll probably use the Locate Cursor and Set Graphics Mode commands more often than the others. The following sections demonstrate various system prompts and text files that put these ANSI commands to work.

Info: If you're picky about such things, note that DOS's ANSI.SYS file is only a subset of the full ANSI command set. ANSI stands for American National Standards Institute, and they've defined a whole slew of ANSI codes for doing many amazing feats. Full-powered ANSI device drivers are available through computer clubs, on-line networks and shareware warehouses. Two worth looking into are NANSI.SYS and ZANSI.SYS.

Spicing Up the DOS Prompt

DOS really wants you to include ANSI commands in its prompt. Otherwise, why make $E part of the PROMPT command? Each of the following PROMPT commands has a different effect on your system prompt. Type them in, and then experiment on your own if you want a colorful—or crazy—system prompt.

475

Info: For each of these sample prompts, the commands pg are assumed to be part of your original prompt. If not, substitute pg in the examples below with your own, special PROMPT commands.

If you tire easily of a black and white system prompt, try the following:

```
PROMPT $e[1;37;44m$p$g
```

The escape sequence sets the high-intensity attribute, white foreground color, and blue background color. Type CLS to clear the screen and you have a highly-touted custom bright-white-on-blue-background command environment.

```
PROMPT $e[1;33;41m$p$g
```

The above PROMPT command is also popular, giving you a bright-yellow-on-red background.

If you're using a program that displays multiple lines of information, try the following very colorful and interesting prompt:

```
PROMPT $e[33;40m$d$_$e[35m$t$_$e[36m$p$g$e[m
```

This is a basic Date-Time-Path prompt. The following breaks it down into its individual elements:

$e[33;40m	Set the color to yellow on black
d_	Display the date and a new line
$e[35m	Set the foreground color to magenta (black is still the background color)
t_	Display the time and a new line
$e[36m	Set the foreground color to cyan
pg	Display the currently logged drive and directory and a greater-than sign
$e[m	Reset all attributes; white-on-black text

No one can argue that DOS is dull after that command!

The problem with using the ANSI cursor movement commands in a prompt is that they can wreck the display. Consider the following PROMPT command, which always places the system prompt at the top of the screen:

```
PROMPT $e[1;1H$e[K$p$g
```

Here are the commands:

$e[1;1H	"Home" the cursor, moving it to the upper left of the screen
$e[K	Delete to the end of the line (which erases the top line on the screen)
pg	The standard system prompt

Type the CLS command and maybe a few DIR commands. While it looks cool, it's really impractical. The same holds true if you use the escape sequence $e[25;1H to keep the prompt at the bottom of the screen. After a time, the novelty wears thin.

The following prompt command is the Super Prompt. It makes use of the interesting Save Cursor Position and Restore Cursor Position commands. This solves the problem of the static prompt, while still giving you an interesting screen display:

```
PROMPT $e[s$e[H$e[7m$e[K$v: Logged to $p$e[1;53H$d @ $t$e[m$e[u$g
```

Here are the individual elements used to create the prompt:

$e[s	Save the cursor position
$e[H	Move to position 1, 1 (the upper left corner of the screen)
$e[7m	Set the inverse attribute on (black-on-white characters)
$e[K	Erase the line (which also sets the attributes for all text on that line to inverse)
$v	Display the DOS version, "MS-DOS Version 5.00"
: Logged to	Display the text (a space follows "to")

$p	Display the logged drive and path
$e[1;53H	Move to column 53 on the top line of the display
$d	Display the date
@	Display an At Sign with a space on either side
$t	Display the time
$e[m	Turn off the inverse attribute; normal text
$e[u	Restore the cursor position
$g	Display a greater-than prompt

The effect of this prompt is a banner across the top of the screen. It tells you the DOS version, the logged path, and then right-justifies the date and time (by positioning the cursor at column 53, above). After that display is created, the cursor is restored to its previous position so the prompt (>) can be displayed. In the end, the banner remains static at the top of the screen, but the prompt flows with the text.

You can add color to this prompt by changing two commands:

First, change the $e[7m command to the colors you want to use for displaying the banner at the top of the screen. For example, to display bright yellow on red, substitute $e[1;33;41m for $e[7m.

Second, change the $e[m command to the colors you want to use for the rest of the screen. For example, $[e37;42m, which sets white on green text. (Actually, it looks kind of nice.)

You can change the color of each item displayed in the banner by specifying a new color between them. The following shows how you could sandwich in the color commands:

```
$v       : Logged to        $p$e[1;53H     $d     @             $t
$v$e[37m : Logged to $e[34m$p$e[1;53H$e[30m$d$[5m @ $e[0;35m$t
```

Make sure you get in that last command, $e[0;35m. That turns off the blinking @ sign, and keeps you from having fits from looking at a flashing display.

Some Interesting Batch Files

ANSI commands can really make batch files look sharp. The following is the MOVE.BAT file mentioned in Chapter 21. Note how it's been improved by the use of ANSI color and attribute commands:

```
 1: @ECHO OFF
 2: REM MOVE FILES FROM %1 TO %2
 3: IF "%1"=="" GOTO WARNING
 4: IF "%2"=="" GOTO WARNING
 5: ECHO ←[5mMoving Files...←[m
 6: COPY %1 %2 >NUL
 7: DEL %1 <C:\BATCH\YES >NUL
 8: ECHO Files moved
 9: GOTO END
10: :WARNING
11: ECHO ←[7mPlease specify a source and destination filename←[m
12: :END
```

Line 5 has been edited to add the ANSI commands to flash the text. Note how the un-flash command is issued at the end of the ECHO command.

Line 11 has been edited to display the text in inverse video. If you like, you could add color to the commands—but don't go overboard with it!

Info: Refer to the start of this chapter for information on entering ANSI commands into your text editor or word processor. Remember, if you're using a word processor to save in an unformatted, non-document, DOS or ASCII text format.

The following batch file uses the cursor positioning commands to display a menu on the screen. Create it in the MS-DOS Editor and name it MAIN.BAT:

```
 1: @ECHO OFF
 2: CLS
 3: ECHO ←[4;16HMain Menu
 4: ECHO ←[7;10H1. Run word processor
 5: ECHO ←[9;10H2. Run spreadsheet
 6: ECHO ←[11;10H3. Check your mail
```

```
7: ECHO ←[13;10H4. Exit
8: PROMPT $e[17;12HEnter choice:
```

This batch file clears the screen and then displays "Main Menu" and four menu items, using Locate Cursor ANSI commands. Enter the batch file and save it to disk as MAIN.BAT. Run MAIN at the DOS prompt when you're done.

See how the PROMPT command is integrated into the menu structure? Because the PROMPT command is positioned properly on the screen, it naturally looks as if you're running a "real" menu program. (It's still the same old DOS prompt.)

Info: If you wanted to complete such a menu structure, you could write batch files named 1.BAT, 2.BAT and so on, and have them carry out whichever commands each menu item represents. End each batch file with the commands necessary to rerun MAIN.BAT.

The CLS command in line 2 could be replaced with the ANSI command to clear the screen. But better than that, re-edit MAIN.BAT and change line 2 to read as follows:

```
ECHO ←[2J←[=1h
```

Save the file and return to DOS. Now type MAIN and see what happens.

The ANSI command ←[2J clears the screen. But the command ←[=1h activates the 40-column mode on most color displays, making the menu text fill the screen (which is why the menu commands were positioned toward the left on the 80 column screen).

Displaying text in the 4-column format makes the menu easier to read and less imposing for some people. To restore the screen at the DOS prompt, use the MODE Co80 command. The ANSI escape sequence to restore the 80 column color display is ←[=3h. To restore your system prompt, type in your favorite PROMPT command at the "Enter choice:" prompt.

Further examples of interesting ANSI batch files are given at the end of this chapter.

Text Files Worth Looking At

It's easier to put ANSI commands into a text file and then TYPE that file at the keyboard or have a batch file TYPE it for you. For example, the previous MAIN.BAT program could keep its ANSI commands and menu layout in a text file named MAIN.TXT. To do so, the following steps should be taken:

1. COPY MAIN.BAT to MAIN.TXT.

2. Use the MS-DOS Editor to edit MAIN.TXT.

Remove the first @ECHO OFF batch file, and then remove the word ECHO from the following lines. Delete the final line containing the PROMPT command. In the end, the MAIN.TXT file should look like this:

```
←[2J←[=1h
←[4;16HMain Menu
←[7;10H1. Run word processor
←[9;10H2. Run spreadsheet
←[11;10H3. Check your mail
←[13;10H4. Exit
```

3. Save MAIN.TXT and exit.

4. Edit the MAIN.BAT program.

Delete all the ECHO commands (lines 2 through 7). Replace them with the command TYPE MAIN.TXT.

MAIN.BAT should now look like this:

```
@ECHO OFF
TYPE MAIN.TXT
PROMPT $e[17;12HEnter choice:
```

Any time you have several ANSI commands to issue at once, it's usually a good idea to store them all in a text file and then TYPE the text file from your batch file. This runs the commands a bit quicker than using the ECHO command in a batch file—although a drawback is that it's one extra file on the hard disk to edit.

The following ASCII text file is worth saluting. The numbers in curly brackets indicate how many spaces you're supposed to type; do not enter the curly brackets or the numbers they contain.

```
←[1m
←[4;10H←[2J
←[5;10H←[37;44m * * * * * * * * *←[41m  {27}  ←[33;40m=
←[6;10H←[37;44m  * * * * * * * * *  ←[47m  {27}  ←[33;40m=
←[7;10H←[37;44m * * * * * * * * * *  ←[41m  {27}  ←[33;40m=
←[8;10H←[37;44m  * * * * * * * *  ←[47m  {27}  ←[33;40m=
←[9;10H←[37;44m * * * * * * * * * *  ←[41m  {27}  ←[33;40m=
←[10;10H←[37;44m  * * * * * * * *  ←[47m  {27}  ←[33;40m=
←[11;10H←[37;44m * * * * * * * * * *←[41m  {27}  ←[33;40m=
←[12;10H←[47m  {46}  ←[33;40m=
←[13;10H←[41m  {46}  ←[33;40m=
←[14;10H←[47m  {46}  ←[33;40m=
←[15;10H←[41m  {46}  ←[33;40m=
←[16;10H←[47m  {46}  ←[33;40m=
←[17;10H←[41m  {46}  ←[33;40m=
←[m
```

Save this file using the name FLAG.TXT. At the DOS prompt, type the following:

```
TYPE FLAG.TXT
```

The above command would make a nice patriotic end to an AUTOEXEC.BAT file, or you can use the ANSI commands and screen colors to create a custom banner for your system.

ANSI Keyboard Tricks

The second half of the CON device is the keyboard. ANSI commands can be used to change the way your keyboard behaves, assigning new characters to some keys or making certain keys display strings of text—including DOS commands.

There are two different ANSI keyboard commands:

Keyboard Key Reassignment

Keyboard String Assignment

Both commands use a similar format, and both end with a little "p".

Keyboard Key Reassignment

The Keyboard Key Reassignment command allows you to assign any ASCII character to any key on the keyboard. The format is:

```
←[old;newp
```

Old is the ASCII code for the key to redefine. (ASCII codes are covered in Chapter 5 and in Appendix A.)

New is the ASCII code to assign to the key defined by old.

To issue this ANSI command, you can put an ECHO statement into a batch file, but a quick-and-dirty way is to use the PROMPT command. For example:

```
PROMPT $e[65;69p
```

ASCII code 65 equals the letter "A" and 69 is the code for the letter "E". After the above command, pressing the A key will cause an E to be displayed. Type upper-case A several times to confirm this, and then type your favorite PROMPT command to reset the system prompt.

Info: Since the ASCII code 65 represents capital A, only the upper case A is converted to E. To convert both upper and lower case letters, specify their numbers as well.

Note that since ASCII only affects DOS, the switch won't be present in any of your applications or programs that don't use DOS's keyboard functions.

To restore the original character, specify the first value twice, as in:

```
PROMPT $e[65;65p
```

Tip: An easier way to do things is to specify the characters in double quotes. For example, the following ANSI escape sequence will cause "E" to appear when the "A" key is pressed:

```
←["A";"E"p
```

A much more useful example is typing in foreign languages; swapping often used foreign characters to some seldom used keys can be much more useful (and less annoying) than using KEYB to redefine the entire keyboard. Consider the following two commands which could be used in a batch file:

```
ECHO ←[96;164p
ECHO ←[126;165p
```

The first ECHO command maps the ñ character to the ' (accent grave) key; the second one maps the Ñ character to the ~ (tilde) key. You could put those two lines in AUTOEXEC.BAT or in a batch file on their own. They give you access to those special keys often used in Spanish, without redefining the entire keyboard.

Some keys on the keyboard lack ASCII codes—among these, the function keys. These keys are represented in the ANSI keyboard commands as two values: The first is usually zero, the second is a code representing a special scan code value of the key. Several of the more interesting key's scan codes are listed in Appendix J.

As an example, the following command assigns the "blank" character (code 255) to Alt-F1. Alt-F1's scan code is 104:

```
ECHO ←[0;104;255p
```

Pressing Alt-F1, represented above as 0;104 now produces the blank character. If you're using the blank as a way to name files (with secret "spaces" in them), then Alt-F1 is much easier to type than Alt-2-5-5.

Keyboard String Reassignment

The ANSI Keyboard String Reassignment command is basically the same as the Keyboard Key Reassignment command. The difference is that strings of characters are assigned to a single key, as opposed to one character. The format is:

```
←[key_code;"string"p
```

Key_code is the ASCII code or a scan-code value for a key on the keyboard. If it's an ASCII key, then the ASCII code is used. If it's a function key or other non-ASCII key, then its code value is specified, preceded by zero and a semicolon (see below).

String is a string of characters, or a single character, enclosed in quotes.

The following two ECHO commands can be used to reassign the Q key to the "Qu" combination, and q to the "qu" combination:

```
ECHO ←[81;"Qu"p
ECHO ←[113;"qu"p
```

Since you often type a Q followed by a U, the two batch file commands above will cut down on your typing.

Info: To reassign the keys to their original values, use the following two batch-file commands:

```
ECHO ←[81;81p
ECHO ←[113;113p
```

The most popular use of this command is in assigning DOS commands to function keys. The function key scan codes that can be used with the ANSI keyboard reassignment commands are listed below:

Key	Normal	Shifted	Control	Alt
F1	0;59	0;84	0;94	0;104
F2	0;60	0;85	0;95	0;105
F3	0;61	0;86	0;96	0;106
F4	0;62	0;87	0;97	0;107
F5	0;63	0;88	0;98	0;108
F6	0;64	0;89	0;99	0;109
F7	0;65	0;90	0;100	0;110
F8	0;66	0;91	0;101	0;111
F9	0;67	0;92	0;102	0;112
F10	0;68	0;93	0;103	0;113
F11	0;133	0;135	0;137	0;139
F12	0;134	0;136	0;138	0;140

When you reassign a function key, remember that DOS uses the function keys F1 through F6, and DOS key uses F7, Alt-F7, F8, F9, and Alt-F10. Keeping that in mind, consider the following:

```
ECHO ←[0;84;"COPY "p
```

The above batch-file command assigns the COPY command (followed by a space) to Shift-F1 (0;84). Pressing Shift-F1 now causes COPY to be quickly displayed on the screen, ready for you to name the file to be copied.

```
ECHO ←[0;85;"DIR";13p
```

The above command assigns the DIR command to Shift-F2. See the ";13" at the end? That's the ASCII code for the Enter key. Tacking that on to the end of the reassignment string causes Enter to automatically be "pressed" after DOS "types" the command.

The following batch file can be used to assign DOS commands to the Function keys Shift-F1 through Shift-F10. Enter it using the MS-DOS Editor:

```
@ECHO OFF
REM Reassign Shift-F1 through Shift-F10
ECHO Reassigning keys...
ECHO ←[0;84;"COPY "p
ECHO ←[0;85;"DIR";13p
ECHO ←[0;86;"CLS";13p
ECHO ←[0;87;"FORMAT "p
ECHO ←[0;88;"CD \";13p
ECHO ←[0;89;"CD ..";13p ECHO ←[0;90;"DEL "p
ECHO ←[0;91;"PATH C:\DOS;C:\UTIL;C:\BATCH";13p
ECHO ←[0;92;"PROMPT $p$g";13p
ECHO ←[0;93;"DOSSHELL";13p
ECHO Done!
```

You can replace some of the above commands with the names of programs on your system, or customize the function key assignments any way you see fit. Save this file as FKEYS.BAT, and then run it whenever you want to reassign the function keys to be more useful to you in DOS.

Info: Remember, these function-key reassignments won't affect your other applications. Your WordPerfect function keys are read using different internal programming code and will not be "erased" by ANSI keyboard reassignment commands.

Tip: Here's a jewel that should have been included with DOSKEY. Consider adding the following line to your AUTOEXEC.BAT file if you use the DOSKEY command:

```
ECHO ←[0;68;"DOSKEY /MACROS";13p
```

DOSKEY uses Alt-F10 to erase your macro definitions, just as it uses Alt-F7 to erase the command history. But while DOSKEY uses F7 to display the command history, F10 does nothing. The above command assigns F10 to "DOSKEY /MACROS" to display the list of your macros—which is the way it should have been all along.

Summary

To give your system access to the ANSI commands you install the ANSI.SYS device driver using the DEVICE configuration command in CONFIG.SYS.

All ANSI commands start with an escape sequence, the Escape character, ASCII 27 or Ctrl-[, followed by a left bracket. This book shows that as "←[".

ANSI commands are sent to DOS using the PROMPT command, or by listing a text file containing ANSI commands with the TYPE command, or by ECHOing ANSI commands in a batch file.

ANSI's screen commands can position the cursor, erase the display, change the color of text and its attributes, and change the screen mode.

You can use ANSI's screen commands to spice up a dull system prompt, or to add zest to boring little batch files.

ANSI's keyboard commands can reassign a single character to a single key, or a whole string of text—complete with Enter key—to a key on the keyboard.

CHAPTER 24

Advanced File Manipulation

In DOS, file manipulation is done using the COPY, REN, and DEL commands. Advanced file manipulation involves dealing with both files and devices. DOS allows you to move information between its devices in a variety of manners, and there are interesting and useful things you can do with devices to better exploit the power of DOS.

This chapter answers the following questions:

- What are devices used for?

- How can DOS deal with devices other than the disk drives?

- What are the standard I/O devices?

- How can output of a DOS command be sent to another device?

- What does >> do?

- Of what use is input redirection?

- How is the pipe character used in DOS?

- What is a filter and how does it modify output?

DOS and Devices

DOS sees everything in the PC as a device: The disk drives, keyboard, printer, serial port—everything is a device. This is good because DOS is device oriented. It treats all devices the same; unlike an operating system that may only work with disk drives, DOS works equally well the disk drives, printer, screen, and keyboard.

Device Names and I/O

Device are used by DOS for input and output (I/O). For example, the CON device supplies DOS with input from the keyboard; output is sent from DOS to the display. Disk drives are the classic I/O devices, allowing DOS to both store information (output) and retrieve information (input). The printer is a DOS device, but it can only be used for output; DOS cannot receive input from the printer.

DOS refers to each device by name. Each of them are listed in the following table, along with their I/O capabilities:

Device Name	I/O	Device
NUL	x x	Null device (empty)
CON	x x	Console, screen (output), and keyboard (input)
AUX	x x	First serial port
PRN	x	First printer
CLOCK$	x x	System clock
A	x x	First floppy drive
B	x x	Second floppy drive
C	x x	First hard drive
D, E, F...	x x	Additional hard drives
COM1	x x	First serial port
LPT1	x	First printer port
LPT2	x	Second printer port
LPT3	x	Third printer port
COM2	x x	Second serial port
COM3	x x	Third serial port
COM4	x x	Fourth serial port

The three basic DOS devices are CON, AUX, and PRN. CON is the device DOS uses for standard input and output; it's where DOS expects its input to come from (the keyboard) and where it sends the output (the screen). AUX is a generic name for the first serial port (COM1) and PRN is the name for the first printer (LPT1). The disk-drive letters are all device names, as are any additional serial (COM) or printer (LPT for Line Printer) devices. (The CLOCK$ device is internal, and it cannot be used like the other devices.)

The benefit of DOS being device oriented is that it treats all its devices equally. You can tell DOS to use the printer or a file for output instead of using the standard output device; DOS can receive input from a file or a communications port just as it would from the standard input device; DOS can take the output of any one device and redirect it to another device. The way DOS deals with its devices opens up lots of possibilities, each of which is explored in this chapter.

Using Devices

Most DOS commands move or copy information from one device to another. The best example is the COPY command. COPY doesn't copy "files." Instead, it copies information from one device to another. Normally, the device is a disk drive, but because DOS is device-oriented, you can COPY information from one device to any other device in the system.

Info: Disk drives are special devices. Information on disk drives is stored as files, which makes that device different from other devices. Although you cannot store a "file" on the keyboard, text generated at the keyboard can be treated as if it were coming from a file. As far as DOS is concerned, there is no difference. But keep in mind that files are unique and DOS is primarily geared toward working with them.

Just as the COPY command copies a file from the hard drive to a floppy, it can copy that file from a disk drive to another device—say, the printer:

```
COPY COWS.TXT PRN
```

The above command copies the file COWS.TXT to the printer, the PRN device. The end result is that the file is printed—you generate a hard copy of the text file.

You can copy any file to the printer, as long as it's a formatted text file. The results for non-text files are the same as when you use the TYPE command on them—unpredictable. Also, you should use your applications to print formatted files such as word processing documents; COPYing them to the printer probably won't yield the results you're looking for.

While you can copy any formatted text file from a disk drive to the printer, the opposite is not true:

```
COPY PRN LPTINPUT
```

The PRN device is an output-only device; it's just an "O"—no "I." Because it doesn't generate text, you cannot use it for input and the above command would fail:

```
0 file(s) copied
```

One of the most universal devices is the standard device, CON:

```
COPY COWS.TXT CON
```

The above command copies the COWS.TXT file to the CON device, which is the screen for all output. The net effect of the above command is identical to the command TYPE COWS.TXT—with the addition of the "1 file(s) copied" message at the end.

Because the CON device is also used for input, the following command works:

```
COPY CON NEWTEXT
```

The file NEWTEXT is created using input from the CON device—the keyboard. All the text you type is actually stored in a buffer (one of the same ones you create using the BUFFERS configuration command; see Chapter 19). Text is written to disk every time the buffer fills or when you end input (signified by entering the Ctrl-Z character).

Info: The COPY CON "command" is a quick-and-dirty way to generate text files and short batch files. On each line you do have access to the standard DOS editing keys: F1 through F5, Esc, Backspace, and Enter. (DOSKEY, if loaded, will be inactive during COPY CON).

The only drawback to COPY CON is that once you press Enter to end a line, you cannot return to it for editing. To end all input, press Ctrl-Z or F6, and then press Enter.

The following command activates the DOS "typewriter mode," turning your several-thousand-dollar PC into a several-hundred-dollar word processor:

```
COPY CON PRN
```

The above command copies input from the CON device (the keyboard) to the PRN device (output). (Each time you press Enter, a line is sent to the printer.) To end the typewriter mode, press Ctrl-Z or F6 then Enter.

Tip: To eject a page from the printer as you're typing, press the Ctrl-L key, and then Enter.

An interesting device is the NUL device. NUL is the empty device, a black hole in your computer. It's primarily used as a dummy device for testing programs or for suppressing the output of some DOS commands.

As an output device, information you send or copy to the NUL device goes nowhere:

```
C:\>COPY COWS.TXT NUL
        1 file(s) copied
```

The above command successfully copied the COWS.TXT file to the NUL device. Yet, because the NUL device isn't anywhere, there isn't a duplicate copy of the file to be found.

Info: As an output device, NUL is primarily used for output redirection, covered later in this chapter.

NUL can also be used for input. The results are predictable:

```
C:\>COPY NUL TESTFILE
        0 file(s) copied
```

Because there is no information in NUL, a file isn't generated. However, unlike the PRN device, NUL is a full I/O device. It can be used to generate zero length files, and this is covered later in this chapter.

The AUX device intrigues quite a few DOS enthusiasts, especially those into communications. If you have a modem, you're used to copying files and information using the serial port. But note that, without exception, all major communications programs circumvent DOS and access your PC's serial hardware directly.

It's possible to send information from a file to the serial port and, therefore, to another computer or a modem. But in practice it's really limited. As a test, create a file on disk using the following instructions. In keeping with the device theme, use COPY CON to create a file that contains the modem commands to dial your own phone number—or the phone number for the Time:

```
C:\TEMP>COPY CON PHONE#
ATDT555-1212
^Z
        1 file(s) copied
```

Above, a file named PHONE# is created, containing the modem commands "ATDT" followed by the phone number everyone uses on TV and in the movies. To copy that phone number to a modem hooked up to your first serial port, you first need to set up the serial port for use with DOS. The following command configures the serial port for 1200 Baud operation:

```
C:\TEMP>MODE COM1:1200

COM1: 1200,e,7,1,-
```

Now you send the phone number to your modem:

```
C:\TEMP>C:\TEMP>COPY PHONE# AUX
        1 file(s) copied
```

Info: If you get a "Write fault" error message, then a modem may not be connected to your COM1 port; try COM2 for some internal modems. Also, you may have to use the command twice on some systems and with some modems.

A better way to dial the phone/modem using the computer is covered later in this chapter.

The CTTY Command, Revisited

The CTTY command is used to change the standard input and output device (CON) to something else. Usually it's the AUX device, primarily because the communications port is the only "active" input/output device in the system.

If you like, you can connect your PC to another (and it doesn't have to be a PC, I've done it with a Mac) using a null modem cable. On the second PC, run a communications program and set the communications to 9600 Baud, 8-N-1. On the DOS end, use the following MODE command to set similar communications statistics on your system:

```
MODE COM1:9600,N,8,1
```

Then type:

```
CTTY AUX
```

You can now run DOS from the remote computer. All DOS commands will work, but applications—including DOS Shell and the MS-DOS Editor—will not.

There's not much you can do with CTTY AUX, other than pull a few directories and some file-manipulation commands. On the remote computer, type CTTY CON to restore the system to normal.

I/O Redirection

When DOS displays information, it uses the standard output device—the display. When DOS receives information, it assumes the standard input device—the keyboard. But DOS isn't hard wired into using the CON device for all its standard I/O. Using some special symbols, you can redirect the input or output of DOS from or to a file or another device. This is known as I/O redirection.

Redirected Output, >

The output redirection symbol is >, the greater-than symbol. It tells DOS to redirect the output of the DOS command to the device specified. For example, type the following command:

```
DIR > DIRTEXT
```

After pressing Enter you won't see anything. DOS has taken the output of the DIR command and redirected it to a file named DIRTEXT. The file is created in the current directory, and if a file named DIRTEXT already exists it will be overwritten. To see DIRTEXT, type the following:

```
TYPE DIRTEXT
```

There's the directory! Stored in a file, you can now manipulate the directory using a text editor, or you can save it for any other purpose. Try the following:

```
CLS > CLEAR
```

This redirects the output of the CLS command to a file named CLEAR. But what is the output of the CLS command? To find out, TYPE the CLEAR file:

```
TYPE CLEAR
```

Info: The output of the CLS command is the ANSI escape sequence for clearing the screen, ←[2J. When TYPEd to the screen from a file, it still clears the screen. However, if ANSI.SYS isn't installed, you'll see only ←[2J displayed (yet, CLS does still clear the screen when ANSI.SYS isn't installed—weird, no?).

Because a device name wasn't specified, DOS created a file for output redirection. However, when you specify a device, DOS sends the output to that device:

```
DIR > PRN
```

The above command sends the output of the DIR command to the printer. This is much more effective than using the Ctrl-P toggle (DOS's Echo-to-Printer function, covered in Chapter 10).

One of the problems of redirecting output to the printer—especially a laser printer—is that you need to lean over and press the Form Feed button to see the page. Instead of doing that, send a form-feed character to the printer with the following command:

```
ECHO ^L > PRN
```

The ^L character is the form-feed character, produced by typing Ctrl-L on the command line. Normally, the ECHO command would spit out a Ctrl-L character on the screen. Above, that output is redirected to the printer, and the end result is an ejected page.

Tip: Create a batch file, EJECT.BAT with the following as its contents:

```
@ECHO ^L > PRN
```

Whenever you want to see what you're printing or eject a page from the laser printer, run EJECT.BAT.

When used with the TYPE command, output redirection creates a duplicate of the text file:

```
TYPE DIRTEXT > DIRTEXT2
```

The above TYPE command lists the contents of DIRTEXT, but output redirection stores the contents in the file DIRTEXT2—a new file DOS creates. You could also use output redirection to get a hard copy of the file, as in:

```
TYPE DIRTEXT > PRN
```

However, the following command will work just as well:

```
COPY DIRTEXT PRN
```

An interesting device for output redirection is the NUL device, although it's used most commonly in batch files to suppress the output of some DOS commands (see the next section). Otherwise, a curious use for the oddball NUL device can be used to produce zero-length files with output redirection. Try the following command:

```
TYPE NUL > ZERO
```

When used in the above format, the NUL device generates an immediate end-of-file character, Ctrl-Z. The result is a zero-length file that appears in the directory as follows:

```
ZERO          0 04-04-93  12:32p
```

Using > in Batch Files

Output redirection opens up many opportunities for batch files. The most common technique is to use the NUL device to suppress the output of some DOS commands:

```
COPY C:\BATCH\*.BAT D:\ > NUL
```

The above COPY command copies all your batch files from the C:\BATCH subdirectory to drive D. What output redirection does is to suppress the list of files the COPY command produces, as well as the final "xx file(s) copied" message. This cleans up the batch file, causing it to run "silent" and avoiding some messages that may confuse the user.

I/O Redirection and the Path

Maintaining several different search paths can be done by assigning new environment variables to the path. This was demonstrated earlier in this book, for example:

```
SET OLDPATH=%PATH%
PATH=C:\WINDOWS;C:\WINWORD;C:\PCTOOLS;C:\DOS
...
REM Other stuff goes here...
...
PATH=%OLDPATH%
```

If you're maintaining several paths, or you don't like using environment space, then consider using I/O redirection to create a path batch file. Consider this command:

```
PATH > C:\BATCH\SETPATH1.BAT
```

The output of the PATH command is redirected to a file SETPATH1.BAT. Later, that batch file is run by means of the CALL command:

```
CALL C:\BATCH\SETPATH1
```

How does this work? Because the output of the PATH command is a path command itself:

```
C:\>PATH
PATH=C:\DOS;C:\UTIL;C:\BATCH
```

Putting that output into a new batch file allows you to use the CALL command to reset the path. Likewise, you can create several SETPATH-type batch files and use CALL to change the path to whatever is convenient.

I/O Redirection and Your Modem

If you have a modem hooked up to your PC, you can send commands to it using the ECHO command and output redirection. First, you must set DOS to deal with the modem. The following command initializes COM1 to 1200 Baud:

```
MODE COM1:1200
```

Now you can talk to the modem using the following command:

```
ECHO ATZ > COM1
```

This sends the command "ATZ" (modem reset) to a Hayes-compatible modem hooked up to your first serial port.

The following batch file, DIAL.BAT, uses this aspect of output redirection to dial a phone number. Enter this batch file using the MS-DOS Editor. Pay special attention to the output redirection commands:

```
 1: @ECHO OFF
 2: REM Dial the phone batch file
 3: IF "%1"=="" GOTO ERROR
 4: ECHO Make sure your modem is on-line and ready to go.
 5: PAUSE
 6: MODE COM1:1200 > NUL
 7: ECHO Dialing %1
 8: ECHO ATDT%1 > COM1
 9: ECHO Wait for the phone to ring, then
10: PAUSE
11: REM Disconnect the modem
12: ECHO AT > COM1
13: GOTO END
14: :ERROR
15: ECHO Please specify a phone number after DIAL
16: :END
```

Save the file as DIAL.BAT, preferably in your BATCH subdirectory. At the DOS prompt, run DIAL.BAT by following it with a phone number to dial:

```
C:\BATCH>DIAL 555-1212
Make sure your modem is on-line and ready to go.
Press any key to continue . . .
```

Press the Spacebar when your modem is ready.

```
Dialing 555-1212
Wait for the phone to ring, and then
Press any key to continue . . .
```

When the phone rings, pick up your handset and then press the Spacebar to hang up the modem.

Redirected Output, Append >>

One drawback to using redirected output is that it always destroys any existing file you create. For example, suppose you were using redirected output to keep a log (such as a phone log) with the DIAL.BAT program. The following line could be added after line 8:

```
ECHO Dialed the number %1 > PHONE.LOG
```

The problem is that PHONE.LOG would always contain the last number dialed; output redirection would consistently overwrite the original file.

The solution s to use redirected output/append, which is represented by two greater-than symbols, >>. Type the following:

```
DIR > DIRTEXT
```

This outputs the current directory to the file DIRTEXT. If you already had a DIRTEXT file on disk—it's gone! Now type:

```
DIR >> DIRTEXT
```

501

Instead of erasing DIRTEXT, output redirection has appended the new directory listing to the end of the DIRTEXT file. Use the TYPE command to verify the two directory listings held in the single DIRTEXT file.

In the DIAL.BAT program, you can use output redirection/append to maintain your phone log:

```
ECHO Dialed the number %1 >> PHONE.LOG
```

All the phone numbers dialed will now be appended to the PHONE.LOG file, maintaining a record of your calls dialed using DIAL.BAT.

An example of using output redirection/append in a batch file is when you change directories. Some batch files use CD to hop all over the drive. But you never really know in which directory the user first ran the batch file. The directory can be saved by redirecting the CD command as follows:

```
CD > ORGDIR
```

This places the current directory into the file ORGDIR. But the output of the CD command isn't formatted like a DOS command— unlike the PATH command. CD may display:

```
C:\SYSTEM\BORLAND\SKPLUS
```

That's not a command or filename—it's a pathname. However, if you place a CD command before it, you can then append a pathname to that CD command and, lo, you'll have a DOS command.

Change to your BATCH file subdirectory and enter the following to create the text file CDCMD:

```
C:\BATCH>COPY CON CDCMD
CD ^Z
        1 file(s) copied
```

Type CD, a space, then Ctrl-Z or F6. This file, CDCMD, can now be used to help restore the current path. To do so, add the following code to the start of your batch file:

```
@ECHO OFF
COPY C:\BATCH\CDCMD %TEMP%\ORGDIR.BAT > NUL
CD >> %TEMP%\ORGDIR.BAT
```

The net effect here is that the file CDCMD ("CD" followed by a space) is copied to a file ORGDIR.BAT. The current path is then appended to that file using the >> symbols. After the COPY and CD commands above, a workable DOS command in is created elsewhere on disk, in a file named ORGDIR.BAT. To return to the original subdirectory, stick the following command at the end of the batch file:

```
CALL %TEMP%\ORGDIR
```

Remember to use the proper path to CDCMD in your batch files; above C:\BATCH is assumed.

Redirected Input, <

Redirected input is a bit trickier than redirected output—and partially dangerous. When you redirect input, DOS expects all input to come from the device you specify; the keyboard will be totally ignored. So, if the file or device specified for input lacks the necessary keystrokes, your computer will hang. Still, redirected input does have its place and is quite useful.

To work with redirected input, you first need to know what type of input a DOS command or program will accept. You must then determine exactly how much input is required and specify all those keystrokes, usually in a file. For example, the command DEL *.* prompts with a message "Are you sure?" and waits for a Y or N key press, followed by Enter. You can supply DEL with Y and Enter by placing them both in a file. The following creates the YES file for that purpose:

```
C:\BATCH>COPY CON YES
Y

^Z
        1 file(s) copied
```

Type a Y, Enter, Enter and then Ctrl-Z.

The file YES contains both a Y and Enter (a carriage return). To delete all the files in a directory in a batch file, you could use the following command:

```
DEL *.* < C:\BATCH\YES
```

DEL *.* asks "Are you sure" and waits for a Y from the keyboard. But input redirection supplies input from the YES file instead. Above, YES is assumed to be in the C:\BATCH directory. The command could further be silenced use output redirection to the NUL device as follows:

```
DEL *.* < C:\BATCH\YES > NUL
```

Info: This technique was used in the MOVE.BAT file, which was discussed in Chapter 21.

To make the best possible use of redirected input, it helps to create some standard input files on your system. These can be tossed into your BATCH subdirectory and used by other batch files for input to DOS commands. Some good files to create in addition to YES are ENTER, ENTERN, and NO.

The ENTER file contains a single Enter key stroke. Here's how to create it:

```
C:\BATCH>COPY CON ENTER

^Z
        1 file(s) copied
```

Just type Enter, and then Ctrl-Z or F6. This could be used for a DOS command or program that requires you to press Enter to continue—but not for the FORMAT command. FORMAT also asks for a volume label. When that happens and there are no more key strokes in the ENTER file, your system will hang (eternally waiting for characters that will never appear). Reset to continue when that happens.

The ENTERN file contains an Enter key stroke, followed by a press of the N key and Enter again:

```
C:\BATCH>COPY CON ENTERN

N
^Z
         1 file(s) copied
```

Finally, as a complement to the YES file, a NO file can be created containing a single N key stroke:

```
C:\BATCH>COPY CON NO

N
^Z
         1 file(s) copied
```

You can create additional files to supply input to DOS commands or programs. Note that input redirection only works with programs that use DOS's input and output functions. This rules out using I/O redirection with major applications and most utility programs.

When you use input redirection, remember to specify a full pathname to the file containing input. Also, carefully review your keystrokes and consider all the possibilities. Aside from simple key presses, input redirection can be used to create scripts for DOS's DEBUG program, which is covered in the next chapter.

Pipes and Filters

Pipes and filters deal with I/O redirection, but more along the lines of modifying output than redirecting it. A pipe is a character—the vertical bar (|), which may or may not have a space in the middle. A filter is a type of program. Filters are built to modify standard input and output, making adjustments and fine tuning. DOS comes with three filter programs, FIND, MORE, and SORT.

Info: You must define a TEMP environment variable in order for DOS to use the pipe character.

The SORT Filter

To understand how the pipe works, you need to know the limitations of output redirection and how useful filters can be. The most interesting filter is the SORT filter which, as its name suggests, sorts things. Type the following at the DOS prompt:

```
SORT
```

You're now running the SORT program. True, SORT is really a filter, but it's designed to filter standard I/O, which is your keyboard and screen. Type the following:

```
BUSH
REAGAN
CARTER
FORD
NIXON
JOHNSON
KENNEDY
```

Press Ctrl-Z and Enter to end input. The SORT command then displays:

```
BUSH
CARTER
FORD
JOHNSON
KENNEDY
NIXON
REAGAN
```

By itself, the SORT filter takes standard input (up until the end-of-file marker, Ctrl-Z), sorts it, and then displays the result as standard output. But normally SORT is used in conjunction with I/O redirection. To continue with this example, re-type the list of presidents using the MS-DOS Editor. Save the file as PREZEZ.

To display the sorted list of names in the PREZEZ file, the following command could be used:

```
SORT < PREZEZ
```

Above, the input for the SORT filter is provided by the file PREZEZ using input redirection. The output still goes to the standard output device, but that too can be changed:

```
SORT < PREZEZ > PREZSORT
```

Now the input is supplied by the file PREZEZ and the output sent to the file PREZSORT.

Before DOS version 5, the SORT filter was the only way you could display a sorted directory listing. But think about how that works for a second: The DIR command displays text which must be piped (major hint) through the SORT filter. Would the following command work?

```
DIR > SORT
```

Above, the output of the DIR command is sent to a file named SORT on disk. How about this:

```
SORT < DIR
```

Again the answer is no; SORT looks for input from a file named DIR on disk.

To pipe the output of a DOS command through a filter you need the pipe (|) character. Type the following:

```
DIR | SORT
```

The output of the DIR command is piped through the SORT filter, and a sorted directory list is displayed. Unlike the DIR command's /O switch, everything in the output is sorted: Directory information, disk information, sizes and so forth.

If you wish to redirect the sorted list to a file, you can further use I/O redirection:

```
DIR | SORT > SORTEDIR
```

Above, the directory is sorted and sent off to a file SORTEDIR on disk.

The SORT filter also has optional switches which allow you to control the sort. The /R switch is used to reverse the order of the sort. Type the following command:

```
TYPE PREZEZ | SORT /R
```

Above, the PREZEZ file is TYPEd and piped through the SORT filter with the /R switch specified. The list of presidents will be sorted in reverse order.

The /+n switch is used to sort the text at a certain column, specified by n. To test this, edit PREZEZ file to appear as below. Make sure you enter the proper number of spaces for each column of information:

```
BUSH     GEORGE   Republican   1988
REAGAN   RONALD   Republican   1980
CARTER   JAMES    Democrat     1976
FORD     GERALD   Republican   1974
NIXON    RICHARD  Republican   1968
JOHNSON  LYNDON   Democrat     1963
KENNEDY  JOHN     Democrat     1960
```

Each president's first last name begins on column 1, their first names at column 10, their political parties at column 19, and the years they were elected or took office at column 32. Save the file to disk and return to DOS.

To sort the file by the presidents' first names, the following SORT command is used:

```
TYPE PREZEZ | SORT /+10
```

To sort by parties, substitute 19 for 10 above. If you want to reverse the sorting order, add the /R switch. When using the file as redirected input, use the following format:

```
SORT /+32 /R < PREZEZ
```

Tip: Using a filter always works quicker with redirected input than when you use the pipe.

COMMAND: SORT (External/Filter)
            Function: The sorting filter.
            Format: SORT /R /+n

By itself, SORT sorts standard input from the console, displaying the alphanumerically sorted result to the console. Normally, SORT is used with I/O redirection or the pipe to sort a formatted text file.

/R is an optional switch used to reverse the sort.

/+n is an optional switch used to sort the list at a specific column, as specified by *n*.

Characters are sorted according to information specified with the COUNTRY command in CONFIG.SYS. Upper and lower case letters are considered the same.

Note that any file used for input to the SORT filter must be less than 64K in size.

SORT is usually used with I/O redirection or the pipe in the following formats:

```
SORT switches < filename

COMMAND | SORT switches
```

The MORE Filter

The MORE filter is used to place a "more" prompt at the bottom of the screen after each screenful of text is displayed. Just as the DIR command's /P switch gives you a "more" prompt, the MORE filter can be used to add a "more" prompt to any DOS command that displays text.

For example, suppose the file MEANDER contains about one jillion lines of text. To view it a screenful at a time, you would type the following:

```
MORE < MEANDER
```

The MORE filter reads in the text from the MEANDER file. After each screenful of text, the following is displayed at the bottom of the screen:

```
---More---
```

Press the Spacebar to continue the display.

Info: If you've changed the size of your screen using the MODE command (and you have the ANSI.SYS device driver installed), the MORE command will recognize this and pause at the appropriate line on the screen.

The MORE filter can be used with the pipe as follows:

```
TYPE MEANDER | MORE
```

Using input redirection is faster, but sometimes the only way to use the MORE filter is with a pipe. For example:

```
DIR | SORT | MORE
```

The above command takes the output of the DIR command, sorts it, and then displays the result using the MORE filter to pause between each screen.

COMMAND: MORE (External/Filter)
              Function: Pauses the display after a screenful of text.
              Format: MORE

The MORE filter counts the number of lines displayed. After a screenful, it displays "--- More---" and waits for you to press a key to continue. MORE is usually used with I/O redirection or the pipe in the following formats:

```
MORE < filename

TYPE filename | MORE

COMMAND | MORE
```

The FIND Filter

The FIND filter is interesting and quite powerful. It locates lines in a formatted text file or a DOS command that contains the text you specify.

The general format of the FIND filter is as follows:

```
FIND "text" filename
```

Text is text you want to locate in a file. It can be anything, although it must be enclosed in double quotes. If double quotes are in the text, then they must be specified twice, "".

Filename is a single file for FIND to scan, looking for matching text. More than one filename can be specified, although none of them can contain wildcards.

Enter the following command:

```
FIND "ECHO" \AUTOEXEC.BAT
```

Press Enter and you'll see all the lines in AUTOEXEC.BAT that use the ECHO command. (If you didn't see anything, try typing ECHO in lower case.)

```
-------- \AUTOEXEC.BAT
@ECHO OFF
```

The FIND filter displays its results by printing the file name and then any lines found with the matching text. The optional /N switch can be used to display the line number along with the line:

```
C:\>FIND /N "DEVICE" \CONFIG.SYS

-------- \CONFIG.SYS
[8]DEVICE=C:\MOUSE\MOUSE.SYS
[9]DEVICE=C:\DOS\ANSI.SYS
[10]DEVICE=C:\DOS\RAMDRIVE.SYS /A
[11]DEVICE=C:\DOS\SETVER.EXE
```

If you didn't see any DEVICE commands, then try using the /I switch to force the FIND command to match upper and lower case letters:

```
FIND /I /N "DEVICE" \CONFIG.SYS
```

Although the FIND filter only scans one file at a time, you can use it with the FOR command to scan a group of files using a wildcard. Log to your BATCH directory and type the following command:

```
FOR %B IN (*.BAT) DO FIND /I "ECHO" %B
```

The above FOR command scans each batch file for the text "ECHO." The /I switch is used to match both upper and lower case.

Info: The display tends to scroll off the screen; however, you cannot pipe the output through the MORE filter; MORE only works on each instance of the FIND command FOR processes. To see everything, you would have to redirect/append all output to a file and then input the file to the MORE filter.

The /C switch was used in Chapter 21 in the BACKTEST.BAT program. FIND's /C switch only counts the lines of text containing the matching string. The command in BACKTEST.BAT was:

```
FIND /C "A " %TEMP%\ARCHIVE
```

The output of the ATTRIB command lists the Archive attribute as capital A followed by a space. The above FIND command simply counts all occurrences of A-space in the ARCHIVE file. The output is displayed in summary style, as below:

```
---------- C:\TEMP\ARCHIVE: 845
```

As a filter, you can use FIND to sift through the output of a DOS command. For example:

```
DIR | FIND "<DIR>"
```

The above command displays all the subdirectories in the current directory. For example:

```
DOS    <DIR> 03-18-91 9:33p
BATCH  <DIR> 09-20-90 11:52p
UTIL   <DIR> 09-20-90 11:37p
TEMP   <DIR> 09-20-90 11:14a
```

To see how many subdirectories are in the current directory, you can use the following:

```
C:\>DIR | FIND /C "<DIR>"
10
```

Remember the TIME command? You now know what it takes to extract the current time using I/O redirection and the FIND command. Type the following:

```
TIME | FIND "is" < C:\BATCH\ENTER
```

Be sure you specify the proper directory for your ENTER file (created earlier in this chapter). Also, note that that's a little "is" above, to match "is" in the TIME command's output. The end result of the above command looks something like this:

```
Current time is 10:03:35.61a
```

You can further use I/O redirection to create a log file, which you can place in a batch file. Consider adding the following two commands to your AUTOEXEC.BAT file as an example:

```
ECHO System Booted >> LOGFILE
TIME | FIND "is" < C:\BATCH\ENTER >> LOGFILE
```

Each time you start your computer, the current time will be appended to the file LOGFILE. Other batch files that do certain chores for you could contain similar commands. Your batch file that runs the BACKUP program may have the following commands toward the end:

```
ECHO System backup completed >> LOGFILE
TIME | FIND "is" < C:\BATCH\ENTER >> LOGFILE
```

LOGFILE keeps a record of all your activities on the computer.

COMMAND: FIND (External/Filter)
             Function: Locates a string of text in a file
             Format: FIND switches "text" filename

Text is text to locate in a file, which is enclosed in double quotes. Text cannot contain the characters |, <, or >, and if a double quote appears in text it must be specified twice.

Filename is the name of a formatted text file FIND will scan. It cannot contain a wildcard, although you can specify more than one individual file and the FIND command will scan each of them.

Switches are optional switches used to modify the FIND command's output. Without the switches, the FIND command displays all lines in the file that contain matching text. Otherwise, the switches do the following:

/C directs the FIND command to display a line count indicating the number of lines containing text. Only the filename and line count are displayed.

/I directs the FIND command to ignore any differences in upper or lower case in the text.

/N directs the FIND command to list the line number before displaying a line of matching text.

/V directs the FIND command to display only those lines not containing matching text.

As a command, FIND uses the following format:

```
FIND switches "text" filename
```

As a filter, FIND uses this format:

```
COMMAND | FIND switches "text"
```

To scan a group of files, use the FIND and FOR commands as follows:

```
FOR %v IN (set) DO FIND switches "text" %v
```

Summary

DOS gives a name to each of its devices. The standard I/O device is CON, the console, which consists of the screen (output) and keyboard (input). PRN is the first printer device, and AUX is the first serial port. Disk drive devices are given single letters, from A through Z.

DOS's file (or information) manipulation commands can be used with devices as well as filenames. You can copy a file to the console via the CON device, to the printer via PRN, and so on. You can copy between any two devices capable of output or input.

The output redirection symbol, >, is used to redirect DOS's output from the standard output device (the console) to another file or device. If the file doesn't exits, DOS creates it; if it does exist, the new file overwrites it.

The output redirection append symbol, >>, also redirects DOS's output. However, if the named file exists, DOS will append the new text to it.

The input redirection symbol, <, is used to redirect DOS's input from a device other than the console, either a file or some other device capable of generating input. This can be tricky, however, in that the redirected input must supply or anticipate all the proper keystrokes. If not, keyboard control may not return.

The pipe symbol, |, is used to pipe the output of a DOS command through another DOS command or through a special program or filter.

A filter is a program that accepts standard input, modifies it, and then displays the result as standard output. You can use the I/O redirection symbols or the pipe to modify the output of a DOS command or file through a filter. DOS comes with three filters, SORT, MORE, and FIND.

The SORT filter is used to sort lines of text in a formatted text file. The text is sorted in alphanumeric order, reverse order, or at a specified column offset.

The MORE filter is used to pause display of long text by showing a "more" prompt at the bottom of each screen.

The FIND filter locates lines of text containing specified characters in a formatted text file. The output of a DOS command can be piped through the FIND filter to locate specific text.

CHAPTER 25

DEBUG

DEBUG is a great little program, full of mystery and bursting with power. But DEBUG is dangerous: It's really a programmer's tool, relatively unchanged from the early days of DOS and personal computing. While DEBUG can do interesting things, show you parts of your computer you can't otherwise see, and let you create interesting programs and effects, it's not to be used carelessly.

This chapter answers the following questions:

- How does DEBUG look at and change memory?

- What interesting things can be done with DEBUG and memory?

- How does DEBUG modify raw information on disk?

- How can DEBUG modify a file on disk?

- How can DEBUG be used to create a COM program file?

- What is disassembly?

What Does DEBUG Do?

DEBUG is a multifaceted tool—a programmer's buddy. It's primitive, but that simplicity is power. Basically, DEBUG lets you do the following:

Look at and edit memory (individual bytes)

Examine and change the microprocessor's registers

Load portions of disk into memory for examination or editing

Save portions of memory to disk

Create assembly language programs and save them to disk

Run assembly language and COM programs

Disassemble COM programs

DEBUG gets its name from the word "bug" (if you can believe that). The original moth or insect that found its way crawling into an early computer caused problems that have since been generically referred to as bugs. Fixing a program is "getting the bugs out." The original purpose of DEBUG was to debug a program, finding out what went wrong and allowing a programmer to fix it. This is why DEBUG contains so many low-level routines.

Info: DEBUG has its basis in early microcomputer programs that served the same purpose. One of them is DDT, which was used on CP/M computers in the late '70s and early '80s. DDT was named after the now-banned pesticide.

With DEBUG you can "look under the hood" and see what makes your computer tick. Of course, unless you're well versed in the subject of computer operations, know programming, or are intimate with the technical aspects of a PC, DEBUG is less than useful. This chapter will show you what DEBUG can do and how to make it productive for you. It also opens the door to some of the inner workings of your PC—and it's fun.

Running the DEBUG Program

DEBUG is a program, DEBUG.EXE, usually located in your DOS subdirectory. To run the DEBUG program, type DEBUG at the DOS prompt:

```
C:\>DEBUG
-
```

DEBUG's prompt is the hyphen—not too friendly. You enter DEBUG's commands at the hyphen prompt. Each command is typically one letter long, followed by optional parameters and values. The most important commands to know now are Help and Quit.

The Help command is a single question mark. It displays a list of all DEBUG's commands and their command format. Type the question mark and press Enter. You'll see a list similar to the following:

```
assemble                        A [address]
compare                         C range address
dump                            D [range]
enter                           E address [list]
fill                            F range list
go                              G [=address] [addresses]
hex                             H value1 value2
input                           I port
load                            L [address] [drive] [firstsector]
                                                        [number]
move                            M range address
name                            N [pathname] [arglist]
output                          O port byte
proceed                         P [=address] [number]
quit                            Q
register                        R [register]
search                          S range list
trace                           T [=address] [value]
unassemble                      U [range]
write                           W [address] [drive] [firstsector]
                                                        [number]
allocate expanded memory        XA [#pages]
deallocate expanded memory      XD [handle]
map expanded memory pages       XM [Lpage] [Ppage] [handle]
display expanded memory status  XS
```

This list isn't informative. Instead, it serves only as a reminder of the command letters and format. Note that each command is one or two letters, upper or lower case.

To quit DEBUG, the Q command is used. That returns you to DOS and leaves DEBUG alone. (Don't return to DOS just yet.)

If you make a mistake typing a command, DEBUG tells you where the mistake is as follows:

```
-Y
 ^ Error
```

The caret points to the offending part of the command you entered, followed by the word "Error." When this happens, check your typing or refer to the Help Command list for the proper command format.

Hexadecimal

All numbers entered in DEBUG are hexadecimal, base-16 counting. When a DEBUG command requires an optional value, it must be entered in hexadecimal or "hex." This can really blow your mind, because as a human you use base-10 counting. For using DOS, knowing hexadecimal isn't important. But occasionally it does crop up (as in DEBUG and, in the next chapter, with the MEM command).

In hexadecimal, the numbers range from 0 through 15 as opposed to 0 through 9 in base 10. The values 11 through 15 are represented by the letters A through F, respectively. So a hexadecimal number will have both letters and numbers.

Info: An example of a hexadecimal number you've been seeing all along is a disk's serial number. It contains the numbers 0 through 9 and the letters A through F.

In the decimal counting system, each position in a number is a multiple of ten. Thus number 125 is one 100, two 10s, and five 1s. In hexadecimal counting, each position in a number is a multiple of 16, which means that, in addition to containing letters, hexadecimal values will be much larger than their decimal look-a-likes: The hexadecimal number 125 is one 265s, two 16s, and five 1s—293 in decimal.

Hex number	Decimal value
10	16
50	80
80	128
100	256
200	512
400	1024
1000	4096

The table at the end of this section shows how to calculate hexadecimal values, translating them into decimal values. But for using DEBUG, just lift your mind out of the decimal gutter and accept the numbers as entered. Actually, if you've been using computers for some time, you'll recognize a few common hexadecimal values right off:

Decimal number	Hex value
10	A
20	14
25	19
50	32
100	64
1000	3E8

Note that "interesting" numbers in decimal have rather unimpressive hexadecimal values. All of this is linked to the binary (base 2) system, by the way. In fact, programmers use hexadecimal because it's a handy abbreviation for binary.

To calculate a decimal equivalent, take each character in the hexadecimal number and multiple it by the proper decimal value in the table. For example, the number 1A76 is figured as follows:

```
1 = 4096
A = 2560
7 = 112
6 =   6
```

The total is 6774 decimal.

	4,096's	256's	16's	1's
1	4096	256	16	1
2	8192	512	32	2
3	12288	768	48	3
4	16384	1024	64	4
5	20480	1280	80	5
6	24576	1536	96	6
7	28672	1792	112	7
8	32768	2048	128	8
9	36864	2304	144	9
A	40690	2560	160	10
B	45056	2816	176	11
C	49152	3072	192	12
D	53248	3328	208	13
E	57344	3584	224	14
F	61440	3840	240	15

Table 25-1. Hexadecimal Values

DEBUG the Memory Peeker

DEBUG is capable of wreaking much havoc, but as long as you carefully follow the instructions in this chapter you will do no damage. For example, the following sections deal with looking at memory—just peeking around. Later, you'll actually change memory, which could have unusual (but nothing permanent) effects. (You'll be alerted if there's any potential for true PC assault.)

The Dump Command

To view the contents of memory, you use the rather inelegantly named Dump command.

Info: "Dump" is a classic computer term, originating in the old days when big computers used to perform a core dump when something went wrong. A core dump contained a copy of all the computer's memory, just as if it had dumped its soul out on paper. The term is also used to describe what the Print Screen key does—a screen dump. (Not very flattering.)

At the hyphen prompt, press D and enter. You'll see something like Figure 25-1. Keep in mind that all values displayed are in hexadecimal.

```
-D

09E7:0100   00  00 00 00 00 00 00 00-00 00 00 00 00 00 33 B8   .............3.
09E7:0110   00  F0 83 34 B2 00 B2 09-00 00 99 00 34 00 D6 09   ...4........4...
09E7:0120   00  00 00 00 00 00 00 00-00 00 00 00 00 00 00 00   ................
09E7:0130   00  00 00 00 00 00 00 00-00 00 00 00 00 00 00 00   ................
09E7:0140   00  00 00 00 00 00 00 00-00 00 00 00 00 00 00 00   ................
09E7:0150   00  00 00 00 00 00 00 00-00 00 00 00 00 00 00 00   ................
09E7:0160   00  00 00 00 00 00 00 00-00 00 00 00 00 00 00 00   ................
09E7:0170   00  00 00 00 00 00 00 00-00 00 00 00 00 00 00 00   ................
```

Figure 25-1. The output of the Dump command.

The Dump command shows you the contents of memory and the value of each byte at a specific location (address) in memory. What you see on your screen will be different from that above. But each of the three columns will display the same type of information:

The first column displays the location in memory. It's given as two values; the first is a segment address and the second is an offset within that segment. In Figure 25-1, the segment address is 09E7 and the offsets range from 100 through 170. In computerese, you're looking at the 9E7th 16-byte segment in memory, offsets 100 through 170 hex—which is exactly 128 bytes of memory.

The middle column displays the values for each byte in memory. Sixteen bytes across are shown in the column, with a dash separating the seventh and eighth bytes. A byte can contain any value from zero (00) through 255 (FF). Most of the bytes in Figure 25-1 contain zero, but a few contain other values. The exact location of those bytes is their column position plus the offset value.

The third column displays the ASCII characters represented by the sixteen bytes in the middle column. Non-ASCII and control characters are shown as a dot. In Figure 25-1, the characters "3" and "4" can be seen.

The Dump command can be used to view any 128-byte chunk of memory. For example, the very bottom of memory is segment zero offset zero. To view that segment, type in the following Dump command:

```
D 0:0
```

Again, 128 bytes are displayed in the same format. If you press D again, you'll see another 128 bytes. On your screen will be the first 256 bytes in memory.

The Dump command can display any number of bytes at any specific location. The following command displays the 256 bytes at segment 40, offset 0:

```
D 40:0 100
```

What you see on your screen now is just so many bytes. But to the computer, there is some important information there. This memory location, segment 40, is where DOS and your PC store information such as the amount of memory installed, a list of all equipment in the computer, and the last several keys you've pressed. Of course, everything is a byte value, which makes it a moot point to look for specific items.

Locating the Environment

The Dump command is an interesting way to explore the innards of your computer, but unless you can be impressed with byte values, it's of little value. However, the Dump command can be used to locate your PC's environment. That, at least, contains readable text strings you will recognize. Let's go environment hunting...

Start by quitting and then re-launching Debug. Type Q to quit, and then type DEBUG again at the DOS prompt. At DEBUG's hyphen prompt, type D0 (the Dump command followed by a zero). That displays the first 128 bytes in what's called the program segment prefix.

Info: Every program DOS runs has a program segment prefix (PSP). It contains all sorts of interesting tidbits (and tidbytes) about the program running, options typed on the command line, and DOS information for the program.

Nestled in among the bytes displayed is the segment address of your PC's environment, where the PATH, PROMPT and other environment variables are stored. The address is held at offset 2C (hex) in the current segment. You could locate that value by counting to "2C" as you read each byte value on the screen. Instead, use the power of the computer to help you find it. Type:

```
D 2C L2
```

The command displays two bytes (L2, length two) in memory at offset 2C. What you see on your screen will be different, but my screen shows the following two bytes:

```
2D 04
```

Those bytes represent the segment address of the environment in memory. But they're backwards! (This is the way all PC microprocessors store data.) To get the true segment address, you must swap the bytes you see on your screen and use them with the Dump command. For example, above 2D 04 changes into the following Dump command:

```
D 042D:0
```

Swap the bytes on your screen and enter them after the Dump command, followed by a colon and a zero. Press Enter to see the environment.

```
042D:0000  54 45 4D 50 3D 43 3A 5C-54 45 4D 50 00 50 41 54   TEMP=C:\TEMP.PAT
042D:0010  48 3D 43 3A 5C 44 4F 53-3B 43 3A 5C 42 41 54 43   H=C:\DOS;C:\BATC
042D:0020  48 3B 43 3A 5C 55 54 49-4C 00 4D 50 41 54 48 3D   H;C:\UTIL.MPATH=
042D:0030  43 3A 5C 44 4F 53 3B 43-3A 5C 42 41 54 43 48 3B   C:\DOS;C:\BATCH;
042D:0040  43 3A 5C 55 54 49 4C 00-43 4F 4D 53 50 45 43 3D   C:\UTIL.COMSPEC=
042D:0050  43 3A 5C 44 4F 53 5C 43-4F 4D 4D 41 4E 44 2E 43   C:\DOS\COMMAND.C
042D:0060  4F 4D 00 50 52 4F 4D 50-54 3D 24 50 24 47 00 00   OM.PROMPT=$P$G..
042D:0070  00 00 00 00 00 00 00 00-00 00 00 00 00 00 00 00   ................
```

Figure 25-2. The environment in memory.

Look to the third column and see if you recognize the environment variables and their strings. What you're looking at is a copy of the master environment stored in memory for use by DEBUG. There's really nothing useful that can be done here, other than looking at something familiar.

Zapping the Screen

DEBUG's Dump command can look at memory anywhere in your PC. This includes reserved memory and ROM. Type the following Dump command:

```
D FE00:0
```

What you see on your screen is ROM, in particular, your computer's BIOS, which is located at segment FE00. You may recognize a copyright notice in the third column on the screen or the letters "IBM." But this is ROM and cannot be changed. To find some interesting memory to manipulate, video RAM can be used.

Info: Your PC's video memory starts at segment B800 if you have a color system, or B000 if you have monochrome. This chapter assumes you have color, so the value B800 is used in the following DEBUG commands. If you have a monochrome system, substitute B000 instead.

Using DEBUG to view video memory is hard because DEBUG scrolls the screen. To start off "on top," quit DEBUG by typing Q, and then at the DOS prompt type CLS to clear the screen and then DEBUG to again enter DEBUG.

To change bytes in memory, the Enter command, E, is used. The Enter command allows you to enter new bytes at the memory location you specify. To put an "A" on the screen, ASCII code 65 or 41 hex, type the following:

```
E B800:0 41
```

Press Enter and an "A" magically appears in the upper left corner of the screen. You've just poked the value 41 hex into the video-memory location B800:0.

If you follow the E command with a string in quotes, that string will be poked into memory. Type the following:

```
E B800:0 "Hello world!"
```

Hlowrd? It doesn't make sense, but it certainly is psychedelic.

What happened was that you only poked every odd character into video memory as a displayable character. The even characters are interpreted by your video adapter as character attributes, similar to the attributes set by the ANSI Set Graphics Mode command. Re-enter the command as follows:

```
E B800:0 "Hpeplplpop pwpoprplpdp!p"
```

Every other character is a little "p", which is equivalent to the attribute code for black-on-white text. Press Enter and you'll see the text properly displayed.

DEBUG's Fill command is used to fill memory with a specific byte or pair of bytes. The format is:

```
F segment:offset-length byte(s)
```

Segment:offset is the location in memory.

Length is the number of bytes to fill.

Byte(s) is either a single-byte value or a pair of bytes. If a pair, then the Fill command puts each byte in every other memory location.

Type the following command:

```
F B800:0 A0 41 70
```

This fills A0 (160) bytes of video memory with the bytes 41 hex (ASCII "A") and 70 hex (ASCII "p"). Press enter and the top line of the screen is filled with the letter A in inverse text.

The entire screen is FA0 bytes long. To fill the entire screen with inverse A's, use the following command:

```
F B800:0 FA0 41 70
```

Try the following for an exciting effect:

```
F B800:0 FA0 21 CE
```

Press Enter, and then, after you can't stand it anymore, press Q to quit DEBUG and type CLS at the DOS prompt.

DEBUG the Disk Editor

DEBUG can be used to examine and edit information on disk. You specify the disk drive and number of sectors, and DEBUG copies the information on those sectors into memory. Once in memory, you can edit the information in the sectors using the Dump, Enter, and Fill commands. After making your modifications, you have the option of writing the information back out to disk—but this is the scary part and should be used only when you're certain of what you're doing.

Reading Disk

To load sectors from disk into memory the Load command is used. This is a perfectly safe command and will only copy information from disk into memory. The format is:

```
L address disk sector count
```

Address is the segment and offset in memory where you want to store the information read from disk. Usually the value 100 is specified.

Disk is a value from zero through 25 representing drives A through Z, respectively. Remember, 0 is drive A.

Sector is the starting sector on disk to be loaded. Disks come in different formats, which means each disk has a different sector count. For this chapter, only the first few sectors on disk are loaded.

Count is the number of sectors to load into memory. Remember that each sector uses 512 bytes of memory.

You can load in sectors from any disk in your system. But for this chapter, you should use a test diskette. If you created a TEST DISK for the earlier chapters of this book, retrieve it now for experimentation with the DEBUG command. Otherwise, use the FORMAT command to format a diskette in drive A, and then copy a few files to that diskette (such as AUTOEXEC.BAT and CONFIG.SYS). Put the diskette in drive A, and then start DEBUG.

```
C:\>DEBUG
-
```

Looking around a disk can be as boring as looking around memory, unless you know what it is you're looking at and where to find it. An interesting thing to view on disk is the root directory. But for each disk size, the root directory is at a different location on disk. The following table gives the starting sector of the root directory for each of the four popular diskette sizes:

Diskette Size	Root Sector (hex)
360K	5
720K	7
1.2M	F
1.4M	13

Given the size of your test diskette in drive A, substitute the proper value from above into the following Load command:

```
L 100 0 size 1
```

This reads, "Load into memory address 100 from the diskette in drive A (0), the sector number size, one sector only please." If drive A is a 1.2M floppy, you'd type the following command:

```
L 100 0 F 1
```

Press Enter after typing the appropriate command. Drive A will spin as the root directory's first sector is read by DEBUG. Next, use the Dump command to see what you've loaded into memory. A sample is shown in Figure 25-3.

```
09E7:0100   54 45 53 54 20 44 49 53-4B 20 20 28 00 00 00 00   TEST DISK  (....
09E7:0110   00 00 00 00 00 00 AB 58-85 16 00 00 00 00 00 00   .......X........
09E7:0120   41 55 54 4F 45 58 45 43-42 41 54 20 00 00 00 00   AUTOEXECBAT ....
09E7:0130   00 00 00 00 00 00 0A 7C-82 16 02 00 F2 01 00 00   .......|........
09E7:0140   43 4F 4E 46 49 47 20 20-53 59 53 20 00 00 00 00   CONFIG  SYS ....
09E7:0150   00 00 00 00 00 00 52 AD-83 16 03 00 C8 01 00 00   ......R.........
09E7:0160   00 00 00 00 00 00 00 00-00 00 00 00 00 00 00 00   ...............
09E7:0170   00 00 00 00 00 00 00 00-00 00 00 00 00 00 00 00   ...............
```

Figure 25-3. The floppy diskette's root-directory sector in memory.

You should see filenames in the third column. That's how filenames look as they're stored on disk, but here you're looking at them in memory. If you were bold (which you won't be in this chapter), you could make editing changes using the E command, and then write those changes out to disk. If you know what you're doing, interesting tricks can be done here. But instead of messing with that, the following section shows you how to modify something less dangerous with rather humorous consequences.

Modifying Disk with the Write Command

Keep the test diskette in drive A. Use the following command to load in the diskette's boot sector. This command works for all sizes of diskettes:

```
L 100 0 0 1
```

Sector zero, the boot sector, is loaded from the diskette in drive A at memory address 100. The boot sector is very important to all diskettes, particularly the hard drive. Messing with it can be disastrous. But here you're going to have fun with it.

The diskette in drive A is a data diskette. As such, if you start the computer with that diskette in the drive, DOS displays the following message:

```
Non-System disk or disk error
Replace and press any key when ready
```

531

Recall from Chapter 17 that the boot sector is actually a program, loaded when the computer first starts. On DOS diskettes, the program searches out the file IO.SYS and loads it into memory. On non-DOS diskettes, such as the one you have stuck into drive A, the program displays the above message. Using DEBUG, you're now going to carefully change that message to say something else.

The boot sector is 512 bytes long, which translates to 200 hex. To display the boot sector in memory, use the following Dump command:

```
D 100 L200
```

This command displays the 200 hex (512) bytes at address 100, which is where the boot sector was loaded into memory. Press Enter.

Near the bottom of the screen, on the right hand side, you'll see the ASCII representation of the boot-disk error message. The message actually starts at offset 2A0 and extends through the byte value 00, located at offset 2E5 (row 2E0, fifth column).

You can replace that string of text with any other string you like, provided two things: The new string is the same length or shorter than the current string, and the string ends with the byte value 00. For example, type the following Enter command:

```
E "Boy! Did you goof!" 0d 0a "Remove me and press any key!" 0d 0a 0
```

The "0d 0a" are the carriage return and line feed characters, which display any text following on the next line. Text in quotes is literally poked into memory. To view the changes, type the following command:

```
D280
```

Press Enter and you'll see the last 128 bytes of the boot sector. Verify that the string above (or whichever string you entered) ends before offset 2E5. (You may see the tail end of the old message still in memory; verify that the byte value at row 2E0 column 5 is still a 00.)

If you've overshot, then quit DEBUG and start over; reload the sector and then use the E command to enter a new message. Otherwise, the sector looks good and you can save it to disk using the Write command.

The Write command, W, has the same format as the L command. The difference is that memory is written to disk. To write the boot sector back to the floppy disk in drive A, carefully type the following command:

```
W 100 0 0 1
```

You're writing one sector of information from memory location 100 to the diskette in drive A. Doubly verify your typing; there should be only zeros and ones in that command. Press Enter and the sector is written back to the floppy drive.

Quit DEBUG with the Q command to return to DOS. Now keep the diskette in drive A and reset your system. After the PC does its memory check, you'll see the following message displayed by the data diskette in drive A:

```
Boy! Did you goof!
Remove me and press any key.
```

Remove the test diskette and press any key to boot from your hard drive.

DEBUG the Programmer

DEBUG is a gem with many facets. In one of its personalities, DEBUG serves as a program editor, allowing you to build and take apart programs. Building programs, however, isn't that simple. You must know how DOS operates internally, as well as know how the microprocessor works. All computer programming isn't that terrible, but DEBUG never promised to be easy.

Building the GETKEY.COM Program

Using DEBUG you can tell the computer exactly what to do. You can build a program in memory and run it in memory. If you like what you've done, then you can tell DEBUG to save that section of memory to a program file on disk.

The following are instructions for creating a useful little program, GETKEY.COM. Yes, it's a "real" program, with a COM extension. As a program, GETKEY is used to read a key from the keyboard. It then takes that key's ASCII value and returns it to DOS as a return code. That return code can be evaluated in a batch file using the IF-ERRORLEVEL command. This makes the GETKEY.COM program excellent for creating interactive batch files.

Start creating GETKEY.COM by entering DEBUG (if you're not already in DEBUG).

```
C:\>DEBUG
-
```

The command to start creating programs is Assemble. This puts you in DEBUG's mini-assembly language mode, where you can enter special instructions for the microprocessor. The instructions are called mnemonics, and you don't need to memorize them here.

Type the A command:

```
-A
xxxx:0100 _
```

Debug displays the current segment and offset 100, the memory location where you'll start writing your program. Above "xxxx" is used to represent whichever segment you see on your screen. Type the following assembly language mnemonics; double check your typing before pressing Enter:

```
MOV AH,8
INT 21
AND AL,5F
MOV AH,42
INT 21
```

Press Ctrl-C after entering "INT 21." Your screen should look something like this:

```
xxxx:0100 MOV AH,8
xxxx:0102 INT 21
xxxx:0104 AND AL,5F
xxxx:0106 MOV AH,42
xxxx:0108 INT 21
xxxx:010A ^C
-
```

This assembly language program waits for a key from the keyboard (standard input). It converts lower-case letters into upper case for easier identification, and then sends that key's ASCII value back to DOS as an ERRORLEVEL value, which can be used in a batch file.

To save the program to disk, you need to tell DEBUG two things: How long the file is (in bytes) and its name. This program is 10 bytes long, which is the number "A" in hexadecimal. You tell that to DEBUG by using the RCX command. Type RCX, Enter, and then A and Enter again:

```
-RCX
CX 0000
:A
-
```

To name the file GETKEY.COM, use the Name command N:

```
-N GETKEY.COM
-
```

To save the file to disk, the Write command is used. But because a filename is specified, you need only to type W by itself. DOS will figure out where to place the file on disk, and in which sector. (It's only when you deal with raw sectors on disk that you specify options after the Write command.) Type W and Enter:

```
-W
Writing 0000A bytes
```

The file is now created and saved on disk in the current directory. It may be a good idea to move it to your UTIL or utility subdirectory, or a convenient directory on the path. (Delete the original if you move it.)

To run GETKEY, quit DEBUG and then type GETKEY at the DOS prompt:

```
C:\>GETKEY
_
```

Like the PAUSE command, GETKEY sits there, hovering until you press a key. Press Enter and another DOS prompt appears. What you didn't see is what the return code GETKEY just sent DOS. If you typed Enter, and then the return code was 13, the ASCII value of the Enter key.

To better see how GETKEY can be put to use, use the MS-DOS Editor to enter the following batch file, KEYTEST.BAT. Note how it uses the IF-ERRORLEVEL test to determine which key you pressed:

```
 1: @ECHO OFF
 2: :LOOP
 3: ECHO Type an A or a B:
 4: GETKEY
 5: IF ERRORLEVEL 67 GOTO LOOP
 6: IF ERRORLEVEL 66 GOTO BPRESSED
 7: IF ERRORLEVEL 65 GOTO APRESSED
 8: GOTO LOOP
 9: :BPRESSED
10: ECHO You pressed the B key 11: GOTO END
12: :APRESSED
13: ECHO You pressed the A key
14: :END
```

Save this file to disk, preferably in your BATCH subdirectory, as KEYTEST.BAT. To run the program type KEYTEST at the DOS prompt, press the A or B key (case is unimportant). For example, if you pressed the B key, you'd see:

```
C:\>KEYTEST
Type an A or a B:
You pressed the B key
C:\>
```

536

Here is a description of how KEYTEST.BAT works:

Line 1 turns ECHO OFF.

Line 2 contains the LOOP label, used with the GOTO in line 8 to scan for input.

Line 3 prompts the user to type an A or a B, immediately followed by line 4, which gets input from the keyboard. GETKEY returns the ASCII code for a key you press on the keyboard, returning lowercase letters as upper case. (Refer to Appendix A for the ASCII characters and their codes.)

Lines 5 through 7 evaluate the character input using IF-ERRORLEVEL commands. IF-ERRORLEVEL passes the test if the errorlevel is equal to or greater than the code returned. Line 5 tests for 67 (ASCII C) or above and, if found, the GOTO command loops back to line 2 where the user is prompted again. Line 6 tests for "B" (ASCII 66) and, if found, GOTO branches to the label BPRESSED at line 9. Line 5 tests for "A" (ASCII 65) and, if found, GOTO branches to APRESSED at line 12. If any other key was pressed, execution falls through to line 8, which branches back to the LOOP label at line 2.

Line 9 is executed when the "B" key is pressed. Line 10 displays "You pressed the B key" and line 11 branches to the END label at line 14, finishing the program.

Line 12 is executed when the "A" key is pressed. Line 13 displays the confirmation message, and then the program ends with line 14.

Tip: To test for Y-key press, such as when asking a Y/N question, use the IF ERRORLEVEL test with GETKEY.COM as follows:

```
:LOOP
GETKEY
IF ERRORLEVEL 89 IF NOT ERRORLEVEL 90 GOTO Y_PRESSED
GOTO LOOP
```

This code narrows down the options for the IF test to Y (ASCII 89) and no other value. If Y is pressed, execution branches to the Y_PRESSED label. Otherwise, the commands between LOOP and GOTO LOOP are executed until an upper- or lowercase Y is pressed.

The BOOT.BAT Program

The computer can be reset by whacking the Big Red Switch or pressing Ctrl-Alt-Delete. But you can also reset the computer with software. You can use DEBUG to create a program that resets the computer. Rather than write a program in a manner similar to GETKEY.COM, the following is a batch file that does something a little different.

To reset the computer, first a low-memory address is poked with the two hex-byte values 12 and 34. Next, the system is reset by executing an instruction way at the tip-top of memory. This can be done by a program, or it can be done by typing in the commands directly to DEBUG. Start the DEBUG program from the DOS prompt and type the following commands:

```
E 40:72 34 12
```

This pokes the values 12 and 34 into the proper memory address. Next, type:

```
G=FFFF:0
```

G is the Go command. It tells the computer to go to memory location FFFF:0000 and execute the instructions there, resetting your computer. Press Enter to reset.

These two commands are fairly nifty but clumsy to type when you want a software reset. If you used input redirection, you could force-feed them into DEBUG. Doing so would require two files: a batch file to start redirection and a text file containing the two necessary commands. But why not combine them both?

Use the MS-DOS Editor to enter the following file. Save it to disk as BOOT.BAT:

```
1: @ECHO OFF
2: GOTO BEGIN
3:
4: E 40:72 34 12
5: G=FFFF:0
6:
7: :BEGIN
8: DEBUG < C:\BATCH\BOOT.BAT
```

Save the file to disk, preferably in your BATCH-file directory. Note that line 7 contains the name of this file and must indicate the proper subdirectory on your system where the file is located. Also, be mindful of the blank lines, 3 and 6. They are important.

This program is rather cannibalistic. It uses itself as the input for I/O redirection—which looks clumsy—yet everything works.

Line 1 starts by turning ECHO OFF. Line 2 branches to the BEGIN label at line 7. Then, in line 8, the batch file feeds itself to DEBUG. Here's what happens in DEBUG:

DEBUG doesn't understand @ECHO OFF, so it interprets it as an error. Likewise for GOTO BEGIN—DEBUG reads that as garbage. Line 3 is a carriage return (Enter), which clears DEBUG's head and gives you a blank hyphen prompt. Then lines 4 and 5—which are the two commands required to reset the system—are fed to DEBUG. Because the system boots after line 6, the rest of the program is never completed.

You can include this program in any other batch file in which you want the system to reset. Simply list BOOT as a command by itself. You don't need to CALL BOOT because the computer won't be returning. And you can always type BOOT at the DOS prompt to reset the system. Do so now if you like:

```
BOOT
```

DEBUG as Disassembler

This section is for the utterly curious only. DEBUG can disassemble files on disk, let you view them for editing on the byte level, or just peek around and see how a program works. This isn't as magic as it reads; DEBUG disassembles programs into assembly language and machine code, which can be viewed readily only by those versed in assembly-language programming.

The Microprocessor Registers

When you typed the assembly language mnemonics earlier in this chapter, you were really giving instructions directly to the microprocessor. The microprocessor uses special high-speed memory locations called registers, in which it stores information.

Enter DEBUG and type the Register command, R:

```
-R
AX=0000  BX=0000  CX=0000  DX=0000  SP=FFEE  BP=0000  SI=0000 DI=0000
DS=09E7  ES=09E7  SS=09E7  CS=09E7  IP-0100 NV UP EI PL NZ NA PO NC
09E7:0100 62 DB 62
```

Some of the values you see on your screen will be different, but the general display is the same. You're looking at your microprocessor's registers. Displayed are the values of each, along with other information that would only make an assembly language programmer happy.

Info: Actually, you're seeing the 8086-compatible registers for your microprocessor. The 80286s look somewhat similar, but the 80386s are twice as large and there's several additional registers, which DEBUG doesn't show.

Take note of the CX register. This is the register you modified when you saved GETKEY.COM to disk. When the Write command is used to save a filename to disk, it uses the hexadecimal value stored in the CX register to determine the file's size. (The file is always assumed to start at offset 100.)

To change a register such as the CX register, the R command is used, immediately followed by the register name:

```
RCX
```

After entering the command, DEBUG displays the current contents of the register, and then gives you a change to enter a new value. Keep in mind that all values must be entered in hexadecimal.

Tracing a Program's Execution

You can see how these registers work by loading in a COM file, and then stepping through it one line at time. For example, why not load the GETKEY.COM file into memory? After all, you're the programmer who created it.

To load in a COM file you must first name it. This is done with the Name command, N. Type:

```
N C:\UTIL\GETKEY.COM
```

Specify the proper pathname for GETKEY.COM; above, C:\UTIL is assumed. Press Enter. This only names the file, telling DEBUG which program to save with the Write command—or which one to load with the Load command. Type L:

```
-L
-
```

It appears as if nothing happened, but DEBUG has just loaded your program. To prove it, type the Register command again:

```
-R
AX=0000  BX=0000  CX=000A  DX=0000  SP=FFEE  BP=0000  SI=0000 DI=0000
DS=09E7  ES=09E7  SS=09E7  CS=09E7  IP-0100 NV UP EI PL NZ NA PO NC
09E7:0100 B408 MOV AH,08
```

Note how the CX register reflects the size of the program just loaded. Above, GETKEY.COM is A (10) bytes long. At the bottom of the output you see the first command you entered, the first instruction to the microprocessor in the GETKEY.COM program file. "MOV AH,08" means to move the value 08 (hex) into the register AH. To see that happen, use the Proceed command; press the P key:

```
-P
AX=0800  BX=0000  CX=000A  DX=0000  SP=FFEE  BP=0000  SI=0000 DI=0000
DS=09E7  ES=09E7  SS=09E7  CS=09E7  IP-0102 NV UP EI PL NZ NA PO NC
09E7:0102 CD21 INT 21
```

Note how the AX register changes (right below the R command). It now reads 0800. You have moved the value 08 into the upper half of the AX register. The next instruction is INT 21. Press the P command to process it.

After pressing P, the computer waits. The two instructions you've just stepped through tell DOS to wait for a character from the keyboard. Type the "a" key (lowercase).

```
AX=0861  BX=0000  CX=000A  DX=0000  SP=FFEE  BP=0000  SI=0000 DI=0000
DS=09E7  ES=09E7  SS=09E7  CS=09E7  IP-0104 NV UP EI PL NZ NA PO NC
09E7:0104 245F  ANDAL,5F
```

The key you just pressed is saved in the AX register. The value 61 above and on your screen is the hexadecimal value for the ASCII code for the letter a (little A). The command on the bottom of the screen, AND AL,5F, is used to convert lowercase to uppercase. Press P to proceed:

```
-P
AX=0841  BX=0000  CX=000A  DX=0000  SP=FFEE  BP=0000  SI=0000 DI=0000
DS=09E7  ES=09E7  SS=09E7  CS=09E7  IP-0106 NV UP EI PL NZ NA PO NC
09E7:0106 B44C  MOVAH,4C
```

The 61 in the AX register has changed to 41, which is now the hexadecimal code for capital A. The command now visible at the bottom of the screen is the Quit to DOS function, MOV AH,4C. Press P twice more to quit to DOS:

```
-P
AX=4C41  BX=0000  CX=000A  DX=0000  SP=FFEE  BP=0000  SI=0000 DI=0000
DS=09E7  ES=09E7  SS=09E7  CS=09E7  IP-0108 NV UP EI PL NZ NA PO NC
09E7:0108 CD21  INT21
-P

  Program terminated normally
  -
```

One step at a time, that's how the program works. If you ever get into programming, you'll find all this fascinating. If not, then it just shows another wondrous thing DEBUG can do—take programs apart and look at them.

Quit DEBUG using the Q command to return to DOS. (You don't need to save the GETKEY.COM program; it's already on disk.)

Summary

DEBUG is a multifaceted program you can use as a tool to do the following:

Look at memory

Change memory

Load disk into memory, where it can be changed

Save memory to disk

Load a program into memory

Save a program from memory

Create a program in memory and then save it to disk

The only drawback to DEBUG is its cryptic commands—usually one letter and followed by hexadecimal values. The commands covered in this chapter are listed below:

Command	Function
?, Help	Displays a Help screen, a summary of all DEBUG's commands
Q, Quit	Quits DEBUG, returns to DOS
D, Dump	Displays a chunk of memory at a specific segment and offset. If the L option is added, it displays a chunk of memory for the length specified.
E, Enter	Changes bytes at a given memory location
F, Fill	Fills a range of bytes in memory with a specific byte value or a pair of bytes.

L, Load   Loads sectors from disk into memory. If a file is named (using the Name command), the file is loaded into memory at offset 100.

W, Write   Writes sectors from memory to disk. If a file is named, it's written to disk with its size specified in the CX register.

A, Assemble   Enters DEBUG's mini-assembler, where you can enter assembly-language mnemonics and create little COM files.

N, Name   Names a file on disk to load, or the name of a file in memory to save. A full pathname can follow N to save the file in another directory.

G, Go   Causes the computer to go to a specific memory address and execute the instructions found there. In this chapter, the G command is used to go to the ROM location that stores the computer's reset instructions.

P, Proceed   Steps through an assembly-language program loaded into memory.

R, Register   Displays the current set of microprocessor registers and their values. If followed by the name of a register, it's used to change the register's contents.

CHAPTER 26

Memory Management

For years PC owners suffered under DOS. A new 80386 PC could have megabytes of memory installed, but DOS had to be compatible with all PCs, including older 8088's that could only access one megabyte of memory. Because of this, users with advanced computers suffered. DOS 5 changed all that, and now allows you to take advantage of memory in your PC, giving you more RAM in which to run DOS and your applications.

This chapter answers the following questions:

- How is memory organized in the typical PC?

- What is the difference between extended and expanded memory?

- What is extended memory good for?

- How can you see which programs are in memory?

- What is the HMA?

- What's the difference between the XMS and EMS?

- How are upper-memory blocks created?

- What can go into a UMB?

- How do the DEVICEHIGH and LOADHIGH commands differ?

Your PC's Memory

When you work with memory on a PC, you let the jargon genie out of the bottle. To make things easier, and to make the task of using the memory managers more manageable, the following sections explain how memory in a PC works and what the different types of memory are called. Any new terms are defined in the text.

The Memory Map

A memory map is a graphic representation of your computer's memory. They were very popular in the early days of personal computing. Using programs similar to DEBUG, you could change key values in memory, causing the computer to do interesting things.

Since treating the PC like a "fun" computer is frowned upon, DOS's memory maps are used to show you where and how memory is used in your computer. Figure 26-1 shows you the memory map of the two basic types of PCs: the older 8088- or 8086-based PC, and 80286 and later PCs.

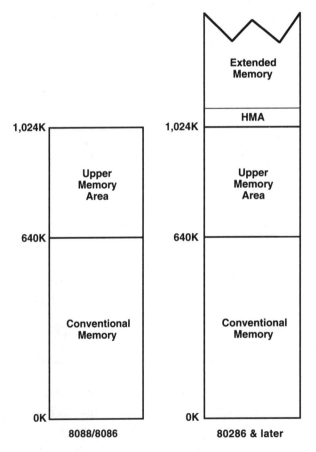

Figure 26-1. PC/XT and 80286 memory maps.

Info: There is a great difference between the 8086 and 80286 and how they use memory; the 80286 could access up to 16 megabytes of memory—way beyond the limited 1,024K addressable by the 8086. The 80386 and later microprocessors can access up to four gigabytes of memory. For the basic memory map, however, the "picture" of an 80286 and a 80386 system's memory is nearly identical.

DOS and your programs run in what's called conventional memory. It's the first 640K of RAM—or less, if you don't have the full amount installed—and that's all you have for running DOS and your programs.

Info: Conventional memory is the basic 640K of RAM. It's also called DOS memory or low DOS memory.

The remainder of the basic one megabyte of memory is reserved for "future expansion" by IBM. That area, referred to as the upper-memory area, is used for video memory and ROM: the video BIOS; hard disk BIOS; PC system BIOS; the BASIC programming language (on IBM machines); and any other hardware—such as a network adapter—you may add to your system.

Info: The upper-memory area is the top 384K of memory, used for ROMs, BIOSs, and video RAM. It's also called reserved memory or high DOS memory.

Because DOS and all computers that run DOS are compatible with the original 8088, the split of 640K for conventional memory and 384K for the upper-memory area is solid. This is why the 640K line is often called a "brick wall"; there is no way your software can get around that wall to use any extra memory in the computer.

When the 80286 microprocessor was introduced in the PC/AT, it offered a potential of 16 megabytes of memory. That memory, any extra RAM in the PC above the one megabyte mark of the old 8088/8086, is called extended memory. The same memory on a '386 or later PC is also called extended memory. Below the one megabyte mark, the memory map is still the same as an 8088/8086, with that same brick wall at 640K.

DOS cannot run programs in extended memory. In order to do so, it must activate the 80286 or '386 microprocessor's protected mode. But DOS is an 8088/8086 operating system. To run DOS, the 80286 and later microprocessors must run in the real mode. In that mode, they cannot access extended memory. This leaves 80286 or later PC owners in a quandary: What can be done with all that extra memory—and all the unused potential of the advanced microprocessors?

Info: So why not rewrite DOS as a protected-mode operating system? One major reason: It wouldn't be compatible with the original DOS, thus preventing millions of older PC owners from using the new DOS and making all current DOS software obsolete. How is that true? Because OS/2 is the rewritten, protected-mode version of DOS. And few like it.

Extended memory can be used under DOS, but only for data storage. Programs such as RAM disks, print spoolers, and disk caches can use extended memory for their buffers (memory storage). Some applications, such as Lotus 1-2-3 and Windows, can use extended memory, but only by running special DOS Extender software. Still, for DOS applications, there is only the 640K of conventional memory in which to work.

One way to put extended memory to work directly under DOS is by using the HIMEM.SYS device driver. HIMEM.SYS converts the first 64K of extended memory into the high-memory area, the HMA. PC's with extended memory can use that extra 64K of RAM to store some special applications, such as DOS itself or Windows. (Using the HMA under DOS is covered later in this chapter.)

Using the Basic 640K

When you think about it, 640K is a lot of memory. That's 655,360 bytes—more characters than there are in this book. At the time of the PC's introduction, most personal computers had only 64K of RAM. So 640K was ten times as much. Yet, after only a few short years, software developers introduced applications that ate up all that RAM.

The problem isn't the full 640K of RAM—that's still a lot. The problem lies in the many other items DOS places into conventional memory. The following is a list of those items, showing their use of memory from 0K up through the potential full 640K of RAM.

The Interrupt Vectors

At the very bottom of memory is 1K of special information for the microprocessor. It's also used by DOS and the BIOS.

The Communications Areas

DOS and the BIOS store interesting and miscellaneous information in the low-memory communications areas. Information such as the screen size, video mode, memory in the computer, system time, keys typed at the keyboard, and other fun stuff is located here.

IO.SYS

DOS's first program, IO.SYS, is loaded into memory just above the communications areas.

MSDOS.SYS

The second DOS program, MSDOS.SYS, sits in memory right on top of IO.SYS. The computer hasn't fully booted and yet, more than 40K of the basic 640K is gone.

DOS System Data

Above MSDOS.SYS, DOS stores its various FILES and BUFFERS, which are defined in CONFIG.SYS.

Device Drivers

A heavy memory toll is taken by device drivers loaded by CONFIG.SYS. The MOUSE.SYS driver may gobble up 14K; ANSI.SYS some 4K; and each RAMDrive you start takes up 1K. If the RAMDrive program creates a RAM drive in conventional memory, subtract its size from the total as well.

INSTALLed Programs

If you use the INSTALL command to run memory-resident programs in CONFIG.SYS, subtract their size from your total RAM as well.

COMMAND.COM

After CONFIG.SYS runs, COMMAND.COM is loaded. The resident portion of COMMAND.COM takes up about 4K of RAM; the rest (the transient portion) is loaded into upper memory and doesn't really subtract from your total RAM.

COMMAND.COM's Environment

Any environment variables used by DOS are placed into the 256 bytes set aside by COMMAND.COM for its environment.

Memory-Resident Programs

Any memory-resident programs you run (those, for example, in AUTOEXEC.BAT) sit fat in memory. These includes pop-up utilities, memory-resident programs, screen blankers, and DOS programs such as KEYB, MIRROR, PRINT, and so on.

Your Applications

Finally, after all the above material is loaded into memory, you can load your applications. At this time, your 640K of conventional memory has been whittled down to maybe 580K—if you're lucky. But with a lot of device drivers and memory-resident programs (network drivers especially), you may end up with less than 500K.

Your Application's Data

On top of your application, you need RAM to store your data. A 512K WP.EXE file will barely squeeze into memory. But where does that leave RAM for your Pulitzer-prize winning article on the rain forests (which vanish almost as fast as RAM in a PC)?

Memory is a precious commodity. There are two solutions to getting at more of it under DOS: The first is expanded memory, which is available to all types of PC. The second is DOS 5's memory-management tricks, some of which work on an 80286-based PC, but all of which really shine on '386 systems. (Expanded memory is covered in the next section; DOS 5's memory management is covered later in this chapter.)

Expanded Memory

The first solution to the PC's memory crises was expanded memory. Expanded memory is not extended memory; extended memory is memory above the one megabyte mark in a 80286 or later microprocessor. Expanded memory is simply extra memory in a PC—like an extra hard drive, although it's all RAM.

The expanded-memory solution was devised by Lotus, whose users wanted more memory for their huge spreadsheets. Intel, pioneers the PC's microprocessors, joined in the act, followed by Microsoft, makers of DOS. Together, they forged a standard for expanded memory, the LIM EMS—the Lotus-Intel-Microsoft Expanded Memory Specification. The latest version of this specification is one called LIM 4.0 EMS.

EMS is both a hardware and software standard. On the hardware side, EMS defines up to 32 megabytes of extra memory a PC can use. It's installed into 8088/8086 and 80286 computers by means of an EMS-compatible expansion card. The '386 family of microprocessors have advanced memory management built in; they can convert existing extended memory into expanded memory.

On the software side, EMS memory is controlled by an Expanded Memory Manager (EMM), a device driver installed in your CONFIG.SYS file. It controls the EMS hardware and allows your software access to the expanded memory.

Expanded memory itself works a lot like your disk drives. In the upper-memory area, the EMM driver designates a 64K area of unused memory as the page frame. The page frame is further divided into four 16K windows. In each window is kept a copy of 16K worth of expanded memory located somewhere on the expanded memory card.

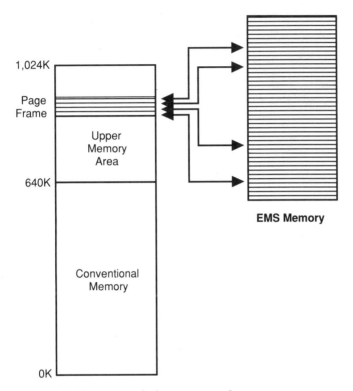

Figure 26-2. How expanded memory works.

EMS-compatible software accesses expanded memory through the windows in the page frame. Your application will ask the EMM driver to copy memory to or from the page into EMS memory. This may seem awkward; after all, accessing up to 32 megabytes of EMS memory 16K at a time is like building your garage out of toothpicks. But consider that a 100M hard drive is accessed by DOS 512 bytes at a time—and that memory is faster than disk—and you can see how useful EMS memory can become.

With version 4.0 of EMS, the page frame has been expanded to include some 384K of conventional memory in addition to the 64K page frame. This allows programs such as Software Carousel and DESQview to quickly swap full programs in and out of memory, permitting you to run more than one application at a time on any computer. (The DOS Shell application only swaps programs out to disk, not EMS memory.)

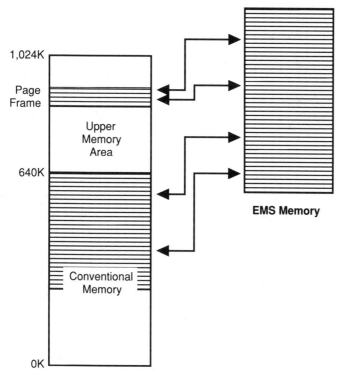

Figure 26-3. Version 4.0 of EMS lets you swap out even more memory.

Which to Use?

Under DOS, more applications will use expanded memory for data storage. Most graphics applications want expanded memory; Lotus 1-2-3 can use up to four megabytes of it; WordPerfect would like 512K, thank you; and if you look up "memory" or "expanded memory" in most user manuals, you'll find something expanded memory can be used for.

Extended memory is required by a few applications, notably Windows. (Internally, Windows actually converts extended into expanded memory, but Windows likes to do the converting itself.)

If you have an 8088/8086-based system, you can add and use only expanded memory. An advantage to LIM 4.0 EMS is that it can swap out up to 384K of conventional memory, making the PC more useful in some circumstances. To do this, try to disable all but 256K (or less, if possible) of your PCs conventional memory. (This is done by flipping switches on the motherboard.) Then, fill in what's missing using the EMS hardware's backfilling technique. This is covered in your EMS hardware manual.

Info: Backfilling is what makes software such as Software Carousel and DESQview work on an 8088 and 80286 system: Use EMS memory to fill in conventional memory. If you already have conventional memory, disable some of it and let the rest come from the EMS hardware.

If you have an 80286-based system, then you probably have 640K of RAM and at least 384K of extended memory. Any additional memory you add to the computer's motherboard becomes extended memory. But to get the most from DOS, you should add expanded memory to the system, just as you would an 8088 PC. The expanded memory is especially useful in exploiting some of the advanced memory management DOS offers.

If you have a '386 system (80386, 386SX or 486), you have the best of everything. All the memory in your computer is extended memory. However, by using software drivers you can convert some or all of it over for use as expanded memory. Having a '386 system is the key to fully exploiting the memory power of DOS and your applications.

The MEM Command

You can look at raw memory using the DEBUG command. But that's like ordering from a menu that has only prices; you don't know what those values actually represent. The MEM command can show you how much memory you have as well as which parts of memory are used for what.

Before the MEM command, the only way to see how much memory was used in your PC was with the CHKDSK command. As part of CHKDSK's hocus-pocus, it displayed used and available memory statistics. Type CHKDSK at the DOS prompt:

```
C:\>CHKDSK
Volume DOS 5   created 09-21-1990 1:26p
Volume Serial Number is 1676-8638

  42366976 bytes total disk space
     73728 bytes in 2 hidden files
     96256 bytes in 45 directories
  26275840 bytes in 900 user files
  15921152 bytes available on disk

      2048 bytes in each allocation unit
     20687 total allocation units on disk
      7774 available allocation units on disk

    655360 total bytes memory
    560096 bytes free
```

This PC, a 386SX system with two megabytes total memory, has the full 640K available as conventional memory. Of that amount, almost 547K is unused. (640K equals 655,360 bytes; 547K equals 560,128 bytes.)

Using CHKDSK this way is clumsy. The MEM command, introduced with DOS 4, was created specifically to give a more detailed report of what's going on in memory. MEM has three optional switches, but when used by itself, it displays a summary of information about memory:

```
C:\>MEM

    655360  bytes total conventional memory
    655360  bytes available to MS-DOS
    560096  largest executable program size

   1210720  bytes total contiguous extended memory
   1310720  bytes available contiguous extended memory
```

Above, the MEM command reports the same two memory values returned by CHKDSK, 655360 and 560096. Additionally, MEM properly reports the remaining 1.3 megabytes of extended memory in this system. If any expanded memory is available, MEM reports that as well.

When used with its optional switches, MEM will also tell you which programs are loaded into memory as well as their specific locations. The first two switches are /PROGRAM and /DEBUG, which can be abbreviated /P and /D respectively. These are really switches for programmers, although you may find the display interesting. Type the following command:

```
MEM /PROGRAM | MORE
```

Info: The MORE filter is used to pause the long display after each screen.

Information about memory is displayed in four columns: An address, or memory location (in hex); the name of the program or "owner" of that area of memory; the size of the program (again, in hex); and the type of program. At the bottom of the display is the same memory summary produced when the MEM command is used without an optional switch.

Figure 26-4 may look similar to what you see on your screen. Notice some of the device drivers loaded into memory: MOUSE, ANSI, and SETVER. Below them you can see COMMAND.COM and then DOSKEY loaded into memory. Even the MEM command shows up in the display.

The MEM command with it's /DEBUG switch displays a more detailed list of what's in memory—truly information for the computer guru type. There is very little practical information displayed by MEM /DEBUG for the typical DOS user. But you can use the switch when you really want to impress your friends.

```
Address        Name           Size        Type
───            ───            ───         ───

000000                        000400      Interrupt Vector
000400                        000100      ROM Communication Area
000500                        000200      DOS Communication Area

000700         IO             000A60      System Data

001160         MSDOS          00A410      System Data

00B570         IO             0097C0      System Data
               MOUSE          0039E0       DEVICE=
               ANSI           001060       DEVICE=
               SETVER         000190       DEVICE=
                              000640       FILES=
                              000100       FCBS=
                              004280       BUFFERS=
                              0001C0       LASTDRIVE=
014D40         COMMAND        001160      Program
015EB0         MSDOS          000040      — Free —
015F00         COMMAND        000400      Environment
016310         MEM            0000C0      Environment
0163E0         DOSKEY         001020      Program
017410         MEM            0176F0      Program
02EB10         MSDOS          0714E0      — Free —


    655360 bytes total conventional memory
    655360 bytes available to MS-DOS
    560096 largest executable program size

   1310720 bytes total contiguous extended memory
   1310720 bytes available contiguous extended memory
```

Figure 26-4. Typical output of the MEM /PROGRAM command.

The /CLASSIFY switch is the most practical of all the MEM command's switches. That switch, which can also be abbreviated as /C, is used to give a brief listing of the files in memory, their sizes in decimal, and any programs that have been loaded high into upper-memory blocks. (Upper memory blocks are covered later in this chapter. Type the following command:

```
MEM /C
```

What you see will look similar to Figure 26-5. The output is much cleaner than MEM /PROGRAM's output. The filenames in memory are more clear, and their sizes in decimal and kilobyte values give you a better understanding of how much memory is being used: DOS eats up 64K on this system; three device drivers gobble up 19K; the memory-resident program DOSKEY chows down another 4K. That's not monstrous. Some PCs will fare far worse (is yours one of them?).

```
Conventional Memory :

    Name              Size in Decimal        Size in Hex

    MSDOS             65776     ( 64.2K)         100F0
    MOUSE             14816     ( 14.5K)          39E0
    ANSI               4192     (  4.1K)          1060
    SETVER              400     (  0.4K)           190
    COMMAND            5472     (  5.3K)          1560
    DOSKEY             4128     (  4.0K)          1020
    FREE                 64     (  0.1K)            40
    FREE                192     (  0.2K)            C0
    FREE             560096     (547.0K)         88BE0

Total  FREE :        560352     (547.2K)

Total bytes available to programs :        560352    (547.2K)
Largest executable program size :          560096    (547.0K)

    1310720 bytes total contiguous extended memory
    1310720 bytes available contiguous extended memory
```

Figure 26-5. The output of MEM /CLASSIFY.

The next few chapters will go over the ways DOS has to increase the amount of memory available to your programs. As a preview, you're going to first eliminate the 50K DOS occupies, then wrest loose the 19K (or whatever amount) taken by device drivers and the 4K (or whatever) used by memory resident programs.

COMMAND: MEM (External)

Function: Reports the contents of memory, memory statistics.

Format: MEM switches

By itself, the MEM command gives you a summary of the memory in, used, and available in your system. This includes conventional, extended, and expanded memory.

Switches are optional switches used with the MEM command. There are three switches, with only one at a time specified after the MEM command:

/CLASSIFY or /C is used to give a brief summary of the programs in conventional memory and the upper-memory area. Program sizes are listed in decimal, kilobytes, and hexadecimal.

/DEBUG or /D gives a complete and highly detailed summary of memory. Program names, area names, sizes and addresses in hex, and type of memory is completely summarized.

/PROGRAM or /P gives a complete report on the contents of memory, although not in as much detail as the /DEBUG report.

Optimizing Memory

DOS's memory-management magic has one priority: freeing up as much of conventional memory as possible. With some configurations of DOS, it's possible to get back the full 640K—even more with third-party memory managers. Everything works one step at a time and there are definite rules that need to be followed. You already know the terms; what comes next is learning the commands.

Info: The following memory commands will only work on 80286 or later PCs. If you have an older system, you should look into third-party memory management products that are compatible with DOS 5.

Creating the HMA

The first step in cleaning up conventional memory is to give DOS an extra 64K bank of memory in which to play. That bank is available only on 80286 or later PCs with at least 350K of extended memory. It's actually the first 64K of extended memory, which is referred to as the High Memory Area or HMA. (See Figure 26-1.)

The HMA comes into existence thanks to a quirk in the 80286. That microprocessor can look at memory in 64K chunks. When you get near the 1,024K boundary, the 64K chunk will either wrap around back to 0K, as it does in the 8086, or it will advance into the first 64K of extended memory. When the 64K bank branches up into extended memory, it can be used directly by DOS to store programs or data.

To create the HMA you use the HIMEM.SYS device driver. HIMEM.SYS actually serves two functions: First, it sets up a method of accessing extended memory called the Extended Memory Specification, or XMS; second, HIMEM.SYS creates the HMA and allows DOS to use it.

To use HIMEM.SYS, place a line such as the following in your CONFIG.SYS file:

```
DEVICE=C:\DOS\HIMEM.SYS
```

Remember to specify a proper pathname; HIMEM.SYS should be in your DOS subdirectory; above, C:\DOS is assumed.

HIMEM.SYS can be followed by an optional parade of switches. These are all listed in the reference section. The only time you'll probably ever use them is if some hardware or software manual suggests you do so.

Place HIMEM.SYS as close to the start of your CONFIG.SYS file as possible. Only special hard-disk device drivers should come before it. (If you're using any expanded memory managers on your 80286 system, they should be installed immediately after HIMEM.SYS.)

After making the changes to CONFIG.SYS, save the file to disk and reset. (If DOS's SETUP program installed DOS on your system, then HIMEM.SYS may already be installed.)

Info: If you're familiar with Windows, you may recognize HIMEM.SYS as one of Windows' memory-management device drivers. However, this may bring some confusion as to which HIMEM.SYS to use. After all, both come from Microsoft— probably from the same lab.

The answer is to always use memory-management software that comes with your applications before running DOS's memory managers. The reason is that, although both HIMEM.SYS programs come from Microsoft, the one that came with Windows was tested and guaranteed to work with Windows. Use it.

After resetting, notice a new message displayed as DOS boots:

```
HIMEM: DOS XMS Driver, Version 2.76 - 10/31/90
XMS Specification Version 2.0
Copyright 1988-1990 Microsoft Corp.

Installed A20 handler number 1.
64K High Memory Area is available
```

This is HIMEM.SYS's startup message, which lets you know the XMS is installed and DOS now has 64K extra memory (the HMA) to use. But that memory isn't added to the basic 640; instead, it can only be used by those programs that know about it, primarily DOS and Windows.

Getting DOS Out of the Way

Once HIMEM.SYS is installed, you can use the HMA it creates to store DOS's own programs, IO.SYS and MSDOS.SYS—the DOS kernel. This is done using the DOS configuration command.

Info: The format of the DOS configuration command is shown in Chapter 19.

To move DOS into the HMA, place the following command in your CONFIG.SYS file:

```
DOS=HIGH
```

That line can go before or after the DEVICE command that installs HIMEM.SYS, although it seems more comfortable to place it after, as in:

```
DEVICE=C:\DOS\HIMEM.SYS
DOS=HIGH
```

Save the changes to CONFIG.SYS, exit to DOS, and then reset your system.

As the system boots, you won't see any new messages displayed. Yet, the effect of loading DOS into the HMA becomes vividly evident when you type the MEM command:

```
C:\>MEM

    655360 bytes total conventional memory
    655360 bytes available to MS-DOS
    614336 largest executable program size

   1310720 bytes total contiguous extended memory
         0 bytes available contiguous extended memory
   1245184 bytes available XMS memory
    MS-DOS resident in High Memory Area
```

First off, you'll notice extra conventional memory. In the sample output above, there is now a total of 614,336 bytes free conventional memory. The gain of 54,240 bytes is made by moving DOS's kernel into the HMA. That one command alone is responsible for the largest increase in conventional memory—and everything still works.

All the contiguous extended memory is gone, according to the above output. It's been put under the control of HIMEM.SYS, which is why 1,245,184 bytes show up above as available XMS memory. The missing 65,536 bytes? That's the 64K High Memory Area.

The last line above tells you that DOS is loaded into the HMA. That's how you get so much extra conventional memory—a relatively huge amount compared with previous versions of DOS.

Loading High

With DOS moved into the HMA, you have some 53K extra conventional memory. But you can do better still; those pesky device drivers and memory-resident programs are still sitting heavy in conventional memory. To remove them, you need to do two things:

Create upper-memory blocks, or UMBs.

Move the device drivers and memory-resident programs into those UMBs.

Info: The following memory commands will work only on 80386 or later PCs. If you have an 80286 system, you should look into third-party memory management products that will do the same or similar tricks.

Creating Expanded Memory

To create UMBs you use the EMM386.EXE memory device driver that comes with DOS. Note that EMM386.EXE is a device driver, despite its EXE file extension. (It also doubles as a command-line program.) Don't make the mistake of typing "EMM386.SYS".

The EMM386 device driver is actually an expanded memory manager, one specifically designed for '386 PCs. Its primary function is to convert extended memory into expanded memory, which is more useful to most DOS applications. The format for EMM386 is as follows:

```
DEVICE=pathname\EMM386.EXE memory options
```

Pathname is the drive and directory where EMM386.EXE is located. Usually this will be your DOS subdirectory.

Memory is a value indicating the amount of extended memory EMM386 will convert into expanded memory. Values for memory range from 16 through 32768 for 16K through 32M. The default for memory is 256 for 256K.

Options are switches and optional parameters that customize the way the EMM386.EXE device driver behaves.

Suppose you have one megabyte of extended memory, yet your applications, on average, may request only some 512K of expanded memory. To convert 512K of extended memory into expanded memory, the following command can be installed into your CONFIG.SYS file:

```
DEVICE=C:\DOS\EMM386.EXE 512
```

If you want that much expanded memory, insert the above command into your CONFIG.SYS file. If you want more expanded memory, specify a larger value; no value will give you the default 256K.

Info: How much expanded memory should you convert? It's up to your applications and their requirements. A good plan of attack is to convert all of extended memory into the more useful expanded memory. There is one exception—if you're using a RAM drive or disk cache. That software performs better in extended memory, so set aside just enough extended memory for those programs to run, and give the rest over to EMM386.EXE for conversion to expanded memory.

If you don't want any expanded memory (such as when running Windows) skip installing the EMM386.EXE device driver for now. A Windows solution is provided in the next section.

The position of the EMM386.EXE device driver is important; it must go after the DEVICE configuration command that installs HIMEM.SYS. So now the core memory drivers in CONFIG.SYS should look something like this:

```
DEVICE=C:\DOS\HIMEM.SYS
DOS=HIGH
DEVICE=C:\DOS\EMM386.EXE 512
```

Of course, your CONFIG.SYS file may have a different DOS subdirectory, and you may specify another value after EMM386.EXE for a different amount of expanded memory.

After saving the changes, exit to DOS and then reset your system. When the computer starts, you'll see the EMM386.EXE device driver's startup message, right after HIMEM.SYS's message:

```
MICROSOFT Expanded Memory Manager 386  Version 4.20.06X
(C) Copyright Microsoft Corporation 1986, 1990

EMM386 successfully installed.

    Available expanded memory . . . . . . . .    512 KB

    LIM/EMS version . . . . . . . . . . . .      4.0
    Total expanded memory pages . . . . . . .    56
    Available expanded memory pages . . . . .    32
    Total handles . . . . . . . . . . . . .      64
    Active handles  . . . . . . . . . . . .      1
    Page frame segment  . . . . . . . . . .      D000 H

EMM386 Active.
```

Most of this information is technical in nature. Basically, you have 512K (or whatever value you specified) of expanded memory, LIM 4.0 EMS compatible. Extended memory is still available. In fact, when you type the MEM command, you'll see the new amount of expanded memory in the display:

```
C:\>MEM

   655360 bytes total conventional memory
   655360 bytes available to MS-DOS
   605920 largest executable program size

   917504 bytes available EMS memory
   524288 bytes free EMS memory

  1310720 bytes total contiguous extended memory
        0 bytes available contiguous extended memory
   622592 bytes available XMS memory
   MS-DOS resident in High Memory Area
```

You'll note that the total amount of conventional memory available (the "largest executable program size") is now a few bytes less than what it was. That's memory now used by the EMM386.EXE driver. (But the trade-off will be worth it later; keep reading.)

The bytes-free EMS memory value is 512K, the value you specified. The larger value above it reflects 384K of additional EMS memory—the old upper-memory area—which EMM386.EXE also converts. The amount of available XMS memory is now 512K less than its previous value. Remember: EMM386 doesn't create expanded memory, it converts extended into expanded memory.

Your applications that need expanded memory now have it. Programs that need extended memory have it as well. What's missing from the picture is the solution for "loading high"—moving your device drivers and memory-resident programs out of conventional memory. This is done by telling the EMM386.EXE device driver to create upper-memory blocks, which can be done whether or not you want to convert extended into expanded memory.

The Command Line EMM386

EMM386 is also a DOS command, thanks to its EXE extension. As a DOS command, you can use EMM386 to turn expanded-memory support on or off, as well as specify support for a Weitek coprocessor. The format is:

```
EMM386 status Weitek
```

Status is either ON, OFF, or AUTO: ON turns expanded-memory support on; OFF turns it off; and AUTO keeps it off, turning it on only when a program makes the request.

Weitek is either W=ON or W=OFF, to turn support for a Weitek coprocessor either on or off, respectively. This switch has effect only if you have a Weitek coprocessor installed.

Note that you cannot use EMM386 as a DOS command if you've created UMBs. This is covered in the next section.

Creating Upper-Memory Blocks

Two of EMM386.EXE's options are the /RAM and /NOEMS switches. They both create the upper-memory blocks in the upper-memory area. But what are upper-memory blocks?

When IBM designed the original PC, they set aside the top 384K of memory for future expansion. At the time of the PC's introduction, about 40K of that reserved-memory area was used by the PC's BIOS and the BASIC programming language (on a ROM chip). If you had an IBM monochrome (MDA) display, another 4K of the upper-memory area was used for video memory; if you had a CGA display, you used up to 32K of the upper memory area. This left huge unused holes in upper memory— holes that weren't used for anything.

As the PC matured, more and more stuff found its way into the upper-memory area: The hard-disk controller/BIOS; more video RAM—up to 96K of it with EGA and VGA—plus a few kilobytes for their BIOS; Network and other additional BIOS or ROMs; as well as a 64K page frame when you use expanded memory. Still, there's quite a lot of space left up there, as seen in Figure 26-6.

Using the advanced memory-management techniques of the '386 chip, you can fill those unused holes in the upper-memory area with usable RAM. That's what creates the UMB. While you cannot run DOS programs in that memory (it's not contiguous with the basic 640K), you can run device drivers and memory-resident programs—as many as will fit.

Both the /RAM and /NOEMS switches direct EMM386.EXE to create the UMBs. The /RAM switch is used if you're converting extended memory into expanded memory. The /NOEMS switch is used only to create the UMBs; it tells EMM386.EXE not to convert any expanded memory.

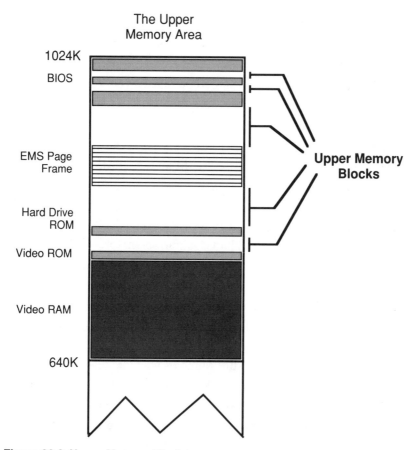

Figure 26-6. Upper-Memory Blocks.

If you're using the EMM386.EXE device driver to convert extended into expanded memory, then edit your CONFIG.SYS file and tack on the /RAM switch to the EMM386.EXE command. That will create your UMBs:

```
DEVICE=C:\DOS\EMM386.EXE 512 /RAM
```

If you don't need any expanded memory, but would like to free up conventional memory by creating UMBs, edit your CONFIG.SYS file and insert the EMM386.EXE device driver. Specify the /NOEMS switch to create your UMBs and nothing else:

```
DEVICE=C:\DOS\EMM386.EXE /NOEMS
```

Info: /NOEMS is the Windows-compatible switch.

Save the changes to CONFIG.SYS and reset. You'll notice the EMM386.EXE device driver now displays additional upper-memory block information as it boots:

```
Total upper memory available  . . . . . .    31 KB
Largest Upper Memory Block available  . .    31 KB
Upper memory starting address . . . . . .   C800 H
```

You're now ready to use the two special DOS commands that will load device drivers and memory-resident programs into the UMBs.

Tip: If you're using the /NOEMS switch, you'll notice the total upper-memory-available value will be greater than that of when you use the /RAM switch. The reason is that EMM386.EXE uses memory bank D for its page frame. It assumes bank E is used for BIOS, which is only the case in a few PCs (notably PS/2s and some laptops).

If you want to increase the number of UMBs available by 64K, and you're certain your PC lacks any BIOS or ROMs in bank E, start EMM386 with the following switch:

```
M9
```

Or the more English-like version:

```
FRAME=E000
```

For example:

```
DEVICE=C:\DOS\EMM386.EXE 512 FRAME=E000 /RAM
```

The above command will give you 64K extra UMBs. This is only necessary when you're using the /RAM switch, and only if you're certain there is nothing else in bank E.

Activating the UMBs

In addition to creating the upper-memory blocks, you also need to tell DOS about them. This is done by means of the DOS configuration command's UMB option.

Because you already have DOS=HIGH in your CONFIG.SYS file, edit it to read:

```
DOS=HIGH,UMB
```

The UMB option tells DOS to maintain its internal links to upper memory after the computer has booted. Without that option, you cannot use the DEVICEHIGH and LOADHIGH commands, which actually transfer your device drivers and memory-resident programs into the UMBs.

Info: You must add the UMB switch to use the upper-memory blocks, even if you're using the /NOEMS switch on EMM386.EXE.

Edit your CONFIG.SYS file, make the change to the DOS configuration command, and then return to DOS. There is no need to reset just yet.

Using the DEVICEHIGH Command

To load device drivers into UMBs, you substitute the DEVICEHIGH command for DEVICE. For example, you can free up 4K of RAM by loading the ANSI.SYS device driver high with the following command:

```
DEVICEHIGH=C:\DOS\ANSI.SYS
```

Save that change to CONFIG.SYS and reset. ANSI.SYS will now be loaded into an upper-memory block. You can confirm this using the MEM command with its /CLASSIFY switch, as seen in Figure 26-7. Type:

```
MEM /C | MORE
```

570

Conventional Memory :

Name	Size in Decimal		Size in Hex
MSDOS	12416	(12.1K)	3080
HIMEM	1184	(1.2K)	4A0
EMM386	8400	(8.2K)	20D0
MOUSE	14816	(14.5K)	39E0
SETVER	400	(0.4K)	190
COMMAND	3392	(3.3K)	D40
DOSKEY	4128	(4.0K)	1020
FREE	64	(0.1K)	40
FREE	192	(0.2K)	C0
FREE	610112	(595.8K)	94F40

Total FREE :   610368   (596.1K)

Upper Memory :

Name	Size in Decimal		Size in Hex
SYSTEM	163840	(160.0K)	28000
ANSI	4192	(4.1K)	1060
FREE	28512	(27.8K)	6F60

Total FREE :   28512   (27.8K)

Total bytes available to programs (Conventional+Upper) : 638880 (623.9K)
Largest executable program size :   610112 (595.8K)
Largest available upper memory block :   28512 (27.8K)

     917504 bytes total EMS memory
     524288 bytes free EMS memory

    1310720 bytes total contiguous extended memory
          0 bytes available contiguous extended memory
     589824 bytes available XMS memory
            MS-DOS resident in High Memory Area

Figure 26-7. The output of MEM /CLASSIFY with ANSI.SYS loaded high.

There are now two areas of memory described by MEM /CLASSIFY. The first is conventional area and the second is the upper-memory area. In the upper memory area you'll find the ANSI device driver. Notice how the overall value for available conventional memory is now some 4K larger.

Just about any device driver can be loaded high. But there are some rules; the most important rule is that you should load the larger device drivers first. In the output of the MEM /CLASSIFY command, locate your device drivers and order them in CONFIG.SYS, loading them from largest to smallest. For example, in Figure 26-7, the MOUSE.SYS device driver is largest at 14.5K, ANSI comes next at 4.1K, and finally SETVER at 0.4K. Load them in that order:

```
DEVICEHIGH=C:\MOUSE\MOUSE.SYS
DEVICEHIGH=C:\DOS\ANSI.SYS
DEVICEHIGH=C:\DOS\SETVER.EXE
```

Another problem may be expanding device drivers. These are drivers that load into memory at one size, and then balloon up after they're loaded. To deal with them, you need to specify the size option with the DEVICEHIGH configuration command.

As an example, consider the BALLOON.SYS device driver. It initially uses 200 bytes of memory, but after it's loaded it steals another 5,132 bytes. If you use DEVICEHIGH with BALLOON.SYS, it may not fit into the assigned UMB and it could crash the system.

To fix the problem, obtain the device driver's true size by using the MEM / CLASSIFY command. Locate the size of the driver in memory and in hexadecimal. For example, the following could be the output of the MEM /CLASSIFY command showing the BALLOON.SYS device driver in conventional memory:

```
BALLOON          5332      (  5.2K)        14D4
```

BALLOON uses 14D4 hex-bytes of memory. To load it high with the DEVICEHIGH configuration command's size option, you would use the following:

```
DEVICEHIGH SIZE=14D4 C:\FLOAT\BALLOON.SYS /NOPOP
```

The size option and size in hex are hugged around the equal sign, followed by the size of the device driver as reported by MEM /CLASSIFY—and in hexadecimal. That's followed by the pathname of the device driver and any optional switches.

The size option is used for device drivers that bloat up after being loaded, but it cannot fix all problems. Some device drivers cannot be loaded high or will "misbehave." When that's the case, you can experiment with the loading order (remember: larger device drivers go first) or just live with them in conventional memory.

Info: If DEVICEHIGH cannot load a device driver into a UMB, it will load it into low memory. The only way to discover this is to use the MEM /CLASSIFY command.

Here is a list of DOS device drivers approved for loading high with the DEVICEHIGH command:

```
DISPLAY.SYS          DRIVER.SYS
EGA.SYS              PRINTER.SYS
RAMDRIVE.SYS         SETVER.EXE
SMARTDRV.SYS
```

Info: The common MOUSE.SYS device driver can also be loaded high.

In the case of RAMDrive and SMARTDrive, note that the "brains" of the driver are loaded high; the RAM drive or cache is still placed in conventional, extended, or expanded memory—wherever you specify.

The following is the final result of the CONFIG.SYS file changes made to my test system:

```
DEVICE=C:\DOS\HIMEM.SYS
DOS=HIGH
DEVICE=C:\DOS\EMM386.EXE 512 /RAM

DEVICEHIGH C:\MOUSE\MOUSE.SYS
```

```
DEVICEHIGH C:\DOS\ANSI.SYS
DEVICEHIGH C:\DOS\SETVER.EXE
```

The MEM command now shows a total of 625,360 bytes available conventional memory. That's a good amount, but it can get better.

Using the LOADHIGH Command

Memory-resident programs and DOS utilities can be loaded into upper-memory blocks using the LOADHIGH command. The format is:

```
LOADHIGH program options
```

Program is the name of a memory-resident program, just as you'd type it on the command line or have it listed in a batch file.

Options are any options, filenames, or switches that normally follow the program on the command line or in a batch file.

Essentially, you just stick the LOADHIGH command in front of your memory-resident program, usually in your AUTOEXEC.BAT file. Note that LOADHIGH can be abbreviated as LH.

The following command is used to load the DOSKEY program into a UMB:

```
LH DOSKEY /INSERT
```

DOSKEY is loaded high, and its /INSERT switch is specified. Other than that, nothing's unusual. (Note that you need only to load the first DOSKEY command high; additional DOSKEY commands, such as those used to define macros, do not need to be loaded high.)

The following command loads the venerable SideKick application high:

```
LH SK
```

No sweat.

Review your AUTOEXEC.BAT file and scan for memory-resident programs to load high. Edit AUTOEXEC.BAT and stick LOADHIGH or LH in front of those commands. Here is a list of DOS programs that are approved for loading high with the LOADHIGH command:

APPEND.EXE	MODE.COM
DOSKEY.COM	MIRROR.COM
DOSSHELL.COM	NLSFUNC.EXE
GRAPHICS.COM	PRINT.EXE
KEYB.COM	SHARE.EXE

Unlike DEVICEHIGH, LOADHIGH doesn't worry about ballooning memory-resident programs. (The design of a memory-resident program is different than that of a device driver, which eliminates some problems.) Of course, not every memory-resident program will be happy in upper memory; if you experience any problems, reload the program low.

Info: As with DEVICEHIGH, if a memory-resident program won't load high, or there isn't enough free UMB memory, the LOADHIGH command will load it low.

After loading the DOSKEY program high in the test system's CONFIG.SYS and then resetting, the final value is the grand total of available conventional memory:

```
629504 largest executable program size
```

That's an improvement of 69,408 bytes over the old amount.

You may not be using very many device drivers or memory-resident programs. Yet, if you're an old-time DOS user, you may have a few of them laying around in your closet—put away during the height of the RAM crisis. If so, bust 'em out and dust 'em off! By taking advantage of DEVICEHIGH and LOADHIGH, you can now use the software you paid for—and still have memory left over for your DOS applications.

Info: In addition to DOS, there are lots of third-party memory managers, a few of which will do a better job than DOS of cleaning up and controlling memory. Two good ones for the '386 are 386MAX and QEMM. For 80286 systems, QRAM and MOVE'EM are program loaders you can use to get some '386 benefits out of DOS 5 on your 80286 system.

Summary

Memory management on a PC involves freeing up as much of the basic 640K conventional memory as possible. This can be done easily under DOS—providing you have an 80386 or later PC. If you have an 80286, some of the tricks are limited. But if you have an 8088, you're out of luck!

The PC can have three types of memory: conventional (the basic 640K); expanded (or extra memory used by DOS programs); and extended (extra memory in an 80286 or later PC).

The MEM command is used to tell you what's in memory and how much space it occupies. The /PROGRAM and /DEBUG switches display a highly detailed view of memory; the /CLASSIFY switch lists programs and sizes in decimal as well as hexadecimal, and it also shows you UMB usage.

The first step to DOS memory management is HIMEM.SYS. It creates the High Memory Area (HMA), the first 64K of extended memory in 80286-or-later machines with extended memory installed. HIMEM.SYS also establishes the XMS, the extended memory specification, for dealing with extended memory in the system.

The second step is to load DOS into the HMA with the DOS=HIGH command in your CONFIG.SYS file.

If you have a '386 system, you can use the EMM386.EXE device driver to create expanded memory. EMM386.EXE converts a given amount of extended memory, turning it into expanded memory for those applications that need it.

EMM386.EXE is also used to create upper-memory blocks (UMBs) in the upper-memory area. These are blocks of usable RAM into which DOS can transfer device drivers and memory-resident programs. The UMBs are created using EMM386.EXE's /RAM switch or the /NOEMS switch. The DOS=UMB configuration command is also required to access UMBs.

The DEVICEHIGH command is used to load device drivers into UMBs. Large device drivers should be loaded first. Any expanded device drivers should be loaded with the size option, followed by the driver's expanded size in hexadecimal.

The LOADHIGH command (or LH) is used to load memory-resident programs.

CHAPTER 27

Other Ways to do DOS

DOS does only so much; everything else comes from outside in the form of third-party programs and enhancers. Several of these truly enhance the performance of DOS, so much so that they're called extended DOS environments. This chapter tells you about them and how to integrate them into your system, as well as other ways of "doing" DOS.

This chapter answers the following questions:

- What lies beyond DOS and what can extend the power of DOS?

- What is shelling?

- How can one program run another?

- What do the different menu systems offer?

- What is the advantage of DESQview over Windows?

- How does Windows fit into the PC?

- How can Windows' performance be improved?

Shelling

Two funky DOS terms are kernel and shell. The kernel is the core of DOS, the IO.SYS and MSDOS.SYS programs that sit low in memory (or high in the HMA) and control DOS's basic, primal functions. The shell is COMMAND.COM, the command interpreter, where you communicate with DOS and tell it what to do for you. (Because the command interpreter surrounds the kernel, it's called the shell.)

Info: COMMAND.COM is the supplied DOS shell. But other shells can be used, the only popular one being J.P. Software's 4DOS, which is much more powerful than COMMAND.COM, but visually similar.

Beyond the command line interface lie other shells, basically shells-on-shells. These include menu programs and graphical user interfaces (GUIs) that purportedly make DOS easier to use. If you know DOS, you may find them annoying or redundant. Still, for some PC users, they're easier to use than DOS, and often offer extra tools that DOS lacks. But everything starts with COMMAND.COM.

Running the Command Processor

DOS automatically looks for and runs COMMAND.COM when you start your system. It's expected to be in the root directory of the boot disk unless you use the SHELL configuration command, which tells DOS to look elsewhere. (Also, the SHELL command is how you load alternative command processors, such as 4DOS.)

As a shell, COMMAND.COM gives you a command line and all the internal DOS commands. The external commands are programs on disk—one of which is actually COMMAND.COM.

By typing COMMAND at the DOS prompt, you run another copy of the command processor—another shell. For example, type COMMAND at the DOS prompt and you'll see the following:

```
C:\>COMMAND

Microsoft (R) MS-DOS(R) Version 5.00
 (C)Copyright Microsoft Corp 1981-1991.

C:\>
```

That second DOS prompt is actually produced by the new command processor, which you've just loaded into memory. The first command processor is still there, but it's suspended. And it takes up some 3.3K of memory.

Why create another command processor? Part of doing so is "just because"; it shows you what DOS is capable of—not just with COMMAND.COM but with most applications. You can leave a program suspended in memory and go off to run something else. As long as there's memory for the second program, it's no problem. The name of this technique is generally referred to as shelling.

You've just shelled into a second copy of COMMAND.COM. Other than having several fewer kilobytes conventional memory, everything looks the same. However, the new copy of COMMAND.COM has its own environment. It's possible to change this environment and then return to the original COMMAND.COM with its environment intact.

Info: This is a good way to test out new prompts and environment variables without messing up the originals.

For example, change your system prompt:

```
PROMPT [$P]
```

That changes your prompt to the type OS/2 "text window" system prompt. Now add an environment variable:

```
SET SHELL=I AM IN A SHELL
```

Use the SET command by itself to confirm your changes to the environment.

The changes affect only the current COMMAND.COM. To return to the original COMMAND.COM and restore the original environment, you type the EXIT command:

```
EXIT
```

After pressing Enter, you'll see your original prompt. Type the SET command to see that the SHELL variable is gone; it was never part of the original environment. You've just "quit" the second copy of COMMAND.COM and returned to the original.

Shelling Out to DOS

Running COMMAND.COM is a good way to show all DOS users how shelling out to DOS works; everyone has a copy of COMMAND.COM handy. But other applications are capable of the same feat. Most of the big hitters have a "Shell to DOS" or "Run program" command. They let you either shell to another copy of COMMAND.COM or type a DOS command which the application will then run. Both of these are similar to running a second copy of COMMAND.COM at the DOS prompt.

The follow is a list of a few popular applications and their commands and keystrokes required to shell to DOS. Some of these will pop you directly out into another copy of the command processor; others will ask you to specify a program to run:

Application	Command	Keystrokes
DOS Shell	Command Prompt	Shift-F9
QBASIC	SHELL	SHELL
WordPerfect	Shell, Go to DOS	Ctrl-F1, 1
Lotus 1-2-3	System	/S
Telix	Shell to DOS	Alt-J
XTree	eXecute	Alt-X

If the application allows you to type only the name of a program to run (such as XTree) and what you really want to do is run DOS, then type COMMAND.COM. Essentially, that's the same thing as shelling to DOS—but enter a full pathname if COMMAND.COM isn't on your path.

Be careful if your communications program offers a shell-to-DOS feature; often that disables on-line communications. In fact, when you shell to DOS, the program is always suspended, hanging tight in memory; in WordPerfect, the printing will stop once you shell to DOS.

Info: If you want programs to continue to run after you've shelled to DOS, then what you really want is a multitasking system, a few of which are covered later in this chapter.

The advantages of shelling to DOS are that it's possible to access two programs in memory without quitting one of them. Provided both fit in RAM, you can shell from one application to another, get some data, and then quit the second application (or type EXIT) to return to the first application.

As an example, I use WordPerfect's Shell command to run the BACK.BAT program at the end of the day: BACK.BAT backs up all the documents for this project to floppy diskettes. When it's done running, control returns right to WordPerfect.

DOS Menu Systems

You bought your PC to run applications, and DOS is designed to make that easier for you. Some users can use DOS all day, others will prefer professional menu systems that make running applications one-key simple. Also, there are certain situations where a level of security is required and a menu program becomes necessary.

Third-Party Shells and Menus

Writing menus or "shells" for DOS is a common pastime. There are dozens on the market, from simple one-key application runners to complex shells that provide extra utilities, sizzle, and pop. A few of the more popular are listed below:

Deskmate

Deskmate is Tandy's solution for making their DOS-compatible systems easier for the newcomer to use. Since Deskmate is compatible with all DOS computers, you can visit a Radio Shack store and pick up your own copy. Deskmate offers some simple get-started programs of its own, which you'll quickly tire of but can then integrate with your own applications. Deskmate lacks in utility power.

DOS Shell

DOS Shell comes with DOS, which is the best argument anyone can make for it. It offers DOS utilities, does a few things DOS cannot, and also lets you create lists of programs to run. The task-swapping feature allows you to switch easily between several running programs at once, which is a bonus over some of the other shells described in this section.

Direct Access

Direct Access is the father of all menu systems. It's simple, offers password protection, several levels of menus, and time logging that lets you keep track of who does what and for how long. Most software stores use Direct Access on their in-store demo computers.

Magellan

Lotus' Magellan is more of a hard-disk information tool than a true shell. While you can run applications from Magellan (in most cases, simply by selecting the proper data file and pressing a key), its true strength lies in its ability to locate files containing specific text, to view files "in context" (as the applications would display them), and as an information-organization tool. You can create a single menu for launching applications, but there are no submenus.

PC Shell

PC Shell is part of the PC Tool's package of utilities-and-just-about everything-else for the PC. The shell is big on using DOS, organizes files, and comes packed with useful utilities. However, it offers only one pull down menu which contains a list of programs you can run.

Norton Commander

The Norton Commander is the "power users" shell, offering lots of disk tools and file-manipulation abilities. Basically, the Commander extends your control over DOS and your file system. You can install your own applications on pull-down menus for quick-launching them.

Build Your Own

It's possible to create your own menu system using batch files and all the DOS tricks and secrets revealed in this book. The general strategy is as follows:

1. Create your menu screens using ANSI commands.

2. Create menu batch files that display the screens and change the DOS prompt to allow for input.

3. Write batch files that run submenus or applications. After running the applications, the batch files return control to the main batch file menu.

A start to this approach was shown in Chapter 23. The menu screen was created using an ANSI text file and the DOS prompt modified to ask for input. Since the menu contained numbered items, corresponding numbered batch files need to be created:

```
1.BAT
2.BAT
3.BAT
...etc.
```

Each of these batch files could display a submenu of items or run an application directly. Often, if you're running your system with batch files anyway, then all that's needed is to rename a few of the key batch files as above.

The drawback to this approach is that DOS is limited in what it can do. You can obtain batch-file enhancers (or create them in DEBUG if you're good) to spice things up a bit. But eventually roadblocks will occur, the most important of which is the lack of security a batch-file menu system offers.

And don't forget the time required. Often when you're done, you'll find you've created a system identical to what Direct Access offers—but where that program only costs some $65 through mail order, you've spent 100 hours of your time creating your own. How much is your time worth?

DOS Environments

Beyond the simple menus and shells are more complex DOS environments. Where the menus may display a list of programs to run or add power to DOS's file commands, the environments supplement DOS's power with extra muscle.

DESQview

DESQview is the offspring of IBM's early TopView program, which allowed you to run several DOS applications at once on a PC. Unlike shelling to DOS, where you ran several applications under TopView all of them ran at once, each in its own little text window on the screen.

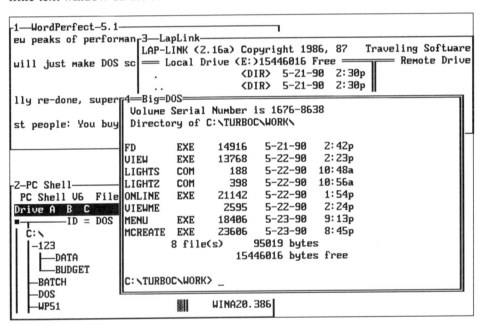

```
┌1─WordPerfect─5.1───────────────────────┐
│eu peaks of performan┌3─LapLink─────────────────────────────────────
│                     │LAP-LINK <2.16a> Copyright 1986, 87    Traveling Software
│will just make DOS sc│══ Local Drive <E:>15446016 Free ═══════════ Remote Drive
│                     │  .                <DIR>  5-21-90   2:30p ║
│                     │  ..               <DIR>  5-21-90   2:30p ║
│lly re-done, super┌4═Big═DOS═══════════════════════════════════════┐
│                  │Volume Serial Number is 1676-8638              │
│st people: You buy│Directory of C:\TURBOC\WORK\                    │
│                  │                                               │
│                  │FD       EXE    14916   5-21-90   2:42p         │
│                  │VIEW     EXE    13768   5-22-90   2:23p         │
│                  │LIGHTS   COM      188   5-22-90  10:48a         │
│┌2─PC Shell────────│LIGHTZ   COM      398   5-22-90  10:56a         │
│  PC Shell V6  File│ONLINE   EXE    21142   5-22-90   1:54p         │
│ Drive A  B  C     │VIEWME           2595   5-22-90   2:24p         │
│ ▪──────ID = DOS   │MENU     EXE    18406   5-23-90   9:13p         │
│  C:\              │MCREATE  EXE    23606   5-23-90   8:45p         │
│    ─123           │        8 file(s)      95019 bytes            │
│      ├─DATA       │                   15446016 bytes free        │
│      └─BUDGET     │                                               │
│    ├─BATCH        │C:\TURBOC\WORK> _                               │
│    ├─DOS          │                                               │
│    └─WP51         │       ▓▓▓     WINA20.386│
└──────────────────┴───────────────────────┘
```

Figure 27-1. A typical DESQview screen.

The problem with TopView was timing: It could only run programs in conventional memory—meaning you could run as many applications as would fit simultaneously in 640K of RAM. But at its introduction, most applications had just crossed over the 256K-minimum requirement.

DESQview took TopView's base and added LIM 4.0 EMS memory support. This allowed several programs to be swapped in and out of memory quickly, and let some of them remain in memory to be run simultaneously. With the introduction of the '386 microprocessor, full multitasking was achieved. With DESQview/386, any number of applications can be loaded and run simultaneously in memory.

In DESQview, each application runs in its own window, although it's a text window and not graphics. Most users will "zoom" the window out to fill the screen, which gives the impression that you're not running a DOS environment at all. But by pressing the special "DESQ key" (usually Alt), the DESQview menu pops up and you can start another program or switch to a program already running in memory.

DESQview is ideal solution if you have lots of expanded memory or a '386 system with lots of memory. If you need to access and run several programs at once, and those are all text-based programs, then consider DESQview as a powerful means to extend DOS's power.

Info: At present, DESQview and Windows are dueling it out in the battle of the DOS environments. Windows usually wins, but DESQview is a much better solution for those without graphics-based or Windows software.

GeoWorks

GeoWorks is a GUI for DOS, based on an earlier program that proved quite successful on the Apple II and Commodore 64 computers. But don't think GeoWorks is cheap or immature; its a capable graphical operating system, one that can enhance the power of any DOS computer without too terrible a price in hardware.

GeoWorks is fast and pretty to look at. Some users may prefer its interface over Windows, and its built-in applications are definitely useful. What GeoWorks lacks, however is Windows marketing and popularity. On low-end machines, GeoWorks is much better at using resources and lacks Windows' confusing modes.

Windows

Windows is being touted as DOS's future. But whichever crystal ball you look into, you'll always see DOS sitting there in the center. Windows is pushed hard and heavy on the PC user, but keep in mind that it's not the only game in town. One disadvantage is that Windows is taxing on the typical PC's resources. On the upside, Windows is tremendously popular and a lot of applications require it.

There's nothing much that can be said about running Windows here that isn't said in more detail in Windows-specific books; however, two points worth covering are ways to run Windows and how to optimize its performance.

Running Windows

Windows has three modes of operation:

The real mode is Windows mode of operation on 8088 systems or 80286 or later systems with less than 250K of extended memory. In this mode, Windows can run only one program at a time, although it can switch between several open programs at once. To get the most out of Windows in the real mode, add as much expanded memory as possible to your system.

The standard mode is Windows mode of operation on 80286 systems with at least 250K of memory. In the standard mode, Windows programs can run simultaneously. But not DOS programs; start up a DOS application and all the Windows programs screech to a halt. More extended memory helps, but to boost performance further you should consider creating a disk cache or running some applications from a RAM drive.

The 386 enhanced mode is Windows top-flight performance mode. It works on 80386-or-later systems with at least two megabytes total memory. In the 386 enhanced mode, all Windows and DOS programs can run simultaneously. The more memory you have, the smoother things run.

Info: If you're running Windows in the 386 enhanced mode, note that the file WINA20.386 must be in the root directory of your boot drive. That file tells Windows that although DOS is already using the 386 microprocessor's A20 line, it's okay for Windows to use it too. Otherwise, Windows will refuse to run.

Windows will always try to start in the best possible mode for your system. If you don't meet the memory requirements, then Windows drops down to the next lowest mode and attempts to start it. You can force Windows to try to run in a specific mode by using the following command line switches:

WIN /R   The real mode

WIN /S   The standard mode

WIN /3   The 386 enhanced mode

In some instances, such as when you've converted extended into expanded memory using the QEMM or 386MAX memory managers, you must specify WIN /3 to run Windows in the 386 enhanced mode.

It's best to start Windows using a batch file, or by setting everything up properly at the end of your AUTOEXEC.BAT file. Windows would like to have a TEMP environment variable, which is convenient because you probably already use one for DOS, but Windows is taxing on the search path.

Nearly all Windows programs, including Windows itself, want to be on your path. For example, if you own both Windows and Word for Windows, then your Windows path may look like this:

```
PATH=C:\WINDOWS;C:\WINWORD;C:\DOS;C:\BATCH;C:\UTIL
```

Of course, if you're just running Windows, then you can lop off the C:\BATCH and C:\UTIL subdirectories; you'll be using Windows' own utilities on your system. But if you add a few other applications, then they too may want on the path. The end result: monster path!

One way to make the path shorter is to use the SUBST command, reassigning subdirectories to drive letters. For example:

```
SUBST W: C:\WINDOWS
SUBST X: C:\WINWORD
SUBST T: C:\TOOLKIT
SUBST P: C:\PAGEMAKER
...etc.
```

This allows you to create a path that contains only drive letters. Another solution may be to set a special path only when Windows runs. The following is a batch file that can be used to start Windows:

```
@ECHO OFF
SET PATH=C:\WINDOWS;C:\WINWORD;%PATH%
C:
CD \WINDOWS
WIN %1 %2 %3 %4 %5
SET PATH=%MPATH%
```

First, the PATH is extended to contain the Windows and WinWord subdirectories; the old path is appended using the %PATH% environment variable. Windows is then run, but note how command-line parameters are used to pass certain switches to Windows.

After Windows runs, the batch file finishes by resetting the path. Above, the MPATH environment variable (which is probably set to the original PATH back in AUTOEXEC.BAT.) is used. (Refer to Chapter 20 for more information.)

Special Windows environment batch files can also be created. For example, if you want to run Windows in the real mode, say in a DESQview window (which is possible and rather curious to do), you can write the following batch file, WINR.BAT:

```
@ECHO OFF
SET PATH=C:\WINDOWS;C:\WINWORD;%PATH%
C:
CD \WINDOWS
WIN /R %1 %2 %3 %4 %5
SET PATH=%MPATH%
```

The only real difference in this batch file is that Windows is started with the /R switch, keeping it in the real mode and avoiding conflicts with DESQview. A slight modification of this batch file is required to run Word for Windows in a DESQview window. The following batch file, WINWORD.BAT, does the job:

```
@ECHO OFF
SET PATH=C:\WINDOWS;C:\WINWORD;%PATH%
C:
CD \WINWORD
WIN WINWORD /R
SET PATH=%MPATH%
```

Above, Windows is started by specifying the WINWORD.EXE program file, and then the /R switch to keep Windows in the real mode. After a few moments, Windows pops up in a DESQview window running Word for Windows.

Info: You don't need to force the real mode in Windows if you're just using DOS. In fact, the above batch file could be used on any DOS system to run Word for Windows; simply omit the /R switch on the line that starts Windows.

Windows Optimization Secrets

Windows is power hungry. No matter how mighty your system, Windows seems to want more. But the answer to feeding Windows' power urge doesn't require tossing more expensive hardware at your system. Instead, there are a few Windows-optimization secrets you should try. At the most, these solutions involve adding more RAM to your system. And at the least, they'll improve other applications you run as well.

Use DOS's Memory Management

The first step to boosting Windows' power is to give yourself as much conventional memory as possible. Using DOS's memory-management commands to free conventional memory helps a lot. If you have an 80286, third-party memory managers can be used to load device drivers and memory-resident programs into upper memory.

Use SMARTDrive

Both Windows and DOS come with the SMARTDrive disk cache. When Windows installs, it will create a disk cache in CONFIG.SYS using SMARTDRV.SYS, usually giving it quite a hefty size. The only time you'll want to reduce that size is when it eats up too much extended memory, preventing Windows from running in the standard or 386 enhanced modes. Otherwise, create a large cache to help improve Windows' performance.

Use a RAM drive

RAM drives are only of minor help to Windows. If you can fit all of one Windows application on a RAM drive, then it will run super fast. But you're talking about a hefty RAM drive, maybe using up to three megabytes of extended memory. Instead, consider putting some of that memory to use as a larger disk cache and giving the rest back to Windows as usable RAM.

Create a swap file

If you're running Windows in the 386 enhanced mode, you can speed up disk operations by creating a large, permanent swap file. Normally, Windows uses a disk swap file, but that temporary swap file isn't as effective at improving disk performance as the permanent swap file. To create it, you must exit Windows, and then start Windows with the following command:

```
WIN /R SWAPFILE
```

That command puts Windows into the real mode and runs the SWAPFILE program. In that program, first delete any current swap files, and then create a new one. Windows will suggest a fairly large size—almost half the free space on your hard drive. Adjust that size; for example, a one-megabyte permanent swap file is great. Next click OK, quit Windows, and restart.

As a large, contiguous file on disk, the permanent swap file should improve disk performance right away.

Run Windows from a network

If your PC is hooked up to a network, run Windows from the file server. You'll need to adjust your path to reflect the proper location of Windows' files. Refer to your system administrator for all the right commands.

Clean up memory

Aside from loading your device drivers high, consider removing any memory-resident programs that don't directly affect Windows. For example, it's possible to run some memory-resident programs, such as SideKick 2.0, in a non-memory-resident mode. If so, then create a Windows' PIF file and run SideKick in its own window as a non-resident program. That will also better fit into the Windows motif.

About the only device drivers Windows really needs are the following:

Device driver	Function
HIMEM.SYS	Rules over extended memory, sets up the HMA for both DOS and Windows
EMM386.EXE	Creates upper-memory blocks. Uses the /NOEMS switch when you run Windows. Also, uses DOS's EMM386.EXE— not the EMM386.SYS file that came with Windows
MOUSE.SYS	Loads the mouse driver into memory; Windows needs a mouse. (You can also use MOUSE.COM in AUTOEXEC.BAT.)
EGA.SYS	Used only on PCs with an EGA video system; it forces Windows (as well as DOS Shell) to properly recognize the EGA's different text and graphics screens
SMARTDRV.SYS	Creates the SMARTDrive disk cache
RAMDRIVE.SYS	Creates a RAM drive

Windows will also like your BUFFERS set to at least 20. Note that with SMARTDRV.SYS installed, you won't need to set BUFFERS to a higher value. Also, set FILES to 32—a good, general value.

Perform regular disk maintenance

Hard-disk optimization, defragmentation, and backing up are often central to keeping any computer system operating in top condition. But when you do disk maintenance on a Windows system, do the maintenance either before or after you run Windows. Why? Windows creates a host of temporary files and if you delete them too early, the system may hang. Also, doing disk optimization while running any multitasking software is a risky thing.

Add more memory

As a last resort, you can add more memory to your system—expanded memory for 8088 and 80286 systems, and extended memory for '386 systems. This will help feed Windows RAM appetite.

Info: You can also boost Window's speed by adding a math coprocessor to your system. While that's usually very expensive (more than a few megabytes of RAM or a second hard drive in most cases), it does improve Windows somewhat.

Windows is not thought of as being "peppy." But there are definitely ways to make it less lethargic.

Summary

Running additional copies of the command processor, COMMAND.COM, is referred to as shelling. You type the EXIT command to quit COMMAND.COM and return to the previous program (or copy of COMMAND.COM).

Some applications offer the ability to shell out to DOS or to run another application. If the only option is to specify a program name, then specifying COMMAND.COM will shell you out to DOS.

DOS menu systems can be used to simplify the way applications are run, to organize them on your system, and to augment the power of DOS.

DOS environments are used to extend the power of DOS.

DESQview allows you to run several programs at once in text windows. When compared with Windows, DESQview gives you similar power, doesn't require a mouse or graphics, and runs the programs you're already using (including Windows software).

GeoWorks is an inexpensive Windows-alternative. It's a graphical-based environment and comes with its own set of applications. The advantage of GeoWorks is that it runs equally well on any PC, no matter what the microprocessor or graphics system.

Windows is the premier DOS environment, extending the power and function of DOS without making things overly complex. Windows works on all types of PCs, but it really shines on 386 systems, where it can run DOS and Windows applications at the same time.

The major drawback to Windows is its drain on system resources: Windows wants a fast microprocessor, a fast hard drive, graphics, and lots of memory. There are ways to optimize Windows performance without buying new hardware, but often, to make Windows really shine, you need a computer with more muscle.

PART SIX

Troubleshooting

This part of the book is a wrap up, covering items that have yet to be covered and also concentrating on dealing with disk mishaps, general troubleshooting, as well as a list of common DOS ails and their remedies. There are only two chapters here:

Chapter 28 deals with disaster, but more importantly, it explains how to prevent it. Several interesting and useful DOS disaster-relief utilities are discussed, as well as preventive medicine and recovery strategies.

Chapter 29 provides helpful information on using DOS and your PC. Various symptoms are presented and their causes and cures discussed.

Dealing with Disaster

Nothing is perfect. Actually, the computer comes close and it's the human element that causes most of the problems. Using a PC on a daily basis means you'll occasionally delete a file you didn't want to or, worse, format a disk that had important data on it you now want to recover. DOS comes with a battery of utilities that will help you to both prevent and cure some common PC ills. While these tools shouldn't encourage sloppiness, they will help you sleep better at night.

This chapter answers the following questions:

- What is the Emergency Boot Diskette strategy?

- Why shouldn't you use the RECOVER command?

- How can the RESTORE command be better than UNDELETE or UNFORMAT?

- Is the MIRROR command the prevention or the cure?

- What is "delete tracking?"

- How does the FORMAT command's /F switch replace five other switches?

- Can a disk be unformatted?

- How are files recovered after they've been deleted?

Creating an Emergency Boot Diskette

One of the best strategies you can use with your computer is to create an Emergency Boot Diskette. This is a diskette from which you can boot your computer, one which has all your basic needs and disaster recover tools on it—Just In Case. Even creating a boot diskette with the basic DOS boot files on it is enough. But the strategy of the Emergency Boot Diskette goes many, many steps further.

Building the Diskette

Fetch a new, unformatted diskette that matches the highest capacity of your system's A drive—for the Emergency Boot Diskette you don't want to skimp on size. Format that diskette and copy DOS's boot files to it. Enter the following command:

```
FORMAT A: /S
```

The /S switch causes DOS to copy the system files—IO.SYS, MSDOS.SYS, and COMMAND.COM to that diskette.

After formatting the diskette, remove it and write on a label "Emergency Boot Diskette." Peel and stick the label on the diskette. Put the diskette back in the drive.

You now have a workable boot diskette. If the hard drive ever fails, you can start the computer using that diskette. But why stop there?

Copy your CONFIG.SYS and AUTOEXEC.BAT files to the Emergency Boot Diskette.

```
COPY C:\CONFIG.SYS A:\
COPY C:\AUTOEXEC.BAT A:\
```

Once there, edit each file using the MS-DOS Editor. For CONFIG.SYS, do the following:

Delete any unneeded commands or device drivers.

For example, you probably won't need ANSI.SYS on the Emergency Boot Diskette. Also, consider removing any RAM drives or disk caches, or any other device drivers that are not absolutely necessary to run the computer.

Device drivers you may consider retaining are: HIMEM.SYS, EMM386.EXE, SETVER.EXE, EGA.SYS, MOUSE.SYS, and any important third-party device drivers, such as disk drive configuration drivers and memory managers.

Edit the paths of those remaining device drivers to reflect a location on drive A.

The hard disk may be gone, in which case the Emergency Boot Diskette won't be able to load your device driver from it. If this happens, edit the CONFIG.SYS file on drive A to reflect a pathname for the device on drive A. For example, you would change:

```
DEVICE=C:\DOS\HIMEM.SYS
```

To read:

```
DEVICE=A:\HIMEM.SYS
```

You can optionally create subdirectories for your device drivers or other files. But because only a few files will be copied to the Emergency Boot Diskette, there's no need to fuss with a subdirectory structure.

Note each device driver's name

Keep a list of the names of the device drivers you retain—or simply print your A:\CONFIG.SYS file when you've finished editing it.

Edit the SHELL configuration command

COMMAND.COM is now on drive A; edit the SHELL configuration command in CONFIG.SYS to reflect that, or just delete that line.

For your AUTOEXEC.BAT file on the Emergency Boot Diskette, make the following changes:

Delete any unnecessary commands

This includes any memory-resident or pop-up utilities, JOIN or SUBST commands, or any hard-drive maintenance done in your AUTOEXEC.BAT file. The purpose of the Emergency Boot Diskette isn't to give you your normal system; it's a lean system designed to help you recover your hard drive. You don't need all the puffy, frilly programs you normally would have.

Edit the paths of the remaining commands to reflect drive A.

As with A:\CONFIG.SYS, any programs used in A:\AUTOEXEC.BAT will now be located on the Emergency Boot Diskette.

Note each command's name

Keep a list of the external commands you use in AUTOEXEC.BAT. Later you'll need the list to copy those programs to the floppy diskette.

Change your PATH to reflect drive A

Edit the PATH command to include drive A's root directory and any other subdirectories you may be using on drive A. Remove any subdirectories on the hard drive; if it's crashed, DOS won't be able to access those files anyway.

Edit any shells or environments that end AUTOEXEC.BAT

Remove the WIN or DV or DOSSHELL command at the bottom of AUTOEXEC.BAT; you want to use DOS—not some fancy environment—for file recovery.

Once you've made the changes, copy the necessary device drivers and programs from the hard drive to the Emergency boot diskette. For example, on my system I'm copying the following files:

```
HIMEM.SYS
SETVER.EXE
DOSKEY.COM
```

Your system may require more or fewer files; and you will be adding additional disaster-recovery programs as your read through this chapter.

To whatever files you copy as required by CONFIG.SYS or AUTOEXEC.BAT, add the following:

```
DEBUG.EXE
FDISK.EXE
FORMAT.COM
SYS.COM
```

600

These three files might be needed to restart or reconfigure a zapped hard drive: DEBUG for low-level formatting; FDISK for partitioning; and FORMAT for the high-level format.

The SYS.COM program also might come in handy. If someone accidentally erases the two boot files IO.SYS and MSDOS.SYS, then SYS will put them back on the hard drive without the needing to reformat.

Info: CHKDSK.EXE could be on the list, but usually in the case of major disk failure, running CHKDSK does more harm than good. Copy CHKDSK if you like; but use other recovery tools before resorting to it.

Testing the Diskette

To make sure everything is up to par, keep the Emergency Boot Diskette in drive A and reset your computer.

After a few moments (somewhat longer than normal because you're booting from a floppy diskette), the system will come alive. Make sure everything works. Note any errors or "Bad command or filename" messages. Then reset the system to boot from the hard drive, edit CONFIG.SYS or AUTOEXEC.BAT, and try it all over again.

Keep the Emergency Boot Diskette handy.

Some Simple Recovery Tools

DOS has three commands that can provide you with some disaster relief. These are what I call the R-word tools: RECOVER, REPLACE and RESTORE. They aren't as marvelous as some of the newer recovery tools, but they can be beneficial under certain circumstances.

The RECOVER Command

The RECOVER command has a promising name but a disappointing outcome. What it purports to do is to scan your disk for questionable sectors and then recover files, piecing them together as best it can. But what it really does is less than useful and, in fact, can be quite deadly.

For example, suppose your floppy disk in drive A was acting up and you were losing data rapidly. You could attempt to recover it by issuing the following command:

```
C:\>RECOVER A:
The entire drive will be reconstructed,
directory structures will be destroyed.
Are you sure (Y/N)?
```

If you press Y in answer to that charming message, the RECOVER program would scan drive A—no matter what. It looks for errors if they're there or not, and recovers files that are probably okay in the first place. Each file is given a name FILExxxx.REC where the xxxx is a number from 0001 on up. After that, you copy the recovered files to a usable diskette. Then your job is to decipher the contents of each file and (if you recognize it) give it back its original name.

If your problem is with only one file, then you can recover it using the following command:

```
RECOVER filename
```

filename is the name of a single file to recover; it cannot contain wildcards.

For example, if you wanted to recover that questionable FLAKEY file, you would type:

```
C:\>RECOVER A:FLAKEY
```

Press any key to begin recovery of the file(s) on drive A:

Press the Spacebar and the RECOVER command seeks out A:FLAKEY and attempts to rebuild it. After the process is complete, you may see the message:

```
4096 of 4096 bytes recovered
```

Unlike the general disk recovery, the file will retain its original name. But a problem is that missing pieces or doubtful sectors of the disk may have been replaced by the RECOVER program using "blank" data. Don't expect the file to be perfect.

RECOVER is truly a deadly command and should never be used at any time. In fact, using RECOVER on your hard drive would be devastating: All subdirectories would be erased and any data in them lost. Instead of resorting to RECOVER, consider the following alternatives:

Use the RESTORE command to grab back an old copy of the file from a backup-diskette set.

Use an advanced disk utility to recover the file or repair the disk or both.

Attempt to copy the file to another diskette; if that doesn't work, rename the file to something uncommon and hide it using the ATTRIB command. (This is the "sweep it under the rug" method.)

COMMAND: RECOVER (External)
                 Function: Quasi-data recovery.
                 Format: RECOVER drive: filename

RECOVER attempts to restore disks or files with missing pieces. The results are less than spectacular and this command should be avoided.

Drive is a drive letter, following a colon, indicating a drive for RECOVER to repair. Every file on the drive will attempt to be rescued and placed in the root directory with the name FILExxxx.REC. This happens until all files have been "recovered" or the root directory fills.

Filename is the name of a specific file to recover; it cannot contain wildcards. RECOVER will scan the disk, picking up whatever pieces of filename it can find and patching it back together.

The REPLACE Command

The REPLACE command isn't a disaster-relief command, but it can come in handy when updating your hard drive. What REPLACE does is to compare two directories of files. Files with matching names but with older dates are sought out and replaced by their newer counterparts.

REPLACE is the ideal software update command. For example:

```
REPLACE A:\*.* C:\ /S /U
```

After the above command, DOS will scan the list of filenames on drive A and compare those with all files in all subdirectories on drive C. If any matches are found, DOS will replace the older files on drive C with the newer ones on drive A.

Note that the above command will only replace matching files between drives A and C; any files on drive A that don't exist on drive C will not be copied. Also, REPLACE only searches subdirectories on drive C, not drive A.

Info: The REPLACE command was instrumental with earlier installation programs that updated DOS. Other applications may use REPLACE to assist you in updating.

COMMAND: REPLACE (External)

                Function: Updates software from one disk to another

                Format: REPLACE filename [pathname switches]

Filename is the source filename, group of files specified by a wildcard, a drive letter or pathname. Filename indicates the source files, those which you want to copy to a destination to update older files.

Pathname is the destination directory, which contains the files to be updated. If pathname is omitted, the currently logged drive and directory are assumed.

Switches are optional switches used to customize the way the REPLACE command behaves. They are as follows:

/A is used when you want to add files specified by the source filename which don't exist in the destination pathname. If the /A switch isn't specified, REPLACE updates only matching filenames. Note that the /A switch cannot be used with the /S or /U switches.

/P is used to display a prompt whenever a file is copied or replaced on the destination.

/R allows the REPLACE command to replace read-only files in the destination pathname. Without the /R switch, the REPLACE command will halt if a read-only file is to be replaced.

/S is used to direct the REPLACE command to scan for matching files on all subdirectories on the destination pathname.

/W causes a prompt to be displayed before the REPLACE operation begins, which allows you time to insert a diskette or to cancel the REPLACE command by pressing Ctrl-C.

/U is used by REPLACE to compare the dates of any matching files. If the date of the destination is earlier than the source, the file is replaced. If not, it's skipped.

The RESTORE Command

The BACKUP command's counterpart, RESTORE, is probably the best traditional tool you can use for disaster recovery—provided you back up regularly. You can replace any single file that you've accidentally deleted or "munged" by using the following command:

```
RESTORE A: pathname
```

Above, "A:" is assumed to be the drive containing the first backup diskette. Pathname is the full pathname of the file, or group of files specified with a wildcard. After entering the above command, RESTORE will scan through the backup diskettes and look for all possible matches with pathname. When found, they'll be restored to the hard drive—but only to their original location (drive and subdirectory).

Often using RESTORE is the quickest and best way to recover part or all of an accidentally deleted subdirectory tree. The format is:

```
RESTORE A: pathname\*.* /S
```

Above, pathname is the name of the directory. The "*.*" and /S will assure that all files in all subdirectories are restored to their original locations. But keep in mind that the files will be in their same condition as when the last backup took place; the more recent the backup, the better the recovery.

Info: The format of the RESTORE command is given in Chapter 21.

If you're building an Emergency Boot Diskette, consider copying the RESTORE.EXE command to it. However, if you're using a third-party backup program, copy its "restore" command (or the whole application, if it will fit) to your Emergency Boot Diskette.

Copying RESTORE is important: If your hard drive goes, then you're left with a stack of backup diskettes and no application to restore them to the hard drive. If you have your RESTORE command on the Emergency Boot Diskette, it's one less thing to worry about.

Tip: If you're using a third-party program and it generates any backup logs, copy them to your Emergency Boot Diskette as well. If you're running your backup via a batch file, incorporate the copying routines into the batch file. For example:

```
ECHO Insert the Emergency Boot Diskette in drive A
PAUSE
COPY *.DIR A:
```

Above, *.DIR matches all the backup logs produced by PC Backup from Central Point Software. Other backup software may have different log file names, all of which can be matched with the proper wildcards.

An Ounce of Prevention

Dealing with disaster isn't that bad if you're fully prepared for disaster. The MIRROR command that comes with DOS is similar to those home-emergency kits advertised for earthquakes, hurricanes or tornados. Like the home-emergency kits, MIRROR won't do anything to stop a disaster. But when the inevitable Act Of God occurs, MIRROR will assist you in a speedy recovery.

Using the MIRROR Command

The MIRROR command is prevention. It does several things for you and can be used in varying degrees. But note that MIRROR does no data recovery by itself. Instead, the things MIRROR does are interpreted by other DOS commands that will bring back dead or mangled files or disks.

MIRROR concentrates its efforts in three areas:

Total hard-drive recovery

> MIRROR records important information about your hard drive—including its partition and boot-sector information—into a file named PARTNSAV.FIL. The information in that file can be used by the UNFORMAT command to help recover the hard drive in case it's ever trashed. (This needs to be done only once.)

Hard-drive and diskette unformatting

> When run daily, MIRROR makes a copy of important information about a disk, including its directory structure. That information is kept in a file, MIRROR.FIL, which can be used by the UNFORMAT command to fully reconstruct a reformatted disk.

Single-file recovery

> MIRROR's delete-tracking feature keeps a running record of files deleted in a file named PCTRACKR.DEL. If you ever need to use the UNDELETE command to recover the file, it examines PCTRACKR.DEL and can recover the file more quickly and often more accurately than you can without it.

To get the MIRROR command to assist with disk and file recovery, you must use it every day. But note that the single MIRROR command operates in varying degrees. The following three sections describe the MIRROR command's three different modes of operation.

Info: Don't let the power of the MIRROR command fool you into being sloppy: You should still be careful when you use DOS—especially with the FORMAT and DEL commands. And nothing beats a good, regular backup routine.

MIRROR and Hard Disk Recovery

Every hard-disk owner needs the MIRROR command to save important information about the hard drive, its boot information and the partition tables. This information is invaluable should the disk become damaged. And you will never need to update the information, unless you run the FDISK program to change the disk's statistics or if you add another hard drive to your system.

Place your Emergency Boot Diskette in drive A, and then on your hard drive, type the MIRROR command with its optional /PARTN switch:

```
C:\>MIRROR /PARTN

Disk Partition Table saver.

The partition information from your hard drive(s) has been read.

Next, the file PARTNSAV.FIL will be written to a floppy disk. Please
insert a formatted diskette and enter the name of the diskette drive.

What drive? A
```

Press Enter to save the partition information on drive A. MIRROR responds with the message:

```
Successful.
```

A file named PARTNSAV.FIL has now been created and placed on your Emergency Boot Diskette. If disaster should ever befall the hard drive, the UNFORMAT command can be used with PARTNSAV.FIL to recover the hard drive more accurately than had this not been done.

Info: The UNFORMAT command is covered later in this chapter.

MIRROR and Disk Unformatting

Whenever you reformat a disk, DOS doesn't erase the entire disk. Instead, only the FAT and root directory are actually erased and replaced with new, blank copies. The rest of the disk is merely scanned, verifying that each sector can still contain data (which is why the reformat takes as long as a new format). So, although you think you've zapped an entire diskette by reformatting it, you've only erased part of it. It's this aspect that MIRROR allows you to exploit.

Info: If you use the FORMAT command with the optional /Q (quick) switch, it will not verify the disk, speeding up the reformat. However, the /U (unconditional) switch will always force FORMAT to completely erase the disk. If you FORMAT a disk using the /U switch, recovery is not possible—even with MIRROR.

Formatting new diskettes out of the box always formats the entire diskette, but this point is not up for debate, because the subject here is data recovery.

How the MIRROR command helps is by reading the FAT and root directories from a designated disk, saving that information in a file named MIRROR.FIL. The file is kept in the disk's root directory, but physically it's located near the end of the disk—out of reach of FORMAT's potential destruction. By using the MIRROR.FIL file, DOS's UNFORMAT command can quickly and almost always successfully rescue any diskette you've accidentally reformatted.

The format of the MIRROR command used to help recover a reformatted disk is:

```
MIRROR drive(s) [/1]
```

Drive(s) is a single-disk drive letter or several drive letters, each followed by a colons. MIRROR will save the FAT and root directory information for each drive in a MIRROR.FIL file placed on that disk. Note that there's no need to use MIRROR on SUBSTed or JOINed drives. If a drive isn't specified, MIRROR creates a MIRROR.FIL file for the current drive.

/1 (one, not L) is an optional switch used to maintain only one copy of the MIRROR.FIL on a disk at a time. Without the /1 switch, the old MIRROR.FIL file is maintained as a backup copy, MIRROR.BAK.

The MIRROR command is best used in your AUTOEXEC.BAT file, which means it will run every day and keep an accurate copy of your disk information.

```
MIRROR C:
```

The above command creates a MIRROR.FIL file for drive C. (If you had any additional hard drives in your system, you could add them after "C:" above.)

When your AUTOEXEC.BAT file runs, you'll see the following displayed:

```
Creates an image of the system area.

Drive C being processed.

The MIRROR process was successful.
```

For floppy diskettes you should use the MIRROR command directly: Insert the floppy diskette into the appropriate drive and type MIRROR followed by that drive letter at the DOS prompt. As an example, locate the Test Diskette you may have created in a previous chapter. Insert that diskette into Drive A and type the following:

```
MIRROR A:
```

Keep the Test Diskette handy for some further demonstrations in a later chapter.

Remember that MIRROR by itself is only prevention—and, by all means, it shouldn't encourage carelessness. The UNFORMAT command is what the MIRROR.FIL file will use to make disk reconstruction easier.

MIRROR and File Recovery

The MIRROR command's final effort at preventive medicine is its delete-tracking feature, which monitors files deleted from disk. MIRROR saves information about the deleted files in a file in the root directory named PCTRACKR.DEL (which has a set system attribute). The UNDELETE command can then use that information to quickly, and often flawlessly, recover the file.

Info: Generally, UNDELETE can resurrect files by itself; using MIRROR's delete tracking only expedites the process. Also, note that the UNDELETE command is most successful with files recently deceased. Even with delete tracking turned on, UNDELETE cannot recover last week's old sales report (which is what makes the RESTORE command a useful tool).

To initiate delete tracking, start MIRROR as you normally would, specifying drive letters on which MIRROR will perform its anti-formatting magic. After those drive letters, you specify the drives you want MIRROR to monitor for delete tracking using MIRROR's optional /T switch. The format is:

```
/Tdrive[-files]
```

The /T switch initiates delete tracking for a single drive, as specified by *drive*. You must specify the /T switch or each system drive that you want to monitor. For example, if you have three hard drives, you would use the following MIRROR command:

```
MIRROR C: D: E: /TC /TD /TE
```

The first three drive letters tell MIRROR to create a MIRROR.FIL file for each drive, saving important information about those drives in case of an accidental reformat. The three /T switches are used to initiate delete tracking on each of the three drives.

Info: As with MIRROR's disk-unformatting command, do not use MIRROR's delete tracking on SUBSTed or JOINed drives.

The *-files* part of the /T switch is optional. It's a number from 1 through 999 that tells MIRROR how many deleted files to monitor for delete tracking. The higher the number, the more files MIRROR will track and the better the chance of recovery. But a large number can eat up disk space, allowing the PCTRACKR.DEL file to grow in size. If you don't specify a value, a default is chosen based on your disk size:

Disk size	-files value	File size (max)
360K	25	5K
720K	50	9K
1.2M	75	14K
1.4M	75	14K
20M	101	18K
32M	202	36K
32M+	303	55K

The default value is usually best. But if you wanted to specify a smaller value for a large disk (to save on disk space), you could specify one as in:

```
MIRROR C: /TC-100
```

Above, the MIRROR command is activated on drive C. Delete tracking will monitor only 100 files, which makes the PCTRACKR.DEL file a little smaller than it may be otherwise. Note that the hyphen after the /T and drive letter is required.

Info: When you initiate MIRROR's delete tracking, it creates a read only, hidden, and system attribute file named MIRORSAV.FIL in the root directory of the drive you're monitoring. Only when you delete a file is PCTRACKR.DEL created, usually at the size indicated by the above table.

The only drawback to using the delete-tracking feature is that it will slow down disk access somewhat. If that's a problem, you can turn delete tracking off using the MIRROR command's /U (uninstall) switch:

```
C:\>MIRROR /U
```

Deleting-tracking software removed from memory.

Do not use the MIRROR /U command if you have loaded other memory-resident programs "on top of" MIRROR (after MIRROR in your AUTOEXEC.BAT file). Doing so could crash your system.

Tip: It's okay to remove memory-resident programs from memory, but only when you "back them out of the garage," peeling them out of memory in the opposite order in which they were loaded. This holds true even if you're loading the programs high into a UMB.

Loading MIRROR High

MIRROR is a memory-resident program and as such it gobbles up conventional memory, sometimes up to 7K of memory. (Not much, but every little byte counts.)

If you're using an 80386-or-later PC, and have created upper-memory blocks, you can load MIRROR into one. Normally this would be done using the LOADHIGH command. But MIRROR is very, very smart; just starting MIRROR on a system where UMBs have been created will cause MIRROR to load itself high automatically. You don't need to specify the LOADHIGH command at all.

Info: Refer to Chapter 26 for more information on loading high and UMBs.

Formatting & Unformatting

The FORMAT command is necessary and useful. But like any tool, hammer, saw, or anvil, when used improperly it can cause damage. Accidentally formatting a floppy disk is a bother. Accidentally formatting a hard drive is worth sticking your head through a plate glass window or kicking a small furry animal. But there are ways to prevent such mishaps, and better ways to deal with them when they happen.

The following two sections cover two equal and opposite commands: FORMAT and UNFORMAT. One does, the other undoes. It works so well that at times you think both files would cancel each other out on disk.

The FORMAT Command

The FORMAT command is used to prepare a disk for use. It's smart enough to know which type of drives you have in your system and it will always format a disk out to its maximum assumed size. To do this, you simply specify the proper drive letter and FORMAT builds you a data diskette.

There are times when you'll want to customize or further manipulate, going beyond the standard "no frills" format. For example, you may want to format a diskette to a smaller size or to a format used by an older version of DOS; you may want to format a system or boot diskette; or you may want to quick-format a diskette or do an unconditional full reformat. To perform any of these feats, you can use some of the FORMAT command's cavalcade of optional switches.

The FORMAT command has 11 optional switches—more than any other DOS command. For easy handling, the switches can be grouped into three categories:

General Disk Switches

System Disk Switches

Diskette Size Switches

General Disk Switches

The General Disk Switches are /V, /Q, and /U. The /V switch is used to specify a volume label, in which case FORMAT won't ask you for one after the disk is formatted. The /Q switch is used to quick-format already formatted diskettes, more like a quick-erase than a full format. And the /U switch starts an unconditional format, totally erasing a disk or formatting it to another size. Note that /Q and /U cannot be used together.

The follow FORMAT command uses the /V switch to automatically assign a volume label to the formatted disk:

```
FORMAT A: /V:DATADISK
```

The above command formats the diskette in drive A (to its full capacity) and gives the diskette the volume label "DATADISK." Note that any additional diskettes you format each will be given the same name. If the volume label contains a space, enclose it in double quotes:

```
FORMAT A: /V:"DATA DISK"
```

The /Q switch is the quick-format switch. When specified, DOS will examine the diskette, determine its size, and then quick-format it. This involves only erasing the FAT and root directories; FORMAT will not verify the rest of the disk. So only use the /Q switch on already formatted diskettes where you're certain that the diskette is good.

For example, assuming that drive A contains an already formatted 1.2M diskette, you could enter the following FORMAT command:

```
C:\>FORMAT A: /Q
Insert new diskette for drive A:
and press ENTER when ready... Enter pressed here

Checking existing disk format.
Saving UNFORMAT information.
QuickFormatting 1.2M
Format complete.
```

The above operation takes maybe eight seconds. After that, you can optionally type a volume label and quick-format any additional diskettes.

Info: The "UNFORMAT information" saved is used by the UNFORMAT command for data recovery when it unformats the diskette. This is not the same information saved by the MIRROR command; MIRROR's information is supplemental and helps the UNFORMAT work more accurately.

The /U switch is nearly the opposite of the /Q switch. It performs an unconditional format of the disk, fully erasing the entire diskette's contents or reformatting a diskette to another size.

You can use the /U switch in one of two situations—when you want to be totally certain that the diskette is fully erased, or when you're formatting a diskette of lower capacity in a high-capacity drive.

Note: Always format diskettes out to their full capacity: high-capacity diskettes and high capacity or lower-capacity diskettes at low capacity. Use the /U switch when reformatting a low capacity diskette in a high-capacity drive. Note that using the /U switch means that the diskette cannot be recovered using the UNFORMAT command. So be careful!

System Disk Switches

Two of FORMAT's parade of switches could be considered System Disk Switches. The first, /S, is used to transfer the system files to a formatted diskette thus making a boot disk. The second switch, /B, is used to reserve room for the system files, which can be added at a later time.

The /S switch is used to make a system diskette, one you can boot. Specifying /S tells FORMAT to copy the two hidden system files (IO.SYS and MSDOS.SYS) to the diskette after formatting. Also copied is COMMAND.COM, which completes the diskette as a boot disk. Note that those files total about 118K of disk space.

The /B switch is a holdover from earlier versions of DOS. It created two holding places for the IO.SYS and MSDOS.SYS files so that they could successfully be copied to the diskette at a later time using the SYS command. Starting with DOS 5, this has no longer been a concern; you can use the SYS command at any time to create a system disk.

Diskette Size Switches

The Diskette Size Switches are the most confusing and redundant of FORMAT's switches. The /F switch is the only switch you really need and it formats a diskette out to the exact size specified. The other five switches are holdovers from previous versions of DOS.

The /F switch sets the form factor (the number of tracks and sectors) for a diskette; this is actually the diskette's formatted capacity. The /F switch is followed by a required size value as follows:

```
/F:size
```

Values for *size* depend on the size of diskette you want to format. Currently, there are eight diskette formats supported by DOS, each of which can have size values according to the following table:

Diskette size	Size values
160K	160, 160K, 160KB
180K	180, 180K, 180KB
320K	320, 320K, 320KB
360K	360, 360K, 360KB
720K	720, 720K, 720KB
1.2M	1200, 1200K, 1200KB, 1.2, 1.2M 1.2MB
1.4M	1440, 1440K, 1400KB, 1.44, 1.44M, 1.44MB
2.8M	2880, 2880K, 2880KB, 2.88, 2.88M, 2.88MB

You can use upper- or lowercase letters after the size values, or you can use none at all. The most popular of these will be the commands to format a 360K diskette in a 1.2M drive or a 720K diskette in a 1.4M drive:

```
FORMAT A: /F:360
```

The above command is used to format a 360K diskette in a 1.2M drive. Note that you may have to specify the /U switch, especially if the FORMAT command returns a "Not ready" message.

```
FORMAT A: /F:720
```

The above command formats a 720K diskette in a 1.4M drive. If you receive a "Not ready" message, then add the /U switch.

The remaining diskette size switches are holdovers from previous versions of DOS. Each customizes the format as follows:

/N:sectors formats a diskette with the specified number of sectors. This switch was used exclusively with the /T switch to create 720K diskettes in 1.4M drives.

/T:tracks formats a diskette with the specified number of tracks. This switch was used with the /N switch to create a 720K diskette as follows:

```
FORMAT A: /N:9/T:80
```

Use the /F:720 switch instead.

/1 formats a single-sided diskette, which was the diskette format prior to DOS 2.0. The two formats created are the 160K and 180K sizes, along with the assistance of either the /4 or /8 switches. Use the /F:160 or /F:180 switches instead.

/4 formats a 360K diskette in a 1.2M drive. (No other switches are needed, although you should use the /F:360 switch instead.)

/8 formats an eight-sector diskette, which was the rage with DOS 1.0. (160K and 320K diskettes were eight-sectored.) You cannot use the /V switch if you specify /8.

After reading the above five holdovers, it's easy to understand the /F switch. In case you're curious, the following table shows you which switches are used to create the various diskette formats. The top row indicates the size of your drive (maximum capacity) and the left column indicates the size of the diskette you want to format.

	360K	720K	1.2M	1.4M	2.8M
160M	/F:160 /1/8	—	/F:160 /4/1/8	—	—
180M	/F:180 /1	—	/F:180 /4/1	—	—
320M	/F:320 /8	—	/F:320 /4/8	—	—
360M	—	—	/F:360 /4	—	—
720M	—	—	—	/F:720 /N:9/T:80	/F:720 /N:9/T:80
1.4M	—	—	—	—	/F:1.44

Table 28-1. Diskette sizes and FORMAT switches.

The two values in each cell represent the /F switch (preferred) and the other switches required to create the format.

COMMAND: FORMAT (External)
               Function: To format disks, preparing them for use.
               Format: FORMAT drive switches

Drive is the letter of the drive containing the disk to be formatted. It must be specified.

Switches are optional switches following the drive letter. They are:

/1 formats a single-sided (either a 160K or 180K) diskette in a 5 1/4-inch drive. (Use either the /F:160 and /F:180 switches instead.)

/4 formats a 360K diskette in a 1.2M drive. (Use the /F:360 switch instead.)

/8 formats an eight-sector (either a 160K or 320K) diskette in a 5-1/4-inch drive. (Use either the /F:160 or /F:320 switches.)

/B reserves room on the diskette for the DOS system files, IO.SYS and MSDOS.SYS. This switch is no longer needed under DOS 5, but it is maintained for compatibility reasons.

/F formats a diskette to the specified size value, following /F and a colon. Size values are listed in a table earlier in this chapter.

/N specifies the number of sectors used to format a diskette. The /N switch was used with /T to format a 720K diskette in a 1.4M drive; use the /F:720 switch instead.

/Q quick-formats an already formatted diskette. The diskette isn't verified, so make sure it's a good diskette. Also, the /Q switch cannot be used when you're specifying a new size for the diskette, or when you're first formatting a diskette out of the box.

/S transfers the system files, IO.SYS and MSDOS.SYS, as well as COMMAND.COM to the new diskette. The /S switch creates a system or boot diskette.

/T specifies the number of tracks used to format the diskette. This switch was formerly used with the /N switch to format a 720K diskette in a 1.4M drive; use the /F:720 switch instead.

/U causes FORMAT to unconditionally format the diskette, totally erasing its contents and formatting it to a new size (if specified). A diskette reformatted with the /U switch cannot be unformatted by the UNFORMAT command.

/V automatically assigns to the diskette a volume label which is specified after /V and a colon. If the label contains a space, enclose it in double quotes.

Always format diskettes out to their full capacity. If you want to format a lower capacity diskette, then buy such a diskette; formatting a high-capacity diskette to a lower capacity is a waste of material, and it will be rendered incompatible with the low-capacity drives.

The UNFORMAT Command

Proving once again that what can be done can be undone, the UNFORMAT command is used to rescue a diskette accidentally reformatted. This must be done as soon as possible after the reformat in order to ensure that all files are successfully rescued. (And if you reformat using the /U switch, recovery will not be possible at all.)

The reason that the UNFORMAT command works is that DOS never fully reformats a diskette. Only the boot sector, FAT and root directories are cleared out and replaced with new values. The rest of the disk is merely scanned, primarily to identify any bad sectors. The majority of your files and information is still intact on 90 percent of the diskette, so recovery is possible although it isn't overly simple.

Info: Never use the UNFORMAT command as an excuse to be negligent.

When DOS reformats a diskette, is saves special UNFORMAT information in the latter part of the disk. This can be seen by means of the following message when you format a diskette:

```
Saving UNFORMAT information.
```

By itself, that information will be enough to recover the diskette should you want to unformat it. If you've run the MIRROR program on the diskette before reformatting it, that adds further protection and will improve the job the UNFORMAT command does.

To test the UNFORMAT command, format a diskette in drive A, or obtain one that you wouldn't mind reformatting as a test. (Do not use the Emergency Boot Diskette!) After formatting the diskette (if necessary), copy a few files to it—all the files in your root directory would be nice. (If you wish to further demonstrate the power of the UNFORMAT command, create a few subdirectories on the disk and put a few files into them as well.)

After you've put a few files on the diskette, use the MIRROR command as follows:

```
C:\>MIRROR A:

Drive A being processed.

The MIRROR process was successful.
```

Now you can use that diskette to test the UNFORMAT command and later the UNDELETE command as well.

Tip: You can verify the files on your test diskette with the following command:

```
TREE A: /F
```

Redirect that command's output to the printer for comparison after the unformatting is complete.

Now format the diskette. Type the following:

```
FORMAT A:
```

Don't bother with any switches, although you can use the /Q switch if you're in a hurry. Continue to watch as the disk is "formatted," entering an optional volume label when the time comes. Type N when asked if you want to format another.

Use the DIR command to verify that the data on the disk is gone. (It will be—or is it?)

Testing the UNFORMAT Command

The UNFORMAT command has three different formats (or "unformats"). It can be used to ensure that diskettes can be unformatted, to unformat diskettes, and to unformat hard drives.

The first mode of the UNFORMAT command is used to test the potential for unformatting a diskette. (Remember, this must be done before any data is written to the accidentally reformatted disk.) The format is:

```
UNFORMAT drive: /J /TEST /L /P
```

Drive is the drive letter, followed by a colon, indicating the disk to be unformatted. It must be specified.

The switches /J /TEST /L /P are optional. They're used to preview the unformat. Note how some of them use the MIRROR.FIL file and others will ignore it.

/J is used to test the MIRROR.FIL unformatting information and verify its date.

/TEST is used to perform a "dry run" through the unformat. Note that when /TEST is specified, the UNFORMAT command will ignore any information in the MIRROR.FIL file.

/L is used to list files found on the formatted diskette as well as on subdirectories. Without the /L switch, UNFORMAT only lists subdirectories and fragmented files.

/P is used to echo all the UNFORMAT command's output to a printer (LPT1).

The only oddball (actually orphan) switch here is the /J switch, which is incompatible with all but the /P switch. Specifying the /J switch won't cause UNFORMAT to rebuild the disk, but it will give you an idea of how much to trust the MIRROR.FIL file. Type the following:

```
UNFORMAT A: /J
```

The UNFORMAT command will ask you to insert the disk to rebuild in drive A. Press Enter. What you see next will be a dry-run of the recovery process using the MIRROR.FIL file.

Look for the dates and times in the middle of the screen. They give you an idea of how recent the MIRROR.FIL file and, if more than one file was found, they give you the option of using either one. If the last date is close, then you can use the MIRROR.FIL file for disk reconstruction.

Press Esc to cancel the UNFORMAT test.

The other test switches, /TEST and /L, will ignore MIRROR.FIL. Type the following:

```
UNFORMAT A: /TEST /L
```

With the disk you need to rebuild inserted in drive A, press Enter. Read the screen, and then type Y and Enter to continue.

```
Simulation only

Searching disk...
xx% searched, xx subdirectories found.
```

The disk scan will take a while, the percentage indicator rising from 1 to 100 percent. After that's done, you'll see a summary of the directories and files recovered. Since the /L switch is specified, all files found will be displayed. Without the /L switch, only subdirectories and fragmented files will be displayed.

Don't be disappointed by the results—especially if there are no files to be found in the root directory. Also, note that the subdirectories off the root are recovered using names like SUBDIR.1 and so on. This is only the UNFORMAT command at work; remember that MIRROR wasn't involved with this test. With MIRROR, your chances for recovery of the root directory are greatly improved.

Press Esc or Ctrl-C to cancel the test.

Info: So why ignore the MIRROR.FIL file? Because it may be old. If so, you won't want to trust the information in it. In that case, you can direct the UNFORMAT command to rebuild the diskette without recognizing the MIRROR.FIL information.

Unformatting the Diskette

To unformat a disk, you use UNFORMAT as follows:

```
UNFORMAT drive: /U
```

Drive indicates the disk to be rebuilt. It's a drive letter followed by a colon, and it must be specified.

/U tells UNFORMAT to rebuild the disk but ignore the MIRROR.FIL file. By default UNFORMAT uses MIRROR.FIL, but if you have an older MIRROR.FIL file and don't trust it, specify the /U switch. (The /J switch will alert you to the date of the MIRROR.FIL file; see above.)

Since your sample unformatting diskette has a good MIRROR.FIL file on it, you won't need to use the /U switch. Type the following:

```
UNFORMAT A:
```

The UNFORMAT program starts by asking you to insert the proper disk. Press Enter when the disk is ready. You'll see:

```
Restore the SYSTEM area of your disk by using the image file created
by the MIRROR command.

    WARNING!            WARNING!

This command should be used only to recover from the inadvertent use
of the FORMAT command or the RECOVER command. Any other use of the
UNFORMAT command may cause you to lose data! Files modified since
the MIRROR image file was created may be lost.

Searching disk for MIRROR image.

The last time the MIRROR or FORMAT command was used was at 08:34 on
01-28-92. The prior time the MIRROR or FORMAT command was used was
at 08:32 on 01-28-92.

If you wish to use the last file as indicated above, press L. If you
wish to use the prior file as indicated above, press P. Press ESC to
cancel UNFORMAT.

—
```

Press L to use the most recent MIRROR.FIL file.

```
The MIRROR image file has been validated.

Are you sure you want to update the system of your drive A (Y/N)?
```

Press Y. The disk will grind away.

```
The system area of drive A has been rebuilt.

You may need to restart the system.
```

The final message is only valid for boot disks, such as drive C. Otherwise, pull a directory of drive A to see how well UNFORMAT has done its job. If you made a hard copy of the TREE command's output, do that again and compare the results. The diskette should be fully recovered.

This was just a test, so the results are spectacular. In "real life," they may not be. Especially if new files have been written to the diskette, reconstruction may take awhile and be less successful. UNFORMAT has a special problem with fragmented files and can only recover the first part of the file. If that happens, you'll be asked whether you want to recover and truncate the file or if you wish to delete it.

Unformatting Hard Drives

Unformatting or rescuing a trashed hard drive involves two steps. The first step is to verify the partition information saved using MIRROR in the PARTNSAV.FIL file. This will repair any "Invalid drive specification" errors you may see, especially when accessing logical drives.

Info: The PARTNSAV.FIL file needs to be created only once—or if you ever change your disk's partition information. A copy should be saved on your Emergency Boot Diskette.

To recover the hard disk's partitions or to verify the partitions, you would type in the following command:

```
UNFORMAT /PARTN
```

The UNFORMAT command will ask you to insert the diskette containing the PARTNSAV.FIL file on it. Insert your Emergency Boot Diskette into drive A or B, and then type that drive letter and press Enter.

Information about the PARTNSAV.FIL file will be displayed, along with the technical information it recorded about your drive. Press Q to quit or 1 to restore the partition, if required.

Tip: To see what the current partition information is, use the following command:

```
UNFORMAT /PARTN /L
```

You can copy this information down or redirect it to the printer for later comparison with the UNFORMAT /PARTN command.

The next step in hard-disk recovery (or the first step if the partition information on the drive hasn't been damaged) is to rebuild the hard disk. This follows the same procedure covered in the previous section for reconstructing a floppy diskette. Specify the switches as necessary, depending on whether or not the MIRROR file is up to date.

Update the Emergency Boot Diskette

Obtain your Emergency Boot Diskette and place it into your A drive. Now copy the UNFORMAT command to that drive:

```
COPY C:\DOS\UNFORMAT.COM A:
```

Substitute the proper pathname for UNFORMAT.COM; above C:\DOS is assumed.

In general, the UNFORMAT command works—and works well. To keep things that way, follow these simple rules:

Use the MIRROR command on regularly used and important floppy disks; use it on the hard drive every day.

Be careful with the FORMAT command!

Use the FORMAT command's /Q switch whenever possible

Use the UNFORMAT command on a diskette before you've had a chance to write any new data to that diskette.

The sooner you unformat, the better your chances are of a full, safe recovery.

Undeleting Files

When you delete a file with the DEL command, DOS does two things: First, it edits the directory listing on disk, replacing the first character of the file with the byte value 229 (the Greek letter sigma). It then finds the file's first entry in the FAT and replaces it with zeros, meaning that part of disk is available for other files.

What the DEL command doesn't do is totally zap the file physically from disk. The file itself sits on the disk intact (or in fragmented pieces); only the FAT shows that nothing is there. Even the filename and directory entry still exists, save for the first character in the filename.

A file can be recovered quite easily, albeit technically. First, the recovery utility scans the directory for filenames starting with byte 229. Once found, it can use information in the "deleted" directory entry to locate where the file would be in the FAT and, from that, rebuild the chain in the FAT and compare it with the disk. If no new file has written over the old information, the file can be recovered. All the user needs to do is supply the first character in the filename.

The MIRROR command's delete-tracking feature makes this operation even easier. As you delete files, a copy of the deleted file's pathname and directory entry is saved in the PCTRACKR.DEL file. The UNDELETE command will automatically look for PCTRACKR.DEL and recover all the files it can match. With delete tracking, recovery of delete files is fast and smooth. Without it, recovery is still possible, but you must supply the first character of the filename.

The UNDELETE Command

Before using the UNDELETE command to recover files, you can tell it to scan for any deleted files that can be recovered. The format is:

```
UNDELETE pathname /LIST [/DOS|/DT]
```

Pathname is an optional drive, directory, or filename which UNDELETE scans, looking for deleted files. If a pathname isn't specified, UNDELETE assumes the current directory.

/LIST is optional and used to display a list of all deleted files and their chances of recovery. When specified, UNDELETE displays only deleted filenames; no files will be recovered.

The /DOS or /DT switches can be used with /LIST to determine how UNDELETE evaluates deleted files, and whether or not delete tracking will be used for recovery. If /DOS is specified, UNDELETE reports on files that DOS could rescue without delete tracking; the /DT switch tells UNDELETE to use the delete-tracking information.

Place your test diskette in drive A and log to it. If delete tracking hasn't been started for that drive, do so now. Type:

```
MIRROR A: /TA
```

Once delete tracking is installed, delete one file from that diskette.

To evaluate how that file and others can be recovered, type the following command:

```
UNDELETE /LIST
```

The UNDELETE command displays a status of the current directory. If delete tracking is installed, you'll see a list of files that have been deleted and stored in the PCTRACKR.DEL file. A summary of the files DOS reports deleted will also be displayed. Look for your filename in the list. Note that delete tracking has told UNDELETE the full file's name, which will come in handy during recovery.

Info: If you have delete tracking installed, the output of the UNDELETE /LIST command is identical to the output when the /DT switch is also specified.

To see the information as displayed without delete tracking installed, type the following command:

```
UNDELETE /LIST /DOS
```

The directory is scanned and a list of files may be displayed. Note that the deleted files will have a ? (question mark) instead of the first character in their name. A single asterisk (*) preceding a file means that part of the file may have been overwritten; proceed with caution. A double asterisk (**) before a file means that the file's data on disk has probably been overwritten and recovery is definitely not possible.

To recover the files, use the UNDELETE command in the following format:

```
UNDELETE pathname /ALL [/DOS|/DT]
```

All the switches are optional; by itself, UNDELETE will attempt to use MIRROR's delete tracking to successfully recover all deleted files in the current directory.

Pathname is an optional drive, directory, or filename which UNDELETE will recover. If pathname isn't specified, UNDELETE recovers all files from the current directory, prompting as it finds each one.

/ALL tells UNDELETE to automatically recover all files possible in the current directory; if the first character in the filename cannot be identified, a "#" is used in its place.

/DOS tells UNDELETE to ignore delete tracking and use only DOS's information to recover files. Note that when /ALL is specified, /DOS causes UNDELETE to prompt for confirmation and the first character of the filename anyway. This switch is the default if delete tracking isn't installed.

/DT tells UNDELETE to use the delete tracking feature, as well as to prompt for confirmation of each file (even when the /ALL switch is specified). Note that you cannot specify both the /DOS and /DT switches.

To recover your file from drive A, type the following UNDELETE command:

```
UNDELETE
```

Nothing else is needed because delete tracking is installed. After you press Enter, you'll see something like the following:

```
Directory A:\
File Specifications: *.*

    Deletion-tracking file contains    1 deleted files.
    Of those,  1 files have all clusters available,
               0 files have some clusters available,
               0 files have no clusters available.

    MS-DOS directory contains xxxx deleted files
    Of those, xxxx files may be recovered.
Using the deletion-tracking file.

    COWS   TXT   522 2-25-93 11:30a ...A Deleted: 4-12-92 4:38p
All of the clusters for this file are available. Undelete (Y/N)?
```

Since delete tracking keeps the original file's name, there's nothing further for you to do; Press Y and the file is fully recovered.

If you haven't used delete tracking, or the PCTRACKR.DEL file is old, you can use DOS's internal file tracking to help recover the file. (Use the /DOS switch to force UNDELETE to ignore PCTRACKR.DEL.) The only drawbacks to using DOS is that you'll have to supply the first letter of the filename, and there are times when DOS is uncertain as to whether a file can be recovered. In the latter case, you'll need to make the call on whether to recover or not. (Chances are usually good that you can.)

Info: The UNDELETE command is handy, but not an excuse for being lazy. Even with delete tracking installed, be careful with the DEL command. Note that the UNDELETE command cannot restore subdirectories. Also, the chances of recovery for files decreases with the number of new files added or old files changed since the file was deleted.

Be sure to copy UNDELETE.EXE from your DOS subdirectory to your Emergency Boot Diskette.

Completing the Emergency Boot Diskette

Pull a directory of the Emergency boot diskette and see how many bytes are remaining. If you have the room consider copying some of the following files to that diskette. These aren't required, but they may come in handy:

Filename	Size in bytes
MEM.EXE	39,818
EDIT.COM	413
QBASIC.EXE	254,847

Note that the MS-DOS Editor requires both the EDIT.COM file and QBASIC.EXE. This takes up a whopping 255,260 bytes! You may consider copying EDLIN.EXE instead at 12,642 bytes or use your own favorite text editor if it will fit.

Beyond these DOS files, consider adding some important third-party utilities— if they can fit. Some utilities take up lots of room, so it may be a good idea to put them on their own boot diskettes. Carefully label those diskettes and put them in an easy-to-find place, along with the Emergency Boot Diskette. Like the household-emergency kit, it will be there whenever you need it.

Tip: Another thing that may come in handy is your system's CMOS memory. If possible, bring up your PC's CMOS listings, either by running a program named SETUP or by pressing a special key combination. (Refer to your hardware manual.)

Once the CMOS statistics are on the screen, turn on your printer and press the Print Screen key. Keep a copy of the CMOS output in case your system ever crashes; you may need to restore those values.

Note that Print Screen may not work when your CMOS memory listing is displayed. If so, copy down the important information: memory sizes, speed and ROM settings, video, and especially the disk-drive configurations and hard-drive type.

Summary

DOS has lots of utilities to assist you in times of panic. To make all of them useful, you should create an Emergency Boot Diskette. That should be a system diskette (bootable), and have all your important CONFIG.SYS and AUTOEXEC.BAT programs on it (but few frivolous device drivers or memory-resident programs). Additionally, you'll want the following:

The RESTORE command, or the third-party equivalent you use—and any backup disk logs.

The PARTNSAV.FIL file, created by the MIRROR command.

The UNFORMAT command and UNDELETE commands.

The following files: FDISK, FORMAT, DEBUG, SYS, and any other disk utilities you see fit to keep around.

The MIRROR command handles three things: Saving hard-disk partition information; creating an image of a disk's boot area, which can then be used to restore or unformat the disk; and delete tracking, which monitors deleted files and allows DOS to quickly and accurately recover them.

The FORMAT command has more switches than any other DOS command. The /Q switch is used to quickly reformat a diskette, and should be used whenever possible; the /U switch unconditionally formats a diskette, and is best used when reformatting a diskette to a different size or formatting a low-capacity diskette in a high-capacity drive; the /F switch is used to specify a different capacity diskette than that the drive normally formats.

The UNFORMAT command is used to undo an accidental reformat of a disk. UNFORMAT can rescue nearly all files in all subdirectories, but not files in the root directory. To make the best use of UNFORMAT, the MIRROR command must be used on the drive and used recently.

The UNDELETE command brings deleted files back from the dead. It works fine under DOS, but works much smoother when the MIRROR command's delete-tracking feature has been activated.

CHAPTER 29

Symptoms, Causes, and Cures

This chapter is different from every other chapter in this book. Rather than list a few brief questions at the start of the chapter, everything is a question here. The questions are followed by possible causes and solutions. It's all presented according to topic, and the topics are listed below:

- Booting

- Disk Trouble

- Memory & Memory Management

- Video

- The Printer

- CONFIG.SYS

- Batch Files & AUTOEXEC.BAT

- Applications

- Miscellany

Booting

Generally speaking, boot problems are hardware related. Especially if your computer beeps several times before it starts or if it doesn't start at all, have an expert look at the hardware.

The hard drive won't boot in the morning

Usually this is a sign of an old hard drive. It may boot after a time, but it's a good reason to keep regular backups and consider buying a new hard drive.

"Not a system disk..."

Check the A drive: the door may be closed and a non-boot disk may be in the drive.

If the hard drive tells you it's not a system disk, try to boot from a floppy drive and access the hard drive. If you can, then use the SYS command to copy the system to the hard drive:

```
SYS C:
```

If this doesn't work, break out your Emergency Boot Disk and its tools for hard-disk recovery. Also consider third-party disk utilities.

"Invalid Drive Specification"

For a hard drive, it indicates a possible error in the partition table. Use the FDISK program to verify (view only) the partitions available:

1. Start FDISK.

2. Select option 4, Display Partition Information.

3. Verify that the hard drive is properly partitioned.

If you have more than one hard drive, select the FDISK option "Change current fixed disk drive" option to examine other physical drives in the system.

If the problem happens on a computer someone else set up, verify that the SUBST command wasn't used to artificially create the drive and then the drive was removed.

"Bad or missing Command Interpreter"

This message will stop your heart. If it happens at boot time, it indicates either a missing COMMAND.COM program in the root directory, or that the SHELL command has specified an incorrect pathname for COMMAND.COM.

After the system boots, the message indicates that COMMAND.COM was unable to load using the COMSPEC environment variable. Verify that COMSPEC is set properly. If you're using the SHELL configuration command, remember to specify a pathname to COMMAND.COM. Refer to Chapter 19.

AUTOEXEC.BAT won't run

If you're using the SHELL configuration command, remember to specify the /P switch after COMMAND.COM. Verify that AUTOEXEC.BAT is located in the root directory of the boot disk.

Disk Trouble

A diskette is suddenly unusable

You probably zapped it with a magnet. Magnets are everywhere and they work hard at reorganizing magnetic particles, just like those that keep the data on your floppy diskettes. Note that there is a magnet in your phone handset and some of your favorite tools may also have magnets in them.

The same disk you've used for years suddenly won't work

Disks wear with time. This used to happen a lot before hard drives became popular and everything was on floppies. If you have important information on floppy diskettes, make backups or DISKCOPY them frequently. Disks wear with use; if you use a disk daily, replace it every three months.

You can't switch floppy diskettes; the computer always asks to reinsert the same diskette

You're using the FASTOPEN command. Remove it from AUTOEXEC.BAT, or it might be installed by means of the INSTALL configuration command in CONFIG.SYS. Use the SMARTDrive disk cache instead of FASTOPEN to speed disk access.

"Invalid media, Track 0 bad..."

You've attempted to format a low-capacity diskette in a high-capacity drive.

The error also occurs when you attempt to reformat a high-capacity diskette that was originally formatted at a lower capacity. The disk may still be good, and you can still format it: Buy a bulk eraser at an electronics store and magnetically erase the diskette. It should format just fine after that, providing that the diskette is still usable.

Memory & Memory Management

What are the basic files used to set up memory management?

If you have an 80286 system, here are the primary two commands you want in your CONFIG.SYS file:

```
DEVICE=C:\DOS\HIMEM.SYS
DOS=HIGH
```

You cannot use the DOS configuration command's UMB option, nor are the DEVICEHIGH and LOADHIGH commands operable on a '286 system.

For 80386 and later systems, the core commands are:

```
DEVICE=C:\DOS\HIMEM.SYS
DOS=HIGH,UMB
DEVICE=C:\DOS\EMM386.EXE mem umb
```

Mem is the amount of extended memory you want to convert into expanded.

Umb is your UMB creation switch: If you're converting extended memory, use the /RAM switch; if you don't want any expanded memory, use the /NOEMS switch.

After creating UMBs, you can use the DEVICEHIGH command to load device drivers into upper-memory blocks. The LOADHIGH/LH command does the same thing for memory-resident programs.

Note that the DOS subdirectory here is assumed to be C:\DOS.

How can third-party memory managers be integrated into DOS?

Quite well. Both QEMM/386 and 386MAX take the place of HIMEM.SYS and EMM386.EXE. You can use the DOS=HIGH command, and if you use the UMB option, you can use DEVICEHIGH and LOADHIGH to load programs into UMBs. QEMM/386 and 386MAX have their own loading-on high routines, which you may prefer over DOS's. Also, their installation programs take a lot of guesswork out of memory management.

On the 80286, the program QRAM (pronounced "cram") can be used with an LIM 4.0 EMS card to give you some 386 features. The steps go like this:

1. Load the HIMEM.SYS device driver.

2. Set DOS=HIGH,UMB.

3. Load your expanded memory manager (EMM.SYS or its equivalent)

4. Load QRAM.

5. Use DEVICEHIGH and LOADHIGH to move device drivers and memory-resident programs into UMBs.

Some 80286 systems come with special hardware that allows them access to UMBs without all the fancy footwork. If your system has the NEAT or AT/386 CHIPSet from Chips and Technologies, it may already be compatible with DOS's memory management. Refer to your hardware manual.

How should I unload programs that are in UMBs?

If you need to unload a memory-resident program, unload them in order. This works the same as if you were unloading them from conventional memory. Even though the program may sit in its own cozy UMB, a memory-resident program may hook into other memory-resident programs before it hooks into DOS. Removing one out of sequence—even if it's in a UMB—will crash the system.

Video

I can't see any games or graphics on my monitor

You have an old MDA video system, which can only display text. Graphics and games are not possible on your system.

It's easy to upgrade: just purchase a new monitor and graphics adapter card. Remember to set whatever DIP switches are required inside the computer, or run a SETUP program to make your system compatible with the new graphics adapter and monitor.

Can I run CGA graphics on my Hercules card?

There is a program in the public domain called SIMCGA.COM, which does an adequate job of fooling software into thinking your Hercules card is a color-graphics adapter. But this only skirts around the issue. Ask yourself: Do I need a color system? If you do, then buy one. Don't toy with half solutions.

What are the commands to change the number of lines and columns on the screen?

If your video system can support more (or less) than 80 columns by 25 rows, then some software particular to that hardware may be available. For example, the Paradise Professional VGA card comes with a menu-driven program, VGAPROF, that makes switching modes easy. If you lack access to such a utility, you need to do the following:

1. Load the ANSI.SYS device driver in your CONFIG.SYS file.

2. Use the MODE command to change video modes as follows:

MODE Command	Screen result
MODE CO80	80 columns by 25 rows, the standard
MODE CO40	40 columns by 25 rows
MODE CON: cols=40	40 columns
MODE CON: cols=80	80 columns
MODE CON: lines=25	25 rows
MODE CON: lines=43	43 rows
MODE CON: lines=50	50 rows

You can mix and match the lines and columns parameters, specifying both at once if you like.

The Printer

Nothing will Print

You may have specified the wrong printer port, or your printer may be hooked up to the wrong port.

Another thing to check is conflicting printer ports. If you have two printer ports installed in your system, one must be LPT1 and the other LPT2. If both are set to LPT1, for example, DOS can't make up its mind and decides that you don't have any printer ports installed. Verify that each printer port is set up properly in your system.

Everything prints double spaced

You need to throw a switch on the printer. The switch tells the printer to add a carriage return character for all line feeds the computer sends. DOS does this automatically, so turn that switch on the printer OFF.

Printing is haphazard and random

Your printer is probably not compatible with your software. Verify that your printer is on the list of those supported by your application. If so, reinstall that printer driver. If not, check to see if your printer is compatible with any printers supported, and then configure the printer accordingly.

I see lots of M's and colons

Your software is attempting to print PC graphics and your printer doesn't support the IBM Extended-ASCII character set. Try using an IBM-compatible printing mode, or select a character set that displays the Extended-ASCII characters.

CONFIG.SYS

Most errors in CONFIG.SYS are typing. When you make a typo, CONFIG.SYS displays an error message and tells you which line contains the questionable command. In addition to misspellings, check to be sure you've listed proper pathnames and filename extensions.

Individual device drivers may give their own errors. The most common of these involve device drivers that can't find the hardware they are to drive, such as a missing mouse or malfunctioning memory.

Batch Files & AUTOEXEC.BAT

The following is a list of error messages you may encounter when running batch files:

Batch file missing

Batch files are read from disk one line at a time; the file is opened, a line read, and then it's closed. But DOS remembers the batch file name and where it exists on disk.

The error message means that the batch file you're running can no longer locate itself to load in the next command. This may happen if you accidentally deleted or renamed the batch file, if the batch file contains unusual characters (it was made by a word processor and saved improperly), or if you've change diskettes.

FOR cannot be nested

> The FOR command cannot be used twice on the same command line. For example:

```
FOR %A IN (*.*) DO FOR %B IN (*.BAK) DO WHATEVER
```

> Try to figure out another way to implement the FOR command.

Label not found

> This error message will halt a batch file instantly. The GOTO statement has indicated a label that doesn't exist. Verify that the label exists, check your spelling, make sure the label starts with a colon.

Out of environment space

> This error message can happen with the PATH, PROMPT, or SET commands. There simply isn't enough room left in the environment. To create more environment space, use COMMAND.COM's /E switch in the SHELL configuration command in your CONFIG.SYS file. Specify a value larger than 256, the default.

Syntax Error

> This is a general type of error, which has a number of causes:

> 1. You forgot to use two equal signs in an IF comparison command.

> 2. You forgot to enclose an environment variable in double quotes.

> 3. You forgot the IN or DO parameters of the FOR command.

> 4. You only specified one percent sign with the FOR command's variable.

> As a solution, consider running the batch file with ECHO on. The "Syntax Error" message will appear right after the wayward line on the screen.

The batch file can't find an environment variable

Remember not to pad the equal sign with spaces when you use the SET command; the spaces become part of the variable and its contents, which often isn't what you want.

An environment variable won't ECHO at the DOS prompt

Environment variables are only expanded when a batch file runs; you cannot access them at the DOS prompt.

How do you trap for an ERRORLEVEL value?

ERRORLEVEL matches all values greater than or equal to the value you specify:

```
IF ERRORLEVEL 3 ...
```

Above, all values from 3 to 255 will match the statement, and the IF command will be true. To narrow down the options, you can use several IF ERRORLEVEL commands in a row. However, the following format will always pin down the IF command:

```
IF ERRORLEVEL X IF NOT ERRORLEVEL X+1 ...
```

The above format will always prove true for only the value X. For example:

```
IF ERRORLEVEL 3 IF NOT ERRORLEVEL 4 ...
```

Applications

My BACKUP.BAT file keeps running over and over and over...

When BACKUP.BAT runs, it probably has a line running the BACKUP.EXE which simply states:

```
BACKUP
```

If BACKUP.BAT is in the current directory, or in a directory on the path before the directory containing BACKUP.EXE, then that's why BACKUP.BAT runs over and over and over. Consider naming either BACKUP.BAT or BACKUP.EXE to something else. Personally, I name my backup batch files BACK.BAT.

My application says "Wrong DOS Version" or that I should upgrade to DOS 2.0—what does that mean?

Quite a few applications check the DOS version number. That's because they are designed to take advantage of features available in, say, DOS 3.3 over DOS 3.1 or DOS 2.11. These programs may only test to make sure you're using a specific version of DOS, and then assume that if you don't have that version you have an earlier version. In the end, the program refuses to run—despite the fact that DOS 5 is more than compatible with the earlier versions.

To fool the program into running under DOS 5 you can use the SETVER command. SETVER is two flavors in one program: The first is a device driver, which must be loaded in CONFIG.SYS. The second is as a command line program.

As a device driver SETVER loads the DOS application and version table into memory. That table has a list of programs and their preferred DOS version numbers. (You'll see it in a moment.) To load SETVER, use the following command in CONFIG.SYS:

```
DEVICE=C:\DOS\SETVER.EXE
```

Note that SETVER is an EXE program, not a SYS file. There are no options. Also, C:\DOS is assumed above; specify your own DOS directory or the proper location for SETVER.EXE.

Once loaded, you can use the SETVER command to view the version-number table:

```
SETVER
```

A list of applications and their preferred version numbers is displayed. To add an application to the list, specify it after SETVER along with the DOS version number. For example, suppose the ARCHAIC.EXE program wanted to run under DOS 3.2. You would use the following command:

```
SETVER ARCHAIC.EXE 3.2
```

This places the file ARCHAIC.EXE into the version table, along with its preferred DOS version, 3.2. Note that you don't need to specify a full pathname to the program; the filename is all that's needed.

You can remove programs from the list as you update to newer versions that support DOS 5. Simply specify the /DELETE switch instead of a DOS version number after the program's name.

COMMAND: SETVER (External)
             Function: To fool older DOS programs into running under newer versions.
             Format: SETVER program version
                     SETVER program /delete [/quiet]

By itself, SETVER displays the current version table. You'll see a list of program names and their preferred DOS version number. When a program runs and requests a version number, SETVER fools it into thinking it's running under that version of DOS.

Program is the name of a COM or EXE file, but only the filename and extension, not the full pathname.

Version follows program and lists the preferred version of DOS program would like to run under in the format X.XX.

/Delete is used to remove a program from the version table, for example, when a program is updated to directly support DOS 5 or later.

/Quiet is an optional switch suppressing the message produced when the /delete switch is used.

Summary

Where do you go from here? One suggestion: Keep using DOS and keep exploring. Consider all the possibilities. This book has tons of suggestions and shows how all DOS commands work. Try a few and see if you can use them in your system.

Consider reading magazines on DOS—especially the Help or Tricks sections. They'll show you some interesting things you can do with DOS, ways to get more power from DOS, and some unexpected surprises.

User groups and computer clubs are good places to find and share information about DOS and using your PC. Also consider national on-line networks or bulletin boards. One secret I use are these public domain/shareware software houses. For a few dollars a diskette, you can get nifty programs, tips, and hints.

When you explore anything new, here are some general steps you may want to take:

1. Play with it first—after all, this is what you want to do anyway.

2. Read the manual. Or just skim it.

3. Play with it some more.

4. Try to use it.

5. Go back and read the manual again.

Going back to the manual after using the program awhile has an interesting effect—now you understand what the manual is trying to say. The person who wrote the manual already knows the program, so most manuals are written assuming you know the software too. After you've played with it awhile, you'll be qualified to read the software manual, and will probably pick up lots of interesting tips and information.

The same "secret" can be applied to DOS: Explore awhile on your own, and then return to this book to brush up on some hints or review some points you might have missed the first time through.

Good luck with your computer and DOS!

CHAPTER 30

DOS Command Reference

DOS Commands

APPEND	DISKCOMP	LOADFIX	SETVER
ASSIGN	DISKCOPY	LOADHIGH/LH	SHARE
ATTRIB	DOSKEY	MEM	SUBST
BACKUP	EDLIN	MIRROR	SYS
BREAK	EMM386	MKDIR/MD	TIME
CHCP	EXE2BIN	MODE	TREE
CHDIR/CD	EXIT	MSHERC	TRUENAME
CHKDSK	EXPAND	NLSFUNC	TYPE
CLS	FASTOPEN	PATH	UNDELETE
COMMAND	FC	PRINT	UNFORMAT
COMP	FDISK	PROMPT	VER
COPY	FORMAT	QBASIC	VERIFY
CTTY	GRAFTABL	RECOVER	VOL
DATE	GRAPHICS	RENAME/REN	XCOPY
DEBUG	HELP	REPLACE	
DEL/ERASE	JOIN	RESTORE	
DELOLDOS	KEYB	RMDIR/RD	
DIR	LABEL	SET	

APPEND

Type:	External, APPEND.EXE
Function:	Creates search path for DOS and applications to look for data files.
Format:	APPEND pathname;pathname... /x /path /e

By itself, APPEND displays the current data directory search path. The format and purpose of the command is similar to the PATH command.

Pathname;pathname... is a list of subdirectories, separated by semicolons, which DOS and your applications will now search through to locate data files.

/x is used to extend APPEND's power to your applications. When /x:on is specified, your application can search APPENDed directories in the same way as DOS. When /x:off is specified, your application will not be able to search the APPENDed directories (although you can still specify a full pathname to any file).

/path is used when you specify a data file with a full pathname. When /path:on is specified, DOS will continue to look through the APPENDed directories even when you specify full pathnames. When /path:off is specified, DOS will not examine the directories when you specify a full pathname. /path:on is the default.

/e directs APPEND to place its data-directory search path into DOS's environment, using the APPEND variable. Otherwise, APPEND stores its data directory in its own memory storage.

A single semicolon following APPEND deletes the current data-directory search path.

See Chapter 20.

ASSIGN

Type:	External, ASSIGN.COM
Function:	Reassigns input and output from one drive to another.
Format:	ASSIGN olddrive:=newdrive: [/STATUS]

ASSIGN is an older DOS command, used to reassign input and output from one drive to another—typically from a floppy drive to the hard drive.

650

Without any options, ASSIGN displays the current status of any assigned drives. Olddrive is either A: or B:, representing drive A or B.

Newdrive is another drive letter. After issuing the ASSIGN command, all I/O requirements for olddrive will be sent to newdrive.

/STATUS is used to display a list of reassigned drives. It can be abbreviated to /STA or /S.

As an example, if some program always wanted to use drive B, but you have only drive A, you could enter ASSIGN B:=A: to redirect the request. Additional disk reassignments can be made by listing more than one drive pair after ASSIGN.

Do not use disk utilities or the BACKUP, DISKCOPY, FORMAT, JOIN, LABEL, RESTORE, OR SUBST commands on an assigned drive.

Refer to the SUBST or JOIN commands for further information on assign drives and subdirectories.

ATTRIB

Type: External, ATTRIB.EXE
Function: To examine or change a file's attributes.
Format: ATTRIB ± A ± R ± H ± S filename /S

ATTRIB by itself displays the attributes for all files in the current directory (assuming *.* for the filename option).

± A is used to set or reset the Archive attribute; + sets the attribute and - resets it. (This holds for all the following options.)

± R is used to set or reset the Read-only attribute.

± H is used to set or reset the Hidden attribute.

± S is used to set or reset the System attribute.

Filename is an optional filename, wildcard, or the name of a subdirectory. When specified, ATTRIB shows the attributes for that filename, group of files, or subdirectory.

/S is the subdirectory switch. When specified, ATTRIB carries out its duties in all the subdirectories under the current subdirectory, matching whichever files and setting or resetting whichever attributes are specified.

See Chapter 17.

BACKUP

Type: External, BACKUP.EXE
Function: Archives files from the hard disk to floppy diskettes.
Format: BACKUP source-drive switches

Source is the source filename, pathname, or a group of filenames specified with a wildcard.

Drive is a floppy-drive letter and colon. It indicates the drive to which the source files will be backed up.

Switches are the optional switches for the BACKUP command. They are:

/A Adds files to an existing backup-disk set. When /A is specified, the contents of the existing backup disk will not be erased; the new files will be added.

/D Archives only those files created after a specified date. This switch is used in conjunction with the /T switch.

/F Allows you to backup to diskettes of a different size than the drive you're using. The size values are the same as those for the /F switch used with the FORMAT command; see FORMAT.

/L Creates a backup-log file. /L is followed by an optional path for the log file. If a pathname isn't specified, the log file BACKUP.LOG is placed in the root directory.

/M Archives only files with their Archive attribute set. The Archive attribute will be reset after the backup. See the ATTRIB command.

/S Archives all files in all subdirectories under the source.

/T Archives files created after a specified time. This switch is used with /D to narrow the field of files to be copied. This switch must be used with the /D switch.

See Chapter 21.

BREAK

Type: Internal
Function: Controls extended Ctrl-C and Ctrl-Break checking.
Format: BREAK status

Without any options, the BREAK command displays the current break status:

```
BREAK is on
```

Or:

```
BREAK is off
```

Status is either ON or OFF, which turns extended break checking either on or off, respectively.

This BREAK command has a counterpart in CONFIG.SYS, which does essentially the same thing. The command line BREAK can be used to override the CONFIG.SYS BREAK configuration command at any time.

See Chapter 19.

CHCP

Type: Internal
Function: Changes code pages.
Format: CHCP codepage

By itself, CHCP displays the currently active code page, as defined by the COUNTRY.SYS command in CONFIG.SYS. (Otherwise, the default 437 U.S.A code page is used.)

Codepage is a three-digit code-page value, indicating the new code page to use. A list of code page values is given in Appendix C.

Refer to Chapter 22 for more information on code pages as well as the NLSFUNC command and COUNTRY configuration command.

CHDIR/CD

Type: Internal

Function: To change to a new directory/display the pathname of the current directory.

Format: CHDIR [drive:]pathname

            CD [drive:]pathname

Without any options, CD displays the name of the current drive and directory.

Drive is optional. If specified, CD displays the current directory for that drive. If followed by a pathname, CD will change directories on that drive to the one specified by pathname. You will not, however, be logged to that drive.

Pathname is the name of the directory to change to.

See Chapter 14.

CHKDSK

Type: External, CHKDSK.EXE

Function: Displays disk statistics, lost chains, and fragmented files.

Format: CHKDSK drive: pathname /F /V

Without any parameters, CHKDSK checks the current drive.

Drive is the letter of a drive for CHKDSK to check. It cannot be an assigned (SUBST'd) or JOINed drive, and the drive letter must be followed by a colon.

Pathname is a filename or wildcard; CHKDSK will report if the files are contiguous or split into noncontiguous blocks.

/F is used to fix any lost chains or clusters. CHKDSK always reports their presence, but by specifying the /F switch will they be removed to files for cleanup.

/V is the verbose switch. When specified, CHKDSK displays the full pathname of every file and directory on disk as it's being processed.

See Chapter 21.

CLS

Type: Internal
Function: To clear the screen.
Format: CLS

After typing CLS, the screen will clear and a new DOS prompt will appear at the top of the display.

See Chapter 9.

COMMAND

Type: External, COMMAND.COM
Function: DOS's command interpreter.
Format: COMMAND.COM pathname device /E:size /P /C /MSG

By itself, COMMAND runs another copy of the command interpreter.

Pathname is the location of COMMAND.COM on disk. It must be specified when using the SHELL configuration command to load COMMAND.COM.

Device is used to specify a DOS device other than the keyboard and screen that COMMAND.COM will use for input and output. This option is usually omitted.

/E is used to specify a new size for the DOS environment in the format /E:size. Values for size range from 160 through 32768, with the default value 256.

/P is used to make the command interpreter permanent; it cannot be quit using the EXIT command. When used with the SHELL configuration command, the /P switch directs COMMAND.COM to look for and run a batch file named AUTOEXEC.BAT in the root directory of the boot disk.

/C is used with COMMAND.COM at the DOS prompt to run another program. The text following /C is passed to the new command interpreter and executed. (This was the old way of calling batch files before the CALL command.)

/MSG is used to load COMMAND.COM's disk-based messages into memory. It only needs to be specified when running DOS from a floppy-based system.

See Chapters 19 and 27, and the EXIT command.

COMP

Type: External, COMP.EXE
Function: Compares two files.
Format: COMP filename1 filename2 /A /C /D /L /N=lines

Filename1 is the name of a file or group of files on disk.

Filename2 is the name of a file to compare with filename1, or a group of files to compare to a matching group. If filename2 is omitted, COMP assumes it to have the same name as filename1 but to be in the current directory.

/A directs COMP to display any differences between two files as ASCII characters. (The default is hexadecimal bytes.)

/C tells COMP to ignore the differences between upper- and lower-case characters when making the comparison.

/D directs COMP to display any differences between the two files as decimal values.

/L causes COMP to display differing bytes by line number as opposed to byte offset.

/N is used to limit the number of lines compared in a text file. The line count immediately follows /N=. Note that /N causes two files to be compared even if they aren't the same size.

If filename1 and filename2 are of different sizes, the comparison is halted. Also, if more than ten differences are found between the two files, the comparison is halted. (Use the FC command to compare files of different sizes and in more detail.)

See Chapter 15, and the FC command.

COPY

Type: Internal
Function: To duplicate a file or to copy a file to another drive or subdirectory.
Format: COPY source[+source] [destination] [/a]/b][/v]

Source is the file to be copied, or a device to be copied from. If the file isn't in the current directory then it will be copied to the current directory.

656

[+source] are any additional files that will be concatenated (stuck to) the first source for creation of the copy.

Destination is the destination pathname for the file, or a device to which output is sent. If a new filename isn't specified, the destination will have the same name as the original file. If destination already exists, it will be overwritten.

/A and /B are two optional switches, either of which may follow the source or destination. These tell DOS how to copy the files and whether to treat them as ASCII (text) files or as binary (non-ASCII) files. You can specify the /A switch after text files and the /B switch after binary files.

/V is an optional switch that forces the COPY command to doubly verify that the contents of the duplicate are identical to the original. If you specify /V, the COPY command will take slightly longer to complete the copying, due to the verification. (Turning the VERIFY command on will have the same effect.)

See Chapter 15 for information about the XCOPY and VERIFY commands.

CTTY

Type: Internal
Function: Specifies an I/O device for DOS.
Format: CTTY device

Device is the name of a DOS device, usually AUX or COM1 through COM4. After using the CTTY command, DOS will expect all input and send all output from device.

The default device for DOS is the CON. To return control to the console after the CTTY command (from the remote device) type:

```
CTTY CON
```

See Chapter 24.

DATE

Type: Internal
Function: Displays the date/sets a new date.
Format: DATE mm-dd-yy

Mm-dd-yy is optional and represents the current month, day, and year, each separated by a hyphen. DOS is aware of the proper number of days in each month. If you enter an incorrect value, the message "Invalid date" is displayed, and you're prompted for the date again. If mm-dd-yy is omitted, the DATE command prompts for the date.

Note that the format mm-dd-yy is used for only certain code pages. If you've set up DOS to work in another country or under another language, the date format will change accordingly.

See Chapter 9.

DEBUG

Type: External, EBUG.EXE
Function: Programmer's utility, memory tool.
Format: DEBUG filename options

Filename is an optional file to be loaded into DEBUG for byte-level editing. COM program files are usually specified. EXE files should be renamed to BIN files before loading.

Options are any options, switches, or parameters that would regularly follow the filename at the DOS prompt.

DEBUG's internal commands are given in Appendix G.

See Chapter 25.

DEL/ERASE

Type: Internal

Function: To delete files.

Format: DEL pathname [/P]

ERASE pathname [/P]

Pathname is the name of the file to delete.

/P is an optional switch. When specified, DOS prompts you before it deletes each file.

See Chapter 15.

DELOLDOS

Type: External, DELOLDOS.EXE

Function: To remove a previous copy of DOS and its files.

Format: DELOLDOS

DELOLDOS runs a program that removes old DOS files after DOS 5 is initially installed. After running, DELOLDOS removes itself from your DOS directory; it can be run only once. This file will not appear at all on some systems.

DIR

Type: Internal

Function: To display files on disk.

Format: DIR pathname /P /W /B /L /S /A:attrib /O:sort

Without any options, the DIR command displays a list of all files in the current directory.

Pathname is an optional drive letter, pathname, wildcard, or individual filename. DIR will list only those files matching the pathname description.

/P is the pause or page switch. When specified, the DIR command will list a screenful of files, and then pause for you to press any key before continuing.

/W is the wide switch. When specified, the DIR command displays only directories and filenames in a five-column format. No information on size, date, or time is displayed.

/B is the brief switch. When specified, the DIR command lists only directories and filenames in one column.

/L is the lower case switch. When specified, the DIR command displays all filenames in lower case.

/S is the subdirectory switch. When specified, the DIR command will seek out the files indicated and display them in all subdirectories under the current directory.

/A is the attribute switch, followed by letters indicating file attributes to match or exclude from the directory listing. The letters are:

A—Archive attribute

D—Directory attribute

H—Hidden attribute

R—Read-only attribute

S—System attribute

If a hyphen precedes an attribute letter, then all files except for that attribute are displayed. More than one letter can be combined after the /A switch but they must not be separated by spaces.

/O is the sort-order switch, followed by letters indicating the order of the sort:

D—Date and time, oldest first

E—Alphabetically by file extension

G—Directories first

N—Alphabetically by filename

S—By size, smallest first

/O:N is the default. Placing a hyphen before a letter reverses the sort for that letter. Specifying more than one letter sorts on more than one level, but note that no spaces should come between the letters.

See Chapters 11 and 17.

DISKCOMP

Type: External, DISKCOMP.COM
Function: To compare two floppy diskettes.
Format: DISKCOMP drive1 [drive2] /1 /8

Drive1 is the drive letter containing the first disk to be compared. If drive1 isn't specified, DOS assumes the current drive (which must be a floppy drive).

Drive 2 is optional. If specified, it indicates the drive containing the second diskette for comparison. Both drive1 and drive 2 must be of the same size and capacity. If drive 2 isn't specified, DOS assumes drive1 for both diskettes and will prompt you to swap them.

/1 directs DISKCOMP to compare only the first side of each disk. This switch is used for compatibility with older diskette formats.

/8 directs DISKCOMP to compare only the first eight sectors of each disk. As with /1 this switch is used for compatibility with older diskette formats.

After the comparison, DISKCOMP will let you know if the two diskettes are identical or it will tell you which side and track contains differing information. Note that two diskettes can contain the same files but may not compare identically.

DISKCOPY

Type: External, DISKCOPY.COM
Function: Makes a duplicate of floppy diskettes.
Format: DISKCOPY drive1 [drive2] /1 /V

Drive1 is the drive letter containing the source diskette, the one to be copied. If drive1 isn't specified, the current drive is assumed. Drive1 must be a floppy drive.

Drive 2 is optional. If specified, it indicates the drive containing the target or destination diskette (the duplicate). Both drive1 and drive 2 must be of the same size and capacity. If drive 2 isn't specified, DOS assumes drive1 for both diskettes and will prompt you to swap them.

/1 directs DISKCOPY to copy on the first side of the diskette. This switch is used for compatibility with older diskette formats.

/V activates double verification, ensuring that the duplicate is the same as the original. Specifying the /V switch will slow the DISKCOPY somewhat.

DISKCOPY makes exact duplicates of diskettes by copying them at the track and sector level. In some instances, this is the only way to duplicate some floppies (as opposed to using XCOPY A:*.* B:\ /E /S).

DOSKEY

Type: External, DOSKEY.COM
Function: Adds extra editing abilities, command history, and macros to the command line.
Format: DOSKEY /reinstall /bufsize=size [/insert|/overstrike]
            DOSKEY name=command

/reinstall is optional. When specified, a new memory-resident copy of DOSKEY will be loaded and the old one disabled. This can be used, for example, to reset the buffer size or when running a second copy of COMMAND.COM.

/bufsize is used to set the size of DOSKEY's command history and macro buffer. Normally the buffer is set at 512 bytes. Using the size parameter after /bufsize, you can set the buffer to any size from 256 bytes on up.

/insert and /overstrike set the initial editing mode for DOSKEY. You can only specify one or the other, with /overstrike being the default. When /insert is specified, new characters are always inserted into the command line. After DOSKEY is initially installed, you use the second format to create macros:

Name is the name assigned to the macro. It can be from one to any number of characters, except for those forbidden in a filename. Note that that name can be the name of a DOS command or a program name.

Command is the DOS command line, command, or program to assign to name, complete with whatever optional parameters are required. Note that some optional parameters must be specified using special characters. If command isn't specified, then the macro name is removed from memory.

All of DOSKEY's editing keys and function keys are listed in Appendix D. See Chapter 22.

DOSSHELL

Type: External, DOSSHELL.COM
Function: To run the DOS Shell program.
Format: DOSSHELL /B [/T|/G]:res[n]

/B directs DOSSHELL to use plain black-on-white graphics, which show up best on some laptops.

/T directs DOSSHELL to start in the text mode.

/G directs DOSSHELL to start in the graphics mode.

Res and n optionally follow /T or /G to set a graphics resolution depending on your graphics hardware. Res can equal L, M, or H for low, medium, or high resolution. N is equal to the number of the low, medium, or high-resolution-mode display option. Values for n can be 1 or 2 and differ with the graphics hardware. To see which are which, select the Options menu, Display item in DOSSHELL. Values for n are listed after the different screen-resolution options.

See Chapter 16.

EDIT

Type: External, EDIT.COM
Function: To run the MS-DOS Editor.
Format: EDIT pathname /B /G /H /NOHI

Pathname is the name of a text file to edit. If pathname doesn't exist, it will be created for editing. If pathname is omitted, EDIT will prompt you for a name when you save the file or before you quit.

/B directs the Editor to use plain black on white graphics, which show up better on some laptops.

/G activates faster screen writes on CGA systems; don't use this switch if your CGA monitor produces "snow."

/H starts the editor in high-text resolution, displaying as many lines on the screen as your graphics system is capable of.

/NOHI disables the 16-color mode in which the Editor is normally used. If your text looks funny or if you can't see some colors, use the /NOHI switch. Do not use this switch with COMPAQ laptop PCs.

In order to use the Editor, the QBASIC.EXE program must be on your path. See Chapter 12.

EDLIN

Type: External, EDLIN.EXE

Function: To run the old MS-DOS line editor.

Format: EDLIN pathname [/B]

Pathname is the name of a formatted-text file on disk to edit. It is required.

/B is used to load the file using the binary format; when specified, EDLIN ignores the traditional Ctrl-Z end-of-file marker and loads the file into memory based on its real disk size.

Information on using Edlin and a summary of its commands is given in Appendix E.

EMM386

Type: External, EMM386.EXE

Function: As a DOS command, EMM386 is used to turn expanded memory support on or off, as well as specify support for a Weitek coprocessor.

Format: EMM386 status Weitek

Status is either ON, OFF, or AUTO: ON turns expanded memory support on; OFF turns it off; and AUTO keeps it off, turning it on only when a program makes the request.

Weitek is either W=ON or W=OFF, turning support for a Weitek coprocessor either on or off, respectively. This switch has effect only if you have a Weitek coprocessor installed.

You cannot use EMM386 as a DOS command if you've created UMBs. Also, refer to the EMM386.EXE device driver later in this reference.

See Chapter 26.

EXE2BIN

Type: External, EXE2BIN.EXE
Function: To convert EXE files into COM files.
Format: EXE2BIN filename.EXE [filename.BIN]

EXE2BIN is a programmer's tool, used after compiling a program file. Compilers traditionally give programs the EXE extension. Some files can be converted into COM files, which load faster than EXE files but must be 64K or less in size (and not use an internal stack).

Filename.EXE is the name of an EXE program to convert into a binary-image or COM-format file.

Filename.BIN is optional; it's the name of the new file created by EXE2BIN. DOS will assume the BIN extension, which you can later change to COM or change directly by specifying COM in the new filename.

Tip: DOS can only tell the difference between a COM and EXE file after it's loaded from disk. If you like, you can rename any COM file to EXE or viceversa—although, internally, true COM formatted files will load faster.

EXIT

Type: Internal
Function: To quit the command processor.
Format: EXIT

The EXIT command quits a shelled copy of COMMAND.COM and returns to the previous application or copy of COMMAND.COM.
See Chapter 27.

EXPAND

Type: External, EXPAND.EXE
Function: To decompress or expand packed files on the original DOS distribution diskettes.
Format: EXPAND filename.XX_ [filename.XXX]

Filename.XX_ is a compressed file on the DOS distribution diskettes. It can be a single file or group of files specified with a wildcard. Traditionally, the final character of the filename's extension is an underscore character (_).

Filename.XXX is optional. It can specify a path to which to copy the decompressed files, or the new name for a single decompressed file. In the latter case, if filename.XXX is omitted, DOS assigns the decompressed file a proper name based on the original.

Note that there is no COMPRESS command corresponding to EXPAND.

FASTOPEN

Type: External, FASTOPEN.EXE
Function: Improves access to previously opened files.
Format: FASTOPEN drive=files /X

Drive is a disk-drive letter, followed by a colon. It indicates the hard drive that FASTOPEN will monitor. (Do not specify floppy drives with this command.)

Files are the number of filenames of which FASTOPEN will keep track. Values range from 1 through 999, with 34 the default.

More than one drive=files combination can be used to have FASTOPEN monitor more than one hard drive on your system.

/X directs DOS to keep FASTOPEN's buffer in expanded memory, if available. Otherwise, the buffer is kept in conventional memory.

Rather than use FASTOPEN, consider running the SMARTDrive disk cache instead. Refer to Chapter 21.

FC

Type: External, FC.EXE

Function: To compare files in detail.

Format: FC /A /B /C /L /LBn /N /T /W /lines filename1 filename2

/A directs FC to display only the first and last lines in a section of text that differs from filename1 to filename2.

/B is used only when comparing binary (non-text) files. No other switches may be used when the /B switch is specified.

/C directs FC to ignore the differences between upper- and lower-case letters when comparing files.

/L directs FC to compare files line by line. FC will attempt to re-synchronize lines after encountering a mismatch.

/LBn sets the size of FC's internal line buffer to the value specified by n. Normally 100 lines are kept in the buffer.

/N directs FC to number the lines it displays.

/T causes FC to treat tabs as individual characters. Normally, FC expands tabs out to the corresponding number of space characters.

/W compresses "white space" characters, translating more than one tab or space into a single tab or space character.

/lines specifies the number of lines to match in order for FC to consider the two files re-synchronized. Lines is equal to the number of lines.

Filename1 is the source file for the comparison.

Filename2 is the target file for the comparison.

The FC command provides a more detailed and less error-prone method of comparing two files than the COMP command.

FDISK

Type: External, FDISK.EXE
Function: Partitions hard drive, prepares it for use by DOS.
Format: FDISK

The FDISK program examines, changes, deletes, or adds DOS partitions on hard drives. It's the second step in preparing a hard drive for use.

See Chapter 17.

FORMAT

Type: External, FORMAT.COM
Function: To format disks, preparing them for use.
Format: FORMAT drive [/1 /4 /8 /B /F /N /Q /S /T /U /V]

Drive is the letter of the drive containing the disk to be formatted. It must be specified.

/1 formats a single-sided (either a 160K or 180K) diskette in a 5-1/4-inch drive. (Use either the /F:160 or /F:180 switches instead.)

/4 formats a 360K diskette in a 1.2M drive. (Use the /F:360 switch instead.)

/8 formats an eight-sector (either a 160K or 320K) diskette in a 5-1/4-inch drive. (Use either the /F:160 or /F:320 switches instead.)

/B reserves room on the diskette for the DOS system files, IO.SYS and MSDOS.SYS. This switch is no longer needed under DOS 5, but it is maintained for compatibility reasons.

/F formats a diskette to the specified size value, following /F and a colon. Size values are:

Diskette size	/F values
160K	160, 160K, 160KB
180K	180, 180K, 180KB
320K	320, 320K, 320KB
360K	360, 360K, 360KB
720K	720, 720K, 720KB
1.2M	1200, 1200K, 1200KB, 1.2, 1.2M 1.2MB
1.4M	1440, 1440K, 1400KB, 1.44, 1.44M, 1.44MB
2.8M	2880, 2880K, 2880KB, 2.88, 2.88M, 2.88MB

/N specifies the number of sectors used to format a diskette. The /N switch was used with /T to format a 720K diskette in a 1.4M drive; use the /F:720 switch instead.

/Q quick-formats an already formatted diskette. The diskette isn't verified, so make sure it's a good diskette. Also, the /Q switch cannot be used when you're specifying a new size for the diskette, or when you're first formatting a diskette out of the box.

/S transfers the system files, IO.SYS and MSDOS.SYS, as well as COMMAND.COM to the new diskette. The /S switch creates a system or boot diskette.

/T specifies the number of tracks used to format the diskette. This switch was formerly used with the /N switch to format a 720K diskette in a 1.4M drive; use the /F:720 switch instead.

/U causes FORMAT to unconditionally format the diskette, totally erasing its contents and formatting it to a new size (if specified). A diskette reformatted with the /U switch cannot be unformatted by the UNFORMAT command.

/V automatically assigns a volume label to the diskette, which is specified after /V and a colon. If the label contains a space, enclose it in double quotes. The /V and /8 switches are incompatible.

See Chapters 17 and 28.

GRAFTABL

Type: External, GRAFTABL.COM
Function: Loads code-page information into your graphics adapter.
Format: GRAFTABL codepage [/status]

By itself, GRAFTABL will load into memory and assume your current code page—those characters defined as Extended ASCII codes 128 through 255. Note that GRAFTABL uses about 1.2K of RAM (and it can be loaded high).

Codepage is an optional three-digit number, specifying a code page to use. The code-page value must have been already defined using the COUNTRY.SYS command in CONFIG.SYS, and it can only be changed using the CHCP command. (GRAFTABL merely loads the characters.)

/STATUS is an optional switch that directs GRAFTABL to display the current code page in use.

GRAPHICS

Type: External, GRAPHICS.COM
Function: Allows certain printers to accurately render the graphic screen's contents.
Format: GRAPHICS printer pathname /R /B /LCD /PRINTBOX:size

Printer identifies your printer or one with which it's compatible. Values are as follows:

Printer	Model/compatibility
color1	IBM Color Printer/One-color ribbon
color4	IBM Color Printer/RGB ribbon
color8	IBM Color Printer, CMY ribbon
deskjet	The HP DeskJet
graphics	IBM Personal Graphics Printer
graphicswide	IBM Personal Graphics Printer/wide carriage

670

hpdefault	All Hewlett Packard or PCL-compatible printers
laserjet	HP LaserJet
laserjetii	HP LaserJet II
paintjet	HP PaintJet
quietjet	HP QuietJet
quietjetplus	HP QuietJet Plus
ruggedwriter	HP Rugged Writer
ruggedwriterwide	HP Rugged Writer/wide carriage
thermal	IBM PC-convertible Thermal Printer
thinkjet	HP ThinkJet

Pathname is the full pathname location of the GRAPHICS.PRO file on your system, usually found in the DOS subdirectory.

/R directs GRAPHICS to render the graphic screen dump in reverse—white on black, how it appears on the screen.

/B is used with the color4 and color8 printer types to print the screen background in color.

/LCD directs GRAPHICS to have the image printed at a liquid-crystal-display aspect ratio instead of the 3:4 aspect ratio of the CGA graphics screen.

/PRINTBOX sets the size of the print box—the area on the page where graphics are printed. Values for size are STD and LCD. To find proper values for your printer, use the Editor to view the contents of the GRAPHICS.PRO file, locating your printer and then its PRINTBOX value.

HELP

Type:	External, HELP.EXE
Function:	To display help for all DOS commands.
Format:	HELP command

671

Command is optional. When specified, HELP displays helpful information about the command, as well as the command's format. When omitted, HELP lists summary information about all DOS commands.

Note that HELP has its own screen page/pausing routine; there is no need to pipe its output through the MORE filer.

All DOS commands have an optional /? switch, which displays helpful information particular to that command.

See Chapter 9.

JOIN

Type: External, JOIN.EXE
Function: Takes a disk drive and assigns it to another drive as a subdirectory.
Format: JOIN drive pathname [/D]

Drive is the drive letter of the drive you want to assign to a subdirectory. After JOINing, the drive will not be accessible (except as the assigned subdirectory).

Pathname is the full pathname of the directory to which the drive will be joined. If the directory doesn't exist, DOS creates it. If it does exist, it should be totally empty.

/D is used to un-JOIN the drive. When the /D switch is used, the pathname isn't specified. After using the /D switch, you can once again access the drive.

Do not use the following commands in a subdirectory that has been JOINed:

BACKUP	FDISK	RECOVER
CHKDSK	FORMAT	RESTORE
DISKCOMP	LABEL	SYS
DISKCOPY	MIRROR	

See Chapter 20.

KEYB

Type: External, KEYB.COM
Function: Defines another keyboard layout for use in DOS.
Format: KEYB kb codepage pathname /E /ID

Without any options, KEYB displays the two-letter code for the keyboard layout you're using, along with code-page information. KEYB is memory resident and if it's not in memory, the KEYB command by itself will let you know.

Kb is a two-letter code representing the country, language, or region of a keyboard layout you want to install.

Codepage is an optional code-page value for KEYB to use.

Pathname is the full pathname for the KEYBOARD.SYS file on your system, or a similar file containing keyboard definitions.

/E is only required if you're using the Enhanced-101 keyboard with an older, 8088 model PC.

/ID is used to specify the code value for a foreign-language keyboard on a PC. This is a hardware keyboard that's used in another country, such as the U.K., France, or Italy. /ID is followed by a colon and the keyboard's three-digit ID number.

Values for kb, codepage, and /ID are given in Appendix C.

See Chapter 22.

LABEL

Type: External, LABEL.EXE
Function: To change or delete a disk's volume label.
Format: LABEL drive label

Drive is the drive letter followed by a colon, of the disk whose label you want to add, change, or delete. If omitted, the current drive is assumed.

Label is a new label to apply to the disk. If omitted, the LABEL command will prompt for a new label. Note that the new label cannot contain the following characters:

" / \ [ ] : * | < > + = ; , ? ( ) & ^

See Chapter 13.

LOADFIX

Type: External, LOADFIX.COM
Function: To load programs above the first 64K of memory.
Format: LOADFIX filename

Filename is the name of a program that will not run in the lower 64K of memory. If you run a program and get the message "Packed file corrupt," then run the program again, putting the LOADFIX command before its name at the DOS prompt.

Since DOS can now be loaded high, this means some applications will have their starting address low in memory—much lower than before was possible. This goofs some programs up, in which case the LOADFIX command can be used to ease the program in at a higher address.

LOADHIGH/LH

Type: Internal
Function: To load device drivers into UMBs.
Format: LOADHIGH program options
            LH program options

Program is the name of a memory-resident program, just as you'd type it on the command line or have it listed in a batch file. It must be a memory-resident program.

Options are any options, filenames, or switches that would normally follow the program on the command line or in a batch file.

See Chapter 26.

MEM

Type: External, MEM.EXE
Function: Reports the contents of memory, memory statistics.
Format: MEM switches

By itself, the MEM command gives you a summary of the memory in, used, and available in your system. This includes conventional, extended, and expanded memory.

674

Switches are optional switches used with the MEM command. There are three switches, only one of which can specified after the MEM command at a time:

/CLASSIFY or /C is used to give a brief summary of the programs in conventional memory and the upper-memory area. Program sizes are listed in decimal, kilobytes, and hexadecimal.

/DEBUG or /D gives a complete and highly detailed summary of memory. Program names, area names, sizes and addresses in hex, and type of memory is completely summarized.

/PROGRAM or /P gives a complete report on the contents of memory, although it is not as detailed as the /DEBUG report.

See Chapter 26.

MIRROR

Type: External, MIRROR.COM
Function: Preventive medicine for disk drives.
Format: MIRROR /PARTN
           MIRROR drive(s) [/1] /Tdrive[-files]
           MIRROR /U

/PARTN directs MIRROR to record and save boot-and-partition-table information from your hard drive(s) into a file PARTNSAV.FIL, which is stored on a floppy diskette.

Drive(s) is a single disk-drive letter or several drive letters, each followed by a colon. MIRROR saves the FAT and root directory information for each drive in a MIRROR.FIL file placed on that disk. Note that there's no need to use MIRROR on SUBSTed or JOINed drives. If a drive isn't specified, MIRROR creates a MIRROR.FIL file for the current drive.

/1 (one, not L) is an optional switch used to maintain only one copy of the MIRROR.FIL on a disk at a time. Without the /1 switch, the old MIRROR.FIL file is maintained as a backup copy, MIRROR.BAK.

/T initiates delete tracking for a single drive, as specified by drive. Each hard drive must have its own /T switch. The value files indicates the number of files for delete tracking to monitor on that drive. If files isn't specified, MIRROR assumes a certain default based on the disk size.

/U deactivates delete-tracking and unloads MIRROR from memory.

See Chapter 28.

MKDIR/MD

Type: Internal

Function: To create or make a new subdirectory.

Format: MKDIR pathname

           MD pathname

Pathname is the name of the new directory to create. The naming rules are the same as for naming a file. Unless otherwise specified, the new directory is created under the current directory.

See Chapter 14.

MODE

Type: External, MODE.COM

Function: Sets the operational mode for several areas of the computer.

Function1: Configure the printer

Format: MODE LPTx: COLS=cols LINES=lines RETRY=r

X is the printer port, 1 through 3.

Cols are the number of columns on the printer, or characters per line). Values for cols are 80 and 132.

Lines indicates the vertical line spacing, or number of lines per inch. Values for lines are 6 and 8.

R determines how the computer will react if the printer port times-out. Values for r are:

B, Return a "busy" status

E, Return an error

N, Take no action

P, Continue trying

R, Return ready

COLS=, LINES=, and RETRY= all may be removed, although you must separate the values with commas.

Function2: Configure the serial port.

Format: MODE COMx: BAUD=b PARITY=p DATA=d STOP=s RETRY=r

X is the serial port, 1 through 4.
B is the Baud rate. Values are:

11 for 110 Baud	24 for 2400 Baud
15 for 150 Baud	48 for 4800 Baud
30 for 300 Baud	96 for 9600 Baud
60 for 600 Baud	19 for 19,200 Baud
12 for 1200 Baud	

P is the Parity, which can be the letters N for none, E for even, O for odd, M for Mark, or S for Space.

D specifies the word size. Values are 5, 6, 7, and 8.

S specifies the number of stop bits: 1, 1.5 or 2.

R determines how the computer will react if the serial port times-out. This is used primarily when the serial port is connected to a printer. For r you can specify the following letters:

B, Return a "busy" status
E, Return an error
N, Take no action
P, Continue trying
R, Return ready

BAUD=, PARITY=, WORD=, STOP= and RETRY= may be omitted, although you must separate the values with commas.

Function3: To obtain the status of a device.

Format: MODE device [/status]

Device is the name of a DOS device, CON for the console, COMx for the serial port x, or LPTx for the printer port x.

/status is used to display the status of a redirected printer port. It may be abbreviated as /sta.

Function4: To redirect printing.

Format: MODE LPTx=COMx

LPTx is the printer to which output will be redirected. x ranges from 1 through 3 for the first through third printer ports.

COMx is the serial port to which your printer is attached. X ranges from 1 through 4 for the first through fourth serial ports.

The MODE command to configure the serial port should be used before this command.

Function5: To set up and select a code page for the console or printer.

Format: MODE device CODEPAGE PREPARE=codepage pathname

MODE device CODEPAGE SELECT=codepage

MODE device CODEPAGE REFRESH

MODE device CODEPAGE /status

Device is a device that uses a code page, either COM or an LPT printer port.

Codepage is the number of a code page to use. Valid code pages are shown in Appendix C.

Pathname is the location of a code-page information file (CPI extension) to support certain printers. The CPI files are listed in Appendix C.

/status is used to display the codepages selected and prepared for the indicated device.

CODEPAGE PREPARE is used to prepare the device for a code page.

CODEPAGE SELECT is used to select a code page for a device.

CODEPAGE REFRESH re-installs code pages that may have been corrupted.

Function6: To configure the display.

Format: MODE adapter [,N]

MODE CON: COLS=columns LINES=rows

Without any options, MODE CON displays information about the console device.

Adapter indicates the basic type of display adapter you have installed. Values are:

Adapter	Type
40	40 column display
80	80 column display
bw40	40 column monochrome display
bw80	80 column monochrome display
co40	40 column color display
co80	80 column color display
mono	monochrome display

Columns are the number of columns on the display (characters per line). Values for columns are 40 and 80.

N or rows specifies the number of lines on the screen. Values can be 25, 43, and 50, with 25 the default. In order to support the 43- or 50-line mode, you need a compatible graphics adapter and the ANSI.SYS device driver must be installed in your CONFIG.SYS file.

Function7: To configure the keyboard, set the typematic rate.
Format: MODE CON: RATE=r DELAY=d

R is the rate at which a key, when held down, will repeat. Values range from 1 through 32 for 2 through 30 characters a second, respectively. The default value is about 20.

D sets the delay—the time after you press the key up until the time it repeats. Values range from 1 through 4 for .25 through 1 second, respectively. The default value is 2.

You must set both the RATE and DELAY values for the typematic.

See Chapter 20.

MSHERC

Type: External, MSHERC.COM
Function: Allows Hercules graphics-card users graphics support in QBASIC.
Format: MSHERC /HALF

/HALF is used to run the Hercules graphics card in its half mode, such as when a color monitor is also installed in the system. /HALF is optional and if not specified, the Hercules card runs in the full mode.

NLSFUNC

Type: External, NLSFUNC.EXE
Function: Adds "natural language support" to DOS.
Format: NLSFUNC pathname

Pathname is the full pathname of the COUNTRY.SYS file, usually in your DOS subdirectory.

See Chapter 22.

PATH

Type: Internal
Function: Sets a search path which DOS uses to locate programs.
Format: PATH directory;directory;...

Without any options, the PATH command displays the current search path.

Directory is the full pathname of a subdirectory containing programs to which you always want to have access. More than one subdirectory can be specified by separating each with a semicolon.

When PATH is followed by a single semicolon, the search path is reset to zero (no directories).

See Chapter 20.

PRINT

Type: External, PRINT.EXE
Function: DOS's background text-file printer.
Format: PRINT /B:size /D:device /M:ticks2 /Q:size /S:ticks3 /T /U:ticks1
            PRINT filename [/C|/P]

The first format is used when you first start the PRINT command; the second is used after PRINT has been loaded into memory.

/B specifies the size of the print buffer. The size value follows /B and ranges from 512 through 16384 for a 512 byte through 16 kilobyte buffer. The default is 512 bytes.

/D specifies the device PRINT is to monitor for printing. Any COM or LPT device can be listed after the /D switch.

/M tells PRINT how many clock ticks (1/18th seconds) to print a character on the printer. Values after /M can range from 1 through 255, with the default being 2.

/Q indicates the number of files PRINT holds in its printing queue. Values range from 4 through 32, with 10 as the default.

/S specifies the number of clock ticks to allocate to PRINT while it's running in the background. Values range from 1 to 255, with 8 as the default. Larger values improve printing time, but decrease overall system performance.

/T is used to remove all files from the queue.

/U specifies the number of clock ticks PRINT is to wait for the printer to become available (not-busy). Values range from 1 through 255 with 1 as the default.

Filename is the name of a text file or group of files to print. It must be a formatted ASCII file. More than one filename may be specified at the DOS prompt (up to 13).

/C is used to clear, or remove, the named file from the print queue.

/P is used to add the named file to the print queue.

PROMPT

Type: Internal
Function: To change the DOS prompt.
Format: PROMPT text

Text is any text to be used as the DOS prompt. Special commands can also be included.

See Chapter 20.

QBASIC

Type: External, QBASIC.EXE
Function: To run the BASIC programming language.
Format: QBASIC [filename.BAS /B /EDITOR /G /MBF /NOHI /RUN]

By itself, QBASIC runs and presents you with input screens for writing BASIC-language programs. Refer to a book specific on BASIC programming for additional instructions.

Filename.BAS is the name of a BASIC program file to load for editing when QBASIC starts. The BAS filename extension is assumed. To run that program, also specify the /RUN switch.

/B directs QBASIC to use only black-and-white text, which shows up better on some laptop displays.

/EDITOR causes QBASIC to run only its editor mode. This is the switch that the EDIT command uses to start the MS-DOS editor. When /EDITOR is specified, the filename is loaded as a text file for editing; the BAS filename extension is not assumed.

/G directs QBASIC to write directly to the screen. If you have CGA graphics system that doesn't produce "snow," specify this switch.

/MBF automatically converts some of BASIC's built-in math functions to use special, extended "floating point" functions.

/NOHI disables the 16-color mode. Do not use this switch on COMPAQ laptop PCs.

/RUN directs QBASIC to load the named file and immediately run it.

RECOVER

Type: External, RECOVER.EXE
Function: Disk and file recover.
Format: RECOVER drive: filename

Drive is a drive letter following a colon, indicating a drive for RECOVER to repair. Every file on the drive will attempt to be rescued and placed in the root directory with the name FILExxxx.REC. This happens until all files have been "recovered" or the root directory fills.

Filename is the name of a specific file to recover; it cannot contain wildcards. RECOVER will scan the disk, picking up whatever pieces of filename it can find and patching it back together.

The results of the RECOVER command are less than spectacular and use of this command should be avoided.

See Chapter 28.

RENAME/REN

Type: Internal

Function: To rename files; give them a new name.

Format: RENAME oldname newname

            REN oldname newname

Oldname is the file's original name. If the file isn't in the current directory, then a full path must be specified.

Newname is to be the file's new name; it's the filename only—not a path. Newname must follow the standard DOS file-naming rules, as listed in Appendix F. See Chapter 15.

REPLACE

Type: External, REPLACE.EXE

Function: Updates software from one disk to another.

Format: REPLACE filename [pathname /A /P /R /S /W /U]

Filename is the source filename, group of files specified by a wildcard, a drive letter, or a pathname. Filename indicates the source files, those which you want to copy to a destination to update older files.

Pathname is the destination directory, which contains the files to be updated. If pathname is omitted, the currently logged drive and directory are assumed.

/A is used when you want to add files specified by the source filename which don't exist in the destination pathname. If the /A switch isn't specified, REPLACE only updates matching filenames. Note that the /A switch cannot be used with the /S or /U switches.

/P is used to display a prompt whenever a file is copied or replaced on the destination.

/R allows the REPLACE command to replace read-only files in the destination pathname. Without the /R switch, the REPLACE command will halt if a read-only file is to be replaced.

/S is used to direct the REPLACE command to scan for matching files on all subdirectories on the destination pathname.

/W causes a prompt to be displayed before the REPLACE operation begins, which allows you time to insert a diskette or to cancel the REPLACE command by pressing Ctrl-C.

/U is used by REPLACE to compare the dates of any matching files. If the date of the destination is earlier than the source, the file is replaced. If not, it's skipped.

See Chapter 28.

RESTORE

Type: External, RESTORE.EXE
Function: Restores files from diskettes created by the BACKUP command.
Format: RECOVER drive pathname /A /B /D /E /L /M /N /S /P

Drive is the floppy-drive letter and colon where RESTORE can locate the backup diskettes.

Pathname is the pathname of the file or group of files to be restored. (If the entire drive or a subdirectory branch needs to be restored, the optional /S switch should be added; see below.)

/A restores files after a specific date. The date follows the /A switch and is in the same format used by the DATE command on your computer.

/B restores files on the backup diskettes with dates before the date specified.

/D causes RESTORE to display a list of files that match the specified pathname on the backup diskettes. The files will not be restored.

/E restores files on the backup diskettes with a time earlier than the specified time. /E is used with the /B switch to further narrow the range of files restored.

/L restores files on the backup diskettes with a time later than the specified time. /L is used with the /A switch to narrow the range of files restored.

/M restores only the original version of files that have been modified after the last backup. Essentially, this switch will undo all changes since the last incremental backup.

/N restores only files that exist on the backup-diskette set but not on the hard drive. This is a great way to recover lost files or parts of the tree structure.

/S restores all files in all subdirectories under the pathname. The /S switch will recreate subdirectories as needed.

/P causes the RESTORE command to prompt you when a file is restored over one that already exists on the hard drive, providing that file has its Read-only or Archive attribute set.

See Chapters 21 and 28.

RMDIR/RD

Type: Internal

Function: To remove or delete a subdirectory.

Format: RMDIR pathname

            RD pathname

Pathname is the name of the directory you want to remove. It must be empty (contain no files or subdirectories), and you cannot be logged to it.

See Chapter 14.

SET

Type: Internal

Function: To view the environment; create or delete environment variables.

Format: SET variable=contents

Without any options, the SET command displays the current contents of the environment.

Variable is the name of the environment variable. It can be any length and can contain any characters except an equal sign. Short descriptive variable names are best. Variable is converted to upper case when placed into the environment.

Contents become the string assigned to variable. It can be any length and can contain any characters (except for an equal sign). If variable already exists, then contents replaces its current contents.

When contents are omitted, the variable is removed from the environment.

See Chapter 20.

SETVER

Type: External, SETVER.EXE
Function: To fool older DOS programs into running under newer versions.
Format: SETVER program version
           SETVER program /delete [/quiet]

By itself, SETVER displays the current-version table, as stored in memory by the SETVER device driver. You'll see a list of program names and their preferred DOS version number. When a program runs and requests a version number, SETVER fools it into thinking that it's running under that version of DOS.

Program is the name of a COM or EXE file, only the filename and extension, not the full pathname.

Version follows program and lists the preferred version the DOS program would like to run under in the format X.XX.

/delete is used to move a program from the version table, for example, when a program is updated to directly support DOS 5 or later.

/quiet is an optional switch suppressing the message produced when the /delete switch is used.

Note that SETVER must be installed as a device driver before using the SETVER command at the DOS prompt.

See Chapter 29.

SHARE

Type: External, SHARE.EXE
Function: Allows file sharing and file locking on your hard drive.
Format: SHARE /F:space /L:locks

/F is an optional switch used to allocate memory for SHARE. The default value for space is 2048 for 2K of memory.

/L specifies the maximum number of files DOS can lock, preventing more than one application from modifying them at a time. The default value for locks is 20.

SHARE can be used with multitasking-DOS and networking environments. However, you should only use SHARE if an application requests it. SHARE used to be required for large partitioned (greater than 32M) hard drives under DOS 4. Starting with DOS 5, SHARE is no longer a requirement. If none of your applications require it, don't use it.

SUBST

Type:　　　External, SUBST.EXE
Function:　Assigns a disk-drive letter to a subdirectory.
Format:　　SUBST drive pathname [/D]

Drive is the drive letter to be assigned to a subdirectory. It's in the range from the next highest unused drive letter in the system, through the highest drive letter defined by the LASTDRIVE configuration command (in CONFIG.SYS).

Pathname is the full pathname of the subdirectory.

/D is used to unsubstitute a drive. When specified, the pathname isn't required.

Do not use the following commands on SUBSTed drive:

BACKUP	FDISK	RECOVER
CHKDSK	FORMAT	RESTORE
DISKCOMP	LABEL	SYS
DISKCOPY	MIRROR	

See Chapter 20.

SYS

Type:　　　External, SYS.COM
Function:　Transfers the system (boot) files to a disk.
Format:　　SYS [pathname] drive

Pathname is optional. It indicates the location of a boot disk's system files, which SYS will copy to the designated drive. Without a pathname, DOS assumes the current drive (and as long as it's a boot disk, it's okay).

Drive is a drive letter indicating a disk to which you want to transfer the system files. After using the SYS command, the IO.SYS, MSDOS.SYS, and COMMAND.COM files will have been copied to the drive, making it a boot disk.

TIME

Type:	Internal
Function:	Displays the time/sets a new time.
Format:	TIME hh:mm:ss[a|p]

Hh:mm:ss is optional and represents the current hour, minute, and second (although you really need only the current hour and minute). The hour (hh) value is assumed to be in military, or 24-hour, format unless you add an A or P to the end of time, representing A.M. or P.M., respectively.

If you enter an invalid time format, the message "Invalid time" is displayed, and you're prompted for the date again. If hh:mm:ss is omitted, the TIME command prompts for the current time.

See Chapter 9.

TREE

Type:	External, TREE.COM
Function:	To display the subdirectory structure for a drive.
Format:	TREE [drive:]pathname [/A /F]

Without any parameters, the TREE command displays the subdirectory structure from the currently logged directory down through any subdirectories it has.

Drive specifies a disk drive you wish the TREE command to examine. If not specified, DOS assumes you mean the current drive.

Pathname specifies the starting directory. The TREE command will display the subdirectory structure from that pathname downward. If not specified, DOS assumes the current directory.

/A is the ASCII switch. When specified, the TREE command's output is produced using ASCII characters.

/F is the Files switch. When specified, the TREE command lists any files found in the subdirectories.

See Chapter 14.

TRUENAME

Type: Internal
Function: Displays a file's true pathname.
Format: TRUENAME filename

Filename is the name of a file. If the file is on a SUBSTed or JOINed drive, TRUENAME will give that file's actual location (it's physical location as opposed to its logical location).

Note that TRUENAME is an undocumented command which was first included with DOS 4.

TYPE

Type: Internal
Function: Displays a file's contents.
Format: TYPE filename

Filename is the name of a file to display.

The TYPE command displays any file you specify. It works best with formatted text or ASCII files.

See Chapter 11.

UNDELETE

Type:	External, UNDELETE.EXE
Function:	To recover deleted files.
Format:	UNDELETE pathname [/ALL|/LIST] [/DOS|/DT]

When used by itself, UNDELETE scans and attempts to recover deleted files in the current directory. This command works best with MIRROR's delete-tracking feature installed.

Pathname is an optional drive, directory, or filename which UNDELETE scans, looking for deleted files. If a pathname isn't specified, UNDELETE assumes the current directory.

/ALL tells UNDELETE to automatically recover all files possible in the current directory; if the first character in the filename cannot be identified, a "#" is used in its place.

/LIST displays a list of all deleted files and their chances of recovery. When specified, UNDELETE only displays deleted filenames; no files will be recovered. The /ALL and /LIST switches cannot be used at the same time.

/DOS tells UNDELETE to ignore delete tracking and only use DOS's information to recover files. Note that when /ALL is specified, /DOS causes UNDELETE to prompt for confirmation and the first character of the filename anyway. This switch is the default is delete tracking isn't installed.

/DT tells UNDELETE to use the delete-tracking feature, as well as to prompt for confirmation on each file (even when the /ALL switch is specified). Note that you cannot specify both the /DOS and /DT switches.

See Chapter 28.

UNFORMAT

Type:	External, UNFORMAT.EXE
Function:	To recover reformatted diskettes.
Format:	UNFORMAT drive: /J /TEST /L /P
	UNFORMAT drive: /U
	UNFORMAT /PARTN

Drive is the drive letter followed by a colon, indicating the disk to be unformatted. Drive must be specified.

/J is used to compare the MIRROR.FIL unformatting information with the UNFORMAT information DOS stores on disk. Use /J as a preview to verify the MIRROR.FIL file and decide whether or not you can trust it for unformatting.

/TEST is used to perform a "dry run" of the unformat. Note that when /TEST is specified, the UNFORMAT command will ignore any information in the MIRROR.FIL file.

/L is used to list files found on the formatted diskette as well as subdirectories. Without the /L switch, UNFORMAT lists only subdirectories and fragmented files.

/P is used to echo all the UNFORMAT command's output to a printer (LPT1).

/U tells UNFORMAT to rebuild the disk but ignore the MIRROR.FIL file. By default, UNFORMAT uses MIRROR.FIL, but if you have an older MIRROR.FIL file and don't trust it, specify the /U switch. (The /J switch will alert you to the date of the MIRROR.FIL file; see above.)

/PARTN is used to restore the hard-drive partition information saved by the MIRROR command. UNFORMAT will ask you to insert the diskette containing PARTNSAV.FIL file.

See Chapter 28.

VER

Type:	Internal
Function:	Displays the DOS version number.
Format:	VER

See Chapter 9.

VERIFY

Type:	Internal
Function:	Controls extended verification of disk writes.
Format:	VERIFY status

Without any options, the VERIFY command displays the current status:

```
VERIFY is on
```

Or:

```
VERIFY is off
```

Status is either ON or OFF, which turns double verification of disk writes either on or off, respectively.

Turning VERIFY ON will slow down all disk writes somewhat. If you want to be specific, you can use the /V switch with either the COPY or XCOPY commands.

VOL

Type: Internal
Function: Displays a disk's volume label and serial number.
Format: VOL drive

Drive indicates the drive containing the disk you want to examine. If omitted, VOL returns the label and serial number for the current drive.

See Chapter 9.

XCOPY

Type: External, XCOPY.EXE
Function: A better COPY command; moves subdirectory structures in addition to files; moves a group of files at once instead of one at a time; can move files based on their Archive attribute or on or after a certain date.
Format: XCOPY source destination /A /D /E /M /P /S /V /W

Source is the source filename, pathname, or a group of filenames specified with a wildcard.

Destination is the target pathname to which XCOPY will duplicate the source file(s). If destination is omitted, XCOPY assumes you mean the currently logged drive and directory.

/A copies only files with their Archive attribute set. This switch does not affect the Archive attribute after he files are copied. (See the /M switch.)

/D copies only those files created after a specified date. The format for the date is the same as for the DATE command.

/E copies subdirectories, even if they're empty. (Used with the /S switch.)

/M copies only files with their Archive attribute set. After the XCOPY command, the Archive attribute will be reset.

/P causes XCOPY to display a prompt "(Y/N)" before copying each file.

/S copies subdirectories under the source as well as all files in those subdirectories. (See the /E switch.)

/V turns on verification; as each file is copied, it will be verified against the original. This somewhat increases the amount of time XCOPY takes.

/W displays an initial pause message before XCOPY begins to copy files.

Filters

FIND

Type: External, FIND.EXE
Function: Locates a string of text in a file or the output of a DOS command.
Format: FIND [/C /I /N /V] "text" filename

/C directs the FIND command to display a line count indicating the number of lines containing text. Only the filename and line count are displayed.

/I directs the FIND command to ignore any differences in upper or lower case in the text.

/N directs the FIND command to list the line number before displaying a line of matching text.

/V directs the FIND command to display only those lines not containing matching text.

Text is text to locate in a file and is enclosed in double quotes. Text cannot contain the characters |, < or >, and if a double quote appears in text it must be specified twice.

Filename the name of a formatted text file FIND will scan. It cannot contain a wildcard, although you can specify more than one individual file and the FIND command will scan each of them.

As a command, FIND uses the following format:

```
FIND switches "text" filename
```

As a filter, FIND uses this format:

```
command | FIND switches "text"
```

To scan a group of files, use the FIND and FOR commands as follows:

```
FOR %v IN (set) DO FIND switches "text" %v
```

MORE

Type: External, MORE.COM
Function: Pauses the display after a screenful of text.
Format: MORE

The MORE filter counts the number of lines displayed. After a screenful, it displays "--- More ---" and waits for you to press a key to continue. MORE is usually used with I/O redirection or the pipe in the following formats:

```
MORE < filename

TYPE filename | MORE

command | MORE
```

SORT

Type: External, SORT.EXE
Function: The sorting filter.
Format: SORT /R /+n

By itself, SORT sorts standard input from the console, displaying the alphanumerically sorted result to the console. Normally, SORT is used with I/O redirection or the pipe to sort a formatted text file.

/R is an optional switch used to reverse the sort.

/+n is an optional switch used to sort the list at a specific column, as specified by n.

Characters are sorted according to information specified with the COUNTRY command in CONFIG.SYS. Upper- and lower-case letters are considered the same.

SORT is usually used with I/O redirection or the pipe in the following formats:

```
SORT switches < filename

command | SORT switches
```

In the above instances, the file used for input must be less than 64K in size.

For additional information on using filters and the pipe command, see Chapter 24.

Batch File Commands

All batch file commands are internal.

CALL

Function: Runs a second batch file and then returns control to the first.
Format: CALL batch_file

Batch_file is the name of a batch-file program. It's followed by any options or required parameters of the batch file—just as if it were entered on the command line.

After batch_file is executed, control returns to the current batch file, at the line following the CALL command.

ECHO

Function: Displays text, controls the echo state.

Format: ECHO [ON|OFF] text

By itself, the ECHO command displays the current state of echoing—either on or off—in a batch file.

When followed with either ON or OFF, ECHO in a batch file will turn on or turn off the echoing of the batch file's commands.

Text is optional text to be echoed to the display.

To echo a blank line, follow ECHO immediately with a period, as in "ECHO."

FOR

Function: Performs a single DOS command on a group of files.

Format: FOR var IN (set) DO command

Var is a FOR variable. At the DOS prompt it starts with one percent sign, followed by a letter of the alphabet. In a batch file, var is preceded by two percent signs. Var is used to represent each file matched by the set.

Set is a group of file names, pathnames, or wildcards.

Command is a DOS command. You can specify var in the command just as you would any single file in the set. Remember to specify either one or two percent signs before var as required.

GOTO

Function: Branches batch file execution to a label elsewhere in the batch file.

Format: GOTO label

Label is required. It's a one-to-eight letter label elsewhere in the batch file to which GOTO sends batch-file execution.

The format for label elsewhere in the batch file starts with a colon. You can specify as many characters after the colon as you like, but only the first eight (up to a space character) are part of the label.

Note that the colon can also be used to replace the REM command, seeing that DOS ignores all text after a colon in a batch file.

IF

Function: Test for certain conditions in a batch file, executing an optional DOS command if the conditions are true.

Format: IF [NOT] %var%==text command

IF [NOT] errorlevel value command

IF [NOT] exist filename command

[NOT] is optional and used to reverse the results of the test.

%var%==text is used to test an environment variable, var, against a word or string, text. If the two compare, command is executed. Note that there are two equal signs used. It's also a good idea to enclose both %var% and text in double quotes.

Errorlevel is used to compare a DOS command or program's return code with the specified value. If the return code is greater than or equal to value, the command is executed.

Exist is used to test for the existence of filename. Filename can be a single file, pathname, or a group of files specified with wildcards. If filename exists, command is executed.

Command is a DOS command, program name, or batch-file command.

PAUSE

Function: Pauses a batch file, waits for any key to continue.

Format: PAUSE text

Text is optional text the PAUSE command will display. However, when ECHO is turned OFF (as it is in most batch files), the text will not be displayed.

REM

Function: Allows for remarks in a batch file.

Format: REM comments

Comments are optional comments after the REM command. Those comments are not executed by DOS nor are they displayed when ECHO is turned off.

698

SHIFT

Function: Shifts the values of command line "left" of position.

Format: SHIFT

After the SHIFT command, variables %1 through %9 are shifted into variables %0 through %8. If a command-line parameter after %9 exists, it's shifted into %9. Additional parameters can be shifted with additional SHIFT commands.

For additional information on batch files, see Chapter 18.

CONFIG.SYS Commands

BREAK

Function: To monitor extended Ctrl-C or Ctrl-Break checking.

Format: BREAK=status

Status is either ON or OFF, which turns extended break checking either on or off. Turning extended break checking on will slow down the system a bit. The command line BREAK command can be used to change break checking at the DOS prompt.

Suggestion: Don't use.

BUFFERS

Function: To allocate memory for DOS to use when reading files from disk.

Format: BUFFERS=buffs,read_ahead

Buffs is the number of buffers, ranging from 1 to 99. If BUFFERS aren't specified, DOS chooses a value from between 2 to 15, depending on your memory and disk-drive configuration.

Read_ahead is an optional value from 1 through 8, used for special "read ahead" type of buffering. If both buffs and read_ahead are used, a comma must separate them.

Suggestion: BUFFERS=32

If you're using the SMARTDrive disk cache, set BUFFERS to a value of 20.

COMMENT

Function: Allows for comments in your CONFIG.SYS file.

Format: COMMENT comments

Comments are comments or notes to yourself explaining the CONFIG.SYS file. COMMENT is an undocumented command in CONFIG.SYS, which was included but not documented starting with DOS 4.

Suggestion: Use REM instead.

COUNTRY

Function: To tell DOS formatting information for specific countries and languages.

Format: COUNTRY=country,codepage,pathname

Country is a three-digit code representing the country, region, or language under which DOS will format the date and time, upper/lower case conversions, alphabetical sorting order, punctuation rules, and currency symbol.

Codepage is a three-digit code representing an Extended-ASCII character set. When specified, DOS will be able to load that character set into memory and use it, which allows some special foreign-language characters to be displayed under DOS. When codepage isn't specified, DOS uses the United States code page.

Pathname is the full pathname of the COUNTRY.SYS file, usually kept in your DOS subdirectory. COUNTRY.SYS contains the information the COUNTRY command needs to set its country code and code-page values.

Suggestion: Properly configured by the SETUP program when you installed DOS; only add or change if necessary.

DEVICE

Function: To load a device driver.

Format: DEVICE=pathname options

Pathname is the full pathname of a device driver. You should always include the drive letter, subdirectory, and the filename extension in the pathname.

Options are any options, parameters, or switches as required by the device driver. A list of DOS-supplied device drivers is provided later in this reference.

Suggestion: Use as necessary, refer to Chapter 19.

DEVICEHIGH

Function: To load a device driver into a UMB.

Format: DEVICEHIGH [size=hex] pathname options

Pathname is the full pathname of a device driver.

Options are options, parameters, or switches as required by the device driver.

Size is required only for expanding device drivers. The size of the driver is obtained from the MEM /C command, and specified after the equal sign as a hex value.

Suggestion: Use instead of DEVICE; refer to Chapter 26.

DOS

Function: To load DOS's kernel into the HMA.

Format: DOS=location,umbs

Location is either high or low. It specifies the location for DOS and whether it will be loaded into the HMA or conventional memory. If location is high, then DOS is loaded into the HMA. If location is low, DOS is loaded into conventional memory. The default is low.

Umbs is either umb or noumb. It specifies whether DOS should maintain links to the upper-memory blocks created by the EMM386.EXE device driver. If umb is specified, DOS maintains the links, and device drivers and memory-resident programs can be loaded into upper-memory blocks. If noumb is specified, device drivers and memory-resident programs cannot be "loaded high." noumb is the default. Note that this option only has effect on 80386 and later computers.

The DOS command requires that the HIMEM.SYS device driver be loaded elsewhere in CONFIG.SYS.

Suggestion: DOS=HIGH,UMB

DRIVPARM

Function: To specify parameters for block devices—typically disk drives.

Format: DRIVPARM /C /D:drive /F:size /H:heads /I /N /S:secs /T:tracks

/C is optional, and should be specified when the disk drive added can detect if its door is open or closed.

/D is required and indicates the physical-drive number. Values for the drive range from 0 through 255 for drives A through whatever. For example, if you were installing an external floppy drive D, /D:3 would be used.

/F indicates the form factor or size and capacity of the drive. Values for size are:

Size	Drive type/form factor
0	360K (or less), 5-1/2-inch
1	1.2M, 5-1/3-inch
2	720K, 3-1/2-inch
3	undefined
4	undefined
5	Hard drive
6	Tape drive
7	1.4M, 3-1/2-inch
8	Read/Write optical disk
9	2.8M, 3-1/2-inch

/H is optional and specifies the number of heads on the device. Values for heads range from 1 through 99, with the default depending on the type of drive (specified with /F).

/I forces some older disk controllers to recognize the 3-1/2-inch disk drives.

/N is used to indicate a nonremovable block device, such as a hard drive.

/S indicates the number of sectors per track for the device. Values for secs range from 1 through 99, with the default depending on the type of drive (specified with /F).

/T indicates the number of tracks per disk that each side the block device supports. Default values for tracks depend on the type of drive (specified with /F).

Suggestion: Use if necessary.

FCBS
Function: To set aside memory for use with file-control blocks (FCBs).
Format: FCBS=n

N is the number of file-control blocks to create. Values range from 1 through 255, with 4 as the default.

Suggestion: Use FILES instead.

FILES
Function: To tell DOS how many files it can have open at a time.
Format: FILES=n

N is the total number of files DOS can access at one time. Values for n range from 8 through 255, with 8 as the default.

Suggestion: FILES=32

INSTALL
Function: To load a memory-resident program into memory.
Format: INSTALL filename options

Filename is the full pathname of a memory-resident program. It must be a memory-resident program (or "TSR") or the results could be unpredictable. Also, it must be an "INSTALL configuration command approved" memory-resident program (which should be stated in the program's manual).

Options are any options or switches that could follow the filename at the DOS prompt.

Suggestion: Use LOADHIGH instead (if possible).

LASTDRIVE

Function: To tell DOS which drive letter will be the highest drive letter allowed in your system.

Format: LASTDRIVE=drive

Drive is a drive letter, ranging from A through Z. Valid values range from the highest lettered drive in your system, up through Z.

Suggestion: LASTDRIVE=Z

REM

Function: To include comments in your CONFIG.SYS file, or to "comment out" certain configuration commands.

Format: REM comments

Comments are notes or instructions to be included in your CONFIG.SYS file.

Suggestion: Use as necessary.

SHELL

Function: To specify a command interpreter for DOS.

Format: SHELL=pathname options

Pathname is the full pathname of a command interpreter to use with DOS. Normally, COMMAND.COM is used.

Options are any options that would follow the command processor.

Suggestion: SHELL=C:\DOS\COMMAND.COM C:\DOS /E:512 /P

Above, C:\DOS is assumed to be the location of COMMAND.COM; be sure to specify the proper directory for your system.

STACKS

Function: To set aside memory for DOS's internal interrupts.

Format: STACKS=stacks,size

Stacks are the number of stacks to create. Values for stacks can be the number 0 and numbers from 8 through 64. The default is 9 unless you have an original 8088-based IBM PC, in which case 0 is used.

Size is the size of each stack, in bytes. Values for size can be 0 and the numbers in the range from 32 through 512. The default is 128 unless you have an original 8088-based IBM PC, in which case 0 is used.

Suggestion: STACKS=0,0

SWITCHES

Function: To suppress extended keyboard functions on Enhanced-101 keyboards.

Format: SWITCHES=/K

/K is not an optional switch; it's the full format of the SWITCHES configuration command. If you use the above command, be sure to specify the /K switch if ANSI.SYS is used; refer to the ANSI.SYS device driver.

Function: To allow the WINA20.386 file to be removed from the root directory.

Format: SWITCHES=/W

You must combine the above command with a modification to your Windows' SYSTEM.INI file. In the section titled [386Enh], add a DEVICE command such as: DEVICE=C:\WINDOWS\WINA20.386. Be sure to specify the proper WINDOWS directory.

Suggestion: Use if necessary.

For additional information on CONFIG.SYS, see Chapter 19.

Device Drivers

All device drivers are installed using the DEVICE configuration command. Below are the device drivers included with DOS. Each is assumed to be in a C:\DOS subdirectory in the example formats; be sure to specify the proper DOS subdirectory for your own system.

ANSI.SYS	EMM386.EXE	SETVER.EXE
DISPLAY.SYS	HIMEM.SYS	SMARTDRV.SYS
DRIVER.SYS	PRINTER.SYS	
EGA.SYS	RAMDRIVE.SYS	

Note: COUNTRY.SYS and KEYBOARD.SYS are not device drivers and should never be used with the DEVICE configuration command.

ANSI.SYS

Function: Installs extended keyboard and screen control using the ANSI standard.

Format: DEVICE=C:\DOS\ANSI.SYS /K /L /SCREENSIZE /X

All ANSI.SYS's switches are optional.

/K maintains compatibility with the SWITCHES=/K configuration command. /K suppresses ANSI.SYS's monitoring of keys on the Enhanced-101 keyboard that don't exist on earlier models. Specify this switch only if you're using the SWITCHES configuration command.

/L forces ANSI.SYS to restore the number of rows and columns on the screen after an application quits. This switch should be specified only if you're using the MODE command to change the number of rows and columns on the screen.

/SCREENSIZE is used to set the physical size of your screen. It's followed by a row and column value in the following format:

```
/SCREENSIZE:(row,column)
```

The default values for row and column are 25 and 80, respectively. Note that /
SCREENSIZE can be abbreviated to just /S.

/X allows ANSI to redefine duplicate keys on the Enhanced-101 keyboard. The
duplicate keys are the arrow keys and cursor movement keys between the typewriter
keys and numeric keypad.

DISPLAY.SYS

Function: Provides code-page support for EGA, VGA, and LCD displays.

Format: DEVICE=C:\DOS\DISPLAY.SYS CON:=(type,codepage,n,m)

Type identifies your display adapter. Values for type can be EGA or LCD. EGA
includes the VGA display. CGA and MONO could also be specified, but those
devices do not support code-page switching.

Codepage is the hardware code page supported by your video system. It's a
three-digit number specifying a country or language character set to use. Valid
values are listed in Appendix C.

N indicates the number of code pages supported by your hardware. Values range
from 0 through 6 and are hardware-dependent; EGA displays support 6, LCD
displays support 1.

M indicates the number of subfonts supported. Values are 2 for EGA systems and
1 for LCD.

DRIVER.SYS

Function: To create logical floppy drives.

Format: DEVICE=C:\DOS\DRIVER.SYS /C /D:n /F:ff /H:h /S:s /T:t

/C is optional, and should be specified when the disk drive added can detect if
its door is open or closed.

/D is required and indicates the physical floppy-drive number. Values for n range
from 0 through 127 for the first through 127th floppy drives. Note that hard drives
and other drive types (defined by DRIVPARM) are not included in the count. Drive
A is 0, B is 1, and an external floppy drive is 2.

/F indicates the form factor or size and capacity of the drive. Values for ff are:

ff	Drive	type/form	factor
0	360K (or less),	5 -1/2-inch	
1	1.2M,	5 -1/3-inch	
2	720K,	3-1/2-inch	(the default)
7	1.4M,	3-1/2-inch	
9	2.8M,	3 -1/2-inch	

The /H, /S and /T switches are all optional, required only if you don't use the /F switch.

/H specifies number of heads on the drive, with values for h ranging from 1 through 99, with a default of 2.

/S indicates the number of sectors per track for the drive, with values for s ranging from 1 through 99, with the default depending on the type of drive.

/T indicates the number of tracks per disk side, with values for t ranging from 1 through 999. The default is either 80 or 40, depending on the type of drive.

This device driver is used exclusively to create logical floppy drives. Use the DRIVPARM command to add external drives of all types to your system.

EGA.SYS

Function: To restore the display after switching between graphics and text modes.

Format: DEVICE=C:\DOS\EGA.SYS

The EGA.SYS driver is required only on EGA graphics systems that run either the DOS Shell program or Windows.

EMM386.EXE

Function: To convert extended to expanded memory on '386 systems and to create UMBs.

Format: DEVICE=C:\DOS\EMM386.EXE mode mem options /NOEMS / RAM

Mode is either OFF, ON, or AUTO, turning expanded memory support off or on, or setting it to automatic. The default is AUTO.

Mem indicates the amount of extended memory to convert into expanded memory. Values for mem indicate the number of kilobytes to convert, and range from 16 through as much extended memory as is available. The default is 256 for 256K.

Options represent a whole procession of optional switches. For the most part these switches will not be used. Only if your hardware or software manual suggests so should you specify them. Note that none of these are preceded by a slash:

w=[on|off]   Turns support for the Weitek coprocessor on or off.

mx   Gives the page-frame address. Values for x are listed below:

x	address	x	address
1	C000	8	DC00
2	C400	9	E000
3	C800	10	8000
4	CC00	11	8400
5	D000	12	8800
6	D400	13	8C00
7	D800	14	9000

The page frame can also be selected by using the following format:

```
frame=address
```

Values for address are listed in the above table.

a=altregs   Specifies the number of fast alternative registers to use. Values for altregs range from zero through 254, the default is 7.

h=handles   Specifies the number of EMS handles to use. Values for handles range from two to 255, with 64 as the default.

d=nnn   Indicates the amount of RAM needed for DMA (direct memory access) buffering. Values for nnn are in kilobytes and range from 16 through 256, with 16 as the default.

/NOEMS is used to create UMBs while not converting any extended memory into expanded memory.

/RAM creates UMBs in addition to converting extended into expanded memory. You cannot specify both the /NOEMS and /RAM switches.

HIMEM.SYS
Function: To control all extended memory, establish the XMS, and create the HMA.

Format: DEVICE=C:\DOS\HIMEM.SYS options

Options are a whole slew of optional switches. Specify them only if your hardware or software manual requests that you do so.

/HMAMIN=m   Indicates a minimum program size for programs using the HMA. Values for m range from 0 through 63; 0 is the default.

/NUMHANDLES=n   Specifies the number of extended-memory blocks that can be used simultaneously. Values for n range from 1 through 128; 32 is the default.

/INT15=nnn   Allocates memory for the interrupt 15 interface to extended memory. Values for nnn are in kilobytes and range from 64 through 65535, 0 is the default.

/MACHINE:xxx   Selects an A20 line handler to be used, depending on your computer. Values for xxx are codes or numbers representing different PCs, as listed in the following table:

code	type	Machine
1	at	IBM PC/AT
2	ps2	IBM PS/2
3	ptlcascade	Phoenix Cascade BIOS
4	hpvectra	Hewlett Packard Vectra A and A+
5	att6300plus	AT&T 6300 Plus
6	acer1100	Acer 1100
7	toshiba	Toshiba 1600 and 1200XE
8	wyse	Wyse 286, 12.5 MHz
9	tulip	Tulip SX
10	zenith	Zenith ZBIOS
11	at1	IBM PC/AT
12	at2	IBM PC/AT (alternative delay)
12	css	CSS Labs
13	at3	IBM PC/AT (alternative delay)
13	philips	Philips
14	fasthp	Hewlett Packard Vectra

/A20CONTROL:status   Determines whether or not HIMEM.SYS will control the A20 line. Status is either ON or OFF, with ON as the default.

/SHADOWRAM:status   Control shadow RAM, which HIMEM.SYS can turn on or off. Status is either ON or OFF, with OFF as the default if you have less than two megabytes of RAM.

/CPUCLOCK:status   Allows HIMEM.SYS to deal with clock speed changes. Status is either ON or OFF, with OFF as the default.

PRINTER.SYS

Function: Provides code-page support for IBM- and Epson-compatible printers.

Format: DEVICE=C:\DOS\PRINTER.SYS LPTx:=(type,codepage,n,m)

X is the number of the printer port. Values for x range from 1 through 3. Note that only some IBM or Epson-compatible printers are supported by this command, and they should be hooked up to the proper printer port.

Type identifies your printer. Values for type are listed in the following table, along with their printer names:

Type	Printer
4201	IBM 4201 Proprinter "family"
4201	IBM 4201 Proprinter XL
4208	IBM 4207 IBM Proprinter X24 & XL24
4208	IBM 4208 IBM Proprinter X24 & XL24
5202	IBM 5202 Quietwriter III

Codepage is a hardware code page supported by the printer. It's a three digit number specifying a country or language character set to use. Valid code-page values are listed in Appendix C.

N indicates the number of code pages supported by your hardware.

RAMDRIVE.SYS

Function: To create a RAM drive.

Format: DEVICE=C:\DOS\RAMDRIVE.SYS size sector entries [/E|/A]

Size is the size of the RAM drive. Values for size range from 16 through 4096 for a 16K through 4 megabyte RAM drive. A 64K RAM drive is created if you don't specify a size value. Note that you must have enough memory available to create a RAM drive of a given size.

Sector is the secto[...]
256, or 512. If you dor[...]
specify a size value if [...]

Entries indicates th[...]
for entries range from 2[...]
Note that you must spec[...]

/E is used to setup th[...]

/A is used to setup th[...]

Either /E or /A can be[...]
is created in conventional[...]

RAM drives are assign[...] [...]ter than that of the last hard drive in your
system. Each RAMDRIVE.SYS command creates a new RAM drive. Refer to the
LASTDRIVE configuration command to make sure you have available drive letters
for all your RAM drives.

SETVER.EXE

Function:　To load the program-version table into memory for use with
　　　　　　SETVER as a DOS command.

Format:　　DEVICE=C:\DOS\SETVER.EXE

The version table is modified using the SETVER command at the DOS prompt.
Note that SETVER is an EXE program, not SYS.

SMARTDRV.SYS

Function:　To create a disk cache.

Format:　　DEVICE=C:\DOS\SMARTDRV.SYS max min /A

Max is the size of the cache in kilobytes. Values for max range from 128 through
8192 for a 128K through 8M cache. If max isn't specified, a 256K cache is created.

Min is the minimum size for the cache. Values for min range from 0 though the
value specified for max.

/A is used to create the cache in expanded memory. If /A isn't specified, the cache is created in extended memory.

Unlike RAMDRIVE.SYS, you should specify only SMARTDRV.SYS once in your CONFIG.SYS file.

APPENDIX A

ANSI Commands

Note that all values in an ANSI command are text—not numeric. The value "23" is the "2" and "3" character, not character code 23. Also, in this appendix, "←" represents the Escape character, ASCII 27, 1B hex, Ctrl-[or ^[.

Screen Commands, Cursor Positioning

Locate Cursor

Move the cursor to a specific row and column:

`←[row;col]H`

Row is a row number from 1 through however many rows are defined using the MODE command. The default is 1.

Col is a column number from 1 through however many columns are defined using the MODE command. The default is 1.

If both parameters are omitted, the cursor is sent to the upper left corner of the screen.

Position Cursor

Move the cursor to a specific row and column:

`←[row;col]f`

Position Cursor works identically to Locate Cursor, but the command ends with a little f.

Move Cursor Up

Moves the cursor up one line.

←[nA

N is the number of lines to move the cursor up. The default is one. If the cursor is at the top line, this command is ignored.

Move Cursor Down

Moves the cursor down one line.

←[nB

N is the number of lines to move the cursor down. The default is one. If the cursor is at the bottom line, this command is ignored.

Move Cursor Right

Moves the cursor right one column.

←[nC

N is the number of columns to move right. The default is one. If the cursor is at the far right column, this command is ignored.

Move Cursor Left

Moves the cursor left one column.

←[nD

N is the number of columns to move left. The default is one. If the cursor is at the far left column, this command is ignored.

Device Status Report

Displays the current cursor position, formatted.

←[6n

After issuing the above command, ANSI.SYS displays the cursor's position using the following format:

←[rr;ccR

RR is a two-digit number representing the current row, *cc* is a two-digit number representing the current column.

Do not use this command as part of a PROMPT command.

Save Cursor Position

Saves the cursor's present location.

←[s

The cursor position is restored using ←[u.

Restore Cursor Position

Restores the cursor position saved by the Save Cursor Position command.

←[u

Restores the cursor to its position as saved by ←[s.

Screen Commands, Erasing

Erase Display

Clears the screen.

←[2J

This command clears the screen and locates the cursor at the upper left corner.

Erase Line

Erases the line the cursor is on.

←[K

The line is erased from the cursor's position to the end of the line.

Screen Commands, Graphics and Color

Set Graphics Mode

Sets the attributes; foreground and background color of text displayed after the command is issued.

$\leftarrow$[*nm*

N is one or more attribute or color values. More than one value for *n* can be displayed, in which case each are separated by semicolons.

Attribute Values

0	Normal text
1	High-intensity
2	Low-intensity
4	Underline on (monochrome displays only)
5	Blinking on
7	Inverse video on
8	Invisible text

Color Values

	Foreground	Background
Black	30	40
Red	31	41
Green	32	42
Yellow	33	43
Blue	34	44
Magenta	35	45
Cyan	36	46
White	37	47

Set/Reset Mode

Changes the display text and graphics modes:

←[=*mode*h

Mode takes on the following values, which set the screen mode accordingly:

Screen Mode Values

0	Monochrome text, 40 x 25
1	Color text, 40 x 25
2	Monochrome text, 80 x 25
3	Color text, 80 x 25
4	Medium resolution graphics (four color), 320 x 200
5	Same as 4, but with color burst disabled
6	High resolution graphics (two color), 640 x 200
13	Color graphics, 320 x 200
14	Color graphics (16 color), 640 x 200
15	Monochrome graphics, 640 x 350
16	Color graphics (16 color), 640 x 350
17	Color graphics (2 color), 640 x 480
18	Color graphics (16 color), 640 x 480
19	Color graphics (256 color), 320 x 200

Character Wrap ON

Allows characters displayed after the far right column to be displayed on the next line.

←[=7h

The above command enables character wrap, which is the default.

Character Wrap OFF

Disables character wrap.

←[=7l

The above command causes all characters displayed after the far right column on the screen to be displayed in that column.

Note that the final character in the command sequence is a lowercase L, not a one.

Keyboard Commands

Keyboard Key Reassignment

Reassigns the ASCII character produced by a key.

←[*old*;*newp*

Old is an ASCII code for a key to redefine. It can also be a single character in double quotes.

New is the ASCII code that will be produced when the key for old is pressed. It can also be a single character in double quotes.

To reverse the assignment, swap new and old.

Keyboard String Reassignment

Assigns a string of text to a key on the keyboard.

←[*key_code*;"*string*"p

Key_code is an extended keyboard code (scan code) of a key on the keyboard, which starts with a zero.

String is a string of characters that will be produced whenever the key is pressed. It's usually enclosed in quotes, although ASCII values may be specified outside of the quotes, and must be separated by semicolons.

The following table lists the extended keyboard codes for the function keys on the PC's keyboard:

	Normal	Shifted	Control	Alt
F1	0;59	0;84	0;94	0;104
F2	0;60	0;85	0;95	0;105
F3	0;61	0;86	0;96	0;106
F4	0;62	0;87	0;97	0;107
F5	0;63	0;88	0;98	0;108
F6	0;64	0;89	0;99	0;109
F7	0;65	0;90	0;100	0;110
F8	0;66	0;91	0;101	0;111
F9	0;67	0;92	0;102	0;112
F10	0;68	0;93	0;103	0;113
F11	0;133	0;135	0;137	0;139
F12	0;134	0;136	0;138	0;140

Also refer to Appendix J for additional scan code values.

ASCII Table

Standard ASCII Codes

0 ^@	32	64 @	96
1 ^A	33 !	65 A	97 a
2 ^B	34 "	66 B	98 b
3 ^C	35 #	67 C	99 c
4 ^D	36 $	68 D	100 d
5 ^E	37 %	69 E	101 e
6 ^F	38 &	70 F	102 f
7 ^G	39 '	71 G	103 g
8 ^H	40 (	72 H	104 h
9 ^I	41)	73 I	105 i
10 ^J	42 *	74 J	106 j
11 ^K	43 +	75 K	107 k
12 ^L	44 ,	76 L	108 l
13 ^M	45 -	77 M	109 m
14 ^N	46 .	78 N	110 n
15 ^O	47 /	79 O	111 o
16 ^P	48 0	80 P	112 p
17 ^Q	49 1	81 Q	113 q
18 ^R	50 2	82 R	114 r
19 ^S	51 3	83 S	115 s
20 ^T	52 4	84 T	116 t
21 ^U	53 5	85 U	117 u
22 ^V	54 6	86 V	118 v
23 ^W	55 7	87 W	119 w
24 ^X	56 8	88 X	120 x
25 ^Y	57 9	89 Y	121 y
26 ^Z	58 :	90 Z	122 z
27 ^[	59 ;	91 [	123 {
28 ^\	60 <	92 \	124	
29 ^]	61 =	93]	125 }
30 ^^	62 >	94 ^	126 ~
31 ^_	63 ?	95 _	127

Control Code Meanings

Code	Ctrl-char	Abbr.	Meaning
0	^@	NUL	Null
1	^A	SOH	Start of heading
2	^B	STX	Start of text
3	^C	ETX	End of text
4	^D	EOT	End of transmission
5	^E	ENQ	Enquiry
6	^F	ACK	Acknowledge
7	^G	BEL	Bell
8	^H	BS	Backspace
9	^I	HT	Horizontal Tab
10	^J	LF	Linefeed
11	^K	VT	Vertical Tab
12	^L	FF	Form feed
13	^M	CT	Carriage Return
14	^N	SO	Shift out
15	^O	SI	Shift in
16	^P	DLE	Data link escape
17	^Q	DC1	Device control 1
18	^R	DC2	Device control 2
19	^S	DC3	Device control 3
20	^T	DC4	Device control 4
21	^U	NAK	Negative acknowledge
22	^V	SYN	Synchronous idle
23	^W	ETB	End transmission block
24	^X	CAN	Cancel
25	^Y	EM	End of medium
26	^Z	SUB	Substitute
27	^[	ESC	Escape
28	^\	FS	File separator
29	^]	GS	Group separator
30	^^	RS	Record separator
31	^_	US	Unit separator

IBM Extended ASCII Codes, Standard 437 Code Page

128Ç	160á	192└	224α
129ü	161í	193┴	225ß
130é	162ó	194┬	226Γ
131â	163ú	195├	227π
132ä	164ñ	196─	228Σ
133à	165Ñ	197┼	229σ
134å	166ª	198╞	230µ
135ç	167º	199╟	231τ
136ê	168¿	200╚	232Φ
137ë	169⌐	201╔	233Θ
138è	170¬	202╩	234Ω
139ï	171½	203╦	235δ
140î	172¼	204╠	236∞
141ì	173¡	205═	237φ
142Ä	174«	206╬	238ε
143Å	175»	207╧	239∩
144É	176	208╨	240≡
145æ	177	209╤	241±
146Æ	178	210╥	242≥
147ô	179│	211╙	243≤
148ö	180┤	212╘	244⌠
149ò	181╡	213╒	245⌡
150û	182╢	214╓	246÷
151ù	183╖	215╫	247≈
152ij	184╕	216╪	248°
153Ö	185╣	217┘	249·
154Ü	186║	218┌	250•
155¢	187╗	219█	251√
156£	188╝	220▄	252ⁿ
157¥	189╜	221▌	253²
158₧	190╛	222▐	254∎
159ƒ	191┐	223▀	255

Code Page Information

The following codes are used by the COUNTRY configuration command and the KEYB command:

Country/Language	Country Code	Keyboard Code	Code Pages
Australia	—	us	437,850
Belgium	032	be	437,850
Brazil	055	—	850,437
Canadian-French	002	cf	863,850
Czechoslovakia	042	cz	850,852
Czech.-Slovak	042	sl	850,852
Denmark	045	dk	865,850
English (Int'l)	061	—	437,850
Finland	385	su	437,850
France	033	fr	437,850
Germany	049	gr	437,850
Hungary	036	hu	852,850
Italy	039	it	437,850
Latin America	003	la	437,850
Netherlands	031	nl	437,850
Norway	047	no	865,850
Poland	048	pl	852,850
Portugal	351	po	860,850
Spain	034	sp	437,850
Sweden	046	sv	437,850
Swiss-French	041	sf	437,850
Swiss-German	041	sg	437,850
United Kingdom	044	uk	437,850
United States	001	us	437,850
Yugoslavia	038	yu	852,850

Countries missing values are limited to either the COUNTRY configuration command or the KEYB command. If a country/language has all the values, then it can be used with both commands.

Keyboard (KEYB) ID Values

The following are the codes for different hardware keyboard arrangements as used with the KEYB command (Chapter 22).

Country/Language	Codes
France	120,189
Italy	141,142
United Kingdom	166,168

Mode Command Code Pages

The following code pages are used with the CHCP, GRAFTABL, and MODE commands and the DISPLAY.SYS and PRINTER.SYS device drivers to configure the CON or LPTx devices:

Country/Language	Codes
Canadian-French	863
Multilingual	850
Nordic	865
Portuguese	850
United States	437
Slavic	852

The following code-page information (CPI) files are used with various IBM-compatible equipment:

4201.CPI	IBM Proprinter, Proprinter XL
4208.CPI	IBM Proprinter X24 & XL24
5202.CPI	IBM Quietwriter III
EGA.CPI	EGA display
LCD.CPI	The IBM PC Convertible laptop display

DOSKEY Commands

Standard DOS Editing Keys

Key	Function
F1	Display the next character in the template
Right arrow	Display the next character in the template
F2, *char*	Display the template up to the character *char*
F3	Display the remaining characters in the template
F4, *char*	Delete characters in the template up to the character char
F5	Store the current line as the template; start over
F6	Ctrl-Z character
Backspace	Move back one character in the template
Left arrow	Move back one character in the template
Delete/Del	Delete the next character in the template
Insert/Ins	Insert characters in the template
Esc	Cancel the line/changes, start over
Enter	End input

DOSKEY Editing Keys

Key	Function
Left arrow	Moves the cursor left one character
Right arrow	Moves the cursor right one character
Ctrl-Left arrow	Moves the cursor left one word
Ctrl-Right arrow	Moves the cursor right one word
Home	Moves the cursor to the start of the command
End	Moves the cursor to the end of the command
Ctrl-End	Delete from the cursor to the end of the command
Ctrl-Home	Delete from the cursor to the start of the command
Backspace	Deletes the character to the left of the cursor
Del	Deletes the current character
Ins	Toggles insert/overwrite (overwrite mode is always active unless DOSKEY was started with the /INSERT switch)
Ctrl-T	Command separator

Command History/Macro Keys

Key	Function
Up arrow	Recall previous command line
Down arrow	Recall next command line
PgUp	Recall the first command line
PgDn	Recall the last command line
F7	List command line history w/line numbers
Alt-F7	Erase command line history
F8	Scan history for matching text
F9	Select command by number
Alt-F10	Erase all macros

Macro Command Characters

Macro Command	Represents
$B	|, pipe character
$G	>, greater-than character
$L	<, less-than character
$T	[¶], Ctrl-T character (command separator)
$$	$, dollar sign
$1 through $9	Command line parameters
$*	All parameters

EDLIN

Running EDLIN

EDLIN is DOS's line editor, the old editor everyone had to use before the MS-DOS editor came along. It's clunky and awkward, but it's smaller in size than the Editor (plus QBASIC) and quite popular, despite is homeliness.

To start EDLIN, you must specify a file to edit:

```
EDLIN filename
```

If filename doesn't exist, EDLIN will create it. Upon saving a newer version of filename, the old version will be renamed filename.BAK.

Unlike text editors, a line editor is command driven. When you start EDLIN, you'll see its prompt, the asterisk, *. This is a command prompt; not the place where you type the text you're going to edit. To start editing text, enter a line number to edit or issue the I (insert) command.

The E (exit) command is used to quit EDLIN and return to DOS. E saves the file you're working on and makes a backup file of the original. The Q, quit, command also leaves EDLIN, but abandons any modifications made to the file. (You'll be prompted before actually quitting.)

EDLIN's Commands

Command	Function
Insert Line Commands	
I	Inserts a new line at the current line. When creating a new file, I inserts line 1.
nI	Inserts a new line number *n*.
.I	Inserts a new line at the current line.
#I	Inserts a new line at the bottom of the file.
+nI	Inserts a new line *n* lines down from the current line number.
-nI	Inserts a new line *n* lines up from the current line number.
Editing Commands	
n	Selects line *n* for editing.
-n	Selects line *n* lines up for editing.
+n	Selects line *n* lines down for editing.
.	Selects current line for editing.
List Commands	
L	Lists the 11 lines before the current line, the current line, and 11 lines after the current line.
xL	Lists 23 lines starting with line *x*.
,yL	Lists the 11 lines before line *y*, line *y*, and the 11 lines after line *y*.
x,yL	Lists the lines from *x* through *y*.
P	"Page" or print from the current line down 23 lines.
,yP	Print from the current line through line *y*.
x,yP	Print from line *x* through line *y*.

Delete Commands

D	Deletes the current line.
xD	Deletes line x.
x,yD	Deletes lines x through y.
,yD	Deletes all lines from the current line through line y.
x,.D	Deletes all lines from x through the current line.

Copy and Move Commands

x,y,zC	Copies the block of lines from x through y and places them at line number z.
x,x,zC	Copies the single line x to line number z.
x,y,zM	Moves the block of lines from x through y and places them at line number z.
x,x,zM	Moves line x to line number z.

Search and Replace Commands

S string	Searches for the characters string.
x,ySstring	Searches for the characters string between lines x and y.
x,y?Sstring	Searches for the characters in string between lines x and y, stops and prompts "OK?" for each occurrence. Pressing Y continues the search, N cancels.
Rstr1^Zstr2	Replaces all occurrences of *str1* with *str2*. ^Z is Ctrl-Z.
x,yRstr1^Zstr2	Replaces all occurrences of *str1* with *str2* in the range of lines from x through y.
x,y?Rstr1^Zstr2	Replaces all occurrences of *str1* with *str2* in the range of lines from x through y. When *str1* is found, replace stops as asks "OK?" Pressing Y replaces, pressing N cancels.

Disk Commands

---

nA	Appends lines from the disk file into memory. (This command only works if the file being edited is too big to fit into memory.)
nT	Transfers text to disk starting with line *n*. If *n* is omitted, the current line is used.
nW	Writes a specific number of lines to disk. (Used only for files too large to fit into memory at once.)

Quitting Commands

E	Ends edit, saves file, renames original file to *.BAK.
Q	Cancels edit, does not save changes.

APPENDIX F

DOS File Naming Rules

Pathnames

A pathname is the full name of a file, starting with the drive letter, colon, all subdirectories (each separated by a backslash), the filename and extension.

The only limitation on a pathname is that the entire name (including drive letter, colon, and filename/extension) can be no more than 63 characters long.

Filenames

The format of a filename (and for the name of a directory) is the 8-dot-3 format, as follows:

filename.ext

Filename is from 1 to 8 characters long.

Ext is an optional extension from 1 to 3 characters long, separated from filename by a period.

Characters not allowed as part of a filename are:

" / \ [ ] : * | < > + = ; , ?

Also not allowed are spaces and any ASCII control code (decimal 31 or less).

Characters allowed as part of a filename include all letters of the alphabet (upper and lower case are considered the same), numbers, and the following symbols:

' ~ ! @ # $ % ^ & ( ) - _ { } '

Included in the above are all Extended ASCII characters (128 of them!).

Device Names

Device Name	Device
NUL	Null device (empty)
CON	Console, screen (output) and keyboard (input)
AUX	First serial port
PRN	First printer
CLOCK$	System clock
A	First floppy drive
B	Second floppy drive
C	First hard drive
D, E, F...	Additional hard drives
COM1	First serial port
LPT1	First printer port
LPT2	Second printer port
LPT3	Third printer port
COM2	Second serial port
COM3	Third serial port
COM4	Fourth serial port

Disk Labels

A disk label is essentially a file name. However, a disk label cannot contain the following characters:

" / \ [ ] : * | < > + = ; , ? ( ) & ^

Note that (,), & and ^ are valid in a filename, but not in a disk label.

DEBUG Commands

All values are in hexadecimal.

Command	Function
A *address*	Enter assembly language commands/create a program in memory. *Address* is optional, if omitted; 100 is assumed.
C *blk1 l blk2*	Compare block of memory *blk1* with *blk2* with length l.
D *address r*	Dump memory contents at address for range *r*. Address is optional and if omitted the current address is assumed.
E *address list*	Enter bytes at memory-location address. List is an optional list of information to place at address, which can be ASCII text enclosed in double quotes.
F *address r list*	Fill memory starting at address for the range *r* with the byte values specified in list.
G *=address*	Go, or start executing instructions, at memory-location address.
H *n1 n2*	Add two values, *n1* and *n2*, and then subtract them. The two results are displayed on the following line.
I *port*	Input one byte from the specified port.
L *address d s1 n*	Load into memory at address from disk *d* (where 0 is drive A) the data starting a sector s1 for *n* sectors. If a program name has been specified with the N command, L alone loads that program into memory.

M *r address*	Moves the bytes in the range *r* to memory-location address.
N *pathname*	Names the program specified by pathname. Using the L or W command will cause that file to be loaded or saved, respectively.
O *port n*	Outputs the byte *n* to the port *port*.
P *address n*	Proceed, or execute the following instruction—such as an INT, CALL, or LOOP instruction. Address specifies the optional location of the instruction and *n* is a repeat count.
Q	Quit.
R *register*	Change the contents of the 8088 register register. Enter the new value on the following line.
S *r list*	Searches for the bytes in list in the range *r*.
T *address n*	Trace or execute the single instruction at address. N is a repeat count.
U *address*	Unassemble the machine code at address. Address may optionally be a range of memory locations or a specific address followed by a range value.
W *address d s1 n*	Write the data at address to disk *d* (where 0 is drive A) to sector *s1* for a sector count of *n*. If a program name has been specified with the N command, W alone writes that program to disk.
XA *x*	Allocates *x* pages of expanded memory.
XD *h*	De-allocates the pages created with XA using the handle *h*.
XM *l,p,h*	Maps the logical expanded-memory page l to the physical page *p*, using handle *h*.
XS	Displays expanded memory status.

Editing the Help File

DOS's HELP command uses a special file on disk, DOSHELP.HLP. This appendix explains how you can edit that file to add your applications or special batch-file commands, which can then be used with the HELP command.

The DOSHELP.HLP file can be edited using a text editor. The rules are:

- Lines starting with an @ (At Sign) are comments not displayed by the HELP command.

- Lines starting with a text character are command descriptions, which are displayed when the HELP command is used by itself.

- Lines starting with spaces are considered a continuation of the following line (for multiline descriptions). As a hint, use the same indenting found with the other commands in the DOSHELP.HLP file.

You should insert new text into the DOSHELP.HLP file in alphabetical order.

To take full advantage of the HELP command, your application should recognize the /? switch. Otherwise, the HELP command will tell you "Help not available for this command" when it's specified after HELP at the DOS prompt.

ERRORLEVEL Exit Values

Several external DOS commands send return codes, or ERRORLEVEL values, back to DOS when they're done. Those programs that return codes are listed here, along with their ERRORLEVEL values. The IF batch-file command can be used to examine the ERRORLEVEL values and take action based on them

BACKUP

0	Normal exit
1	No files found to back up
2	File sharing conflicts. Not all files were backed up
3	Ctrl-C was pressed, halting the backup
4	Error, program stopped

DISKCOMP

0	Normal exit
1	The diskettes didn't compare
2	Ctrl-C was pressed, halting the compare
3	Hardware error (diskette missing, etc.)
4	Initialization error

DISKCOPY

0	Normal exit
1	A read/write error occurred during the copy
2	Ctrl-C was pressed, halting the copy
3	Hardware error
4	Initialization error

FORMAT

0	Normal exit
3	Ctrl-C was pressed, halting the format
4	Error, program stopped
5	User pressed N to stop the format

GRAFTABL

0	Normal exit
1	The character table in memory has been replaced by the new table
2	File error
3	Improper parameter specified, nothing done
4	Incorrect DOS version

KEYB

0	Normal exit
1	Bad keyboard code, code page value, or general syntax error
2	Keyboard definition file not found or bad
4	CON device error
5	Unprepared code page request

REPLACE

0	Normal exit
2	Source file(s) not found
3	Source or target path was not found
5	Read/write access denied. (Change the files with ATTRIB.)
8	Not enough memory to run REPLACE
11	Bad parameter found or invalid format used

RESTORE

0	Normal exit
1	No files found to restore
3	Ctrl-C was pressed, halting the restore
4	Error termination, program stopped

SETVER

0	Normal exit
1	Unknown switch specified
2	Unknown filename specified
3	Not enough memory
4	Improper DOS version number (format)
5	Program entry could not be found
6	DOS system not found
7	Invalid drive specified
8	Too many parameters specified
9	Parameters missing
10	Error reading system file
11	Version table is corrupt
12	DOS system files do not support version tables
13	No space left in version table
14	Error writing system file

XCOPY

0	Normal exit
1	No files found to copy
2	Ctrl-C was pressed, halting the copy
4	Initialization error/not enough memory or disk space/syntax error
5	Write error/disk write protected

Keyboard Scan Code Values

Key	Normal	Shift	Control	Alt
ESC	1	—	—	—
1	2	—	—	0;120
2	3	—	—	0;121
3	4	—	—	0;122
4	5	—	—	0;123
5	6	—	—	0;124
6	7	—	—	0;125
7	8	—	—	0;126
8	9	—	—	0;127
9	10	—	—	0;128
0	11	—	—	0;129
-	12	—	—	0;130
=	13	—	—	0;131
Backspace	14	—	—	—
Tab	15	0;15	0;148	0;165
q	16	—	—	0;16
w	17	—	—	0;17
e	18	—	—	0;18
r	19	—	—	0;19
t	20	—	—	0;20
y	21	—	—	0;21

u	22	—	—	0;22
i	23	—	—	0;23
o	24	—	—	0;24
p	25	—	—	0;25
[	26	—	—	—
]	27	—	—	—
Enter	28	—	—	0;166
Ctrl	29	—	—	—
a	30	—	—	0;30
s	31	—	—	0;31
d	32	—	—	0;32
f	33	—	—	0;33
g	34	—	—	0;34
h	35	—	—	0;35
j	36	—	—	0;36
k	37	—	—	0;37
l	38	—	—	0;38
;	39	—	—	—
"	40	—	—	—
Left shift	42	—	—	—
\	43	—	—	—
z	44	—	—	0;44
x	45	—	—	0;45
c	46	—	—	0;46
v	47	—	—	0;47
b	48	—	—	0;48
n	49	—	—	0;49
m	50	—	—	0;50
,	51	—	—	—
.	52	—	—	—
/	53	—	0;149	0;164
Right shift	54	—	—	—

PrtSc	55	—	0;150	0;114
Alt	56	—	—	—
Spacebar	57	—	—	—
Caps Lock	58	—	—	—
F1	0;59	0;84	0;94	0;104
F2	0;60	0;85	0;95	0;105
F3	0;61	0;86	0;96	0;106
F4	0;62	0;87	0;97	0;107
F5	0;63	0;88	0;98	0;108
F6	0;64	0;89	0;99	0;109
F7	0;65	0;90	0;100	0;110
F8	0;66	0;91	0;101	0;111
F9	0;67	0;92	0;102	0;112
F10	0;68	0;93	0;103	0;113
F11	0;133	0;135	0;137	0;139
F12	0;134	0;136	0;138	0;140
Num Lock	69	—	—	—
Scroll Lock	70	—	—	—
Home	0;71	55	0;119	—
Up	0;72	56	0;141	—
PgUp	0;73	57	0;132	—
Gray -	0;74	—	0;142	—
Left	0;75	52	0;115	—
Keypad 5	0;76	—	0;143	—
Right	0;77	54	0;116	—
Gray +	0;78	—	0;144	—
End	0;79	49	0;117	—
Down	0;80	50	0;145	—
PgDn	0;81	51	0;118	—
Ins	0;82	48	0;146	—
Del	0;83	46	0;147	—

Gray keys:	Normal	Shift	Control	Alt
Home	224;71	224;71	224;119	224;151
Up	224;72	224;72	224;141	224;152
PgUp	224;73	224;73	224;132	224;153
Left	224;75	224;75	224;115	224;155
Right	224;77	224;77	224;116	224;157
End	224;79	224;79	224;117	224;159
Down	224;80	224;80	224;145	224;154
PgDn	224;81	224;81	224;118	224;161
Ins	224;82	224;82	224;146	224;162
Del	224;83	224;83	224;147	224;163

MS-DOS Editor Commands

The Menu Commands

A menu item is available only when highlighted. For example, unless you've selected any text, you cannot use the Cut, Copy, or Clear menu items in the Edit menu.

The File Menu

The File menu deals with the text you edit and disk, saving it to disk, loading a new file into the Editor, printing the file, and quitting back to DOS.

Command	Function
New	Start editing a new file; clear away any present file and prompt to save it
Open	Open (load) a text file on disk into memory, prompt to save any file already in memory
Save	Quick-save the file in the editor to disk
Save As	Save the file in the editor to disk under a new name
Print	Print selected text or the entire file
Exit	Quit the Editor and return to DOS

The Edit Menu

The Edit menu items deal with selected text and a holding area called the clipboard. Text is first selected using the keyboard or mouse, and then copied or cut into the clipboard. From there, it can be pasted back into the file at the cursor's position.

Command	Function
Cut	Delete the selected text, copying it to the clipboard
Copy	Copy the selected text into the clipboard
Paste	Paste text from the clipboard into the document
Clear	Delete selected text

The Search Menu

The Search menu items allow you to locate text in the file and optionally change that text to something else.

Command	Function
Find	Locate text in the file, from the cursor's position to the end of the file
Repeat Last Find	Locate the next occurrence of text found using the Find command
Change	Locate text in the file and change that text to something else (search and replace)

The Options Menu

The Options menu controls the way the Editor behaves and appears on the screen.

Command	Function
Display	Change the Editor's colors; specify whether or not scroll bars are used; set the tab stops
Help Path	Enter a location for the Editor's help files

The Help Menu

The Help menu lets you get help for the Editor and its commands and functions.

Command	Function
Getting Started	Runs the overview of the Editor's helpful information
Keyboard	Displays information on how to use the keyboard
About	Displays information about the Editor

The Key Commands

General Key Commands

Command	Function
Alt	Activate the menu
F1	Help

Using the Help System/Survival Guide/Dialog boxes

Enter	Select highlighted item
Esc	Quit help, return to the Editor
Tab	Move to the next highlighted topic
Shift-Tab	Move to the previous highlighted topic
Letter	Move to the next highlighted topic beginning with letter
Shift-letter	Move to the previous highlighted topic beginning with letter
Alt-F1	Re-display the last help screen
Ctrl-F1	Go to the next help topic
Shift-Ctrl-F1	Go to the previous help topic

Using the Menus

Alt	Activate the menu
Alt-letter	Activate the menu beginning with letter
Right arrow	Move to the next menu to the right
Left arrow	Move to the next menu to the left
Down/Enter	When a menu title is activated, drop down the menu
Down	Move down through the menu items
Up	Move up through the menu items
Enter	Select the highlighted menu item
Esc	Cancel the menu; return to the Editor

Editing, Moving the Cursor

Note that these keys are similar in many respects to the WordStar editing keys.

Right arrow	Move the cursor right one character
Ctrl-D	Move the cursor right one character
Left arrow	Move the cursor left one character
Ctrl-S	Move the cursor left one character
Up arrow	Move the cursor up one line
Ctrl-E	Move the cursor up one line
Down arrow	Move the cursor down one line

Ctrl-X	Move the cursor down one line
Ctrl-Right	Move the cursor right one word
Ctrl-F	Move the cursor right one word
Ctrl-Left	Move the cursor left one word
Ctrl-A	Move the cursor left one word
Home	Move the cursor to the start of the line
Ctrl-Q,S	Move the cursor to the start of the line
End	Move the cursor to the end of the line
Ctrl-Q,D	Move the cursor to the end of the line

When typing Ctrl-Q,S or Ctrl-Q,D, first type the Ctrl-Q. You'll see ^Q appear on the right side of the status bar. Then type an S or D. (It's actually a two-keystroke combination.)

Command	Function
Ctrl-Enter	Move the cursor to the first character on the next line
Ctrl-J	Move the cursor to the first character on the next line
Ctrl-Q,E	Move the cursor to the first line in the window
Ctrl-Q,X	Move the cursor to the last line in the window
PgDn	Move down one screenful of text
Ctrl-C	Move down one screenful of text
PgUp	Move up one screenful of text
Ctrl-R	Move up one screenful of text
Ctrl-Home	Move to the start of the file
Ctrl-Q,R	Move to the start of the file
Ctrl-End	Move to the end of the file
Ctrl-Q,C	Move to the end of the file
Ctrl-Up arrow	Scroll the text up one line
Ctrl-W	Scroll the text up one line
Ctrl-Down arrow	Scroll the text down one line
Ctrl-Z	Scroll the text down one line

Ctrl-PgUp	Scroll the text left one screen
Ctrl-PgDn	Scroll the text right one screen

Deleting Text

Del	Delete the character at the cursor
Ctrl-G	Delete the character at the cursor
Ctrl-Backspace	Delete the character at the cursor
Backspace	Delete the character to the left of the cursor
Ctrl-H	Delete the character to the left of the cursor
Ctrl-T	Delete the word at or to the right of the cursor
Ctrl-Y	Delete the current line
Ctrl-Q,Y	Delete from the cursor to the end of the current line

Special Keys	**Note:** In insert mode, the cursor is a flashing underline; in overstrike mode the cursor is a large flashing block.

Ins	Switch from insert mode to overstrike mode
Ctrl-V	Switch from insert mode to overstrike mode
Ctrl-P	Special character prefix key

After typing a Ctrl-P, the next Ctrl character you type will be "literally" inserted into the text. This is primarily used to insert special characters into the text, such as the Escape character used with ANSI commands.

Selecting Text/Copying, Cutting, Pasting

To select text using the keyboard: Hold down either Shift key, and then move the cursor over the text using the cursor-movement key commands.

To select text using the mouse: Position the mouse cursor over the text's start, then press the mouse button and drag over the desired text. Release the mouse button when done.

The selected text is then marked as a block, shown in inverse (white-on-black) on the screen.

Command	Function
Ctrl-Ins	Copy the selected text to the clipboard (Copy menu item)
Shift-Del	Cut the selected text to the clipboard (Cut menu item)
Ctrl-Y	Cut current line
Ctrl-Q,Y	Cut current line from the cursor position to the end
Shift-Ins	Paste cut or copied text from the clipboard (Paste menu item)
Del	Deletes all selected text (Clear menu item)

Finding/Replacing

Command	Function
Ctrl-Q,F	Find text (Find menu item)
F3	Repeat last find command (Repeat Last Find menu item)
Ctrl-L	Repeat last find
Ctrl-Q,A	Search and replace text (Change menu item)

APPENDIX L

PROMPT Commands

Command	Displays
$$	$, dollar sign character
$b	I, pipe character
$d	The date (according to the system clock)
$e	The ESCape character, ASCII 27
$g	>, greater-than character
$h	Backspace (erase previous character)
$l	<, less-than character
$n	The currently logged disk drive (letter)
$p	The current path (disk drive and subdirectory)
$q	=, equal sign character
$t	The time (according to the system clock)
$v	DOS version
$_	Carriage return/line feed (new line)

Index

A Library of Technical References from M&T Books

NetWare User's Guide
by Edward Liebing

Endorsed by Novell, this book informs NetWare users of the services and utilities available, and how to effectively put them to use. Contained is a complete task-oriented reference that introduces users to NetWare and guides them through the basics of NetWare menu-driven utilities and command line utilities. Each utility is illustrated, thus providing a visual frame of reference. You will find general information about the utilities, then specific procedures to perform the task in mind. Utilities discussed include NetWare v2.1 through v2.15. For advanced users, a workstation troubleshooting section is included, describing the errors that occur. Two appendixes, describing briefly the services available in each NetWare menu or command line utility are also included.

Book only   Item #071-0 $24.95

Blueprint of a LAN
by Craig Chaiken

Blueprint of a LAN provides a hands-on introduction to microcomputer networks. For programmers, numerous valuable programming techniques are detailed. Network administrators will learn how to build and install LAN communication cables, configure and troubleshoot network hardware and software, and provide continuing support to users. Included are a very inexpensive zero-slot, star topology network, remote printer and file sharing, remote command execution, electronic mail, parallel processing support, high-level language support, and more. Also contained is the complete Intel 8086 assembly language source code that will help you build an inexpensive to install, local area network. An optional disk containing all source code is available.

Book & Disk (MS-DOS)   Item #066-4 $39.95
Book only   Item #052-4 $29.95

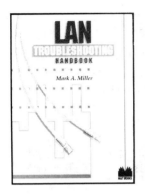

LAN Troubleshooting Handbook
by Mark A. Miller

This book is specifically for users and administrators who need to identify problems and maintain a LAN that is already installed. Topics include LAN standards, the OSI model, network documentation, LAN test equipment, cable system testing, and more. Addressed are specific issues associated with troubleshooting the four most popular LAN architectures: ARCNET, Token Ring, Ethernet, and StarLAN. Each are closely examined to pinpoint the problems unique to its design and the hardware. Handy checklists to assist in solving each architecture's unique network difficulties are also included.

Book & Disk (MS-DOS)	**Item #056-7**	**$39.95**
Book only	**Item #054-0**	**$29.95**

Building Local Area Networks with Novell's NetWare
by Patrick H. Corrigan and Aisling Guy

From the basic components to complete network installation, here is the practical guide that PC system integrators will need to build and implement PC LANs in this rapidly growing market. The specifics of building and maintaining PC LANs, including hardware configurations, software development, cabling, selection criteria, installation, and on-going management are described in a clear "how-to" manner with numerous illustrations and sample LAN management forms. *Building Local Area Networks* gives particular emphasis to Novell's NetWare, Version 2.1. Additional topics covered include the OS/2 LAN manager, Tops, Banyan VINES, internetworking, host computer gateways, and multisystem networks that link PCs, Apples, and mainframes.

Book & Disk (MS-DOS)	**Item #025-7**	**$39.95**
Book only	**Item #010-9**	**$29.95**

NetWare Supervisor's Guide
by John T. McCann, Adam T. Ruef, and Steven L. Guengerich

Written for network administrators, consultants, installers, and power users of all versions of NetWare, including NetWare 386. Where other books provide information on using NetWare at a workstation level, this definitive reference focuses on how to administer NetWare. Contained are numerous examples which include understanding and using NetWare's undocumented commands and utilities, implementing system fault tolerant LANs, refining installation parameters to improve network performance, and more.

Book only   **Item #111-3**   **$29.95**

LAN Protocol Handbook
by Mark A. Miller, P.E.

Requisite reading for all network administrators and software developers needing in-depth knowledge of the internal protocols of the most popular network software. It illustrates the techniques of protocol analysis—the step-by-step process of unraveling LAN software failures. Detailed are how Ethernet, IEEE 802.3, IEEE 802.5, and ARCNET networks transmit frames of information between workstations. From that foundation, it presents LAN performnce measurements, protocol analysis methods, and protocol analyzer products. Individual chapters thoroughly discuss Novell's NetWare, 3Com's 3+ and 3+Open, IBM Token-Ring related protocols, and more!

Book only   **Item 099-0**   **$34.95**

Using QuarkXPress
by Tim Meehan

Written in an enjoyable, easy-to-read style, this book addresses the needs of both beginning and intermediate users. It includes numerous illustrations and screen shots that guide readers through comprehensive explanations of QuarkXPress, its potential and real-world applications. Using QuarkXPress contains comprehensive explanations of the concepts, practices, and uses of QuarkXPress with sample assignments of increasing complexity that give readers actual hands-on experience using the program.

Book/Disk	**Item #129-6**	**$34.95**
Book only	**Item #128-8**	**$24.95**

An OPEN LOOK at UNIX
A Developer's Guide to X
by John David Miller

This is the book that explores the look and feel of the OPEN LOOK graphical user interface, discussing its basic philiosophy, environment, and user-interface elements. It includes a detailed summary of the X Window System, introduces readers to object-oriented programming, and shows how to develop commercial-grade X applications. Dozens of OPEN LOOK program examples are presented, along with nearly 13,000 lines of C code. All source code is available on disk in 1.2 MB UNIX cpio format.

Book/Disk	**Item #058-3**	**$39.95**
Book only	**Item #057-5**	**$29.95**

Turbo C++ by Example
by Alex Lane

Turbo C++ by Example includes numerous code examples that teach C programmers new to C++ how to skillfully program with Borland's powerful Turbo C++. Detailed are key features of Turbo C++ with code examples. Includes both Turbo Debugger and Tools 2.0—a collection of tools used to design and debug Turbo C++ programs, and Turbo Profiler. All listings available on disk in MS/PC-DOS format.

Book/Disk (MS-DOS)	**Item #141-5**	**$36.95**
Book only	**Item #123-7**	**$26.95**

1-800-533-4372 (in CA 1-800-356-2002)

Small-Windows
A Library of Windowing Functions for the C Language
by James Hendrix

Here is an extensive library of C language functions for creating and manipulating display windows. This manual and disk package contains 41 windowing functions, 18 video functions written in assembly, and menu functions that support both static and pop-up menus. Small Windows is available for MS-DOS systems, and Microsoft C Versions 4.0/5.0, Turbo C 1.5, Small C, and Lattice C 3.1 compilers. Documentation and full C source code are included.

Manual & Disk   **Item #35-6**   **$29.95**

Small Assembler
by James Hendrix

Small Assembler is a full macro assembler that was developed primarily for use with the Small C compiler. This manual presents an overview of the Small Assembler, documents the command lines that invoke programs, and provides appendixes and reference materials for the programmer. The accompanying disk includes both the executable assembler and full source code.

Manual & Disk   **Item #024-9**   **$29.95**

Small-Tools User's Manual
by James Hendrix

This package of programs performs specific modular operations on text files such as editing, formatting, sorting, merging, listing, printing, searching, and much more. Small-Tools is supplied in source code form. You can select and adapt these tools to your own purposes. Documentation is included.

Manual & Disk   **Item #02-X**   **$29.95**

The One Minute Memory Manager
Every PC user's Guide to Faster More Efficient Computing
by Phillip Robinson

Readers will learn why memory is important, how and when to install more, and how to wring the most out of their memory. Clear, concise instructions teach users how to manage their computer's memory to multiply its speed and ability to run programs simultaneously. Tips and techniques also show users how to conserve memory when working with popular software programs.

Book only: **Item #102-4**   **$24.95**

Windows 3.0: A Developer's Guide
Jeffrey M. Richter

This example-packed guide is for all experienced C programmers developing applications for Windows 3.0. This book describes every feature, function, and components of the Windows Application Programming Interface, teaching programmers how to take full advantage of its many capabilities. Diagrams and source code examples are used to demonstrate advanced topics, including window subclassing, dynamic memory mamagement, and software installation techniques.

Book/Disk (MS-DOS)   **Item #164-4**   **$39.95**

Book   **Item #162-8**   **$29.95**

Windows 3.0 By Example
by Michael Hearst

Here is a hands-on guide to Windows 3.0. Written for all users new to Windows, this book provides thorough, easy-to-follow explanations of every Windows 3.0 feature and function. Numerous exercises and helpful practice sessions help readers further develop their understanding of Windows 3.0

Book only   **Item #180-6**   **$26.95**

1-800-533-4372 (in CA 1-800-356-2002)

ORDER FORM

To Order:

Return this form with your payment to M&T books, 501 Galveston Drive, Redwood City, CA 94063 or **call toll-free 1-800-533-4372 (in California, call 1-800-356-2002).**

ITEM #	DESCRIPTION	DISK	PRICE

Subtotal	
CA residents add sales tax ___%	
Add $3.50 per item for shipping and handling	
TOTAL	

Charge my:

❑ **Visa**

❑ **MasterCard**

❑ **AmExpress**

❑ **Check enclosed, payable to M&T Books.**

CARD NO. _____

SIGNATURE _____ EXP. DATE _____

NAME _____

ADDRESS _____

CITY _____

STATE _____ ZIP _____

M&T GUARANTEE: If your are not satisfied with your order for any reason, return it to us within 25 days of receipt for a full refund. Note: Refunds on disks apply only when returned with book within guarantee period. Disks damaged in transit or defective will be promptly replaced, but cannot be exchanged for a disk from a different title.

8025